lonely planet

Costa Rica

Arenal &
Northern
Lowlands
p239

Northwestern
Costa Rica
p189

Central Valley
& Highlands
p101

Caribbean
Coast
p136

Península
de Nicoya
p285

San José
p60

Central
Pacific Coast
p347

Southern
Costa Rica &
Península de Osa
p405

Ashley Harrell,
Jade Bremner, Brian Kluepfel

Contents

COFFEE SACKS,
MONTEVERDE P191

STIG STOCKHOLM PEDERSEN/GETTY IMAGES ©

OGPHOTO/GETTY IMAGES ©

PARQUE NACIONAL VOLCÁN
IRAZÚ P122

ALFREDO MAIQUEZ/GETTY IMAGES ©

Contents

CART WHEEL, SARCHÍ P112

Contents

HUMMINGBIRD IN BOSQUE
NUBOSO MONTEVERDE P210

REFUGIO NACIONAL DE
VIDA SILVESTRE GANDOCA-
MANZANILLO P186

Contents

KRYSSIA CAMPOS/GETTY IMAGES ©

CAPUCHIN MONKEYS,
PARQUE NACIONAL MANUEL
ANTONIO P384

Welcome to Costa Rica

Centering yourself on a surfboard or yoga mat, descending into bat-filled caves or ascending misty volcanic peaks, hiking, biking or ziplining – your only limit is your return date.

The Peaceful Soul of Central America

If marketing experts could draw up an ideal destination, Costa Rica might be it. The 'rich coast' has earned its name and stands apart from its Central American neighbors on the cutting edge of so many trends: surfing, farm-to-table restaurants, and sustainable tourism. Developing infrastructure is balanced by green energy such as wind and hydro. One of the world's most biodiverse countries, with half a million species – from insects to the giant anteaters that devour them – it also protects one-quarter of its wild lands through law.

Outdoor Adventures

Rainforest hikes and brisk high-altitude trails, rushing white-water rapids and warm-water, world-class surfing: Costa Rica offers a dizzying suite of outdoor adventures in every shape and size – from the squeal-inducing rush of a canopy zipline to a sun-dazed afternoon at the beach. National parks allow visitors to glimpse life in both rainforest and cloud forest, simmering volcanoes offer otherworldly vistas, and reliable surf breaks are suited to beginners and experts alike. Can't decide? Don't worry: given the country's size, you can plan a rela-'vely short trip that includes it all.

The Wild Life

Such wildlife abounds in Costa Rica as to seem almost cartoonish: keel-billed toucans ogle you from treetops and scarlet macaws raucously announce their flight plans. A keen eye will discern a sloth on a branch or the eyes of a caiman breaking the surface of a mangrove swamp, while alert ears will catch rustling leaves signaling a troop of white-faced capuchins or the haunting call of a howler monkey. Blue morpho butterflies flit amid orchid-festooned trees, while colorful tropical fish, sharks, rays, dolphins and whales thrive offshore – all as if in a conservationist's dream.

The Pure Life

A recent study showed that many Costa Ricans live longer, healthier lives than people on the rest of the planet, and it all comes down to *pura vida* (pure life), a term you'll hear everywhere. Before you dismiss it as marketing banter (and it *is* a big marketing phrase), listen to how it's used. It means hello, goodbye, everything's cool, same to you. It never has a negative connotation. You may enter the country not believing it, but after a week you'll be saying it, too, unconsciously: *pura vida, mae*. Relax and enjoy the ride.

Why I Love Costa Rica

By Brian Kluepfel, Writer

We New Yorkers never really ease up. In Costa Rica, there's no choice. I learned to surf. I enjoyed a *gallo pinto* breakfast with rich, dark local coffee. And I found lots of people living the expat dream: yoga practitioners, organic farmers, surfer chefs and mountain bikers. As a birder, I was amazed daily: I picked one hotel because two trogans were perched on a branch outside, and my raft tailed a cormorant down raging rapids in Sarapiquí. But my favorite moment was when a new Tico friend texted me: 'Hey, man, you're in Costa Rica. Relax!"

For more about our writers, see p544

Above: Catarata del Toro waterfall (p114), Bajos

Costa Rica

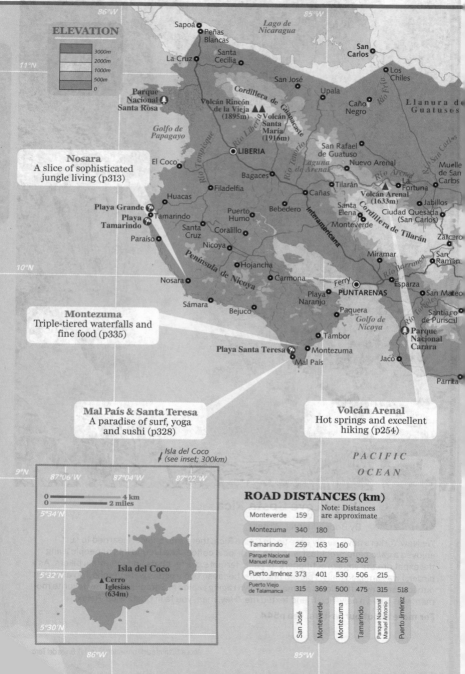

ELEVATION

3000m
2000m
1000m
500m
0

Nosara
A slice of sophisticated jungle living (p313)

Montezuma
Triple-tiered waterfalls and fine food (p335)

Mal País & Santa Teresa
A paradise of surf, yoga and sushi (p328)

Volcán Arenal
Hot springs and excellent hiking (p254)

Lago de Nicaragua

Cordillera de Guanacaste

Volcán Rincón de la Vieja (1895m)
Volcán Santa María (1916m)

LIBERIA

Volcán Arenal (1633m)

Cordillera de Tilarán

Golfo de Papagayo

Península de Nicoya

Golfo de Nicoya

PUNTARENAS
Ferry

Isla del Coco (see inset; 300km)

PACIFIC OCEAN

Sapoá · Peñas Blancas · La Cruz · Santa Cecilia · San Carlos · San José · Upala · Los Chiles · Caño Negro · *Llanura de Guatuses* · Parque Nacional Santa Rosa · El Coco · Bagaces · San Rafael de Guatuso · Nuevo Arenal · Muelle de San Carlos · Huacas · Filadelfia · Tilarán · La Fortuna · Jabillos · Playa Grande · Tamarindo · Cañas · Santa Elena · Ciudad Quesada (San Carlos) · Playa Tamarindo · Puerto Humo · Bebedero · Monteverde · Zarcero · Santa Cruz · Coralillo · Paraíso · Nicoya · Miramar · San Ramón · Hojancha · Carmona · Esparza · San Mateo · Nosara · Playa Naranjo · Paquera · Santiago de Puriscal · Sámara · Bejuco · Tambor · Parque Nacional Carara · Playa Santa Teresa · Montezuma · Jacó · Mal País · Parrita

Rio Tempisque · Rio Liberia · Rio Tenorio · Laguna de Arenal · Rio Arenal · Rio San Carlos · Rio Frío · Interamericana · Rio Barranca · Rio Turrubares · Cerro Iglesias (634m)

Isla del Coco

0 — 4 km
0 — 2 miles

ROAD DISTANCES (km)

Note: Distances are approximate

	San José	Monteverde	Montezuma	Tamarindo	Parque Nacional Manuel Antonio	Puerto Jiménez
Monteverde	159					
Montezuma	340	180				
Tamarindo	259	163	160			
Parque Nacional Manuel Antonio	169	197	325	302		
Puerto Jiménez	373	401	530	506	215	
Puerto Viejo de Talamanca	315	369	500	475	315	518

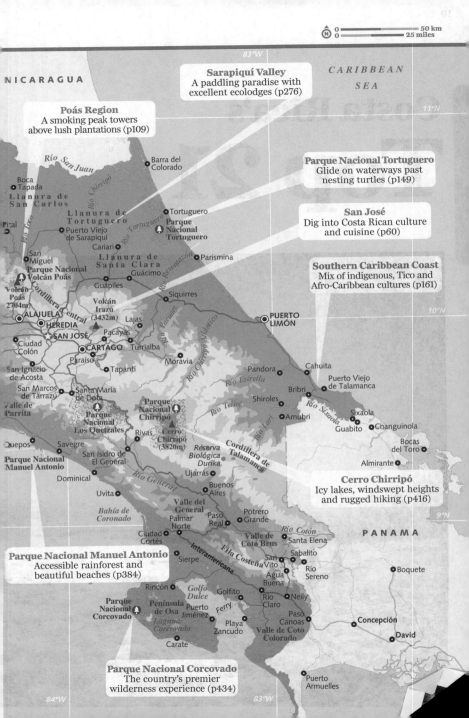

Sarapiquí Valley
A paddling paradise with
excellent ecolodges (p276)

CARIBBEAN
SEA

NICARAGUA

Poás Region
A smoking peak towers
above lush plantations (p109)

83°W

11°N

Barra del
Colorado

Parque Nacional Tortuguero
Glide on waterways past
nesting turtles (p149)

Boca
Tapada

Río San Juan

Río Chirripó

Llanura de
San Carlos

Llanura de
Tortuguero

Tortuguero

San José
Dig into Costa Rican culture
and cuisine (p60)

Pirial

Puerto Viejo
de Sarapiquí

Parque
Nacional
Tortuguero

San
Miguel

Cariari

Parismina

Southern Caribbean Coast
Mix of indigenous, Tico and
Afro-Caribbean cultures (p161)

Parque Nacional
Volcán Poás

Llanura de
Santa Clara

Guácimo

Volcán
Poás
2704m)

Guápiles

Cordillera Central

Siquirres

10°N

Volcán
Irazú
(3432m)

ALAJUELA

Lajas

HEREDIA

SAN JOSÉ

Pacayas

PUERTO
LIMÓN

Ciudad
Colón

CARTAGO

Turrialba

Paraíso

Moravia

San Ignacio
de Acosta

Tapantí

Cahuita

Pandora

San Marcos
de Tarrazú

Santa María
de Dota

Río Estrella

Puerto Viejo
de Talamanca

Bribrí

Valle de
Parrita

Shiroles

Río Telire

Parque
Nacional
Los Quetzales

Río Lari

Amubri

Sixaola

Guabito

Changuinola

Parque
Nacional
Chirripó

Rivas

Cerro
Chirripó
(3820m)

Reserva
Biológica
Durika

Cordillera de
Talamanca

Bocas
del Toro

Quepos

Savegre

San Isidro de
El General

Almirante

**Parque Nacional
Manuel Antonio**

Dominical

Río General

Ujarrás

Cerro Chirripó
Icy lakes, windswept heights
and rugged hiking (p416)

Buenos
Aires

Uvita

Valle del
General

Bahía de
Coronado

Palmar
Norte

Paso
Real

Potrero
Grande

9°N

Río Cotón

PANAMA

Ciudad
Cortés

Interamericana

Valle de
Coto Brus

Santa Elena

Parque Nacional Manuel Antonio
Accessible rainforest and
beautiful beaches (p384)

Sierpe

Fila Costeña

San
Vito

Sabalito

Río
Sereno

Boquete

Rincón

Golfo
Dulce

Golfito

Agua
Buena

Parque
Nacional
Corcovado

Península
de Osa

Puerto
Jiménez

Ferry

Río
Claro

Neily

Concepción

Laguna
Corcovado

Playa
Zancudo

Paso
Canoas

David

Valle de Coto
Colorado

Carate

Puerto
Armuelles

Parque Nacional Corcovado
The country's premier
wilderness experience (p434)

84°W

83°W

Costa Rica's
Top 21

Mal País & Santa Teresa

1 In the little surf towns of Mal País and Santa Teresa (p328), the sea is replete with wildlife and the waves are near-ideal in shape, color and temperature. The hills are lush and the coastline long, providing a perfect backdrop for the pink and orange sunsets. From the bustling, dusty intersection that divides the towns, you can head north into yogic paradise and foodies' bliss or south to the less hectic old-school vibe of Malpa, ending in a fishing village, a hidden zipline, and the gateway to Costa Rica's original national park. Below: Santa Teresa

Parque Nacional Tortuguero

2 Canoeing the canals of Parque Nacional Tortuguero (p149) is a boat-borne safari: here, thick jungle meets the water and you can get up close with shy caimans, river turtles, crowned night herons, monkeys and sloths. In the right season, under cover of darkness, watch the awesome, millennia-old ritual of turtles building nests and laying their eggs on the black-sand beaches. Sandwiched between extravagantly green wetlands and the wild Caribbean Sea, this is among the premier places in Costa Rica to watch wildlife. Below: Green basilisk lizard

N K/SHUTTERSTOCK/GETTY IMAGES ©

JD GREBBIN/SHUTTERSTOCK ©

3

Volcán Arenal & Hot Springs

3 While the molten night views are gone, this mighty, perfectly conical giant (p254) is still considered active and worthy of a pilgrimage. Shrouded in mist or bathed in sunshine, Arenal has several beautiful trails to explore and, at its base, you're just a short drive away from its many hot springs. Some of these springs are free, and any local can point the way. Others range from inexpensive Tico favorites to pricier over-the-top resorts to isolated ecstasy – dip your toes into the romantic Eco Termales, for starters.

Parque Nacional Corcovado

4 Muddy, muggy and intense, the vast, largely untouched rainforest of Parque Nacional Corcovado (p434) is anything but a walk in the park. Here travelers with a flexible agenda and a sturdy pair of rubber boots thrust themselves into the unknown and come out the other side with the story of a lifetime. And the further into the jungle you go, the better it gets: the country's best wildlife-watching, most desolate beaches and most vivid adventures lie down Corcovado's seldom-trodden trails.

Top right: Scarlet macaw

Parque Nacional Manuel Antonio

5 Although droves of visitors pack Parque Nacional Manuel Antonio (p384) – the country's most popular (and smallest) national park – it remains an absolute gem. Capuchin monkeys scurry across its idyllic beaches, brown pelicans dive-bomb its clear waters and sloths watch over its accessible trails. It's a perfect place to introduce youngsters to the wonders of the rainforest, and as you splash around in the waves you're likely to feel like a kid yourself. There's not much by way of privacy, but it's so lovely that you won't mind sharing.

White-Water Rafting

6 The dedicated adrenaline junkie could easily cover some heart-pounding river miles in the span of a few days in this compact country. For those not burning to do them all, pick a river, any river: Pacuare (p128; pictured below), Reventazón, Sarapiquí, Tenorio. Any of them are fun runs, with rapids ranging from Class I to Class V, and all have smooth stretches that allow rafters to take in the luscious jungle scenery and animal life amid the glorious gorges. All you need is a lifejacket, a helmet and some *chutzpah*.

Southern Caribbean Coast

7 By day, lounge in a hammock, cruise by bike to snorkel off uncrowded beaches, hike to waterfall-fed pools and visit the remote indigenous territories of the Bribrí and Kéköldi. By night, dip into zesty Caribbean cooking and sway to reggaetón at open-air bars cooled by ocean breezes. The villages of Cahuita, Puerto Viejo de Talamanca (pictured right) and Manzanillo, all outposts of this unique mix of Afro-Caribbean, Tico and indigenous culture, are the perfect, laid-back home bases for such adventures on the Caribbean's southern coast (p161).

Wildlife-Watching

8 World-class parks, long-standing dedication to environmental protection and mind-boggling biodiversity enable Costa Rica to harbor scores of rare and endangered species. Simply put, it's one of the best wildlife-watching destinations on the globe. Visitors hardly have to make an effort; no matter where you travel, the branches overhead are alive with critters, from lazy sloths and mischievous monkeys to a brilliant spectrum of tropical birds. And in case there's some animal you happen to miss, the country is replete with rescue centers, such as the Jaguar Centro de Rescate (p181). Left: Three-toed sloth

Montezuma

9 If you dig artsy-rootsy beach culture, enjoy rubbing shoulders with neo-Rastas and yoga fiends, or have always wanted to spin fire, study Spanish or lounge on sugar-white coves, find your way to Montezuma (p335). Strolling this intoxicating town and rugged coastline, you're never far from the rhythm of the sea. From here you'll also have easy access to the famed Cabo Blanco and Curú reserves, and can take the tremendous hike to a triple-tiered waterfall. Oh, and when your stomach growls, the town has some of the best restaurants in the country.

Bosque Nuboso Monteverde

10 Turning their backs on the Korean War in the 1950s, the Quakers came, saw, and protected this 105-sq-km cloud-forest paradise straddling the continental divide. They're still here, teaching and living modestly, while Monteverde Cloud Forest (p210) and its three neighboring preserves provide a misty escape into a mysterious Neverland shrouded in mist, draped with mossy vines, sprouting with ferns and bromeliads, gushing with creeks, blooming with life and nurturing rivulets of evolution. Neighboring Santa Elena Reserve provides an even mellower respite.

Sarapiquí Valley

11 Sarapiquí (p276) rose to fame as a principal port in the nefarious old days of United Fruit dominance. It later sank into agricultural anonymity, only to be reborn as a paddlers' mecca thanks to the frothing, serpentine mocha magic of its namesake river. These days it's still a rafters' paradise, dotted with fantastic ecolodges and private forest preserves that will educate you about pre-Columbian indigenous life, get you into that steaming, looming, muddy jungle, and bring you up close to local wildlife. Top: Poison-dart frog

Surfing

12 Point break, beach break, reef break, left, right: even if these terms mean nothing to you, no worries. Costa Rica's patient instructors and forgiving beaches (p318) welcome the beginner, but for the experienced there are challenges aplenty: untamed Pacific outposts named for sorcerers (Witch's Rock) and *yanqui* military adventurers alike (Ollie's Point). The bath-like waters mean no wetsuits required, and rental shops and requisite gear are easy to come by. Hey, they didn't film *Endless Summer II* here for nothing, dude.

CHRISTER FREDRIKSSON/GETTY IMAGES ©

JOHN (PAN GRESSO)/LONELY PLANET ©

Quetzal Spotting

13 Considered divine by pre-Columbian cultures of Central America, the beautiful quetzal was sought after for its long, iridescent-green tail feathers, which adorned the headdresses of royalty (it's Guatemala's national bird and the name of its paper currency). This unusual, jewel-toned bird remains coveted in modern times – but now as a bucket-list sighting for birdwatchers. Fortunately, though the quetzal's conservation status is listed as near threatened, it's commonly sighted in San Gerardo de Dota (p409) and at lodges like Mirador de Quetzales, especially during its breeding season in April and May.

Nosara

14 Nosara (p313) is a heady mix of surf culture, jungled microclimates and yoga bliss, where three stunning beaches are stitched together by a network of swerving, rutted roads that meander over coastal hills (after years of promises, the road from the central peninsula is finally being paved). Visitors can stay in the alluring surf enclave of Playa Guiones – where there are some fabulous restaurants and a drop-dead-gorgeous beach – or in romantic, rugged and removed Playa Pelada. Thousands of nesting sea turtles invade nearby beaches, which you can visit by appointment.

Ziplining in the Rainforest Canopy

15 Canopy tours are one place you literally have to let yourself go. Steady those knees and do it! Few things are more purely joyful than clipping into a high-speed, high-altitude cable and zooming through the teeming jungle. This is where kids become little daredevils and adults become kids. Invented in Monteverde in the 1990s, zipline outfits quickly began cropping up in all corners of Costa Rica. The best place to sample the lines is still Monteverde (p191), where the forest is alive, the mist fine and swirling, and the afterglow worth savoring.

Poás Region

16 An hour northwest of the capital, Poás (p109) is a fairy-tale land of verdant mountains and hydrangea-lined roadsides. Although 2017 activity has closed the volcano itself, it's still a spectacular, sulfurous behemoth, well worth a look – even from a distance – particularly on cloudless mornings. The winding approach drive takes you past strawberry farms and coffee plantations. And over at La Paz Waterfall Gardens, visitors hike to storybook waterfalls and encounter rescued monkeys, tropical birds and wild cats, including three jaguars.

MATTEO COLOMBO/GETTY IMAGES ©

Playa Sámara

17 Some expat residents call Playa Sámara (p321) the black hole of happiness, which has something to do with that crescent of sand spanning two rocky headlands, the opportunity to surf, stand-up paddle board, surf cast or fly above migrating whales in an ultra-light plane, and the plethora of nearby all-natural beaches and coves. All of it is easy to access on foot or via public transportation, which is why it's becoming so popular with families, who enjoy Sámara's manifest ease and tranquility.

San José

18 The heart of Tico culture lives in San José (p60), as do university students, intellectuals, artists and politicians. While it's not the most attractive capital in Central America, it has some graceful neo-classical and Spanish-colonial architecture, leafy neighborhoods, museums housing pre-Columbian jade and gold, nightlife that goes until dawn, and sophisticated restaurants. Street art – both officially sanctioned and guerrilla – adds unexpected pops of color and public discourse to the cityscape. For the seasoned traveler, Chepe, as it's affectionately known, has its charms.

17

18

Paddling in the Golfo Dulce

19 Getting out into the Golfo Dulce (p449) brings kayakers and stand-up paddlers into contact with the bay's abundant marine life – orcas and humpback whales calve in the warm waters, and spotted and bottlenose dolphins breach the surface. Comprising 17 protected reserves and 3% of Costa Rica's landmass, the tropical biome is home to half the country's flora and fauna, and four species of sea turtle visit the area. The gulf's maze of mangrove channels is another world completely, offering a chance to glide past herons, crested caracaras, snakes and sloths.

Cerro Chirripó

20 The view of wind-swept rocks and icy lakes from the rugged peak of Cerro Chirripó (p416), the country's highest summit, may not resemble the Costa Rica of the postcards, but the two-day hike above the clouds is one of the most satisfying excursions in the country. A pre-dawn expedition rewards hardy hikers with the real prize: a chance to catch the fiery sunrise and see both the Caribbean Sea and the Pacific Ocean in a full and glorious panorama from 3820m up.

Coffee Plantations of the Central Valley

21 Take a country drive on the scenic, curvy back roads of the Central Valley, where the hillsides are a patchwork of agriculture and coffee shrubbery. If you're curious about the magical brew that for many makes life worth living, tour one of the coffee plantations and learn how Costa Rica's golden bean goes from plant to cup. A couple of the best places for a tour are Finca Cristina (p124) in the Orosi Valley and Café Britt Finca near Barva, although a couple of convenient caffeinated circuits have sprung up near La Fortuna.

Need to Know

For more information, see Survival Guide (p503)

Currency
Costa Rican colón (₡)
US dollar ($)

Language
Spanish, English

Visas
Most nationalities do
not need a visa for stays
of up to 90 days. Check
the visa requirements
for your country at www.
costarica-embassy.org.

Money
US dollars accepted
almost everywhere and
dispensed from most
ATMs; carry colones
for small towns, bus
fares and rural shops.
Credit cards generally
accepted.

Cell Phones
3G and 4G systems
are available, but those
compatible with US
plans require expensive
international roaming.
Prepaid SIM cards
are cheap and widely
available.

Time
Central Standard Time
(GMT/UTC minus six
hours)

When to Go

Tamarindo
GO Nov–Apr

San José
GO Dec–Apr

Puerto Limón
GO Jan–Apr

**Parque Nacional
Manuel Antonio**
GO Dec–Feb

Puerto Jiménez
GO Feb, Mar, Sep & Oct

▮ Tropical climate, rain year-round
▮ Tropical climate, wet and dry seasons

High Season
(Dec–Apr)

➡ 'Dry' season still
sees some rain;
beach towns fill with
domestic tourists.

➡ Accommodations
should be booked
well ahead; some
places enforce
minimum stays.

Shoulder
(May–Jul & Nov)

➡ Rain picks up
and the stream of
tourists starts to
taper off.

➡ There may still be
crowds; students in
Europe and North
America on holiday.

➡ Roads are muddy
and rivers begin to
rise, making off-the-
beaten-track travel
more challenging.

Low Season
(Aug–Oct)

➡ Rainfall is highest,
but storms bring
swells and the best
surfing conditions.

➡ Rural roads can
be impassable due to
river crossings.

➡ Accommodations
prices lower
significantly.

➡ Some places
close entirely; check
before booking!

Useful Websites

Anywhere Costa Rica (www.anywhere.com/costa-rica) Excellent destination overviews.

Essential Costa Rica (www.visitcostarica.com) The Costa Rica Tourism Board website has planning and destination details.

Yo Viajo (www.yoviajocr.com) Enter two destinations anywhere in the country and view the bus schedule and fare.

Guanacaste Costa Rica (www.caturgua.com)The bilingual magazine of the region's tourism board has cultural articles, recipes, helpful maps.

The Tico Times (www.ticotimes.net) Costa Rica's English-language newspaper.

Lonely Planet (www.lonelyplanet.com/costa-rica) Destination information, hotel bookings, traveler forum and more.

Important Numbers

Costa Rica country code	506
International access code	011
International operator	00
Emergency	911

Exchange Rates

Australia	A$1	₡453
Canada	C$1	₡453
Euro zone	€1	₡674
Japan	¥100	₡525
New Zealand	NZ$1	₡419
UK	£1	₡740
USA	US$1	₡575

For current exchange rates, see www.xe.com.

Daily Costs

Budget: Less than US$40

➡ Dorm bed: US$8–15

➡ Meal at a *soda* (inexpensive eatery): US$3–7

➡ DIY hikes without a guide: free

➡ Travel via local bus: US$2 or less

Midrange: US$40–100

➡ Basic room with private bathroom: US$20–50 per day

➡ Meal at a restaurant geared toward travelers: US$5–12

➡ Travel on an efficient 1st-class shuttle van like Interbus: US$50–60

Top End: More than US$100

➡ Luxurious beachside lodges and boutique hotels: from US$80

➡ Meal at an international fusion restaurant: from US$20

➡ Guided wildlife-watching excursion: from US$40

➡ Short domestic flight: US$50–100

➡ 4WD rental for local travel: from US$60 per day

Arriving in Costa Rica

Aeropuerto Internacional Juan Santamaría (San José) Buses (about US$1.50) from the airport to central San José run hourly all day. Taxis charge from US$30 and depart from the official stand; the trip takes 20 minutes to an hour. Interbus runs between the airport and San José accommodations (US$17 per adult, children under 2 free if sharing a seat). Many rental-car agencies have desks at the airport, but it's advisable to book ahead.

Aeropuerto Internacional Daniel Oduber Quirós (Liberia) Buses run to the Mercado Municipal (around US$1, 30 minutes, hourly) between 5am and 9pm Monday to Saturday, less frequently on Sunday. Taxis between the airport and Liberia are about US$20. There are no car-rental desks; make reservations in advance and your company will meet you at the airport with a car.

Getting Around

Air Inexpensive domestic flights between San José and popular destinations such as Puerto Jiménez, Quepos and Tortuguero will save you the driving time.

Bus Very reasonably priced, with extensive coverage of the country, though travel can be slow and some destinations have infrequent service.

Shuttle Private and shared shuttles such as Interbus and Gray Line provide door-to-door service between popular destinations and allow you to schedule to your needs.

Car Renting a car allows you to access more remote destinations that are not served by buses, and frees you to cover as much ground as you like. Cars can be rented in most towns. Renting a 4WD vehicle is advantageous (and essential in some parts of the country); avoid driving at night.

PLAN YOUR TRIP NEED TO KNOW

For much more on **getting around**, see p519

First Time Costa Rica

For more information, see Survival Guide (p503)

Checklist

➡ Check the validity of your passport, the visa situation and government travel advisories

➡ Organize travel insurance

➡ Check flight restrictions on luggage and camping or outdoors equipment

➡ Check your immunization history

➡ Contact car-insurance provider about foreign coverage

➡ If you plan to rent a car, bring driver's license and a copy of your insurance policy

What to Pack

➡ Bathing suit

➡ Camera

➡ Flip-flops, hat, hiking boots

➡ Sunglasses

➡ Sunscreen – it's expensive in Costa Rica

➡ Refillable water bottle

➡ Bug repellent with DEET

➡ Phone charger

➡ Waterproof case for passport

➡ Flashlight or headlamp

➡ Poncho

➡ Binoculars

➡ First-aid kit

➡ Small day pack

Top Tips for Your Trip

➡ In Costa Rica, things have a way of taking longer than expected. Make space for leisurely meals, don't overschedule, learn to relax into delays and take these opportunities to get to know the locals.

➡ Avoid driving at night – pedestrians, animals and huge potholes are difficult to see on Costa Rica's largely unlit roads. Also keep an eye out for impatient drivers passing on two-lane roads.

➡ Take public transit. There's no better way to get to know the country or its people.

➡ If you need directions, ask a few different people.

➡ It's often cash only in remote areas. Keep a stash of colones or dollars, because ATMs do run out.

What to Wear

Although the coastal areas are sunny, hot and humid, calling for a hat, shorts and short sleeves, you'll want to pack a sweater and lightweight jacket for popular high-elevation destinations such as Volcán Irazú and Monteverde. If you plan to hike up Chirripó, bring lots of layers and a hat and gloves. Additionally, while hiking through the rainforest is often a hot and sweaty exercise, long sleeves and lightweight, quick-drying pants help keep the bugs away. A lightweight rain poncho comes in handy in quite a few places.

Sleeping

Book ahead if you're visiting during high season, especially during the Christmas, New Year and Easter (Semana Santa) holidays. Prices skyrocket during those weeks, too.

Hotels These range from small, family-run affairs to boutique and larger establishments.

B&Bs There's a variety of B&Bs throughout the country, reflecting the diversity of the landscape as well as the proprietors.

Hostels You'll find a great bunch of hostels in the more popular locales. 'Resort' hostels are almost hotel level in terms of quality and amenities.

Apartments and villas All levels of short-term rental apartments, villas and, increasingly, entire homes are available.

Money

US dollars accepted almost everywhere and dispensed from most ATMs; carry colones for small towns, bus fares and rural shops. Credit cards are generally accepted.

For more information, see p510.

Bargaining

➡ A high standard of living along with a stream of international tourist traffic means that the Latin American tradition of haggling is uncommon in Costa Rica.

➡ Negotiating prices at outdoor markets is acceptable, as is bargaining when arranging informal tours or hiring long-distance taxis.

Tipping

Restaurants Your bill will usually include a 10% service charge. If not, you might leave a small tip.

Hotels Tip the bellhop/porter US$1 to US$5 per service and the housekeeper US$1 to US$2 per day in top-end hotels, less in budget places.

Taxis Tip only if some special service is provided.

Guides Tip US$5 to US$15 per person per day. Tip the tour driver about half of what you tip the guide.

Language

Spanish is the national language of Costa Rica, and knowing some very basic phrases is not only courteous but also essential, particularly when navigating through rural areas. That said, a long history of North American tourists has made English the country's unofficial second language. With the exception of basic *sodas* (inexpensive eateries), local buses, and shops catering exclusively to locals, travelers can expect bilingual menus, signs and brochures.

Etiquette

While Ticos are very laid-back as a people, they are also very conscientious about being *bien educado* (polite). A greeting when you make eye contact with someone, or more generally maintaining a respectful demeanor and a smile, will go a long way.

Asking for help Say *disculpe* (literally translated as 'sorry') to get someone's attention, *perdón* (also literally translated as 'sorry') to apologise.

Visiting indigenous communities Ask permission to take photos, particularly of children, and dress more modestly than you would at the beach.

Surfing Novices should learn the etiquette of the lineup, not drop in on other surfers, and be aware of swimmers in their path.

Hitchhiking Picking up hitchhikers in rural areas is common. If you get a ride from a local, offer a small contribution towards the cost of the fuel.

Topless sunbathing It isn't customary for women to sunbathe topless in public.

What's New

Uber & out

Though Uber was introduced here in 2015, due to taxi-syndicate pressures (including nationwide strikes), Uber drivers are still fined and have even had their cars seized by police.

New Alajuela restaurant zone

El Patio is a cluster of chic restaurants, including the excellent Valedi Food. (p108)

Container Platz

About a dozen mini-businesses have sprung to life in brightly painted shipping containers in Santa Ana. The effort earns high marks for innovation and reasonably priced, artisanal fast food. (p88)

Rooftop bar at El Presidente

A new rooftop cocktail bar is the talk of San José, with incredible city views and an exquisite, open-air garden. (p75)

Selina hostels

A new empire of backpacker hostels has opened across many destinations, including San José, Jacó, Manuel Antonio, Puerto Viejo de Talamanca, Santa Teresa, Tamarindo and La Fortuna. (www.selina.com)

Fuego

This new craft brewery is the first to open in Dominical, and it serves a really fantastic guanabana-infused Hefeweizen. (p396)

Jacó Walk

Jacó's gone classy with this dainty new square, to which most of the towns' best restaurants have recently relocated. It's adorned in multicolored bricks, potted plants and pretty lights, and all the restaurants offer outdoor seating. (p361)

Batsù garden

A garden designed specifically for bird-watching and photography, Batsù is a new attraction in San Gerardo de Dota (a place where not much changes). There are a great many hummingbirds, parakeets, flycatchers, tanagers and more, along with some wonderfully natural backdrops. (p409)

Airborne arts

It's now possible to learn trapeze in the middle of the Costa Rican countryside, with a view of a 100m waterfall, with world-renowned acrobat couple Jonathon Conant and Christine Van Loo. They've constructed a circus-themed paradise near the remote town of Las Tumbas, a bit north of Dominical. (p391)

Improvements to the Interamericana & Ruta 4

Between Cañas and Liberia, the Interamericana is now four lanes. A final 27km connection between San Carlos and Chilamate – the Vuelta Kooper, which cuts north–south driving distances by 60km – opened in August 2017. One day after it opened, it (briefly) flooded.

Changes at Cerro Chato

Popular volcano hike Cerro Chato has been closed to the public due to a combination of safety concerns and political wrangling. You can still get near there on a hike, but not summit. Sigh.

For more recommendations and reviews, see lonelyplanet.com/costa-rica

If You Like...

Beaches

Playa Manuel Antonio With mischievous monkeys, perfect sand and turquoise water, this beach is worth the park fee. (p385)

Playa Grande This seemingly endless beach is good for strolling and frequented by leatherback turtles and surfers. (p298)

Playa Guiones Backed by lush vegetation, these gentle waves are ideal for swimming, surfing or just frolicking. (p313)

Playa Negra Cahuita's wild black-sand beach doesn't draw many surfers, making it great for swimming. (p162)

Parque Nacional Marino Ballena The long, rugged, coconut-strewn beaches of Ballena feel like an isolated desert island. (p401)

Playa Rajada Rajada's white-sand beaches and languid, Jacuzzi-esque waves embrace you at the southern end of Bahía Salinas. (p236)

White-Water Rafting & Kayaking

Río Pacuare Take on runs of Class II to IV rapids on the country's best white water. (p128)

Río Sarapiquí This less-frequented river is a great place to raft or learn how to kayak. (p277)

Golfo Dulce Lucky kayakers can paddle out with dolphins and explore sea caves. (p449)

Canales de Tortuguero Excellent for kayaking through canals to get close to birds and wildlife. (p149)

Río Savegre Gentle rapids that pick up in the rainy season; trips depart from Quepos. (p371)

MATTHEW MICAH WRIGHT/GETTY IMAGES ©

Playa Negra, Puerto Viejo de Talamanca (p170)

Surfing

Salsa Brava This Caribbean break has the country's biggest surf – in December waves get up to 7m. (p170)

Pavones One of the longest left-hand breaks on Earth draws the goofy-footed from near and far. (p455)

Dominical Countless foreigners show up here to surf – and can't bring themselves to leave. (p389)

Playa Guiones The best beach break in the Central Peninsula, especially when there's an off-shore wind. (p313)

Playa Grande Costa Rica's most reliable break draws hordes – luckily, it's so big it never seems crowded. (p298)

Playa Hermosa Several beautiful beach breaks for pros, a stone's throw from Jacó's beginner breaks. (p368)

Playa Sámara One of the best places to learn, with mellow instructors and gentler waves. (p321)

Wildlife-Watching

Rancho Naturalista More than 250 species of bird have been seen from the balcony of this avian-crazy lodge. (p133)

Wilson Botanical Garden This private reserve attracts many specialty birds of southern Costa Rica, including rare high-altitude species. (p423)

Península de Osa Although they're rare in the country, scarlet macaws frequent the skies around Parque Nacional Corcovado. (p405)

Parque Nacional Los Quetzales Named for its banner attraction, the flamboyantly colored ceremonial bird of the Maya. (p411)

Top: Collared aracari, Sarapiquí Valley (p276)

Bottom: Manta ray, Reserva Biológica Isla del Caño (p429)

Monteverde & Santa Elena
Keep your eyes peeled for keel-billed toucans, three-wattled bellbirds and motmots. (p191)

Parque Nacional Tortuguero
Herons, kites, ospreys, kingfishers, macaws: the bird list is a mile long at this wildlife-rich park. (p149)

Caño Negro The steamy Nicaraguan borderlands host waterfowl like nesting anhingas, purple gallinules and Amazon kingfishers. (p267)

Boca Tapada If you're lucky, both scarlet and great green macaws – symbol of conservationists' success – can be seen here. (p275)

Hiking

Parque Nacional Chirripó Up and up: the trail to the top of Costa Rica is a thrilling (chilly) adventure. (p416)

Parque Nacional Corcovado
These challenging trails provide a supreme look at the wonders of the rainforest. (p434)

Monteverde Cloud Forest
Utterly fantastic for day hikes, with walks through cloud-forest gorges among plant and animal life. (p210)

Parque Nacional Volcán Tenorio The trails circumnavigate volcanoes and misty waterfalls, with frequent blue-morpho-butterfly sightings. (p216)

Volcán Barva A little tough to get to, but what a reward: crater lakes and quiet cloud forest. (p140)

Diamante Falls Sleep behind waterfalls in a cave outside of Dominical. (p389)

Luxury Spas & Resorts

El Silencio Hanging at the edge of a canyon, this is a slice of Zen in the cloud forest. (p114)

La Paloma Lodge A posh delight in Costa Rica's wildest corner, this jungle lodge is far off the grid. (p430)

Hotel Villa Caletas Guests enjoy seclusion, personalized service and breathtaking sunsets atop a Pacific cliff just north of Playa Herradura. (p359)

Peace Lodge Surrounded by trails near the Volcán Poás, this storybook resort and rescue center enchants. (p109)

Eco Termales These exclusive, sand-bottomed, varying-temperature baths of Fortuna swallow you up after a rough day's hiking or biking. (p243)

Ecolodges

Casa Corcovado Jungle Lodge
Osa's first top-certified ecolodge is removed from civilization, near the wilds of Corcovado. (p434)

Villa Blanca Cloud Forest Hotel & Nature Reserve With the highest sustainability rating, Villa Blanca offers plush ecological digs. (p115)

Pacuare Lodge This posh, riverfront lodge transcends the need for electricity with high style and adventure. (p142)

Arenas del Mar The best ecolodge near Manuel Antonio, this architectural stunner has private Jacuzzis overlooking the coast. (p379)

Ecolodge San Luis One of the highest-rated ecolodges of the region, with Monteverde just outside the door. (p202)

Maquenque This sustainability-minded gem in the riverine lowland, borderland paradise is a birding hot spot. (p276)

Diving & Snorkeling

Isla del Coco The only world-class dive spot in Costa Rica, in a hammerhead-filled sea. (p458)

Isla del Caño Reliable visibility, sea turtles, barracudas and, if you're lucky, humpback whales. (p429)

Isla Murciélago Manta rays, bull sharks and even humpback whales migrate through these waters. (p230)

Playa Manzanillo In September and October this Caribbean beach has the best snorkeling in the country. (p329)

Fishing

Golfo Dulce Boats from little Puerto Jiménez and Golfito often return with fish that challenge world records. (p449)

Caño Negro Abundant tarpon, snook and gar, and no-frills fishing ventures make this a low-key Northern Lowlands option. (p267)

Quepos Plenty of captains lead fishing ventures into the waters off Quepos, which offer a shot at marlin and sailfish. (p371)

San Gerardo de Dota Excellent trout-fishing in the clear upper regions of the Río Savegre. (p409)

Playa Grande Epic surf casting brings in big fish from rocks that get thrashed with waves. (p298)

Laguna de Arenal Troll in the shadow of the big volcano at this lake full of rainbow bass and machacas. (p260)

Month by Month

January

Every year opens with a rush, as North American and domestic tourists flood beach towns to celebrate. January sees dry days and occasional afternoon showers.

✪ Fiesta de la Santa Cruz

Held in Santa Cruz in the second week of January, this festival centers on a rodeo and bullfights. It also includes a religious procession, music, dances and a beauty pageant.

☆ Jungle Jam

Calling all Deadheads: the biggest musical event to hit Jacó stretches over several days and venues outside of the main event, set in the jungle just outside town. Held in mid-January. (p363)

✪ Las Fiestas de Palmares

Ten days of boozing, horse shows and other carnival events take over the tiny town of Palmares in the second half of the month. There's also a running of the bulls – um, opt out.

February

February has ideal weather and no holiday surcharges. The skies above Nicoya are particularly clear, and it's peak season for some species of nesting turtle to do their thing.

☆ Envision Festival

Held in Uvita in late February, this is a festival with a consciousness-raising, transformational bent, bringing together fire dancers and performance artists, yoga, music and spiritual workshops. Also takes place during the first week of March in Dominical. (p398)

✪ Fiesta de los Diablitos

Replete with colorful masks, this festival re-enacts an epic battle between Spaniards (the *toro*, or bull) and indigenous Boru people (the *diablitos*, or 'little devils'). See p32 for dates.

✪ Fiesta Cívica de Liberia

A beauty pageant and a carnival atmosphere complete with horseback riding and traditional food enliven Liberia at the end of February.

March

Excellent weather continues through the early part of March, though prices shoot up during Semana Santa, the week leading up to Easter and North American spring break.

✪ Día del Boyero

A colorful parade, held in Escazú on the second Sunday in March, features painted *carretas* (oxcarts, the national symbol) and includes a blessing of the animals. Plaid shirt and cowboy hat optional. (p71)

✪ Feria de la Mascarada

During Feria de la Mascarada, begun in 2002, people don massive colorful masks (weighing up to 20kg) to dance and parade around the town square of Barva. Usually held during the last week of March. (p119)

April

Easter and Semana Santa can fall early in April, which means beaches fill and prices spike. Nicoya and Guanacaste are dry and hot, with little rain.

🎎 Día de Juan Santamaría

Commemorating Costa Rica's national hero (the main airport is named for him), who died in battle against American colonist William Walker's troops in 1856, this day of celebration on April 11 includes parades, concerts and dances.

May

Attention, budget travelers: wetter weather begins to sweep across the country in May, heralding the country's low season. So, although conditions are pleasant, prices drop.

🎎 Día de San Isidro Labrador

Visitors can taste the bounty of San Isidro and nearby villages during the nation's largest agricultural fairs, in honor of the growers' patron saint, on May 15. Don't miss the chance to see soccer-playing priests.

June

The Pacific Coast gets fairly wet during June, though this makes for good surfing. This time of year has lots of discounted rates.

🎎 Día de San Pedro & San Pablo

Celebrations with religious processions are held in villages of the same name on June 29. They honor the martyrdom of Catholic saints Peter and Paul.

☆ Festival de las Artes (FIA)

This multidisciplinary, multiday festival featuring international artists takes flight all across San José and has recently been moved to June to July. (p71)

July

Mostly wet, especially on the Caribbean coast, but July also occasionally enjoys a brief dry period that Ticos call *veranillo* (summer). Expect rain, particularly late in the day.

🎎 Día de Guanacaste

Celebrates the 1824 annexation of Guanacaste from Nicaragua. There are rodeos, bullfights, cattle shows and general bovine madness. Held on July 25.

🎎 Fiesta de La Virgen del Mar

Held in Puntarenas and Playa del Coco on the Saturday closest to July 16, the Festival of the Virgin of the Sea involves colorful, brightly lit regattas and boat parades.

August

The middle of the rainy season doesn't mean that mornings aren't bright and sunny. Travelers who don't mind some rain will find great hotel and tour deals.

🎎 La Virgen de los Ángeles

The patron saint of Costa Rica, the Black Virgin or Black Madonna, is celebrated with an important procession from San José to Cartago on August 2.

September

The Península de Osa gets utterly soaked during September, which is the heart of the rainy season and what Ticos refer to as the *temporales del Pacífico*. It's the cheapest time to visit the Pacific.

🎎 Costa Rican Independence Day

The center of the Independence Day action is the relay race that passes a 'Freedom Torch' from Guatemala to Costa Rica. The torch arrives at Cartago on the evening of the 14th, when the nation breaks into the national anthem.

October

Many roads become impassable as rivers swell and rain falls in one of the wettest months in Costa Rica. Lodges and tour operators are sometimes closed until November.

🎎 Día de la Raza

Columbus' historic landing on Isla Uvita has traditionally inspired a small carnival in Puerto Limón on October 12, with street parades, music and dancing.

November

The weather can go either way. Access to Parque

Nacional Corcovado is difficult after several months of rain, though the skies clear by month's end.

✰✰ Día de los Muertos

Families visit graveyards and have religious parades in honor of the dead on November 2.

December

The beginning of the month is a great time to visit but things ramp up toward Christmas and reservations become crucial.

✰✰ Festival de la Luz (Festival of Light)

San José comes to life as it marks the beginning of the Christmas season on the second Saturday of the month, with marching bands, floats, and colorful light displays and artworks throughout downtown (www.festivaldelaluz.cr).

✰✰ Fiesta de los Diablitos

Men booze up and don wooden devil masks and burlap sacks, then re-enact the fight between the indigenous and the Spanish. (In this rendition, Spain loses.) Held in Boruca from December 30 to January 2 and in Rey Curré from February 5 to February 8. (p420)

✰✰ Las Fiestas de Zapote

In San José between Christmas and New Year's Eve, this weeklong celebration of all things Costa Rican (rodeos, cowboys, carnival rides, fried food and booze) draws tens of thousands to the bullring in the suburb of Zapote every day. (p71)

Top: Dancers, Costa Rican Independence Day (p31)

Bottom: Masked revellers, Fiesta de los Diablitos

Itineraries

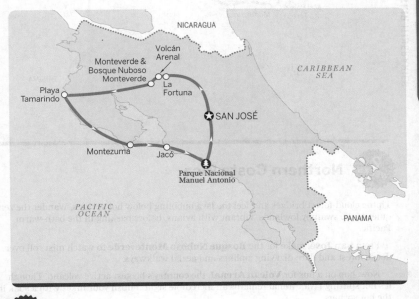

Essential Costa Rica

2 WEEKS

This is the trip you've been dreaming about: a romp through paradise with seething volcanoes, tropical parks, warm-water beaches and ghostly cloud forests.

From **San José**, beeline north to **La Fortuna**. After a refreshing forest hike on the flanks of **Volcán Arenal**, soak in the country's best hot springs. Then do the classic jeep-boat-jeep run across Lake Arenal to **Monteverde**, where you might encounter the elusive quetzal on a stroll through the **Bosque Nuboso Monteverde**.

Next: beach time. Head west to the biggest party town in Guanacaste, **Playa Tamarindo** (or head to Mal País/Santa Teresa) and enjoy the ideal surf, top-notch restaurants and rowdy nightlife.

Continuing south, visit waterfalls and linger a bit in chilled-out **Montezuma**, where you can connect via speedboat to **Jacó**, another town with equal affection for surfing and partying. Spend half a day busing to Quepos, the gateway to **Parque Nacional Manuel Antonio**. A full day in the park starts with some jungle hikes and wildlife-watching and ends with a picnic and a dip in the park's perfect waters.

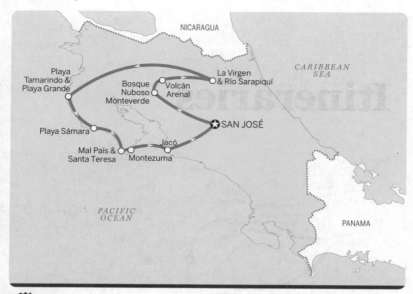

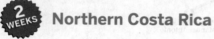

2 WEEKS **Northern Costa Rica**

Tiptoe cloud-forest bridges and feel the lava bubbling below hot springs. Wander the zen quiet of the swampy lowlands, vibrant with avians, before basking in the bath-warm Pacific.

From **San José**, make for the **Bosque Nuboso Monteverde** to watch mist roll over dense forest and dare dizzying ziplines and aerial walkways.

Now, hop on a bus for **Volcán Arenal**, the country's biggest active volcano. Though it's not spitting lava, Arenal remains an incredible sight. Finish your hikes with a soak in the hot springs.

Leave the tourists behind at the lowland ecolodges of Caño Negro or Boca Tapada. After a couple of days connecting with easygoing Ticos, make for **La Virgen** to raft the white water of **Río Sarapiquí**.

Beach time! First stop: **Playa Tamarindo**, to party, sample some of the country's best cuisine and learn to surf. During turtle season, **Playa Grande** hosts hordes of nesting leatherbacks.

Take a bus south to enjoy the sand and contemporary cuisine at **Playa Sámara** or swells at **Mal País** and **Santa Teresa**. Wind down with yoga in Nosara or **Montezuma** and head back by boat and bus to San José via **Jacó**, where you can enjoy some last rays of sunshine and a decadent meal.

2 WEEKS Pacific Coast Explorer

Here jungle touches ocean and fresh fish practically leap onto your plate.

Kick things off with **Parque Nacional Carara**, and spend a few hours hiking up and down the coast. Then head south to **Quepos**, a convenient base for the country's most popular national park, **Parque Nacional Manuel Antonio**. Here the rainforest sweeps down to meet the sea, providing a refuge for rare animals, including the endangered squirrel monkey.

Continue south, stopping at roadside *ceviche* stands, and visit **Hacienda Barú National Wildlife Refuge** for some sloth-spotting, or keep heading south to **Dominical** in search of waves. For deserted beaches, continue on to **Uvita**, where you can look for whales spouting offshore at **Parque Nacional Marino Ballena**.

From Uvita, move south to the far-flung **Península de Osa**, where you'll journey through the country's top national park for wildlife-viewing. Emerge at the northern end in lush, remote **Bahía Drake**, where you'll swim in paradisiacal coves. Return to civilization via ferry through Central America's longest stretch of mangroves to **Sierpe**, home to ancient stone spheres.

2 WEEKS Southern Costa Rica

Hands down the best itinerary for adventurers, this is the wilder side of Costa Rica.

Either head down the Pacific coast or fly into **Puerto Jiménez**, gateway to Península de Osa. Here you can spend a day or so kayaking the mangroves and soaking up the charm.

The undisputed highlight of the Osa is **Parque Nacional Corcovado**, the crown jewel of the country's national parks. Spend a few days exploring jungle and beach trails with a local guide, whose expert eyes will spot tapirs and rare birds; trekkers willing to get down and dirty can tackle a through-hike of the park.

Return to Puerto Jiménez and travel up the Pacific Costanera Sur to **Uvita**, where you can surf, snorkel and look for whales at **Parque Nacional Marino Ballena**.

Then it's off to the mountains. Link together buses for **San Gerardo de Rivas**, where you can spend a day acclimating to the altitude and hiking through the **Cloudbridge Nature Reserve**. End the trip with an exhilarating two-day adventure to the top of **Cerro Chirripó**, Costa Rica's highest peak.

10 DAYS Caribbean Coast

Latin beats change to Caribbean rhythms as you explore the 'other Costa Rica.'

Hop an eastbound bus out of **San José** for Cahuita, capital of Afro-Caribbean culture and gateway to **Parque Nacional Cahuita**. Decompress in this mellow village before moving on to **Puerto Viejo de Talamanca**, the Caribbean's center for nightlife, cuisine and all-round good vibes.

From Puerto Viejo, rent a bicycle and ride to Manzanillo, jumping-off point for snorkeling, kayaking and hiking in **Refugio Nacional de Vida Silvestre Gandoca-Manzanillo**.

To fall further off the map, grab a boat from **Moín** to travel up the canal-ribboned coast to **Tortuguero**, where you can watch nesting green and leatherback turtles. But the real reason you're here is to canoe the mangrove-lined canals of **Parque Nacional Tortuguero**, Costa Rica's mini-Amazon.

After spotting your fill of wildlife, head back to San José via water taxi and bus through the tiny town of Cariari and then **Guápiles**, an ideal base for gazing at open farmland and exploring **Parque Nacional Braulio Carrillo**.

10 DAYS Central Valley

The Central Valley circuit – centering on volcanoes, waterfalls and strong cups of coffee – explores the spiritual core of the country, all sans the madding crowds.

Begin at **San Isidro de Heredia** for a close encounter with rescued baby sloths and toucans and a taste of the region's chocolate history. Hike around **Volcán Irazú**, at 3432m the largest and highest active volcano in Costa Rica, and peer right into its crater. With geological and culinary wonders covered, raft your way along the **Río Pacuare**, one of the country's best white-water runs and with some of Central America's most scenic rafting.

Move on to **Monumento Nacional Arqueológico Guayabo**, the country's only significant archaeological site, protecting ancient petroglyphs and aqueducts. Finally, swing south into the heart of the **Valle de Orosi**, Costa Rican coffee country, and take the caffeinated 32km loop passing the country's oldest church and endless green hills. End on a spiritual note at Costa Rica's grandest colonial-era temple, the Basílica de Nuestra Señora de Los Ángeles in **Cartago**.

Top: Volcán Arenal (p254)

Bottom: Bahía Drake (p427)

CAMPPHOTO/GETTY IMAGES ©

Off the Beaten Track: Costa Rica

BOCA TAPADA AREA

Travel through a Tico heartland of pineapple plantations to discover the pristine rainforest of Refugio Nacional de Vida Silvestre Mixto Maquenque. (p275)

LA GAVILANA HERBS & ART

This bake shop and gallery offers two-day 'extreme hikes' between El Castillo and San Gerardo (near Santa Elena) that traverse old-growth forests and raging rivers. (p259)

PLAYA PALO SECO

A dirt road through palm plantations winds up at a 6km finger of isolated black-sand beach, and nearby mangroves to explore by boat. (p371)

MATAPALO

Not far off the Costanera Sur, but surprisingly lightly trodden, Matapalo doesn't have much more than kilometers of gray-sand beach and wild waves for the more experienced surfing set. (p388)

Map labels:
NICARAGUA
Lago de Nicaragua
La Cruz
San Carlos
Los Chiles
Upala
Parque Nacional Santa Rosa
Golfo de Papagayo
Liberia
Laguna de Arenal
Bagaces
El Coco
Cañas
Tilarán
LA GAVILINA HERBS & ART
Ciudad Quesada (San Carlos)
Tamarindo
Paraíso
Nicoya
Puntarenas
Paquera
Golfo de Nicoya
Parque Nacional Carara
Mal País
Montezuma
Jacó
PLAYA PALO SECO
PACIFIC OCEAN

PARISMINA

This far-flung spit of sand between canal and Caribbean Sea has only the barest bones of tourist-oriented infrastructure and not a lot of action besides turtle conservation and kayaking the local canals. (p148)

SELVA BANANITO

One of the country's most secluded and delightful ecolodges offers wildlife encounters, delicious meals and comfy cabins made from recycled hardwood atop Caribbean-style stilts. (p162)

PARQUE INTERNACIONAL LA AMISTAD

The country's deepest, most impenetrable wilderness lies in this vast park that spans both Costa Rica and Panama. Encompassing numerous life zones, the forest's diversity is truly awesome. (p424)

LUNA LODGE

Up a winding road into the mountains, this remote ecolodge borders Parque Nacional Corcovado and is run by an infectiously passionate conservationist. (p439)

La Fortuna (p242)

Plan Your Trip

Activities

Miles of shoreline, endless warm water and an array of national parks and reserves provide an inviting playground for active travelers. Whether it's the solitude of absolute wilderness, family-oriented hiking and rafting adventures, or surfing and jungle trekking you seek, Costa Rica offers fun to suit everyone.

Best Outdoors

Best Beginner Surf Beaches

Playa Tamarindo,

Playa Jacó

Playa Sámara

Best Epic Hikes

Cerro Chirripó

Corcovado through-hike

Best Dive Sites

Isla del Coco

Isla del Caño

Best Wildlife-Watching

Parque Nacional Corcovado

Best Rainforest for Families

Parque Nacional Manuel Antonio

Best White Water

Río Pacuare

Hiking & Trekking

Hiking opportunities around Costa Rica are seemingly endless. With extensive mountains, canyons, dense jungles, cloud forests and two coastlines, this is one of Central America's best and most varied hiking destinations.

Hikes come in an enormous spectrum of difficulty. At tourist-packed destinations such as Monteverde, trails are clearly marked and sometimes paved. This is fantastic if you're traveling with kids or aren't confident about route-finding. For long-distance trekking, there are many more options in the remote corners of the country.

Opportunities for moderate hiking are typically plentiful in most parks and reserves. For the most part, you can rely on signs and maps for orientation, though it helps to have some navigational experience (your phone compass might come in handy). Good hiking shoes, plenty of water and confidence in your abilities may enable you to combine several shorter day hikes into a lengthier expedition. Tourist information centers at park entrances are great resources for planning your intended route.

If you're properly equipped with camping essentials, the country's longer and more arduous multiday treks are at your disposal. Costa Rica's top challenges are scaling Cerro Chirripó, traversing Corcovado and penetrating deep into the heart of La Amistad. While Chirripó can be undertaken independently, local guides are required for much of La Amistad and for all of Corcovado.

Surfing

Point and beach breaks, lefts and rights, reefs and river mouths, warm water and year-round waves make Costa Rica a favorite surfing destination. For the most part, the Pacific coast has bigger swells and better waves during the latter part of the rainy season, but the Caribbean cooks from November to May. Basically, there's a wave waiting to be surfed at any time of year.

For the uninitiated, lessons are available at almost all of the major surfing destinations – especially popular towns include Jacó, Dominical, Sámara and Tamarindo on the Pacific coast. Surfing definitely has a steep learning curve, and it can be dangerous if the currents are strong. With that said, the sport is accessible to children and novices, though it's advisable to start with a lesson and always inquire locally about conditions before you paddle out.

Throughout Costa Rica, waves are big (though not massive), and many offer hollow and fast rides that are perfect for intermediates. As a bonus, this is one of the few places on the planet where you can surf two different oceans in the same day. Advanced surfers with plenty of experience can contend with some of the world's most famous waves. Top ones include Ollie's Point and Witch's Rock, off the coast of the Santa Rosa sector of the Área de Conservación Guanacaste (featured in *Endless Summer II*);

Mal País and Santa Teresa, with a groovy scene to match the powerful waves; Playa Hermosa, whose bigger, faster curls attract a more determined (and experienced) crew of wave-chasers; Pavones, a legendary long left across the sweet waters of the Golfo Dulce; and the infamous Salsa Brava in Puerto Viejo de Talamanca, for experts only.

Wildlife-Watching & Birding

Costa Rica's biodiversity is legendary, and the country delivers unparalleled opportunities for bird- and wildlife-watching. Most people are already familiar with the most famous, yet commonly spotted, animals. You'll recognize monkeys bounding through the treetops, sloths clinging to branches and toucans gliding beneath the canopy. Young children, even if they have been to the zoo dozens of times, typically love the thrill of spotting creatures in the wild.

For slightly older visitors, keeping checklists is a fun way to add an educational element to your travels. If you really want to know what you're looking at, pick up wildlife and bird guides before your trip – look for ones with color plates for easy positive IDs (Rainforest Publications produces easy-to-store laminated foldouts of birds, flowers and fauna).

Parque Nacional Corcovado (p434)

A quality pair of binoculars (starting at US$200 to US$300) is highly recommended and can really make the difference between far-off movement and a veritable face-to-face encounter (some guides and lodges can lend you a pair). For expert birders, a spotting scope is essential, and multi-park itineraries will allow you to quickly add dozens of new species to your all-time list. Optics are heavy and expensive, though, so consider that when packing.

How to Make it Happen

Costa Rica is brimming with avian life at every turn, but sometimes it takes an experienced guide to help you notice it.

Aratinga Tours (☏2574-2319; www.aratinga-tours.com) 🖉 Some of the best bird tours in the country, led by ornithologist Pieter Westra.

Birding Eco Tours (☏in USA 614-932-1430; www.birdingecotours.com) An international bird-tour company with highly entertaining and qualified guides in Costa Rica.

Tropical Feathers (☏2771-9686; www.costaricabirdingtours.com) Local owner and guide Noel Ureña has over 16 years' experience leading birding tours.

TOP SPOTS FOR WILDLIFE

Parque Nacional Corcovado (p434) At the heart of the Península de Osa, this is the country's richest wildlife area.

Parque Nacional Tortuguero (p149) Canals and waterways provide excellent birdwatching.

Refugio Nacional de Vida Silvestre Caño Negro (p267) Expansive wetlands provide a refuge for reptiles and avians.

Monteverde & Santa Elena (p191) These reserves provide insight into the cloud-forest ecosystem.

Boca Tapada Area (p275) The steamy rivers near the Nicaraguan border are a birders', as well as a fishers', delight.

Diver, Isla del Coco (p458)

Windsurfing & Kitesurfing

Laguna de Arenal is the nation's undisputed windsurfing (and kitesurfing) center. From December to April winds are strong and steady, averaging 20 knots in the dry season, often with maximum winds of 30 knots, and windless days are a rarity. The lake has a year-round water temperature of 18°C (64°F) to 21°C (70°F), with 1m-high swells. For warmer water (but more inconsistent winds), try Puerto Soley in the less-visited Bahía Salinas.

White-Water Rafting & Kayaking

White-water rafting has remained one of Costa Rica's top outdoor pursuits since the '80s. Ranging from family-friendly Class I riffles to nearly unnavigable Class V rapids, the country's rivers offer highly varied experiences.

First-time runners are catered for year-round, while seasoned enthusiasts arrive en masse during the wildest months from June to October. There is also much regional variation, with gentler rivers located near Manuel Antonio along the central Pacific coast, and world-class runs along the Río Pacuare in the Central Valley. Since all white-water rafting in Costa Rica requires the presence of a certified guide, you will need to book trips through a reputable tour agency. No matter the run, you'll get totally soaked and tossed about, so pack a sense of humor, but no fancy clothes or jewelry.

River kayaking has its fair share of loyal fans. The tiny village of La Virgen in the northern lowlands is the unofficial kayaking capital of Costa Rica and the best spot to hook up with other paddlers. The neighboring Río Sarapiquí has an impressive variety of runs that cater to all ages and skill levels.

With 1228km of coastline, two gulfs and plentiful mangrove estuaries, Costa Rica is also an ideal destination for sea kayaking. This is a great way for paddlers to access remote areas and catch glimpses of rare birds and wildlife. Access varies considerably, and is largely dependent on tides and currents.

DANITA DELIMONT/GETTY IMAGES ©

Red-eyed tree frog (p497)

How to Make it Happen

June to October are considered peak season for river rafting and kayaking, though some rivers offer good runs all year. Government regulation of outfitters is shoddy, so ask lots of questions about your guide's water-safety, emergency and medical training. If you suspect they're bluffing, move along – there are plenty of legit outfits.

River kayaking can be organized in conjunction with white-water-rafting trips if you are experienced; sea kayaking is popular year-round.

Aguas Bravas (p247) In La Virgen, this is the best outfitter on Costa Rica's best white water.

Costa Rica Expeditions (☎2521-6099; www.costaricaexpeditions.com) This outfitter handles small groups and offers rafting trips that cater to foodies.

Exploradores Outdoors (p170) This outfit offers one- and two-day trips on the Ríos Pacuare, Reventazón and Sarapiquí.

Green Rivers (p278) A young and fun Sarapiquí-based outfit working out of the Posada Andrea Cristina.

Gulf Islands Kayaking (☎in Canada 250-539-2442; www.seakayak.ca) Tours on offer include five days of sea kayaking in Corcovado.

H2O Adventures (p373) Arranges two- and five-day adventures on the Río Savegre.

Pineapple Tours (p391) Exciting half-day kayak trips go through caves and mangrove channels.

Ríos Tropicales (☎2233-6455, in USA 866-722-8273; www.riostropicales.com) Multiday adventures on the Río Pacuare and two days of kayaking in Tortuguero.

Canopy Tours

The most vibrant life in the rainforest takes place at canopy level, but with trees extending 30m to 60m in height, the average human has a hard time getting a look at what's going on up there. You will find canopy tours everywhere in Costa Rica, and many of them will also have a zipline or two to whiz along for a small additional charge. The most elaborate facilities also have Superman cables (which allow you to fly like the Man of Steel) and Tarzan swings.

Some companies have built elevated walkways through the trees. SkyTrek (p199) near Monteverde and Rainmaker Aerial Walkway (p373) near Quepos are two of the most established operations. A somewhat newer option is Diamante Eco

TOP FIVE SPOTS TO RIDE WATER

Turrialba (p134) Home to the country's most popular rafting rivers, the Pacuare and Reventazón.

La Virgen (p278) The base town for rafting and kayaking on the Río Sarapiquí.

Parque Nacional Manuel Antonio (p384) A tourist mecca that offers family-friendly rafting year-round.

Parque Nacional Tortuguero (p149) Boasts 310 sq km of wildlife-rich and kayak-friendly lagoons and canals.

Bahía Drake (p427) Extensive mangrove patches are optimally explored by kayak.

Surfer's Map

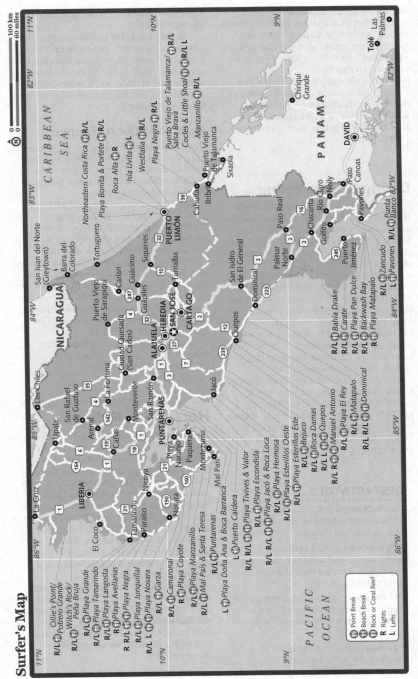

Adventure Park (p293) in Guanacaste, which offers dual ziplines, allowing guests to ride side by side. Canopy Mal País (p329) allows you to surf and zipline at the same time – sort of! – within spitting distance of the Pacific.

You can also take a ski lift–style ride through the treetops on aerial trams run by Rainforest Adventures (p513) near Braulio Carrillo or Veragua Rainforest Research & Adventure Park (p144) near Puerto Límon.

Diving & Snorkeling

The good news is that Costa Rica offers body-temperature water with few humans and abundant marine life. The bad news is that visibility is low because of silt and plankton, and soft corals and sponges are dominant.

However, if you're looking for fine opportunities to see massive schools of fish, as well as larger marine animals such as turtles, sharks, dolphins and whales, then jump right in. It's also worth pointing out that there are few places in the world where you could feasibly dive in the Caribbean and the Pacific on the same day – though why not take your time?

The Caribbean Sea is better for novice divers and snorkelers, with the beach towns of Manzanillo and Cahuita particularly well suited to youngsters. Puerto Viejo de Talamanca lays claim to a few decent sites that can be explored on a discovery dive. Along the Pacific, Isla del

Caño ups the ante for those with solid diving experience.

Isla del Coco is the exception to the rule – this remote island floating in the deep Pacific is regarded by veteran divers as one of the best spots on the planet. To dive the wonderland of Coco, you'll need to visit on a liveaboard and have logged some serious time underwater.

How to Make it Happen

Generally, visibility isn't great during the rainy months, when rivers swell and their outflow clouds the ocean. At this time, boats to offshore locations offer better viewing opportunities.

The water is warm – around 24°C (75°F) to 29°C (84°F) at the surface, with a thermocline at around 20m below the surface where it drops to 23°C (73°F). If you keep it shallow, you can skin-dive.

If you're interested in diving but aren't certified, you can usually complete a one-day introductory course that will allow you to do one or two accompanied dives. If you love it – and most people do – certification courses take three to four days and cost around US$350 to US$500.

To plan a trip to Isla del Coco, get in touch with the liveaboard operation Undersea Hunter (p459).

Horseback Riding

Though horseback-riding trips are ubiquitous throughout Costa Rica, quality and care for the horses vary. Rates range from US$25 for an hour or two to more than US$100 for a full day. Overnight trips with pack horses can also be arranged and are a popular way of accessing remote destinations in the national parks. Riders weighing more than 100kg (220lb) cannot be carried by small local horses. Always ask to see the horses beforehand, because some shady operators send out malnourished and mistreated animals.

Reliable outfitters with healthy horses include Hacienda El Cenizaro (p234) in La Cruz, Discovery Horseback Tours (p363) and **Serendipity Adventures** (☑2556-2222, in USA & Canada 877-507-1358, toll free from UK 808 281-8681; www.serendipity adventures.com).

White-water rafting (p43)

Mountain Biking & Cycling

Although the winding, potholed roads and aggressive drivers can be a challenge, cycling is on the rise in Costa Rica. Numerous less-trafficked roads offer plenty of adventure – from scenic mountain paths with sweeping views to rugged trails that take riders through streams and past volcanoes.

The best long-distance rides are along the Pacific coast's Interamericana, which has a decent shoulder and is relatively flat, and on the road from Montezuma to the Reserva Natural Absoluta Cabo Blanco on the southern Península de Nicoya. The hills around Bahia Salinas in the northwest are good fun, too.

Mountain biking has taken off in recent years and there are good networks of trails around Corcovado and Arenal, as well as more rides in the central mountains.

Yoga

Something about yoga and Costa Rica just go together: whether people come here solely to relax or to beat up their bodies in the surf or on the trails, nothing seems to be a better cure-all than a session on the mat. Along the beaches, schools are catering to this need better than ever (and the fantastic views at many places are part of the allure). Drop in for a class or stay for a week; you'll leave with body and mind refreshed. Some favorites:

Anamaya Resort (p340)

Bodhi Tree (p315)

Blue Osa Yoga Retreat (p441)

Casa Zen (p330)

Danyasa Yoga Arts School (p391)

Downtown Yoga (Map p68; ☏7272-0690; www.downtownyogacostarica.com; cnr Calle 15 & Av 7, San José; drop-in class US$10)

Nosara Wellness (p314)

Shooting Star Studio (p455)

Yoga Studio at Nautilus (p330)

Monteverde (p191)

Plan Your Trip

Travel with Children

In a land of such dizzying adventure and close encounters with wildlife, waves, jungle ziplines and enticing mud puddles, it can be challenging to choose where to go. Fortunately, your options aren't limited by region, and kids will find epic fun in this accessible paradise that parents will enjoy too.

Best Regions for Kids

Península de Nicoya

Excellent beaches and family-friendly resorts make this an ideal destination for families. This is a great place for kids (and their folks) to take surfing lessons.

Northwestern Costa Rica

The mysterious and ghostly cloud forests of Monteverde pique children's imaginations about the creatures that live there, while the area's specialty sanctuaries let them see bats, frogs, butterflies and reptiles up close.

Central Pacific Coast

Easy trails lead past spider monkeys and sloths to great swimming beaches at Parque Nacional Manuel Antonio, a busy but beautiful piece of coastal rainforest.

Caribbean Coast

The whole family can snorkel all day in the relatively tranquil waters of Manzanillo or Cahuita and set out on a night adventure to see nesting turtles.

Costa Rica for Kids

Mischievous monkeys and steaming volcanoes, mysterious rainforests and palm-lined beaches – Costa Rica sometimes seems like a comic book made real. The perfect place for family travel, it's a safe, exhilarating tropical playground that will make a huge impression on younger travelers. The country's myriad adventure possibilities cover the spectrum of age-appropriate intensity levels – and for no intensity at all, some kids might like the idea of getting their hair braided and beaded by a beachside stylist in Puerto Viejo de Talamanca. Whatever you do, the warm culture is extremely welcoming of little ones.

In addition to amazing the kids, this small, peaceful country has all the practicalities that rank highly with parents, such as great country-wide transportation infrastructure, a low crime rate and an excellent health-care system. But the reason to bring the whole family is the opportunity to share unforgettable experiences such as spotting a dolphin or a sloth, slowly paddling a kayak through mangrove channels, or taking a night hike in search of tropical frogs.

Children's Highlights

Wildlife-Watching

You can't not spot wildlife in Costa Rica – coatis cause regular traffic jams around Laguna de Arenal and scarlet macaws loudly squawk in tropical-almond trees down the central Pacific coast. Stay a day or two at a jungle lodge, and the wildlife will come to you.

Parque Nacional Manuel Antonio, Pacific coast (p384) Tiny and easily accessible; a walk through this park usually yields sightings of squirrel monkeys, stripy iguanas and coatis.

Parque Nacional Cahuita, Caribbean coast (p168) Seeing white-faced capuchins is almost guaranteed along the beach trail; go with a guide and you'll probably see sloths, too.

Parque Nacional Tortuguero, Caribbean coast (p149) Boat tours through Tortuguero canals uncover wildlife all around, but staying in any jungle lodge outside the village will reveal the same.

Chilamate Rainforest Eco Retreat, Sarapiquí Valley (p280) In the valley's steamy rainforest, this family-friendly lodge has miles of trails for easy wildlife-spotting hikes.

Turtle-Watching, Pacific and Caribbean coasts One of Costa Rica's truly magical experiences is watching sea turtles lay their eggs under the cover of night.

Beaches

Playa Pelada, Nosara area (p313) This low-key beach has little wave action and big, intriguing boulders.

Playa Carrillo, near Sámara (p325) South of family-friendly Sámara, this beach can be all yours during the week and convivially crowded with Tico families on the weekends.

Parque Nacional Manuel Antonio, Pacific coast (p384) Beach visits are usually enlivened by monkeys, coatis and iguanas.

Parque Nacional Marino Ballena, Pacific coast (p401) A yawning stretch of white-sand, jungle-fringed beach, a sand spit shaped like a whale's tail at low tide, and the chance to see whales spouting offshore.

Playa Negra, Cahuita (p162) This black-sand, blue-flag beach (meeting Costa Rica's highest ecological standards) has plenty of space to plant your own flag.

Playa Manzanillo, Mal País and Santa Teresa (p329) Beautiful, jungle-backed beach from here to Punta Mona (about as far south as you can go before you have to start bushwhacking).

Adventures

Mangrove tours Kayaking or canoeing through the still waters of mangrove canals can turn up waterbirds, caimans, sleeping bats and sloths. Try Parque Nacional Marino Ballena (p401), around Puerto Jiménez and Tortuguero.

Surfing lessons For surfing lessons specifically tailored to kids, check out One Love Surf School (p171) on the Caribbean coast; kids' lessons are also offered at beginner beaches in Jacó and Tamarindo.

White-water rafting Family-friendly rafting and 'safari trips' happen year-round on Ríos Sarapiquí, Savegre and Pejibaye.

Volcán Irazú, northeast of Cartago (p122) Peer into a volcano's crater at this national park with a kilometer of trails suitable for children.

Planning

Although Costa Rica is in the heart of Central America, it's a relatively easy place for family travel, making pre-departure planning more similar to that required for North America or Europe than, say, Honduras.

Fresh strawberries, Alajuela (p104)

Eating with Kids

➡ If you're traveling with an infant or small child, stock up on formula, baby food and snacks before heading to remote areas, where shops are few and far between.

➡ Kids love refreshing *batidos* (fresh fruit shakes) and the variety of novel tropical fruits may appeal to older kids.

➡ Many restaurants have kids' menus, but these tend to offer international rather than Costa Rican food.

Getting There & Around

➡ Children under the age of 12 receive a discount of up to 25% on domestic flights, while on some carriers children under two fly free (provided they sit on a parent's lap).

➡ Children aged three and up pay full fare with most bus companies.

➡ Car seats for infants are not always available at car-rental agencies, so bring your own or make sure you double (or triple) check with the agency in advance.

Casado (p53), a typical Costa Rican meal

Plan Your Trip

Eat & Drink Like a Local

Traditional Costa Rican fare, for the most part, is comfort food, consisting largely of beans and rice, fried plantains, and the occasional slab of chicken, fish or beef. Recently, locals have started to experiment more with the country's fresh, exotic and plentiful produce. The results have been inspiring and delicious.

The Year in Food

Food festivals are concentrated at the end of the rainy season, but the tropical Eden that is Costa Rica produces exotic and incredible fruits and vegetables and vends them in farmers markets year-round.

Rainy season (October & November)

Deliciously ripe mangoes and *mamon chino* (rambutan), plus agricultural celebrations such as the Fiesta del Maíz (Festival of Corn) and the Feria Nacional de Pejibaye (National Peach Palm Market).

Christmas (December)

Tamales, prepared with masa (corn meal soaked in lime), pork, potatoes and garlic and steamed in banana leaves, become a very big deal at this time of year.

Coffee harvest (September to January)

Many seasonal laborers from Nicaragua head down to pick *grano de oro* (the golden grain).

Dare to Try

Museo de Insectos (p69) This bug museum has its own kitchen, where guests are served meal worms and crickets with lots of salt and oregano.

Mondongo Tripe intestines are a *campesino* (farmers) favorite in Costa Rica, and they are served surprisingly spicy.

Meat on a stick Is it pork? Chicken? Beef? Who cares. On roadsides and at local fiestas, this mysterious Tico delicacy is just as good as it smells, even after the vendor uses a paintbrush to apply spicy sauce.

Green Treats

Sibu Chocolate (p120) In San Isidro de Heredia, the history of chocolate illuminates and satisfies.

Feria Verde de Aranjuez (p93) San José's 'green market,' and an all-around winner for breakfast, produce, smoothies, everything.

Punta Mona (p187) The sprawling garden at this secluded eco-retreat near Manzanillo has one of the world's largest collections of edible tropical plants.

Costa Rica Cooking (p245) Help to whip up your own meal in La Fortuna, based on local and almost entirely organic produce.

Food Experiences

Cheap Treats

Guanabana Also known as soursop, this sweet and sticky fruit should be purchased wherever you find it, and eaten with your hands.

Patí A flaky, Caribbean-style turnover filled with meat, onions, garlic and spicy goodness.

Street mango Sold in plastic bags with salt, lime juice and sometimes chili powder, this is the ultimate refreshment.

Pipa fría Find a vendor with a machete and an ice chest and they'll hack off the top of a coconut, stick a straw in it, and you're good to go, with a frosty, sweet treat.

Pejivalle The roasted peach-palm fruit is a roadside standard, delicious warm and salted, although Ticos like to add a dab of mayonnaise.

Local Specialties

Breakfast for Ticos is usually *gallo pinto* (literally 'painted rooster'), a stir-fry of last night's rice and beans. When combined, the rice gets colored by the beans, and the mix obtains a speckled appearance. Served with eggs, cheese or *natilla* (sour cream), *gallo pinto* is generally cheap, filling and sometimes downright tasty. If you plan to spend the whole day surfing or hiking, you'll find that *gallo pinto* is great energy food.

Considering the extent of the coastline, it's no surprise that seafood is plentiful, and fish dishes are usually fresh and delicious. While it's not traditional Tico fare, *ceviche* is on most menus, usually made from *pargo* (red snapper), *dorado* (mahi-mahi), octopus or tilapia. The fish is marinated in lime juice with some combination of chilis, onions, tomatoes and herbs. Served chilled, it is a delectable way to enjoy fresh seafood. Emphasis is on 'fresh' here – it's raw fish, so if you have reason to believe it's not fresh, don't risk eating it. Sushi is also finding a place in many towns.

Food is not heavily spiced, unless you're having traditional Caribbean-style cuisine. Most local restaurants will lay out a bottle of Tabasco-style sauce, homemade salsa or Salsa Lizano, the Tico version of Worcestershire sauce and the 'secret' ingredient of *gallo pinto*. Some lay out a tempting jar of pickled hot peppers as well.

Most bars also offer the country's most popular *boca* (snack), *chifrijo*, which derives its name from two main ingredients: *chicharrón* (fried pork) and frijoles (beans). Diced tomatoes, spices, rice, tortilla chips and avocado are also thrown in for good measure. Fun fact about *chifrijo*: in 2014 a restaurant owner named Miguel Cordero claimed he officially invented it. He brought lawsuits against 49 businesses and demanded a cool US$15 million in damages. So far he has not been able to collect.

Caribbean cuisine is the most distinctive in Costa Rica, having been steeped in indigenous, *criollo* (Creole) and Afro-Caribbean flavors. It's a welcome cultural change of pace after seemingly endless *casados*. Regional specialties include *rondón* (whose moniker comes from 'run-down,' meaning whatever the chef can run down), a spicy seafood gumbo; Caribbean-style rice and beans, made with red beans, coconut milk and curry spices; and *pati*, the Caribbean version of an *empanada* (savory turnover), the best street food, bus-ride snack and picnic treat.

Ceviche (lime-marinated seafood)

MARCOS HONMA/GETTY IMAGES

A midday lunch (served between 11:30am and 2:30pm) at most *sodas* (lunch counters) usually involves a *casado* (set meal; literally, 'married'), a cheap, well-balanced plate of rice, beans, meat, salad and sometimes *plátanos maduros* (fried sweet plantains) or *patacones* (twice-fried plantains), which taste something like french fries.

For dinner (6pm to 9pm), a *casado* is on offer at most restaurants. Upscale Tico establishments may serve *lomito* (a lean cut of steak) and dishes like *pescado en salsa palmito* (fish in heart-of-palm sauce). Some of the more forward-thinking eateries in San José may drop an experimental vegetable plate in front of you.

How to Eat & Drink

When to Eat

Breakfast for Ticos is taken in the early morning, usually from 6am to 8am, and consists of *gallo pinto*. Many hotels offer a tropical-style continental breakfast, usually consisting of toast with butter and jam, accompanied by fresh fruit. American-style breakfasts are also available in many eateries and are, needless to say, heavy on the fried foods and fatty meats.

Where to Eat

The most popular eating establishment in Costa Rica is the *soda*. These are small, informal lunch counters dishing up a few daily *casados*. Other popular cheapies include the omnipresent fried- and rotisserie-chicken stands.

A regular *restaurante* is usually higher on the price scale and has slightly more atmosphere. Many *restaurantes* serve *casados,* while the fancier places refer to the set lunch as the *almuerzo ejecutivo* (literally 'executive lunch').

For something smaller, *pastelerías* and *panaderías* are shops that sell pastries and bread, while many bars serve *bocas* ('mouthfuls'; snack-sized portions of main meals).

Vegetarians & Vegans

Costa Rica is a relatively comfortable place for vegetarians to travel. Rice and beans, as well as fresh fruit juices, are ubiquitous, but there's a lot more than that. The Happy Cow has a handy list of veggie restaurants nationwide (www.happycow.net/north_america/costa_rica). Visit farmers markets to sample what's in season: Costa Rica is a growers' paradise.

Most restaurants will make veggie *casados* on request and many places are now including them on the menu. These set meals usually include rice and beans, cabbage salad and one or two selections of variously prepared vegetables or legumes.

With the high influx of tourism, there are also many specialty vegetarian restaurants or restaurants with a veggie menu in San José and tourist towns. Lodges in remote areas that offer all-inclusive meal plans can accommodate vegetarians with advance notice.

Vegans, macrobiotic and raw-food-only travelers will have a tougher time, as there are fewer outlets accommodating those diets, although this is slowly changing. If you intend to keep to your diet, it's best to choose a lodging where you can prepare food yourself. Many towns have *macrobióticas* (health-food stores), but the selection varies. Fresh vegetables can be hard to come by in isolated areas and will often be quite expensive, although farmers markets are cropping up throughout the country.

Habits & Customs

When you sit down to eat in a restaurant, it is polite to say *buenos días* (good morning), *buenas tardes* (good afternoon) or *buenas noches* (good evening) to the waitstaff and any people you might be sharing a table with – and it's generally good form to acknowledge everyone in the room this way. It is also polite to say *buen provecho,* which is the equivalent of *bon appetit,* at the start of the meal.

THE GALLO PINTO CONTROVERSY

No other dish in Costa Rica inspires Ticos quite like their national dish of *gallo pinto,* that ubiquitous medley of rice, beans and spices. You might even hear Costa Ricans refer to themselves as '*más Tico que gallo pinto*' (literally, 'more Costa Rican than *gallo pinto*'). Exactly what type and amount of this holy trinity makes up authentic *gallo pinto* is the subject of intense debate, especially since it is also the national dish of neighboring Nicaragua.

Both countries claim that *gallo pinto* originated on their soil. Costa Rican lore holds that the dish and its iconic name were coined in 1930 in the neighborhood of San Sebastián, on the southern outskirts of San José. Nicaraguans claim that it was brought to the Caribbean coast of their country by Afro-Latinos long before it graced the palate of any Costa Rican.

The battle for the rights to this humble dish doesn't stop here, especially since the two countries can't even agree on the standard recipe. Nicaraguans traditionally prepare it with small red beans, whereas Costa Ricans swear by black beans. And let's not even get into the subtle complexities of balancing cilantro, salt and pepper.

Nicaragua officially holds the world record for making the biggest-ever pot of *gallo pinto.* On September 15, 2007, a seething vat of it fed 22,000 people, which firmly entrenched Nicaragua's name next to *gallo pinto* in the *Guinness Book of World Records.* Costa Rica responded in 2009 by cooking an even more massive avalanche of the stuff, feeding a small crowd of 50,000. Though the event was not officially recognized as setting any records, that day's vat of *gallo pinto* warmed the hearts and bellies of many a proud Tico.

Above: Typical food including *gallo pinto*

Right: Cocoa fruit

JALIAREZG/GETTY IMAGES ©

Regions at a Glance

Where will your passion take you? Wildlife-watchers will be in heaven here, with an array of biospheres supporting a multitude of colorful species, including the resplendent quetzal, rainbow-hued frogs, the elusive jaguar and nesting sea turtles. Surfers need no intro to the plentiful and varied surf spots, and even rookies will find plenty of beginner breaks. If surfing's not your thing, you can take to the ocean, lakes or rivers in kayaks or white-water rafts. Hikers can traverse the thick, humid jungle of remote Corcovado, summit the country's highest peak, Cerro Chirripó, or just meander through cloud forests, around the rims of steaming volcanoes and along beachside trails on day hikes.

San José

Culture
Entertainment
Food

Museums

Gritty, no-nonsense San José doesn't offer much in the way of architectural beauty, but this is the only place with a dense concentration of museums, exhibiting everything from pre-Columbian gold frogs to the hottest multimedia installations by local contemporary artists.

Live Music

This is where you come to catch chamber music, international touring bands and up-and-coming local talent. The National Theater is a solid place to start.

Fine Restaurants

Argentinian, vegetarian, Asian-fusion and classic French cuisine shine in superb San José venues, bringing welcome diversity to *gallo pinto*–weary palates.

p60

Central Valley & Highlands

Geography
Adventure
Landscapes

Highlands

The picturesque highlands of Costa Rica are often overlooked in favor of its beaches. But here cows wander along twisting mountain roads, and villages boast organic farmers markets and parks with psychedelic topiaries.

White Water

World-class white water awaits on the Río Pacuare, which is well worth a run for its cascade of thrilling rapids through a stunningly beauteous jungle gorge.

Volcanoes

Volcanoes range from the wild and moderately active (Turrialba) to the heavily trafficked (Poás, now active and temporarily closed), showing off crater lakes and misty moonscapes. If you're lucky, one may send up smoke during a visit.

p101

Caribbean Coast

Culture
Ecology
Turtles

Afro-Caribbean

Set apart geographically and culturally from the rest of Costa Rica, the Caribbean coast has a distinct Afro-Caribbean feel all of its own. Taste it in the coconut rice, hear it in the local *patois* and live it in superchill Cahuita.

Wildlife

The waterlogged coast along the Caribbean teems with sloths, three of Costa Rica's four monkey species, crocodiles, caimans, poison-dart frogs, manatees, tucuxi dolphins and over 375 bird species.

Nesting beaches

On this wild coast, turtle nesting is serious business. In Parismina and Tortuguero, the leatherback, green and hawksbill turtles return to their natal beaches to nest.

p136

Northwestern Costa Rica

Places to Stay
Outdoors
Landscapes

Ecolodges

The number of groovy, independent ecolodges means you can choose from cute B&Bs to spectacular working *fincas* (farms) or biological stations ensconced in natural forest, all far from the crowds.

Watersports

Lose yourself in aquamarine rivers, ride perfect lefts that crash on wild beaches, or ride the wind on the most epic bay you've never heard of. And all of the water's walk-in (or fall-in) warm.

Cloud Forests

Northwestern cloud forests – studded with cathedral trees, which shelter valuable watersheds – birthed the ubiquitous canopy tour. You'll be in awe of *bosques* on volcanic slopes and along the wild coast.

p189

Arenal & Northern Lowlands

Culture
Wildlife
Outdoors

Local Culture

This is where you'll discover real-life Costa Rica – face to face with cows and pigs on working *finca* homestays, on tours through rainforest preserves, and while paddling inky lagoons or mocha rivers with lifelong resident guides.

Birds

The humid swamps and lowland hills are thick with vegetation and teeming with hundreds of species of bird, from storks and egrets to toucans and macaws.

Watersports & Fishing

Whether you plan to paddle frothing white water shadowed by looming forest, wish to carve inland lakes by kayak, or just want to hop a motorboat to spot caimans or reel in tarpon, this is your Neverland.

p239

Península de Nicoya

Outdoors
Food
Yoga

Surf & Dive

It's almost impossible to believe there are so many waves on one spectacular, rugged peninsula. Below the surface, don't expect Caribbean clarity, but the mantas, bull sharks and pelagics will bend your brain.

Food

The creative, international kitchens that dot this intrepid coast source ingredients from local *fincas* and fishers, and the savory dishes are prepared with *savoir faire*. Nicoya is one of the 'blue zones' of the world, with many residents living into their 90s and beyond thanks in part to the traditional staple diet. Dig in.

Yoga

Nosara and Santa Elena are standouts with multiple studios, many with hard-to-beat vistas.

p285

Central Pacific Coast

Outdoors
National Park
Beaches

Surfing

From the pros-only Playa Hermosa to the beginner-friendly Dominical, the famous breaks of the Pacific coast bring blissful swells and tons of variety.

Manuel Antonio

Manuel Antonio, Costa Rica's most popular national park, is a kid-friendly, beach-lined delight. Sure, there are crowds of people, but they're outnumbered by monkeys, coatis and tropical birds.

Marino Ballena

It's a bit of a hike to get to this national park, but those who find themselves on its empty beaches can scan the sparkling horizon for migrating whales. There's even a whale and dolphin festival (www.festivaldebal lenasydelfines.com) in September.

p347

Southern Costa Rica & Península de Osa

Mountain Peak
Outdoors
Culture

Cerro Chirripó

Scaling ancient trails to the wind-swept peak of Chirripó is an adventure into a wholly different Costa Rica. The sunrise view from above the clouds is the brilliant highlight of this three-day excursion.

Hiking

Jaguars, jungle trails and wild beaches: this is among the world's most biologically intense patches of green. Hiking Corcovado is a sublime trip into untamed tropical rainforest.

Indigenous Costa Rica

Traveling deep into the mountains or jungle of the Osa allows you to meet some of Costa Rica's indigenous citizens, and see how they keep the country's ancient traditions alive.

p405

Thermal springs in Parque Nacional Rincón de la Vieja (p227)

Jade jewelry at Museo Nacional de Costa Rica (p63)

On the Road

San José

POP 2,158,898 / ELEV 1170M

Best Places to Eat

➡ Park Café (p83)

➡ La Esquina de Buenos Aires (p82)

➡ Saúl Bistro (p88)

➡ Cocina Eclectica (p88)

➡ Maxi's By Ricky (p87)

➡ Café de Los Deseos (p80)

Best Places to Stay

➡ Hotel Grano de Oro (p76)

➡ Hostel Bekuo (p76)

➡ Hotel Presidente (p75)

➡ Selina San José (p72)

➡ Studio Hotel (p79)

Why Go?

Chances are San José wasn't the top destination on your list when you started planning your Costa Rica trip, but give this city a chance and you might be pleasantly surprised. It's true that Chepe – as San José is affectionately known – doesn't make a great first impression, with its unremarkable concrete structures and honking traffic, but it's well worth digging deeper to discover the city's charms.

Take your time exploring historic neighborhoods such as Barrio Amón, where colonial mansions have been converted into contemporary art galleries, and Barrio Escalante, the city's gastronomic epicenter. Stroll with Saturday shoppers at the farmers market, join the Sunday crowds in Parque La Sabana, dance the night away to live music at one of the city's vibrant clubs, or visit the museums of gold, jade, art and natural history, and you'll begin to understand the multidimensional appeal of Costa Rica's largest city and cultural capital.

When to Go

➡ Rainy season usually lasts from mid-April through December, and is therefore a great time to look for deals and beat the crowds. Beware of October, which usually sees heavy rains for days at a time.

➡ The city's climate is considerably cooler than on the coasts, especially at night; daytime temps generally vary between 21°C and 27°C (70°F to 80°F).

➡ The best time to visit is around the Christmas holidays, when the Ticos' festive cheer reaches its height with the Festival de la Luz (p71) and Las Fiestas de Zapote (p71).

➡ Any season is good for exploring the capital's cultural attractions.

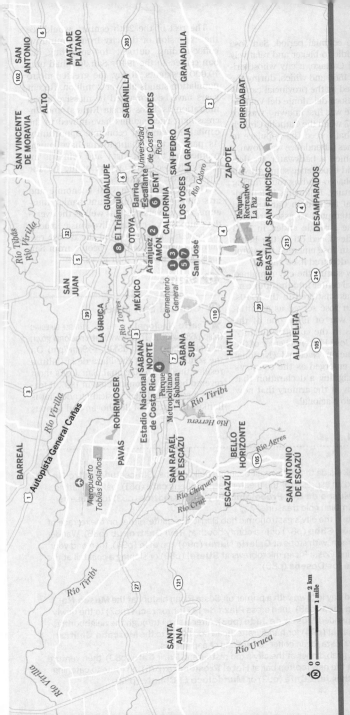

San José Highlights

1 Teatro Nacional (p92)
Savoring performances amid the beaux-arts interior.

2 Feria Verde de Aranjuez (p93) Poking around the Saturday farmers market in search of locally grown treats.

3 Barrio Amón (p66)
Visiting colonial mansions that have been converted into coffee shops, art galleries and music venues.

4 Estadio Nacional de Costa Rica (p93) Attending a soccer match or concert in the legendary, clam-shaped arena.

5 Museo de Jade (p63)
Exploring the vast universe of carved stone and ceramic treasures.

6 Barrio Escalante (p69)
Indulging your taste buds at fun bars and fine eateries.

7 Museo de Oro Precolombino y Numismática (p63) Admiring

Costa Rica's artistic traditions, past and present.

8 Really Experience Community (p70) Learning about the struggles of less fortunate city residents on a respectful and engaging tour.

History

For much of the colonial period, San José played second fiddle to bigger and relatively more established Cartago, a city whose origins date back to 1563 and which, during the colonial era, served as the provincial capital. Villanueva de la Boca del Monte del Valle de Abra – as San José was first known – was not founded until 1737, when the Catholic Church issued an edict that forced the populace to settle near churches (attendance was down).

The city remained a backwater for decades, though it did experience some growth as a stop in the tobacco-trading route during the late 18th century. Following independence in 1821, rival factions in Cartago and San José each attempted to assert regional supremacy. The struggle ended in 1823 when the two sides faced off at the Battle of Ochomongo. San José emerged the victor and subsequently declared itself capital.

Despite its new status, the city remained a quiet agricultural center into the 20th century. The calm was shattered in the 1940s, when parts of San José served as a battlefield in the civil war of 1948, one of the bloodiest conflicts in the country's history. Out of that clash, José Figueres Ferrer of the Partido de Liberación Nacional (National Liberation Party) emerged as the country's interim leader – signing a declaration that abolished the army at the armory that now serves as the Museo Nacional.

The rest of the 20th century would see the expansion of the city from diminutive coffee-trading outpost to sprawling urban center. In the 1940s San José had only 70,000 residents. Today, the greater metro population stands at over 2 million. Recent years have been marked by massive urban migration as Ticos (Costa Ricans) and, increasingly, Nicaraguans have moved to the capital in search of economic opportunity. As part of this, shantytowns have mushroomed on the outskirts, and crime is increasingly becoming a part of life for the city's poorest inhabitants.

The city remains a vital economic and arts hub, home to important banks, museums and universities – as well as the everyday outposts of culture: live-music spaces, art centers, bookstores and the corner restaurants where *josefinos* (people from San José) gather to chew over ideas.

◉ Sights

◉ Central San José

★ Teatro Nacional
NOTABLE BUILDING
(Map p68; ☎ 2010-1110; www.teatronacional.go.cr; Av 2 btwn Calles 3 & 5; US$10; ☺ 9am-7pm) On the southern side of the Plaza de la Cultura resides the Teatro Nacional, San José's most revered building. Constructed in 1897, it features a columned neoclassical facade that is flanked by statues of Beethoven and famous

---

SAN JOSÉ IN...

One Day

Begin with a peek inside the city's most beautiful building, the 19th-century **Teatro Nacional** (p62) and an espresso at the theater's atmospheric **cafe** (p81), before heading into the nearby **Museo de Oro Precolombino y Numismática** (p63) to peruse its trove of pre-Columbian gold treasures.

Take lunch within the city's gastronomic hub Barrio Escalante, either on the terrace of **Kalú Café & Food Shop** (p87) or in a comfy booth at **Rávi Gastropub** (p86). Wander historic Barrio Amón, with stops at **Galería Namu** (p94) and **eÑe** (p94), then end your afternoon sampling Costa Rican microbrews at **Stiefel** (p89) or sipping a cocktail at the fabulous **Café de los Deseos** (p80).

Two Days

Start your second day in town with a primer on Costa Rican history at the **Museo Nacional de Costa Rica** (p63), then cross **Plaza de la Democracia** (p67) to the newly relocated and expanded **Museo de Jade** (p63). After a stroll through the neighboring **Mercado Artesanal** (p94) for handicrafts, head northwest to the **Mercado Central** (p63) to shop for Costa Rican coffee, cigars and cheap snacks.

In the evening, grab dinner at the city's top restaurant, **Park Café** (p83), then venture east for a drink at the new rooftop bar at **Hotel Presidente** (p75), en route to catching a local band at either **Jazz Café** (p92) or **Mundoloco El Chante** (p92).

17th-century Spanish dramatist Calderón de la Barca. The lavish marble lobby and auditorium are lined with paintings depicting various facets of 19th-century life. The hourly tours (p70) here are fantastic, and if you're looking to rest your feet, there's also an excellent onsite cafe (p81).

The theater's most famous painting is *Alegoría al café y el banano,* an idyllic canvas showing coffee and banana harvests. It was produced in Italy and shipped to Costa Rica for installation in the theater, and the image was reproduced on the old ₡5 note (now out of circulation). It seems clear that the painter never witnessed a banana harvest because of the way the man in the center is awkwardly grasping a bunch (actual banana workers hoist the stems onto their shoulders).

★ Museo de Jade
MUSEUM

(Map p68; ☑2521-6610; www.museodeljadeins.com; Plaza de la Democracia; US$15; ☉10am-5pm) This museum houses the world's largest collection of American jade (pronounced 'ha-day' in Spanish), with an ample exhibition space of five floors offering seven exhibits. There are nearly 7000 finely crafted, well-conserved pieces, from translucent jade carvings depicting fertility goddesses, shamans, frogs and snakes to incredible ceramics (some reflecting Maya influences), including a highly unusual ceramic head displaying a row of serrated teeth. The new museum cafe, Grano Verde, serves sandwiches, salads and smoothies. Children aged five and under have free entry to the museum.

★ Museo de Oro Precolombino y Numismática
MUSEUM

(Map p68; ☑2243-4202; www.museosdelbancocentral.org; Plaza de la Cultura, Avs Central & 2 btwn Calles 3 & 5; adult/student/child US$11/8/free; ☉9:15am-5pm) This three-in-one museum houses an extensive collection of Costa Rica's most priceless pieces of pre-Columbian gold and other artifacts, including historical currency and some contemporary regional art. The museum, located underneath the Plaza de la Cultura, is owned by the Banco Central and its architecture brings to mind all the warmth and comfort of a bank vault. Security is tight; visitors must leave bags at the door.

Mercado Central
MARKET

(Map p68; Avs Central & 1 btwn Calles 6 & 8; ☉6:30am-6pm Mon-Sat) Though *josefinos* mainly do their shopping at chain supermarkets, San José's crowded indoor markets retain an old-world feel. This is the main market, lined with vendors hawking everything from spices and coffee beans to *pura vida* souvenir T-shirts made in China. It's all super cheap, and likely made in China or Nicaragua.

In December Mercado Central sometimes has extended hours and is open on Sundays.

Mercado Borbón
MARKET

(Map p68; ☑2223-3512; www.facebook.com/mercadoborbon; cnr Av 3 & Calle 8; ☉5am-6pm Mon-Sat) The Mercado Borbón focuses on produce, though it sells a bit of everything. (Be aware: the streets can get sketchy around the Borbón. Keep a close watch on your bag.)

Museo Nacional de Costa Rica
MUSEUM

(Map p64; ☑2257-1433; www.museocostarica.go.cr; Calle 17 btwn Avs Central & 2; adult/child US$9/4; ☉8:30am-4:30pm Tue-Sat, 9am-4:30pm Sun) Entered via a beautiful glassed-in atrium housing an exotic butterfly garden, this museum provides a quick survey of Costa Rican history. Exhibits of pre-Columbian pieces from ongoing digs, as well as artifacts from the colony and the early republic, are all housed inside the old Bellavista Fortress, which historically served as the army headquarters and saw fierce fighting (hence the pockmarks) in the 1948 civil war. It was here that President José Figueres Ferrer announced, in 1949, that he was abolishing the country's military. Among the museum's many notable pieces is the fountain pen that Figueres used to sign the 1949 constitution.

Don't miss the period galleries in the northeast corner, which feature turn-of-the-20th-century furnishings and decor from when these rooms served as the private residences of the fort's various commanders.

Museo de los Niños & Galería Nacional
MUSEUM

(Map p64; ☑2258-4929; www.museocr.org; Calle 4, north of Av 9; adult/child US$3.80/3.50; ☉8am-4:30pm Tue-Fri, 9:30am-5pm Sat & Sun; ☗) If you were wondering how to get your young kids interested in art and science, this unusual museum – actually two museums in one – is an excellent place to start. Housed in an old penitentiary built in 1909, it is part children's museum and part art gallery. Small children will love the hands-on exhibits related to science, geography and natural history, while grown-ups will enjoy the unusual juxtaposition of contemporary art in abandoned prison cells.

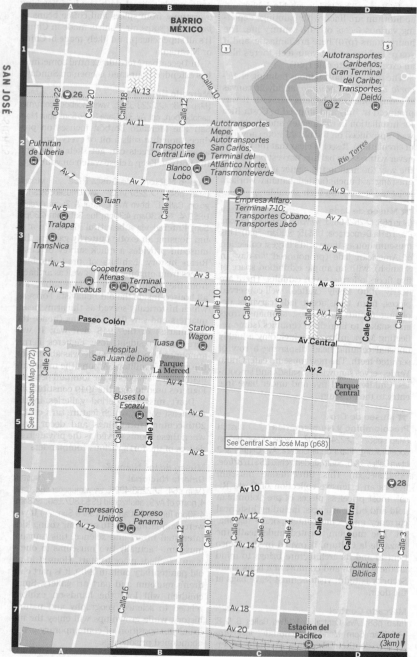

BARRIO MÉXICO

Calle 10

Calle 22
Calle 20
Calle 18
Av 13
Av 11
Calle 12

Pulmitan de Liberia

Av 7

Transportes Central Line

Blanco Lobo

Autotransportes Mepe; Autotransportes San Carlos; Terminal del Atlántico Norte; Transmonteverde

Autotransportes Caribeños; Gran Terminal del Caribe; Transportes Deldú

Río Torres

Av 9

Av 7

Tuan
Av 5
Tralapa
TransNica
Av 3

Av 7

Calle 14

Empresa Alfaro; Terminal 7-10; Transportes Cobano; Transportes Jacó

Av 7
Av 5

Av 3

Coopetrans Atenas
Nicabus
Terminal Coca-Cola
Av 1

Av 3

Av 1

Calle 10
Calle 8
Calle 6
Calle 4
Calle 2
Calle Central
Calle 1

Av 3
Av 1
Av Central

Paseo Colón

Calle 20

Station Wagon
Tuasa
Hospital San Juan de Dios
Parque La Merced
Av 4

Av 2

Parque Central

Buses to Escazú
Calle 16
Calle 14
Av 6

Av 8

See La Sabana Map (p72)

See Central San José Map (p68)

Av 10

28

Empresarios Unidos
Expreso Panamá
Av 12

Calle 12
Calle 10
Av 12
Calle 8
Calle 6
Calle 4
Av 14

Calle 2
Calle Central
Calle 1
Calle 3

Av 16

Clínica Bíblica

Calle 16

Av 18

Av 20

Estación del Pacífico

Zapote (3km)

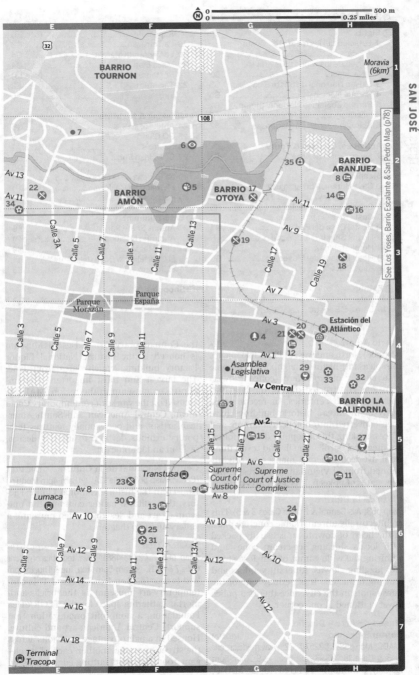

SAN JOSÉ

Moravia
(6km)

N 0 _____ 500 m
0 _____ 0.25 miles

BARRIO
TOURNON

BARRIO
AMÓN

BARRIO
OTOYA

BARRIO
ARANJUEZ

BARRIO LA
CALIFORNIA

See Los Yoses, Barrio Escalante & San Pedro Map (p78)

32

108

Av 13

Av 11

Calle 3A
Calle 5
Calle 7
Calle 9
Calle 11
Calle 13

Calle 17
Calle 19

Av 9

Av 11

Av 7

Parque
Morazán

Parque
España

Calle 3
Calle 5
Calle 7
Calle 9
Calle 11

Av 3

Estación del
Atlántico

Asamblea
Legislativa

Av 1

Av Central

Av 2

Calle 15
Calle 17
Calle 19
Calle 21

Supreme
Court of
Justice

Supreme
Court of Justice
Complex

Av 6

Transtusa

Lumaca

Av 8

Av 8

Av 10

Av 10

Av 12

Calle 5
Calle 7
Calle 9
Calle 11
Calle 13
Calle 13A

Av 12

Av 10

Av 14

Av 16

Av 18

Terminal
Tracopa

7

6

5

34

22

8
14
16

19

18

35

20
21
4
12
1

29
33
32

27

15

10

11

9

23
30
13

25
31

24

San José

Sights

Activities, Courses & Tours

Sleeping

Eating

Drinking & Nightlife

Entertainment

Shopping

Barrio Amón AREA
(Map p68) North and west of Plaza España lies this pleasant, historic neighborhood, home to a cluster of *cafetalero* (coffee grower) mansions constructed during the late 19th and early 20th centuries. In recent years, many of the area's historic buildings have been converted into hotels, restaurants and offices, making this a popular district for an architectural stroll. You'll find everything from art-deco concrete manses to brightly painted tropical Victorian structures in various states of upkeep. It is a key arts center.

Plaza de la Cultura PLAZA
(Map p68; Avs Central & 2 btwn Calles 3 & 5) This architecturally unremarkable concrete plaza in the heart of downtown is usually packed with locals slurping ice-cream cones and admiring the wide gamut of San José street life: juggling clowns, itinerant vendors and cruising teenagers. It is perhaps one of the safest spots in the city since there's a police tower stationed at one corner.

Museo de Arte y Diseño Contemporáneo MUSEUM
(MADC; Map p68; ☎2257-7202; www.madc.cr; cnr Av 3 & Calle 15; US$3, Tue free; ⏲9:30am-5pm Tue-Sat) Commonly referred to as MADC, the Contemporary Art & Design Museum is housed in the historic National Liquor Factory building, which dates from 1856. The largest and most important contemporary-art museum in the region, MADC is focused on the works of contemporary Costa Rican, Central American and South American artists, and occasionally features temporary exhibits devoted to interior design, fashion and graphic art.

Central Nacional de la Cultura LANDMARK
(Cenac; Map p68; Calle 11A; ⏲8am-4pm Mon-Fri) Housed in the historic National Liquor Factory, this cultural center contains the museum of art and design, a video museum, a gallery and two theaters.

TEOR/éTica GALLERY
(Map p68; ☎2233-4881; www.teoretica.org; cnr Calle 7 & Av 11; ⏲9am-5pm Mon, Tue & Thu, to 6pm Wed, to noon Fri, 10am-4pm Sat) FREE This contemporary-art museum is the bricks-and-mortar gathering space for the TEOR/éTica Foundation, a nonprofit organization that supports Central American art and culture. Housed in a pair of vintage mansions across the street from one another, each of its elegant rooms exhibits cutting-edge works by

established and emerging figures from Latin America and the rest of the world.

Parque Nacional   PARK
(Map p64; Avs 1 & 3 btwn Calles 15 & 19) One of San José's nicest green spaces, this shady spot lures retirees to read newspapers and young couples to smooch coyly on concrete benches. At its center is the Monumento Nacional, a dramatic 1953 statue that depicts the Central American nations driving out North American filibuster William Walker. The park is dotted with myriad monuments devoted to Latin American historical figures, including Cuban poet, essayist and revolutionary José Martí, Mexican independence figure Miguel Hidalgo and 18th-century Venezuelan humanist Andrés Bello. Across the street, to the south, stands the **Asamblea Legislativa** (Legislative Assembly; cnr Av 8 & Calle 33), which also bears an important statue: this one a depiction of Juan Santamaría – the young man who helped kick the pesky Walker out of Costa Rica – in full flame-throwing action.

Parque Zoológico
Nacional Simón Bolívar   ZOO
(Map p64; 2256-0012; www.fundazoo.org; Av 11 btwn Calles 7 & 9; adult/child US$5/3.70; 8:30am-4pm Mon-Fri, 9am-4:30pm Sat & Sun;) It may seem ironic to visit a zoo in one of the most biologically rich countries in the world, but this is a popular spot with local families who pour in on weekends to peek at the animals. It's rough around the edges – the cages are cramped and a few travelers have complained of the animals' filthy living spaces – but for small children it can serve as a basic primer on the area's wildlife.

If you have time for a day trip, a much better option is Zoo Ave outside Alajuela.

Spirogyra Jardín de Mariposas   GARDENS
(Map p64; 2222-2937; www.butterflygardencr. com; Barrio Amón; adult/child US$7/4; 9am-2pm Mon-Fri, to 3pm Sat & Sun; ; to El Pueblo) Housing more than 30 species of butterfly – including the luminescent blue morpho – in plant-filled enclosures, this small butterfly garden is a great spot for kids. Visit in the morning to see plenty of fluttering. The garden is 150m east and 150m south of Centro Comercial El Pueblo, which can be reached on foot (about a 20- to 30-minute walk from downtown), by taxi or by bus.

Plaza de la Democracia   PLAZA
(Map p68; Avs Central & 2 btwn Calles 13 & 15) Between the Museo Nacional and the Museo de Jade is the stark Plaza de la Democracia, which was constructed by President Oscar Arias in 1989 to commemorate 100 years of Costa Rican democracy. The concrete plaza is architecturally dull, but some of its elevated terraces provide decent views of the mountains surrounding San José (especially at sunset). On its western flank is an open-air crafts market (p94).

Catedral Metropolitana   CATHEDRAL
(Map p68; 2221-3820; Avs 2 & 4 btwn Calles Central & 1) East of Parque Central, the Renaissance-style Catedral Metropolitana was built in 1871 after the previous cathedral was destroyed in an earthquake. The graceful neoclassical interior has colorful Spanish-tile floors, stained-glass windows, and a Christ figure that was produced by a Guatemalan workshop in the late 17th century. On the north side of the nave, a recumbent Christ that dates back to 1878 draws devout Ticos, who arrive here to pray and deposit pleas scribbled on small slips of paper.

Estación del Ferrocarril
de Costa Rica   HISTORIC BUILDING
(Estación Atlántico; Map p64; 2542-5800; www. incofer.go.cr; cnr Av 3 & Calle 21) Less than a block to the east of the Parque Nacional is San José's historic train station to the Atlantic, which was built in 1908. Nowadays offering weekday train service to Heredia and Cartago, it's a remarkable example of tropical architecture, with swirling art nouveau–inspired beams and elaborate stonework along the roofline.

Parque Morazán   PARK
(Map p68; Avs 3 & 5 btwn Calles 5 & 9) Southwest of Parque España is Parque Morazán, named for Francisco Morazán, the 19th-century general who attempted to unite the Central American nations under a single flag. Once a notorious center of prostitution, the park is now beautifully illuminated in the evenings. At its center is the **Templo de Música** (Music Temple), a concrete bandstand that serves as an unofficial symbol of San José.

Parque Central   PARK
(Map p68; Avs 2 & 4 btwn Calles Central & 2) The city's central park is more of a run-down plaza. At its center is a grandiose bandstand that looks as if it was designed by Mussolini: massive concrete arches support a florid roof capped with a ball-shaped decorative knob.

Parque España   PARK
(Map p68; Avs 3 & 7 btwn Calles 9 & 11) Surrounded by heavy traffic, Parque España may be

Central San José

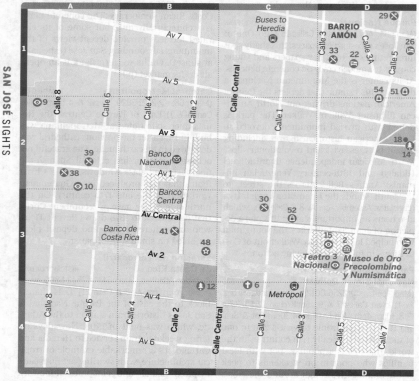

small, but it becomes a riot of birdsong every day at sunset when the local avian population comes in to roost. In addition to being a good spot for a shady break, the park is home to an ornate statue of Christopher Columbus that was given to the people of Costa Rica in 2002 by his descendants, commemorating the quincentenary of the explorer's landing in Puerto Limón.

Edificio Metálico
LANDMARK

(Map p68; cnr Av 5 & Calle 9) One of downtown San José's most striking buildings, this century-old, two-story metal edifice on Parque España's western edge was prefabricated in Belgium, then shipped piece by piece to San José. Today it functions as a school and local landmark.

Casa Amarilla
HISTORIC BUILDING

(Map p68; Av 7 btwn Calles 11 & 13) On Parque España's northeast corner, this elegant colonial-style yellow mansion (closed to the public) houses the Foreign Affairs Ministry.

The ceiba tree in front was planted by John F Kennedy during his 1963 visit to Costa Rica. If you walk around to the property's northeast corner, you can see a graffiti-covered slab of the Berlin Wall standing in the rear garden.

La Sabana & Around

Parque Metropolitano La Sabana
PARK

(Map p72) Once the site of San José's main airport, this 72-hectare green space at the west end of Paseo Colón is home to a museum, a lagoon and various sporting facilities – most notably Costa Rica's National Stadium (p93). During the day, the park's paths make a relaxing place for a stroll, a jog or a picnic.

Museo de Arte Costarricense
MUSEUM

(Map p72; ☑2256-1281; www.musarco.go.cr; east entrance of Parque La Sabana; ☺9am-4pm Tue-Sun; 🅿 FREE This Spanish-style structure served as San José's main airport terminal until

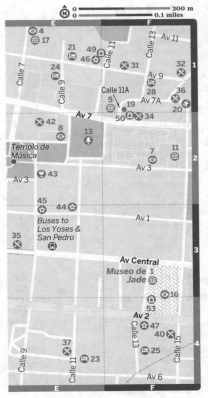

1955. The recently remodeled museum features regional art and other exhibits.

**Museo de Ciencias
Naturales La Salle** MUSEUM
(☑2232-1306; www.museolasalle.ed.cr; Sabana Sur; adult/child US$2/1.60; ⊙8am-4pm Mon-Sat, 9am-5pm Sun; ⊛) This natural-history museum near Parque La Sabana's southwest corner has an extensive collection of taxidermic animals and birds from Costa Rica and far beyond, alongside animal skeletons, minerals, preserved specimens and a vast new collection of butterflies. Kids in particular will appreciate this place.

◎ Escazú & Santa Ana

**Refugio Herpetologico
de Costa Rica** ANIMAL SANCTUARY
(☑2282-4614; www.refugioherpetologico.com; Carretera John F. Kennedy, Santa Ana; adult/child US$20/10; ⊙9am-4pm Tue-Sun) Costa Rica is full of wild reptiles, but for people who prefer meeting things with scales under controlled circumstances, there's the Refugio Herpetologico. On display are a bunch of snakes, turtles, caimans and a large crocodile, which can be viewed through a window, swimming underwater. There are also some resident spider and capuchin monkeys, plus a couple of ocelots.

◎ Los Yoses, Barrio Escalante & San Pedro

Barrio Escalante AREA
(Map p78) Formerly a residential enclave, the streets of this increasingly hip neighborhood are now lined with dozens of restaurants, cafes, bakeries and bars. The largest concentration of eateries stretches along Calle 33 and has been dubbed Paseo Gastronómico La Luz (La Luz Restaurant Promenade) in honor of a small grocery store that used to stand on the street's corner facing Avenida Central. Crowds of foodies descend on Barrio Escalante on weekend evenings, when finding parking becomes a very tall order.

Museo de Insectos MUSEUM
(Insect Museum; Map p78; ☑2511-8551, 2511-5318; www.facebook.com/insectosucr/; San Pedro; US$3; ⊙8am-noon & 1-4:45pm Mon-Fri) Reputedly Central America's largest insect museum, this place has an extensive collection assembled by the Facultad de Agronomía (agronomy faculty) at the Universidad de Costa Rica. After viewing the specimens, visitors are invited to a room with a kitchen to sample meal worms, scarabs and crickets. A little salt and oregano does wonders.

Curiously, the museum is housed in the basement of the music building, a brutalist structure painted an incongruous shade of Barbie pink.

🏃 Activities

Parque Metropolitano La Sabana has a variety of sporting facilities, including tennis courts, volleyball, basketball and baseball areas, jogging paths and soccer pitches. Beyond that, you can hit the links at **Parque Valle del Sol** (☑ext 3 2282-9222; www.vallesol.com; 1.7km west of HSBC Bank, Santa Ana; 9 or 18 holes US$48-67, golf carts US$23-32; ⊙6am-6pm Tue-Sun, 8am-6pm Mon), hike to a bunch of awesome windmills at **Las Eólicas** (The Windmills; Santa Ana) FREE or learn salsa with **Merecumbé San Pedro** (Map p78; ☑2224-3531; cnr Av 8 & Calle 65) or

Central San José

Escazú (Map p82; ☎8884-7553, 2289-4774; www.facebook.com/merecumbe.escazu.3/; cnr Av 26 & Calle Cortés).

☞ Tours

The city is small and easily navigable. If you're looking for a walking tour that will guide you to key sites, there are plenty on offer.

★**Barrio Bird Walking Tours**   WALKING
(Map p68; ☎6280-6169; www.toursanjose costarica.com; tours from US$29) Knowledgeable and engaging guides show visitors San José's famous and not-so-famous sights, providing history and insight on the city's architecture, markets and urban art. Specialized tours also cater to foodies and culture enthusiasts.

★**Really Experience Community**   TOURS
(Triángulo de la Solidaridad Slum Tour; ☎2297-7058; www.boywithaball.com; US$12-25 per person, $100 minimum group rate) Nonprofit Boy with a Ball wants to be clear: Really Experience Community is not your average slum tour. It may seem exploitative, but visiting El Triángulo, a squatter development of 2000 people north of San José, is anything but. Promising young residents lead tours, introducing guests to neighbors and community entrepreneurs. No cameras are allowed, but the conversations make a lasting impression. Note that this tour has a minimum cost of $100, making it ideal for groups. Boy With a Ball requires that you book at least three days in advance.

Teatro Nacional   CULTURAL
(Map p68; ☎ext 1114 2010-1100; www.teatrona cional.go.cr/Visitenos/turismo; Av 2 btwn Calles 3

& 5; tours US$10, under 12yr free; ☺9am-5pm) On this fascinating tour, guests are regaled with stories of the art, architecture and people behind Costa Rica's crown jewel. The best part is a peek into otherwise off-limits areas, such as the Smoking Room, which feature famous paintings, lavish antique furnishings and ornate gold trim. Tours are offered every hour on the hour in Spanish and English, to a maximum of 15 people.

ChepeCletas
TOURS

(Map p68; ☑8849-8316; www.chepecletas.com; Sat morning walking tours US$10 per person) This dynamic Tico-run company offers excellent private tours focusing on history, culture, food markets, coffee and nightlife. Its ever-changing menu of offerings also includes informative walks around San José on Saturday mornings and free bike tours on Wednesdays at 7pm (and occasionally on Sunday mornings as well).

Costa Rica Art Tour
TOURS

(☑8359-5571, in USA 877-394-6113; www.costa ricaarttours.com; per person US$150) This small outfit run by Molly Keeler conducts private tours that offer an intimate look at artists in their studios, where you can view (and buy) the work of local painters, sculptors, printmakers, ceramicists and jewelers. Lunch and San José city hotel pickup is included in the price. Reserve at least a week in advance. Discounts are available for groups.

Swiss Travel Service
WALKING

(Map p64; ☑2282-4898, 8310-7636; www.swiss travelcr.com; price dependent on group size) This long-standing agency offers a four-hour afternoon city tour of San José that hits all the key sites. Not offered on Mondays.

Carpe Chepe
TOURS

(☑8347-6198; www.carpechepe.com; guided pub crawls US$20; ☺8pm Fri & Sat) For an insider's look at Chepe's nightlife, join one of these Friday- and Saturday-evening guided pub crawls, led by an enthusiastic group of young locals. A shot is included at each of the four bars visited. There are other offerings as well, including a hop-on-hop-off nightlife bus, food tours, a craft-beer tour and free walking tours of San José. Note that the tours may not run on time and can feel a bit disorganized.

⚜ Festivals & Events

Día del Boyero
CULTURAL

(☺Mar) On the second Sunday of March, Escazú holds this popular event honoring Cos-

ta Rica's *boyeros* (oxcart drivers). Dozens of attendees from all over the country decorate traditional, brightly painted carts and form a colorful (if slow) parade.

Día de San José
RELIGIOUS

(St Joseph's Day; ☺19 Mar) San José marks the day of its patron saint with Mass in some churches.

Festival de las Artes
PERFORMING ARTS

(FIA; ☑2248-3240; www.facebook.com/festival delasartescr) About every other year, San José becomes host to this biennial citywide arts showcase that features theater, music, dance and film. It's usually held for two weeks in March or April, but the month can vary. Keep an eye out for information in the daily newspapers.

International Book Fair
LITERATURE

(www.feriadellibrocostarica.com; Antigua Aduana; ☺Aug or Sep) Thousands descend on Costa Rica's capital for this massive, multiday literary event, which includes readings, book sales and presentations from internationally renowned authors.

Desfile de los Boyeros
CULTURAL

(Oxcart Parade; Paseo Colón; ☺Nov) This parade of oxcarts down Paseo Colón is a celebration of the country's agricultural heritage.

Festival de la Luz
RELIGIOUS

(Festival of Light; www.festivaldelaluz.cr; ☺Dec) December brings San José's big Christmas parade, marked by elaborate costumes and floats, and an absurd amount of plastic 'snow.'

Las Fiestas de Zapote
CULTURAL

(www.fiestaszapote.com; Zapote; ☺late Dec-early Jan) Between Christmas and New Year, this week-long holiday celebration of all things Costa Rican annually draws in tens of thousands of Ticos to the bullring in the suburb of Zapote, just southeast of San José.

🛏 Sleeping

Accommodations in San José run the gamut from simple but homey hostels to luxurious boutique retreats. If you're flying into or out of Costa Rica from here, it may be more convenient to stay in Alajuela, as the town is minutes from the international airport.

Reservations are recommended in the high season (December through April), particularly the two weeks around Christmas and Semana Santa (Holy Week, the week preceding Easter).

La Sabana

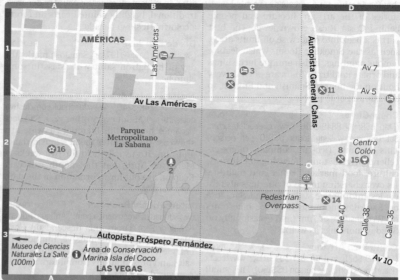

La Sabana

◎ Sights

1 Museo de Arte Costarricense	D2
2 Parque Metropolitano La Sabana	B2

◎ Sleeping

3 Apartotel La Sabana	C1
4 Gaudy's	D2
5 Hotel Grano de Oro	E3
6 La Rosa del Paseo	E2
7 Mi Casa Hostel	B1

◎ Eating

8 Las Mañanitas	D2
9 Lubnan	F3
10 Machu Picchu	E2
11 Más X Menos	D1
12 Pali	F2
13 Park Café	C1
Restaurante Grano de Oro	(see 5)
14 Soda Tapia	D3

◎ Drinking & Nightlife

15 Club Vertigo	D2

◎ Entertainment

16 Estadio Nacional de Costa Rica	A2
17 Sala Garbo	E3

🛏 Central San José

Most of downtown's better sleeping options are located east of Calle Central, many of them in historic Victorian and art-deco mansions. Many of the top-end hotels accept credit cards.

★ Hostel Casa del Parque HOSTEL $
(Map p64; ☎2233-3437; www.hostelcasadel parque.com; Calle 19 btwn Avs 1 & 3; dm US$14, d with/without bathroom US$49/39; 🛜) A vintage art-deco manse from 1936 houses this cozy and welcoming spot on the northeastern edge of Parque Nacional. Five large, basic private rooms (two with private bathroom), a newer seven-bed dormitory and an older 10-bed dormitory upstairs have parquet floors and simple furnishings. Enjoy some sun on the plant-festooned outdoor patio and take advantage of the shared kitchen.

The bilingual young owner is a good source of local dining information.

★ Selina San José HOSTEL $
(Map p68; ☎4052-5147; www.selina.com/san-jose; cnr Calle 13 & Av 9; dm US$10-15, r from US$40; 🐾🛜) Ensconced in a rad space within centrally ocated Barrio Otoya, this hostel is part of the Selina backpacker empire now

stretching across the lower Americas. Seemingly overnight, it has become the go-to hangout for young travelers, and brings in top local artists and musicians to adorn the place and perform live sets. It's loud here, and people like it that way.

Beds are comfy, the atmosphere is convivial and the space is inspired, with a reception desk built out of an old Volkswagon. There's a delicious restaurant too.

Casa Ridgway
GUESTHOUSE $

(Map p64; ☑2222-1400, 2233-6168; www.casaridgwayhostel.com; cnr Calle 15 & Av 6A; incl breakfast dm US$17, s/d without bathroom US$24/38; P☺🛜) This small, peaceful guesthouse on a quiet side street is run by the adjacent Friends' Peace Center, a Quaker organization promoting social justice and human rights. There is a small lounge, a communal kitchen and a lending library filled with books about Central American politics and society. No smoking or alcohol is allowed, with quiet hours from 10pm to 6am.

Costa Rica Backpackers
HOSTEL $

(Map p64; ☑2221-9761, 2221-6191; www.costaricabackpackers.com; Av 6 near Calle 21; dm US$12-16, d without bathroom US$35; P@🛜🏊) This popular hostel has 19 basic but clean dormitories and 14 private rooms with shared

bathrooms surrounding a spacious hammock-filled garden and a free-form pool. Two bars, a restaurant and chill-out music enhance the inviting, laid-back atmosphere. Other benefits include a communal kitchen and TV lounge, free luggage storage, internet access, an onsite travel agency and low-cost airport transfers ($26).

Hostel Shakti
HOSTEL $

(Map p64; ☑2221-4631; www.hostelshakti.com; cnr Av 8 & Calle 13; incl breakfast dm/s/d US$18/30/40; P❄@🛜) This lovely little guesthouse uses bold colors and natural materials to create an oasis of calm and comfort amid the chaos of San José. Three dorms and four private rooms are dressed up with eclectic furnishings and colorful bedding. There is a fully equipped kitchen, but you might not need it as the onsite restaurant (p80) is healthy, fresh and amazing.

Costa Rica Guesthouse
GUESTHOUSE $

(Map p64; ☑2223-7034; www.costa-rica-guesthouse.com; Av 6 btwn Calles 21 & 25; d incl breakfast with/without bathroom US$50/40; P@🛜) This 1904 guesthouse has simple, graceful rooms with spacious bathrooms and hallways lined with Spanish tiles. Furnishings are basic (creaky beds), but it's a tranquil, couple-friendly spot. There's a small internet lounge, an outdoor patio and an enclosed parking area out back. Laundry service (per kg US$3) is available.

Casa Botanica de Aranjuez
HISTORIC HOTEL $$

(Map p64; ☑8818-1894; www.facebook.com/pg/casabotanicaaranjuez; Calle 19; r incl breakfast from US$60; 🛜) Set in a century-old wooden home in Barrio Aranjuez, this charming place to stay is owned by a local biologist and adorned with his personal art collection. There are five uniquely decorated units of varying sizes, some with private or shared kitchens. There's also a basement gallery and event space where San José's movers and shakers are known to gather.

Hostel Pangea
HOSTEL $$

(Map p68; ☑2221-1992; www.hostelpangea.com; Av 7 btwn Calles 3 & 3A, Barrio Amón; dm US$14, d with/without bathroom US$55/35, ste from US$70; P@🛜🏊) This industrial-strength hostel – 25 dorm beds and 25 private rooms – has been a popular 20-something backpacker hangout for years. It's not difficult to see why: it's smack in the middle of the city and comes stocked with a pool and a rooftop restaurant-lounge with stellar views. Needless to say, it's a party spot.

Rooms are tidy, mattresses firm and the shared bathrooms enormous and clean. The hostel's five suites have king-size beds and flat-screen TVs. Other perks include free internet, luggage storage and 24-hour airport shuttles (from US$14).

Hotel Aranjuez
HOTEL $$

(Map p64; ☑ 2256-1825; www.hotelaranjuez.com; Calle 19 btwn Avs 11 & 13; r incl breakfast US$32-95; P @ 🛜) This hotel in Barrio Aranjuez consists of five nicely maintained vintage homes that have been strung together with a labyrinth of gardens and connecting walkways. The 35 spotless rooms come in various configurations, all with a lockbox and a cable TV. The hotel's best attribute, however, is the lush garden patio, where a legendary breakfast buffet is served every morning. Though the architecture can be a bit creaky and the walls thin, the service is efficient and the hotel is a solid, family-friendly option. Rooms in the newer apartment-building annex half a block away lack the charm and sense of community of the main hotel, but annex guests still have access to the bounteous breakfast and pleasant common areas across the street.

Luz de Luna
BOUTIQUE HOTEL $$

(Map p78; ☑ 2225-4919; www.luzdelunahotelboutique.com; Calle 33 btwn Avs 3 & 5; r US$46-75; 🛜) A converted old mansion, this boutique hotel, restaurant and cafe is in a prime location: the heart of Barrio Escalante's Paseo Gastronómico La Luz district and its up-and-coming restaurants. Foodies who like to relax will appreciate this sanctuary and self-described 'lunar complex' for its lush gardens, hardwood floors and occasional pre-Columbian statues.

Hotel Posada del Museo
GUESTHOUSE $$

(Map p64; ☑ 2258-1027; www.hotelposadadelmuseo.com; cnr Calle 17 & Av 2; s/d/tr/q incl breakfast US$40/51/65/79; @ 🛜) Managed by an amiable, multilingual couple, this architecturally intriguing, 1928-vintage inn is diagonally across from the Museo Nacional. French doors line the entrances to each of the rooms, no two of which are alike. Some rooms accommodate up to four people, making this a family-friendly option. Light sleepers, take note: the hotel is adjacent to the train tracks.

Hemingway Inn
HOTEL $$

(Map p68; ☑ 2257-8630; www.hemingwayinn.com; cnr Calle 9 & Av 9; incl breakfast s US$40-68, d US$57-85; 🛜🖥) This family-owned, funky little spot in Barrio Amón offers 17 simple, comfortable and unique rooms in a rambling *cafetalero* (coffee growers) house dating back to the 1920s. The garden, shared kitchen and wall murals lend the inn a relaxed and friendly ambience, and room prices include a full made-to-order breakfast. As a rare perk, pets can be accommodated with prior notice.

Kaps Place
GUESTHOUSE $$

(Map p64; ☑ 2221-1169; www.kapsplace.com; Calle 19 btwn Avs 11 & 13; incl breakfast s US$35-45, d/tr US$55/65, apt US$100-140; P @ 🛜) On a residential street in Barrio Aranjuez, this homey guesthouse has 20 rooms of various configurations spread over two buildings. Guests have access to patios decorated in colorful mosaics, three shared kitchens, a

---

SAN JOSÉ FOR KIDS

Chances are if you're in Costa Rica on a short vacation you'll be headed out to the countryside fairly quickly. But if for some reason you're going to be hanging out in San José for a day – or two or three – with your kids, know that it's not a particularly kid-friendly destination. There is lots of traffic and the sidewalks are crowded and cracked, making it difficult to push strollers or drag toddlers around. Although the city offers relatively few things specifically for children, here are a few activities they will likely enjoy.

Near Parque La Sabana, the Museo de Ciencias Naturales La Salle (p69) will impress youngsters with its astounding array of skeletons and endless cases full of stuffed animals, while the Museo de los Niños (p63) is a sure hit for children who just can't keep their hands off the exhibits. Young nature-lovers will enjoy getting up close to butterflies at the Spirogyra Jardín de Mariposas (p67) or checking out the exotic animals at the Parque Zoológico Nacional Simón Bolívar (p67). Just a little further afield (an easy day trip from San José) is the wonderful zoo and wildlife-rescue center Zoo Ave (p109), where you can enjoy native birds and monkeys in a more naturalistic setting.

If you're spending more than a week in the city, note that many Spanish-language academies offer special custom-made lessons for teens.

games room with ping-pong, pool and foosball tables, a big-screen TV lounge with a huge DVD library, and free phone calls to 60 countries. Recently the owner opened Kaps Cafe (p81), a lovely little eatery serving both guests and nonguests.

Hotel Fleur de Lys
HOTEL **$$**

(Map p68; ☑2223-1206; www.hotelfleurdelys.com; Calle 13 btwn Avs 2 & 6; incl breakfast r from US$76, junior/master ste US$126/156; P🅿🄰@🔊) Impeccably maintained, this century-old, bright-pink Victorian mansion houses 30 spotless wood-paneled rooms with firm beds, ceiling fans and wicker furnishings. A small onsite bar provides a welcome cocktail or smoothie, and on Fridays there is live music. The staff are attentive and the location central (note the proximity of the train tracks). German, French and English are spoken.

Hotel Colonial
HOTEL **$$**

(Map p68; ☑2223-0109; www.hotelcolonialcr.com; Calle 11 btwn Avs 2 & 6; s/d/ste incl breakfast US$71/82/110; P🅿🄰@🔊🄰) An intricately carved baroque-style carriage door and an arched poolside promenade usher guests into this 1940s Spanish-style inn. The 16 rooms and one suite are either whitewashed or painted an earthy mustard yellow color, with dark wood furnishings and bright bedspreads. Those on higher floors have sweeping views of the city and outlying mountains, while three ground-level rooms are wheelchair-accessible.

Bells' Home Hospitality
HOMESTAY **$$**

(☑2225-4752; www.homestay-thebells.com; s/d incl breakfast US$35/60, dinner US$10) This recommended agency is run by the bilingual Marcela Bell, who has operated the business for more than 30 years. She can arrange stays in more than a dozen homes around San José, including her own. Each one has been personally inspected and they are all close to public transportation. Airport pickup is also available.

Hotel Kekoldi
HOTEL **$$**

(Map p68; ☑2248-0804; www.kekoldi.com; Av 9 btwn Calles 5 & 7; r incl breakfast US$60-98; 🔊) This airy art-deco building in Barrio Amón has 10 high-ceilinged rooms of various sizes, painted in pastel shades and equipped with cable TV. The best ones face the street or backyard and are drenched in natural light; interior rooms are less appealing. Common spaces include a cheerful breakfast room and a garden for lounging, and bathrooms were recently updated.

Hotel Don Carlos
HOTEL **$$**

(Map p68; ☑2221-6707; www.doncarloshotel.com; Calle 9 btwn Avs 7 & 9; incl breakfast s/d US$79/90, ste s/d US$90/102; P🅿@🔊🄰) Built around an early-20th-century house that once belonged to President Tomás Guardia, this welcoming Barrio Amón inn exudes a slightly campy colonial-era vibe. Its 32 rooms surround a faux-pre-Columbian sculpture garden with a sundeck and a small kiddie-depth pool. All rooms have a cable TV, a lockbox and a hairdryer; upstairs units are generally nicer than the mustier ones downstairs. Don't miss the Spanish-tile mural, just outside the onsite restaurant, which beautifully depicts central San José in the 1930s.

La Rosa del Paseo
BOUTIQUE HOTEL **$$**

(Map p72; ☑2257-3225; http://larosadelpaseo.com; Paseo Colón btwn Calles 28 & 30; s/d/ste from US$70/80/90; P🅿@🔊) 🅿 Don't let the Paseo Colón location and the small facade fool you: this sprawling Victorian-Caribbean mansion (built in 1910 by the coffee-exporting Montealegre family) has 18 spacious rooms reaching way back into an interior courtyard far from the city noise. The recently revamped hotel still maintains the original tile floors and other historic details, including antique oil paintings and sculptures. Rooms are simple, with polished-wood floors and period-style furnishings. There's a wonderful front sitting room where guests can listen to vintage vinyl discs on the phonograph, and the garden, where breakfast is served each morning, is filled with heliconias and bougainvilleas.

★ Hotel Presidente
BOUTIQUE HOTEL **$$$**

(Map p68; ☑2010-0000, in USA 1-877-540-1790; www.hotel-presidente.com; Av Central; r US$100-189; P🅿🄰🔊) 🅿 Recent revamping has turned this formerly drab hotel into a glorious boutique stay. The new lobby offers tons of inlaid brick and antique adornments, and a red spiral staircase leads to a rooftop garden and hip new cocktail bar. The central location remains ideal, as do the 71 well-appointed rooms, the best of which feature Jacuzzis and stunning city views.

The hotel's rooftop cocktail bar (p89) is the talk of San José, with incredible city views and an exquisite garden.

🛏 La Sabana & Around

You'll find everything from hostels to vintage B&Bs in the neighborhoods that surround Parque Metropolitano La Sabana.

Gaudy's
HOSTEL $

(Map p72; ☎ 2248-0086; www.backpacker.co.cr; Av 5 btwn Calles 36 & 38; dm US$13, r with/without bathroom US$39/35; ᴘ@🛜) Popular among shoestring travelers for years, this homey hostel inside a sprawling modernist house northeast of Parque La Sabana has 13 private rooms and two dormitories. The owners keep the design scheme minimalist and the vibe mellow, with professional service and well-maintained rooms. There's a communal kitchen, a TV lounge, a pool table and a courtyard strung with hammocks.

Mi Casa Hostel
HOSTEL $

(Map p72; ☎ 2231-4700; www.micasahostel.com; Las Américas; incl breakfast dm US$13, r with/without bathroom from US$38/35; ᴘ@🛜) This converted modernist home in La Sabana has polished-wood floors, vintage furnishings and over a dozen eclectic guest rooms to choose from, including one large dorm and another room that's wheelchair-accessible. Mellow communal areas are comfortably furnished, and the shared kitchen is clean and roomy. There is a pleasant garden, a pool table, free internet, and a laundry service.

Colours Oasis Resort
BOUTIQUE HOTEL $$

(☎ 2296-1880, in USA & Canada 866-517-4390; www.coloursoasis.com; cnr Triángulo de Pavas & Blvr Rohrmoser; r US$55-200; 🛜🏊) This longtime LGBT-friendly hotel occupies a sprawling Key West–style complex in the elegant Rohrmoser district (northwest of La Sabana). Rooms and mini-apartments have modern furnishings and impeccable bathrooms. Facilities include a TV lounge, pool, sundeck and Jacuzzi, as well as an international restaurant, ideal for evening cocktails.

Apartotel La Sabana
HOTEL $$

(Map p72; ☎ 2220-2422; www.apartotel-lasabana.com; Calle 48; d/apt/f incl breakfast from US$85/101/141; ᴘ❄@🛜🏊) This lovely and well-maintained apartment complex 150m north of Rostipollos has 32 units in various configurations that draw long-term business travelers as well as families. Apartments (with or without kitchen) are accented with wood furnishings and folk art. The interior courtyard has a nice pool, and free shuttle service is offered both from and to the airport.

★ Hotel Grano de Oro
BOUTIQUE HOTEL $$$

(Map p72; ☎ 2255-3322; www.hotelgranodeoro.com; Calle 30 btwn Avs 2 & 4; d US$197-372, ste US$390-593; ᴘ❄@🛜) It's easy to see why honeymooners love it here. Built around a sprawling early-20th-century Victorian mansion, this elegant inn has 39 demure 'Tropical Victorian' rooms furnished with wrought-iron beds and rich brocade linens. Some rooms boast private courtyards with gurgling fountains, and a rooftop garden terrace offers two bubbling Jacuzzis. The whole place sparkles with tropical flowers and polished-wood accents.

If you want to experience the Costa Rica of a gilded age, this is the place to do it. Also the restaurant (p86) is incredible.

🛏 Los Yoses, Barrio Escalante & San Pedro

Locals use several prominent landmarks when giving directions, including Spoon restaurant, the Fuente de la Hispanidad fountain and Más x Menos supermarket.

★Hostel Bekuo
HOSTEL $

(Map p78; ☎ 2234-1091, in USA 1-813-750-8572; www.hostelbekuo.com; Av 8; dm US$11-13, d from US$30; 🛜) For pure positive energy, you won't find a nicer hostel in San José. This restful spot, in a hip area of Los Yoses just a block south of Av Central, feels extremely homey, thanks to frequent backyard BBQs, a living room with piano and guitar, and a kitchen equipped with good knives, appliances and an inviting work space.

The airy modernist structure has nine unique and colorful rooms with high-quality beds and mattresses (including four dormitories, one reserved especially for women), along with large tiled bathrooms, an expansive TV lounge dotted with beanbags, and an interior courtyard slung with hammocks. Well-traveled owner Brian Van Fleet and his staff go the extra mile for guests, with colorful and well-conceived information displays and evening outings designed to show visitors the best of San José's nightlife. Yet this remains a place where you can get a good night's sleep; quiet time is respected from 10:30pm onwards.

Hostel Urbano
HOSTEL $

(Map p78; ☎ 2281-0707; www.hostelurbano.com; Calle 39; dm US$12, d with/without bathroom US$39/33) Within easy walking distance of the university and its nightlife, yet right on the bus line into downtown San José, this immaculate hostel is in a 1950s home opposite Parque Kennedy in San Pedro. Guests feel instantly welcome, with its open floor plan, spacious backyard, pool table, modern internet facilities and a kitchen-dining area nice enough for a dinner party.

TALK LIKE A TICO

San José is loaded with schools that offer Spanish lessons (either privately or in groups) and provide long-term visitors to the country with everything from dance lessons to volunteer opportunities. Well-established options include the following:

Costa Rican Language Academy (Map p78; ☎ 2280-1685, in USA 866-230-6361; www.spanishandmore.com; Calle Ronda, Barrio Dent)

Institute for Central American Development Studies (ICADS; ☎ 2225-0508; www.icads.org; Calle 87A, Curridabat; month-long courses with/without homestay US$1990/915)

Personalized Spanish (☎ 2278-3254, in USA 786-245-4124; www.personalizedspanish.com; Tres Ríos)

Already speak Spanish? To truly talk like a Tico, check out the **Costa Rica Idioms** app, available for iOS. It's quite basic but defines local lingo and uses each term in a sentence. *Tuanis, mae!* (Cool, dude!)

Smaller rooms, which are often rented out as private doubles, are also ideal for groups of three or four friends traveling together. Even the larger 12- and 16-bed dorms manage not to feel claustrophobic, thanks to the thoughtful placement of well-constructed modern bunks. The owners have also opened a small coffee shop next door and a second hostel in Los Yoses.

Hostel Casa Yoses HOSTEL $
(Map p78; ☎ 2234-5486; www.casayoses.hostel.com; Av 8, Los Yoses; incl breakfast dm US$10-15, d with/without bathroom US$38/33; P @ 🛜) A mellow place, this Spanish Revival–style house from 1949 is perched on a hill that offers lovely views of the valley from the front garden. Here you'll find 10 rooms (three of them dorms) of varying decor and style, all of which are spotless, with wooden floors and tiled hallways. There is a shared kitchen, an attached bar, La Sospecha, with a pool table and foosball, and even an area for BBQs. The owners speak Spanish, English and French.

Hotel Ave del Paraíso HOTEL $$
(Map p78; ☎ 2283-6017, 2225-8515; www.hotelavedelparaiso.com; Paseo de la Segunda Republica; s/d incl breakfast US$68/79; @ 🛜) 🍴 Decorated with beautiful mosaic tiles, this hotel run by an artsy family is set back from the busy street just far enough to permit a good night's sleep. There's a wonderful restaurant and bar, Café Kracovia (p86), owned by the same family. The university is just a two-minute walk east.

Hotel Milvia B&B $$
(☎ 2225-4543; www.hotelmilvia.com; cnr Calle 75 & Av 1; s/d incl breakfast US$59/69; @ 🛜) Owned by a well-known Costa Rican artist and former museum director, this lovely Caribbean-style building offers a homey retreat from the city. Nine eclectic rooms, all dotted with bright artwork, surround a pleasant courtyard with a trickling fountain. An upstairs terrace provides views of the mountains.

Hotel 1492 Jade y Oro B&B $$
(Map p78; ☎ 2280-6265, 2225-3752; www.hotel1492.com; Av 1 btwn Calles 29 & 33; r incl breakfast from US$50; P 🛜) On a quiet Barrio Escalante side street you'll find this 10-room B&B in a Spanish-style house built in the 1940s by the Volio family. The rooms vary in size, but all are nicely accented, with Portuguese tile work and some original furnishings. Breakfast is served in a charming rear garden.

Hotel Le Bergerac BOUTIQUE HOTEL $$$
(Map p78; ☎ 2234-7850; www.bergerachotel.com; Calle 35 btwn Avs Central & 8; d standard/superior/deluxe/grande incl breakfast US$109/132/160/177; P @ 🛜) This Los Yoses standard-bearer features 25 rooms, most with a private garden patio, in a whitewashed building tranquilly removed from the main street. Though sizes and configurations vary, all rooms are comfortable and sunny with wooden floors and floral bedspreads, and equipped with an immaculate bathroom, a cable TV, a telephone and a safe. The onsite restaurant has a bar.

🛏 Escazú & Santa Ana

Escazú and Santa Ana are stylish suburbs with accommodations ranging from sleek boutique inns to homey B&Bs – but there's not much in these parts for the budget traveler. Street addresses aren't always given;

Los Yoses, Barrio Escalante & San Pedro

Los Yoses, Barrio Escalante & San Pedro

call directly or check hotel websites for directions (which are invariably complicated).

Santa Ana is situated three kilometers west of Escazú, and on the road between the two you'll find a few out-of-the-way spots to stay and eat.

Tiger's Den
B&B $

(☎ 8667-3591, 4033-4632; www.tigersdenbnb.com; La Paco, San Rafael de Escazú; r US$35-50; ❊ ☎) This comfy B&B in residential Escazú is a quiet, homey escape run by Tiger, an attentive former nurse and personal trainer who makes art and cooks brilliantly (meals cost US$10). Guests here are frequently medical and dental tourists, and Tiger can cater to their diets. Prices drop for longer stays, and the host prefers a minimum three-night commitment. Ask Tiger for directions.

★ **Studio Hotel** BOUTIQUE HOTEL **$$**
(☑2282-0505; www.costaricastudiohotel.com; 750m south of Fórum 1; r from $96; P✳🕏🏊) This boutique stay wins for so many reasons: it's comfy, close to good restaurants and the airport, reasonably priced and decked out in Costa Rican artwork. It also doubles as a gallery, with 90 works from some of the country's greatest talents, including painter Francisco Amighetti. Guests can (and should) book art tours of the hotel ($15 per couple).

Posada El Quijote B&B **$$**
(☑2289-8401; www.quijote.cr; Calle del Llano; d standard/superior/deluxe/studio apt incl breakfast US$85/99/109/109; P➔✳🕏) This Spanish-style hillside *posada* (guesthouse) in Bello Horizonte rates as one of the area's top B&Bs. Homey standard rooms have wooden floors, throw rugs, cable TV and hot-water bathrooms; superior and deluxe units have a patio or a private terrace. Guests are invited to drink at the honor bar, then soak up sweeping Central Valley views on the patio. A backyard swing set and trampoline make this place especially fun for families with kids.

Costa Verde Inn INN **$$**
(☑2228-4080, in USA 1-800-773-5013; www.costaverdeinn.com; Av 34, Escazú; s/d/tr incl breakfast US$60/70/80, d apt from US$90; P@🕏🏊) This homey stone inn is surrounded by gardens that contain a hot tub, a mosaic-tiled swimming pool, a BBQ area and a sundeck with wi-fi. Sixteen rooms of various sizes have king-size beds, comfy rocking chairs and folk-art accents. Five apartments come with a fully equipped kitchen. A generous Tico breakfast is served on the outdoor terrace. Weekly rates are available.

Hotel Mirador Pico Blanco HOTEL **$$**
(☑2289-6197; www.facebook.com/picoblancoinn; Calle Salitrillos; d standard/ste US$40/50; P) A sleepy stone inn high in the hills, Pico Blanco is perched on a ridge 3km southeast of central Escazú. It has seen better days, but its 15 rooms are comfortable, with tile floors, cable TV and clean, if slightly worn, bathrooms. For the money, you won't find more extravagant metropolitan views. A small onsite restaurant cooks up traditional meals.

Villa Escazú B&B **$$**
(☑2289-7971; www.hotels.co.cr/villaescazu; Av 36; s/d incl breakfast US$49/55; P🕏) This wooden chalet with a wraparound veranda is surrounded by gardens and fruit trees. The two quaint, wood-paneled rooms feature local artwork, comfy couches and a shared bathroom. Breakfast is served on the outdoor balcony. There's a two-night minimum stay: reserve well in advance. It's 900m west of Banco Nacional.

Out of Bounds B&B **$$**
(☑2288-6762; www.bedandbreakfastcr.com; Carretera John F Kennedy; d US$70-90; P✳🕏) This friendly, contemporary inn 1km west of Costa Rica Country Club has seven simple rooms with blond-wood floors; large, comfortable beds; painted sinks with folk-art motifs; mini-refrigerators and in-room coffeemakers. Two units come with air-con and two are wheelchair accessible. A broad outdoor deck with pleasant views is stocked with rocking chairs for lounging.

Casa de las Tías B&B **$$$**
(Map p82; ☑2289-5517; www.casadelastias.com; Av F Delgado; r US$102-136; P🕏🏊) In a quiet area of San Rafael, this yellow-and-turquoise Cape Cod–style house (complete with picket fence) has five immaculate, individually decorated rooms, all with private bathrooms. The house is adorned with crafts that friendly, helpful owners Xavier and Pilar have picked up on their travels in Latin America, lending the place a cozy, intimate feel.

Hotel Alta Las Palomas HOTEL **$$$**
(☑2282-4160, in USA 888-388-2582; www.thealtahotel.com; Carretera John F. Kennedy, btwn Santa Ana & Escazú; d/ste from US$203/277, per extra person US$20; P@🕏🏊) This graceful Mediterranean-style villa has 23 whitewashed rooms decked out in terracotta tiles, contemporary wood furnishings and expansive bathrooms equipped with hair dryers and robes. Upstairs balconies offer stunning views of the surrounding hills, and the onsite restaurant, La Luz, serves up fresh Mediterranean fare in an elegant setting. An upstairs parlor often hosts classical music performances.

🍴 Eating

From humble corner stands dishing out gut-filling *casados* (set meals) to contemporary bistros serving fusion everything, in cosmopolitan San José you'll find the country's best restaurant scene. Dedicated foodies should also check out the dining options in Los Yoses and San Pedro, as well as Escazú and Santa Ana.

Top-end restaurants are often busy on weekend evenings; make a reservation.

✖ Central San José

In downtown San José, long-standing neighborhood *sodas* (lunch counters) mix effortlessly with contemporary cafes and Asian-fusion eateries. One of the best places for a budget-priced lunch is the Mercado Central, where you'll find a variety of *sodas* serving *casados*, tamales, seafood and everything in between.

★ Café de los Deseos
CAFE $

(Map p64; ☎2222-0496; www.facebook.com/Cafedelosdeseos; Calle 15 btwn Avs 9 & 11; mains US$5-12; ☺11:30am-10pm Tue-Thu, to 11pm Fri & Sat; 🛜) Abuzz with artsy young bohemians, this colorful Barrio Otoya cafe makes a romantic spot for drinks (from wine to cocktails to smoothies), *bocas* (handmade tortillas with Turrialba cheese, salads, teriyaki chicken, individual pizzas), and tempting desserts. Walls are hung with the work of local artists and rooms are adorned with hand-painted tables, beaded curtains and branches entwined with fairy lights.

Maza Bistro
BISTRO $

(Map p64; ☎2248-4824; www.facebook.com/MazaBistro/; Calle 19, on Parque Nacional; mains US$8, brunch US$10; ☺9am-6pm Tue-Sun; 🍴) At this charming, alfresco restaurant attached to Hostel Casa del Parque (p72), brunch is served all day, with dishes like *huevos pochados* (a Latino version of eggs benedict) and braised beef shank *au jus* with pickled vegetables and a fried egg. The burgers combine three kinds of meat and are also a big hit, along with daily veggie options.

★ Café Rojo
CAFE $

(Map p68; ☎2221-2425; cnr Av 7 & Calle 3; coffee US$1.50-4, mains US$7-10; ☺noon-7pm Mon-Thu, to 8pm Fri & Sat, noon-7pm Sun; 🍴) This quaint cafe with a cactus out front uses the fresh produce of Costa Rica to create innovative lunch specials, such as Vietnamese noodle bowls and sandwiches with pork meatballs or caramel chicken, and mind-blowingly delicious salads. Vegans will find plenty to like here, as will coffee enthusiasts. All the flavorings and syrups for drinks are homemade, and the iced ginger coffee is divine.

Restaurante La Criollita
COSTA RICAN $

(Map p68; ☎2256-6511; Av 7 btwn Calles 7 & 9; breakfast from US$6, casados US$8-10; ☺6am-9pm) This homey local spot, popular with office types, dishes out a changing menu of simple Costa Rican specialties, such as stewed chicken or grilled fish. The setting is pleasant and the service efficient, and you can order a glass of Chilean or Spanish wine (US$4) to accompany your meal.

Café Miel
CAFE $

(Map p68; www.facebook.com/cafemielcostarica; Av 9 btwn Calle 11 & 13; coffee US$1-5, pastries US$2; ☺9am-6pm Mon-Fri, 2-6pm Sat) This tiny cafe opened to such wild success in 2014 that the owners quickly opened two more nearby. What's its secret? In addition to adorable and homey interiors, it's the artisanal products from the cafes' chefs and bakers. The mushroom *empanadas* are divine, as is the locally sourced coffee.

La Ventanita Meraki
FAST FOOD $

(Map p64; ☎2221-8016; www.facebook.com/laventanitameraki; cnr Av 3 & Calle 21, in front of the train station; mains US$5-8; ☺11am-midnight Tue-Thu, to 2am Fri & Sat, noon-8pm Sun) Ventanita means 'little window' in Spanish and Meraki means 'artistry' in Greek. Put them together and it's an accurate moniker for this fusion hole-in-the-wall: a to-go window in front of downtown's train station that serves innovative street food. Expect elaborate spins on typical fare, along with sandwiches like pumpkin butter cheese madness, and Twinkie *frito* (fried Twinkie) for dessert.

Café La Mancha
CAFE $

(Map p68; ☎2221-5591; www.facebook.com/pg/cafelamancha; Steinvorth buildling, Calle 1; coffee US$3-5; ☺10am-7pm Mon-Sat) Hidden away in a courtyard within the historic Steinvorth building, this new third-wave coffee shop is the passion project of a local photographer with a fondness for the golden bean. From *cortado* (espresso mixed with warm milk) to chemex, La Mancha offers all the latest in coffee technology and holds coffee-related workshops. The tranquil setting, replete with lovely photographs and plant life, is a welcome respite from the chaotic city streets.

Restaurante Shakti
VEGETARIAN $

(Map p64; ☎2222-4475; cnr Av 8 & Calle 13; mains US$5-10; ☺7:30am-7pm Mon-Fri, to 5pm Sat; 🍴) This informal neighborhood health-food outpost has simple, organic-focused cooking and freshly baked goods. Favorites include veggie burgers, along with various fish and chicken dishes, but most people come for the vegetarian *plato del día* (meal of the day) – only US$6 for soup, salad, main course and fruit drink (or US$8 with coffee and dessert thrown in)!

Alma de Café   CAFE $

(Map p68; 📞 2010-1119; www.teatronacional. go.cr/Cafeteria; Av 2 btwn Calles 3 & 5, Teatro Nacional; mains US$6-11; ⏰ 9am-7pm Mon-Sat, to 6pm Sun) One of the most beautiful cafes in the city, this atmospheric spot evokes early-20th-century Vienna. In other words, it's a perfect place to sip a cappuccino, enjoy a crepe or quiche and take in the lovely ceiling frescoes and rotating art exhibitions. The spiked coffee concoctions are an excellent midday indulgence.

Talentum   CAFE $

(Restaurante Tournant; Map p64; 📞 2256-6346; www.galeriatalentum.com; Av 11 btwn Calles 3 & 3A; lunch specials US$8-10; ⏰ gallery 11am-6pm Mon, to 7pm Tue-Fri, 11am-4pm Sat; restaurant 11:30am-6pm Mon, to 10pm Tue-Fri, 1-10pm Sat) This vibrant, quirky cultural space in a renovated mansion runs the gamut from cafe to art gallery. Sporting local artwork inside and out, with cozy seating on vintage couches and an outdoor deck, it's a fun place for a midday break. The ever-changing cultural agenda includes book signings, films, anatomical drawing classes and occasional live music.

Café Té Ría   CAFE $

(Map p68; 📞 2222-8272; www.facebook.com/CafeTe RiaenAmon; cnr Av 7 & Calle 13; mains US$6, cakes US$1.50-3; ⏰ 10:30am-7:30pm Mon-Fri, noon-7:30 Sat; 🛜📶🐾) This petite, pet-friendly cafe in Barrio Amón is adorned with local art and replete with homey goodness. It's a perfect place to work over a few cups of morning coffee, then stay for a fresh salad, delicious sandwiches or a mouthwatering pastry. Vegetarians are well served.

Café del Barista   CAFE $

(Map p64; 📞 2221-4712; www.cafedelbarista.com; Av 9 btwn Calles 19 & 21; buffet lunch US$8; ⏰ 7am-6pm Mon-Fri, 9am-6pm Sat) This corrugated-roofed, warehouse-like space in Barrio Aranjuez brews up a great cup of gourmet coffee (and makes a halfway decent cinnamon roll too). During the week, there's a delicious buffet lunch from 11am to 1:30pm.

Café Mundo   ITALIAN $$

(Map p68; 📞 2222-6190; cnr Av 9 & Calle 15; mains US$8-36; ⏰ 11am-10:30pm Mon-Fri, 5-11:30pm Sat; 📶) This longtime Italian cafe and expat favorite is set on a sprawling terrace in a vintage Barrio Otoya mansion. It's a perfect spot to enjoy a glass of wine and good (if not earth-shattering) pizzas and pastas within sight of a splashing outdoor fountain. Don't miss the good-value *plato del día* (US$8) at lunchtime on weekdays.

Kula   CAFE $$

(Map p68; 📞 8583-0786; cnr Calle 15 & Av 7; mains $7-12; ⏰ 10:45am-5:45pm) This sunny yellow cafe is newly perched in a second-story space, its plant-draped windows framing a particularly scenic corner of Barrio Amón. The food is fresh and inventive; highlights include a *pejibaye* (peach palm fruit) and heart of palm salad, and mouthwatering *arepas* filled with mushrooms and cheese. Don't miss the *churro* truffles for dessert.

El Patio del Balmoral   INTERNATIONAL $$

(Map p68; 📞 2222-5022; www.balmoral.co.cr; Av Central btwn Calles 7 & 9; mains US$8-27; ⏰ restaurant 6am-10pm; terrace bar 4-10pm Mon-Thu, to 11pm Fri & Sat) Filled with chattering gringos and suited Ticos, this all-purpose cafe-restaurant is a good place to chill out while taking in the pedestrian action on Av Central. Bonus: on sunny days the restaurant opens its retractable roof. The upstairs terrace bar hosts live bands on Tuesday through Friday nights.

Alma de Amón   LATIN AMERICAN $$

(Map p68; 📞 2222-3232; www.facebook.com/Al madeAmon/; Calle 5 btwn Avs 9 & 11; small plates US$6-9, large plates US$10-18; ⏰ 6am-10pm Mon-Wed, to midnight Thu-Sat, 6-11am Sun) With dishes from nearly a dozen Latin countries and considerable Caribbean influence, this restaurant is a solid option in Barrio Amón. Popular menu items include *mofongo* (a Puerto Rican dish with fried plantains) and *coxinhas* (Brazilian croquettes with chicken). The bartender shakes up spicy and delicious cocktails; El Chapulin has tequila, ginger beer, lime and sugar-cane syrup.

Q Café   CAFE $$

(Map p68; 📞 4056-5604; 2nd fl, cnr Av Central & Calle 2; mains US$8-20; ⏰ 7am-8:30pm Mon-Fri, 8am-8pm Sat, 9am-7pm Sun) A sleek, monochromatic cafe with excellent views of the ornate Correo Central building, this modern 2nd-floor spot near the heart of San José's pedestrian zone is perfect for coffee drinks (including delicious iced mochas) and pastries. Try the *empanadas*, which go well with the cafe's homemade hot sauce.

Kaps Cafe   CAFE $$

(Map p64; 📞 2221-1169; www.kapsplace.com; Calle 19 btwn Avs 11 & 13; mains US$7-15; ⏰ 7am-8pm Mon-Sat, 7-10am Sun; 📶) A lovely little eatery linked to the eponymous hostel (p74), with yummy coffee plus creative pastries and sandwiches. Especially great carrot cake.

★ La Esquina de Buenos Aires

ARGENTINE $$$

(Map p68; ☎2223-1909; www.laesquinadebuenos aires.com; cnr Calle 11 & Av 4; mains US$15-29; ☺11:30am-3pm & 6-10:30pm Mon-Thu, 11:30am-11pm Fri, 12:30pm-11pm Sat, noon-10pm Sun; ☑) White linens and the sound of old tango evoke the atmospheric bistros of San Telmo, as does the menu, featuring grilled Argentine cuts of steak, house-made *empanadas* and an extensive selection of fresh pastas in exquisite sauces. The excellent South American–centric wine list and attentive service make this an ideal place for a date. Reservations recommended.

La Terrasse

FRENCH $$$

(Map p64; ☎8939-8470; chef.patricia.frenchcui sine@gmail.com; Calle 15 btwn Avs 9 & 11; mains US$17-32) Hidden away in the living room of a 1925 Barrio Otoya home, this intimate French restaurant regularly welcomes well-heeled locals with something to celebrate. Gracious Gerald plays host while his wife, the talented chef Patricia, reveals her fine sensibilities in thick, creamy soups and cheeses, hearty meat dishes and imaginative presentation. Order French wine and a few dishes to share.

Tin Jo

ASIAN $$$

(Map p64; ☎2221-7605; www.tinjo.com; Calle 11 btwn Avs 6 & 8; mains US$11-19; ☺11:30am-2:30pm & 6-10pm Mon-Thu, 11:30am-2:30pm & 6-11pm Fri, noon-3:30pm & 6-11pm Sat, noon-9pm Sun; ☑) The interiors of this popular Asian standard-bearer are a riot of pan-Asian everything, just like the menu. Expect a wide range of fare from various regions – from *kung pao* shrimp to crunchy shrimp rolls to pad thai – as well as an extensive vegetarian menu.

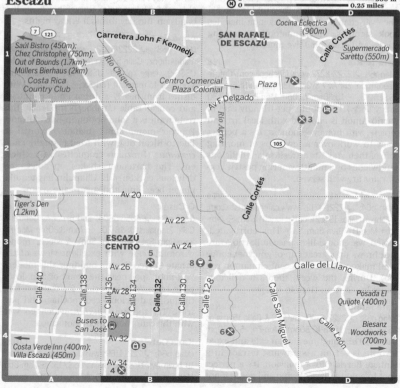

Escazú

✖ La Sabana & Around

There's a good mix of upscale international cuisine and fast food around the park. Supermarkets include **Más X Menos** (Map p72; ☑2248-1396; www.masxmenos.co.cr; cnr Autopista General Cañas & Av 5; ⊘7am-midnight Mon-Sat, to 10pm Sun; ℗) and **Palí** (Map p72; ☑2256-5887; www.pali.co.cr; Paseo Colón btwn Calles 24 & 26; ⊘8am-8pm Mon-Sat, 8:30am-6pm Sun; ℗).

Soda Tapia   SODA **$**
(Map p72; ☑2222-6734; www.sodatapia.com; cnr Av 2 & Calle 42; mains US$4-10, desserts US$2-7; ⊘6am-2am Sun-Thu, 24hr Fri & Sat; ℗🖶) An unpretentious '50s-style diner with garish red-and-white decor, this place is perpetually filled with couples and families noshing on grilled sandwiches and generous *casados*. If you have the nerve, try the monstrous 'El Gordo,' a pile of steak or chicken, onions, cheese, lettuce and tomato served on Spanish bread. Save room for dessert: ice-cream and fruit sundaes are the specialty.

La Sorbetera de Lolo Mora   DESSERTS **$**
(Map p68; ☑2256-5000; Mercado Central; desserts US$2-5; ⊘9:30am-5:45pm Mon-Sat) Head to the main market for this century-old local favorite that serves up fresh sorbet and cinnamon-laced frozen custard. Do as the locals do and order *barquillos* (cylindrical sugar cookies that are perfect for dipping).

Mariscos Poseidon   SEAFOOD **$**
(Map p68; ☑2221-8589; Mercado Central Annex; mains US$5-12; ⊘9am-6pm Mon-Fri, to 5pm Sat) The congenial Doris runs this narrow, blue-and-yellow seafood joint in the cen-

tral market's northern wing. The *ceviche mixto* appetizer (fish, shrimp and octopus marinated in lime juice) is tasty and cheap, as are the generous portions of seafood-studded rice.

Lubnan   LEBANESE **$$**
(Map p72; ☑2257-6071; www.facebook.com/lubnancr; Paseo Colón btwn Calles 22 & 24; mains US$8-25; ⊘11am-3pm & 6pm-midnight Tue-Fri, noon-4pm & 6pm-midnight Sat, 11am-5pm Sun; ℗) This atmospheric Lebanese place is a great date spot, with creamy hummus, flavorful tabbouleh and an array of succulent meats – some cooked, some deliciously raw. Waiters wear fezzes and a live belly-dancing performance goes down every Thursday at 8:30pm. DJs perform on Saturday nights.

Machu Picchu   PERUVIAN **$$**
(Map p72; ☑2222-7384; Calle 32 btwn Avs 1 & 3; mains US$9-22; ⊘11am-10pm Mon-Sat, to 6pm Sun; ℗🛜🖶) This locally renowned Peruvian restaurant does Andean right. A popular spot for a leisurely Sunday lunch, it has an encyclopedic menu featuring Peruvian classics such as *pulpo al olivo* (octopus in olive sauce), *ají de gallina* (a nutty chicken stew) and *causa* (chilled potato terrines stuffed with shrimp and avocado). The pisco sours here are deliciously powerful.

Las Mañanitas   MEXICAN **$$**
(Map p72; ☑2248-1593; Calle 40 btwn Paseo Colón & Av 3; mains US$6-17; ⊘11:30am-10pm Mon-Sat) At this authentic Mexican place near the park, well-rendered specialties include tacos in sets of four – corn tortillas accompanied by chicken, steak, sea bass or *carne al pastor* (spiced pork). Fans of *mole poblano* (central Mexico's famous chili and chocolate sauce) will also want to try it here, as the restaurant's owner hails from Puebla.

★ Park Café   EUROPEAN **$$$**
(Map p72; ☑2290-6324; www.parkcafecostarica.blogspot.com; Calle 48; tapas US$6-12, mains US$17-35; ⊘5-9:15pm Tue-Sat) At this felicitous fusion of antique shop and French restaurant, Michelin-starred chef Richard Neat offers an exquisite menu of smaller sampling plates (Spanish tapas–style), normal-sized mains, and a thoughtful wine list. The romantic candlelit courtyard is eclectically decorated with Asian antiques imported by Neat's partner, Louise France. It's near Parque La Sabana's northeast corner (100m north of Rostipollos restaurant).

Escazú

E. ROJAS/GETTY IMAGES ©

1. Parque Morazán (p67)

The park's Templo de Música hosts musical and other cultural performances and is an unofficial symbol of San José.

2. Teatro Nacional (p62)

The city's most revered building is lined with paintings; tours of the theatre are fascinating.

3. Colorful murals (p75)

Tile paintings outside Hotel Don Carlos.

4. Museo Nacional de Costa Rica (p63)

The Sphere at the National Museum of Costa Rica.

AL MERCADO

¿QUÉ LE VENDO, CHOLITA?.. ¿QUÉ QUIERE, ENCANTO?
..¡MIRE QUÉ CEBOLLITAS, ESPÍ QUÉ NABOS!

The tantalizing menu includes classic flavor combinations – carpaccio of beef with mustard dressing – alongside innovative offerings such as crab ravioli with asparagus and ginger cappuccino, crispy leg of duck with cucumber-mint salad or Gorgonzola gnocchi with prune-stuffed pork fillet, all prepared with passion and flair by Neat himself. An eight-table limit enhances the intimate atmosphere.

Restaurante Grano de Oro   FUSION $$$
(Map p72; ☑ 2255-3322; www.hotelgranodeoro. com; Calle 30 btwn Avs 2 & 4; lunch mains US$15-29, dinner mains US$19-42; ☉ 7am-10pm) Known for its Costa Rican–fusion cuisine, this stately, flower-filled restaurant is one of San José's top dining destinations. The menu features unique specialties such as sea bass breaded with toasted macadamia nuts or seared duck crowned with caramelized figs, and there's an encyclopedic international wine list. For dessert, don't miss the coffee cream mousse. Dinner reservations recommended.

✖ Los Yoses, Barrio Escalante & San Pedro

Succulent Turkish sandwiches, Caribbean-style *rondón* (seafood gumbo), wood-fired pizzas – you can find every type of cuisine imaginable in this corner of the city. Just north of Los Yoses, Calles 33 and 35 in Barrio Escalante are prime foodie destinations, boasting several fine restaurants within a few city blocks.

**Mantras Veggie Cafe
and Tea House**   VEGETARIAN $
(Map p78; ☑ 2253-6715; www.facebook.com/man trasveggiecafe; Calle 35 btwn Avs 11 & 13; mains US$8-10; ☉ 8:30am-5pm; ☑) Widely recognized as the best vegetarian restaurant in San José (if not all of Costa Rica), Mantras draws rave reviews from across the foodie spectrum for meatless main dishes, salads and desserts so delicious that it's easy to forget you're eating healthily. It's in Barrio Escalante, and there's a great brunch on Saturdays and Sundays.

Café Kracovia   CAFE $
(Map p78; ☑ 2253-9093; www.cafekracovia.com; Paseo del la Segunda Republica; snacks US$4-10, mains US$8-14; ☉ 10:30am-9pm Mon, to 11pm Tue-Sat; ☞) With several distinct spaces, from the low-lit, intimate downstairs to the outdoor garden courtyard, this hip cafe has something for everyone. Contemporary artwork and a university vibe create an appealing ambience for lunching on crepes, wraps, salads, Polish food and craft beer. It's 500m north of the Fuente de la Hispanidad traffic circle, where San Pedro and Los Yoses converge.

★ Olio   MEDITERRANEAN $$
(Map p78; ☑ 2281-0541; www.facebook.com/Res taurante.olio; cnr Calle 33 & Av 3; tapas from US$7, dishes US$12-22; ☉ 11:30am-11pm Mon-Wed, to midnight Thu & Fri, 6pm-midnight Sat; ☑) This cozy, Mediterranean-flavored gastropub in a century-old brick building in Barrio Escalante serves a long list of tempting tapas, including divine stuffed mushrooms, goat-cheese croquettes and pastas. The enticing drinks list includes homemade sangria and a decent selection of beers and wine. It's a romantic spot for a date, with imaginative, conversation-worthy quirks of decor and beautiful patrons.

★ Rávi Gastropub   GASTROPUB $$
(Map p78; ☑ 2253-3771; www.facebook.com/ ravicostarica; cnr Calle 33 & Av 5; mains US$9-18; ☉ noon-11pm Tue-Thu, to midnight Fri & Sat) This cool corner pub in Barrio Escalante is awash in bright murals, with seating in cushy blue booths, intimate back rooms or on the convivial bar stools up front. A menu of *bocas*, sandwiches, pizzas and more is served with craft brew on tap and homemade fruit sodas served in cute little bell jars.

At lunchtime, pick from the rotating menu of appetizers and main dishes and throw in a homemade soda, all for US$10.

Sofia Mediterráneo   MEDITERRANEAN $$
(Map p78; ☑ 2224-5050; www.facebook.com/Sofia Mediterraneo; cnr Calle 33 & Av 1; mains US$8-22; ☉ 6-11pm Tue-Fri, noon-11pm Sat, noon-5pm & 6:30-9pm Sun; ☑) This Barrio Escalante gem serves a superb mix of authentic Mediterranean specialties, including house-made hummus, tortellini, grilled lamb and a rotating selection of daily specials, accompanied by sweet, delicate baklava for dessert. The restaurant doubles as a community cultural center where owner Mehmet Onuralp hosts occasional themed dinners featuring musicians, chefs and speakers from around the world.

Al Mercat   GASTRONOMY $$
(Map p78; ☑ 2221-0783; http://almercat.com; Av 13, Barrio Escalante; US$8-25; ☉ noon-5pm Tue & Wed, noon-5pm & 6:30-10pm Thu-Sat, noon-3pm Sun; ☑) This exquisite Barrio Escalante restaurant serves whatever is fresh from the market. Family-style dishes of corn and sweet potato *chalupas* or grilled vegetables with smoked chese are fresh and flavorful,

and although vegetarians are well served, meat eaters will appreciate the fine cuts of meat. The service here is impeccable and the atmosphere is enlivened by vertical gardens.

More recently, the chef has added smaller and less expensive plates to the menu, such as tacos and *ceviche*.

El Buho   VEGETARIAN $$
(Map p78; ✆2224-6293; www.facebook.com/El BuhoVegetariano; Av 5, 25m east of Calle 3; mains US$10-18; ⊗11:30am-8pm Mon-Fri; ✍) Drawing health-food devotees from the nearby university and further afield, this buzzing San Pedro eatery just off Calle de la Amargura serves a variety of vegan, vegetarian and gluten-free treats, from eggplant croquettes to stir-fries, and mushroom casseroles to passion-fruit cookies.

El Portón Rojo   PIZZA $$
(Map p78; ✆2224-4872; www.facebook.com/Piz zaElPortonRojo; cnr Av 10 & Calle 43; pizzas small US$8-10, large US$16-18; ⊗noon-3pm & 5:30-11pm Tue-Sat, 5:30pm-11pm Mon, noon-5pm Sun) Serving up some of the best pizza and sangria in the Los Yoses area, this hip restaurant doubles as a gallery. Funky local art sells right off the brick walls, and a steady influx of customers from Hostel Bekuo (p76) keeps things lively.

Restaurant Whapin   CARIBBEAN $$
(Map p78; ✆2283-1480; cnr Calle 35 & Av 13; mains US$10-28; ⊗11am-9pm) For a taste of the Caribbean without leaving San José, try this corner spot in Barrio Escalante painted Rasta red, yellow and green. Steamy bowls of *rondón* (seafood gumbo), rice and red beans, and fish simmered in spicy coconut sauce go well with *agua de sapo*, a zesty sweet ginger drink. Don't forget the fried plantains and seasonal crisp breadfruit.

Kalú Café & Food Shop   INTERNATIONAL $$$
(Map p78; ✆2253-8426, 2253-8367; www.kalu. co.cr; cnr Calle 31 & Av 5; mains US$15-21; ⊗noon-10pm Tue-Fri, 9am-10pm Sat, 9am-4pm Sun; ✍) Sharing a sleek space with Kiosco SJO (p94) in Barrio Escalante, chef Camille Ratton's exceptional cafe serves a global fusion menu of soups, salads, sandwiches, pastas and unconventional delights such as the fish taco trio filled with mango-glazed salmon, red-curry prawns and macadamia-crusted tuna. Don't miss the mind-meltingly delicious passion-fruit pie.

Lolo's   PIZZA $$$
(Map p78; ✆2283-9627; pizzas US$14-24; ⊗6pm-midnight Mon-Sat) Fans of bohemian chic will appreciate this quirky pizzeria, hidden in a mustard-yellow house (No 3396) along the railroad tracks north of Av Central in Barrio Escalante. The vibrantly colorful, low-lit interior, hung with an eclectic collection of plates and other knickknacks, creates an artsy, romantic setting for sangria and pizzas fired up in the bright-red oven out back.

🍴 Escazú & Santa Ana

These two suburbs are home to a great many upmarket restaurants, as well as some fine farmers' markets and plenty of gourmet grocery stores, including **Automercado** (Map p82; ✆2588-1812; Atlantis Plaza, Calle Cortés, San Rafael de Escazú; ⊗7am-10pm Mon-Sat, 8am-9pm Sun), **Más X Menos** (Map p82; ✆2228-2230; Centro Comercial Escazú, Carretera John F Kennedy, San Rafael; ⊗6:30am-midnight Mon-Sat, to 10pm Sun) and **Supermercado Saretto** (✆2228-0247; www.saretto.cr; Av Central, San Rafael; ⊗8am-9pm).

Buena Tierra   CAFETERIA $
(Map p82; ✆2288-0342; www.facebook.com/Cafe OrganicoBuenaTierra; cnr Calle 134 & Av 34; mains US$6-8; ⊗9am-5:30pm Mon-Fri, 8am-2pm Sat; ✍) With tree-trunk tabletops and huge windows, this friendly organic cafe and health-food store in Escazú Centro is a good place to detox. The sandwiches are sublime and coffee is delicious. The cafe also organizes a Wednesday-morning organic farmers market (8am to 11am).

Chez Christophe   BAKERY $
(✆2228-2512; Calle Convento; pastries US$2-5; ⊗7am-7pm Tue-Sat, 8am-5pm Sun) If you have a hankering for a coffee éclair, croque monsieur or plain (but transcendent) croissant, linger here. French *tostadas* are reserved for Sunday, but every other day this authentic French bakery offers freshly baked breads and pastries, as well as espresso and a full breakfast and lunch menu. It's just south of Centro Comerical El Paco in San Rafael.

★ Maxi's By Ricky   CARIBBEAN $$
(✆2282-8619; Calle San Rafael, Santa Ana; appetizers US$1.50-8, mains US$9-30; ⊗noon-midnight) If you can't get to the Caribbean coast, this restaurant is a good substitute. Manzanillo native Ricky transported his lip-smacking restaurant to the Central Valley in 2014 and everybody started showing up to feast on the traditional rice-n-beans, Caribbean chicken and *rondón* soup. The latest addition to the menu: small plates, so everybody can try a little of everything. Delish! It's tricky to find: ask locally for directions.

SAN JOSÉ EATING

★ **Cocina Eclectica** INTERNATIONAL **$$**
(☎8529-2509; www.facebook.com/CocinaEclec
TicaEscazu/; Trejos Montealegre, Escazú; meal
US$12-20; ⊙noon-8pm) The Escazú residence
of Joanna Stein, identifiable only by a small
'J' on the door, might not seem like a res-
taurant. In fact it's much more. All day long,
dressed in an apron and inked with dozens
of tattoos, the self-taught cook pirouettes
around her well-stocked kitchen preparing
her personal vision of haute cuisine with
local produce and exotic ingredients. When
guests arrive, she works out their dietary
needs and desires, considers what's available
and inspiring, and commences her labor of
love. Our visit involved a soul-warming soup
of cardamom, carrot and quinoa, delicious
home-cured trout *ceviche*, and hearty chick-
en *chicharrón* with pear butter and fried po-
tatoes. Dessert was homemade passion-fruit
ice cream. The experience cost just US$12.
Joanna also rents rooms in her lovely abode
for US$20 to US$35 a night.

Saúl Bistro MEDITERRANEAN **$$**
(☎2228-8685; www.facebook.com/SaulBistroCosta
Rica; Calle Real; appetizers US$10-16, mains US$11-
25; ⊙7am-10pm Sun-Thu, to midnight Fri & Sat)
There are life-sized plastic zebras in the dining room at this snazzy open-air restaurant
that appeared (and became a sensation)
in 2015. An extension of Saúl Mendez, the
Guatemala-based empire of men's fashion,
the restaurant is adorned with curious art,
bubbling fountains and vertical gardens, and
it serves delicious Mediterranean cuisine, savory crepes, fine wine and exquisite cocktails.
It's quite the scene; recently a newer location
opened in fabulous Barrio Escalante (p69).

Container Platz GASTRONOMY **$$**
(☎6050-1045; www.facebook.com/ContainerPlatz;
Calle 5, Santa Ana; mains US$6-15; ⊙11:30am-10pm
Mon-Thu, 11am-midnight Fri & Sat, 11am-8pm Sun)
In this recently launched gastronomic exper-
iment, about a dozen mini-businesses have
sprung to life in brightly painted shipping
containers in Santa Ana. The effort earns
high marks for innovation and reasonably
priced, artisanal fast-food, with everything
from a circus-themed nacho place to a *chur-
ros* factory and a '*hummuseria*' that serves
delectable pita triangles with its homemade
hummus. Communal picnic tables foster a
sense of camaraderie, as does the craft-beer
container.

La Posada de las Brujas COSTA RICAN **$$**
(Map p82; ☎2228-1645; off Av 30, btwn Calles San
Miguel & 128, Escazú; mains US$6-24; ⊙11am-mid-
night Tue-Sat, to 10pm Sun; P▣) This open-air
steak house is Escazú's finest family option.
Spacious indoor and outdoor seating accommodates large groups, and big eaters are well
served with heaping plates of rice, beans,
fried plantains and a meat of their choice.
An onsite menagerie (think goats, rabbits, a
donkey and tropical birds) and two trampo-
lines will be big hits with kids.

Casona de Laly COSTA RICAN **$$**
(Map p82; ☎2288-1507; cnr Av 26 & Calle 1, Esca-
zú; US$7-34; ⊙11am-11pm Mon-Sat, to 9pm Sun;
P) This Escazú staple recently reopened
with a fresh new look but exactly the same
delicious Costa Rican menu that everybody
has always showed up for, including hearty
casados, grilled meats and luscious seafood
soup. There's now a light-up sign outside,
along with a small parking lot, a bunch of
flat-screens and a small bar in the corner.

Three other Lalys have opened in neigh-
boring suburbs, but this original location
remains the favorite.

Nuestra Tierra COSTA RICAN **$$**
(Map p68; ☎2258-6500; cnr Av 2 & Calle 15, Esca-
zú; mains US$6-22; ⊙6am-midnight; ▣) Tour-
isty but fun, this bustling eatery maintains
a calculatedly rustic atmosphere, with pic-
nic-style tables, mounted bull's heads and
strings of metal cups dangling from the rafters. Cheery waiters deliver well-prepared if
pricey Tico food, from tasty pork tamales to
wooden platters piled with heaping *casados*.
A fine spot for lunch and sangria after a visit
to the nearby museums.

Tiquicia COSTA RICAN **$$**
(☎2289-7330; Calle Cuesta Grande, Escazú; bocas
US$5-17, mains US$13-23; ⊙noon-11pm Tue-Thu,
to midnight Fri & Sat, to 9pm Sun) This long-
running hilltop restaurant 5km south of Es-
cazú Centro serves up bounteous platters,
accompanied by live folk music on week-
ends. Yes, the food is only so-so, but you're
not here to eat, you're here to admire the
extravagant views of the Central Valley. It's
tricky to find; call for directions.

alTapas Bar TAPAS **$$**
(☎2282-4871; www.facebook.com/tapeandorico/;
Radial Santa Ana, 150m north of the Red Cross, Santa
Ana; tapas US$10-25; ⊙noon-2am Wed-Sat, to 11pm
Sun; ☎) Owned by four brothers, this Spanish
tapas restaurant is over-the-top hospitable,
offering guests a complimentary glass of *cava*
(sparkling Catalonian wine) and a flavorful
mini-croquette at the start of the meal, best
followed by dishes such as local oysters, oc-

GAY & LESBIAN VENUES

The city is home to Central America's most thriving gay and lesbian scene. As with other spots, admission charges vary depending on the night and location (from US$5 to US$10). Some clubs close on various nights of the week (usually Sunday to Tuesday) and others host women- or men-only nights; inquire ahead or check individual club websites for listings. Many clubs are on the south side of town, which can get rough after dark. Take a taxi.

La Avispa (Map p64; ☎2223-5343; www.laavispa.com; Calle 1 btwn Avs 8 & 10; ☺8pm-6am Thu-Sat, 5pm-6am Sun) A lesbian disco bar that has been in operation for more than three decades, La Avispa (the Wasp) has a bar, pool tables and a boisterous dance floor that's highly recommended by travelers.

BO Club (Map p64; ☎2221-0500; cnr Calle 11 & Av 10; ☺8pm-6am Fri & Sat) A club that features everything from classic disco to electronica, as well as special themed nights. It's on the south side of town.

Pucho's Bar (Map p64; ☎2256-1147; cnr Calle 11 & Av 8; ☺8pm-2am Tue-Sat) This gay male outpost is more low-rent (and significantly raunchier) than some; it features scantily clad go-go boys and over-the-top drag shows.

topus in garlic and expertly prepared paella. The decor is austere but classy, with a large wooden bar dominating the space.

🍷 Drinking & Nightlife

Chepe's artsiest and most sophisticated drinking venues are concentrated north and east of the center, in Barrio Amón and Barrio Escalante. For a rowdier, younger scene, head to Barrio la Californiaor Calle la Amargura (p90).

Best for cityscapes and cocktails are the rooftop bar at Hotel Presidente (p75) and the upstairs terrace at El Patio del Balmoral (p81). People-watching rocks at Café de los Deseos (p80) in Barrio Otoya and at Mercado La California.

🍸 Central San José

On weekends, these streets of La California in central San José are packed with 20-something revelers puffing cigarettes and pondering where to head for the next *chili guaro* (an increasingly popular shot with sugar-cane liquor, hot sauce and lime juice). Meanwhile, young professionals hit up the fancier cocktail bars.

★**Stiefel**   PUB
(Map p68; ☎8850-2119; www.facebook.com/ StiefelPub; Av 5; ☺6pm-2am Mon-Sat) Two dozen-plus Costa Rican microbrews on tap and an appealing setting in a historic building create a convivial buzz at this pub half a block from Plaza España. Grab a pint of Pelona or Maldita Vida, Malinche or Chichemel;

better yet, order a flight of four miniature sampler glasses and try 'em all!

Azotea Calle 7   COCKTAIL BAR
(Map p68; ☎2010-0000; www.facebook.com/pg/ azoteacalle7; Calle 7, Hotel Presidente; ☺4-10pm Sun-Wed, to midnight Thu-Sat) Featuring stylish indoor and verdant outdoor spaces, along with a sweeping view of the city, this rooftop cocktail bar fills nightly with Hotel Presidente (p75) guests and well-heeled professionals. Great craft cocktails, too.

Mercado La California   BEER GARDEN
(Map p64; www.facebook.com/MercadoLaCali fornia/; Calle 21; cocktails US$5-15, beer US$3; ☺6pm-3:30am Thu-Sat, 4pm-1:30am Sun) Inspired by Madrid's 'Mercado San Miguel,' El Mercadito (as the locals say) is a recent addition to the up-and-coming Barrio La California. The line regularly snakes down the block from the entrance to this nightlife plaza's food kiosks, cocktail stands and craft-beer vendors, and the people in that line are often stunning to behold.

The plaza is lit up and lively, with seating areas for hanging out and feasting on gourmet tacos, pizza and BBQ-pork sandwiches.

Bebedero   COCKTAIL BAR
(Map p68; ☎2221-3815; www.facebook.com/ bebederoCR; Calle 1; ☺6pm-2am Wed-Sat) This glitzy, recently established cocktail den in the historic Steinvorth Building is brought to you by the mixologist/chef team from Maza Bistro (p80), and they nail it every time. Beverages are artfully concocted with rare liquors, house-made bitters and even

healing teas straight from the jungle. The tapas menu includes luscious local oysters and stuffed *pejibaye* (peach palm fruit). Reservations recommended.

Antik
CLUB

(Map p64; Av 10; cover US$10; ☺11:30am-3pm & 6-11pm Tue-Thu, 11:30am-3pm & 6pm-6am Fri, 6pm-6am Sat) Set in a historic mansion that once belonged to a Venezuelan general, Antik offers a tri-level experience, with a basement catering to the EDM crowd, a main level pizza restaurant and an upper floor featuring Latin dance rhythms and a sweet balcony with city views. There are a couple of bars offering craft beer and excellent, reasonably priced cocktails. The music often continues until dawn.

Craic Irish Pub
PUB

(Map p64; cnr Av 2 & Calle 25A; ☺6pm-2am Mon-Sat) This popular pub in Barrio La California serves a wide variety of beers accompanied by burgers, fries and other bar snacks. It also has a foosball table.

Chubbs
SPORTS BAR

(Map p68; ☑2222-4622; 2nd fl, Calle 9 btwn Avs 1 & 3; ☺11am-2am) In the heart of the San José tourist belt, this little sports bar has reasonably priced drinks, tasty burgers and a stack of TVs displaying the game. It's popular with expats and has unsurprisingly opened a second location on the old road between Santa Ana and Escazú.

La Concha de la Lora
BAR

(Map p64; ☑2222-0130; www.facebook.com/la conchalora; Calle 21 btwn Avs Central & 1; ☺9pm-4am Tue & Thu-Sun) An enthusiastic young crowd packs in here nightly for foosball, good bar snacks, DJs spinning everything from Latin music to Jimi Hendrix, and occasional live bands and reggae nights. Low cover charges (free to US$6) help maintain the upbeat mood.

🍷 La Sabana & Around

The city's two most famous clubs throb in the western and northern stretches of the city, and a handful of bars surround each one.

★ Castro's
CLUB

(Map p64; ☑2256-8789; cnr Av 13 & Calle 22; ☺1pm-4am) Chepe's oldest dance club, this classic Latin American disco in Barrio México draws crowds of locals and tourists to its large dance floor with a dependable mix of salsa, *cumbia* and merengue.

Club Vertigo
CLUB

(Map p72; ☑2257-8424; www.vertigocr.com; Paseo Colón btwn Calles 38 & 40; cover US$6-15; ☺10pm-dawn Fri & Sat) Located on the ground floor of the nondescript Centro Colón office tower, the city's premier club packs in Chepe's beautiful people with a mix of house, trance and electronica. Downstairs is an 850-person-capacity sweatbox of a dance floor; upstairs is a chill-out lounge lined with red sofas. Dress to the nines and expect admission charges to skyrocket on guest-DJ nights.

🍷 Los Yoses, Barrio Escalante & San Pedro

Calle La Amargura (Sorrow St) is the more poetic name for Calle 3, north of Av Central. However, it should be called Calle de la Cruda (Street of Hangovers) because it has the highest concentration of bars of any single street in town, and many of these are packed with customers (mainly university students) even during daylight hours. Places come and go, but Terra U (Map p78; ☑2283-7728; www. facebook.com/TerraUSanPedro; Calle La Amargura; ☺10:30am-2:30am Mon-Sat, 3pm-2am Sun) is a longtime party spot. The area gets rowdy in the wee hours: watch out for drunks and pickpockets.

Wilk
BREWERY

(Map p78; www.facebook.com/wilkcraftbeer; cnr Calle 33 & Av 9; ☺4pm-1am Tue-Sat) This Escalante pub attracts a mixed crowd of Ticos and Gringos who share an appreciation for craft brews and seriously delicious burgers (veggie included). The wide selection includes 27 craft beers on tap, including inventive concoctions of Costa Rica Craft Brewing and Treintaycinco. On each month's first Thursday, a crowd gathers to watch a local brewmaster invent a new beer.

Roots Cool and Calm
BAR

(The House of Reggae; Map p78; ☑2253-1953; www. facebook.com/rootscoolandcalm; Av 8; ☺7pm-2am Mon-Sat, to midnight Sun) The dreadlocked set crowds this cool Los Yoses bar, which brings in DJs from as far afield as Puerto Viejo on the Caribbean coast. It's a sweet spot to get a beer and hang with reggae-loving locals.

Un Lugar Resto-bar
BAR

(Map p78; ☑2225-3979; www.facebook.com/bar unlugar; Calle 33 btwn Avs 11 & 13; ☺5:30pm-midnight Mon-Thu, 5pm-2am Fri & Sat) This small wood-lined bar in Barrio Escalante serves as a neighborhood hangout that draws artsy types and young professionals for cold beer and *bocas*.

Río Bar
BAR

(Map p78; ☑ 2225-8371; Av Central; ☺ 4pm-midnight Mon-Thu, to 2am Fri-Sat) Just west of Calle 43 and the Fuente de la Hispanidad (the official boundary between Los Yoses and San Pedro), this large, popular bar has live bands some nights and flat-screen TVs showing the current game. It's a good spot to watch the rush-hour traffic crawl by in the company of an after-work crowd.

🍸 Escazú & Santa Ana

If you're looking for a spicy cocktail and some house music, 8ctavo Rooftop (p92) is where the beautiful people partake. And just a short drive west you'll find the country's premier brewery, Costa Rica Craft Brewing (p91), along with its popular tasting room. Escazú also has a few dive bars sprinkled around its main plaza, but few are particularly appealing.

★ Costa Rica Craft Brewing
BREWERY

(☑ 2249-4277; www.facebook.com/craftbeercostarica; Calle Cajeta; ☺ 10am-10pm Mon-Wed, to midnight Thu-Sat, noon-6pm Sun) Just when everyone thought it would be Imperial versus Pilsen forever, this artisanal brew pub paved the way for craft beer in Costa Rica. The brewery's newer location in Brasil, a suburb of San José, offers tours and tastings of its fine products, which include staple ales such as Libertas and Segua, along with more experimental barley wines and Russian Imperial stouts. It's out of town; ask locally for directions.

Müllers Bierhaus
BEER GARDEN

(☑ 2228-0914; www.facebook.com/MBierhaus/; in front of the Cerro Alto residence, Guachipelín; ☺ 6-11pm Mon-Wed, to midnight Thu & Fri, 1pm-12:15am Sat, 1-7pm Sun) This family-owned German restaurant and beer garden is popular with expats for its tasty curry sausages and vast selection of booze. More than 50 different brews are on offer, many of them German or otherwise international.

Pub
BAR

(Map p82; ☑ 2288-3062; www.facebook.com/the-pubcr; Av 26 btwn Calles 128 & 130; ☺ 4pm-2am Mon-Sat) This small, friendly pub has a list of about a dozen international beers, more than a dozen local brews and a selection of shots. Well-priced happy-hour drink specials keep things hopping, and a greasy bar menu is available to soak up the damage.

★ Entertainment

Pick up *La Nación* on Thursday for listings (in Spanish) of the coming week's attractions. The free publication GAM Cultural (www.gamcultural.com) and the website San José Volando (www.sanjosevolando.com) are also helpful guides to nightlife and cultural events.

Cinema

Many cinemas show recent Hollywood films with Spanish subtitles and an English soundtrack. Occasionally, films are dubbed over in Spanish (*doblado* or *hablado en español*) rather than subtitled; ask before buying a ticket. Movie tickets cost about US$4 to US$5, and generally Wednesday is cheaper. Check newspaper listings or individual theater websites for schedules.

There are bigger multiplexes in Los Yoses and San Pedro, while the most modern theaters are in Escazú.

Centro de Cine
CINEMA

(Map p68; ☑ 2242-5200; www.centrodecine.go.cr; cnr Calle 11 & Av 9) This pink Victorian mansion houses the government-run film center and its vast archive of national and international flicks. Festivals, lectures and events are held here and in outside venues; check the website for current events.

Sala Garbo
CINEMA

(Map p72; ☑ 2222-1034; www.salagarbo.com; cnr Av 2 & Calle 28) Art-house and classic film screenings.

Cine Magaly
CINEMA

(Map p64; ☑ 2222-7116; www.facebook.com/CineMagaly; Calle 23 btwn Avs Central & 1) Screens the latest releases in a large, recently renovated theater, along with independent films in English. The attached Kubrick Gastro Bar (noon to 10pm Monday to Saturday, from 1pm Sunday) serves up delicious salads, pizza, desserts and an assortment of flavored teas. It's the perfect spot for a sweet treat before or after the movie.

DRINK RESPONSIBLY

Be safe. Enterprising thieves sometimes lurk around popular nightspots, waiting to relieve drunken party people of their wallets. When leaving a bar late at night, keep your wits about you and take a taxi.

Live Music

The best spots to see live, local music in San José are El Lobo Estepario , Mundoloco El Chante and El Sótano. Internationally renowned DJs frequently appear at Club Vertigo (p90) and 8ctavo Rooftop.

★ **Teatro Nacional** THEATER
(Map p68; ☑2010-1100; www.teatronacional.go.cr; Calles 3 & 5 btwn Avs Central & 2) Costa Rica's most important theater stages plays, dance, opera, classical concerts, Latin American music and other major events. The main season runs from March to November, but there are performances throughout the year.

★ **Mundoloco El Chante** LIVE PERFORMANCE
(Map p78; ☑2253-4125; www.facebook.com/MundolocoRestaurante/; Av Central, San Pedro; ☺4pm-2:30am Mon-Thu, from noon Fri & Sat) Grab a craft beer and some vegetarian grub, such as stuffed mushrooms, at this super-cute San Pedro restaurant and bar. Then head to the spacious and comfortable backroom for the entertainment, which rotates from stand-up comedy to dance performances and live music of all kinds. Great acoustics here: it's an ideal place to catch a local band.

El Sótano LIVE MUSIC
(Map p64; ☑2221-2302; www.facebook.com/sotanocr; cnr Calle 3 & Av 11; ☺3pm-2am Mon-Sat) One of Chepe's most atmospheric nightspots, Sótano is named for its cellar jazz club, where people crowd in for frequent performances including intimate jam sessions. Upstairs, a cluster of elegant high-ceilinged rooms in the same mansion have been converted into a gallery space, a stage, and a dance floor where an eclectic mix of groups play live gigs.

BULLFIGHTING

Bullfighting is traditional and fights are held seasonally in the southern suburb of Zapote over the Christmas period. Members of the public, who are often drunk at such events, are encouraged to participate in the action. The bull isn't killed in the Costa Rican version of the sport; however, many bulls are taunted, kicked and otherwise injured as a result of the fights, and animal welfare groups are keen to see the fights stopped.

Jazz Café LIVE MUSIC
(Map p78; ☑2253-8933; www.jazzcafecostarica.com; Av Central; cover US$6-13; ☺6pm-2am Mon-Sat) This intimate San Pedro venue presents a different band every night. Countless performers have taken to the stage here, including legendary Cuban bandleader Chucho Valdés and Colombian pop star Juanes. Its sister club in Escazú (☑2288-4740; Autopista Próspero Fernández, north side; cover US$5-10; ☺6pm-2am) features a similar mix of local and international bands.

El Lobo Estepario LIVE MUSIC
(Map p68; ☑2256-3934; www.facebook.com/loboesepariocr; Av 2; ☺4pm-12:45am Sun-Thu, to 2am Fri & Sat) ☞ This artsy, two-story dive serves up good vegetarian fare and attracts some of the top local talent for live music gigs. The ceiling is also a blackboard, filled nightly with messages and drawings of the patrons' choosing.

8ctavo Rooftop LIVE MUSIC
(☑4055-0588; www.facebook.com/8voRooftop; Autopista Próspero Fernández, Hotel Sheraton San José) See and be seen at this swanky rooftop lounge, where international DJs regularly perform. If you want to show up early and dine first, this place is also a hit for the city views, the eclectic menu and the spicy cocktails. It's right off Hwy 27 on the west side of Escazú.

Pepper Disco Club LIVE MUSIC
(☑2224-1472; Av 4, Zapote) This club is *the* place to see heavy metal, punk and ska bands. Its salsa dancing nights are also good.

Arenas Skate Park LIVE MUSIC
(Map p64; ☑8813-7544; Calle 11 btwn Avs 10 & 12) On Friday and Saturday nights, punk shows are all the rage at this skate park in Barrio Soledad.

El Cuartel de la Boca del Monte LIVE MUSIC
(Map p64; ☑2221-0327; www.facebook.com/elcuartelcr; Av 1 btwn Calles 21 & 23; ☺11:30am-2pm Mon-Fri, 6pm-midnight Mon-Thu, 6pm-2am Fri & Sat) This atmospheric old Barrio La California bar has long drawn cheek-by-jowl crowds for live bands. Friday is a good night to visit, as is Monday, when ladies get free admission and the band cranks out a crazy mix of calypso, salsa, reggae and rock. It's popular with university students, who indulge in flirting, drinking and various combinations thereof.

Auditorio Nacional CONCERT VENUE
(Map p64; ☑2105-0511 ext 511; www.museocr.org; Museo de los Niños, Calle 4) A grand stage for

concerts, dance, theater and plays, affiliated with the Centro Costarricense de Ciencia y Cultura.

Theater

There is a wide variety of theatrical options in San José, including some in English. Local newspapers list current shows. Most theaters are not very large, so performances tend to sell out; get tickets as early as possible.

Teatro Melico Salazar THEATER
(Map p68; ☑2233-5172, 2257-6005; www.teatromelico.go.cr; Av 2 btwn Calles Central & 2) A restored 1920s theater with regular fine-arts performances, including music, theater, ballet and other forms of dance.

Teatro Eugene O'Neill THEATER
(Map p78; ☑2207-7554; www.centrocultural.cr; Calle 37) This theater hosts performances sponsored by the Centro Cultural Costarricense Norteamericano, a cultural center that promotes ties between Costa Rica and the United States. It's north of Avenida Central, in San Pedro.

Little Theatre Group THEATER
(☑8858-1446; www.littletheatregroup.org) This English-language performance troupe has been around since the 1950s and presents several plays a year; call or go online to find out when and where the works will be shown.

Sport

Estadio Nacional de Costa Rica STADIUM
(Map p72; Parque Metropolitano La Sabana) Costa Rica's graceful, modernist 35,000-seat national soccer stadium, constructed with funding from the Chinese government and opened in 2011, is the venue for international and national Division-1 *fútbol* (soccer) games. Its predecessor, dating back to 1924 and located in the same spot in Parque Metropolitano La Sabana, hosted everyone from Pope John Paul II to soccer legend Pelé and Bruce Springsteen over its 84-year history.

Casinos

Gamblers will find casinos in several of the larger hotels. Most of these are fairly casual, but in the nicer spots it's advisable to ditch T-shirts in favor of a button-down shirt as there may be a dress code. Gents: be advised that casinos are frequented by prostitutes, so be wary if you're suddenly the most desirable person in the room.

CULTURAL CENTERS

Alianza Francesa (☑2257-1438; www.alianzafrancesacostarica.com; cnr Calle 5 & Av 7; French course US$330; ⏰8am-6pm Mon-Sat) The Alliance has French classes, a small library and rotating art exhibits in a historic Barrio Amón home.

Centro Cultural de España (☑2257-2919; www.ccecr.org; Rotonda del Farolito, Barrio Escalante; ⏰8am-7pm Mon-Fri) One of the city's most vibrant cultural institutions, this Spanish-run center offers a full roster of events. There is also an audiovisual center and a lending library.

Casino Club Colonial CASINO
(Map p68; ☑2258-2807; www.casinoclubcolonial.com; Av 1 btwn Calles 9 & 11; ⏰24hr) San José's most elegant casino.

Casino del Rey CASINO
(Map p68; ☑2257-7800; www.delreyhotel.com; Hotel del Rey, cnr Calle 9 & Av 1; ⏰24hr) A jam-packed shocking-pink building offering everything from roulette to slot machines and what has to be the highest density of prostitutes in the city.

🔒 Shopping

Whether you're looking for indigenous carvings, high-end furnishings or a stuffed sloth, San José has no shortage of shops, running the gamut from artsy boutiques to tourist traps stocked full of tropical everything. Haggling is not tolerated in stores (markets are the exception).

For the country's finest woodcrafts, it is absolutely worth the trip to Biesanz Woodworks (p94).

★**Feria Verde de Aranjuez** MARKET
(Map p64; www.feriaverde.org; Barrio Aranjuez; ⏰7am-12:30am Sat) For a foodie-friendly cultural experience, don't miss this fabulous Saturday farmers market, a weekly meeting place for San José's artists and organic growers since 2010. You'll find organic coffee, artisanal chocolate, tropical-fruit ice blocks, fresh produce, leather, jewelry and more at the long rows of booths set up in the park at the north end of Barrio Aranjuez.

Don't miss the mouthwatering samples of cured trout and fish dip, which an enthusiastic German expat loves feeding to passersby.

Sin Domicilio Fijo ARTS & CRAFTS
(Map p82; ☑2289-9461; www.facebook.com/sindomiciliofijo; cnr Av 32 & Calle Central; ⊙10am-6pm Tue-Fri, from 9am Sat, to 4pm Sun) In downtown Escazú, this art and design shop is ensconced in a historic, 150-year-old house with adobe walls, near the southwest corner of Escazú's church. It's full of unique handicrafts that make ideal gifts, from dainty footwear to kitchen adornments. There's also a lovely open-air cafe that serves up fresh coffee and tasty meals.

Distrito Carmen ART
(Map p68; ☑2256-0337; www.facebook.com/distritocarmen/; cnr Calle 11 & Av 9) Cool new design store where you can pick up interesting art, clothing, jewelry and other odds and ends created by a couple of dozen local artists.

Cerámical Artistica Salitral CERAMICS
(☑2282-7536; www.facebook.com/ceramica.artisticasalitral; 2km south of Herm gas station, road from Salitral to Santa Ana; ⊙9am-5pm) A long-standing, oversized ceramic store and pottery workshop on the curving country road from Santa Ana to Salitral. There are some great finds here, particularly the candle holders and masks, and the store occasionally offers private pottery lessons (call for details).

Mora Books BOOKS
(Map p68; ☑8383-8385; www.morabooks.com; Calle 5 btwn Avs 5 & 7; ⊙11am-7pm) Dog-eared paperbacks in mostly English but also Spanish, French and German teeter in precarious towers atop crammed shelves at this chaotic jumble of a used bookstore. The best place in town for stocking up on reading material for the road. Hours are hit and miss.

Kiosco SJO ARTS & CRAFTS
(Map p78; ☑2253-8426; cnr Calle 31 & Av 5; ⊙noon-8pm Tue-Fri, from 10am Sat, 10am-4pm Sun) 🍃 With a focus on sustainable design by Costa Rican artisans, this sleek shop in Barrio Escalante stocks handmade jewelry, hand-tooled leather bags, original photography, stuffed animals, fashion and contemporary home decor by established designers. It's pricey, but rest assured that everything you find here will be of exceptional quality.

eÑe ARTS & CRAFTS
(Map p68; ☑2222-7681; laesquina13y7@gmail.com; cnr Av 7 & Calle 11A; ⊙10am-6:30pm Mon-Sat) This hip little design shop across from Casa Amarilla sells all manner of pieces crafted by Costa Rican designers and artists, including clothing, jewelry, handbags, picture frames, zines and works of graphic art.

Galería Namu ARTS & CRAFTS
(Map p68; ☑2256-3412, in USA 800-616-4322; www.galerianamu.com; Av 7 btwn Calles 5 & 7; ⊙9am-6:30pm Mon-Sat year-round, plus 1-5pm Sun Dec-Apr) This fair-trade gallery brings together artwork and cultural objects from a diverse population of regional ethnicities, including Boruca masks, finely woven Wounaan baskets, Guaymí dolls, Bribrí canoes, Chorotega ceramics, traditional Huetar reed mats, and contemporary urban and Afro-Caribbean crafts. It can also help arrange visits to remote indigenous territories in different parts of Costa Rica.

Multiplaza Escazú MALL
(☑4001-7999; www.facebook.com/MultiplazaCostaRica; Autopista Próspero Fernández; ⊙10am-9pm Mon-Sat, to 8pm Sun) Costa Rica's most stylish and massive shopping mall has everything you need (or don't). If you're coming from San José, the mall can be reached by taking any bus marked 'Escazú Multiplaza'.

Mercado Artesanal MARKET
(Crafts Market; Map p68; Plaza de la Democracia, Avs Central & 2 btwn Calles 13 & 15; ⊙9am-5pm) A touristy open-air market that sells everything from handcrafted jewelry and Bob Marley T-shirts to elaborate woodwork and Guatemalan sarongs.

> **WORTH A TRIP**
>
> ## BIESANZ WOODWORKS
>
> Located in the hills of Bello Horizonte in Escazú, the workshop of **Biesanz Woodworks** (☑2289-4337; www.biesanz.com; 33 Calle Pedrero; ⊙8am-5pm Mon-Fri, 9am-2pm Sat) can be difficult to find, but the effort will be well worth it. This shop is one of the finest woodcrafting studios in the nation, run by celebrated artisan Barry Biesanz.
>
> His bowls and other decorative containers are exquisite and take their inspiration from pre-Columbian techniques, in which the natural lines and forms of the wood determine the shape and size of the bowl. The pieces are expensive (from US$45 for a palm-size bowl), but they are unique – and so delicately crafted that they wouldn't be out of place in a museum.

Librería Lehmann BOOKS
(Map p68; ☑2522-4848; www.librerialehmann.
com; Av Central btwn Calles 1 & 3; ⊙8am-6:30pm
Mon-Fri, 9am-5pm Sat, 11am-4pm Sun) Good selection of English-language books, maps and
guidebooks (including Lonely Planet).

Mall San Pedro MALL
(Map p78; ☑4001-7999; http://tumallsanpedro.
com; Boulevard Los Yoses) This busy four-
story mall (often used as a landmark) houses
a multiscreen cinema, a food court, a video
arcade and the usual mix of clothing, phone
and other retailers. It's northwest of Fuente
de la Hispanidad.

ⓘ Orientation

San José's center is arranged in a grid with avenidas (avenues) running east to west and calles
(streets) running north to south. Av Central is the
nucleus of the downtown area and is a pedestrian
mall between Calles 6 and 9. The downtown has
several loosely defined barrios (neighborhoods);
those of greatest interest to tourists are north
and east of Plaza de la Cultura, including Barrio
Amón, Barrio Otoya, Barrio Aranjuez, Barrio Escalante and Barrio La California. The central area
is home to innumerable businesses, hotels and
cultural sites, while the area immediately west of
downtown is home to San José's central market
and many of its bus terminals.

Slightly further west of downtown is La Sabana,
named for its huge and popular park where many
josefinos spend their weekends jogging, swimming, picnicking or attending soccer matches.

A few kilometers southwest is the affluent
outer suburb of Escazú, really three neighborhoods in one: Escazú Centro with its peaceful
central plaza and unhurried Tico ambiance;
the US expatriate enclave of San Rafael, dotted
with strip malls, top-end car dealerships, tract
housing and chain restaurants; and San Antonio,
a hillside mix of humble rural homes, sprawling
estates and spectacular views. Still further
west is the up-and-coming enclave of Santa
Ana, another expat favorite with oodles of green
space, a fantastically warm and dry climate and
new businesses galore.

East (and within walking distance) of the center
are the contiguous neighborhoods of Los Yoses
and San Pedro, the former a low-key residential
area with some nice accommodations, the latter
home to the tree-lined campus of the UCR, the
country's most prestigious university. Marking
the dividing line between Los Yoses and San
Pedro is a traffic roundabout graced by a large
fountain known as the Fuente de la Hispanidad (a
frequently referenced local landmark). North of
Los Yoses is Barrio Escalante, home to some of
San José's trendiest bars and restaurants.

TOURIST POLICE

The establishment in 2007 of the *policía
turística* (tourist police; you'll see them
patrolling in pairs around San José, on
foot, bicycle and even horseback) has
helped prevent petty crimes against
foreigners. These officers can be helpful
in the event of an emergency since most
of them speak at least some English.

If you find yourself the victim of a
crime, you'll have to file a report in
person at the **Organismo de Inves-
tigacíon Judicial** (☑2222-1365, 2295-
3000; Calle 17 btwn Avs 6 & 8; ⊙24hr) in
the Supreme Court of Justice building
on the south side of downtown.

ⓘ Information

DANGER & ANNOYANCES

Though Costa Rica has the lowest crime rate of
any Central American country, crime in urban
centers such as San José is a problem. The
most common offense is opportunistic theft (eg
pickpocketing and mugging). Keep a streetwise
attitude, leave your car empty of valuables in a
guarded lot and never put your bag in the overhead racks on a bus. Men should be aware that
prostitutes are known for sleight-of-hand, and
that they often work in pairs.

Neighborhoods covered by Lonely Planet
are generally safe during the day, though you
should be especially careful around the Coca-
Cola bus terminal (p97) and the red-light district south of Parque Central, particularly at
night. Be advised that adjacent neighborhoods
can vary greatly in terms of safety; inquire
locally before setting out.

Gridlocked traffic, gigantic potholes, noise and
smog are unavoidable components of the San
José experience. Most central hotels are subject
to street noise, no matter how nice they are. Be
skeptical of touts and taxi drivers who try to sell
you tours or tell you that the hotel you've booked
is a crime-infested bordello. Many of them will
say anything to steer you to the places that pay
them commissions.

EMERGENCY

Fire	☑118
Red Cross	☑128
Traffic Police	☑2523-3300, 2222-9245, 2222-9330

VOLUNTEERING

For travelers who want an experience beyond vacation, there are dozens of not-for-profit organizations in San José that gladly accept volunteers.

Central American Service Expeditions (☑8839-0515; www.serviceexpeditions.com) A Costa Rican nonprofit that creates custom volunteer opportunities for families and teens focused on sustainability.

Educational Travel Adventures (☑in USA & Canada 866-273-2500; www.etadventures. com) Arranges a wide variety of volunteer trips, conservation projects and service learning opportunities.

United Planet (☑in USA 1-617-874-8041; www.unitedplanet.org) Places volunteers in programs on global health, education and the environment.

INTERNET ACCESS

Most accommodations offer free wi-fi and/or guest computers. You'll also find plenty of cyber cafes, charging US$0.50 to US$1 per hour.

MEDICAL SERVICES

Clínica Bíblica (☑2522-1000; www.clinicabib lica.com; Av 14 btwn Calles Central & 1; ☺24hr) The top private clinic downtown has a 24-hour emergency room; doctors speak English, French and German.

Hospital Calderón Guardia (☑2212-1000; cnr Calle 17 btwn Avs 7 & 9; ☺24hr) A public hospital in central San José.

Hospital CIMA (☑2208-1000; www.hospital cima.com; Autopista Próspero Fernández; ☺24hr) For serious medical emergencies, head to this hospital in San Rafael de Escazú. Its facilities are the most modern in the greater San José area.

Hospital La Católica (☑2246-3000; www. hospitallacatolica.com; 109, Guadalupe; ☺24hr) Pricey private clinic geared toward medical-tourism patients from abroad.

Hospital San Juan de Dios (☑2547-8000; cnr Paseo Colón & Calle 14; ☺24hr) Free public hospital open 24 hours; expect long waits.

POST

Correo Central (Central Post Office; Map p68; ☑2202-2900; www.correos.go.cr; Calle 2 btwn Avs 1 & 3; ☺6:30am-6pm Mon-Fri, to noon Sat) In a gorgeous historic building near the center of town. Express and overnight services.

TOURIST INFORMATION

Canatur (Cámara Nacional de Turismo; ☑2234-6222; www.canatur.org; Aeropuerto Internacional Juan Santamaría; ☺7am-10pm) The Costa Rican National Chamber of Tourism provides information on member services from a small stand next to international baggage claim.

ⓘ Getting There & Away

San José is the country's transportation hub, and it's likely that you'll pass through the capital a number of times throughout your travels (whether you want to or not).

AIR

International flights leave from Juan Santamaría (SJO) airport outside Alajuela.

Aeropuerto Internacional Juan Santamaría (☑2437-2400; www.fly2sanjose.com) Handles international flights and **NatureAir** (☑2299-6000, in USA 1-800-235-9272; www.natureair. com) domestic flights in its main terminal. Domestic flights on **Sansa** (☑2290-4100; www. flysansa.com) depart from the Sansa terminal.

Aeropuerto Tobías Bolaños (☑2232-2820; Pavas) In the San José suburb of Pavas; services private charter and a few national flights.

BUS

Bus transportation in San José can be bewildering. There is no public bus system and no central terminal. Instead, dozens of private companies operate out of stops scattered throughout the city. Many bus companies have no more than a stop (in this case pay the driver directly); some have a tiny office with a window on the street; others operate from bigger terminals servicing entire regions.

Note that bus schedules and prices change regularly. Pick up a copy of the free (but not always up-to-date) booklet *Itinerario de Buses* from San José's downtown tourist office, or download a PDF version from www.visitcosta rica.com (most easily located in your search engine by typing 'Costa Rica Itinerario de Buses'). Buses are crowded on Friday evening and Saturday morning and packed to the gills at Christmas and Easter.

For buses that run infrequently, it is advisable to buy tickets in advance.

Bus Terminals

Collectively, the following five San José terminals serve Costa Rica's most popular destinations. Chances are you'll be passing through one or more of them during your trip. Be aware that theft is common in many bus terminals. Stay alert, keep your valuables close to you and don't stow anything important (such as passports and money) in the overhead racks or luggage compartment of a bus.

Gran Terminal del Caribe (Calle Central) This roomy station north of Av 13 is the central departure point for all buses to the Caribbean.

Terminal 7-10 (☑ 2519-9740; www.terminal 7-10.com; cnr 7th Av & Calle 10) This newer bus terminal is a base for routes to Nicoya, Nosara, Sámara, Santa Cruz, Tamarindo, Jacó, Monteverde, La Fortuna and a few other places. The four-story facility has a food court, shopping center and parking lot. Although it's located in the *zona roja*, historically a dangerous area of the city, police have stepped up their patrols to reduce crime.

Terminal Coca-Cola (Map p64; Av 1 btwn Calles 16 & 18) A well-known landmark. Numerous buses leave from the terminal and the four-block radius around it to points all over Costa Rica, in particular the Central Valley and the Pacific coast. This is a labyrinthine station with ticket offices scattered all over.

Terminal del Atlántico Norte (cnr Av 9 & Calle 12) A small, rather decrepit terminal serving the Southern Caribbean and Puerto Jiménez.

Terminal Tracopa (Map p64; ☑ 2221-4214; www.tracopacr.com; Calle 5 btwn Avs 18 & 20) Buses to southwestern destinations including Neily, Dominical, Golfito, Manuel Antonio, Palmar Norte, Paso Canoas, Quepos, San Isidro de El General, San Vito and Uvita.

Domestic Bus Companies

Autotransportes Caribeños (☑ 2222-0610; www.grupocaribenos.com; Gran Terminal del Caribe, Calle Central) Northeastern destinations including Puerto Limón, Guápiles, Cariari, Siquirres and Puerto Viejo de Sarapiquí; the Caribeños group encompasses several smaller companies (including Empresarios Guapileños and Líneas del Atlántico), all of which share the same terminal and customer-service phone number.

Autotransportes Mepe (☑ 2257-8129; www.mepecr.com; cnr Av 9 & Calle 12, Terminal del Atlántico Norte) Southern Caribbean destinations including Cahuita, Puerto Viejo de Talamanca, Manzanillo, Bribrí and Sixaola.

Autotransportes San Carlos (☑ 2255-4300; cnr Av 7 & Calle 10, Terminal 7-10) La Fortuna, Ciudad Quesada and Los Chiles.

Blanco Lobo (Map p64; ☑ 2257-4121; cnr Av 9 & Calle 12, Terminal del Atlántico Norte) Puerto Jiménez.

Coopetrans Atenas (Map p64; ☑ 2446-5767; www.coopetransatenas.com; Av 1 btwn Calles 16 & 18, Terminal Coca-Cola) Atenas.

Empresa Alfaro (☑ 2222-2666; www.empresaalfaro.com; cnr Av 7 & Calle 10, Terminal 7-10) Nicoya, Nosara, Sámara, Santa Cruz and Tamarindo.

Empresarios Unidos (Map p64; ☑ 2221-6600; cnr Av 12 & Calle 16) Buses to San Ramón and Puntarenas.

Lumaca (Map p64; ☑ 2552-5280; Av 10 btwn Calles 5 & 7) Cartago.

Metrópoli (Map p68; ☑ 2530-1064; Av 2 btwn Calles 1 & 3) Volcán Irazú.

Musoc (☑ 2222-2422; Calle Central btwn Avs 22 & 24) San Isidro de El General and Santa María de Dota.

INTERNATIONAL BUSES FROM SAN JOSÉ

DESTINATION	BUS COMPANY	COST (US$)	DURATION	FREQUENCY
David (Panama)	Tracopa	21	8½hr	7:30am, noon
Guatemala City (Guatemala)	Tica Bus	86	48hr	3am, 6am, 7am, 12:30pm
Managua (Nicaragua)	Tica Bus	29-42	9hr	3am, 6am, 7:30am, 12:30pm
Managua (Nicaragua)	TransNica	28	8½hr	2am, 4am, 5am, 9am, noon
Managua (Nicaragua)	Central Line	29	8½hr	4:30am, 10am
Managua (Nicaragua)	Nicabus	29	8hr	4:30am, 6:30am
Panama City (Panama)	Expreso Panamá	40	14hr	noon
Panama City (Panama)	Tica Bus	42-58	16hr	noon, 11:55pm
San Salvador (El Salvador)	Tica Bus	65	20hr	3am, 6am, 7:30am, 12:30pm
Tegucigalpa (Honduras)	TransNica	57	16hr	2am

DOMESTIC BUSES FROM SAN JOSÉ

DESTINATION	BUS COMPANY	COST (US$)	DURATION (HR)	FREQUENCY
Cahuita	Mepe	8.64	4	6am, 8am, 10am, noon, 2pm, 4pm, 6pm
Cañas	Pulmitan	4.12	3½	11:40am, 1:30pm, 3:30pm
Cariari	Caribeños	2.97	2½	6:30am, 9am, 10:30am, 1pm, 3pm, 4:30pm, 6pm, 7pm
Cartago	Lumaca	1.04	1	every 15min
Ciudad Neily	Tracopa	13.16	6½-7½	11 daily
Ciudad Quesada	San Carlos	3.34	3	hourly
Dominical & Uvita	Tracopa	9.34	4½-5½	6am, 3pm
Golfito	Tracopa	13.16	6½	6:30am, 7am, 3:30pm
Grecia	Tuan	1.91	1	half-hourly
Guápiles	Caribeños	2.43	1¼	half-hourly
Jacó	Transportes Jacó	4.23	2½	every 2hr 7am-5pm
La Fortuna	San Carlos	4.41	4	12:45pm, 2:45pm
Liberia	Pulmitan	8.03	4½	hourly 6am-8pm
Los Chiles	San Carlos	5.16	5	5:15am, 3pm
Manzanillo	Mepe	11.17	5	noon
Monteverde/ Santa Elena	Transmonteverde	4.97	4½	6:30am, 2:30pm
Montezuma/ Mal País	Cobano	12.42	5½-6	6am, 6:30am, 2pm
Nicoya	Alfaro	7.13	5	5:30, 7:30am, 10am, 1pm, 3pm, 5pm
Palmar	Tracopa	10.32	6	13 daily
Paso Canoas	Tracopa	13.81	7-8	13 daily
Peñas Blancas	Deldú	8.18	6	9 daily
Playa del Coco	Pulmitan	9.87	5½	8am, 2pm, 4pm
Playa Flamingo	Tralapa	10.27	6	8am, 10:30am, 3pm
Playa Nosara	Alfaro	8.11	6	5:30am
Playa Sámara	Alfaro	7.54	5	noon

Pulmitan de Liberia (Map p64; ☎2222-0610; Calle 24 btwn Avs 5 & 7) Northwestern destinations including Cañas, Liberia, Playa del Coco and Tilarán.

Station Wagon (Map p64; ☎2441-1181; Av 2 btwn Calles 10 & 12) Alajuela and the airport.

Terminal Tracopa (p97) Southwestern destinations including Ciudad Neily, Dominical, Golfito, Manuel Antonio, Palmar Norte, Paso Canoas, Quepos, San Isidro de El General, San Vito and Uvita.

Tralapa (Map p64; ☎2223-5876; Av 5 btwn Calles 20 & 22) Several Península de Nicoya destinations, including Playa Flamingo, Playa Hermosa, Playa Tamarindo and Santa Cruz.

Transmonteverde (☎2645-7447; www.facebook.com/Transmonteverde; cnr Av 7 & Calle 10, Terminal 7-10) Monteverde.

Transportes Cobano (☎2221-7479; transportescobano@gmail.com; cnr Av 7 & Calle 10, Terminal 7-10) Montezuma and Mal País.

Transportes Deldú (Calle Central, Gran Terminal de Caribe) Peñas Blancas (Nicaraguan border).

Transportes Jacó (☎2290-2922; www.transportesjacoruta655.com; cnr Av 7 & Calle 10, Terminal 7-10) Jacó.

Transtusa (Map p64; ☎4036-1800; www.transtusacr.com; Calle 13A btwn Avs 6 & 8) Cartago and Turrialba.

DESTINATION	BUS COMPANY	COST (US$)	DURATION (HR)	FREQUENCY
Playa Hermosa	Tralapa	8.90	5	3:30pm
Playa Tamarindo	Alfaro	9.51	5	11:30am, 3:30pm
Playa Tamarindo	Tralapa	8.92	5	7am, 4pm
Puerto Jiménez	Blanco Lobo	15	8	8am, noon
Puerto Limón	Caribeños	5.64	3	hourly
Puerto Viejo de Sarapiquí	Caribeños	4.47	2½	10 daily
Puerto Viejo de Talamanca	Mepe	10.04	4½	6am, 8am, 10am, noon, 2pm, 4pm, 6pm
Puntarenas	Empresarios Unidos	4.57	2½	hourly
Quepos/Manuel Antonio	Tracopa	8.10	3½	every 1-2hr
San Isidro de El General	Musoc	6.41	3	hourly 4:30am-6:30pm
San Isidro de El General	Tracopa	6.36	3	hourly
San Vito	Tracopa	12.03	7	6am, 8:15am, noon, 12:15pm, 4pm
Santa Cruz	Alfaro	9.15	5	7 daily
Santa Cruz	Tralapa	8.97	5	9am, noon, 2pm, 6pm
Santa María de Dota	Musoc	4.16	2	6am, 9am, 12:30pm, 2:30pm, 3pm, 5pm, 7:30pm
Sarchí	Tuan	1.93	1½	11:45pm, 5:30pm, 6:05pm Mon-Fri, noon Sat
Siquirres	Caribeños	2.83	2	hourly
Sixaola	Mepe	12.32	5½	6am, 8am, 10am, 2pm, 4pm
Tilarán	Pulmitan	8.04	4	7:30am, 9:30am, 12:45pm, 3:45pm, 6:30pm
Turrialba	Transtusa	2.40	2	hourly
Volcán Irazú	Metrópoli	8.20 round trip	2	8am

Tuan (Terminal de Buses Grecia; Map p64; ☑ 2494-2139, 2258-2004; cnr Av 5 & Calle 18A) Grecia.

Tuasa (Map p64; ☑ 2442-6900; Av 2 btwn Calles 12 & 14) Alajuela and the airport.

International Bus Companies

International buses get booked up fast. Buy your tickets in advance – and take your passport.

Transportes Central Line (Map p64; ☑ 2221-9115; http://transportescentralline.com; Av 9) Managua (Nicaragua).

Expreso Panamá (Map p64; ☑ 2221-7694; www.expresopanama.com; Terminal Empresarios Unidos, cnr Av 12 & Calle 16) Panama City (Panama).

Nicabus (Map p64; ☑ 2221-2581; cnr Av 1 & Calle 20) Managua (Nicaragua).

Tica Bus (Map p72; ☑ 2296-9788; www.tica bus.com; cnr Transversal 26 & Av 3) Nicaragua, Panama, El Salvador and Guatemala.

TransNica (Map p64; ☑ 2223-4242; www.transnica.com; Calle 22 btwn Avs 3 & 5) Nicaragua and Honduras.

Shuttle Buses

Grayline (☑ 2220-2126; www.graylinecosta rica.com; Av 31) and **Interbus** (☑ 4100-0888; www.interbusonline.com; Av 20) shuttle passengers in air-conditioned minivans from San José to a long list of popular destinations around Costa Rica. They are more expensive than the standard bus services, but they offer door-to-door service and can get you there faster.

ℹ Getting Around

Central San José frequently resembles a parking lot – narrow streets, heavy traffic and a complicated one-way system mean that it is often quicker to walk than to take the bus. The same applies to driving: if you rent a car, try to avoid downtown. If you're in a real hurry to get somewhere that's more than 1km away, take an Uber or a taxi.

If traveling by bus, you'll arrive at one of several bus terminals sprinkled around the western and southern parts of downtown. Some of this area is walkable provided you aren't hauling a lot of luggage and are staying nearby. But, if you're arriving at night, take a taxi, since most terminals are in dodgy areas.

BUS

Local buses are useful to get you into the suburbs and surrounding villages, or to the airport. Most buses run between 5am and 10pm and cost between US$0.40 and US$1.10.

La Sabana To catch a bus heading west from San José towards La Sabana (US$0.40), head for the convenient downtown stop at the southeast corner of Av 3 and Calle 3. Buses returning from Parque La Sabana to downtown follow Paseo Colón, then go over to Av 2 at the San Juan de Dios hospital. They then go three different ways through town before eventually heading back to La Sabana. Buses are marked Sabana–Estadio, Sabana–Cementerio or Cementerio–Estadio. These buses are a good bet for a cheap city tour.

Los Yoses & San Pedro Catch eastbound buses to Los Yoses and San Pedro (US$0.50) from the northeast corner of **Calle Central and Av 9** (Map p68; Av Central). These buses run east along Av 2 and then switch over to Av Central at Calle 29. (Many are easily identifiable by the big sign that says 'Mall San Pedro' on the front window.)

Escazú Buses southwest to Escazú (US$0.65 to US$0.80, 15 to 25 minutes) leave from two different locations: **Av 6** (Map p64) between Calles 14 and 16 (south of the Hospital San Juan de Dios), and Calle 16 between Avs 1 and 3 (near the Coca-Cola terminal). Buses labeled 'San Antonio de Escazú' climb the hill south of Escazú and end near the Iglesia San Antonio de Escazú; those labeled 'Escazú Centro' end in Escazú's **main plaza** (Map p82; Calle 136); others, labeled 'Guachipelín', go west on the Carretera John F. Kennedy and pass the Costa Rica Country Club. All go through San Rafael.

Heredia Regular **buses** (Map p68; Calle 1 btwn Avs 7 & 9) leave from Calle 1 and Av 7.

CAR

It is not advisable to rent a car just to drive around San José. The traffic is heavy, the streets are narrow and the meter-deep curbside gutters make parking nerve-wracking. In addition, break-ins are frequent, and leaving a car – even in a guarded lot – might result in a smashed window and stolen belongings.

If you are renting a car to travel throughout Costa Rica, there are more than 50 car-rental agencies – including many of the global brands – in and around San José. Travel agencies and upmarket hotels can arrange rentals; you can also arrange rentals online and at the airport. Note: If you book a rental car online and the low cost seems too good to be true, it is. Rental agencies are notorious for tacking on hundreds of dollars in mandatory insurance when you arrive. They are also known to lie about this over the phone.

One excellent local option is **Wild Rider** (☑ 2258-4604; Paseo Colón btwn Calles 30 & 32; ⏱ 8am-6pm). They have a fleet of more than 60 very reasonably priced 4WD vehicles (from US$380 per week in high season, including all mandatory insurance coverage). Long-term rentals (four weeks or more) allow a discount of up to 40%. Reserve well in advance.

MOTORCYCLE

Wild Rider rents sports bikes such as the Honda XR-250 or the Suzuki DRZ-400S. Prices start at US$420 per week in high season (including insurance, taxes and helmets).

TAXI

Red taxis can be hailed on the street day or night, or you can have your hotel call one for you.

Marías (meters) are generally used, though a few drivers will tell you they're broken and try to charge you more – especially if you don't speak Spanish. Not using a meter is illegal. The rate for the first kilometer should automatically appear when the meter starts up (at the time of research, the correct starting amount was 610 colones). Make sure the *maría* is operating when you get in, or negotiate the fare up front. Short rides downtown cost US$2 to US$4. There's a 20% surcharge after 10pm that may not appear on the *maría*.

You can hire a taxi and a driver for half a day or longer if you want to do some touring around the area; for such trips, it is best to negotiate a flat fee in advance. Uber has also become a popular form of transport in the city.

Central Valley & Highlands

Best Places to Eat

➡ Valedi Food (p108)

➡ Casa Azul (p121)

➡ Jalapeños Central (p107)

➡ Pizzeria a la leña il Giardino (p125)

➡ Xandari (p108)

Best Places to Stay

➡ Peace Lodge (p109)

➡ Montaña Linda (p125)

➡ Catarata del Toro (p114)

➡ Villa Blanca Cloud Forest Hotel & Nature Reserve (p115)

➡ Casa de Lis Hostel (p132)

➡ Casa Amanecer (p114)

Why Go?

It is on the nontouristy, coffee-cultivated hillsides of the Central Valley that you'll find Costa Rica's heart and soul. This is not only the geographical center of the country but also its cultural and spiritual core. It is here that the Spanish first settled, here that coffee built a prosperous nation, here that picturesque highland villages still gather for centuries-old fiestas. It is also here that you'll get to fully appreciate Costa Rica's country cooking: artisanal cheeses, steamy corn cakes and freshly caught river trout.

Curvy mountain roads force travelers to slow their pace. Quaint and quirky agricultural towns invite leisurely detours to farmers markets and church processions, a refreshing break from the tourist-industrial complex on the coasts. But it's not all cows and coffee – world-class rapids, resplendent quetzals and close encounters with active volcanoes all show off the rich landscape in which Costa Rica's character is rooted.

When to Go

➡ During high season (December to March), the region's elevated altitude and landlocked location mean perfect weather.

➡ Afternoon showers are not uncommon during 'green' season (June to December), but so too are bargains.

➡ The rainy months (June to October) are great for whitewater rafting.

Central Valley & Highlands Highlights

1 Río Pacuare (p134) Paddling down the cascading rapids near Turrialba.

2 Volcán Irazú (p122) Peering into the crater and walking around its edge.

3 San Isidro de Heredia (p120) Learning the history of chocolate, stuffing your belly with goodness, and meeting rescued toucans and sloths.

4 Monumento Nacional Arqueológico Guayabo (p135) Contemplating the aqueducts and petroglyphs at Costa Rica's largest archaeological site.

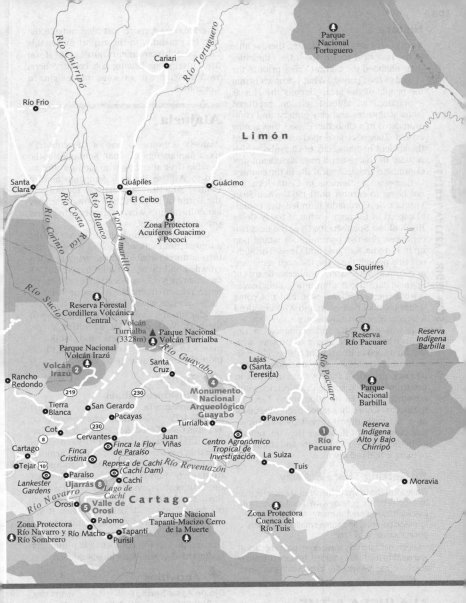

Map labels:

Parque Nacional Tortuguero

Río Chirripó

Río Tortuguero

Cariari

Río Frío

Limón

Santa Clara

Guápiles

El Ceibo

Guácimo

Río Costa Rica

Río Blanco

Río Toro Amarillo

Zona Protectora Acuíferos Guacimo y Pococi

Río Corinto

Siquirres

Río Sucio

Reserva Forestal Cordillera Volcánica Central

Volcán Turrialba (3328m)

Parque Nacional Volcán Turrialba

Río Guayabo

Reserva Río Pacuare

Reserva Indígena Barbilla

Parque Nacional Volcán Irazú

2 Volcán Irazú

Rancho Redondo

(219)

(230)

Santa Cruz

Lajas (Santa Teresita)

4 Monumento Nacional Arqueológico Guayabo

Parque Nacional Barbilla

Reserva Indígena Alto y Bajo Chirripó

Tierra Blanca

San Gerardo

Pacayas

Turrialba

Pavones

Río Pacuare

(8)

Cot

Cervantes

Cartago

Finca Cristina

Finca la Flor de Paraíso

Juan Viñas

Centro Agronómico Tropical de Investigación

La Suiza

1 Río Pacuare

Tejar

(10)

Represa de Cachí (Cachí Dam)

Río Reventazón

Tuis

Paraíso

Cachí

Moravia

Lankester Gardens

8 Ujarrás

Lago de Cachí

Cartago

Río Navarro

Orosi

5 Valle de Orosi

Palomo

Parque Nacional Tapantí-Macizo Cerro de la Muerte

Zona Protectora Cuenca del Río Tuis

Zona Protectora Río Navarro y Río Macho

Río Sombrero

Tapantí Purisil

---

5 Valle de Orosi (p123) Exploring the wilderness, culture and coffee *fincas*.

6 Bajos del Toro (p113) Birdwatching beside a rushing river or hiking to waterfalls.

7 Zarcero (p113) Winding along scenic mountain roads to the home of trippy topiary and organic farming.

8 Ujarrás (p127) Sharing a lazy Sunday afternoon in the park with Tico families beside the ruins of a 17th-century church.

9 Atenas (p110) Relaxing by the square and breathing the clean mountain air.

History

As in other parts of the country, there is little in the historical record about the ethnicities that inhabited the Central Valley prior to the arrival of the Spanish. What is known is that the people of the area – largely the Huetar – practiced an animist religion, produced stone sculptures and clay pottery, and communicated in a Chibchan dialect that is now extinct. They also developed and maintained the ancient highland city of Guayabo, which is today the biggest and most significant pre-Columbian archaeological site in the country.

European settlement in Costa Rica did not begin in earnest until 1563, when Juan Vázquez de Coronado founded the colonial capital of Cartago – what is today Costa Rica's oldest Spanish city. Over the next two centuries, Spanish communities would pop up in Heredia, San José and Orosi. Throughout this period, however, the area remained a colonial backwater, a checkerboard of Spanish farming communities, and *indios bravos* (fierce Indians) who had not come under colonial dominion and who practiced a largely itinerant agriculture.

It was only after independence, in the 1830s, that the area began to prosper with the expanded cultivation of coffee. The *grano de oro* (golden bean) transformed the country, providing the revenue to invest in urban infrastructure such as electricity and pavements, not to mention many baronial mansions. Coffee has since been overtaken as a key agricultural export by pineapples and bananas, but its legacy lives on, reflected in the culture, architecture and traditions of many highland towns.

❶ Getting There & Away

While all of the towns in this area are connected by regular buses, renting a 4WD makes sense if you want to explore the many worthwhile hard-to-reach corners, and some smaller dirt roads are inaccessible by bus.

Locals occasionally wave down passing cars. If you want to hitchhike yourself, beware that there are risks, and always offer to help with gas costs.

ALAJUELA & THE NORTHERN VALLEY

Volcanoes shrouded in mist, undulating coffee *fincas* (plantations), bustling agricultural centers: the area around the provincial capital of Alajuela, 18km northwest of San José, has it all – including Juan Santamaría

International Airport, just 3km outside the city. Its proximity to the airport makes this area a highly convenient transit point if you are entering or leaving the country here, with the chance to see some major sights in Costa Rica.

Alajuela

POP 42,975

Alajuela is home to one of the country's most famous figures: Juan Santamaría, the humble drummer boy who died putting an end to William Walker's campaign to turn Central America into slaving territory in the Battle of Rivas in 1856. Now it's a busy agricultural hub where farmers bring their products to market.

Costa Rica's second city is by no means a tourist 'destination.' Much of the architecture is unremarkable, the streets are often crowded and there isn't a lot to see. But it's an inherently Costa Rican city, and in its more relaxed moments it reveals itself as such – a place where families have leisurely Sunday lunches and teenagers steal kisses in the park. With plenty of amenities, shops, restaurants, supermarkets and banks, it makes an excellent base from which to explore the countryside to the north.

◎ Sights

Museo Histórico Cultural Juan Santamaría   MUSEUM
(☑2441-4775; www.museojuansantamaria.go.cr; Av 1 btwn Calles Central & 2; ⊙10am-5:30pm Tue-Sun) FREE Situated in a century-old structure that has served as both jail and armory, this museum chronicles Costa Rican history from early European settlement through the 19th century, with special emphasis on the life and history of Juan Santamaría and the pivotal mid-1850s battles of Santa Rosa, Sardinal and Rivas. Exhibits include videos, vintage maps, paintings and historical artifacts related to the conflict that ultimately safeguarded Costa Rica's independence.

🏃 Activities

Ojo de Agua Springs   WATER PARK
(☑2441-0655; www.facebook.com/ojodeaguacr; US$2.70, under 3yr free; ⊙7:30am-4:30pm; ⊕) About 6km south of Alajuela, this kitsch water park is packed with local families on weekends. Approximately 20,000L of water gushes from the spring every minute, powering a small waterfall and filling various pools (including an Olympic-size lap pool

complete with diving tower) and an artificial boating lake. It's a seven-minute drive south of San Jose airport, just off Rte 111.

🎓 Courses

Intensa
LANGUAGE

(☑2442-3843, in USA & Canada 866-277-1352; www.intensa.com; 1 week without/with homestay US$355/520; ☺8am-8pm Mon-Fri) Schools in Alajuela and Heredia teach everything from medical to business Spanish. One week of classes includes four lessons of an hour each per day. Prices drop when students study for longer periods.

🎊 Festivals & Events

Juan Santamaría Day
CULTURAL

(☺Apr) The town that gave birth to a poor drummer boy named Juan Santamaría – who helped defeat the US in the Battle of Rivas – erupts in celebration on the victorious anniversary (April 11). This momentous occasion is commemorated with civic events, including a parade and lots of firecrackers.

🛌 Sleeping

Alajuela is so close to the international airport that most hotels and B&Bs arrange airport transfers for a small fee (or for free). If you're driving your own car, note that many places in the center don't have parking, but guarded lots are available. Street noise is a fact of life. A few budget hotels also offer dorm rooms. All top-end hotels accept credit cards, as do most midrange places.

Alajuela Backpackers Boutique Hostel
HOTEL $

(☑2441-7149; www.alajuelabackpackers.com; cnr Av 4 & Calle 4; dm/r/ste US$19/55/70; ❄@🛜) This four-story place with cookie-cutter rooms may feel a tad institutional at first glance, but dig deeper and you'll discover some big pluses: free shuttles to and from the airport, air-conditioned dorms and doubles with en suite bathrooms, and a super-cool 4th-floor bar terrace where you can sip beers while watching planes take off in the distance.

Hostel Maleku
HOSTEL $

(☑2430-4304; incl breakfast dm US$15, s/d without bathroom US$25/38; @🛜) This super-friendly, family-run backpackers' abode has five spick-and-span fan-cooled rooms tucked into a vintage home between the airport and downtown Alajuela (opposite Hospital San Rafael). There's a communal kitchen, plus free storage for items brought from home that you don't need while in Costa Rica (winter coats, bike boxes).

A free airport drop-off service is available hourly between 5am and 5pm.

Villa Pacandé
GUESTHOUSE $

(☑2441-6795; www.villapacande.com; incl breakfast s/d/tr/q from US$35/40/50/65; 🅿@🛜❄) 🏄 Located 3km north of Alajuela center, on the road to Volcán Poás, this Spanish-style home is set in gorgeous grounds festooned with blooms and buzzing with hummingbirds. The nine rooms are simple and comfortable, some offering a lovely view of the garden. This is a perfect choice for your first or last night if you're not interested in exploring Alajuela.

The hotel recently opened a restaurant serving Spanish cuisine, plus sandwiches and pastas.

Casa Antigua Hotel
GUESTHOUSE $$

(☑2441-1024, in USA 213-283-6287; www.casaantiguahotelcr.com; r incl breakfast from US$53; 🛜) Set in tropical gardens and replete with intricate woodwork, hand-painted floor tiles and quirky art, this 12-room guesthouse lures travelers with its proximity to the airport. Even more of a draw, though, is kind-hearted and effusively philosophical owner Hamid, who cooks up delicious Persian meals and offers parking for nonguests (US$7 per day). The hotel's 500m east of Fiesta Casino.

Hotel Los Volcanes
GUESTHOUSE $$

(☑2441-0525; www.hotellosvolcanes.com; Av 3 btwn Calles Central & 2; incl breakfast s/d US$49/62, with air-con US$62/72, without bathroom US$35/46; 🅿❄@🛜) Tranquil and centrally located, this welcoming place in a refurbished 1920s mansion has 15 rooms, from vintage units with period-style furniture and clean shared bathrooms to contemporary rooms with flat-screen TV, air-con and safe. There's an enjoyable courtyard in the back, complete with gurgling fountain. The helpful owners arrange a free airport drop-off at the end of your stay.

Hotel Pacandé
B&B $$

(☑2443-8481; www.hotelpacande.com; Av 5 btwn Calles 2 & 4; incl breakfast r US$55-65, without bathroom US$40; @🛜) This popular, locally run option is spotlessly clean throughout, offering 10 large rooms with wood furnishings, folk-art touches and cable TV. The bright, sunny breakfast nook is a great spot for a morning brew.

Vida Tropical B&B　　　　B&B **$$**
(☏2443-9576; www.vidatropical.com; Calle 3; incl breakfast s/d US$45/68, without bathroom US$36/52; ⓟ@🛜❄) In a quiet residential neighborhood a five-minute walk north of downtown Alajuela, this friendly house has snug, simple guest rooms awash with bright murals; two share a bathroom. The well-tended backyard is perfect for catching some sun in a hammock, and laundry service is available ($5 per load). In the backyard, kids will enjoy two playful pet rabbits.

Water and beer are available at the honor bar and local calls can be made free of charge. Manager Randy is also a reiki master (hour-long sessions from US$50), and he will help arrange airport pickup (US$8) at any hour.

★**Xandari Resort Hotel & Spa**　HOTEL **$$$**
(☏2443-2020, in USA 1-866-363-3212; www.xandari.com; villa d US$300-418, q US$644; ⓟ⊖🛜❄) 🌿 With spectacular bird's-eye views of the Central Valley, this romantic spot is the fanciful creation of an architect-designer couple. Spacious individual villas with ceiling fans are tastefully decorated in vibrant tropical colors, with hand-woven textiles and garden-view showers. The grounds offer 4km of trails, five waterfalls, three pools,

Alajuela

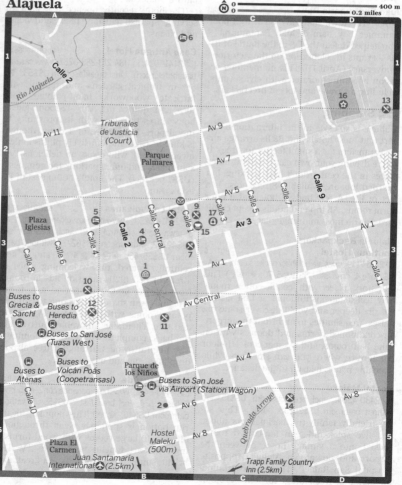

two Jacuzzis, a ping-pong table, a spa and an organic restaurant (p108).

Tacacori Ecolodge
BUNGALOW **$$$**

(☑2430-5846; www.tacacori.com; d incl breakfast US$125, extra person US$20) 🏊 Expat owner Nadine and her sheepdog run this peaceful retreat high above Alajuela. Four spacious bungalows with ultra-modern fixtures and abundant ecofriendly touches (solar hot water, LED lighting, dual-flush toilets) sit on a verdant hillside. Attractively priced 'Hello-Goodbye' packages and 15-minute airport transfers (from US$15) provide an incentive to begin and end your travels here.

Trapp Family Country Inn
INN **$$$**

(☑2431-0776; www.trappfamilycostarica.com; r incl breakfast US$108, additional adult/child 5-11yr US$30/25; ⓟ🅰@🛜🏊) The most attractive option you'll find so close to the airport landing strip, this hacienda-style country inn houses eight terra-cotta-tiled rooms with comfortable beds. The best units have balconies overlooking the inviting turquoise pool and verdant garden laced with bougainvillea and fig trees. Despite its rural feel, it's only 2km from the international airport; free airport transfers are provided.

Hotel Buena Vista
HOTEL **$$$**

(☑2442-8595, in USA 1-800-506-2304; www.hotelbuenavistacr.com; incl breakfast d from US$143, ste US$172, villas US$219; ⓟ🅰@🛜🏊) 🏊 About 5km north of Alajuela, this whitewashed Mediterranean-style hotel, perched on a mountaintop, has panoramic views of the nearby volcanoes. The best of the tastefully decorated rooms have private balconies with valley views; five villas offer private balconies along with wood-beamed ceilings and

minibar. A small trail leads down through a coffee *finca* to the main road.

🍴 Eating & Drinking

For the cheapest meals, head to the enclosed **Mercado Central** (Calles 4 & 6 btwn Avs 1 & Central; ⊙8am-6pm Mon-Sat). Self-caterers can stock up on groceries at the **Palí** (⊙8.30am-9pm), **MegaSuper** (Av Central btwn Calles Central & 2; ⊙8am-9pm Mon-Sat, to 8pm Sun) or **Más X Menos** (Av 1 btwn Calles 4 & 6; ⊙7am-9pm Mon-Sat, to 8pm Sun) supermarkets. There are plenty of major fast-food chains in town and a handful of excellent restaurants.

Alajuela isn't known for its nightlife; aside from dive bars, local hotels and restaurants are the best bet for a nightcap. The 4th-floor terrace bar at Alajuela Backpackers (p105) is the airiest spot in town; Valedi Food (p108) sits in a trendy spot named El Patio, where craft beer is served; and Jalapeños Central pours giant salty margaritas.

★ Jalapeños Central
MEXICAN **$**

(☑2430-4027; www.facebook.com/JalapenosCentralCR; Calle 1 btwn Avs 3 & 5; mains US$4.50-8; ⊙11:30am-9pm Mon-Sat, to 8pm Sun) Offering the best Tex-Mex in the country, this popular 11-table spot will introduce some spice into your diet. The simple and fresh burritos, chimichangas and enchiladas come in a meal deal or on their own, and regardless should be devoured with some of the house-made guacamole and salsa, and washed down with a salty margarita or a giant Coronarita.

Mezcla Cafe & Tienda
CAFE

(☑8333-0449; www.facebook.com/mezclacafe; Calle 1, btwn Avs 5 & 3; coffee from US$2, waffles from US$3.50; ⊙10am-8pm Mon-Sat) The hip

---

Alajuela

Costa Rican owners of this small coffee shop were inspired to open their sleek space, with hardwoods, metallic stalls and clean white walls, after recent trips to Seattle. Part coffee shop and part boutique, it sells creations by local designers – from Frida Kahlo socks and asymmetric jewelry to graphic T-shirts. Browse while enjoying fresh juices and sweet waffles.

El Chante Vegano VEGETARIAN $
(✆8911-4787, 2440-3528; www.elchantevegano.com; mains US$6-10; ⏰11am-8pm Tue-Sun; ✐) Two brothers, their mom and a girlfriend run this eatery specializing in healthy organic food. Vegan treats – including garbanzo and portobello-mushroom burgers, falafel, textured-soy-protein nachos, pasta, pizza and sandwiches like the Veggie Lú (grilled veggies, avocado and sprouts on homemade bread) – are served on an open-air, street-facing patio.

Coffee Dreams Café CAFE $
(✆2430-3970; cnr Calle 1 & Av 3; mains US$5-10; ⏰7am-9pm Mon-Sat, to 7pm Sun; ✐) For breakfast, *bocas* (appetizers) and a variety of *típico* (traditional Costa Rican) dishes, this centrally located cafe is a reliably good place to dine or enjoy a coffee accompanied by one of its rich desserts.

★ **Valedi Food** FUSION $$
(✆4700-5395; www.facebook.com/ValediFOOD; El Patio, Calle 3, btwn Avs 6 & 8; US$4-15; ⏰11am-10pm Mon-Thu, to midnight Fri, 9am-midnight Sat, 9am-9pm Sun; P✿✐✪) ✐ The food is excellent at this hip new, fairy-lit, open-air restaurant featuring simple white walls, wooden benches, hammocks and hanging plants. A build-it-yourself menu of organic, gluten-free and vegan creations includes juicy organic burgers, fresh salmon and slabs of meat, along with your choice of carbs, vegetables and toppings, presented on wooden boards or enamel dinner plates. Wash it down with a fresh juice or sangria. Young kids will enjoy playing in the restaurant's teepee.

Xandari INTERNATIONAL $$$
(✆2443-2020; www.xandari.com; Xandari Resort Hotel & Spa; mains US$12-32; ⏰7-10am, noon-4pm & 6-9pm; ✐) ✐ If you want to impress a date, you can't go wrong at this elegant restaurant with incredible views. The menu is a mix of Costa Rican and international, with plenty of vegetarian options. The restaurant utilizes the resort's homegrown organic produce, supplemented by locally grown organic produce whenever possible – it all makes for tasty *and* feel-good gourmet meals.

★ Entertainment

The perennial Costa Rican soccer champions, Alajuela's own La Liga (Liga Deportiva Alajuelense), have won 29 national championships and play at the **Estadio Morera Soto** (✆2289-0909; tickets from US$8) at the northeastern end of town on Sunday during *fútbol* (soccer) season.

🔒 Shopping

Goodlight Books BOOKS
(✆2430-4083; Av 3 btwn Calles 1 & 3; ⏰11am-6pm Mon-Sat) Book-a-holics, rejoice! Alajuela has one of the best English-language bookstores in the country (if not Central America). Managed by Alajuelense Rosa Carballo, Goodlight offers more than 20,000 well-organized used and new books, a worthwhile stock of difficult-to-find volumes on Costa Rica, a growing supply of Spanish-language titles and a sizable array of books in other European languages.

BUSES FROM ALAJUELA

DESTINATION	BUS COMPANY	COST (US$)	DURATION	FREQUENCY
Atenas	Coopetransatenas	2	1hr	every 30-90min 5:50am-9:45pm Mon-Fri (less frequently Sat & Sun)
Grecia	Transportes Tuan	2	1hr	roughly half-hourly 5am-10pm
Heredia	Tuasa	1.50	45min	every 15min 5:30am-10pm
Juan Santamaría International Airport	Tuasa	1.50	15min	every 10-30min, 24hr
San José	Tuasa	1.50	45min	every 10-30min, 24hr
Sarchí	Transportes Tuan	2	1-1.5hr	roughly half-hourly 5am-10pm
Volcán Poás	Coopetransasi	5 round trip	1hr	departs 9:15am, returns 2:30pm

ZOO AVE

About 10km west of Alajuela, **Zoo Ave** (☑ 2433-8989; www.rescateanimalzooave.org; adult/child US$20/5; ☺ 9am-5pm; 🅿 ♿) is a well-designed animal park with more than 115 types of bird on colorful, squawking display. The tranquil 14-hectare setting is also home to all four species of Costa Rican monkey, reptiles, wild cats and other species, many of which have been rescued and rehabilitated. Though technically a zoo, it is also an important animal-breeding center that aims to reintroduce native animals into the wild; admission fees fund wildlife rescue, rehabilitation, release and conservation programs.

The park's restaurant, Cafe David, serves buffet food ($US11), à la carte dishes like grilled sea bass and penne bolognese, or salads and sandwiches.

ℹ️ Information

Banco Nacional (⊙ 8:30am-3:30pm Mon-Fri) The most centrally located ATM can be found in the main square opposite the church.

Hospital San Rafael (☑ 2436-1001; Calle 4) Alajuela's hospital is a three-story building south of Av 10.

Post office (☑ 2443-2653; cnr Av 5 & Calle 1; ⊙ 8am-5pm Mon-Fri, to noon Sat)

ℹ️ Getting There & Away

Taxis charge between US$6 and US$10 (depending on destination) for the five- to 10-minute drive from Juan Santamaría International Airport into Alajuela.

There is no central bus terminal; instead, a number of small terminals and bus stops dot the southwestern part of the city. Note that there are two Tuasa terminals – **east** (☑ 2442-6900; Calle 8 btwn Avs Central & 1) and **west** (Calle 8 btwn Avs Central & 1) – right across the street from each other. From there, **buses to Grecia and Sarchí** (cnr Calle 10 & Av 1) are a block west; **buses to Atenas** (Calle 10 btwn Avs Central & 2) are one block west and one block south; and **buses to Volcán Poás** (☑ 2442-6900; Calle 8 btwn Avs Central & 2) are a block south. **Buses to San José via the airport** (Av 4 btwn Calles 2 & 4) leave from in front of the Parque de los Niños, on the opposite side of the street.

Coopetransasi (☑ 2449-5141) offers routes around Costa Rica.

Parque Nacional Volcán Poás

Just 37km north of Alajuela by a winding and scenic road is **Parque Nacional Volcán Poás** (☑2482-1226; US$15; ⊙8am-3:30pm), the home of a 2704m active volcano. Violent eruptions hadn't taken place for more than 60 years when rumblings began in 2014; there were further significant eruptions in April and June 2017, and at the time of research the park was closed due to these events.

In previous years it was possible to peer into the crater, measuring 1.3km across and 300m deep, and watch the steaming, bubbling cauldron belch sulfurous mud and water hundreds of meters into the air. This may be possible again in future, but for now the best place to view Poás is from afar, in the scenic, uncluttered countryside. At research time the volcano was smoking – a spectacular sight. The best time to see it is early in the morning, ideally before the clouds creep in around noon.

🛏️ Sleeping & Eating

There are no accommodations inside the park, but the area surrounding the volcano offers a range of options for all tastes and budgets. Some are closed due to recent eruptions, but the Peace Lodge is still open; book before you visit.

⭐ **Poás Volcano Lodge**   LODGE $$$
(☑2482-2194; www.poasvolcanolodge.com; Vara Blanca; incl breakfast garden r US$115-145, lodges US$195-245; 🅿 @ 🛜) For contemporary class in an idyllic rural setting, visit this high-altitude dairy farm, whose 11 suites combine rusticity and elegance; the best have a balcony and private garden and/or fireplace. Spacious common areas include a games room and a library. More than 3km of hiking trails offer quetzal sightings and views of the volcano (and even Nicaragua!) on clear days.

Peace Lodge   LODGE $$$
(☑2482-2720; www.waterfallgardens.com; d standard/deluxe/villa/deluxe villa US$430/510/710/940, additional adult/child US$40/20; 🅿 🛜 🏊) Guests feel they've stepped into a fairy tale at this over-the-top lodge, with its exquisite villas boasting majestic valley views, private decks with Jacuzzis, fireplaces and huge bathrooms with waterfall showers. There's an animal

WORTH A TRIP

LA PAZ WATERFALL GARDENS

The storybook complex of **La Paz Waterfall Gardens** (☑ 2482-2720, reservations 2482-2100; www.waterfallgardens.com; adult/under 13yr US$42/26, package tours from San José US$88/78; ⊙ 8am-5pm; P 🚼) just east of Volcán Poás offers the most easily digestible cultural experience in the Central Valley. Guests walk 3.5km of well-maintained trails to five scenic waterfalls, and can also wander around zoo-like displays including a butterfly conservatory, get up close to hummingbirds and hand-feed toucans. Then, tour a serpentarium and ranarium (frog garden), witness wild cats eating their meals, and devour a plate of your own at one of park's restaurants. It's an ideal spot for families, and you can stay on-site at the Peace Lodge (p109).

rescue center, hiking trails, five giant waterfalls and a trout pond where you can fish for your own lunch. This highly imaginative setting, with its multiple pools and interactive animal experiences (toucan and hummingbird feeding), will have kids over the moon.

Freddo Fresas　　　BREAKFAST, SOUP $
(☑ 2482-2800; dishes breakfast US$3-7, lunch US$6-10; ⊙ 7am-4pm) This homey spot looks as though it was built from oversize Lincoln logs. It's known for heavenly strawberry smoothies (milky ones beat watery ones) and large, piping-hot breakfasts that fuel some serious hikes. For those returning from a hike, a wide soup selection warms the soul. Find Freddo's a couple of blocks north of the cemetery.

★ Colbert Restaurant　　　FRENCH $$
(☑ 2482-2776, 8301-1793; www.facebook.com/restaurantefrancescolbert; Vara Blanca; mains US$8-32; ⊙ noon-8pm Fri-Tue) At this charming restaurant 6km east of Poasito, the toque-clad, mustachioed French chef Joël Suire looks like he's straight out of central casting. Naturally, the menu is loaded with traditional French items such as onion soup, housemade pâté and rabbit with beer sauce. A good wine list is strong on vintages from South America and France.

❶ Information

Before the recent eruptions there was a visitor center near the park entrance with a souvenir shop, a cafe and a small museum. These were closed at research time but may reopen in future.

❶ Getting There & Away

Numerous local companies offer daily tours to the volcano (US$40 to US$100). Check with the companies before you plan your trip to see if the tours are still running after the park's closure in 2017. It's much cheaper, and nearly as easy, to visit the volcano on the daily Coopetransasi bus from Alajuela (US$5 return, 9:15am, 50 minutes). Due to the latest volcanic activity the bus may only reach a certain point; check with the driver before you board. Both the tours and the bus typically reach the area around 10am – right when the clouds start rolling in.

To beat the clouds, your best bet is to hire a car (from US$40 per day) or a taxi (roughly US$35 from Alajuela, US$50 to US$60 from San José) and arrive near the park's entrance. The road from Alajuela to the volcano is well signposted, but at the time of research you could only drive as far as Poás Lodge (4km below the park's entrance), due to the recent eruptions.

Atenas

POP 5000

This small village, on the historic *camino de carretas* (oxcart trail) that once carried coffee beans as far as Puntarenas, is best known for having the most pleasant climate in the world – according to none other than *National Geographic*. It's not too heavy on sights, but springtime is always in the air and the central square is a lovely spot to take in Costa Rican life.

◉ Sights

Monumento al Boyero　　　MONUMENT
(Monument to the Oxcart Driver) **FREE** This iron monument welcomes visitors to Atenas while honoring the Costa Rican oxcart driver. It's 1km before Atenas on the north side of the road.

🛏 Sleeping & Eating

Vista Atenas B&B　　　B&B $$
(☑ 2446-4272; www.vistaatenas.com; r incl breakfast US$85-105; 🛜 🐾) 🌿 Here you can soak up stunning valley views that include four volcanoes – lucky guests may even see smoking craters in the distance. There are comfy rooms and self-catering cabins to choose from, plus a communal swimming-pool terrace. Expat owner Vera has lovingly enhanced the property with ecofriendly touches, including solar-pumped and heated spring water. Kitchenettes are available.

Chicharronera Don Yayo LATIN AMERICAN $
(☑2446-5901; dishes US$7-12; ⊙11am-11pm)
About 1km from the center of Atenas and
within sight of the Monumento al Boyero,
this open-air restaurant specializes in fried
pork dishes, barbecue and grilled meats. It's
a satisfying spot to enjoy a hearty meal and
a cold beer.

**Restaurant La Trocha
del Boyero** COSTA RICAN $$
(☑2446-0533; casados US$9, mains US$9-18;
⊙noon-8:30pm Thu-Tue; ☜) Tico families and
expats crowd the pleasant deck here for the
casados (set meals) on offer, fresh trout (in
season), sirloin and heaping bowls of *chifrijo*
(rice and beans with fried pork, corn chips
and fresh tomato salsa). It's located on a road
off the main road towards Alajuela before the
monument. Look for a sign at the turnoff.

❶ Getting There & Away

Coopetransatenas (☑2446-5767) buses run
from Atenas to Alajuela (US$1.50, 45 to 60 min-
utes, every 30 minutes to 1½ hours from 5.10am
to 8.30pm), with one change in La Garita. **Trans-
portes Morales** (☑2223-5567) buses run to
San José (US$2, 1¼ hours, every 15 minutes to
1½ hours from 6am to 7.30pm). The Atenas area
is quite spread out, and best navigated by car.

Grecia
POP 15,450

The village of Grecia – known as the 'Clean-
est Little Town in Latin America' – is cen-
tered on pleasant **Parque Central**, anchored
by one of the most charming churches in
Costa Rica. Southeast of town are two stun-
ning natural waterfalls.

◉ Sights

Las Cataratas de Los Chorros WATERFALL
(☑7091-2554; US$6; ⊙8am-4pm Mon-Sun)
About 7km southeast of Grecia, north of
Tacares and Flores, are two gorgeous water-
falls and a swimming hole surrounded by
shaded areas and picnic tables. It's a popular
spot for weekending couples. Look for the
sign on Rte 722 heading north of Flores. Just
beyond the sign is a grassy parking lot. Pay
the attendant around US$6 and then walk
approximately 15 minutes along a stony,
sometimes muddy, dirt track to the spectac-
ular falls; the first is 40m high.

CENTRAL VALLEY & HIGHLANDS GRECIA

PARQUE NACIONAL JUAN CASTRO BLANCO

This 143-sq-km **national park** (admission by donation) was created to protect the slopes
of Volcán Platanar (2183m) and Volcán Porvenir (2267m) from logging and mining. The
headwaters for five major rivers originate here, making this one of the most important
watersheds in the country. While federally protected, much of the park is still privately
owned by plantation families – only those parts that have already been purchased by the
government are technically open to travelers.

From the visitor center a 2km trail climbs through pastureland, then descends to Pozo
Verde, a green lake surrounded by mountains. A rougher trail continues 3.5km to Las
Minas, an abandoned mine site (only hikeable with a guide). Shorter trails include the
Universal Trail (only half a kilometer) and the 1.5km Canto de Las Aves (Birdsong) trail.
The park is popular among **anglers** as the five rivers are brimming with trout.

The limited infrastructure and tourist traffic mean your chances of spotting rare **wild-
life** (quetzals, black guans, curassows) are higher than average. Guides can be arranged
through tour agencies and hotels in the area.

Sleeping & Eating
Albergue Ecológico Pozo Verde (☑8872-9808; www.alberguemonterreal.com/eng/
index.html; d incl breakfast US$50-70; ☜) is the only place to stay near the park.

Tucked into a pretty valley about 1km before the park headquarters, **Restaurante
El Congo** (☑8872-9808; www.alberguemonterreal.com/eng/restaurant.html; mains US$10;
⊙9am-5pm Sat & Sun; ☜) is the area's only place to eat.

Getting There & Away
The park entrance is located at the end of a rough 10km road from El Sucre, 20km north
of Zarcero. The road is passable for skilled drivers in 2WD vehicles until the final descent;
if you don't have a 4WD, park on the hilltop 300m before the visitor center.

Catedral de la Mercedes
CHURCH

(☑2494-1616; http://parroquiadegrecia.com) At the heart of town you'll find the incredibly quaint Catedral de la Mercedes, a red metal structure that was prefabricated in Belgium and shipped to Costa Rica in 1897 – and resembles a gingerbread church. It has an airy nave, bright Spanish-tile floors and a Gothic-style altar covered in marble.

Rock Bridge
BRIDGE

About 5km south of Grecia, a bend in the road leads to an 18th-century rock bridge connecting the hamlets of Puente de Piedra and Rincón de Salas. Locals say the only other bridge like this is in China, and legend holds that it was built by the devil. If you park before the entrance you can get closer on foot to see the impressive stone structure.

🍴 Sleeping & Eating

Mangífera Hostel
HOSTEL $

(☑2494-6065; www.mangiferahostel.com; dm/d US$10/38, d without bathroom US$34; P🐾🛜) This cozy hostel, with wooden floors and a friendly ambience, feels instantly welcoming. On the northern side of Parque Central, it has eight rooms, three of which are dorms. There's a shared kitchen and small garden where hummingbirds feed. Laundry service available.

Café Delicias
CAFE $$

(☑2494-2093; www.cafedelicias.com; sandwiches US$5-7, dishes US$7-15; ◷7am-9pm; 🛜) For rich coffee drinks, cinnamon rolls, sandwiches and light meals – as well as free wi-fi – hit this enjoyable spot near the southwestern corner of Parque Central.

ℹ Getting There & Away

Buses for San José and Sarchí stop at the TUAN bus terminal, 150m north of Grecia's central plaza.

San José Around US$3.50, one hour, at least half-hourly from 4.30am to 8:30pm.

Sarchí, connecting to Naranjo US$1, 30 minutes, half-hourly from 5:55am to 11:15pm.

Sarchí
POP 6900

Welcome to Costa Rica's most famous crafts center, where artisans produce the ornately painted oxcarts and leather-and-wood furnishings for which the Central Valley is known. Just about everything is covered in the colorful signature geometric designs – even city hall. Yes, it's a tourist trap, but it's a pretty one. The town is stretched out along a road that weaves through hilly countryside.

Most people just come in for an afternoon of shopping, but if you have time on your hands it's possible to meet different artisans and custom order a creation. In Sarchí Norte you'll find the heart of the village, including a twin-towered church, some restaurants and *pulperías* (corner stores), and what is purported to be the world's largest oxcart.

👁 Sights

Jardín Botánico Else Kientzler
GARDENS

(☑2454-2070; www.elsegarden.com; Sarchí Norte; adult/child US$5.50/3.50; ◷8am-4pm; ♿) This well-tended botanical garden 1.4km north of Sarchí Norte's soccer field has 2km of trails winding through more than 2000 types of clearly labeled plants, including succulents, fruit trees, palms, heliconias and orchids. Regular yoga workshops, plant fairs and talks also take place in the grounds.

🍴 Sleeping & Eating

Hotel Paraíso Río Verde
BUNGALOW $

(☑2454-3003; San Pedro de Sarchí; r from US$45, bungalows from US$60; P🛜🏊) A 5km detour

---

SHOPPING SARCHÍ

Most travelers come to Sarchí for one thing only: *carretas*, the elaborate, colorfully painted oxcarts that are the unofficial souvenir of Costa Rica – and the official symbol of the Costa Rican worker. In Sarchí they come ready for the road (oxen sold separately) or in scaled-down versions. But the area produces plenty of other curios: leather-and-wood furniture (including those incredible rocking chairs that collapse for shipping), wooden tableware and trinkets emblazoned with the colorful mandala design popularized by the *carretas*.

There are more than 200 vendors, and prices and quality vary, so it pays to shop around. Workshops are usually open from 8am to 5pm daily; they accept credit cards and US dollars, and can arrange international shipping. Two of the most respected and popular spots are the **Fábrica de Carretas Eloy Alfaro** (☑2454-4131; http://souvenirscostarica. com; Sarchí Norte; ◷8am-5pm) and the **Fábrica de Carretas Joaquín Chaverri** (☑2454-4411; www.facebook.com/FabricaDeCarretasJoaquinChaverri; Sarchí Sur; ◷8am-5pm).

northeast of Sarchí, this spot in the highland village of San Pedro enjoys nice panoramic vistas of coffee plantations and volcanoes Poás, Barva and Irazú. Two inexpensive doubles (including one with prime morning perspectives on the valley) are complemented by a pair of spacious four-person bungalows with kitchenettes. The optional breakfast costs US$8 per person. As it's only identifiable from the road by a huge German flag painted on wood, finding this secluded place can be tricky. With notice, the owners can provide GPS coordinates or meet you beside the giant oxcart in Sarchí's plaza. Credit cards are not accepted, and wi-fi only works in the outdoor common areas.

Don Lolo BUFFET $$
(☑ 2454-1633; mains US$10-20; ⊙ 8am-3pm) In the upstairs area of Fábrica de Carretas Eloy Alfaro (p112), this *soda* serves up breakfasts, brunch and buffets.

❶ Getting There & Away

If you're driving from San José, from the Interamericana take the signed exit to Grecia and from there follow the road north to Sarchí. If you're coming from the west, take the turnoff north to Naranjo, then head east to Sarchí.

Buses arrive and depart from Sarchí Norte, running to:

Alajuela Around US$2, one to 1½ hours, every 15 to 30 minutes from 5am to 10:30pm.

Grecia Around US$1, 30 minutes, half-hourly from 5:25am to 10:35pm.

San José Around US$2.50, 1½ to 2¾ hours, around every 30 minutes from 5am to 10:30pm, with a change in Alajuela.

Zarcero

POP 13,200

North of Naranjo, the road winds for 20km until it reaches Zarcero's 1736m perch at the western end of the Cordillera Central. This is a gorgeous location: the mountains look as if they've been lifted from landscape paintings and the climate is fresh. But the real reason you're here is to see the country's most surreal shrubbery at Parque Francisco Alvarado.

🛏 Sleeping & Eating

Hotel Zarcero HOTEL $
(☑ 2463-4141; s/d/tr/q from US$21/26/35/43) A couple of blocks up from the church, Hotel Zarcero is the only place to stay in town. There are 15 basic rooms with locally made furnishings.

PARQUE FRANCISCO ALVARADO

In front of the Iglesia de San Rafael, **Parque Francisco Alvarado** was a normal plaza until the 1960s, when a gardener named Evangelisto Blanco became inspired to shave the ordinary topiary into a bizarre series of drippy, abstract shapes. Over the years these morphed into fanciful creatures, weird blobby creations and tunnels of arches you can walk through. Bring your camera.

Rancho Amalia FARMSTAY $$
(☑ 2463-2401, 8994-4288; www.ranchoamalia.com/en; d cabin US$87, extra person $13; ⊙ Dec-May, groups year-round; ❵❧) Attention, horse people: this family-owned mountaintop ranch just 10 minutes south of Zarcero is your dream. On offer are four charming and well-constructed cabins with fireplaces, TVs and full kitchens, a dining hall and elegant stables. The property's horses carry guests across the hillside, through forests and over scenic pastureland surrounded by wildflowers and views of the Central Valley.

Riding tours cost from US$15 per person. Watch out for the barking guard dogs on the way into the property.

Hereford Steak House STEAK $$
(☑ 2463-4309; meals US$5-16; ⊙ 11am-late) When in cowboy country, hit the steak house. With plenty of steer horns, saddles, lassos and other equine memorabilia decorating the walls, this longtime favorite grills up New York strip, filet mignon and other mouthwatering cuts. Alternative options include sandwiches, pastas, burgers and pizzas.

❶ Getting There & Away

Transportes Zarcero (☑ 2451-4080) runs daily direct buses to San José (around US$2.50, two hours, with one change in Alajuela) every hour from 6:10am to 8:10pm. All buses stop along the main street below the square.

Bajos del Toro

A gorgeous road snakes northeast out of Zarcero, climbing steeply through hillsides dotted with family dairy farms, then plunging abruptly into the stunning valley of the Río Toro, surrounded by the lower reaches of the area's cloud-forest ecosystem. If you were looking for a little piece of Costa Rica where everybody knows everybody, then look no further. This small town (full name: Bajos del Toro Amarillo) is rural idyll at its finest. There are no banks. Bring all the cash you'll need.

🛏️ Sleeping & Eating

There are only three hotels in the area, and they're very popular. Be sure to show up with a reservation.

★ Catarata del Toro
CABINA **$$**

(📞2476-0800, 8399-7476; www.catarata-del-toro.com; s/d/t/q incl breakfast US$65/80/105/130) At this roadside spot 6km north of Bajos del Toro, wood-paneled rooms are tucked under A-frame-style eaves. However, the real attraction is the adjacent **waterfall**, a 90m-tall beauty that cascades into a volcanic crater; the waterfall is reached by a steep but well-maintained trail (US$14, free for guests). There's also a restaurant where humming-birds flock to feed alongside the humans.

Bosque de Paz Rain/Cloud Forest Lodge & Biological Reserve
LODGE **$$$**

(📞2234-6676; www.bosquedepaz.com; per person incl 3 meals s US$163-225, d US$123-173; 🅿️🛜) 🏊 A birdwatcher's paradise, this 10-sq-km reserve straddles an important wilderness corridor between Parque Nacional Volcán Poás and Parque Nacional Juan Castro Blanco, with more than 22km of trails in old-growth forest, and an orchid garden. The dozen spacious, terra-cotta-tiled rooms, within earshot of a rushing river, feature large windows with forest views. Vegan diets can be accommodated. Advance reservations recommended.

El Silencio
LODGE **$$$**

(📞2476-0303, reservations 2231-6122; www.elsilenciolodge.com; ste/villas incl breakfast & activity but not tax US$310-660; 🅿️🛜) 🏊 Secluded outside of town, this upscale lodge comprises luxuriously designed *cabina* suites with private deck, rocking chairs, a Jacuzzi and fine mountain views, plus six-person villas with gas fireplaces and full kitchens. There's also a spa, 8km worth of trails (leading to stunning waterfalls) and a health-conscious restaurant serving meals using organic produce grown on site. The wi-fi can be weak in some areas of the lodge.

Soda Restaurante Nené
COSTA RICAN **$**

(📞2476-0631, 2476-0130; mains US$5-8; ⏰9am-6pm) Just south of town, tucked slightly back from the main road, this simple green shack

of a restaurant is flanked by well-stocked trout ponds. Catch your own fish, then enjoy it fried or grilled with garlic at the rustic picnic-bench-style tables. Chicken, squid and tuna fried rice also available.

ℹ️ Getting There & Away

Driving north from the Interamericana through Zarcero, take a right immediately after the church and continue northeast about 15km. Alternatively, take the road due north from Sarchí's central plaza. Both roads are almost entirely paved but involve stomach-churning steep climbs and hairpin turns; a 4WD makes all the difference to your nerves but isn't obligatory.

There's a bus from Grecia at 3pm every day except Thursday. The fare is around US$2.

San Ramón
POP 10,700

The pretty colonial town of San Ramón is no wallflower in the pageant of Costa Rican history. The 'City of Presidents and Poets' has sent five men to the country's highest office, including Rodrigo Carazo, who built a tourist lodge a few kilometers to the north.

Another of Costa Rica's beloved presidents, José Figueres Ferrer, is paid homage in an edifying culture and history center just north of the city's central park.

◉ Sights

José Figueres Ferrer Center for Culture & History
ARTS CENTER

(📞2447-2178; http://centrojosefigueres.org; ⏰10am-6pm Wed-Sat) **FREE** This museum and cultural center celebrates all things José Figueres, the three-time Costa Rican president best known for abolishing the country's army in 1948. The museum has historical exhibits and artistic representations of Figueres on display, and also contains art and music classrooms and performance spaces.

Parque Central
PLAZA

The twin spires of the ash-gray **Iglesia de San Ramón** tower over this pretty square at the center of town.

🛏️ Sleeping

★ Casa Amanecer
B&B **$$**

(📞2445-2100; www.casa-amanecer-cr.com; s/d/ste incl breakfast US$73/82/95; 🅿️🛜) 🏊 A 10-minute drive northeast of San Ramón, this sleekly designed B&B, owned by former Habitat for Humanity volunteers, offers five graceful contemporary rooms with polished-concrete floors and orthopedic beds. Tasty veggie breakfasts are served on the breezy shared terrace. Additional meals and airport transfers (US$85 for up to four people) can be arranged with advance reservation.

Hotel La Posada INN **$$**
(☑2445-7359; www.posadahotel.net; s/d US$45/60, incl breakfast US$50/70; P✳@🀫) ✐
Well-maintained rooms surround a lush, plant-filled courtyard at this pleasant inn, 400m north of the church. Rooms are somewhat baroque-looking, outfitted with massive handcrafted beds that lie somewhere on the design continuum between Louis XIV and African safari. All have mini fridges and cable TV; more expensive units have hot tubs. Some units are wheelchair-accessible, and a few have air-conditioning.

★**Villa Blanca Cloud Forest Hotel & Nature Reserve** LODGE **$$$**
(☑2461-0300, in USA & Canada 1-877-256-8399; www.villablanca-costarica.com; d US$210-275, additional person US$50, child under 6yr free; P@🀫) ✐ Occupying a cloud-forest aerie, this private reserve 18km north of San Ramón is centered on a land and dairy ranch once owned by ex-president Rodrigo Carazo. Its 35 free-standing *casitas* (little houses) come with wi-fi, private terrace, minibar and TV. Additional facilities include a restaurant, a spa (massages from US$60), a yoga center and a movie theater screening films nightly.

The surrounding 800 hectares of primary and secondary cloud forest offer excellent wildlife-spotting opportunities. Bilingual naturalist guides are available for morning and evening cloud-forest walks (US$29), and birdwatching (US$29) and quetzal-spotting (US$79) tours. Certified at the highest level of sustainability, the lodge composts, recycles and follows energy-efficient practices. For kids, there's an arcade and a games room; child-care services are available for a fee. You can also book a place on night hikes and cow-milking and ice-cream-making sessions.

The turnoff is well signposted from the Interamericana, but a 4WD is recommended for the 9km-long potholed road. A taxi from San Ramón costs about US$30.

Tierras Enamoradas LODGE **$$$**
(Lands in Love; ☑2447-9331, in USA 1-408-215-1000; www.landsinlove.com; Hwy 702; d incl breakfast US$132, additional person US$27; P🀫🐾🏊) ✐ Midway between San Ramón and La Fortuna, this well-signposted lodge has eclectic rooms with bright floral motifs, a lounge, an outdoor swimming pool and Jacuzzi, a pet

hotel (US$40 per night) and a plethora of adventure activities, from a canopy tour to canyoning to horseback riding. The restaurant serves an international mix of delicious vegetarian and vegan dishes.

✖ Eating

Merak Fusion and Soda Ata FUSION **$**
(☑2447-3470; cnr Av 8 & Calle 1; US$6-12; ⊙Soda Ata 7am-3pm, Merak 6-10pm; 🀫) Two eateries operate out of this new space with hardwood floors and simple, clean decor. By day it's a *soda*, selling soup and rice dishes; in the evening it becomes a fusion restaurant with creations like Portobello mushrooms and blue cheese, Caribbean squid, and mountain beans and sauerkraut. The menu changes weekly. It's lovely for a sangria, wine or beer, too. Find it southeast of the church.

Mi Choza COSTA RICAN **$$**
(☑2445-1286; cnr Calle 7 & Av 10; mains US$8-20; ⊙11am-11pm) At the southeastern end of town, this lively *cantina* is decked out with mounted steer horns, soccer jerseys and flat-screen TVs. The steaks are large and the service is friendly.

El Rincón Poeta COSTA RICAN **$$**
(☑2447-3942; Calle 1 btwn Avs 2 & 4; mains US$8-17; ⊙11am-10pm) Hidden away off the main street and decorated with historical black-and-white photos of San Ramón, this locally popular spot serves up big platters of *típico* meat, seafood and rice dishes in a dining room filled with sturdy tree-trunk tables or on the pleasant vine-shaded gravel patio up front. It's 150m southeast of the church.

❶ Getting There & Away

San Ramón is served by hourly buses (around US$3, one hour 20 minutes, between 4.30am and 8.15pm) to San José's Empresarios Unidos terminal (p97). Buses also head north to Zarcero via Ciudad Quesada (around US$5, three hours, 5.55am, 1pm and 5.15pm). Bus stops are just northwest of Parque Central; contact **Coopatrac** (☎2460-0638) for info.

HEREDIA AREA

At the southern point of the province, only 11km north of San José, a quaint university city sits in the shadow of the dormant Volcán Barva. Established in 1706, Heredia is known as the 'City of Flowers' due to its verdant flora, which thrive in the area's temperate climate and sporadic rain showers. Dotted with colonial architecture, it's a popular choice for those wanting to learn Spanish.

There's a mini tech industry in Heredia, and Intel opened two new business units in 2015, focusing on engineering, information security and product life cycle, yet the region's most notable industry is still coffee. Base yourself here for an easy gateway to one of Costa Rica's largest swaths of highland forest, Parque Nacional Braulio Carrillo.

❶ Getting There & Away

Buses are a reliable, cheap bet in and around Heredia. Rent a car for more flexibility.

Heredia

POP 135,300

During the 19th century, La Ciudad de las Flores (the City of the Flowers) was home to a *cafetalero* (coffee grower) aristocracy that made its fortune exporting Costa Rica's premium blend. Today the historic center retains some of this well-bred air, with a leafy main square and low-lying buildings, reflecting Spanish-colonial architectural style.

Although only 11km from San José, Heredia is – in personality – removed from the grit and grime of the capital. Universidad Nacional (National University) keeps things a touch bohemian, and on any afternoon you're bound to find the local bars and cafes abuzz with young folk idling away their time. Heredia is also the most convenient base from which to explore little-visited Volcán Barva, within the Parque Nacional Braulio Carrillo.

◉ Sights

Casa de la Cultura   MUSEUM
(☎2261-4485; http://casadelaculturaalfredogonza lezflores.blogspot.co.uk; cnr Calle Central & Av Cen-

tral; ◷8am-8pm) **FREE** Occupying a privileged position on the corner of the plaza just above the church, this low-lying Spanish structure dates back to the late 18th century. At one point it served as the residence of President Alfredo González Flores, who governed from 1913 to 1917. It is beautifully maintained and now houses permanent historical displays as well as rotating art exhibits.

Parque Central   PARK
Heredia was founded in 1706, and in true Spanish-colonial style it has several interesting old landmarks arranged around Parque Central, including an ornate fountain and a bandstand.

El Fortín   TOWER
This tower, constructed in 1876 by order of Heredia's provincial governor, is the official symbol of Heredia. It was declared a national historic monument in 1974, but because of its fragile state it remains closed to the public.

◈ Courses

Centro Panamericano de Idiomas LANGUAGE
(CPI; ☎2265-6306, in USA 1-877-373-3116; www. cpi-edu.com; private lessons from US$30, 20hr of group tuition from US$460, 1-week homestay from US$200) Based in San Joaquín de Flores, just outside Heredia, this popular school also has a teen camp and family programs. There's a maximum of four students per class.

Intercultura   LANGUAGE
(☎2260-8480; www.interculturacostarica.com; cnr Calle 10 & Av 4; private lessons from US$26, 20hr group tuition with/without 1-week homestay from US$570/275) This school also arranges volunteer opportunities and offers cooking and dance classes.

▒ Sleeping

Hotel Las Flores   HOTEL $
(☎2261-8147; www.hotel-lasflores.com; Av 12 btwn Calles 12 & 14; s/d/tr US$17/32/42; ℗❀) A bit of a walk from the action, this spotless no-frills, family-run place has basic, brightly painted rooms with TVs and hot-water showers.

Hotel Valladolid   HOTEL $$
(☎2260-2912, 2260-2905; www.hotelvalladolid. net; cnr Calle 7 & Av 7; s/d incl breakfast US$75/87; ℗❀@❀) This business hotel on a quiet street has 12 bright, clean and business-like tiled rooms with wi-fi, safes, cable TV and private bathrooms with hot water. Credit cards accepted.

Heredia

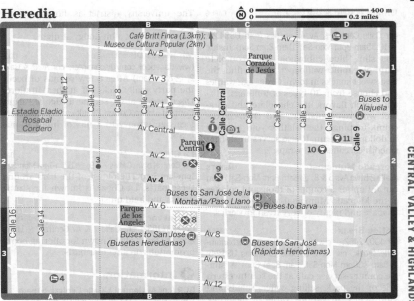

Heredia

◎ Sights
1 Casa de la Cultura............................C2
2 El Fortín C2

◆ Activities, Courses & Tours
3 Intercultura A2

🛏 Sleeping
4 Hotel Las Flores A3
5 Hotel Valladolid..............................D1

✴ Eating
6 Coffee Break..................................B2
7 La Cantina.....................................D1
8 Mercado Municipal..........................B3
9 Ohana Waffle & Coffee Bar................C2

🍷 Drinking & Nightlife
10 El Bulevar Relax.............................D2
11 La Choza D2
   Miraflores Discotheque.................(see 6)

Hotel Chalet Tirol   INN $$$
(☎2267-6222; www.hotelchaleteltirol.com; r US$90-
115; P🅿🛜🐾) This charming hotel channels
the gingerbread quaintness of the Alps. (It
once served as a backdrop for a German
beer advert.) The 15 suites and 20 chalets
have cable TV, room service and a gorgeous
mountain setting; some also have Jacuzzis,
fireplaces or wheelchair-accessible facili-
ties. The in-house restaurant serves French
food (dishes US$5 to US$25) and sometimes
hosts live music on weekends. Find the hotel
northeast of Heredia, 3km north of Castillo
Country Club.

Hotel Bougainvillea   HOTEL $$$
(☎2244-1414, from USA 866-880-5441; www.hb.co.
cr; Santo Domingo; d incl breakfast US$128.50-
154.50, extra person US$17.50; P🅿@🛜🏊) ✧ Set
on 4 hectares about 6km outside town, this
efficient hotel is surrounded by an expansive,
well-manicured garden with old trees, stunning flowers and plenty of statuary. The crisp,
whitewashed rooms have balconies with
views of mountains or the city, and several
private trails wind by the swimming pool and
tennis courts, through forest and orchards.
Credit cards accepted. There's also a tennis
court and gym. Cribs are complimentary.

✕ Eating

In the grand tradition of university towns
worldwide, Heredia offers plenty of spots
for pizza and cheap grub, not to mention a
branch of every fast-food outlet imaginable.
There are a couple of good cafes where you
can enjoy a sandwich too.

Ohana Waffle & Coffee Bar CAFE $
(☑ 2237-8493; www.facebook.com/ohanawaffles; cnr Calle Central & Av 4; waffles from US$4.20; ⊙ 10:30am-9pm Mon-Sat, 11am-8pm Sun) Inside this slim, blue cubbyhole cafe, complete with pineapple wallpaper, you'll find the best sweet snacks in town. Order egg waffles and choose from 50 types of toppings. Mix-and-match flavors like chocolate and caramel with marshmallows and Oreo-cookie-chunk toppings, then slather your creation in dollops of cream. It also serves fresh-fruit smoothies, coffee and wraps.

Mercado Municipal MARKET $
(Calle 2 btwn Avs 6 & 8; ⊙ 6am-6pm Mon-Sat) You can fill up for a couple of thousand colones at the Mercado Municipal, which has *sodas* to spare and plenty of very fresh groceries.

Coffee Break CAFE $
(☑ 4001-2462; www.facebook.com/herbarium-coffeebreak; cnr Av 2 & Calle 2; mains US$2-5; ⊙ 8am-7:30pm Mon-Sat, 9am-8pm Sun) A simple counter-service cafe at the southwestern side of the park, selling coffee, salads and sandwiches (in various varieties including crab meat, chicken, ham and cheese), plus quiches, omelettes and pancakes.

La Cantina LATIN AMERICAN $
(☑ 4034-8774; Calle 9 btwn Avs 3 & 5; mains US$4-7; ⊙ 5-11pm Mon-Sat) This yellow-and-red joint with two bars has patio seating and specializes in *chicharrón* (fried pork), with a killer *chifrijo* (dish of fried pork, beans, rice and avocado). The extensive list of *bocas* (appetizers) and fried bar snacks is worth a nibble as well.

🍷 Drinking & Nightlife

With a thriving student body, the city has no shortage of live music and cultural events.

The university district is hopping most nights of the week. Be aware that downtown Heredia can get a bit dodgy at night.

Miraflores Discotheque CLUB
(www.facebook.com/discomiracr; cnr Av 2 & Calle 2; ⊙ 8pm-6am) After a few rounds of beers, the party really kicks off at the Miraflores Discotheque, at the southern edge of Parque Central above Coffee Break cafe (p118). Here locals get groovy to a mix of international beats.

La Choza BAR
(Av Central btwn Calles 7 & 9; ⊙ 11am-1am Mon-Sat, 1pm-1am Sun) The oldest of the bars around these parts, La Choza is known for strong drinks and loud music.

El Bulevar Relax SPORTS BAR
(☑ 2237-1832; cnr Calle 7 & Av Central; ⊙ 11am-1am; 🛜) Sports bar known for offering boozy promotions on a regular basis.

ℹ️ Information

BCR (cnr Av Central & Calle Central; ⊙ 5am-10pm) Has an ATM dispensing US dollars.
Hospital San Vicente de Paul (☑ 2562-8100; Calle 12) A new hospital south of Av 14.

ℹ️ Getting There & Away

There is no central bus terminal; buses leave from stops scattered between the university and the Mercado Central.

The **San José–bound Rápidas Heredianas bus** (Av 8 btwn Calles Central & 1) is the best option if you're transferring to a Caribbean-bound bus, as it drops you near San José's Terminal Caribeña. The other bus to San José can be found two blocks west (Av 8 btwn Calles 2 & 4). Buses to Barva (Calle 1 btwn Avs 4 & 6), as well as buses to San José de la Montana/Paso Llano (Calle 1 btwn Avs 4 & 6), can be found due north of the San José

BUSES FROM HEREDIA

DESTINATION	COMPANY	COST (US$)	DURATION	FREQUENCY
Alajuela	Tuasa	1	45min	every 15min 6am-10:30pm
Barva	Transportes Barveños LTDA	1	15min	every 15min 4:55am-11pm
San José	Busetas Heredianas	1	30min	every 5-10min 5am-11pm
San José	Rápidas Heredianas	1	30min	every 15min-2hr (longer for early-morning buses) midnight-11:50pm
San José de la Montaña/Paso Llano (for Volcán Barva)	Transportes del Norte	1	60min	every 10min-1hr 4:50am-5:30pm

KID-FRIENDLY CENTRAL VALLEY

Family-friendly attractions abound in the Central Valley. Here are a few spots guaranteed to please kids and adults alike.

Parque Francisco Alvarado (p113) In Zarcero, kids will love zigzagging through rows of bushes sculpted into stegosauruses and other fantastic shapes in these topiary gardens.

Río Pejibaye (p129) Turrialba outfitters lead rafting trips on this Class I–II river that's plenty scenic but not too rough.

Zoo Ave (p109) In La Garita, stroll the grounds alongside peacocks and giant lizards, visit with monkeys or take the canopy tour at this zoo and animal-rescue center.

Parque Nacional Tapantí-Macizo Cerro de la Muerte (p126) Easy hiking trails lead down to sandy beaches where kids can splash in a boulder-strewn river.

Rápidas Heredianas buses near the main drag, Av 4. Buses to Alajuela (cnr Av 1 & Calle 9) are on the northeastern side of town.

Barva

POP 34,600

Surrounded by picturesque mountains only 2.5km north of Heredia, the historic town of Barva is a settlement dating back to 1561. Declared a national monument, the town center is dotted with low-lying 19th-century buildings and is centered on the towering Iglesia San Bartolomé, constructed in 1893. The surrounding area was once popular with the Costa Rican elite: Cleto González Víquez (1858–1937), twice president of Costa Rica (he built the original National Library), was born and raised here. It's a perfect spot for a lazy afternoon stroll.

◉ Sights

Museo de Cultura Popular MUSEUM
(☑2260-1619; Santa Lucía; ⊘8am-5pm Sun) FREE Housed in a restored 19th-century farmhouse 1.5km southeast of Barva, this tiny museum surrounded by well-labeled gardens is run by the Universidad Nacional. Visitors can tour rooms full of antique furniture, textiles, ceramics and other period pieces. On Sunday the on-site restaurant La Fonda serves *casados* (US$8) on its pleasant open-air terrace. The museum is also open by reservation only for groups from 8am to 4pm Monday to Friday. An admission fee is charged on these days; phone to inquire about a price for your group.

⌖ Tours

Café Britt Finca TOURS
(☑2277-1600; www.coffeetour.com; without/with lunch adult US$25/39, student US$20/34; ⊘8am-

5pm, tours 9am, 11am, 1.15pm & 3.15pm) Costa Rica's most famous coffee roaster offers a 90-minute bilingual tour of its plantation that includes coffee tasting and a comedic stage play about the history of coffee (kids will likely dig it). More in-depth tours are available, as are packages including transport from San José; reserve ahead. Drivers won't be able to miss the many signs between Heredia and Barva. A large on-site gift shop and cafe sells coffee, drinks and pastries plus Costa Rica–themed gifts.

✲ Festivals & Events

Feria de la Mascarada CULTURAL
Every year the city hosts the Feria de la Mascarada, a tradition with roots in the colonial era. Participants don massive colorful masks (some weighing 20kg), and gather to dance and parade around the town square. Demons and devils are frequent subjects, but celebrities and politicians also feature (you haven't lived until you've seen a 6m-tall Celia Cruz). Dates vary; inquire locally.

⬛ Sleeping

★**Finca Rosa Blanca** INN $$$
(☑2269-9392, in USA 305-395-3042; www.fincarosablanca.com; Santa Bárbara; d incl breakfast US$360-508; ⓟ@🅐🅔) ✿ Set amid a stunning hillside coffee plantation 6km northwest of Barva, this honeymoon-ready, Gaudí-esque confection of suites and villas is cloaked in fruit trees that shade private trails. The 14 sparkling-white adobe rooms with wood-beamed ceilings and private balconies are lavishly appointed; one tops a tower with 360-degree views, reached by a winding staircase made from a tree trunk.

Shower in an artificial waterfall, take a moonlit dip in the pool or have an organic coffee scrub at the spa. Fuel up at the hotel's restaurant, which serves fresh local produce, including eggs from the chicken coop in the garden for breakfast and Costa Rican fusion dishes like queen sea bass encrusted in homemade chorizo for dinner. Credit cards accepted. At 9am and 1pm, Finca Rosa Blanca offers a 2½-hour tour of its picturesque, 12-hectare organic coffee plantation, processing plant and roasting house. Guests hike the fields, learn the process and taste the delicious results. Outside guests can pay US$40 per person for the same tour.

ⓘ Getting There & Away

Buses travel about every 15 minutes between Heredia and Barva (about US$1, 15 minutes), picking up and dropping off in front of Barva's church. Routes from Barva to Heredia start at 4:45am and run until 10:45pm. The route is operated by **Transportes Barveños** (☎2262-1839).

San Isidro de Heredia

POP 20,500

This scenic, agrarian town northeast of San José offers all the lush greenery of the neighboring Parque Nacional Braulio Carillo, along with undulating drives over the countryside and a couple of the Central Valley's most enjoyable tours. Light afternoon showers nearly every day make San Isidro de Heredia the rainbow capital of Costa Rica, and a fantastic place to grow (and eat) just about anything.

◉ Sights

Toucan Rescue Ranch   ANIMAL SANCTUARY
(☎2268-4041; http://toucanrescueranch.org; donation requested adult/6-10yr US$35/17, under 6yr free; ☉ tours by appointment 9am & 2pm Mon-Sat)
A decade ago, expat Leslie Howle and her husband, Jorge Murillo, started taking in sick and injured toucans. The couple found it hard to turn any animal away and eventually ended up with owls, sloths, monkeys, an otter, an oncilla, a weasel and more. Guests tour their picturesque grounds in the hills of San Isidro de Heredia. Call for directions or to inquire about volunteer opportunities.

⌖ Tours

★**Sibu Chocolate**   FOOD & DRINK
(☎2268-1335; http://sibuchocolate.com; half-day tours per person US$28; ☉ tours 10am Tue-Sat, restaurant 11am-6pm Tue-Sat, to 4pm Sun) 🍮 This divine chocolate tour explains the culture and history surrounding Costa Rica's most decadent export. See cacao's story brought to

life as you sample pre-Columbian-inspired hot chocolate and other treats. Lunch and sumptuous hot chocolate can be enjoyed on the terrace surrounded by lush gardens, and a shop sells goodies to take home. Tours have a four-person minimum; call ahead.

Ingredients, such as herbs, for flavoring the chocolate and restaurant's recipes, are grown organically at the facility. This restaurant and chocolate operation is located just 20 minutes north of downtown San José, around 1.5km off the highway to Guápiles.

🛏 Sleeping & Eating

Toucan Rescue Ranch   B&B $$$
(☎2268-4041; http://toucanrescueranch.org; d incl tour & breakfast US$165, extra person US$30; 🅿🛜) The local animal-rescue center (p120) also provides the best lodgings in town, with two adorable and well-constructed guesthouses just a short walk from the owls, sloths, toucans and other exotic, recovering creatures. It's an incredibly serene setting, with a backdrop of rainforest and rolling hills, and is conveniently located just 35 minutes from San José's international airport. Those staying in the guesthouse will witness the inner workings of the sanctuary and may even see new animals being brought in.

Casa Antigua Café &
Restaurante   COSTA RICAN $
(☎2268-3366; mains from US$7.50; ☉noon-7pm Thu, to 9pm Fri, 8am-9pm Sat, 8am-7pm Sun) Breakfast, lunch and dinner are served in this atmospheric century-old colonial house with hardwood floors, painted ceilings, stained-glass windows, period furniture and detailed alcoving. Order a Baileys espresso and a slice of cake at the counter or enjoy *casados* (set meals), pastas, wraps, hamburgers, crepes and sandwiches in the unique dining rooms, some private – like you're hosting a dinner party. It's on the road east out of San Isidro on the way to San Josecito.

★**Bromelias del Río**   CAFETERIA $$
(☎2268-9901; www.facebook.com/cafeteriayrestaurantebromeliasdelrio; mains US$6-27, pastries from US$2; ☉7am-7pm) Ensconced in a tropical garden by a mountain stream, this bakery-restaurant tempts with spiked coffee drinks (hot mocha with Baileys and chocolate syrup) and decadent sandwiches, some piled high with *lomito* (steak), heart of palm, avocado and gravy. Share a main and save room for dessert. It's 50m off Hwy 32 at the Santa Elena exit to San Isidro.

OFF THE BEATEN TRACK

STAYS AWAY FROM SAN JOSÉ

For many visitors to Costa Rica, a night in San José is practically obligatory at the beginning or end of every trip. But if you have a car, you can instead arrange to stay at one of the following country inns. All lie within an hour's drive of the international airport – and most have incredible mountain scenery.

➡ Just outside Alajuela, Trapp Family Country Inn (p107), Tacacori Ecolodge (p107) and Xandari Resort Hotel & Spa (p106) have verdant settings and are five to 15 minutes from the airport.

➡ The dreamy Finca Rosa Blanca (p119) is less than 30 minutes from the airport check-in.

➡ Vista Atenas B&B (p110), only 30 minutes west of the terminal, is perched so spectacularly high above the valley you'll think you're flying again.

➡ Just 35 minutes east of the airport is Toucan Rescue Ranch (p120), where guests sleep in comfy guesthouses steps away from sloths, owls and toucans.

Casa Azul   SPANISH **$$**
(☑2268-6908, 8376-6493; San Josécito; mains US$12-23; ☺5-10pm Tue-Fri, from noon Sat, noon-4pm Sun) Tucked away just off Hwy 32 in a quaint little blue house adorned with blue curtains, antiques and hardwood floors, this Spanish–Costa Rican fusion restaurant is one of the Central Valley's most romantic spots. Popular dishes include paella, trout, and mouthwatering medallions of *lomito* (tenderloin) that pair well with a bottle of cabernet.

🛈 Getting There & Away

Transportes Arnoldo Ocampo SA buses for San José leave from a stop 100m east of San Isidro de Heredia's central plaza. Buses for Heredia leave from in front of the MegaSuper supermarket, 100m east of the Catholic church.

San José Under US$1, 20 minutes, roughly half-hourly from 4:40am to 9:45pm Monday to Saturday, 5:30am to 9:45pm Sunday.

Heredia Under US$1, 15 minutes, roughly every 20 minutes from 4:50am to 10:15pm.

CARTAGO AREA

The riverbank setting of the city of Cartago was handpicked by Spanish governor Juan Vásquez de Coronado, who said that he had 'never seen a more beautiful valley.' Cartago was founded as Costa Rica's first capital in 1563, and Coronado's successors endowed the city with fine colonial architecture. However, the city was destroyed during a 1723 eruption of Volcán Irazú. Any remaining landmarks were toppled by earthquakes in 1841 and 1910.

Although the city was relegated to backwater status when the seat of government moved to San José in 1823, the surrounding area, particularly the Orosi Valley, flourished during the days of the coffee trade. Today, much of the region continues to be devoted to coffee production. Although Cartago no longer has the prestige of a national capital, it remains a vital commercial hub – not to mention the site of some of the country's most important religious monuments.

🛈 Getting There & Away

Bus stops are scattered around Cartago and routes connect to Turrialba, Orosi and San José. Train services run between San José's Estación del Pacífico and Cartago's downtown station.

Cartago

POP 157,800

Cartago exists mainly as a commercial and residential center, though the beauty of the surrounding mountains helps take the edge off modern life. As in other commercial towns, expect plenty of functional concrete structures. Two worthy exceptions, however, are the striking ruins of the Santiago Apóstol Parish, an ancient site home to a number of churches since 1575, and the bright white Basílica de Nuestra Señora de Los Ángeles. The latter is visible from many parts of the city – it stands out like a snowcapped mountain above a plain of one-story edifices. The city is thrown briefly into the spotlight every August, when pilgrims from every corner of the country descend on the basilica to say their most serious prayers.

⊙ Sights

Mercado Central
MARKET

(Av 1 btwn Calles 2 & 4; ⊙6am-5:30pm Mon-Sat, to noon Sun) This old-school covered market is conveniently located right around the corner from the bus and train stations that serve San José. It's fun just to wander the labyrinth of aisles, where you'll find fresh produce and food items of every description.

Basílica de Nuestra Señora de Los Ángeles
CHURCH

(Calle 15 btwn Avs Central & 1) Cartago's most important site, and Costa Rica's most venerated religious shrine, this basilica exudes Byzantine grace, with fine stained-glass windows, hand-painted interiors and ornate side chapels. Dating from the 1630s, the structure retains an unharmed central relic: La Negrita (the Black Virgin), a small representation of the Virgin Mary, that was found on this spot on August 2, 1635. As the story goes, when the woman who discovered the statuette tried to take it with her, it miraculously reappeared back where she'd found it. Twice. So the townspeople built a shrine around her. In 1824 she was declared Costa Rica's patron Virgin. She now resides on a gold, jewel-studded platform at the main altar. Each August 2, on the anniversary of the statuette's miraculous discovery, pilgrims from every corner of the country (and beyond) walk the 22km from San José to the basilica. Many of the penitent complete the last few hundred meters of the pilgrimage on their knees.

Las Ruinas de la Parroquia
RUINS

(Iglesia del Convento; Calle Central btwn Avs Central & 2) This now-ruined church was built in 1575 as a shrine to St James the Apostle. It was destroyed by the 1841 earthquake, rebuilt a few years later and then destroyed again in the 1910 earthquake. Today only the outer walls remain, but 'the ruins' are a pleasant spot for people-watching. Legend has it that the ghost of a headless priest wanders here.

🛏 Sleeping & Eating

Los Ángeles Lodge
B&B $$

(☑2551-0957, 2591-4169; hotel.los.angeles@hotmail.com; Av 1 btwn Calles 13 & 15; s/d incl breakfast US$35/50; ❄🐾) With balconies overlooking Plaza de la Basílica, this decent B&B stands out with spacious and comfortable rooms, hot showers and breakfast made to order.

La Puerta del Sol
COSTA RICAN $$

(☑2551-0615; Av 1 btwn Calles 13 & 15; mains US$6-13; ⊙8:30am-10pm Mon-Sat, to 9pm Sun) Located downstairs from Los Ángeles Lodge

and decorated with vintage photos of Cartago, this pleasant restaurant has been around since 1957 and serves myriad Tico specialties, from *ceviche* (seafood marinated in lemon) to *casados*, along with breakfasts (rice, beans and eggs), chicken salads, pastas, burgers and sandwiches.

ℹ Information

Banco de Costa Rica (Av Central btwn Calles 5 & 7) and **Banco Popular** (Av 2; ⊙8:45am-4:30pm Mon-Fri, 8.15-11.30am Sat) have ATMs.
Hospital Max Peralta (☑2550-1999; www.ccss.sa.cr/hospitales; Av 6 btwn Calles 2 & 4) Emergency and medical services.

ℹ Getting There & Away

BUS
Bus stops are scattered around town. Destinations include the following:

Orosi (Autotransportes Mata Irola) About US$1, 45 minutes, every 15 to 30 minutes between 5:15am and 10:25pm; departs from Calle 3 between Avs 2 and 4.

San José (Lumaca) About US$1.50, 50 minutes, every 15 minutes between 4:35am and 11pm; departs from the terminal on Calle 6 between Avs 3 and 7.

Turrialba (Transtusa) US$1.60, one hour 20 minutes, every 20 minutes to an hour between 6:15am and 11pm weekdays (less frequently on weekends); departs from Av 4 between Calles 5 and 7.

TRAIN
Train services run between San José's Estación del Pacífico and Cartago's downtown **station** (Av 3 btwn Calles 4 & 6). The one-hour trip costs around US$1. Trains run Monday to Friday from 5:25am to 7:05pm every 30 minutes to an hour in a schedule weighted toward morning and afternoon commuting hours. On Saturday trains run to San José every hour until 1:30pm. See www.incofer.go.cr for up-to-date timetable info.

Parque Nacional Volcán Irazú

Looming on the horizon 19km northeast of Cartago, 3432m Irazú – which derives its name from the indigenous word *ara-tzu* (thunder point) – is the largest and highest active volcano in Costa Rica and one of the few you can currently hike around. In 1723 the Spanish governor of the area, Diego de la Haya Fernández, watched as the volcano unleashed its destruction on the city of Cartago (one of the craters is named in his honor).

Since the 18th century, 15 major eruptions have been recorded. At the time of research the volcano was slumbering peacefully.

The summit is a bare landscape of volcanic ash craters. The principal crater is 1050m across and 300m deep; the adjacent Diego de la Haya Crater is 690m across and 80m deep; and the shallowest, Playa Hermosa Crater, is being colonized by sparse vegetation. There's also a pyroclastic cone, consisting of rocks fragmented by volcanic activity.

🍃 Tours

Tours are arranged by a variety of San José operators and cost US$50 to US$70 for a half-day, and up to US$100 for a full day combined with lunch and visits to sights such as the Lankester Gardens (p124) or the Orosi Valley. Tours from hotels in Orosi (US$30 to US$45) can also be arranged – these may include lunch and visits to the basilica in Cartago or sights around the Orosi Valley.

✕ Eating

Restaurant 1910 COSTA RICAN $$
(☑ 2536-6063; mains US$10-26; ⊗11:30am-9pm Mon-Fri, to 10pm Sat, to 6:30pm Sun; 🅿🛜) On the road to Irazú (Rte 219), 300m north of the Christ statue marking the Guayabo turnoff, is this homey spot with a glass-walled deck. It's overpriced but worth a stop to see its collection of photographs documenting the 1910 earthquake that completed the destruction of colonial Cartago. Expect a long list of Tico specialties and a sumptuous Sunday buffet (adult/child US$20/11).

ℹ Information

The **ranger station** (☑ 2299-5800; park US$15, parking US$2; ⊗8am-3:30pm) at the park's entrance, 1.5km before the summit, is where you pay your entry and parking fees.

ℹ Getting There & Away

A daily bus to Irazú (roughly US$10) departs from San José at 8am and arrives at the summit around 10am. The bus departs from Irazú at 12:30pm, taking just over two hours to return to San José, with one change in Cartago.

A round-trip taxi from Cartago to the summit will cost about US$50; negotiate with drivers to allow you an hour to explore up top.

If you're in a group, renting a car is the best deal, as you can get to the park early, before the skies cloud over and the crowds arrive. From Cartago, take Hwy 8, which begins at the northeastern corner of the plaza and continues 31km to the summit. The road is well signposted.

Valle de Orosi

This straight-out-of-a-storybook river valley is famous for mountain vistas, a lake formed by a hydroelectric facility, a truly wild national park and coffee – lots and lots of coffee. A well-paved 32km loop winds through a landscape of rolling hills terraced with coffee plantations and valleys dotted with pastoral villages, all set against the backdrop of volcanoes Irazú and Turrialba. If you have a rental car (or good legs for cycling) you're in for a treat, though it's still possible to navigate most of the loop via public buses.

The loop road starts 8km southeast of Cartago in Paraíso, heads south to Orosi, then doubles back northeast and west around the artificial Lago de Cachí, passing the historic church at Ujarrás en route back to Paraíso. Alternatively, from Orosi you can branch south into Parque Nacional Tapantí-Macizo Cerro de la Muerte, an end-of-the-road national park with superb river and mountain scenery.

ℹ Getting There & Away

Autotransportes Mata Irola (☑ 2533-1916) runs buses (roughly US$1) every 30 minutes to Paraíso (20 minutes) from 4:15am to 8pm weekdays, 5:30am to 9pm Saturday and Sunday, and to Cartago (45 minutes) from 4:30am to 8pm weekdays, 5:30am to 9pm Saturday and 8:30am to 10pm Sunday. From Cartago you can transfer for buses to San José. The main bus stops sit along Orosi's main street, next to the square.

Paraíso Area

Though the village of Paraíso isn't all that its name implies, it does lead to the wonderful Valle de Orosi beyond. The area's attractions

---

SPANISH SCHOOLS IN THE CENTRAL VALLEY

Spanish schools usually do packages including homestays, meals and daily language lessons.

➡ Adventure Education Center (p132)

➡ Centro Panamericano de Idiomas (p116)

➡ Intensa (p105)

➡ Intercultura (p116)

➡ Spanish by the River (p132)

include the tranquil Lankester Gardens and the spectacular Mirador Orosi.

Sights

Mirador Orosi   VIEWPOINT
(⊙6am-4.30pm) **FREE** Heading south from Paraíso toward Orosi you'll hit Mirador Orosi, a big green space with a jaw-dropping scenic overlook complete with toilets, barbecue facilities, cultivated flowerbeds and a secure parking lot. Bring your camera and food for a picnic.

Lankester Gardens   GARDENS
(✒2511-7939, 2511-749; www.jbl.ucr.ac.cr; adult/student US$10/7.50; ⊙8:30am-4:30pm) The University of Costa Rica runs the exceptional 11-hectare Lankester Gardens, started as a private garden by British orchid enthusiast Charles Lankester in 1917, then turned over to the university for public administration in 1973. Orchids are the big draw here: there are more than 1000 varieties, at their showiest in April. The garden is wheelchair accessible. Find it about 5km west of Paraíso on the road to Cartago; look for a blue sign with an image of an orchid. There's also a Japanese garden, as well as areas full of bromeliads, palms, heliconias and other tropical plants. Guided tours in English and Spanish are available by prior arrangement.

Activities

Finca La Flor de Paraíso   VOLUNTEERING
(✒2534-8003; www.la-flor.jimdo.com; per day US$28) ✐ Immerse yourself in the Central Valley's rural culture with a stay at Finca La Flor de Paraíso, outside Cartago. This not-for-profit organic farm operated by the Association for the Development of Environmental and Human Consciousness (Asodecah) has a volunteer-work program that will allow you to get your hands dirty on projects related to agriculture, reforestation, animal husbandry and medicinal-herb cultivation.

The cost of the volunteer-work program, including room and board (in simple wood *cabinas* and dormitories), is US$25 per day. Vacationers can arrange guided visits (per person US$5, plus snack/lunch US$1.50/2.50) or overnight stays (per person including three meals US$50). Family rates are available; reservations necessary.

Tours

Finca Cristina   TOURS
(✒2574-6426, in US 203-549-1945; www.cafecristina.com; guided tours per person US$15; ⊙by ap-

pointment) Finca Cristina, 2km east of Paraíso on the road to Turrialba at the end of a short dirt track, is an organic coffee farm. Linda and Ernie have been farming in Costa Rica since 1977, and a two-hour tour of their microprocessing plant is a fantastic introduction to the processes of organic coffee growing, harvesting and roasting. The tour finishes with a cup of their delicious coffee.

Getting There & Away

Autotransportes Mata Irola (p123) runs buses (fares around US$1 for a single journey) back and forth between Orosi and Paraíso every 30 minutes. The trip takes about 20 minutes and involves multiple stops. Buses run from Paraíso between 5.40am and 10.50pm weekdays and from 5.55am Saturday and Sunday.

Orosi

POP 9850

Named for a Huetar chief who lived here at the time of the Spanish conquest, Orosi charmed colonists in the 18th century with its perfect climate, rich soil and wealth of water – from hot springs to bracing waterfalls. So, in the typical fashion of the day, the colonists decided to take the property off Orosi's hands. Today the area remains picturesque – and it's a good spot to revel in beautiful scenery and a small-town atmosphere.

Sights

Iglesia de San José Orosi   CHURCH
Orosi is one of the few colonial-era towns to survive Costa Rica's frequent earthquakes, which have thankfully also spared the photogenic village church. Built in the mid-1700s, it is the oldest religious site still in use in Costa Rica. The roof of the church is a combination of thatched cane and ceramic tiling, while the carved-wood altar is adorned with religious paintings of Mexican origin.

Museo de San José Orosi   MUSEUM
(✒2533-3051; adult/child US$1/0.50; ⊙1-5pm Tue-Sat, 9am-5pm Sun) Adjacent to Orosi's church, this small museum displays interesting examples of Spanish-colonial religious art and artifacts, some of which date back to the 17th century.

Activities

Aventuras Orosi   RAFTING
(✒2533-4000; www.facebook.com/aventurasorosicr; rafting per person from US$75; ⊙9am-4pm) Operated by the charming Luis, who served as a guide for the venerable Ríos Tropicales

rafting company for years, this small outfit organizes canopy tours and rafting expeditions as well as custom itineraries. The office is on the main street, south of the park.

Monte Sky   HIKING
(🖉 2228-0010; www.facebook.com/MonteSkyME; day entry US$8, overnight stay from US$35) About 5km south of Orosi, high in the hills off the road to Tapantí, this 536-hectare private reserve teems with 290 bird species and offers hiking trails with waterfalls and jaw-dropping vistas. Day entry includes use of all cabin facilities, including kitchen and barbecue area. Call for directions; a 4WD is recommended for the 3.5km dirt road up to the cabin. The folks at Monte Sky or OTIAC (p126) in Orosi can help arrange a 4WD transfer for your visit. Overnight stays include accommodation in one of the four rooms (sleeping up to 16). Large groups can pre-order meals and get group prices.

🍃 Courses

Montaña Linda runs one of the most affordable Spanish-language schools in the country; check the website for current prices and schedules. Located 300m south of Orosi's plaza.

🛏 Sleeping

Montaña Linda   HOSTEL $
(🖉 2533-3640; www.montanalinda.com; dm US$9, guesthouse s/d/tr/q US$30/30/35/40, s/d/tr/q without bathroom US$15/22/33/40; 🅿 @ 🛜) A short walk southwest of the bus stop, this welcoming, chilled-out budget option has three tidy dorms and eight private rooms surrounding a homey terrace with flowers, hammocks and a wood-heated hot tub. All share a guest kitchen and six bathrooms with hot showers. Owners provide an exceptional information packet highlighting local attractions, including hot springs, waterfalls and more.

Orosi Lodge   INN $$
(🖉 2533-3578; www.orosilodge.com; d/tr US$63/73, chalet d US$100, extra person US$15; 🅿 🛜) This quiet haven, run by a friendly couple, has bright rooms with wood-beamed ceilings, tile floors, minibar, coffeemaker and free organic coffee. Most rooms face a lovely garden courtyard with a fountain, and one is wheelchair accessible. Delicious, wholesome continental or rustic breakfasts are served for US$8 at the colorfully decorated cafe with scenic balcony seating.

Rancho Río Perlas   RESORT $$$
(🖉 2533-3341; www.rio-perlas.com; r for 1/2/3 people incl breakfast US$90/140/210; 🅿 🛜 ♨) With trout-filled lakes, a system of thermal waters and 2km of hiking trails, this picturesque mountain resort is a top sanctuary for locals and visitors looking to escape city life. Nicer rooms offer artificial fireplaces and Jacuzzi tubs. A conference center and chapel make this a popular spot for weddings and other events.

🍴 Eating & Drinking

Batidos La Uchuva   JUICE BAR $
(🖉 8603-8373; batidos US$2-4; ⊙ 9am-5pm Tue-Sat, to 3pm Sun) At this simple stall 100m south of Banco Nacional, owner André whips up flavorful *batidos* (fruit shakes) made with milk, water or yogurt. Choose from his long list of creative combinations, or invent your own.

Panadería Suiza   BAKERY $
(🖉 8706-6777; www.costarica-moto.com/caf-y-panaderia-suiza; pastries from US$1, breakfast US$6-7; ⊙ 6am-5pm Tue-Sat, to noon Sun) Starting at the crack of dawn, ebullient expat Franzisca serves healthy breakfasts and snacks at her main-street bakery, 100m south of Banco Nacional. On offer are sweet and savory pastries, wholegrain breads, and lunch packets for outdoors enthusiasts.

She also rents out two charming cabins (US$40 to US$70), motorcycles (US$55 to US$85 per day) and scooters ($50 per day).

Cafetería 1743   CAFE $
(🖉 2201-6665; snacks from US$2; ⊙ 11am-8pm Tue-Sun) This simple cafe, with white walls, black chairs and blackboards displaying the specials, is a recent addition to Orosi. It sits right on the southwestern corner of the square and sells shakes heaped with cream, fresh smoothies, sandwiches, cakes and plenty of coffee. Pull up a seat on the veranda and watch village life go by.

Rancho Orosi   COSTA RICAN $
(🖉 2533-1061; www.facebook.com/Restaurante RanchoOrosi; mains US$6-13; ⊙ 11am-8pm) Just a few hundred meters out of town, on the road heading south, this simple open-air restaurant has lanterns and dark wooden benches. An English and Spanish menu displays simple and fresh homemade dishes centering on rice and meat, fajitas, spaghetti or trout.

Pizzeria a la leña il Giardino   PIZZA $$
(🖉 2533-2022; pizzas from US$10; ⊙ noon-9pm Thu-Tue) This cute country-style pizzeria has

THERMAL SPRINGS

Being in a volcanic region means that Orosi has the perk of thermal springs. Though not nearly on the scale of the steaming-hot waters found near Fortuna, Orosi does offer a pair of warmwater pool complexes. **Balneario de Águas Termales Orosi** (☑ 2533-2156; www.balnearioaguastermalesorosi.com; US$6; ☺ 7:30am-4pm Wed-Mon) is the more centrally located of the two, with four pools of varying size flanked by grassy expanses and a shaded bar-restaurant terrace. **Los Patios** (☑ 2533-3009; US$6; ☺ 8am-4pm Tue-Sun) is a larger complex 1.5km south of town, whose waters include a 43°C (110°F) therapeutic pool suitable for adults only.

a proper stone pizza oven where the chef makes tasty thin-crust pizzas – the mozzarella, tomato and basil is spot on. The place is decorated with hardwood paneling and farm equipment. Out front is a pretty garden in which to sample some of the many craft beers on offer.

Restaurante Coto COSTA RICAN $$
(☑ 2533-3032; mains US$5-17.50; ☺ 8:30am-9pm) Established in 1952, this family-run eatery on the north side of the soccer field dishes out good *típico* food, particularly the whole fried fish, in a wood-beamed dining room with open-air seating. It's a great place to enjoy mountain views and the goings-on about town.

❶ Information

OTIAC (Orosi Tourist Information; ☑ 2533-3640; ☺ 9am-4pm Mon-Fri, 11am-5pm Sun; 🛜) is run by multilingual long-term residents Toine and Sara. This exceptionally helpful organization functions as an information center, cafe, cultural hall and book exchange. Staff can help arrange tours and are a good source of information about volunteer and teaching opportunities. Find it 200m south of the park and one block west of the main road.

More information on the area is available on the village website: www.orosivalley.com.

❶ Getting There & Away

The drive into Orosi is a pretty one, as Rte 224 from Paraíso snakes down the valley with gorgeous views of the mountains.

Autotransportes Mata Irola buses run between Orosi and Paraíso (roughly US$1, 20 minutes, every 30 minutes from 4.15am to 8pm weekdays and 5.30am to 9pm Saturday and Sunday).

Services to Cartago (45 minutes) run from 4:30am to 8pm weekdays, 5:30am to 9pm Saturday and 8.30am to 10pm Sunday. From Cartago you can transfer for buses to San José.

The main bus stop sits along Orosi's main street, next to the square.

Parque Nacional Tapantí-Macizo Cerro de la Muerte

Protecting the lush northern slopes of the Cordillera de Talamanca, this 580-sq-km **national park** (☑ 2206-5615; adult/6-12yr US$10/5; ☺ 8am-4pm; 🅿) is the wettest in Costa Rica. Known simply as Tapantí, the park protects wild and mossy country that's fed by literally hundreds of rivers. Waterfalls abound, vegetation is thick and the wildlife is prolific, though not always easy to see because of the rugged terrain. In 2000 the park was expanded to include the infamous Cerro de la Muerte (Mountain of Death), a precipitous peak that marks the highest point on the Interamericana and the northernmost extent of *páramo,* a highland shrub and tussock-grass habitat – most commonly found in the Andes – that shelters a variety of rare bird species.

🏃 Activities

Walking and nature-spotting are the main ways to spend your time here. Rain gear is advisable year-round.

Wildlife-Watching

More than 300 bird species have been recorded in the park, including hummingbirds, parrots, toucans, trogons and eagles. The birdwatching opportunities here are world class, as it's possible to spot hundreds of varieties in this small area. Though rarely sighted due to the thick vegetation, monkeys, coatis, pacas, tayras and even pumas, ocelots and oncillas are also present.

Hiking

A well-graded dirt road runs into the park from the information center, dead-ending at a *mirador* (viewing platform) that affords broad views across the valley. Three signed trails branch off from this road: the 1.2km **Sendero Oropéndola**, which heads downhill to a picnic area and then follows the banks of the Río Grande de Orosi for a few hundred meters before looping back uphill; the 1.5km **Sendero La Pava** to La Catarata, which descends from a common trailhead to boulder-strewn river beaches and affords excellent views of a dramatic waterfall across the valley; and the 3km **Sendero Natural Árboles Caídos**, which climbs steeply uphill from the main road before descending to rejoin it further west – there are no services on this route, and hiking shoes and water are musts. Tapantí is not open to backcountry hiking.

Fishing

Fishing is allowed in low season (April to October; permit required; ask at the Information Center for more details), but the 'dry' season (January to April) is generally considered the best time to visit.

🛏 Sleeping & Eating

Kiri Mountain Lodge   LODGE $

(☎8394-6286; www.kirilodge.net; s/d incl breakfast from US$35/45; 🅿🛜) About 2km before the park entrance, surrounded by 50 mossy hectares of land, Kiri has six rustic *cabinas* with intermittent wi-fi and hot water (but no fans), and a restaurant specializing in trout. Trails wind into the nearby Reserva Forestal Río Macho.

Kiri Mountain Lodge
Restaurant   COSTA RICAN $$

(☎8394-6286; casados US$8-12; ⊘7am-8pm) This charming place specializes in trout, which can be caught in several well-stocked ponds and served how you like it. Call ahead to check it's open, as its hours vary.

ℹ Information

Visitors receive a simple trail map upon paying fees at the park entrance, which doubles as the **Information Center** (☎2206-5615; park entrance adult/6-12yr US$10/5; ⊘8am-4pm).

ℹ Getting There & Away

With your own car you can drive the 11km from Orosi to the park entrance; about halfway along, near the town of Purisil, the route becomes a bumpy gravel road (4WD recommended but not required).

Renting a bike in Orosi is another good option; the ride to the park takes about an hour. Buses (about US$1, 30 minutes) only make it as far as Purisil, 5km from the entrance; they leave Orosi at 7:15am, 11:45am, 1:45pm and 4:45pm and return at 8am, noon, 3pm and 5pm. Taxis charge about US$20 to US$30 one way from Orosi to the park.

Orosi to Paraíso

From Orosi, a scenic loop circles the artificial Lago de Cachí. The lake was created following the construction of the Represa de Cachí (Cachí Dam), which supplies San José and the majority of the Central Valley with electricity. About 3km past the dam, at the foot of a long, steep hill, you'll find the abandoned village of Ujarrás and the ruins of its 17th-century church.

◉ Sights

Casa del Soñador   GALLERY

(Dreamer's House; ☎2577-1186, 8955-7799; carvings from US$10; ⊘9am-5pm) **FREE** This artisanal woodworking studio is run by Hermes and Miguel Quesada, sons of renowned Tico carver Macedonio Quesada. The brothers maintain the *campesino* (peasant farmer) tradition of whittling gnarled coffee-wood branches into ornate religious figures and whimsical characters. Their workshop displays sculptures ranging from mystical faces and masks to abstract carvings of all sizes, with pieces available for purchase. The studio is on the main road, 1.5km south of the dam.

Ruins of Ujarrás   RUINS

(☎2299-5918; ⊘8am-4:30pm) **FREE** The village of Ujarrás was damaged by an 1833 flood and then abandoned. All that remains are the crumbling walls of **Iglesia de Nuestra Señora de la Limpia Concepción**, a 1693 stone church once home to a miraculous painting of the Virgin. According to folklore, the relic refused to be moved, forcing clerics to build a church around it. But after floods and earthquakes, the painting conceded to move to Paraíso, leaving the church ruins in a rambling park.

Every year, usually on the Sunday closest to April 14, there is a procession of 3000 to 4000 people from Paraíso to the ruins, where Mass, food and music help celebrate the day of La Virgen de Ujarrás. The church's grassy grounds are a popular picnicking spot on Sunday afternoon, but go in the middle of the week and chances are you'll have them all to yourself. There are bathroom facilities in the park.

To reach the village, turn left off the main road at the 'Ujarrás' sign and wind about 1km gently downhill, passing the well-signposted Restaurant La Pipiola en route.

🧗 Activities

Escalada Cachí
CLIMBING

(☑8867-8259; www.escaladacachi.com; climbing from US$30; ⊙8am-4pm Sat & Sun, by appointment with 4-person minimum Mon-Fri) Escalada Cachí is a fun climbing spot with 39 routes for different abilities. The US$30 fee includes equipment rental, as much climbing as you can crank out, and a soak in a lovely river-diverted pool afterwards. Book ahead of your visit and bring your own lunch/snacks.

Located on a challenging dirt road off Rte 225 when heading north of the town of San Jeronimo, the climbing wall can be tricky to find; call ahead for directions (though note that the route requires a 4WD and a lot of skill) or to get picked up. Alternatively, park where the dirt road branches off and hike the 2.2km down (don't leave anything in your car). Call for detailed directions or you're likely to get lost.

🛏️ Sleeping & Eating

The area is home to two peaceful mountain-top retreats. Private transportation is a must to reach them.

Cabañas de Montaña Piedras Albas
CABINA $$

(☑8697-3218, 8883-6449; d cabinas from US$60; P🐾🍲) These fully equipped, bright wooden *cabinas* in the hills beyond Cachí are a great choice if you're here to really slow down. Accommodations come with kitchen, cable TV and private deck with views, and there are hiking trails. Your own transportation is a must; find the turnoff across the main road from La Casona del Cafetal.

★ Hotel Quelitales
BUNGALOW $$$

(☑2577-2222; www.hotelquelitales.com; junior ste from US$86, ste incl breakfast from US$130; P🐾) 🍃 This idyllically sited collection of contemporary-chic bungalows features spacious rooms with wooden floors, ultra-comfy mattresses, indoor and outdoor solar-powered rain showers, private decks (some with waterfall views) and large wall canvases of the hummingbirds, ladybugs, toucans and other critters for whom the cabins are named. The on-site restaurant serves delicious trout and other Tico specialties.

At the time of research the owner was planning yoga and meditation sessions by the waterfall. Meanwhile, birdwatchers will be in their element – you can spot more than 300 species in this area.

La Casona del Cafetal
COSTA RICAN $$

(☑2577-1414; www.lacasonadelcafetal.com; mains US$8-29; ⊙11:30am-5pm, to 4pm Sun; 🍲) It's all about the beautiful setting at this charming restaurant situated in the middle of a coffee plantation, with calming views of the Lago de Cachí. Specialties include fresh river trout and coffee-laced desserts, plus crepes and flans. It's especially popular with local families on buffet Sundays. There's a small playground, as well as short trails around the lagoon.

The restaurant is near the town of Cachí, on the left-hand side of the road about 2km past the dam when you're heading southeast.

❶ Getting There & Away

This stretch is best explored by car, bicycle, scooter or motorcycle – and it's worth exploring, as this is beautiful countryside. After Ujarrás, the route continues west for a few more kilometers to rejoin the main road at Paraíso.

TURRIALBA AREA

In the vicinity of Turrialba, at an elevation of 650m above sea level, the Río Reventazón gouges a mountain pass through the Cordillera Central. In the 1880s this geological quirk allowed the 'Jungle Train' between San José and Puerto Limón to roll through, and the mountain village of Turrialba grew prosperous from the coffee trade. Later, the first highway linking the capital to the coast exploited this same quirk. Turrialba thrived.

However, things changed by the early 1990s, when the straighter, smoother Hwy 32 through Guápiles was completed and an earthquake shut down the railway for good. Suddenly, Turrialba found itself off the beaten path. Even so, the area remains a key agricultural center, renowned for its strong coffee, ubiquitous cheese and Central America's best white-water rafting. To the north, the area is home to two worthy sites: the majestic Volcán Turrialba and the archaeological site of Guayabo.

❶ Getting There & Away

Regular and reliable buses serve the Turrialba area. But if you'd like the freedom to explore these twisting mountain roads, renting a car is a great idea.

Turrialba

POP 31,100

When the railway shut down in 1991, commerce slowed, but Turrialba nonetheless remained a regional agricultural center where local coffee planters could bring their crops to market. And with tourism on the rise in Costa Rica in the 1990s, this modest mountain town soon became known as the gateway to some of the best white-water rafting on the planet. By the early 2000s, Turrialba was a hotbed of international rafters looking for Class V thrills. For now, the Río Pacuare runs on, but its future is uncertain.

🏃 Activities

Centro Agronómico Tropical de Investigación

GARDENS

(Catie; Center for Tropical Agronomy Research & Education; ☑2556-2700, 2558-2000; www.catie. ac.cr; adult/student/youth US$10/8/6, guided tours US$25-50; ⊙7am-4pm Mon-Fri, 8am-4pm Sat & Sun) Catie's sprawling grounds, 2km east of Turrialba, encompass 10 sq km dedicated to tropical agricultural research and education. Agronomists from all over the world recognize this as one of the most important centers in the tropics. You'll need to make reservations for one of several guided tours through laboratories, greenhouses, a seed bank, experimental plots and one of the most extensive libraries of tropical agriculture literature in the world. Alternatively, pick up a map and take a self-guided walk.

Ecoaventuras

OUTDOORS

(☑2556-7171, 8868-3938; www.ecoaventuras. co.cr; white-water rafting packages per person from US$70) Ecoaventuras offers white-water rafting on the Ríos Pacuare and Pejibaye, along with horseback riding (from US$50) and mountain biking (prices depend on tour length and rider experience). Three-day rafting experiences include all meals, accommodation, equipment and a zipline tour (inquire for prices). It's 100m north and 100m west of the Rawlings Factory.

Costa Rica Ríos

RAFTING

(☑2556-8664, in USA & Canada 888-434-0776; www.costaricarios.com; Calle 1) Offers week-long rafting trips that must be booked in advance.

DAMNING THE RIVERS?

Considered one of the most beautiful white-water-rafting rivers in the world, the wild Río Pacuare became the first federally protected river in Central America in 1985. Within two years, however, Costa Rica's national power company, the Instituto Costarricense de Electricidad (ICE), unveiled plans to build a 200m gravity dam at the conveniently narrow and screamingly scenic ravine of Dos Montañas.

The dam would be the cornerstone of the massive Siquirres hydroelectric project, which would include four dams in total, linked by a 10km-long tunnel. If built, rising waters on the lower Pacuare would not only flood 12km of rapids up to the Tres Equis put-in but also parts of the Reserva Indígena Awari and a huge swath of primary rainforest where some 800 animal species have been recorded.

The project was intended to help ICE keep up with the country's rapidly increasing power demands. But as the proposal moved from speculation to construction, a coalition of local landowners, indigenous leaders, conservation groups and, yep, white-water-rafting outfits organized against it. (Rafael Gallo, of the Fundación Ríos Tropicales, the charitable arm of the venerable rafting company, was a key figure in this fight.)

The group filed for the first environmental impact assessment (EIA) in the region's history – and won. The move required ICE to seek an independent study of the dam's environmental impact and economic feasibility, effectively stalling its construction. In the meantime, organizers were able to draw international attention to the situation. In 2005, residents of the Turrialba area held a plebiscite on the issue of the dam. Of the 10,000 residents polled, 97% gave the project a thumbs down – a resounding 'No.'

Although the nearby Río Reventazón lost a third of its Class V rapids due to the construction of dams, the Pacuare recently saw its greatest victory. On August 29, 2015, President Luis Guillermo Solís signed a decree banning hydroelectric projects of 500 kilowatts or more from the river for the next 25 years. Although the Pacuare seems safe for now, another decree by a future president (with elections looming at the time of research) could again leave it unprotected.

1. La Paz Waterfalls Gardens (p110)
Trails lead visitors to five scenic waterfalls, past birds and other wildlife.

2. Parque Nacional Volcán Poás (p109)
Best viewed from a distance, Volcán Poás steams and smokes following eruptions in 2017.

3. Bang's Mountain Squirrel
Wildlife can be spotted in the serene countryside around Parque Nacional Volcán Poás.

4. Ujarrás (p127)
The crumbling ruins of the Iglesia de Nuestra Señora de la Limpia Concepción, built in 1693.

An eight-day kayaking and canoeing trip costs US$1699 per person (based on double occupancy), while the adventure-tour package, including rafting, ziplining, snorkeling, surfing and mountain biking, costs US$2899 per person (also based on double occupancy). The office is located near Av 6.

Courses

Spanish by the River   LANGUAGE
(☑2556-7380, in USA 1-877-268-3730; www.spanish atlocations.com; 10/30hr per week US$160/300, homestay/hostel bed US$22/12) A five-minute bus ride from Turrialba, this school offers accommodation along with weekly Spanish classes for varying levels of fluency.

Adventure Education Center   LANGUAGE
(☑in USA 800-237-2730; www.facebook.com/AEC SpanishInstitute/; 1 week without/with homestay US$325/490) Combine Spanish classes and white-water rafting at this Turrialba school that also offers medical Spanish. A week's group language instruction entails 20 hours of lessons.

Tours

Loco's   RAFTING
(☑8704-3535, 2556-6035, in USA 707-703-5935; www.whiteh2o.com) Loco's takes guests on wild rides of varying difficulty down the Ríos Pacuare and Reventazón. The outfit also runs camping trips on the Pacuare, plus canyoning and rappelling adventures. A day of rafting starts at around US$70 per person, depending on group size; prices include lunch and transport.

Explornatura   RAFTING
(☑2556-0111, in USA & Canada 866-571-2443; www.explornatura.com/en/; Av 4 btwn Calles 2 & 4) Offers rafting, mountain-biking and horseback-riding tours. A rafting day trip on the Pacuare is US$85 per person, a canyoneering and canopy tour US$75 per person.

Sleeping

In town you'll find a solid mix of budget hostels and midrange hotels. Around the Turrialba area there are some stellar hotels that bring guests close to nature. All can arrange tours and rafting trips.

In Town

★ Casa de Lis Hostel   HOSTEL $
(☑2556-4933; www.hostelcasadelis.com; Av Central; dm/d/tr/q US$14/45/60/70, under 3yr free;

☞) Hands down Turrialba's best value, this sweet, centrally located place is a traveler's dream. Spotless dorms and doubles with comfy mattresses and reading lamps are complemented by a fully equipped kitchen, a volcano-view roof terrace, a pretty back garden, fantastic information displays and a friendly atmosphere. There's free tea and coffee in the mornings, a book exchange and board games. It's near Calle 2.

Hotel Interamericano   HOTEL $
(☑2556-0142; www.hotelinteramericano.com; Av 1; s/d/tr/q US$25/35/50/65, without bathroom US$15/22/33/44; P☞) On the south side of the old train tracks is this basic 20-room hotel, traditionally regarded by rafters as *the* meeting place in Turrialba. The collection of basic rooms includes some with private bathroom, some with shared bathroom and many that combine bunks with regular beds. There's also a new shared kitchen, plus TVs in some of the rooms.

The friendly owner will help book adventure and rafting day trips. The hotel's near Calle 1.

Hotel Wagelia   HOTEL $$
(☑2556-1566; www.hotelwageliaturrialba.com; Av 4 btwn Calles 2 & 4; s/d incl breakfast US$55/80; P☞) Simple, modern and clean rooms come with cable TV and face a quiet interior courtyard. A restaurant serves Tico specialties, while the pleasant terrace bar is a good place for a drink and has wi-fi.

Turrialba B&B   B&B $$
(☑2556-6651; www.turribb.com; Calle 1; d/t/q incl breakfast from US$85/100/115, extra person US$10; P✳☞) If you're seeking a bit of tranquility in downtown Turrialba (a rare commodity!), this B&B may be worth a look for its lovely garden patio with pool table and hammocks. Rooms are spacious, with hardwood furniture, and the living room has a TV and a good collection of paperbacks. There's also a shared kitchen and a small bar. It's north of Av 6.

Around Turrialba

Wagelia Espino Blanco Lodge   LODGE $$
(☑2556-1029, 2556-0616; www.wageliaespinoblan colodge.com; r incl breakfast US$118, extra person US$15; P☞) ✔ High above Turrialba, this 10-bungalow ecolodge sits on 30 hectares of forest land. The quaint and well-constructed cabins are without electricity, TVs or distractions from the serenity of the place, which

also features a small amphitheater, a poets' corner, a charming restaurant (the US$20 buffet includes main, drink and dessert; book ahead) and seven hiking trails of varying difficulty.

The lodge runs three- to four-hour nature tours for US$35 per person including lunch. There's wi-fi in the bar but not in the rooms. From Turrialba, the lodge is about a 20-minute drive north up winding Hwy 230. The roads can be tricky – call for directions.

Turrialtico Lodge
LODGE $$

(☑ 2538-1111; www.turrialtico.com; d incl breakfast US$58-75; P 🛜) Commanding dramatic, sweeping views of the Río Reventazón valley, this Tico-run lodge in an old farmhouse 9km east of Turrialba (off the highway to Siquirres) offers 18 attractive, polished-wood-panel rooms decorated with local artwork. Rooms in the reception building share a large terrace and sitting area, and a pleasant open-air restaurant (mains US$5 to US$18) serves up country cooking.

★ Rancho Naturalista
LODGE $$$

(☑ 8704-3217; www.ranchonaturalista.net; r per person incl 3 meals US$194; P @) About 1.3km south of Tuis and 900m above sea level, this small lodge on 50 hectares of land is a must-do for birdwatchers. More than 450 species have been recorded in the area (250 from the lodge's balcony alone). The 14 homey rooms in the lodge are complemented by a cluster of private *casitas,* surrounded by pretty landscaped grounds.

Birdwatchers can sit on the big wooden veranda with a coffee and watch hummingbirds approach the many feeders. Delicious meals include organic beef and pork from the cows and pigs raised on site. Staff are friendly and the lodge has a knowledgeable billingual private guide, who can be booked from US$50 per trip (price for up to five people) to accompany you along the surrounding trails, or you can walk them yourself.

Casa Turire
HOTEL $$$

(☑ 2531-1111, in USA 877-750-6855; www.hotelcasaturire.com; d standard/ste/master ste incl breakfast US$168/288/452, additional person US$28-62, child under 3yr free, child 4-12yr US$28; P ❄ 🛜 🏊) 🏊 This elegant three-story plantation inn has 16 graceful, well-appointed rooms with high ceilings, wood floors and wrought-iron beds; a massive master suite comes with a Jacuzzi and excellent views of the coffee and macadamia-nut plantations

in the distance. Adding icing to the cake are spa services, a restaurant and bar, horseback riding, birdwatching, and kayaking on the on-site lake. A kids' pool and on-site playground will please younger visitors.

Take the La Suiza/Tuis turnoff from Hwy 10, head south for 2.3km, then follow signs an additional 1.4km down a dirt road to the hotel.

🍴 Eating

Those on a budget will have no problem finding cheap meals in Turrialba; if you're looking to make an evening of it, there's the choice of Asian, fusion, Costa Rican or barbecue food. There are plenty of supermarkets for self-caterers, too.

Maracuyá
CAFE $

(☑ 2556-2021; www.facebook.com/maracuya2012; Calle 2; frozen coffee around US$4, mains US$5-7; ⊙ 2-9:30pm Wed-Mon; ☑) This bright-walled cafe north of Av 10 serves up one of the best coffee treats in the country – a frozen caffeine concoction with gooey *maracuyá* (passion fruit) syrup and crunchy seeds. Dishes include veggie wraps, creative salads, fried chicken and chips, and Latin American favorites such as *patacones* (fried plantains).

La Feria
COSTA RICAN $

(☑ 8378-7979, 2556-0386, 2556-5550; www.facebook.com/RestauranteLaFeria; Calle 6; mains US$5-14; ⊙ 11am-9:30pm Wed-Mon, to 2:30pm Tue; ☑) This unremarkable-looking eatery has friendly service and excellent, reasonably priced home cooking. Sometimes the kitchen gets a bit backed up, but the hearty *casados* (typical dishes with beans, rice, a small salad and a choice of protein) are well worth the wait. Caribbean chicken, salads, pasta and red snapper are also available. Find the place north of Av 4.

Restaurant Betico Mata
BARBECUE $

(☑ 2556-8640; Hwy 10; gallos US$2, mains US$6; ⊙ 11am-midnight Mon-Fri, to late Sat & Sun) This carnivores' delight is at the southern end of town. Its cafeteria style isn't pretty, but you can't beat the good-value *gallos* (open-face tacos on corn tortillas) piled with succulent, fresh-grilled meats including beef, chicken, sausage or pork, all soaked in the special house marinade. It all goes smashingly well with an ice-cold beer.

Check your bill carefully here, as addition errors have been known to happen.

★ **Wok & Roll** ASIAN $$
(☑ 2556-6756; www.facebook.com/Wok-Roll-489
594887746705; Calle 1; mains US$9-16; ⊘11am-
10pm Wed-Mon) Pan-Asian cuisine fills the
menu at this eatery near the main square.
Enjoy sushi rolls and sashimi, teriyaki
or sweet-and-sour chicken, Thai curry,
wontons and other Asian favorites, plus
tempura ice cream for dessert. Wash it all
down with homemade mint lemonade and
honey-sweetened jasmine tea.

More Than Words THAI, ITALIAN $$
(☑ 2556-1362; www.facebook.com/morethanwords
888; small/large pizzas from US$8/15, mains from
US$10; ⊘11am-10pm Tue-Thu, to 11pm Fri, noon-
11pm Sat & Sun) With a large bar at its center,
this restaurant opposite the church in the
main square is the new venture from the
owners of Wok & Roll (p134). Service can be
slow, but the dishes are satisfying. The diverse menu has freshly made pizzas, pasta
dishes, New York steaks and interesting creations like *wantacos* (a hybrid wanton-taco
stuffed with marinated chicken and salad).

Ask about upcoming live events, from
music to comedy.

🍷 Drinking & Nightlife

Loco's Bar and Restaurant BAR
(☑ 2556-3500; www.facebook.com/locosrestau
ranteybar; drinks from US$2, dishes from US$4;
⊘2pm-midnight Sun-Thu, to 2am Fri, noon-2am
Sat) This new bar, from the owners of
Loco's (p132) adventure outfit, is where rafters end up after an adrenaline-fueled day
on the rivers. Things might get lively with
brightly colored cocktails, Jägermeister,
B-52s and tequila shots, but it's a decent
late-lunch and dinner spot, too. Bites include guacamole and nachos, mozzarella
sticks, fajitas, *ceviche* and mixed plates.

ⓘ Information

There's no official tourist office, but most hotels
and rafting outfits can organize tours, accommodation and transportation throughout the
region.

Banco de Costa Rica (cnr Av Central & Calle
3; ⊘9am-4pm Mon-Fri) Has 24-hour ATMs
dispensing dollars and colones.

ⓘ Getting There & Away

A modern bus terminal is located on the western
edge of town off Hwy 10.

San José via Paraíso and Cartago About
US$3, two hours to two hours 20 minutes,
every 15 to 30 minutes from 4:30am to 9pm.

Siquirres, for transfer to Puerto Limón About
US$2.50, two hours, every 30 minutes to two
hours from 5:30am to 6:15pm. Schedules vary
slightly on weekends.

DON'T MISS

WHITE-WATER RAFTING IN THE CENTRAL VALLEY

The Turrialba area is a major center for white-water rafting. Traditionally the two most
popular rafting rivers have been the **Río Reventazón** and the **Río Pacuare**, but the
former has been dramatically impacted by a series of hydroelectric projects, including a
huge 305-megawatt dam currently under construction.

As a result, most organized expeditions from Turrialba now head for the Río Pacuare,
which arguably offers the most scenic rafting in Central America. The river plunges down
the Caribbean slope through a series of spectacular canyons clothed in virgin rainforest,
through runs named for their fury and separated by calm stretches that enable you to
stare at near-vertical green walls towering hundreds of meters above.

Lower Pacuare With Class II–IV rapids, this is the more accessible run: 28km through
rocky gorges, past an indigenous village and untamed jungle.

Upper Pacuare Classified as Class III–IV, but a few sections can go to Class V, depending on conditions. It's about a two-hour drive to the put-in, after which you'll have the
prettiest jungle cruise on earth all to yourself.

The Pacuare can be run year-round, though June to October are considered the best
months. The highest water is from October to December, when the river runs fast with
huge waves. March and April are when the river is at its lowest, although it's still
challenging.

PARQUE NACIONAL VOLCÁN TURRIALBA

Before 2015, Volcán Turrialba's last major eruption was in 1866. At the time of research the 3328m volcano was very active, having erupted multiple times in 2017; the **park** (☎8704-2432, 2557-6262; pnvolcanturrialba@gmail.com; ⊗8am-3:30pm) was closed and the capital put on high alert in the same year. Smoke could be seen in the distance, the smell of sulfur in nearby towns was reported in local news and volcanic-ash advisories were issued. The park remained closed at research time and no information about when it may reopen was available. Warning signs forbade visitors from driving further than 8km shy of the summit. The exclusion zone may be larger or smaller during your visit. Check with locals before you attempt to drive on the volcano and note that the best place to see it may be from afar. Views are best in the mornings, before the clouds pass over.

Getting There & Away

The volcano is only about 15km northwest of Turrialba as the crow flies but more than twice that far by car. From the village of Santa Cruz (13km from Turrialba and connected via public bus – check if buses are running before you set out), an 18km road climbs to the top of the volcano.

Monumento Nacional Arqueológico Guayabo

Nestled into a patch of stunning hillside forest 19km northeast of Turrialba is the largest and most important archaeological site in the country. Guayabo (☎2559-1220; US$5; ⊗8am-3:30pm) is composed of the remains of a pre-Columbian city that was thought to have peaked at some point in AD 800, when it was inhabited by as many as 20,000 people. Today visitors can examine the remains of petroglyphs, residential mounds, a roadway and an impressive aqueduct system – built with rocks that were hauled in from the Río Reventazón along a cobbled 8km road. Amazingly, the cisterns still work, and (theoretically) potable water remains available at the site. In 1973, as the site's importance became evident, Guayabo was declared a national monument, with further protections established in 1980. The site occupies 232 hectares, most of which remains unexcavated. It's a small place, so don't go expecting Mayan pyramids, but it's a fascinating visit nonetheless.

🏃 Activities

The site currently protects the last remaining pre-montane forest in the province of Cartago, and although mammals are limited to squirrels, armadillos and coatis there are plenty of good birdwatching opportunities here. Particularly noteworthy among the avifauna are the oropendolas, which colonize the monument by building sack-like nests in the trees. Other birds include toucans and brown jays – the latter are unique among jays in that they have a small inflatable sac in their chest, which causes the popping sound that is heard at the beginning of their raucous calls.

👉 Tours

Guided tours (in Spanish; from US$20) are available from the monument's front desk. In high season English-speaking guides may be available.

ℹ️ Information

Across the road from the ticket office there's a small information and exhibition center that provides an overview of what the city may have looked like.

ℹ️ Getting There & Away

Normally by car you would head north out of Turrialba and make a right after the metal bridge, but at research time the bridge up to Guayabo was being reconstructed. The road is well signed from there, and all but the last 3km is paved; a 4WD is recommended, though not required, for the final rough section. If this road is closed there's another entrance from the north of the site: small roads and dirt tracks wind their way off Rte 230 northwest of Turrialba – this route is possible using a 2WD, but a 4WD is highly recommended.

Buses to the site were suspended during research but would normally leave from Turrialba (about US$1, one hour); check in Turrialba to see if service has resumed. You can also take a taxi from Turrialba (round-trip fares start at US$30, with an hour to explore the park).

Caribbean Coast

Best Places to Eat

➡ Laszlo's (p177)

➡ El Refugio (p184)

➡ Palenque Luisa Casa de Carnes (p167)

➡ Café Rico (p175)

➡ Mopri (p176)

Best Places to Stay

➡ Casa Verde (p174)

➡ Casa Marbella (p154)

➡ Tree House Lodge (p182)

➡ Hotel Miss Junie (p154)

➡ Pacuare Lodge (p142)

➡ Punta Mona (p187)

Why Go?

The wildness of the Caribbean thwarted 16th-century Spaniards in their quest to settle here and isolated the region for centuries afterwards, making it distinctly different from the rest of Costa Rica. Influenced by indigenous peoples and West Indian immigrants, the Caribbean's culture has blended slowly and organically.

It does take a little more effort to travel here to see the nesting turtles of Tortuguero, raft the Río Pacuare or dive the reefs off Manzanillo, but you'll be glad you made the trip. Nature has thrived on this rugged and rustic coast – many visitors will meet resident sloths, hear the call of howler monkeys and spot alligators on the vast network of canals. Others tuck into the area's unique flavors, such as jerk chicken, grilled snapper and *rondón* (spicy seafood gumbo); listen to the lilt of patois; and laze around on the uncrowded palm-lined beaches.

When to Go

➡ The biggest swells hit the southern Caribbean from December to March, and surfers descend.

➡ Turtle-nesting season from March to October means egg-laying and hatching spectacles in Tortuguero.

➡ December to April is dry season: the most popular but most expensive time to visit. May to December is also warm, but expect some rain.

History

In 1502 Christopher Columbus spent a total of 17 days anchored off the coast of Puerto Limón on what would be his fourth and final voyage to the New World. He dropped anchor at an isle he baptized La Huerta (today known as Isla Uvita), loaded up on fresh water, and never returned.

For Costa Rica's Caribbean coast, this brief encounter foreshadowed the colonization that was to come. But it would be centuries before Europeans would fully dominate the area. Because of the difficult nature of the terrain (croc-filled swamps and steep mountain slopes) and the malaria delivered by relentless fleets of mosquitoes, the Spanish steadfastly avoided it. For hundreds of years, in fact, the area remained the province of indigenous ethnicities – the Miskito in the north and the Cabécar, Bribrí and Kèköldi in the south – along with a mix of itinerant Afro-Caribbean turtle hunters from Panama and Colombia.

It was the building of the railroad, beginning in 1871, that solidified the area's West Indian accent, with the arrival of thousands of former Jamaican slaves in search of employment. The plan was to build a port at the site of a grand old lemon tree (hence the name Puerto Limón) on the Caribbean Sea, so that coffee barons in the Central Valley could more easily export their crops to Europe. The railway was intended to unify the country, but it was a source of segregation as well. Black people were not allowed to vote or travel freely around Costa Rica until 1949. Out of isolation, however, sprang an independent culture, with its own musical and gastronomic traditions, and even its own unique language, a Creole called Mekatelyu – which is still spoken today.

Parks & Reserves

Many refuges and parks line the Caribbean coast. These are some of the most popular.

Parque Nacional Cahuita (p168) A patch of coastal jungle home to armadillos, monkeys and sloths, while the protected reef is one of the most important on the coast.

Parque Nacional Tortuguero (p149) Jungle canals obscure snoozing caimans, while howler, spider and capuchin monkeys traipse overhead. The star attraction, however, are the sea turtles, which nest here from March to October.

Refugio Nacional de Vida Silvestre Gandoca-Manzanillo (p186) A rich rainforest and wetland tucked away along the country's southeastern border, with rivers full of manatees, caimans and crocodiles.

❶ Getting There & Away

When traveling to Puerto Limón and the southern Caribbean, it's easy enough to hop on any of the regular buses from San José. Buses also connect most towns along the coast, from Sixaola, on the Panamanian border, to Puerto Limón. The main roads are in good condition, so driving is also an option.

The north is a little trickier but easy enough with a little planning. Much of the area is only linked up by waterways, making boats the sole means of transport. Puerto Limón, Tortuguero, Parismina and Barra del Colorado all have landing strips, but only Tortuguero has daily commercial flights.

THE ATLANTIC SLOPE

The idea was simple: build a port on the Caribbean coast and connect it to the Central Valley by railroad, thereby opening up important shipping routes for the country's soaring coffee production. Construction began in 1871, through 150km of dense jungle and muddy mountainsides along the Atlantic slope. It took almost two decades to build the railroad, and the first 30km reportedly cost thousands of men their lives. But when the last piece of track was laid down in 1890, the economic forces it unleashed permanently changed Costa Rica (and the rest of Central America, for that matter). It was the dawn of the banana boom, an industry that would dominate life, politics and the environment in the region for almost a century.

Today, the railroad is no longer. Likewise, banana production is not as mighty as it once was, supplanted in many areas by pineapples and African oil palms.

Parque Nacional Braulio Carrillo

Enter this under-explored **national park** (☑2206-5500, 2266-1883; adult/child \$12/5; ⊙8am-3:30pm) and you'll have an idea of what Costa Rica looked like prior to the 1950s, when 75% of the country's surface area was still covered by forest. Here, steep hills cloaked in impossibly tall trees are interrupted only by canyons and cascading rivers. It has extraordinary biodiversity due

Caribbean Coast Highlights

1 Tortuguero
(p151) Sliding silently through jungle canals in search of wildlife or volunteering to protect endangered sea turtles.

2 Río Pacuare
(p170) Rafting the country's most extreme river.

3 Puerto Viejo de Talamanca (p170) Sampling the culinary scene, lazing on the beach and partying.

4 Punta Uva
(p180) Surfing or diving at Punta Uva's pristine, tucked-away cove.

5 Cahuita (p162) Chilling out in rustic bliss, soaking up the Caribbean Creole culture and visiting Cahuita National Park.

6 Manzanillo
(p185) Snorkeling the teeming reefs and adventuring through the dripping jungle.

7 Parque Nacional Braulio Carrillo (p137) Witnessing the dramatic meeting of the murky Río Sucio and the crystal-clear Río Honduras.

8 Bribrí (p184) Visiting cacao farms and indigenous villages.

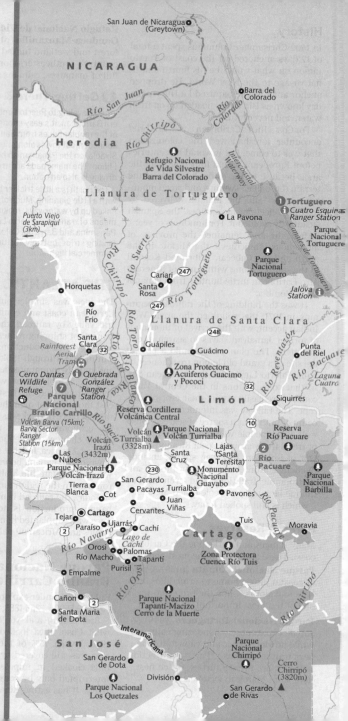

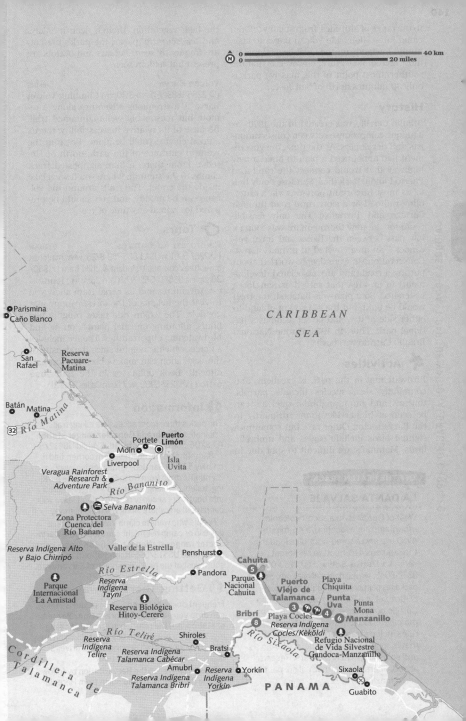

N

0 ————————— 40 km
0 ————————— 20 miles

CARIBBEAN

SEA

Parismina
Caño Blanco

San
Rafael

Reserva
Pacuare-
Matina

Batán   Matina

32 Río Matina

Portete   **Puerto
Moín   Limón**

Liverpool   Isla
                             Uvita
Veragua Rainforest
Research &
Adventure Park   Río Bananito

          Selva Bananito

Zona Protectora
Cuenca del
Río Banano

*Reserva Indígena Alto
y Bajo Chirripó*   Valle de la Estrella

                                    Penshurst

Río Estrella   Cahuita
                     Pandora   **5**
Parque
Internacional   Reserva   Parque   **Puerto   Playa
La Amistad   Indígena   Nacional   Viejo de   Chiquita**
                Tayní   Cahuita   Talamanca
                                              Punta   Punta
          Reserva Biológica   Uva   Mona
          Hitoy-Cerere   **4**   **Manzanillo**
                              Bribrí **6**
                       8 Playa Cocles
Río Teliré   Shiroles *Reserva Indígena
                              Cocles/Kèköldi*
*Reserva
Indígena   Bratsi Río Sixaola Refugio Nacional
Telire*   de Vida Silvestre
       Reserva Indígena   Gandoca-Manzanillo
       Talamanca Cabécar
Amubri   *Reserva*   Yorkín
       Reserva Indígena *Indígena*   Sixaola
       Talamanca Bribrí *Yorkín*
                                    PANAMA
Cordillera de   Guabito
Talamanca

to the range of altitudes, from steamy 2906m cloud forest alongside Volcán Barva to lush, humid lowlands on the Caribbean slope. Its most incredible feature, however, is that the southernmost point of this massive park is only 30 minutes north of San José.

History

Braulio Carrillo was created in the 1970s as a unique compromise between conservationists and developers. At the time, the government had announced a plan to build a new highway that would connect the capital to Puerto Limón. Back then, San José's only link to its most important port was via a crumbling railroad or a slow rural road through Cartago and Turrialba. The only feasible route for the new thoroughfare was along a low pass between the Barva and Irazú volcanoes – an area covered in primary forest. Conservationists were deeply worried about putting a road (and any associated development) in an area that served as San José's watershed. So a plan was hatched: the road would be built, but the 475 sq km of land to either side of it would be set aside as a national park. Thus, in 1978, Parque Nacional Braulio Carrillo was born.

🏃 Activities

Birdwatching in the park is excellent, and commonly seen species include parrots, toucans and hummingbirds; quetzals can be seen at higher elevations, primarily in the Barva sector. Other rare but sometimes sighted birds include eagles and umbrella birds. Mammals are difficult to spot due to

---

OFF THE BEATEN TRACK

LA DANTA SALVAJE

West of Guápiles, in a secret volcanic-mountain-range location, a 45-minute 4WD trip and a three-hour hike lead to the fabulous 410-hectare rainforest reserve **La Danta Salvaje** (📱2750-0012, 8332-8045; www.ladantasalvaje.com; 3-night packages per person US$350) at altitude 800m, set in a Parque Nacional Braulio Carrillo buffer zone. You'll sleep in an atmospheric lodge with no electricity, and rates include transport from Guápiles, meals, jungle hiking, wildlife-spotting and splashing in nearby rivers. Reserve ahead. There's a minimum of six people and a maximum of 12.

---

the lush vegetation, though deer, monkeys and *tepezcuintle* (pacas, the park's mascot) are frequently seen. Jaguars and ocelots are present but seldom seen.

Volcán Barva   HIKING

(📱2266-1883; ⊙8am-3:30pm) Climbing Volcán Barva is a strenuous adventure along a remote but reasonably well-maintained trail. Because of its relative inaccessibility, there's a good chance you'll be alone. Begin at the western entrance of the park, north of Heredia. From there, a 3km signposted track climbs to the summit, where you'll see a lake inside the crater. The trails around the volcano can be muddy, and you should be prepared for rain at any time of year.

☞ Tours

Rainforest Adventures   ECOTOUR

(📱2257-5961, in USA 1-866-759-8726; www.rainforest adventure.com; adult/student & child tram US$60/30, zipline US$50/35; ⊙7:30am-2pm; 🐾) Rainforest Adventures and its aerial tram allow you to visit the heights of the forest canopy in a gondola. The 2.6km ride takes roughly two hours, affording unusual plant-spotting and birdwatching opportunities. The fee includes a guide, which is helpful since the density of the vegetation can make observing animals difficult. Book online or in the **San José office** (📱2257-5961; Av 7 btwn Calles 29 & 31).

ℹ Information

The park's three most accessible hiking trails originate at **Quebrada González ranger station** (📱2206-5500; park entry adult/child US$12/5; ⊙8am-4pm) in the northeastern corner; find it on Hwy 32 (the San José–Guápiles highway), a 25-minute drive from Guápiles. It has safe parking, toilets, drinking water and a ranger-staffed info booth. For security reasons, don't leave your car parked anywhere along the main highway.

People who want to climb Volcán Barva on a day trip or camp overnight can stop by the **Barva Sector ranger station** (📱2266-1883; park entry adult/child US$12/5; ⊙8am-3:30pm), in the southwest of the park, 3km north of Sacramento.

ℹ Getting There & Away

Frequent buses between San José and Guápiles can drop you off at the Quebrada González ranger station, but the return trip is more challenging. While it's possible to flag a bus down on busy Hwy 32, your luck will depend on the driver's discretion and how full the bus is.

Drivers can reach the Barva station by following the decent paved road north from Heredia through Barva village to San José de la Montaña, Paso Llano and Sacramento. From Sacramento, a signposted, 4WD-only trail leads 3km north to the entrance. It is not advisable to drive this stretch in the rain, as the road is a mess of car-swallowing potholes. Public buses from Heredia will only get you as far as Paso Llano, 7km from the park entrance. For a day trip without your own vehicle, you'll need to take an early bus from Heredia. Make sure you're catching a bus that goes all the way to Paso Llano, or you'll be left more than 15km from the park's entrance.

Guápiles & Around

POP 36,500

A pleasant and nontouristy (but not terribly scenic) lowland agricultural town, Guápiles lies at the base of the northern foothills of the Cordillera Central. It serves as a transportation center for the Río Frío banana-growing region and also makes a convenient base from which to explore Parque Nacional Braulio Carrillo – the entrance is a 20-minute drive away – or go ziplining in Veragua Rainforest Research & Adventure Park.

Sleeping

Hotel y Cabinas de Tropico   HOTEL $
(☑ 2710-1882; d from US$30; P ✳ ☎) This motel-style abode isn't glamorous – it's on a side road off Guápiles' main highway (Rte 32) and is frequented by truckers who arrive late and leave early in the morning, but you can't beat it on price or facilities. Clean, simple rooms all have air-con, TV and refriger-

ator. The front desk sells snacks and serves free coffee. It's a 20-minute walk or five-minute drive into the center of town.

Casa Río Blanco B&B   B&B $$
(☑ 8570-8294, 2710-4124; www.casarioblanco.com; s/d/tr/q incl breakfast US$85/85/100/115; P ☎) ✿ One of Costa Rica's original ecolodges, this welcoming place offers four cabins on a 2-hectare hillside above the Río Blanco. Devoid of cable TV and air-con, it's a throwback to earlier days when ecotourism was all about unplugging. Croaking frogs and flickering lightning bugs provide late-night entertainment, while daytime diversions include visits to the nearby swimming hole and national park (p137).

Hotel Country Club Suerre   HOTEL $$$
(☑ 2713-3000; www.suerre.com; r incl breakfast US$110, extra person US$20; P ☺ ✳ ☎ ☀) On the road to Cariari, 1.5km north of the Servicentro Santa Clara, this Holiday Inn–like business resort has 98 spacious, tidy rooms and two restaurants. The meticulously maintained grounds house a casino, a large pool, a gym, shaded tennis courts and a children's play area.

Eating

Soda Yurifer   COSTA RICAN $
(☑ 2710-1721; casados US$4-6; ☺ 24hr; ☎) It has lime-green walls and a cafeteria feel, but this clean, simple *soda* (lunch counter) sells good, cheap *casados* (with chicken, Mexican-style meat or pork, or fajita style), and fried rice with shrimp, beef or both. Top it all off with some pickled vegetables from the large chili jar on each table. Find the place south of Av Central on Calle 5. There are also burgers, hot dogs and sandwiches on the menu.

Restaurante El Yugo de Mi Tata   COSTA RICAN $
(☑ 2711-0090; mains US$5-10; ☺ 24hr) It doesn't look like much, but there's a reason this is truck-stop heaven. Strategically placed just below Hwy 32's tortuous climb into Parque Nacional Braulio Carrillo (13km west of

BUSES FROM GUÁPILES

DESTINATION	COST (US$)	DURATION	FREQUENCY
Cariari (Coopetraca)	1	45min	every 10-20min 4:40am-10pm
Puerto Limón via Guácimo & Siquirres (Tracasa)	5	1-2hr	hourly 4:50am-7:10pm, from 5:30am Sun
Puerto Viejo de Sarapiquí (Guapileños)	2.40	1hr	5am, 8am, 9am, 10:30am, noon, 2:30pm, 4pm & 6:30pm
San José (Guapileños)	2.60	1¼hr	every 15-30min 5am-7:30pm

Guápiles), it's the perfect stop before or after a visit to the national park. A huge and fabulous array of tasty, affordable buffet-style food is available round the clock.

ℹ Orientation

The center of town is about 1km north of Hwy 32, reached by a pair of well-marked turnoffs on either side of Taco Bell. Guápiles' two major streets are one way, running parallel to each other east and west. Most of the services, restaurants, shops and ATMs are on the loop that these streets make through the busy downtown.

ℹ Getting There & Away

Guápiles' modern bus terminal is 800m north of the main highway from the western Taco Bell turnoff.

Siquirres

POP 31,600

The steamy lowland town of Siquirres has long served as an important transportation hub. It sits at the intersection of Hwy 32 (the main road that crosses the Atlantic slope to Puerto Limón) and Hwy 10, the old road that connects San José with Puerto Limón via Turrialba.

There is little reason to stop here unless you're heading to Parismina – in which case this is a good spot to find banking, internet and telephone services. Tip: buy phonecards here; they aren't sold in Parismina. For the purposes of orientation, Siquirres' church – a highly recognizable round, red-domed building – is located west of the soccer field.

History

Even before the highways bisecting the town were built, Siquirres was a significant location, for it was here in the early 20th century that the lines of segregation were drawn. At the time, black people were barred from traveling west of the town without special permission. Accordingly, any train making its way from Limón to San José was required to stop here and change its crew: black people working as conductors and engineers would change places with their Spanish counterparts and the train would continue on its route to the capital. This ended in 1949, when a new constitution outlawed racial discrimination.

Today Siquirres still marks the place where Costa Rica takes a dip into the Caribbean – and not just geographically. This is where Costa Rican *casados* give way to West Indian *rondón* and where Spanish guitar is replaced with the strains of calypso.

🛏 Sleeping & Eating

Pacuare Lodge   LODGE **$$$**
(☑ 4033-0060, in USA & Canada 1-800-963-1195; www.pacuarelodge.com; 3-day, 2-night all-inclusive packages s/d from US$1348/1866; 📶) 🍃 There are two ways into this dream of an ecolodge, both equally adventurous. Most visitors arrive at its remote location on the Río Pacuare by raft, via a thrilling 45-minute guided paddle. Others take a 7km dirt path (only accessible via the hotel's 4WD) to the river, and then climb into a rickety cable car that crosses the water to the lodge.

Outdoor enthusiasts will love the elegant private bungalows overlooking the river, with hardwood floors, solar-heated showers and thatched roofs; some bungalows have infinity pools. Most (aside from family rooms) have no electricity or walls, only screens – all the better to unplug from city life and immerse yourself in nature. Activities include guided hikes in virgin rainforest, ziplining, canyoning and meeting nearby indigenous communities. Unwind at the spa or eat dinner in the treetops on an elevated canopy terrace.

The lodge is currently participating in a panther program: 40 motion-sensor cam-

---

| WORTH A TRIP |

CENTRO TURÍSTICO LAS TILAPIAS

Chito, the enthusiastic owner of **Centro Turístico Las Tilapias** (☑ 2768-9293; 30min canal tours from US$10, cabinas d with fan/air-con US$45/50; ☺ 9am-7pm; 🅿) is a passionate naturalist who spent 20 years building and introducing wildlife into a 5km canal system just outside Siquirres. It's now teeming with exotic nature, from birds, turtles and sloths to monkeys, frogs and more, and Chito runs tours around his thriving canal network. There's also a tasty restaurant-bar here and some charming rustic *cabinas* perched above a lagoon and the canals. Take a taxi or ask locals for careful directions, as it's tricky to find.

BUSES FRON SIQUIRRES

DESTINATION	BUS COMPANY	COST (US$)	DURATION	FREQUENCY
Limón	Tracasa	2.50	1hr	every 20-40min 5am-8:10pm Mon-Sat, 5:30am-8.10pm Sun
San José	Autotransportes Caribeños	3	2hr	every 30min-2½hr 2am-6:50pm
Turrialba	Transtusa	2.50	1hr 50 min	every 1-1½hr 5:30am-7pm Mon, every 2hr 5:30am-6.30pm Tue-Thu, every 1-1½hr 5:30-7pm Fri & Sat & 6am-7pm Sun

eras are set up around the reserve to capture wild-cat activity, and there's a learning center with video footage of recent sightings.

Package deals include transportation to and from San José, a bilingual guide, a rafting tour or ground transportation to the lodge, equipment, meals, most drinks and a hike.

If you absolutely must plug in during your stay, wi-fi and charging points are available in the common areas.

Pacuare River Bar & Grill   COSTA RICAN $
(☑ 7016-3147; www.facebook.com/pacuareriver bar; bar food US$2-8; ⊙ 11am-midnight) Run by bilingual local Johanna and her American partner, Kirk, this Colorado-style bar and restaurant is on Hwy 10 between Turrialba and Siquirres. Enter the laid-back roadhouse through swing doors, grab a drink at the bar, decorated with a snake skin and bull horns, and tuck into tangy *ceviche* (seafood marinated in lemon), fresh beef fajitas or buffalo wings. It's a good place to stop on the way to the Caribbean coast. Look for the kayaks out front.

ⓘ Getting There & Away

Siquirres has two main bus terminals. The one on the southeastern corner of the park serves Limón and San José. Buses for Turrialba leave from a separate terminal on the north side of the park.

Puerto Limón

POP 58,500
Puerto Limón is the biggest city on Costa Rica's Caribbean coast, the capital of Limón province, and a hardworking port that sits removed from the rest of the country. Cruise ships deposit dazed-looking passengers here between October and May, but around these parts, business is measured by truckloads of fruit, not busloads of tourists, so don't expect any pampering.

A general lack of political and financial support from the federal government means

Limón has not aged gracefully: it's an unlovely grid of dilapidated buildings, overgrown parks, and sidewalks choked with street vendors. Crime is more common here than in other Caribbean towns. However, despite its shortcomings, Limón can be a good base for adventurous urban explorers.

History

Until the 1850s the most frequent visitors to Limón were pirates, who used the area's natural deep-water bays as hideouts. At the time, the country's main port was in Puntarenas, on the Pacific coast, but when the railroad arrived in the late 19th century, Limón blossomed into a full-blown trade hub. The city ultimately served as the key export point for the country's newest agribusiness: bananas.

Beginning in 1913, a series of blights shut down many Caribbean *fincas* (farms) and a large portion of the area's banana production moved to the southern Pacific coast. Afro-Caribbean workers, however, couldn't follow the jobs, as they were forbidden to leave the province. Stranded in the least-developed part of Costa Rica, many turned to subsistence farming, fishing or managing small-scale cacao plantations. Others organized and staged bloody strikes against the powerful United Fruit company. Fed up with the status quo, Limón provided key support to revolutionary José Figueres during the 1948 civil war. This act was rewarded the following year when Figueres, who was then president, enacted a constitution that granted black people full citizenship and the right to work and travel freely throughout Costa Rica.

Even though segregation was officially dismantled, Limón continues to live with its legacy. The province was the last to get paved roads and the last to get electricity (areas south of the city weren't on the grid until the late 1970s), and the region has chronically higher crime and unemployment rates than the rest of the country.

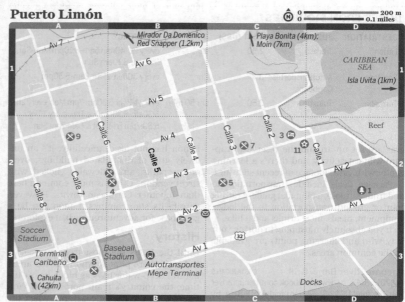

Puerto Limón

Puerto Limón

⊙ Sights

Playa Bonita BEACH
Located 4km northwest of Limón, Playa Bonita has a pleasant sandy beach.

Parque Vargas PARK
The city's waterfront centerpiece won't ever win best in show, but its decrepit bandstand, paths and greenery are surprisingly appealing, all shaded by palms and facing the docks. However, it's best avoided at night.

☞ Tours

Veragua Rainforest Research & Adventure Park ECOTOUR
(☏4000-0949; www.veraguarainforest.com; adult with/without zipline tour US$99/66, child US$75/

58; ⊗8am-3pm Tue-Sun Oct-Apr, large groups only low season; 🚻) 🅿 In Las Brisas de Veragua, this bells-and-whistles rainforest adventure park is nestled into the foothills of the Cordillera de Talamanca. The sprawling complex has guided tours of the forest along elevated walkways, along with such attractions as an aerial tram, a reptile vivarium, an insectarium, and hummingbird and butterfly gardens. At research time the park was converting to solar power. There's also a zipline canopy tour. Installations include a cafeteria and gift shop. Many of the attractions are wheelchair accessible. To get here, take the signed turnoff south from Hwy 32 at Liverpool, 12km west of Puerto Limón.

⚜ Festivals & Events

Día de la Raza
CULTURAL

(Columbus Day; ⊙ Oct 12) When the city can afford it, Puerto Limón celebrates Día de la Raza with a boisterous week of Carnaval festivities, including live music, dancing and a big Saturday parade. During this time, book hotels in advance.

Festival Flores de la Diáspora Africana
CULTURAL

(www.facebook.com/festivaldiasporacr; ⊙ late Aug) While this celebration of Afro-Caribbean culture centers on Puerto Limón, the festival sponsors events throughout the province and in San José.

🛏 Sleeping

Limón offers nothing remotely upscale; it has only budget and midrange options. For something more appealing, head to nearby Playa Bonita.

Hotel Miami
HOTEL $

(📲 2758-0490; hmiamilimon@yahoo.com; Av 2 btwn Calles 4 & 5; s/d US$27/37, with air-con US$40/56; 🅿❄@) For its location on the main drag, this clean, mint-green place feels surprisingly serene, especially in the rooms out back. All 34 tidy rooms are equipped with cable TV and fan. Rooms with air-conditioning have hot water. Welcoming staff, common balconies overlooking the street and a secure setup mean it's the best value in town.

Hotel Playa Bonita
HOTEL $$

(📲 2795-1010; www.hotelplayabonita.com; s/d incl breakfast from US$51/76; 🅿❄🛜🏊) This seaside hotel has simple whitewashed rooms and a breezy, ocean-view restaurant that serves everything from burgers to jumbo shrimp. It's about 5km from downtown Puerto Limón and 2.5km from the entrance to the docks at Moín.

Park Hotel
HOTEL $$

(📲 2798-0555; www.parkhotellimon.com; Av 3 btwn Calles 1 & 2; d incl breakfast US$83; 🅿❄@🛜) Downtown Limón's most attractive hotel has 32 rooms in a faded yellow building that faces the ocean. Tiled rooms are tidy and sport clean bathrooms with hot water; superior and deluxe units come with ocean views and balconies. The hotel also houses the swankiest restaurant in the town center.

✗ Eating

Find cheap eats at the *sodas* in the **central market** (Av 2 btwn Calles 3 & 4; ⊙ 6am-8pm Mon-Fri) and smoothies at **Fruit and Veggies Land** (📲 4702-8653; Calle 7 btwn Avs 2 & 3; smoothies from US$2, meals US$2-5; ⊙ 11am-8pm). You can get groceries at the large **Más X Menos** (cnr Av 3 & Calle 3; ⊙ 7am-9pm, to 8pm Sun), or at the **Palí** (cnr Calle 7 & Av 1; ⊙ 8am-9pm Fri-Mon, to 8:30pm Tue-Thu) next to the Terminal Caribeño.

★ Soda El Patty
CARIBBEAN $

(📲 2798-3407; cnr Av 5 & Calle 7; patí US$1.50, mains US$2-5; ⊙ 7am-6pm Mon-Sat) This beloved nine-table Caribbean eatery, with football memorabilia on the walls, serves up delicious *patí* (flaky beef turnovers stuffed with onion, spices and Panamanian peppers), along with sweet plantain tarts and heaping plates of rice-and-beans (the spicier, more flavorful version of the country's traditional *casado*).

TURTLE BEACH TRAGEDY

The Caribbean's turtle-conservation community suffered a devastating blow on the night of May 30, 2013, when 26-year-old Costa Rican environmentalist Jairo Mora Sandoval was murdered while patrolling a stretch of Moín beach near Puerto Limón. The tragedy shone a light on the challenges facing turtle conservationists. While many communities along the coast have successfully engaged former poachers in guiding and conservation work, turtle eggs continue to be prized on the black market for their supposed aphrodisiac qualities. The remote section of beach where Sandoval was working, near Costa Rica's biggest Caribbean port, is insalubrious, with a history of drug running.

Mora's death sparked strong international and domestic protest, with calls for a beefed-up police presence and stronger conservation measures. In 2016, maximum sentences were given to four poachers found guilty of the murder. The saga has been devastating to Costa Rica's sea-turtle conservation movement, but some bold activists still patrol the beaches on the Caribbean coast.

BUSES FROM PUERTO LIMÓN

DESTINATION	COST (US$)	DURATION (HR)	TERMINAL	FREQUENCY
Bribrí	5	2.5	Autotransportes Mepe	hourly 5am-7pm
Cahuita	3	1-1½	Autotransportes Mepe	hourly 5am-7pm
Guápiles (Tracasa)	4.50	1½	Caribeño	frequent 5am-6:20pm
Manzanillo	5	2	Autotransportes Mepe	every 1-2hr 5am-5:15pm
Puerto Viejo de Talamanca	4	1½-2	Autotransportes Mepe	every 1-2hr 5am-7pm
San José (Autotransportes Caribeños)	7	3	Caribeño	every 30min-1hr 4:30am-7pm
Siquirres (Tracasa)	2.50	1	Caribeño	hourly 5am-7pm
Sixaola	5.50	3	Autotransportes Mepe	hourly 5am-7pm

Macrobiótica Bionatura VEGETARIAN $
(☑2798-2020; Calle 6 btwn Avs 3 & 4; ⊘8am-6:15pm Mon-Fri, to 5:15pm Sat; ☑) This macrobiotic grocery store sells healthy vegetarian foods, vitamins and some things made of soy.

Mirador Da Domenico
Red Snapper CARIBBEAN $$
(☑2758-7613; near Calle Los Miranda; mains US$10-36; ⊘11:30am-midnight; ☑) Head honchos for Limón's new port project often lunch at this scenic half-Italian, half-Caribbean restaurant perched on a mountainside overlooking the city and coastline. The open-air dining room has a bunch of TVs and a convivial vibe, making it an ideal spot to catch a soccer game and devour a whole fried fish. It's on a lane near Calle Los Miranda. Call ahead or ask a local for directions, as it can be tricky to find.

Caribbean Kalisi Coffee Shop CARIBBEAN $$
(☑2758-3249; Calle 6 btwn Avs 3 & 4; mains from US$10; ⊘7am-8pm Mon-Sat, 7:30am-5pm Sun) Belly up to the cafeteria-style counter at this friendly family spot and cobble together a plate of coconut rice, red beans and whatever Caribbean meat and veggie dishes are cooking today. Also recommended in the mornings for its affordable à la carte breakfasts and good *café con leche* (coffee with milk).

Reina's SEAFOOD $$
(☑2795-0879; mains US$9-15; ⊘9am-10pm) On the beach at Playa Bonita, Reina's has loud music, good vibes and plenty of *mariscos* (seafood) and *cerveza* (beer) on the menu.

🍷 Drinking & Nightlife

Rough bars (hangouts for coastal characters: banana workers, sailors and ladies of the night) are dotted around Parque Vargas

and a few blocks west. The more appealing Tsunami Sushi (☑2758-8628; Av 3 btwn Calles 1 & 2; cocktails from US$4, sushi rolls US$2-13; ⊘11am-2am Fri & Sat, 11:30am-11:45pm Tue-Thu) has a good cocktail list and live music. Solo women: don't walk around at night and keep your wits about you in bars. There are better Caribbean towns to go out in.

ℹ️ Information

DANGERS & ANNOYANCES

Though police presence has ramped up noticeably in recent years, pickpockets can be a problem, particularly in the market and along the sea wall. In addition, people do get mugged here, so stick to well-lit main streets at night, avoiding the sea wall and Parque Vargas. If driving, park in a guarded lot overnight and remove everything from the car.

It's worth noting that most of the violent incidents recorded in Limón relate to organized crime and those involved in drug and human trafficking, and do not affect travelers.

INTERNET ACCESS

The internet connection is reasonably good in Limón. Most guesthouses have wi-fi.

MEDICAL SERVICES

Hospital Tony Facio (☑2758-2222) Serves the entire province. It's northeast of the center.

MONEY

If you're traveling onward to Parismina or Tortuguero, Limón is a good opportunity to get cash and phonecards (Parismina has no ATMs, and Tortuguero's one ATM may run out of cash in high season).

Banco de Costa Rica (cnr Av 2 & Calle 1) Exchanges US dollars and has an ATM.

Scotiabank (cnr Av 3 & Calle 2; ⊘9am-5pm Mon-Fri, to 1pm Sat) Exchanges cash and has a 24-hour ATM that dispenses US dollars.

POST

Post office (Calle 4 btwn Avs 1 & 2; ⊙8am-5pm Mon-Fri, to noon Sat)

❶ Getting There & Away

Puerto Limón is the transportation hub of the Caribbean coast.

Cruise ships dock in Limón, but smaller passenger boats bound for Parismina and Tortuguero use the port at Moín, about 7km west of town.

If driving, park your car in a guarded lot at night and don't leave anything on display.

Buses from all points west arrive at **Terminal Caribeño** (Av 2 btwn Calles 7 & 8), just west of the baseball stadium. Buses to all points south depart from the **Autotransportes Mepe Terminal** (☑2758-1572; Calle 6 btwn Avs 1 & 2), on the eastern side of the stadium.

Moín

Most visitors come to Moín for connections to Parismina or Tortuguero. Located 8km northwest of Puerto Limón, the town is a dusty transportation dock for trucks and boat transfers along the connecting canals and rivers.

☞ Tours

Tortuguero Wildlife Tour & Transportation BOATING
(William Guerrero, TUCA; ☑2798-7027, 8371-2323; www.tortuguero-wildlife.com; 1 way tours to Tortuguero from US$35) A small, well-regarded company run by master sloth-spotter William Guerrero and his wife. It's ideal if you want to book a leisurely ride to Tortuguero with plenty of pit stops to see wildlife and have lunch (an optional extra).

All Rankin's Tours BOATING
(☑2709-8101, 2758-4160; www.greencoast.com/allrankin; return trips to Tortuguero from US$70) For leisurely boat rides to Tortuguero, choose these tours run by longtime resident Willis Rankin (who also offers deals for his rustic lodge near Tortuguero's airstrip). On our research trip, the knowledgeable guide spotted sloths, alligators, turtles, toucans, iguanas, monkeys and even a dolphin on the canal; the pretty journey alone is worth the trip.

❶ Getting There & Away

BOAT

The journey by boat from Moín to Tortuguero can take anywhere from three to five hours, depending on how often the boat stops to observe wildlife (many tours also stop for lunch). It's worth taking your time. As you wind through these jungle canals on an Indiana Jones–style adventure, you're likely to spot howler monkeys, crocodiles, two- or three-toed sloths and an amazing array of wading birds, including roseate spoonbills.

Tourist-boat schedules exist in theory only and change frequently depending on demand. If you're feeling lucky, you can just show up in Moín in the morning and pay a premium to get on one of the outgoing tour boats (there's often at least one departure at 10am). You're better off reserving, though, particularly during slower seasons when boats don't travel the route on a daily basis. If the canal becomes blocked by water hyacinths or logjams, the route might be closed altogether. Call ahead for departure times and reservations.

One-way fares generally run between US$35 and US$45 to Tortuguero, US$70 to US$80 return, and between US$25 and US$35 one way to Parismina. **ABACAT** (Asociación de Boteros de los Canales de Tortuguero; ☑8360-7325; boat trips 1 way/return US$35/70) arranges transport on various boats. Try in Tortuguero (p157) for additional operators. There are basic toilet facilities at Moín's dock.

BUS

Tracasa buses to Moín from Puerto Limón (roughly US$1, 20 minutes) depart from Terminal Caribeño hourly from 5:30am to 6:30pm

---

NEW INFRASTRUCTURE FOR CARIBBEAN PORTS

Two major new infrastructure developments are under way in the region around Limón: the construction of a US$1-billion container port in Moín (scheduled for completion in 2018) by the multinational corporation APM, and a Chinese- and Costa Rican–financed US$495-million initiative to widen a 107km section of Hwy 32 between Río Frío and downtown Limón to four lanes, including 26km of bike paths.

While it's estimated that 80% of the country's exports make their way through the Caribbean ports, it is unclear whether the economic benefits of these projects will be shared by the local population. Indeed, plans for the container port sparked massive protests in Limón and Moín by dockworkers-union members, who fear that privatization of the port will undermine rather than improve their standard of living. Others believe that it will bring jobs and infrastructure to the area – only time will tell.

(less frequently on Saturday and Sunday). Get off the bus before it goes over the bridge.

Caribe Shuttle and **Tropical Wind** (☎ 8327-0317, 8313-7164; 1 way/return US$35/70) operate almost-daily shuttles between Tortuguero and Moin in high season.

NORTHERN CARIBBEAN

This is the wettest region in Costa Rica, a network of rivers and canals that is home to diminutive fishing villages and slick sportfishing camps, raw rainforest and all-inclusive resorts – not to mention plenty of wading birds and sleepy sloths.

Most significantly, the area's long, wild beaches serve as the protected nesting grounds for three kinds of sea turtle. In fact, more green turtles are born here than anywhere else in the world.

Parismina

POP 400

For a sense of what Costa Rica's Caribbean coast was like prior to the arrival of mass tourism, jump ship in this sleepy coastal fishing village, wedged between the Canales de Tortuguero and the Caribbean Sea. Bereft of ziplines, it's the sort of spot where elderly men play dominoes on porches and kids splash around in mud puddles.

For those intrepid enough to make the journey, Parismina is also a great place to view turtles and aid in their conservation while avoiding the crowds of Tortuguero. Though fewer turtle species and numbers nest here, it's possible to spot leatherbacks between late February and early October, and green turtles between June and September. Hawksbills have been seen between February and September. There's also a turtle hatchery, at which volunteers can help guard the eggs. Sportfishing is the other traditional tourist draw in this area.

🏃 Activities

Aside from turtle spotting, you can hike, horse ride and learn about coconuts here at Green Gold Ecolodge. Río Parismina Lodge organizes package sportfishing expeditions from the USA.

Asociación Salvemos Las Tortugas de Parismina VOLUNTEERING
(ASTOP, Save the Turtles of Parismina; ☎ 2798-2220; homestays per night incl 3 meals & patrols US$28, registration fee US$35; ☺ by arrangement

Mar-Sep) 🌿 This grassroots turtle-protection organization has strong community support and employs former poachers as 'turtle guides.' It maintains a guarded turtle hatchery on a section of 6km beach. Travelers can volunteer as guards to patrol the beaches alongside local turtle guides. Day volunteers pay a one-time US$35 registration fee, then $10 per patrol (five-patrol minimum).

ASTOP also organizes homestays, offers free internet access and a hangout space for volunteers, and arranges horseback-riding trips, bike rentals, turtle-watching tours and wildlife-viewing excursions by boat.

🛏 Sleeping & Eating

Green Gold Ecolodge LODGE $
(☎ 8647-0691, 8697-2322; dm adult/child US$20/10, incl 3 meals US$50/30) 🌿 About 3km south of the dock, this simple solar- and generator-powered retreat, steps from the beach and surrounded by 36 hectares of jungle, is an authentic rainforest hideaway. Run by the charming (and bilingual) Jason and Juliana, it has rustic but comfortable facilities including eight screened-in upstairs rooms (some with dorm beds), a shared open-air kitchen and shared bathrooms.

Guests can lounge in hammocks on the large porch and gaze at the fruit plants or spot sloths and monkeys in the trees. Jason can arrange activities from hiking, horseback riding and fishing to coconut tours (in which you'll learn about growing, collecting methods and uses). To get there, walk around 40 minutes from the village, arrange for a truck ride from town (around US$10 one way) or arrive by private boat (US$20 from Caño Blanco); reservations recommended. Barbecue meals that include traditional Caribbean fare can be arranged.

Carefree Ranch CABINA $
(☎ 8744-6403; r per person US$12) Opposite the Catholic church at the southern end of town, friendly local Anna runs this clapboard house – bright yellow with green trim – with eight tidy rooms and an inviting, broad front porch. It's about as quaint as things get in Parismina. Tasty home-cooked *casados* (US$7) can be prebooked.

Río Parismina Lodge LODGE $$$
(☎ 210-824-4442, in USA 800-338-5688; www.riop.com; 3-day fishing tours from US$2600; 😊🏊) Top-of-the-line spot on 20 hectares of jungle, with swimming pool, Jacuzzi, English-speaking guides, and both river and ocean boats. Meals, beverages, internal

charter flights, boat, guide, equipment, lures and daily laundry service included in rates.

Soda Rancho La Palma
SODA $

(☏8550-7243; casados US$7; ☺5am-9pm Mon-Sat) Right next to the dock, no-nonsense Doña Amelia serves up fresh and tasty fish and meat *casados,* plus rice and beans cooked in a coconut Creole-style sauce. She also keeps the small plaster statue of the Virgin that is paraded during a boat procession in July.

ℹ Information

There are no banks or post offices in Parismina. Credit cards are not accepted, so make sure you bring enough cash.

There's not much in the way of public internet access in Parismina, but the ASTOP hang-out base is well connected and will let visitors use the wi-fi for a couple of dollars.

While the village has a pay phone, no one in town sells phonecards – bring your own.

ℹ Getting There & Away

Parismina is only accessible by boat or charter flight. The only scheduled boat service is to Caño Blanco (for transfer to Siquirres). Water taxis (US$2, 10 minutes) leave from the Parismina dock at 5:30am, 1:30pm and 5:30pm on weekdays, and at 5:30am, 9am, 1:30pm and 5:30pm on weekends. A bus will be waiting at Caño Blanco's dock to continue the journey to Siquirres (US$2.20, two hours); you'll wait roughly 10 minutes for it to leave. There are toilet facilities and a snack shop at Caño Blanco. The boat and bus drivers only accept the local currency: colones.

For journeys from Siquirres to Parismina, take the bus from Siquirres to Caño Blanco (US$2.20, two hours) leaving at 6am, 9:30am and 2pm. On arrival at Caño Blanco a boat should be waiting at the dock and will take you to Parismina (US$2, 10 minutes).

If you are in, or going to, Tortuguero (via Moín), it's possible to reserve a seat on one of the tourist boats that travel between the two destinations, but planning is essential. Note that it may take 24 to 48 hours to secure transportation (around US$25 to US$35), as Parismina is not a regular stop. Call one of the boat companies in Moín or Tortuguero directly, or ask the friendly folk at Soda Rancho La Palma to help you book.

Parque Nacional Tortuguero

Humid **Tortuguero** (☏2709-8086; www.acto. go.cr; US$15; ☺6am-6pm, last entry 4pm) is a 311-sq-km coastal park that serves as the most important breeding ground of the green sea turtle. With annual rainfall of up to 6000mm in the northern part of the park, it is one of the wettest areas in the country. In addition, the protected area extends into the Caribbean Sea, covering about 5200 hectares of marine habitat. In other words, plan on spending quality time in a boat.

The famed **Canales de Tortuguero** are the introduction to this park. Created to connect a series of lagoons and meandering rivers in 1974, this engineering marvel allowed inland navigation between Limón and coastal villages in something sturdier than a dugout canoe. Regular flights service the village of Tortuguero – but if you fly in, you'll be missing half the fun. The leisurely taxi-boat ride, through banana plantations and wild jungle, is equal parts recreation and transportation.

🏃 Activities

Most visitors come to watch sea turtles lay eggs on the wild beaches. The area is more than just turtles, though: Tortuguero teems with wildlife. You'll find sloths and howler monkeys in the treetops, tiny frogs and green iguanas scurrying among buttress roots, plus mighty tarpons, alligators and endangered manatees swimming in the waters.

Turtle-Watching

The area attracts four of the world's eight species of sea turtle, making it a crucial habitat for these massive reptiles. It will come as little surprise, then, that these hatching grounds gave birth to the sea-turtle conservation movement. The Caribbean Conservation Corporation, the first program of its kind in the world, has continuously monitored turtle populations here since 1955. Today green sea turtles are increasing in numbers along this coast, but the leatherback, hawksbill and loggerhead are in decline.

Most female turtles share a nesting instinct that drives them to return to the beach of their birth (their natal beach) in order to lay their eggs. (Only the leatherback returns to a more general region instead of a specific beach.) During their lifetimes, they will usually nest every two to three years and, depending on the species, may come ashore to lay eggs 10 times in one season. Often, a turtle's ability to reproduce depends on the ecological health of this original habitat.

The female turtle digs a perfect cylindrical cavity in the sand using her flippers, and then lays 80 to 120 eggs. She diligently covers the nest with sand to protect the eggs, and she may even create a false nest in another location in an attempt to confuse predators. She then makes her way back to sea – after which the eggs are on their own. Incubation ranges from 45 to 70 days, after which hatchlings – no bigger than the size of your palm – break out of their shells using a caruncle, a temporary tooth. They crawl to the ocean in small groups, moving as quickly as possible to avoid dehydration and predators. Once they reach the surf, they must swim for at least 24 hours to get to deeper water, away from land-based predators.

Because of the sensitive nature of the habitat and the critically endangered status of some species, tours to see this activity are highly regulated. It is important not to alarm turtles as they come to shore (a frightened turtle will return to the ocean and dump her eggs). In high season, tour groups gather in shelter sites close to the beach and a spotter relays a turtle's location via radio once she has safely crossed the high-tide mark and built her nest. At this time, visitors can then go to the beach and watch the turtle lay her eggs, cover her nest and return to the ocean. Seeing a turtle is not guaranteed, but licensed guides will still make your tour worthwhile with the wealth of turtle information they'll share. By law, tours can only take place between 8am and midnight. Some guides will offer tours after midnight; these are illegal.

Visitors should wear closed-toe shoes and rain gear. Tours cost US$25. Nesting season runs from March to October, with July and August being prime time. The next best time is April, when leatherback turtles nest in small numbers. Flashlights and cameras are not allowed on the beach. Wear nonreflective, dark clothing.

Other Wildlife-Watching

More than 400 bird species, both resident and migratory, have been recorded in Tortuguero – it's a birdwatchers' paradise. Due to the wet habitat, the park is especially rich in waders, including egrets, jacanas and 14 types of heron, as well as species such as kingfishers, toucans and the great curassow (a type of jungle peacock known locally as the *pavón*). The great green macaw is a highlight, most common from December to April, when the almond trees are fruiting. In September and October, look for flocks of migratory species such as eastern kingbirds, barn swallows and purple martins. The Sea Turtle Conservancy conducts a biannual monitoring program in which volunteers can help scientists take inventory of local and migratory species.

Certain species of mammal are particularly evident in Tortuguero, especially mantled howler monkeys, the Central American spider monkey and the white-faced capu-

Around Tortuguero

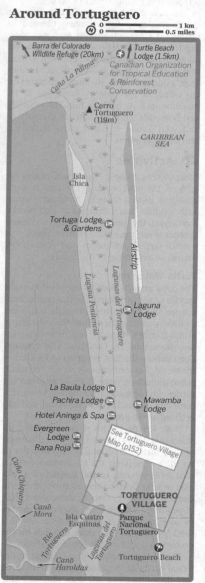

chin. If you've got a reliable pair of binoculars and a good guide, you can usually see both two- and three-toed sloths. In addition, normally shy neotropical river otters are reasonably habituated to boats. Harder to spot are timid West Indian manatees and dolphins, which swim into the brackish canals looking for food. The park is also home to big cats such as jaguars and ocelots, but these are savvy, nocturnal animals – sightings are very rare.

Most wildlife-watching tours are done by boat. To get the best from Tortuguero, be on the water early or go out following a heavy rain, when all the wildlife comes out to sunbathe. It is also highly recommended to take tours by canoe or kayak – these smaller, silent craft will allow you to get into the park's less trafficked nooks and crannies.

Boating

Four aquatic trails wind their way through Parque Nacional Tortuguero, inviting waterborne exploration. **Río Tortuguero** acts as the entranceway to the network of trails. This wide, beautiful river is often covered with water lilies and is frequented by aquatic birds such as herons, kingfishers and anhingas – the latter of which is known as the snakebird for the way its slim, winding neck pokes out of the water when it swims.

Caño Chiquero and **Canõ Mora** are two narrower waterways with good wildlife-spotting opportunities. According to park regulations, only kayaks, canoes and silent electric boats are allowed in these areas. Caño Chiquero is thick with vegetation, especially red guácimo trees and epiphytes. Black turtles and green iguanas like to hang out here. Caño Mora is about 3km long but only 10m wide, so it feels as if it's straight out of *The Jungle Book*. **Caño Haroldas** is actually an artificially constructed canal, but that doesn't stop the creatures – such as Jesus Christ lizards and caimans – from inhabiting its tranquil waters. Canoe rental and boat tours are available in Tortuguero village.

Hiking

Behind Cuatro Esquinas ranger station, the main well-trodden trail is a muddy, 2km out-and-back hike that traverses the tropical humid forest and parallels a stretch of beach. Green parrots and several species of monkey are commonly sighted here. The short trail is well marked. Rubber boots are required and can be rented at hotels and near the park entrance.

> ### PARK ADMISSION FEE
>
> An admission fee (US$15) is charged for each day you visit the main Tortuguero National Park. If you're planning multiple activities within the park, you can save a few colones by concentrating them in a single day; for example, if you go out on a boat tour in the early morning, then hike the walking trail that same afternoon, you'll only pay the admission fee once.

A second hiking option, Cerro Tortuguero Trail, is also available. To reach the trailhead, guests have to take a boat to the town of San Francisco, north of Tortuguero village, where they will disembark at another ranger station and buy a ticket (US$7, plus US$4 for the 15- to 20-minute round-trip boat ride). The trail then takes visitors 1.8km up a hill for a view of the surrounding lagoon, forest and ocean. Casa Marbella (p154) in Tortuguero village can help guests organize the details and even arrange a local guide (from US$35) to take you on the trip.

🛈 Information

Park headquarters is at **Cuatro Esquinas** (📞2709-8086; www.acto.go.cr; ⏰6am-4pm), just south of Tortuguero village. This is a helpful ranger station with maps and info. For canoe tours from this station, new rules limit the number of boats and the amount of time they spend on the canals. Boats are permitted in the park between 6am and 3pm. The early-morning and afternoon tours are best for encountering wildlife and beating the heat. Reserve early for the canal tour, especially in high season.

Jalova Station (⏰6am-4pm) is on the canal at the southern entrance to the national park; it's accessible from Parismina by boat. Although fewer tourists stop here, there's a small visitor center, a short nature trail and a bathroom.

🛈 Getting There & Away

The park entrance is a short walk south of the Tortuguero village (the most common entry point) and is also accessible by boat from Parismina.

Tortuguero Village

POP 1500

Located within the confines of Parque Nacional Tortuguero, accessible only by air or water, this bustling little village with strong Afro-Caribbean roots is best known for attracting hordes of sea turtles (the name

Tortuguero means 'turtle catcher') – and the hordes of tourists who want to see them. While peak turtle season is in July and August, the park and village have begun to attract travelers year-round. Even in October, when the turtles have pretty much returned to the sea, families and adventure travelers arrive to go on jungle hikes, take in the wild national park, and canoe the area's lush canals.

Tortuguero Village

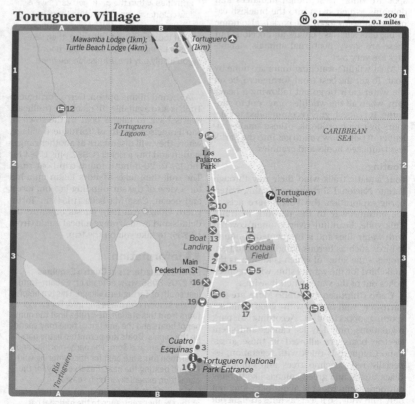

VOLUNTEERING FOR TURTLES

Canadian Organization for Tropical Education & Rainforest Conservation (COTERC; ☑2709-8052; www.coterc.org; dm per week incl 3 meals per day US$275) This not-for-profit organization operates the Estación Biológica Caño Palma, 8km north of Tortuguero village. This small biological research station runs a volunteer program in which visitors can assist with upkeep of the station and research projects, including sea-turtle and bird monitoring, mammal, caiman and snake monitoring, and also a community program.

Sea Turtle Conservancy (STC, formerly Caribbean Conservation Corporation; ☑2297-5510, in USA 352-373-6441; www.conserveturtles.org; museum US$2; ⊙10am-noon & 2-5pm) About 200m north of the village, Tortuguero's original turtle-conservation organization (founded in 1959) operates a research station, visitor center and museum. Exhibits focus on all things turtle related, including a video about the local history of turtle conservation. STC also runs a highly reputable volunteer program.

🏃 Activities

Nonmotorized boat transport offers the best chance of spotting wildlife while exploring the waterways. Numerous businesses rent kayaks and canoes and offer boat tours.

Hikers can follow a self-guided trail, adjacent to Cuatro Esquinas ranger station (p151), that runs parallel to the beach via a well-worn coastal path north from the village to the airport, or walk the beach during daylight hours. Other hiking opportunities exist in and around the park but require the services of a guide.

👉 Tours

Guides post signs all over town advertising their services for canal tours and turtle walks. The most convenient places to arrange tours are at local hotels and at the official Asociación de Guías de Tortuguero kiosk.

Leonardo Tours OUTDOORS
(☑8577-1685; www.leonardotours.wordpress.com; nature walks from US$20; ⊙9am-7pm) With nine years of experience guiding tours in the area, Leonardo Estrada brings extensive knowledge and infectious enthusiasm to his turtle, canoeing, kayaking and hiking tours.

Tinamon Tours TOURS
(☑8842-6561; www.tinamontours.de; 2½hr hikes from US$25, 2-night tour packages per person from US$100) Zoologist and 20-plus-year Tortuguero resident Barbara Hartung offers hiking, canoeing, cultural and turtle tours in German, English, French or Spanish. Packages, including two nights' accommodation, breakfast, a canoe tour and a hike, start at US$100 per person. Note that you'll need to pay the US$15 entrance fee for park hikes.

Riverboat Francesca Nature Tours FISHING
(☑2226-0986; www.tortuguerocanals.com; 2-day sportfishing packages from US$200) A highly recommended company run by Modesto and Fran Watson, Riverboat Francesca offers sportfishing.

Castor Hunter Thomas TOURS
(☑8870-8634; www.castorhunter.blogspot.com; nature tours per person from US$35) Excellent local guide and 44-year Tortuguero resident Castor has led hikes, turtle tours and canoe tours for more than 20 years.

Casa Cecropia FOOD
(☑2709-8196, 8829-8523; 1½hr tour US$20; ⊙tours 10:30am & 4pm) At the entrance to Tortuguero National Park (p149) a little hut offers the perfect indoor activity if it's raining. Biologist Rafael teaches the history of chocolate, including how it's produced, and even lets you have a go at peeling and grinding cacao beans. Then you get to gobble some chocolate and try a delicious chocolatey drink.

Asociación de Guías de Tortuguero TOURS
(☑2767-0836; www.asoprotur.com; ⊙6am-7pm) The most convenient place to arrange tours is at the official Asociación de Guías de Tortuguero kiosk by the boat landing. Made up of scores of local guides, the association offers tours in English, French, German and other languages. Although guides are all certified to lead tours in the park, the quality of the tours can vary. Rates at the time of research were US$25 per person for a two-hour turtle tour and US$20 for a canoe tour. Other options include two-hour walking (US$20), birdwatching (US$35) and fishing (US$80, minimum two people) tours. Tours also involve an extra US$15 admission fee to the park (not required for the fishing tour).

CARIBBEAN COAST TORTUGUERO VILLAGE

🛏 Sleeping

Tortuguero has accommodation options in different places around its waterways; be aware that at the more secluded hotels you may need a boat to get into the main village.

🛏 In Tortuguero Village

In the village you'll find simpler *cabinas* charging US$20 and up for a private room.

Aracari Garden Hostel HOSTEL $
(📞2767-2246; www.aracarigarden.com; dm US$12, r US$22-35; 🛜) This tangerine-colored, newly renovated hostel on the south side of the soccer field has eight sparkling rooms and relaxing shared spaces surrounded by fruit trees. A stay comes with free coffee, a shared open-air kitchen, book exchange and hammocks. The ocean is 50m away and toucans can sometimes be spotted in the trees above.

La Casona CABINA $
(📞2709-8092; www.lacasonatortuguero.com; incl breakfast s/d/tr US$20/35/40; 🛜🍴) Cute rooms with rustic touches, fans and hot showers surround a lovely garden at this family-run spot. Sit back and relax in one of the hammocks and watch hummingbirds, butterflies, iguanas and frogs visit the garden. It's on the north side of the soccer field.

El Icaco HOTEL $
(📞2709-8044; www.hotelelicaco.com; s/d/tr/q US$20/35/45/55; 🛜🍴) This simple lodging offers clean, brightly painted rooms and friendly service. The beachfront location is ideal, and there are plenty of hammocks from which to enjoy it. The hotel also offers access to an off-site swimming pool, along with rental housing for groups and families. Cash only. Breakfast (US$7) is available by prior arrangement.

Cabinas Tortuguero CABINA $
(📞8839-1200, 2709-8114; www.cabinas-tortuguero.com; r US$25-35; 🛜) Down a side street between the boat landing and the park entrance you'll find eight quaint bungalows surrounding a tidy garden at this popular budget spot. Rooms have hardwood floors and fans, and the property features hammocks for lounging, a shared kitchen and laundry service. Inquire about reduced rates in low season.

★ Hotel Miss Junie CABINA $$
(📞2709-8029; www.iguanaverdetours.com; incl breakfast s/d standard US$50/55, superior US$65/75; 🛜) Tortuguero's longest-established lodging, Miss Junie's is set on spacious, palm-shaded grounds strewn with hammocks and wooden armchairs. Wood-paneled rooms in a tropical plantation–style building are tastefully decorated with wood accents and bright bedspreads. Upstairs rooms share a breezy balcony overlooking the canal; the restaurant (p156) downstairs serves delicious food. It's at the northern end of the town's main street.

★ Casa Marbella B&B $$
(📞8833-0827, 2709-8011; http://casamarbella.tripod.com; r incl breakfast US$35-65, extra person US$10; 📧🛜) In the heart of the village, with a spacious and delightful canal-side deck, this B&B owned by naturalist Daryl Loth is one of Tortuguero's most appealing in-town options. Ten simple, well-lit rooms come with ceiling fans, super-clean bathrooms and hearty breakfasts served overlooking the water. It's a two-minute walk north (left) from the village boat landing, but most boats will drop you right at the B&B from the canal. Local tours can be booked by the friendly bilingual check-in staff.

Hotel River View HOTEL $$
(📞8579-9414; 1/2/3/4 people US$25/50/75/100; 🍴🛜) In a prime location on the main street, eight simple, immaculate new rooms with TVs and air-con sit perched above the river. A communal balcony overlooks the water's edge. Breakfast can be arranged in the restaurant downstairs, or there's a bakery right next door.

🛏 Outside the Village

The most upscale lodges and *cabinas* are outside the main village. Those north and west of the village cater to high-end travelers on package deals, although most will accept walk-ins (er, boat-ins) if they aren't full.

★ Rana Roja LODGE $$
(📞2709-8260, 8730-2280; www.ranarojalodge.com; r/cabins per person incl breakfast US$55/75, r per person incl 3 meals US$75; 📧🛜🍴) 🍃 On the opposite site of the canal from Tortuguero village, this jungle hideaway is good value. The immaculate rooms are connected by elevated walkways; some rooms have private terraces and rockers, and all have tiled floors, hot showers and awesome nature views – iguanas, deer and herons are frequently spotted. Free kayaks are available, and the new saltwater pool has a slide. The restaurant serves a nightly buffet. Book a Caribbean dance class at the hotel for US$30.

Toucan & Tarpon Lodge
CABINA **$$**

(📞8408-4239; www.toucanandtarpon.com; s/d/tr/q incl breakfast US$50/60/65/70) Just across the river from Tortuguero village, this place has three simple *cabinas* with solar electricity and Guatemalan textiles. Each room sleeps between two and five people; there are no fans, but the big windows are well ventilated with screens. Other amenities include delicious homemade breakfasts, a communal kitchen with well-stocked spice cabinet, a ping-pong table and free canoe use. There's excellent wildlife-spotting (monkeys, sloths, toucans, armadillos, porcupines, toucans and more) in the surrounding trees. Half-day fishing trips can be arranged for US$350, including refreshments.

La Baula Lodge
LODGE **$$**

(📞2711-3030, 2767-0101; www.labaulalodge.com; s/d/tr incl breakfast US$89/99/109; 📶📺) North of town and across the river, this laid-back, long-running lodge has an unpretentious atmosphere. Rooms have hardwood floors, ceiling fans and hot-water showers. In high season the outdoor dining area features live marimba and Caribbean guitar music. A 300m trail in the grounds offers the chance to spot exotic birds, spider monkeys, iguanas and snakes.

Turtle Beach Lodge
LODGE **$$$**

(📞2241-1419, after hours 8837-6969; www.turtlebeachlodge.com; 1-night, 2-day all-inclusive packages per person s/d/tr/q/child US$284/245/226/210/91; 📺) 🏄 Reached by an Indiana Jones–style boating adventure, this isolated lodge is surrounded by 70 hectares of tropical gardens and rainforest and flanked by beach and river. Spacious wood cabins have tile floors, hardwood furniture and huge screened windows. Guests can explore the network of jungle trails, kayak the adjacent canal, or lounge around the turtle-shaped pool or thatch-roofed hammock hut. Rates include transport, breakfast, buffet lunch and a candlelit dinner in the Turtle Tavern and Restaurant. The lodge is 8km outside Tortuguero village.

Tortuga Lodge & Gardens
LODGE **$$$**

(📞2709-8136, 2257-0766; www.tortugalodge.com; r US$188-296; 📶📺) This elegant lodge is set amid 20 serene hectares of private gardens, directly across the canal from Tortuguero's airstrip. The 27 demure rooms channel a 19th-century safari vibe, with creamy linens, handmade textiles, vintage photos and broad terraces that invite lounging. The grounds come equipped with private trails and a riverside pool, bar and restaurant.

Hotel Aninga & Spa
LODGE **$$$**

(📞2222-6841, 2222-6840; www.aningalodgetortuguero.com; 2-night packages per person s/d US$249/209; 📶📺) 🏄 Sitting 1km north of the village on the opposite side of the canal, Hotel Aninga has a cluster of stilted bungalows connected by a series of boardwalks, along with a bar and a restaurant serving buffet food including Caribbean chicken, beef and pork, veggies and salad, plus pasta.

Nonguests can make appointments at the spa for massages (US$65 to US$120) and other treatments.

Evergreen Lodge
LODGE **$$$**

(📞2222-6841; www.evergreentortuguero.com; 2-night packages per person s/d/tr US$296/243/232; 📶📺) This pleasant place has a rustic feel, with 66 rooms and private bungalows with fans and hot water surrounded by jungle greenery. Guests have access to a pool area, Tortuguero's only canopy tour (US$35), kayaks and an upstairs bar overlooking the river. At the time of research the hotel was renovating a private 1km nature-spotting trail into the park (p149).

Laguna Lodge
LODGE **$$$**

(📞2253-1100, 2709-8082; www.lagunatortuguero.com; s/d/tr incl meals, transfers, tours & activities US$253/223/201; 📶📺) This expansive lodge, liberally decorated with gorgeous mosaic art and trim, has 106 graceful rooms with high ceilings and wide decks lined with Sarchí-made leather rocking chairs. It also has a buffet restaurant, three bars (canal-side, in the rainforest, and poolside), a massage room, a soccer pitch and a Gaudí-esque reception with a giant conch shell on the roof.

Mawamba Lodge
LODGE **$$$**

(📞2709-8181, 2293-8181; www.mawamba.com; 2 nights incl meals, transfers & standard tours s/d/tr US$345/642/792; 📶📺) With pool tables, foosball, a mosaic swimming pool, and butterfly and frog gardens, this lodge sits between the canal and Tortuguero's main turtle-nesting beach, within walking distance of town. Simple wood-paneled rooms have firm beds, good fans and spacious bathrooms with hot water. All are fronted by wide verandas with hammocks and rocking chairs.

Pachira Lodge
LODGE **$$$**

(📞2257-2242, 2256-7078; www.pachiralodge.com; 2-night packages adult/child US$339/170; 📶📺) A sprawling compound set on 14 hectares of land, this 88-room hotel with turtle-shaped pool is a popular family spot. Pristine, brightly painted clapboard bungalows with shared terraces house blocks of rooms that sleep up to four. Cribs and children's beds are available. Rates include transfers, a welcome cocktail and three local tours.

✗ Eating

One of Tortuguero's unsung pleasures is its cuisine: the homey restaurants lure you in with steaming platters of Caribbean-style food, plus international options like pizza and pasta. Most use local produce.

★ Taylor's Place   CARIBBEAN $
(☑8319-5627; mains US$7-14; ☺6-9pm) Low-key atmosphere and high-quality cooking come together beautifully at this backstreet eatery southwest of the soccer field. The inviting garden setting, with chirping insects and picnic benches spread under colorful paper lanterns, is rivaled only by friendly chef Ray Taylor's culinary artistry. House specialties include beef in tamarind sauce, grilled fish in garlic sauce, and avocado and chicken salad.

Fresh Foods   CARIBBEAN $
(☑2767-1063; mains US$3.50-9, smoothies US$3-4; ☺7:30am-9:30pm) In the commercial center of the village, this family-owned restaurant offers breakfasts (omelets, juice, fruit, toast), solid Caribbean meals (chicken and rice) and giant, delicious smoothies in fishbowl glasses. After a long day on the canals, a tasty Caribbean-style filet and a passion-fruit drink really nails it.

Dorling Bakery   BAKERY $
(☑2767-0444; pastries US$2, breakfast US$4-5; ☺5am-8:30pm Mon-Sat, to noon Sun) Thanks to its predawn opening time, this is a good spot to pick up homemade banana bread, lemon and orange cake or cinnamon rolls before an early-morning flight or canal tour.

Sunrise Restaurant   CARIBBEAN $
(mains US$6.50-8; ☺9:30am-9pm Wed-Mon, from 11am low season) Between the dock and the national park, this cozy log cabin–like place will lure you in with the delicious smoky aroma of its grilled chicken and pork ribs. It also serves seafood pasta, fajitas, salad, breakfast and a full Caribbean menu at lunch and dinnertime, with some of the best prices in town.

Soda Doña María   SODA $
(☑8928-8424; dishes US$5-8; ☺11am-8:30pm) Recover from a hike in the park at this riverside *soda*, serving *jugos* (juices), burgers and *casados*. It's about 200m north of the park entrance.

Tutti's Restaurant   ITALIAN $
(☑2709-8117; mains $5.50-9; ☺noon-9pm) The place to come for an Italian fix, Tutti's serves lasagna, penne and spaghetti dishes, and focaccia with cheese. There are also plenty of pizza varieties and loaded calzones – the Caribbean flavor comes with tomato sauce infused with coconut and shrimps, onion and mozzarella. Happy hour (two selected drinks for $10) runs between 3.30pm and 5.30pm.

★ Miss Junie's   CARIBBEAN $$
(☑2709-8029; mains US$9-16; ☺7-9am, noon-2:30pm & 6-9pm) Over the years, Tortuguero's best-known and most delicious Caribbean eatery has grown from a personal kitchen to a full-blown restaurant. Prices have climbed accordingly, but the menu remains true to its roots: jerk chicken, filet mignon, whole snapper and coconut-curry mackerel with rice and beans. It's at the northern end of the main street.

Budda Cafe   EUROPEAN $$
(☑2709-8084; www.buddacafe.com; mains US$10-18, pizzas US$7-9; ☺1-9pm; ☎☑) Ambient club music, Tibetan prayer flags and a river view give this trendy cafe a tranquil vibe. It's a pleasant setting for pizzas, salads, cocktails and crepes (savory and sweet). Grab a table outside for a prime view of the boats going by and, if you're lucky, the yellow-bellied flycatchers zipping across the water.

☕ Drinking & Nightlife

La Taberna Punto de Encuentro   BAR
(☑8877-6515; ☺11am-2am) This popular tavern is mellow in the afternoons but draws the party people after dark with cold beer and blaring reggaetón. The main dance floor has a beautiful open-air view of the river.

① Information

The community's website, Tortuguero Village (www.tortuguerovillage.com), is a solid source of information, listing local businesses and providing comprehensive directions on how to get to the Tortuguero area.

Immediately to the left of the boat landing, the local tour guides' association (p153) is also a good source of tourist information, as is **Tortuguero Keysi Tours** (☑8579-9414; ☺5:30am-6pm).

Several local accommodations have good internet connections, but many can be iffy during heavy rains.

There's one new ATM in town, but bring back-up cash as it may run out of money in high season.

ⓘ Getting There & Away

If you're coming from San José, the two most convenient ways to get to Tortuguero are by air or all-inclusive bus-boat shuttles – though budget travelers can save money by taking public transportation. If you're coming from the southern Caribbean, your best bets are with private boat operators from Moín or shuttle deals from Cahuita and Puerto Viejo.

AIR

The small airstrip is 4km north of Tortuguero village. **NatureAir** (☑ 2299-6000; www.natureair. com) has early-morning flights to/from San José daily during high season. Charter flights land here regularly as well.

BUS & BOAT

The classic public-transit route to Tortuguero is a bit of a faff, taking four to six hours, but is by far the cheapest option. You'll travel by bus from San José to Cariari and then La Pavona, and then by boat from La Pavona to Tortuguero. Alternatively, Tortuguero is easily accessible by private boat from Moín (three to four hours).

From San José & Cariari

From San José's Gran Terminal del Caribe, buy a ticket at the window for one of the early buses (6:10am or 9am) to Cariari (around US$4, two to three hours). In Cariari, buy another ticket from the bus-station window to catch a local **Coopetraca bus** (☑ 2767-7590; US$2.20, 11:30am & 3pm) to La Pavona (one to two hours), where you'll transfer onto the boat (US$3.50, 1pm and 4.30pm) to Tortuguero (around one hour).

On the return trip, boats leave Tortuguero for La Pavona daily at 5am, 9am, 11am and 2pm or 3pm, connecting with Cariari-bound buses at the La Pavona dock.

From Moín

Moín–Tortuguero is primarily a tourist route. While there isn't a scheduled service, boats do cruise these canals frequently. When running, boats typically depart at 10am in either direction, charging US$30 to US$40 for the three- to four-hour trip (US$75 for a return journey). With notice, these same boats can stop in Parismina (one way from either Tortuguero or Moín for US$25 to US$35). Bear in mind that it may take 24 to 48 hours to secure a seat – especially in the low season. For onward transportation beyond Moín, catch a local bus (around US$1, 20 to 30 minutes) to Puerto Limón's bus terminal.

SHUTTLE SERVICES

If you prefer to leave the planning to someone else, convenient shuttle services can whisk you to Tortuguero from San José, Arenal-La Fortuna or the southern Caribbean coast in just a few hours. Shuttle companies typically offer minivan service to La Pavona or Moín, where waiting boats take you the rest of the way to Tortuguero. This is a relatively inexpensive, hassle-free option, as you only have to buy a single ticket, and guides help you negotiate the van-to-boat transfer.

All Rankin's Tours (p147) Round-trip shuttles to Tortuguero from Moín, including excellent nature guides (from US$70).

Caribe Shuttle (☑ 2750-0626; www.caribe shuttle.com) Shuttles from Puerto Viejo (US$75, five hours) and Arenal-La Fortuna (US$60, six hours).

Exploradores Outdoors (p170) More expensive package deals that include transport from San José, Puerto Viejo or Arenal-La Fortuna, a mid-journey Río Pacuare rafting trip, and accommodation in Tortuguero.

Jungle Tom Safaris (☑ 2221-7878; www. jungletomsafaris.com) Offers one-way shuttles between Tortuguero and San José (US$45). All-inclusive one- and two-night packages (US$99 to US$152) can also include shuttles from Cahuita (US$60), Puerto Viejo (US$60) and Arenal-La Fortuna (US$60), as well as optional tours.

Pleasure Ride (☑ 2750-2113, 2750-0290; www.pleasureridecr.com) Shuttles from Puerto Viejo (from US$75, around 1½ hours) and Cahuita (from US$70, around one hour).

Ride CR (☑ 2469-2525; www.ridecr.com) Shuttles from Arenal-La Fortuna (US$55). Minimum two passengers.

Riverboat Francesca Nature Tours (p153) Shuttles from San José to Tortuguero via Moín (from US$75, including lunch) as well as package deals including accommodations.

Terraventuras (p171) Overnight shuttle packages from Puerto Viejo (US$99).

Willie's Tours (p163) Shuttles from Cahuita (from US$70).

ⓘ Getting Around

Water Taxi (☑ 8966-6425; fares from $10) Friendly Colombian boatman Enrique will ferry you around the local waterways. Prices vary depending on the trip.

Barra del Colorado

At 904 sq km, including the frontier zone with Nicaragua, Refugio Nacional de Vida Silvestre Barra del Colorado, or 'Barra' for short, is the biggest national wildlife refuge in Costa Rica. It is also one of the most remote – more so since Costa Rica's commercial airlines suspended service to the area in 2009.

Turtles of the Caribbean

One of the most moving experiences for visitors to the Caribbean coast is turtle-watching on its wild beaches. Witnessing the return of a massive turtle to its natal beach and its laborious nesting ritual feels both solemn and magical. Four species of sea turtle – green, leatherback, hawksbill and loggerhead – nest along the Caribbean coast, and all of them are endangered or threatened.

A Population in Peril

Since it takes many years for sea turtles to mature and reproduce, their populations are quite vulnerable to environmental hazards such as pollution and poaching. Thus conservation efforts are crucial to their survival – these efforts include guarding hatchlings from predators and providing incentives for local communities to protect turtles and their eggs. Volunteer opportunities are plentiful along the Caribbean coast, with tasks ranging from beach patrols, data collection and tagging to moving eggs to hatcheries and hatchling release.

Planning a Tour

Because of the sensitive habitat and critically endangered status of some species, turtle-nesting tours are highly regulated. Groups must be accompanied by licensed guides, who ensure that the turtles are able to lay their eggs in peace and that other nests are left undisturbed. Nesting season runs from March to October, with July and August being the most active period for green turtles. April is another good month, when leatherback turtles arrive.

1. Biologists studying turtle eggs
2. Leatherback turtle hatchlings
3. A hatchling returning to the sea

Depending on when you visit, you may find yourself watching a mother hauling herself onto the beach, laboriously digging a nest with her flippers and hatching dozens of ping-pong-ball-sized eggs, or a parade of new hatchlings on their slow, determined and endearingly clumsy crawl back to the sea.

Turtle-watching tours can be arranged through the Asociación Salvemos Las Tortugas de Parismina (p515) in Parismina and by licensed guides in Tortuguero village.

Doing Time for the Turtles

There are many opportunities for volunteers to help protect sea turtles and the many other creatures that inhabit the Caribbean coast. In most cases, organizations require a minimum commitment of a week. A few options:

Asociación Salvemos Las Tortugas de Parismina (p515) Small, locally run group in Parismina.

Asociación Widecast (p168) Grassroots NGO that has volunteer opportunities in Cahuita and north of the Río Pacuare river mouth.

Canadian Organization for Tropical Education and Rainforest Conservation (p153) Canadian not-for-profit with a research station in Tortuguero.

Sea Turtle Conservancy (p153) Long-time organization with a research station in Tortuguero.

The area has long been a favorite of sport-fishers, who arrive to hook gar, tarpon and snook. Those who aren't into fishing can enjoy the incredible landscape. The Ríos San Juan, Colorado and Chirripó all wind through the refuge and out to the Caribbean Sea through a soggy wetland habitat made up of marshes, mangroves and lagoons. Here you'll find West Indian manatees, caimans, monkeys, tapirs and three-toed sloths, plus a riotous bird population that includes everything from keel-billed toucans to white hawks. There are countless species of waterbird.

Activities

Fishing is the bread and butter of area lodges, which can also organize custom wildlife-watching excursions along mangroves, lagoons and canals (from US$40).

Anglers go for tarpon from January to June and snook from September to December. Fishing is good year-round, however, and other catches include barracuda, mackerel and jack crevalle, all inshore; or bluegill, guapote (rainbow bass) and machaca in the rivers. There is also deep-sea fishing for marlin, sailfish and tuna, though this is probably better on the Pacific. Area lodges are experts at arranging fishing trips; dozens of fish can be hooked on a good day, so 'catch and release' is an important conservation policy of all the lodges.

Tours

Roberto Abram BOATING
(8818-8749; 1hr canal tours from $25) A recommended guide who can be contacted through Casa Marbella (p154) in Tortuguero village; he also leads local river trips originating in Barra del Colorado.

Sleeping

Most of the area's lodging is west of the airstrip, on the south side of the river. **Tarpon Land Lodge** (8818-9921; s/d US$24/32, incl sportfishing & full board US$250/350;) and Río Colorado Lodge are accessible on foot. Other lodges will have a boat waiting when you arrive with a reservation. There are also a few basic family-run *cabinas* between the airstrip and the beach, charging roughly US$30 to US$45 per night.

Río Colorado Lodge LODGE $$$
(2232-4063, in USA 800-243-9777; www.rio coloradolodge.com; fishing packages incl lodging & meals per day US$575;) Owned by a retired Mississippi lawyer, this 18-room lodge is housed in a rambling tropical-style building with breezy rooms connected by covered walkways; there's also a pool table and a deck with satellite TV. Its bar, within walking distance of the landing strip, attracts a local crowd, and regular afternoon happy hours have reinforced its reputation as a party lodge.

GETTING TO NICARAGUA

The northern border of the refuge is the Río San Juan, which is also the border with Nicaragua (many local residents are Nicaraguan nationals). This area was politically sensitive during the 1980s due to the Nicaraguan conflict. Today, however, it's possible to journey north along the Río Sarapiquí and east along the Río San Juan, technically entering Nicaragua. Foreign travelers should carry their passport and the official US$35 permit fee when out fishing.

If you're planning to head further into Nicaragua you can make arrangements with your lodge for a water taxi to take you to the border town of San Juan del Norte – now called San Juan de Nicaragua (or Greytown). It's a tranquil village with few services but an interesting history. At various times over the centuries it's been under the control of the Miskito people, Spanish colonists, British troops and even US Marines. Much of it was destroyed during the Contra-Sandinista conflict of the 1980s.

This is a little-used border crossing, however, so don't make the trip without first checking in with Costa Rican immigration officials (p513). Barra del Colorado has a police checkpoint but does not have a Costa Rican immigration office of its own, meaning that re-entry could be problematic. At the Nicaragua border there is an immigration office; you will have to pay US$2 per boat to enter and US$12 to exit. **Río Indio Ecolodge** (2296-0095; www.therioindiolodge.com; San Juan de Nicaragua; s/d incl meals per person US$232/185;) can help you arrange the finer details of your crossing.

San Juan is linked to the rest of Nicaragua by irregular passenger boats sailing up the Río San Juan to San Carlos, on the Lago de Nicaragua.

Eat breakfast on the veranda overlooking the river, and enjoy hearty American and Tico food for dinner – from pork chops and roast beef to Southern fried chicken and fresh fruit and vegetables. Fishing packages include lodging, meals, an eight-hour fishing trip and happy hour.

Silver King Lodge　　　　LODGE $$$
(☑8447-5988, in USA 877-335-0755; www.silverkinglodge.com; 3-day packages per person US$3850; ✴@⚥🐟) This sportfishing lodge caters to couples, families and friends. Ten huge hardwood rooms have cane ceilings and lots of amenities. Outside, covered walkways lead to a pool, Jacuzzi and sauna. Bounteous meals are served buffet style and an open-air bar whips up cocktails. Rates include equipment, fishing license, air transport to and from San José and one cigar per day. No joke.

❶ Getting There & Away

The cheapest, but most difficult, way to Barra del Colorado is public bus-boat transportation from Cariari. **Coopetraca** (☑2767-7137) buses go from Cariari to the village of Puerto Lindo (roughly US$5, 2½ hours, 4am and 2pm), then you transfer to the boat for Barra del Colorado (around US$6, 20 minutes). Boat and bus drivers will only accept the local currency: colones.

An alternative, much easier, and more scenic way to reach Barra del Colorado is by chartering a boat from Tortuguero. The 90-minute trip starts at US$100 per boat (the price goes up or down depending on gas prices, season and number of passengers). A recommended guide is Enrique (p157), in Tortuguero village; he also does local trips around Tortuguero's waterways.

That said, most folks intent on a remote fishing trip arrive by air charter from San José, arranged by individual lodges.

SOUTHERN CARIBBEAN

The southern coast is the heart and soul of Costa Rica's Afro-Caribbean community. Jamaican workers arrived in the middle of the 19th century, and stayed to build the railroad and work for the United Fruit corporation. Also in this area, to the interior, are some of the country's most prominent indigenous groups – cultures that have managed to remain intact despite several centuries' worth of incursions, first from the Spanish, later from the fruit industry and currently from the globalizing effects of tourism. They principally inhabit the Cocles/Kèköldi, Talamanca Cabécar and Bribrí indigenous territories.

Naturally, this fascinating cultural bubble couldn't remain isolated forever. Since the 1980s the southern coast has seen the arrival of surfers, backpackers and adventurous families on holiday – many of whom have stayed, adding Italian, German and North American flavors to the cultural stew. For the traveler, it's a rich and rewarding experience – with lovely beaches to boot.

Reserva Biológica Hitoy-Cerere

One of Costa Rica's most rugged and rarely visited reserves, 99-sq-km **Hitoy-Cerere** (☑2206-5516; US$5; ◷8am-4pm) sits at the edge of the Cordillera de Talamanca, characterized by varying altitudes, evergreen forests and rushing rivers. This may be one of the wettest reserves in the park system, inundated with 4000mm to 6000mm of rain annually. Be aware that the river can wash away bridges; check with a guide before you visit.

The reserve is surrounded by some of the country's most remote indigenous reserves, which you can visit with a local guide. This virgin habitat is also home to jaguars.

Although there's a ranger station with bathrooms at the reserve entrance, there are no other facilities nearby. A 9km trail leads south to a waterfall, but it's steep, slippery and poorly maintained. When rivers are high, some crossings may be impassable. Jungle boots are recommended.

🏃 Activities

Local Guide　　　　HIKING
(☑8412-8355) Cahuita-based nature guide Richard works with other guides to take adventurous hikers into the Reserva Biologica Hitoy-Cerere; he also leads snorkeling trips, and hikes in Parque Nacional Cahuita (p168).

❶ Getting There & Away

By car (4WD essential) from Cahuita, the journey will take roughly two hours. Head west on Rte 234 towards Finca Concepción – you'll drive on a series of dirt roads passing a spectacular banana plantation. Head through Finca Concepción village past the football field, then take a left at the crossroads and continue to the right. The ranger station will be at the end of a challenging dirt road. Leave your name in the visitors book – you'll likely be the only one in there.

OFF THE BEATEN TRACK

SELVA BANANITO

Selva Bananito Lodge (☑ 2253-8118, 8375-4419; www.selvabananito.com; d all inclusive from US$100, extra person US$10; 🛜), at the foot of Cerro Muchito, at the edge of Parque Internacional La Amistad, is a family-run, 1200-hectare farm that has dedicated the last three decades to developing sustainable ecotourism. While there's no beach access, there's plenty to keep adventurous travelers occupied: tree climbing, birdwatching, waterfall hiking and horseback riding. Rates include activities, three meals and transportation from San José; minimum three-night stay.

Conscious of their environmental impact, the owners employ solar energy, recycled hardwood and biodegradable products. They are deeply committed to preserving the Limón watershed (which provides Puerto Limón's drinking water) and have installed camera traps around their property to record the movements of wild cats and other fauna. They aim to become a wildlife corridor that will allow jaguars to move freely between Parque Internacional La Amistad and the Caribbean coast.

For those driving to the lodge, the turnoff is just south of the Río Vizcaya crossing (about 19km south of Limón). The lodge is about 11km inland on a bumpy, often wet dirt road, suitable for 4WD cars only. Detailed directions are posted on the website, and you can call the lodge for further info. All rooms have mosquito nets. The wi-fi can be very unreliable.

Cahuita

POP 8300

Even as tourism has mushroomed on Costa Rica's southern coast, Cahuita has managed to hold onto its laid-back Caribbean vibe. Dirt roads remain off the main highways, many of the older houses rest on stilts, and chatty neighbors still converse in Mekatelyu.

Cahuita proudly claims the area's first permanent Afro-Caribbean settler: a turtle fisherman named William Smith, who moved his family to Punta Cahuita in 1828. Now his descendants, along with those of many other West Indian immigrants, run the charming eateries and brightly painted bungalows that hug this idyllic stretch of coast.

Situated on a pleasant point, the town itself has a waterfront but no beach. For that, most folks make the five-minute jaunt up the coast to Playa Negra or southeast into neighboring Parque Nacional Cahuita.

👁 Sights

★ Playa Negra   BEACH

At the northwestern end of Cahuita, Playa Negra is a long, black-sand beach flying the *bandera azul ecológica*, a flag that indicates that the beach is kept to the highest ecological standard. This is undoubtedly Cahuita's top spot for swimming and is never crowded. When the swells are big, this place also has a good beach break for beginners.

Playa Blanca   BEACH

At the entrance to the national park. A good option for swimming.

Tree of Life   GARDENS

(☑ 8317-0325, 2755-0014; www.treeoflifecostarica. com; adult/child US$15/7.50; ⊙ tour 11am Tue-Sun 1 Nov-9 Apr) This lovingly maintained wildlife center and botanical garden 3km northwest of town on the Playa Negra road rescues and rehabilitates animals while promoting conservation through educational programs. The rotating cast of residents typically includes kinkajous, peccaries, sloths, monkeys and toucans. There's excellent English-language signage throughout. It's also possible to volunteer here; see the website for information.

👉 Tours

Snorkeling, horseback riding, national-park hiking, chocolate tours and visits to nearby indigenous territories are standard offerings.

Centro Turístico Brigitte   HORSEBACK RIDING

(☑ 2755-0053; www.brigittecahuita.com; Playa Negra) Behind Reggae Bar (p167) in the heart of Playa Negra, this well-signposted backstreet spot does it all, but specializes in horseback tours (hour to full day; US$35 to US$110) and surf lessons (US$35 including board use). Brigitte also rents bicycles (US$8) and offers laundry (US$10 a load) and internet (US$2 per hour) services. Check the website or stop by for full details.

Also offers a couple of basic wood *cabinas* and two private single rooms, and serves a good brekkie.

Cahuita Tours
TOURS

(☑2755-0101, 2755-0000; www.cahuitatours. com; ☺7.30am-noon & 2-5pm) One of the most established agencies in town. Offers snorkeling trips (from US$55 per person), horseback riding (US$85) and hiking tours (from US$50).

Snorkeling House
TOURS

(☑8361-1924; www.snorkelinghouse.com; snorkeling tours adult/child from US$25/15) Local tour guide and conservationist Fernando Brown launches his excellent snorkeling tours in Cahuita national park (p168) from Miss Edith's (p167), his family's restaurant. The tour includes a couple of stops where reef sharks, rays and numerous fish are often spotted, and concludes with a fresh fruit snack.

Mister Big J's
TOURS

(☑8887-4695, 2755-0060; horseback riding from US$45; ☺8am-7:30pm) Offers horseback riding, hiking, snorkeling and other local tours.

Roberto's Tours
FISHING

(☑2755-1148; aventurasrobertotour@gmail.com; full-day fishing tours from US$210) Specializes in sportfishing tours *and* has a restaurant for cooking up your catch.

Willie's Tours
TOURS

(☑2755-1024, 8917-6982; www.williestourscostarica .com; tours from US$20; ☺8am-6pm Mon-Sat) A full-service tour agency that can also arrange further-flung tours and transport. Options include white-water rafting (US$60), a traditional Bribrí lunch and chocolate-making tour (US$59), a Parque Nacional Cahuita hike (US$20) and snorkeling (US$25).

🛏 Sleeping

There are two general areas to stay in Cahuita: the town center (near the national park) and the quieter north of town along Playa Negra. If you're journeying between Playa Negra and the center at night, be streetwise; better yet, bike (with lights) or take a taxi, especially if traveling alone.

🛏 In the Center

Cabinas Tito
BUNGALOW $

(☑8880-1904, 2755-0286; www.cahuita-cabinas-tito.com; d US$40, tr US$55, q US$60-65, 5-person house with kitchen US$100; P🐾) Only 200m northwest of Cahuita, yet surrounded by extensive tropical gardens, this quiet oasis offers six brightly painted, clean and simple *casitas,* plus a family-friendly Caribbean-style house with a kitchen. There's also a resident sloth named Lola, who's been living in one of the trees on the property for five years.

Cabinas Riverside
CABINA $

(☑8893-2252; d with/without kitchen US$30/25; P) This tidy budget place just around the corner from Kelly Creek ranger station offers nine simple rooms with mosquito nets and hot showers; five units that are a bit more expensive also come with kitchens. The grassy yard abuts a swampy area perfect for spotting caimans, monkeys and sloths.

Cabinas Smith 1 & 2
CABINA $

(☑2755-0157, 2755-0068; s/d/tr with fan US$18/ 23/30, s/d/tr/q with air-con US$30/35/40/45; P🐾🛜) These clean rooms spanning two properties between the main drag and the waterfront are run by a friendly older couple with deep local roots. Eight units adjacent to the owners' home have TV, air-con, wi-fi and fridge; five older fan-cooled units around the corner with an outside bathroom are primarily of interest to the budget minded. All share a guest kitchen.

Cabinas Secret Garden
CABINA $

(☑2755-0581; koosiecosta@live.nl; dm/s/d/tr US$12/18/22/30; P🛜) This tiny place with a lush garden has five tiled units with fans, mosquito nets, and hot-water showers in cubicle-style bathrooms, plus one five-bed dorm with cold showers. There's also a nice shared kitchen, and often howler monkeys in the trees nearby.

Spencer Seaside Lodging
CABINA $

(☑2755-0027; s US$18-22, d US$32-42; P) Rooms at this long-standing, locally owned spot are rough around the edges but big – and nothing else at this price level can match the seaside setting within two blocks of the town center with national-park views. Upstairs units have better views as well as a shared terrace strung with hammocks.

★ Alby Lodge
BUNGALOW $$

(☑2755-0031; www.albylodge.com; d/tr/q US$60/ 65/70; P🛜) This fine lodge on the edge of the park has spacious landscaped grounds that attract howler monkeys and birds. Four palm-thatched, raised bungalows (two sleeping three people, two sleeping four) are spread out, allowing for plenty of privacy. High ceilings, mosquito nets and driftwood

Cahuita

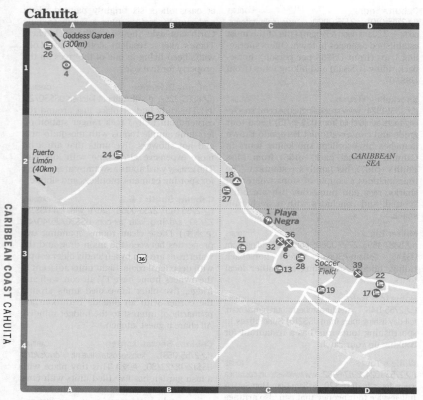

details make for pleasant jungle decor. Rooms also have safes and fans.

A common *rancho* (thatched gazebo) has excellent communal kitchen facilities and an honesty bar with water, beer and Coke.

Kelly Creek Hotel CABINA $$
(☎2755-0007; www.hotelkellycreek.com; s/d/ste US$50/60/70, extra person US$10; 🅿🛜) At this place just outside the national-park entrance, where sloths and caimans hang out, you may be serenaded by the dulcet squawks of the resident parrot. Draw closer and find five graceful wood *cabinas,* some with new bathrooms, that have high ceilings, cream-colored linens and mosquito nets. Local artwork adorns the reception area, and the restaurant serves continental breakfast (US$6).

Bungalows Aché BUNGALOW $$
(☎2755-0119; www.bungalowsache.com; bungalows s US$45, d US$50-55, tr US$60, q US$65;

🅿🛜) In Nigeria, Aché means 'Amen,' and you'll likely say the same thing when you see these three spotless polished-wood bungalows nestled into a grassy yard bordering the national park. Each octagonal unit comes with its own lockbox, mini fridge, kettle and small private deck with hammock.

Ciudad Perdida BUNGALOW $$$
(☎2755-0303; www.ciudadperdidaecolodge.com; incl breakfast d US$95-120, tr US$115-140, q US$190; 🅿🌀🛜) 🍃 In a shady, peaceful spot bordering the national park, but only an eight-minute walk from Cahuita's town center, this eco-conscious lodge offers cute one- and two-room, candy-colored wood bungalows surrounded by landscaped gardens. All include hammocks, ceiling fans, refrigerators and safe boxes. One house has a Jacuzzi, some have kitchens and all have cable TV.

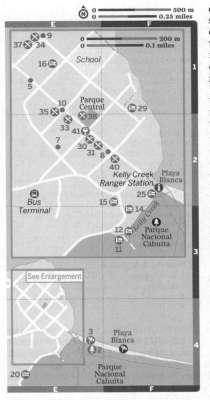

complemented by three kitchen-equipped storybook cottages. Tropical accents include colorful mosaics in the bathrooms and cozy wicker lounge furniture on the private verandas. A lovely pool, honor bar and barbecue area are tucked into the well-manicured garden dotted with fan palms.

Every unit has thoughtful and homey touches, including mini fridge and coffee maker, and staff members go out of their way to help guests explore the area. A winner all around.

Casa Marcellino CABINA $$
(☎8351-1198, 2755-0390; www.casamarcellino.com; d US$85-110, q US$105-130; ☏) In a peaceful garden setting, just inland down a side road between Cahuita and Playa Negra, you'll find this charming cluster of spotless wood cabins with fully equipped kitchens. More expensive units have large bathtubs, plus spacious porches with hammocks and retractable awnings. Monthly and weekly rates are available.

El Encanto B&B B&B $$
(☎2755-0113; www.elencantocahuita.com; incl breakfast s/d/tr/studio/ste US$85/95/115/115/210; P❋☏❄) This pleasant B&B, only about 200m northwest of downtown Cahuita, is set in landscaped grounds dotted with easy chairs and hammocks. Demure bungalows have high ceilings, tile floors and firm beds draped in colorful textiles. The studio and upstairs apartment both have fully equipped kitchens, and the on-site spa and Jacuzzi are super *tranquilo*.

Cabinas Iguana CABINA $$
(☎2755-0005; http://cabinas-iguana.com; d/tr/q US$65/80/95, 5/6 people US$110/120, d with shared bathroom US$25; P☏❄) Set back from the beach on the road marked by the Reggae Bar (p167), this family-run spot features rather worn but nicely shaded simple wood cabins with kitchens. Cabins are of various sizes and are nestled into forested grounds with abundant wildlife. The pool's a pretty place to spot nature.

La Piscina Natural CABINA $$
(☎2755-0146; www.piscina-natural.com; d/tr US$50/65; P☏❄) Run by Cahuita native Walter and expatriate former schoolteacher Patty, this chilled-out gem of a spot near Playa Negra's northern end is a self-proclaimed 'Caribbean Paradise.' The small rooms share access to a huge kitchen and open-air lounge, but the lush grounds, the hammocks next to the gorgeous waterfront and the

🛏 Playa Negra

Camping María CAMPGROUND $
(☎2755-0091; campsites per person US$8, incl tent rental US$10; P☏) Well-spaced campsites share a gorgeous section of waterfront near the northern end of Playa Negra, shaded by coconut palms and a variety of fruit trees. Campers have access to rudimentary cooking facilities, bathrooms with cold-water showers, hammocks, a tree swing and a barbecue area. There are power outlets throughout for phone charging. Maria also rents out her own tents.

There's one private room (US$11), which would be suitable for a group leader.

⭐**Playa Negra Guesthouse** BUNGALOW $$
(☎2755-0127; www.playanegra.cr; d US$70, q US$84, d with air-con US$94; P❋☏❄) Owned by a delightful couple, this meticulously maintained place offers four charming rooms in a Caribbean-style plantation house,

Cahuita

rock-fringed natural ocean-water pool really make this place special.

Hotel La Diosa
BUNGALOW $$$

(☏2755-0055; www.hotelladiosa.net; incl breakfast s US$70, d US$85-115, tr US$105-130; P❉☎🛜🏊) This relaxing spot on Playa Negra offers six well-constructed bungalows, some of which have Jacuzzi tubs, air-conditioning and oceanfront terraces. The grounds include a tranquil pool, a *palapa*-topped restaurant and a meandering walkway to the beach. This is the spot for some serious R&R.

Kenaki Lodge
BUNGALOW $$$

(☏2755-0485; www.kenakilodge.com; d incl breakfast US$90-200; P☎) Opposite Playa Grande, this appealing place is the creation of expatriate Isabelle and Costa Rican tae kwon do master Roberto. Bright, high-ceilinged rooms and elegant bungalows with satellite TV and modern kitchen fixtures surround a spacious landscaped yard and a wooden breakfast deck. Yoga and tae kwon do sessions are available in the open-air dojo.

An extra bed in a room or bungalow is US$20, while an extra person for breakfast is US$10 (children aged six to 11 pay half price for both). The lodge has two bicycles, which can be rented for US$10 per day.

Coral Hill Bungalows
BUNGALOW $$$

(☏2755-0479, 8861-0063; www.coralhillbungalows .com; d incl breakfast US$130; 🛜) Popular with honeymooners, these three immaculate private bungalows in a wildlife-friendly garden setting feature tropical decor: polished-wood floors, bamboo beds, mosquito nets, hand-painted ceramic sinks, African tribal art, and porches with hammocks and leather rocking chairs. Luxuries include rain showers, full breakfasts served by the gracious hosts, and fresh flowers. Follow signs from Reggae Bar.

Hotel Suizo Loco Lodge
BUNGALOW $$$

(☏2755-0349; www.suizolocolodge.com; incl breakfast s/d/tr US$85/115/165, ste d/tr US$140/203; P🛜🏊) Eleven immaculate whitewashed bungalows have king-size beds and folk-art decor at this serene family-friendly lodge (cribs available). All units have safes, mini fridges, solar-heated showers and small private terraces. The perfectly landscaped grounds contain an impressive mosaic-tile pool with a swim-up bar. Plus, there's a tropical/European restaurant. It's around 2km northwest of Cahuita's main center.

Goddess Garden Eco Resort
LODGE $$$

(☏2755-0070, in USA & Canada 800-854-7761; www.thegoddessgarden.com; d 5-night packages incl 3 meals daily US$720; P ⊛ ⊠) Surrounded by old-growth jungle (including an awe-inspiring 'Goddess Tree'), this place at the end of the Playa Negra road is geared toward larger groups and yoga enthusiasts, but independent travelers looking for a peaceful, meditative five- to seven-day immersion experience are also welcome. Rates include four free yoga classes, a one-hour massage and a hike in Cahuita National Park.

✕ Eating

The town offers some of the best Caribbean fare around, along with some surprisingly delicious Italian and French cuisine. There are good options near Playa Negra, too.

Cocoricó   ITALIAN $
(☑ 2755-0409; mains US$7-13; ⊙ 5-10pm Wed-Mon, may be closed low season; 🐾) The menu at this casual spot, decorated with classic movie posters, revolves around pizza, pasta and other Italian-themed mains, but it's better known for its regular film screenings and drink deals. Catch a free movie every night.

Café Cahuita   CAFE, CREPERIE $
(☑ 2755-0323; crepes US$2.50-5.50; ⊙ 7am-6pm Wed-Mon) This friendly main-street spot whips up sweet crepes filled with fresh fruit, chocolate or jam, plus savory varieties like ham and cheese, spinach or gluten free (prepared with plantain flour). It also serves hot and iced coffees and croissants.

Soda Kawe   COSTA RICAN $
(☑ 2755-0233; casados US$7; ⊙ 5:30am-7pm) This humble spot on Cahuita's main street (a few hundred yards from the Kelly Creek park entrance) serves delicious, reasonably priced *casados* cooked over a wood fire, plus hearty breakfasts. It serves *ceviche*, fried rice dishes and fresh fruit juices, too.

Reggae Bar   CARIBBEAN $
(mains US$5.50-12.50; ⊙ noon-10pm; 🐾) Exuding a friendly, laid-back vibe, this *soda* serves sandwiches and pastas on a wooden deck hung with green, red and yellow lampshades in the heart of Playa Negra. Reggae music and waves crashing on the beach across the street enhance the chilled-out atmosphere.

★ Palenque Luisa Casa de Carnes STEAK $$
(☑ 7039-9689; mains US$6-16; ⊙ noon-10pm Mon-Sat; 🐾) In the corner veranda of an old house, this cozy, candle-lit spot specializes in delicious red-wine-covered filet mignon, tenderloin and T-bone steaks. You'll also find plenty of other savory treats, including chicken in

jalapeño or coconut sauce, pork chops, grilled seafood and *ceviche*. Plus there's a veggie section on the menu – with *casados*, pastas, and vegetables in coconut sauce.

★ Restaurant Italiano CahuITA   PIZZA $$
(☑ 2755-0179; pizzas US$11-20; ⊙ 4-9.30pm Fri-Wed; 🐾) This excellent, unpretentious pizzeria is the real deal. Grab a seat at the aluminum tables on the cement back patio and enjoy a surf and insect serenade while you wait for your thin-crusted beauty to emerge from the wood-fired oven. Handmade pastas, grilled meats and gluten-free options are also available.

Chao's Paradise   CARIBBEAN $$
(☑ 6098-4864; seafood mains US$9-15; ⊙ noon-10pm; 🐾) Follow the wafting smell of garlic and simmering sauces to this highly recommended Playa Negra open-air restaurant-bar, where chef Norman has been serving up fresh catches cooked in spicy 'Chao' sauce for more than 20 years. Other dishes include shrimp and octopus in Caribbean sauce, and beef in red-wine sauce. Also has a pool table.

Baraka Bistro   FRENCH, ITALIAN $$
(☑ 2755-0145; www.facebook.com/barakkabistro cahuita; mains US$7-15; ⊙ 11am-9:30pm Tue-Sun) This new cafe-bistro has hardwood floors, sleek white walls, a parasol-shaded outdoor area and blackboards displaying the specials. Here you can enjoy some of the best French and Italian fare in town: the Florentina crepe is stuffed with spinach, cream, chicken and cheese and has an egg cooked into its center, while the filet mignon comes with shrimp and exotic sauce.

The baked fish of the day and the croque monsieur with béchamel sauce, ham and Emmental cheese are also winners. Finish up with the homemade tiramisu.

Restaurant La Fé Bumbata   SEAFOOD $$
(☑ 8323-3497; dishes US$6-14; ⊙ 7:30am-11pm) Chef and owner Walter, a Cahuita native, serves up tall tales and tasty meals – from pancakes to sandwiches to whole snapper – at this reasonably priced spot. There's a laundry list of Tico and Caribbean items, but the main draw is anything doused in the restaurant's spicy-delicious coconut sauce.

Miss Edith's   CARIBBEAN $$
(☑ 2755-0248; mains US$6-16; ⊙ 7am-10pm; 🐾) This long-standing restaurant serves a slew of Caribbean specialties and a number of vegetarian options, such as coconut-milk-and-ginger curry. The service may be

laid-back, and some dishes aren't spectacular, but the spicy jerk chicken and potatoes stewed in garlic are worth the wait. The fresh passion-fruit, lemon-ginger-mint and pineapple juices are good, too.

Sobre Las Olas
SEAFOOD $$$

(☑2755-0109; pastas US$15-18, mains US$15-30; ☺noon-10pm Wed-Mon; ☑) Garlic shrimp, seafood pasta and grilled fish of the day come accompanied by crashing waves and sparkling-blue Caribbean vistas at this sweet spot. Cahuita's top option for romantic waterfront dining, it's only a 400m walk northwest of Cahuita, on the road to Playa Negra.

Drinking & Nightlife

Coco's Bar
BAR

(www.facebook.com/cocosbar.cahuita; ☺noon-late) Low-key Cahuita is home to one insanely loud drinking hole. At the main intersection, you can't miss it: painted Rasta red, gold and green and cranking the reggaetón up to 11. On some nights (usually on weekends) there's also live music.

Splash
BAR

(☑8412-1872; ☺10am-8pm) This day-drinking spot has an outdoor bar with its own swimming pool and often hosts roots and reggae nights, private parties and other special events. The two-for-one happy hour (3pm to 8pm) includes margaritas and Cuba libres. At the time of research the owner was planning to open a pizzeria in the bar.

Information

The town's helpful website, www.cahuita.cr, has lodging and restaurant information, including pictures of many of the town's facilities and attractions. Most cafes, bars and restaurants have wi-fi.

Banco de Costa Rica (☺9am-4pm Mon-Fri) At the bus terminal; has an ATM.

Getting There & Around

The best way to get around Cahuita – especially if you're staying in Playa Negra – is by bicycle. Several places rent bikes, including Mister Big J's (p163) in Cahuita and Centro Turístico Brigitte (p162) in Playa Negra. Most places charge between US$7 and US$10 per day.

BUS

Autotransportes Mepe buses arrive and depart at the bus terminal 200m southwest of Parque Central.

Parque Nacional Cahuita

This small but beautiful park (☑2755-0302, 2755-0461; US$5; ☺Kelly Creek entrance 6am-5pm, Puerto Vargas entrance 8am-4pm) – just 10 sq km – is one of the more frequently visited national parks in Costa Rica. The reasons are simple: it's bursting with wildlife and easily walkable from the nearby town of Cahuita, which provides attractive accommodation. It also has the unusual combination of white-sand beach, coral reef and coastal rainforest, so you can spot an abundance of exotic species on land and underwater all in one day.

Activities

Guided Nature Walks
HIKING

(☑8412-8355; ludrickenrriquemcloud@hotmail.com) Friendly local guide Ludrick McLoud offers fascinating nature walks through Cahuita National Park and snorkeling trips off the coast. He can also arrange guides to Gandoca-Manzanillo wildlife refuge (p186) and Hitoy-Cerere biological reserve (p161).

Asociación Widecast
VOLUNTEERING

(☑in San José 2236-0947; www.latinamericanseaturtles.com) This grassroots NGO offers volunteer opportunities on turtle-protection projects. Participants can assist in patrols, hatchery maintenance, and research and beach clean-up efforts. Rates (US$40 per

BUSES FROM CAHUITA

DESTINATION	COST (US$)	DURATION	FREQUENCY (DAILY)
Manzanillo	2.40	1hr	6am, 9:30am, 11:30am, 1:45pm, 4pm, 6:15pm
Puerto Limón	2.40	1½hr	hourly 6:30am-8:30pm
Puerto Viejo de Talamanca	1.50	½hr	half-hourly 6am-8:30pm
San José	9	4hr (change in Puerto Limón)	every 1-2hr 6am-4pm
Sixaola	4	2hr	hourly 6:30am-8:30pm

day) include training, accommodations, all equipment and three meals per day. Boat transfers are not included.

Hiking

An easily navigable 8km **coastal trail** leads through the jungle from Kelly Creek to Puerto Vargas. At times the trail follows the beach; at other times hikers are 100m or so away from the sand. At the end of the first beach, Playa Blanca, hikers must ford the dark Río Perezoso (Sloth River), which bisects Punta Cahuita. Inquire about conditions before you set out: this river is generally easy enough to wade across, but during periods of heavy rain it can become impassable since it serves as the discharge for the swamp that covers the point.

The trail continues around Punta Cahuita to the long stretch of Playa Vargas. It ends at the southern tip of the reef, where it meets up with a road leading to the Puerto Vargas ranger station. Once you reach the ranger station, it's another 1.5km along a gravel road to the park entrance. From here you can hike the 3.5km back to Cahuita along the coastal highway or catch a ride going in either direction. Buses will stop if you flag them down. They pass around every 30 minutes in each direction; fares are about US$1 – bring change in local currency.

Swimming

Almost immediately upon entering the park, you'll see the beautiful 2km-long **Playa Blanca** stretching along a gently curving bay to the east. The first 500m of beach may be unsafe for swimming, but beyond that the waves are usually gentle (look for green flags marking safe swimming spots). The rocky Punta Cahuita headland separates this beach from the next one, **Playa Vargas**. It is unwise to leave clothing or other belongings unattended when you swim.

Snorkeling

Parque Nacional Cahuita contains one of the last living coral reefs in Costa Rica. While the reef represents some of the area's best snorkeling, it has suffered damage over the years from earthquakes and tourism-related activities. In an attempt to protect the reef from further damage, snorkeling is only permitted with a licensed guide (p161). The going rate to accompany one person is about US$25 to US$30.

You'll find that conditions vary greatly, depending on the weather and other factors. In general, the drier months in the high-

Parque Nacional Cahuita

lands (February to April) are best for snorkeling on the coast, as less runoff results in less silt in the sea. Conditions are often cloudy at other times.

✕ Eating

Right next door to the park, Cahuita offers a wide selection of good Caribbean, Italian and seafood restaurants. If you can't wait, there's a mediocre eatery named **Boca Chica** (☑ 2755-0415; meals US$10-14; ⊘ 11am-5pm, often closed low season) near the Puerto Vargas ranger station at the park's southern entrance.

ℹ Information

Kelly Creek Ranger Station (☑ 2755-0461; admission by donation; ⊘ 6am-5pm) Restrooms are available at the park's northern entrance.

Puerto Vargas Ranger Station (☑ 2755-0302; US$5; ⊘ 8am-4pm) At the park's southern entrance.

ℹ Getting There & Away

It's possible to flag down a local bus traveling on the main road from either end of the park. Buses pass roughly every 30 minutes and will drop you 3.5km away at the other end of the park; fares are about US$1.

PARQUE NACIONAL CAHUITA'S FLORA & FAUNA

Declared a national park in 1978, Cahuita is meteorologically typical of the entire coast (that is to say: very humid), which results in dense tropical foliage, as well as coconut palms and sea grapes. The area includes swampy **Punta Cahuita**, which juts into the sea between two stretches of sandy beach. Often flooded, the point is covered with cativo and mango trees and is a popular hangout for birds such as the green ibis, the yellow-crowned night heron, the boat-billed heron and the rare green-and-rufous kingfisher.

Red land and fiddler crabs live along the beaches, attracting mammals such as crab-eating raccoons and white-nosed *pizotes* (coatis). White-faced capuchins, southern opossums and three-toed sloths also live in these parts. The mammal you are most likely to see (and hear) is the mantled howler monkey, which makes its bellowing presence known. The coral reef represents another rich ecosystem, abounding with sea life.

Buses to San José (about US$9, four hours, every two hours 6am to 4pm) and Puerto Limón (about US$2.40, 1½ hours, hourly 6:30am to 8:30pm) leave from Cahuita's main bus station.

Puerto Viejo de Talamanca

This burgeoning party town is no longer a destination for intrepid surfers only; it's bustling with tourist activity. Street vendors tout Rasta trinkets and Bob Marley T-shirts, stylish eateries serve global fusion, and intentionally rustic bamboo bars pump dancehall and reggaetón. It can get downright hedonistic, attracting revelers wanting to marinate in ganja and *guaro* (a local firewater made from sugarcane).

Despite that reputation, Puerto Viejo manages to hold onto an easy charm. Stray a couple of blocks off the main commercial strip and you might find yourself on a sleepy dirt road, savoring a spicy Caribbean stew in the company of local families. Nearby you'll find rainforest fruit and cacao farms set to a soundtrack of cackling birds and croaking frogs, and wide-open beaches where the daily itinerary revolves around surfing and snoozing. If you're looking to chill a little, party a little and eat a little, you've come to the right place.

◉ Sights

Aiko-logi　　　　　　　WILDLIFE RESERVE
(☑2750-2084, 8997-6869; www.aiko-logi-tours.com; day tours incl transport & lunch US$60, overnight stays per person incl meals US$120; [P]) ✎ Nestled into the Cordillera de Talamanca, 15km outside Puerto Viejo, this private 135-hectare reserve is centered on a former *finca* (farm), on land fringed with dense primary rainforest. It's ideal for birdwatching, hiking and splashing around in swimming holes. Day

tours from Puerto Viejo (or Cahuita) can be arranged, as can overnight tent-platform stays and yoga classes. Reserve.

Finca La Isla　　　　　　GARDENS
(☑2750-0046, 8886-8530; self-guided/guided tours US$6/12; ⊙10am-4pm Fri-Mon; [P]) ✎ West of town, this farm and botanical garden has long produced organic pepper and cacao, along with more than 150 tropical fruits and ornamental plants. Birds and wildlife, including sloths, poison-dart frogs and toucans, abound. Informative guided tours (minimum three people) include admission, fruit tasting and a glass of fresh juice; alternatively, buy a booklet (US$1) and take a self-guided tour. The farm also makes its own chocolate.

🏃 Activities

Exploradores Outdoors is an excellent source of general information on local activities.

Exploradores Outdoors　　　　RAFTING
(☑2222-6262; www.exploradoresoutdoors.com; 1-day rafting trips incl lunch & transportation from US$99) This outfit offers one- and two-day trips on the Ríos Pacuare and Reventazón. Staff can pick you up and drop you off in Cahuita, Puerto Viejo, San José or Arenal, and you're free to mix and match your pick-up and drop-off points. It has an office in the center of Puerto Viejo.

Surfing

Find one of the country's most infamous waves at Salsa Brava – a shallow reef break that's most definitely for experts only. It's a tricky but thrilling ride over sharp coral. Salsa Brava offers both rights and lefts, although the right is usually faster. Conditions are best with a southeasterly swell.

For a softer landing, try the beach break at Playa Cocles (p180), about 2km east of town, where the waves are consistent, white water is abundant for beginners, and the wipeouts are more forgiving. Conditions are usually best early in the day, before the wind picks up. Meanwhile, Punta Uva (p180) has a fun, semi-fickle right-hand point for intermediates, and you can't beat the setting.

Waves in the area generally peak from December to February, but you might get lucky during the surfing mini-season between June and July. From late March to May, and in September and October, the sea is at its calmest. Several surf schools around town charge US$40 to US$50 for two-hour lessons. Locals on Playa Cocles rent boards from about US$20 per day.

One Love Surf School SURFING
([📞]8719-4654; https://onelovecostarica.wordpress.com/about; 2hr surf lessons US$50, 1hr reiki US$50) Julie Hickey and her surfing sons, Cedric and Solomon, specialize in beginners' surf lessons, reiki and Thai massage. She also offers massage and reiki courses from US$300.

Caribbean Surf School SURFING
([📞]8357-7703; 2hr lesson US$50) Lessons by super-smiley surf instructor Hershel Lewis are widely considered the best in town. Recently he started teaching paddle boarding.

Hiking

There are superb coastal hiking opportunities within easy reach. Parque Nacional Cahuita (p168) is 17km north of Puerto Viejo, and Refugio Nacional de Vida Silvestre Gandoca-Manzanillo (p186) is 13km south.

🌊 Courses

Spanish School Pura Vida LANGUAGE
([📞]2750-0029; www.spanishschool-puravida.com; 1/2/3/4 weeks Spanish lessons US$200/380/555/720) Located at the Hotel Pura Vida (p173), this school offers everything from private hourly tutoring (US$15) to intensive five-hours-a-day, multiweek courses.

👉 Tours

Tour operators generally require a minimum of two people on any excursion. Rates may be discounted for larger groups. Gecko Trail Costa Rica (p171) can help you to book.

Gecko Trail Costa Rica TOURS
([📞]2756-8159, in USA & Canada 415-230-0298; www.geckotrail.com; ⊙tours from US$50) This full-service agency arranges local tours as well as transportation, accommodation and excursions throughout Costa Rica, including horseback riding, hikes, rafting, hot-spring visits and spa days. It has an administrative office in Puerto Viejo (inside the Pleasure Ride building), but bookings are made by phone and online.

Terraventuras TOURS
([📞]2750-0750; www.terraventuras.com; ⊙7am-7pm) Offers overnight stays in Tortuguero (US$99), a cultural tour to an indigenous reserve (US$80) and a Caribbean cooking class (US$50), along with the usual local tours. It also has its very own 23-platform, 2.1km-long canopy tour (US$58), complete with Tarzan swing.

CARIBBEAN COAST PUERTO VIEJO DE TALAMANCA

SALSA BRAVA

One of the best breaks in Costa Rica, Salsa Brava is named for the heaping helping of 'spicy sauce' it serves up on the sharp, shallow reef, continually collecting its debt of fun in broken skin, boards and bones. The wave makes its regular, dramatic appearance when the swells pull in from the east, pushing a wall of water against the reef and in the process generating a thick and powerful curl. There's no gradual build-up here: the water is transformed from swell to wave in a matter of seconds. Ride it out and you're golden. Wipe out and you may rocket into the reef. Some mordant locals have dubbed it 'the cheese grater.'

Interestingly, this storied wave helped turn Puerto Viejo into a destination. More than 30 years ago the town was barely accessible. But bumpy bus rides and rickety canoes didn't dissuade dogged surfers from making the week-long trip from San José. They camped on the beach and shacked up with locals, carbo-loading at cheap *sodas*. Other intrepid explorers – biologists, Peace Corps volunteers, disaffected US veterans looking to escape the fallout of the Vietnam War – also materialized during this time, helping spread the word about the area's luminous sunsets, lush rainforests and monster waves. Today Puerto Viejo has a fine paved road, global eateries and wi-fi. Salsa Brava's ferocity, however, remains unchanged.

Puerto Viejo de Talamanca

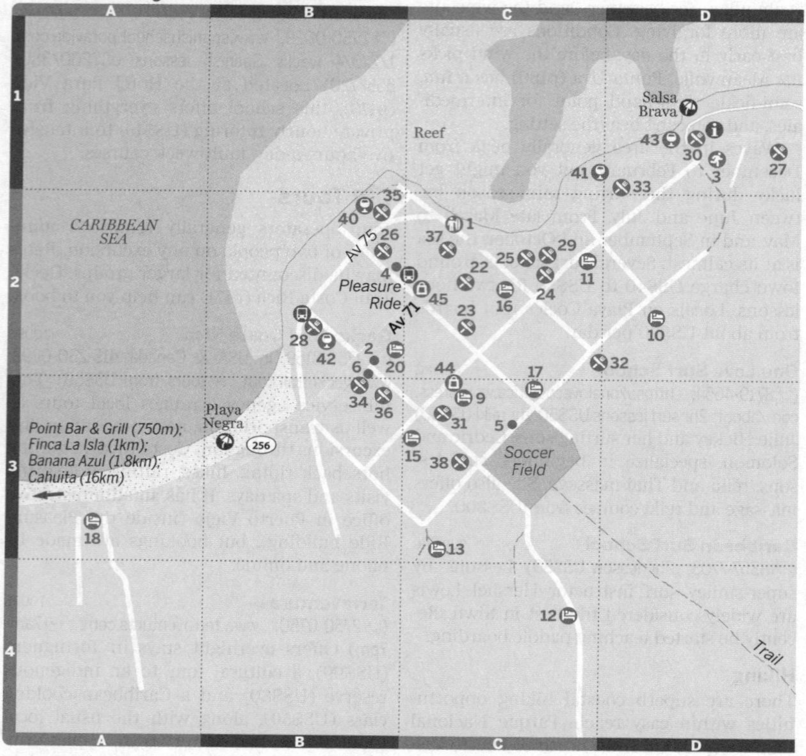

Caribe Shuttle TOURS
(☎2750-0626; www.caribeshuttle.com/puerto-viejo-tours; tours from US$45) This company offers a wide variety of tours in the Puerto Viejo area, and excursions to Bocas del Toro (Panama) and Tortuguero. It also provides transport to San José, northwestern Costa Rica and San Juan del Sur (Nicaragua).

Sleeping

Puerto Viejo has a little bit of everything. Many budget spots have private hot-water bathrooms and internet access. Rates are generally discounted slightly if you pay cash.

Kaya's Place GUESTHOUSE $
(☎2750-0690; www.kayasplace.com; d from US$25, with air-con from US$40, r without bathroom from US$20; P ❄ 📶) Across from the beach at Puerto Viejo's western edge, this funky guesthouse has colorful basic rooms, ranging from dim units with shared cool-water showers to more spacious garden rooms with air-con and hot-water bathrooms. The property also includes a bungalow, a private cabin and three apartments (inquire for prices). A 2nd-floor deck is filled with hammocks with ocean views.

The bar and restaurant serves breakfast (from US$5), plus *casados,* homemade pizzas and excellent craft beer. You can book a brewery tour (US$20) and other activities at reception. There's also a free pool table.

Cabinas Tropical CABINA $
(☎2750-2064; www.cabinastropical.com; s/d/tr US$40/45/55; P ⊖ ❄ 📶) Ten spacious rooms – decorated with varnished wood and shiny tiles – surround a primly landscaped garden at the eastern end of town. The comfortable quarters are just part of the appeal: biologist owner Rolf Blancke leads excellent hikes, birdwatching excursions and tours. Call to check rates; prices vary.

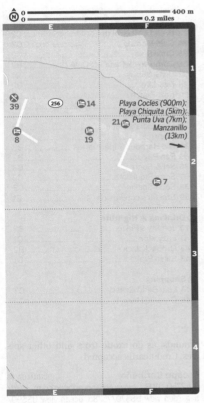

Playa Cocles (900m);
Playa Chiquita (5km);
Punta Uva (7km);
Manzanillo
(13km)

La Ruka Hostel
HOSTEL $

(☎2750-0617; http://larukahostel.com; dm US$12, r with/without bathroom US$46/36; [P][✱]) If the sign 'welcome all sexes, races, colors, religions, languages, shapes and sizes' doesn't lure you in, the friendly greeting from owners Dannie and Dave will. East of town, this hostel has common areas, a shared kitchen, dorms and a couple of private rooms with shared bathroom upstairs, plus a barbecue area, book exchange, and surfboard and snorkel rental.

Hotel Puerto Viejo
CABINA $

(☎2750-0620; www.hotelpuertoviejocostarica.com; d US$40, r per person without bathroom US$16; [P][@][✱]) This crash pad launched by surfer Kurt Van Dyke has been around for 30 years, and consists of a warren of wooden rooms in the middle of town. Units are basic but clean and come equipped with strong fans. There's a huge shared kitchen and bar with a mellow vibe, where the talk is often all about waves.

Hotel Pura Vida
HOTEL $

(☎2750-0002; www.hotel-puravida.com; s/d/tr US$40/45/60, without bathroom US$30/35/45; [P][✱]) This inn opposite the soccer field doubles as a Spanish school and offers mid-range amenities. Breezy, immaculate rooms feature polished wood, bright linens and ceramic-tile floors; many have charming views of the surrounding village. Showers are heated with solar power, and there's a lounge with easy chairs and hammocks. Breakfast (US$7), snacks and chilled beer are available.

Jacaranda Hotel & Jungle Garden
CABINA $

(☎2750-0069; www.cabinasjacaranda.net; s/d/tr from US$35/45/60, air-con extra US$15; [P][✱][✱]) In a blooming garden intersected by walkways, this place near the soccer field has 12 simple wood *cabinas* (sleeping one to four people) with spotless ceramic-tile floors and murals of flowers. There's a small shared kitchen and patio, and yoga classes (US$10) are available. The spa offers massage and bodywork (hotel guests get 15% off treatments).

Lionfish Hostel
HOSTEL $

(☎2750-2143; www.facebook.com/thelionfish hostel; dm US$10, r US$25; [P][✱]) Right off the main street in the center of the action, this hostel is tops for party people. It was started by local surfers and appeals to like-minded adventurers. The dorms are basic and can be stuffy. Facilities include shared kitchen, fans, lockers and hot water. A fried-chicken joint on the first level keeps patrons well fed.

Hostel Pagalú
HOSTEL $

(☎2750-1930; www.pagalu.com; d US$38, dm/d without bathroom US$15/34; [P][✱]) A contemporary hostel with clean, airy doubles and dorms, the latter with lockers and bunk-side reading lamps. There's also a shared, open-air kitchen and a quiet lounge with tables and hammocks, plus a supply of coffee, tea, and spring water for refilling your bottle.

Rocking J's
HOSTEL $

(☎2750-0657; www.rockingjs.com; camping per person US$12, hammocks US$10, dm/d/tr/ste US$15/33/50/70, dm with air-con US$14; [P][✱][✱]) Puerto Viejo's biggest party hostel and 'hammock hotel' has a DJ almost every night in high season. The accommodation is basic: tight rows of tents and hammocks, snug dorms and private doubles share rickety showers in an environment brightened by an explosion of psychedelic mosaics. There are fans in rooms and an on-site restaurant and bar.

Puerto Viejo de Talamanca

Free pickup is available from the bus station if booked ahead. Surfboards, snorkels and bikes are available for rent (US$6), and free yoga lessons take place every morning at 8am.

Cabinas Guaraná CABINA $
(2750-0244; www.hotelguarana.com; s/d/tr/q US$36/45/57/62; P@🕸) Right in town, amid a flourishing tropical garden, brightly painted concrete *cabinas* are decorated with vibrant walls, wooden furniture and colorful folk tapestries. Each one has a small private terrace with hammock. There are mosaics throughout the property, plus a spacious shared kitchen.

Casa Verde CABINA $$
(2750-0015; www.cabinascasaverde.com; d US$59-85, extra person US$20, air-con extra US$10; P❄🕸🏊) Under new ownership, this 17-room wonder has been refurbished and now features tiled walkways winding through gardens hosting tidy accommodation, each with high ceilings, stained-wood furniture, folk-art touches and private terraces with hammocks. The pool is straight out of *Fantasy Island*. A family of sloths lives in the grounds, as do exotic frogs and other species. Credit cards accepted.

Escape Caribeño BUNGALOW $$
(2750-0103; www.escapecaribeno.com; s/d/tr garden view US$70/75/85, ocean view US$90/95/105; P❄@🕸) Charming owners keep these bungalows spotless. Some bungalows sit on the beach side, others in the garden across the road, 500m east of town toward Playa Cocles. More expensive units are in lovely Caribbean-style structures with stained-glass shower stalls; all units have stocked mini fridges, cable TV, fans and hammocks. Breakfast (continental US$5, American US$10) also available.

Coco Loco Lodge BUNGALOW $$
(2750-0281; www.cocolocolodge.com; d US$69-87, with air-con US$92-112; P@🕸) You'll find various options at this quiet hotel. The most charming are the palm-thatched bungalows, featuring shining wooden floors, mini fridges, and coffee makers. All have private terraces with hammocks, offering views of the expansive garden. One large accommodation in the main house is equipped with a kitchen and ideal for a family. Credit cards accepted.

Bungalows Calalú BUNGALOW **$$**
(☑ 2750-0042; www.bungalowscalalu.com; d/tr US$55/65, d/tr/q with kitchen & air-con US$70/90/100; ☑⚙☎❄) A lovely tropical-garden setting, a swimming pool and convenient parking are among the appealing features at this cluster of six bungalows within easy walking distance of town. Cheaper fan-cooled units have private front porches where you can listen to the chorus of chirping birds every morning. Larger family-friendly units come with air-con and kitchen.

Blue Conga Hotel B&B **$$**
(☑ 2750-0681; www.hotelblueconga.com; r US$70-125; ☑☎❄) This backstreet B&B 1km east of town has simple rooms in a two-story, tropical-style building. Best value are the airy upstairs units, with high ceilings, clerestory windows, canopy beds with mosquito nets, handcrafted lamps, private terraces, coffee makers and refrigerators. Rooms downstairs are less inspiring. Breakfast is served on a lovely open-air garden deck, beside the pool.

Banana Azul LODGE **$$$**
(☑ 2750-2035; www.bananaazul.com; incl breakfast cabinas from US$89, r & ste US$109-222; ☑☎❄) Removed from town, this romantic hotel sits astride a blissfully tranquil black-sand beach. Jungle-chic decor (white linens, mosquito nets, bromeliads in the showers) is complemented by fine ocean vistas from upstairs terraces. Of the 22 rooms, the best is the corner Howler Suite, with multidirectional views. There's also a restaurant-bar, and bike and boogie-board rentals. No children under 16.

Cashew Hill Jungle Cottages BUNGALOW **$$$**
(☑ 2750-0256, 2750-0001; www.cashewhilllodge.co.cr; cottages US$90-130, dogs extra US$10; ☑☎❄⚙) On a lush hillside five minutes above town are seven bright, colorful and comfortable cottages sleeping up to six, with full kitchens, loft-style areas and charming rustic touches. All have private decks or patios, with comfy chairs and hammocks. The two-bedroom Playa Negra cabin has exquisite ocean views. A yoga platform hosts classes and there's a laundry service (US$8).

✖ Eating

With the most diverse restaurant scene on the Caribbean coast, Puerto Viejo has the cure for *casado* overkill. You'll find everything from sushi to homemade pizza.

You'll find groceries at the local **Old Harbour Supermarket** (☑ 2750-1908; ⊙ 6:30am-10pm) or incongruous chain-store **Mega-Super** (☑ 2750-0187; ⊙ 8am-9pm). Don't miss the Saturday organic market (p180), where vendors and growers sell snacks typical of the region.

★**Café Rico** CAFE **$**
(☑ 2750-0510; caferico.puertoviejo@yahoo.com; breakfast US$3-8, lunch from US$6; ⊙ 7am-12:45pm Sat-Wed; ☎) Home to some of Puerto Viejo's best house-roasted coffee, and natural smoothies such as probiotic ginger ale, this cozy garden cafe serves breakfast (yogurt and strawberries, omelets) and early lunch (the Hawaiian pineapple sandwich with ham and cheese is tasty). A plethora of other services include wi-fi, a large book exchange, laundry, plus snorkel and bike rentals.

★**Bread & Chocolate** BREAKFAST **$**
(☑ 2750-0723; www.facebook.com/bandcpuerto viejo; cakes US$3.50-4, meals US$6-9; ⊙ 6:30am-6:30pm Wed-Sat, to 2:30pm Sun; ✎) Ever had a completely homemade PB&J (with bread, peanut butter and jelly all made from scratch)? That and more can be yours at this dream of a cafe, serving sandwiches, soups and salads, and of course the treat that gives it its name: chocolate, served as truffles, bars, cakes, tarts and covered nuts, and in cookies (gluten free available).

Coffees are served in individual French presses; mochas come deconstructed so you have the pleasure of mixing your own homemade chocolate, steamed milk and coffee; and everything else – from the gazpacho to the granola to the biscuits – is lovingly and skillfully made in-house.

Soda Riquísimo CARIBBEAN **$**
(☑ 2750-0367; US$4.50-9; ⊙ 7am-10pm; ☎) Typical Caribbean dishes, like jerk chicken served with salad, beans, rice and plantain, are done well at this simple *soda* off the main strip. Reggae plays in the background and the atmosphere is friendly enough, but in this touristy town you can't beat these prices. At weekends the place is packed. It also serves toast, omelets and fruit for breakfast.

Como en mi Casa Art Café CAFE **$**
(☑ 6069-6337; www.comoenmicasacostarica.word press.com; mains US$3.50-6; ⊙ 8am-4pm Wed-Mon, kitchen to 2:30pm; ✎) Owned by a friendly bohemian expat couple, this charming vegetarian cafe champions the 'slow food'

movement and makes everything from scratch, from the jams and the hot sauces to the gluten-free pancakes. Popular items include raw cakes, homemade lentil-bean burgers, and gluten-free avocado wraps, smoothies and chocolate brownies. The walls are covered in local art.

Soda Shekiná
CARIBBEAN $

(2750-0549; mains US$6-10; breakfast 7:30-11:30am, lunch & dinner 11:30am-9pm Thu-Sun) Delicious pancake and fruit breakfasts and Caribbean home cooking can be found at this backstreet eatery with wooden slab tables on an open-air terrace. Lunch and dinner mains are served with coconut rice and beans, salad and caramelized fried bananas. It's just northwest of the soccer field.

De Gustibus
BAKERY $

(2756-8397; www.facebook.com/degustibusbakery; baked goods from US$1; 6.45am-6pm) This bakery on Puerto Viejo's main drag draws a devoted following with its fabulous focaccia, along with slices of pizza, apple strudels, profiteroles and all sorts of other sweet and savory goodies. Eat in or grab a snack for the beach.

Sel & Sucre
FRENCH $

(2750-0636; meals US$4-10; noon-9:30pm Tue-Sun;) Dark coffee and fresh-fruit smoothies offer a nice complement to the menu of crepes, both savory and sweet. These delights are all prepared by the one and only chef Sebastien Flageul, who also owns the hostel next door. Service can be slow, but it's worth the wait.

Dee-Lite
ICE CREAM $

(8419-2023; gelati from US$3, menu items US$1-7; 10am-10pm;) Directly across from the bus stop, this authentic *gelateria* has up to 80 flavors on rotatation, including non-dairy and vegan options. It's the perfect place to cool off after a long, hot bus ride. It also serves crepes, banana splits, pancakes, paninis, pastries, and hot and cold drinks.

Pan Pay
BAKERY $

(2750-0081; dishes US$3-6; 7am-4pm) This popular corner spot on the beachside road in town is excellent for strong coffee, freshly baked goods and hearty wedges of fluffy Spanish omelet served with crisp tomato bread. There are sandwiches and other light meals, but it's the flaky chocolate croissants that'll make you want to jump out of bed in the morning.

★ Mopri
SEAFOOD $$

(2756-8411; mains US$9-20; noon-10pm;) You'd never know it from Mopri's dingy facade and cheap plastic tables, but this place serves some of the best seafood in Puerto Viejo. Choose your star ingredient – whole snapper, calamari, lobster or prawns. Then choose your sauce – Caribbean, Mopri's garlic butter, curry, jalapeño or a lip-smacking salsa. Last, pile on the sides – rice, fried potatoes, plantains, salad, veggies or beans.

It also has a kids' menu and pasta dishes for non-fish eaters, plus wine, beer, juice and coffee to wash it all down.

Stashu's con Fusion
FUSION $$

(2750-0530; mains US$10-14; 5-10pm Thu-Tue;) Stroll 250m out of town toward Playa Cocles to this romantic low-lit patio cafe serving creative cuisine that combines elements of Caribbean, Indian, Mexican and Thai cooking. Macadamia- and coconut-encrusted tilapia and tandoori chicken are just a couple of standouts. Excellent vegetarian and vegan items. Owner-chef Stash Golas is an artist in the kitchen and out.

Miss Lidia's Place
CARIBBEAN $$

(2750-0598; dishes US$7-20; 1-9pm Tue-Sat, 11:30am-8pm Sun) A long-standing favorite for classic Caribbean flavors, Miss Lidia's has been around for years, pleasing the palates and satisfying the stomachs of locals and tourists alike. Fruit-and-veggie lovers will appreciate the ice-cold *batidos* (fresh-fruit drinks) and the delicious assortment of broccoli, green beans, cauliflower, corn-on-the-cob, carrots and mushrooms accompanying most dishes (red snapper, shrimp, chicken etc).

Chile Rojo
ASIAN $$

(8396-3247; US$7-13; noon-11pm;) Craving sushi? Head to this open-air Asian joint on Puerto Viejo's main street overlooking the beach and boats. Bonus raw-fish varieties include soy-infused, Hawaiian-style tuna *poke*, and *ceviche*. Meanwhile, cooked dishes include Thai curries, whole red snapper and yellowfin tuna. Vegetarians can tuck into Middle Eastern delights like tabouleh, fattoush salad and falafel burgers.

At the time of research, deals included two-for-one happy-hour cocktails between 6pm and 10pm.

Bikini Restaurant & Bar
FUSION $$

(2750-3061; mojitos US$3.50, mains US$5.50-14; 5.30-11pm;) If frozen mojitos are your thing, get thee to Bikini. This hip restaurant and bar attracts a crowd of revelers with its affordable cocktails and varied menu. Caribbean dishes, pasta, salads, curries and sushi all pair well with strong drinks and a convivial atmosphere. There are also 32 vegan and vegetarian options.

★ **Laszlo's**　　　　　　　　SEAFOOD $$$
(☑8730-6185; mains US$16; ⊙6-9pm) Whaddya get when you take a champion sport fisherman, born and raised in Transylvania, and transplant him to Puerto Viejo by way of New Jersey? Answer: an amazing, eclectic eatery with no sign and no menu that only opens when owner Laszlo catches enough fish. The day's catch comes with garlic and parsley, homemade French fries and grilled veggies. Yum.

The homemade fruit cocktails are pretty special, too. Beer and wines also available. Find the restaurant two doors away from Exploradores Outdoors (p170).

Koki Beach　　　　　LATIN AMERICAN $$$
(☑2750-0902; http://kokibeach.blogspot.com.au; mains US$10-43; ⊙5-11pm Tue-Sun, sometimes closed low season; 🛜) 🅟 A high-end favorite for drinks and dinner, this sleek eatery at the eastern end of town cranks up the lounge music and sports colorful Adirondack chairs that face the ocean from an elevated platform. There's a decent selection of Peruvian-inflected *ceviches*, plus meat and other seafood dishes. Produce comes from local organic suppliers, but there are slim pickings for vegetarians.

🍷 Drinking & Nightlife

Restaurants often metamorphose into rollicking bar scenes after the tables are cleared. For excellent people-watching over beer, try Bikini Restaurant & Bar. If you want to see and be seen, hit Koki Beach or eat the catch of the day at Laszlo's or Mopri.

Outback Jack's　　　　　　　　BAR
(☑8554-4903; ⊙11am-11pm; 🛜) This Aussie-owned, junk-shop-style bar and grill is decorated with colorful refuse sculptures, bent pieces of metal, painted bikes and other recycled bits. Boards behind the outdoor bar read 'moonshine,' and they ain't kidding: it comes in many varieties, including chocolate, coconut, mango and banana. A daily two-for-one happy hour runs from 11am to 5.30pm, and there's live music in high season.

The adjacent grill sells tacos, steak and fish and chips and cooks fresh shrimp on the barbie (naturally!).

Salsa Brava　　　　　　　　　BAR
(www.facebook.com/SalsaBravaBeachBar; cocktails from US$5; ⊙11am-2am) Specializing in tacos, Caribbean bowls and sweet plantain fries, this popular spot is the perfect end-of-day cocktail stop – hit happy hour from 4pm to 6pm and you'll also catch two-for-one mojitos to enjoy while taking in the sunset over Salsa Brava surf break. On Friday and Sunday the bar brings in DJs for popular reggae nights.

Lazy Mon　　　　　　　　　　CLUB
(☑2750-2116; www.thelazymon.com; signature cocktails from US$5; ⊙noon-2:30am) Run by brothers Khalil and Abasi and their friend Rocky, Puerto Viejo's most dependable spot for live music opened in 2010. Lazy Mon draws big crowds, plays reggae, and serves two-for-one cocktails (4pm to 7pm); sometimes there's even a 'crappy hour' (10pm to midnight). Try Jamakin' Me Crzy, a potent mix of vanilla vodka, orange liquor, mango and coconut cream.

Point Bar & Grill　　　　　SPORTS BAR
(☑2756-8491; www.thepointcostarica.com; Playa Negra; ⊙10:30am-11:30pm; 🛜) If you happen to be traveling during football season (or any other sport season, for that matter), you don't have to miss the big game. Just head to this convivial spot on the beach northwest of town. Decent food, big screens, craft beer and daily drink deals – 'nuff said.

Johnny's Place　　　　　　　CLUB
(☑2750-2000; meals US$5-18; ⊙11am-8pm Mon, Thu & Sun, to 3am Wed, Fri & Sat) Once a beachside clubbing institution, Johnny's slowed after the party started getting out of control in 2015. The place shut down briefly and reopened under new ownership as a classy restaurant (selling *ceviche*, salads, mixed rice and grilled fish) and bar with fancy cocktails. There are still DJs, dancing and occasional revelry on weekends, though.

🛍 Shopping

Lulu Berlu Gallery　　　ARTS & CRAFTS
(☑2750-0394; ⊙9am-9pm) On a backstreet parallel to the main road, this gallery carries folk art, clothing, jewelry, ceramics, embroidered purses and mosaic mirrors, among many other one-of-a-kind, locally made items.

CARIBBEAN COAST PUERTO VIEJO DE TALAMANCA

INVICTUS SARL/ALAMY STOCK PHOTO ©

1. Tortuguero Village (p151)
Cabins and chalets overlook the rainforest.

2. Flora and fauna
Insects in the jungle of Parque Nacional Tortuguero.

3. Canales de Tortuguero (p149)
A series of lagoons and rivers link coastal villages.

4. Manzanillo (p185)
The beachside village is part of the Refugio Nacional de
Vida Silvestre Gandoca-Manzanillo.

BUSES FROM PUERTO VIEJO

DESTINATION	COST (US$)	DURATION	FREQUENCY
Bribrí/Sixaola	1.50/3.35	30/90min	hourly 7am-9pm
Cahuita/ Puerto Limón	1.50/3.60	45min/2hr	hourly 6am-8pm
Manzanillo	1.30	30min	every 2hr 6:30am-6:45pm, less frequently weekends
San José	10.90	5hr	7am, 7:30am, 9am, 11am & 4pm

Organic Market   MARKET
(☺6am-noon Sat) Don't miss the weekly organic market, when local vendors and growers sell snacks typical of the region, particularly tropical produce and chocolate. Arrive before 9am or the best stuff will be long gone.

ℹ Information

DANGERS & ANNOYANCES
Be aware that though the use of marijuana (and harder stuff) is common in Puerto Viejo, it is nonetheless illegal.

As in other popular tourist centers, theft can be an issue. Stay aware, use your hotel safe, and if staying outside of town avoid walking alone late at night.

INTERNET ACCESS
Most bars, cafes, guesthouses and hotels have wi-fi.

MONEY
Banco de Costa Rica (☺9am-4pm Mon-Fri) Two ATMs here work on Plus and Visa systems, dispensing both colones and dollars. Sometimes they run out of cash on weekends, and they can be finicky; if one machine won't let you withdraw cash, try the other.

Banco Nacional (☺9am-4pm Mon-Fri, ATM 6am-10pm daily) Just off the main street near the bridge into town. Dispenses colones only.

TOURIST INFORMATION
Costa Rica Way (☎2750-3031; www.costarica way.info; ☺8am-6pm) Operates a tourist-information center near the waterfront east of town, and lists hotel and restaurant info on its website.

Puerto Viejo Satellite (www.puertoviejosatel lite.com) A good place to look for info on local lodgings, eating and activities.

ℹ Getting There & Around

BICYCLE
A bicycle is a fine way to get around town, and pedaling out to beaches east of Puerto Viejo is one of the highlights of this corner of Costa Rica.

You'll find rentals all over town for about US$10 per day.

BUS
All public buses arrive at and depart from the bus stop along the beach road in central Puerto Viejo. The ticket office is diagonally across the street.

SHUTTLE
An ever-growing number of companies offer convenient van shuttles from Puerto Viejo to other tourist hot spots around Costa Rica and down the coast to Bocas del Toro (Panama). For an exhaustive list, see Gecko Trail's very helpful website (www.geckotrail.com).

Playa Cocles, Playa Chiquita & Punta Uva

A 13km road winds east from Puerto Viejo through rows of coconut palms, alongside coastal lodges and through lush lowland rainforest before coming to a dead end at the sleepy town of Manzanillo. Though well paved, the road is narrow, so if you're driving, take your time and be alert for cyclists and one-lane bridges.

◉ Sights

★ Punta Uva   BEACH
Off a dirt road marked by Punta Uva Dive Center is an idyllic quiet cove that could double for a scene in the Leonardo DiCaprio film *The Beach*. There are usually a couple of locals renting out surfboards on the sand, and the reef to the right of the cove is excellent for snorkeling and surfing (but not at the same time!). When the waves are up, this spot creates a forgiving peeling right-hand wave that's suitable for intermediates.

★ Playa Cocles   BEACH
Playa Cocles has waves for surfers who aren't keen to break skin and bones at nearby Salsa Brava (Costa Rica's biggest break). Instead, it has steep lefts and rights, which

break (and often dump) on the steep sandy beach. During the right tide and swell, the best wave breaks near the island offshore; this spot produces a mellow left-hand longboarder's ride over a deep reef. Conditions are best from December to March, and early in the day before winds pick up.

The organized lifeguard system helps offset the dangers of the frequent riptides.

Jaguar Centro de Rescate   WILDLIFE RESERVE
(☑2750-0710; www.jaguarrescue.foundation; Playa Chiquita; 1½hr tours adult/child under 10yr US$20/free; ☺tours 9:30am & 11:30am Mon-Sat; ⊕) ✐ Named in honor of its original resident, a jaguar, this well-run wildlife-rescue center in Playa Chiquita now focuses mostly on other animals, including sloths, alligators, anteaters, snakes and monkeys. Founded by zoologist Encar and her partner, Sandro, a herpetologist, the center rehabilitates orphaned, injured and rescued animals, for reintroduction into the wild whenever possible.

Volunteer opportunities (US$350 including accommodation) are available with a one-month minimum commitment.

⚡ Activities

The region's biggest draws are surf, sand, wildlife-watching and tanning.

Greg's Surf School   SURFING
(☑8877-4115, 6010-6099; willony@hotmail.com; 1hr/day board rental US$5/20, 1½hr lessons US$40) You'll usually find friendly Manzanillo local Greg set up on the shaded left-hand side of Punta Cocles beach, displaying his selection of surfboards. By prior arrangement he leads surf safaris to the spots with the best conditions in the area.

Indulgence Spa   SPA
(☑2750-0536; www.indulgencespa-salon.com; Playa Cocles; treatments from US$8, massages US$25-85; ☺11am-6pm Mon-Sat) The southern Caribbean's best day spa. It's located at La Costa de Papito (p182).

Punta Uva Dive Center   DIVING
(☑2759-9191; www.puntauvadivecenter.com; Punta Uva; shore/boat dives from US$85/95) Offers fun dives, night dives, PADI courses, snorkeling tours (US$55), SUP tours (US$75) and kayak hire (US$10 per hour). Clearly signposted off the main road in Punta Uva.

☞ Tours

Chocolate Forest Experience   TOURS
(☑2750-0504, 8341-2034; www.caribeanscr.com; Playa Cocles; tours US$28; ☺8:30am-6pm Mon-Sat, tours 10am Mon, 10am & 2pm Tue & Thu, 2pm Fri & Sat) ✐ Playa Cocles–based chocolate producer Caribeans leads tours of its sustainable cacao forest and chocolate-creation lab, accompanied by gourmet chocolate tastings. There's also a shop with a refrigerated chocolate room where visitors can try several varieties of chocolate flavor.

Crazy Monkey Canopy Tour   ADVENTURE
(☑2271-3000, in USA 800-253-6591; www.almondsandcorals.com/activities/crazy-monkey-canopy-ride; per person US$60; ☺10am-2pm) The region's only canopy tour has 13 cables and platforms among the trees, with treetop views of nature and a thatched indigenous village. The 1¼-hour tour finishes on the beach. Located between Punta Uva and Manzanillo, it's operated by Almonds & Corals Lodge (p185).

☷ Sleeping

This stretch of coastline features some of the most charming and romantic accommodations in the country.

☷ Playa Cocles

The broad, 2km, white-sand Playa Cocles lies within easy walking distance east of Puerto Viejo (only 1.5km away), offering proximity to the village and its many restaurants but plenty of peace and quiet, too.

Physis   B&B $$
(☑8866-4405, 2750-0941; www.physiscaribbean.net; incl breakfast d US$85-105, tr US$100-115; ⊛🛜) Comforts abound at this four-bedroom B&B, tucked down a Playa Cocles side road and managed by expatriates Jeremy and Emily. There are free Netflix movies in the smaller downstairs units, satellite TV in the honeymoon suite, and sound systems, dehumidifiers, air-con, mini fridges and super-strong wi-fi throughout. The pretty garden has water features, and nature scenes adorn the bright external walls.

Finca Chica   BUNGALOW $$
(☑2750-1919; www.fincachica.com; bungalows US$65-130; 🛜) Surrounded by lush tropical greenery, four stand-alone wooden houses range from a two-person bungalow to an amazing three-story structure known as

'La Casita del Río' that sleeps up to six. All have fully equipped kitchens, and three have spacious living and dining areas. It's tucked down a dead-end dirt driveway a few hundred meters off the main road.

El Tucán Jungle Lodge
CABINA $$

(☑ 2750-0026; www.eltucanjunglelodge.com; s/d/tr/q US$48/58/68/78; P �🠖) Only 1km off the road, this jungle retreat feels miles from anywhere, making it ideal for birdwatchers. Four clean wooden *cabinas* on the banks of the Caño Negro share a broad patio with hammocks, from which you can observe sloths, monkeys, iguanas, toucans and more. Upon request the welcoming owners serve breakfast (per person US$8) and organize walks in the area.

Hotel Isla Inn
CABINA $$

(☑ 2537-9338, 2750-0109; www.hotelislainn.net; d/f/master ste US$90/190/220; P ✳ ⓦ ⇄) Opposite the lifeguard tower at the main hub of Playa Cocles lies this efficient wooden lodge with expansive rooms, some sleeping up to five. All rooms are equipped with safe, cable TV, hot shower, coffee maker, fridge and handmade wooden furnishings crafted from the slightly curved outer boards that are discarded during lumber processing.

Azánia Bungalows
BUNGALOW $$$

(☑ 2750-0540; www.azania-costarica.com; d incl breakfast US$100, additional person US$25; P @ ⓦ) Ten spacious but dark thatch-roofed bungalows are brightened up by colorful linens at this charming inn set on landscaped jungle grounds. Nice details include woven bedspreads, well-designed bathrooms and wide-plank hardwood floors. A free-form pool and a Jacuzzi nestle into the greenery, and there's an Argentine restaurant and bar. Rooms sleep up to four people.

La Costa de Papito
BUNGALOW $$$

(☑ 2750-0080; www.lacostadepapito.com; d incl breakfast US$128, additional adult/child US$19/9; P ⓦ) Relax in rustic comfort in the sculpture-studded grounds of this popular Cocles outpost, which has timber-and-bamboo bungalows decked out with hand-carved furniture, stone bathrooms straight out of *The Flintstones* and roomy porches draped with hammocks. The restaurant serves Caribbean specialties, while the rustic, palm-thatched Indulgence Spa (p181) offers massage and spa treatments.

🛏 Playa Chiquita

It isn't exactly clear where Playa Cocles ends and Playa Chiquita begins, but conventional wisdom applies the latter name to a series of beaches 4km to 6km east of Puerto Viejo.

⭐ Tree House Lodge
BUNGALOW $$$

(☑ 2750-0706; www.costaricatreehouse.com; d US$250-590, extra person US$50; P) 🍃 Adventurers who like their lodgings whimsical will love these five open-air *casitas,* including a literal 'tree house': a two-story cabin built around a living sangrillo tree, complete with a minigolf course around the trunk. All have kitchens, barbecues, spacious decks with easy chairs and hammocks, and private paths leading to a small white-sand beach.

Houses sleep up to five and have mosquito nets; one has a Jacuzzi.

La Kukula
BUNGALOW $$$

(☑ 2750-0653; www.lakukulalodge.com; d incl breakfast US$110-130; ⇄) 🍃 Three tastefully spaced 'tropical contemporary' bungalows bring guests close to nature with natural ventilation (super-high ceilings and screen walls) and open jungle views from the rain showers. The wood-decked pool is great for bird- and frog-watching. For larger groups a three-bedroom house, with private kitchen and pool, sleeps up to nine. The delicious breakfast features homemade bread and marmalade.

Shawandha Lodge
BUNGALOW $$$

(☑ 2750-0018; www.shawandha.com; d incl breakfast US$147, additional person US$30; P ✳ ⓦ ⇄) Immersed in greenery, with frogs, agoutis and other tropical critters close by, this upscale lodge has 14 private, spacious, nature-themed bungalows painted in earth tones and equipped with large mosaic-tiled bathrooms. A meticulously maintained thatched *rancho* serves as an open-air lounge, and there's a French-Caribbean restaurant. A private path across the road leads to the beach.

Tierra de Sueños
BUNGALOW $$$

(☑ 2750-0378; www.tierradesuenoslodge.com; bungalows incl breakfast US$105-155; P ⓦ) 🍃 True to its name ('land of dreams'), this blissful garden retreat comprises seven adorable wood bungalows with mosquito nets and private decks. The quiet, tropical atmosphere is complemented by regular yoga (US$8/10 for guests/nonguests) on an open-air platform. Laundry (US$10 per load) and bicycle hire (US$8) are available, as is wi-fi (common areas only). Bungalows sleep two to five.

🛏 Punta Uva

In calm seas, Punta Uva has one of the region's most swimmable beaches. It's a quiet spot, embraced by a palm-tree-lined cove. To find the turnoff to the point (about 7km east of Puerto Viejo), look for the Punta Uva Dive Center sign.

Walaba Hostel   HOSTEL $
(☑ 2750-0147; www.walabahostel.hostel.com; tw US$30, dm/s/d without bathroom US$18/21/26; P🤚) Funky, colorful and relatively cheap for Punta Uva, this ramshackle collection of open-air dorms, private rooms (including an 'attic' double reached by a ladder) and small cabins is surrounded by a flowery garden and managed by friendly staff. Guests share ample kitchen facilities, hot and cold showers, and a creaky-floored communal area with games, books and DVDs.

★Cabinas Punta Uva   CABINA $$
(☑ 2759-9180; www.cabinaspuntauva.com; cabinas with/without private kitchen US$90/65; P🤚🐾) Steps from idyllic Punta Uva, this cluster of *cabinas* with tiled bathrooms, polished-wood verandas, hammocks and a shared open-air kitchen is hidden down a dead-end street in a verdant garden setting. Fall asleep to the sound of crashing waves and chirping insects and wake up to the roar of the resident howler monkeys. Wi-fi's available in common areas.

Villas del Caribe   HOTEL $$
(☑ 2233-2200, 2750-0202; www.villasdelcaribe. com; incl breakfast d US$90, villas US$125-185; P❄🤚🛥) With a prime location near the beach, this resort offers lovely, brightly painted rooms, comfortable beds, sitting areas and roomy bathrooms with Spanish tiles. Junior villas also come with kitchenettes, while the two-story villas have ocean views, king-size beds, kitchens and barbecues. All have private decks with hammocks. Select villas have air-conditioning. Wi-fi is available in the bar area.

Casa Viva   BUNGALOW $$$
(☑ 2750-0089; www.puntauva.net; 1-bedroom houses US$100, 2-bedroom houses d/tr/q US$130/ 160/190; P🤚) Beautifully handcrafted by a master carpenter, these enormous, fully furnished hardwood houses, each with tiled shower, kitchen and wraparound veranda, are set on a beachfront property – an ideal spot in which to chill out in a hammock and observe the local wildlife. Ask about weekly and monthly rates. Fans available in rooms.

Korrigan Lodge   BUNGALOW $$$
(☑ 2759-9103; www.korriganlodge.com; d incl breakfast US$115, extra person US$20; P) Nestled into a patch of jungle near the main road, these four thatch-roofed wood-and-concrete bungalows come with minibar, safe, fan, modern bathroom, and private terrace with hammock. All guests have access to free bikes. Breakfast is served in an open-air *rancho* surrounded by gardens.

🍴 Eating

Playa Cocles is close to the lively eating options of Puerto Viejo; after that, the pickings get slim until you approach Punta Uva, which has a cluster of fantastic restaurants.

Pita Bonita   MIDDLE EASTERN $$
(☑ 2756-8173; Playa Chiquita; US$7.50-13.50; ⊙1-9pm Mon-Sat) For Turkish coffee, hummus and the best pita bread in the Caribbean, this Israeli-owned spot is the place. There's also creamy *moutabal* (a roasted-aubergine and tahini dip), spicy *shakshuka* (a Middle Eastern dish with poached eggs and tomato sauce) and fresh tabouli (tomatoes, parsley, mint, bulgur, lemon juice and onion). Find the open-air restaurant across from Tree House Lodge.

There's a good selection of liquor, beer and wines, too.

★Selvin's Restaurant   CARIBBEAN $$
(☑ 2750-0664; www.selvinpuntauva.com; Punta Uva; mains US$12-18; ⊙noon-8pm Thu-Sun) Selvin has been serving Caribbean food since 1982 and his place is considered one of the region's best, specializing in shrimp, sautéed lobster in butter, garlic and onion, T-bone steak, a terrific *rondón* (seafood gumbo) and a succulent chicken *caribeño* (chicken stewed in a spicy Caribbean sauce). Those with a sweet tooth will enjoy the organic chocolate bar and coconut candy.

Pura Gula   INTERNATIONAL $$
(☑ 8634-6404; Punta Uva; mains US$6-16; ⊙2-4pm & 6-10pm) The short but solid menu at this casually elegant eatery includes teriyaki scallops, pad Thai, pasta with macadamia

pesto, and homemade egg flan. Everything's served on a pleasant open-air deck, just off the main road between Playa Chiquita and Punta Uva.

El Refugio ARGENTINE, INTERNATIONAL **$$$**
(☑ 2759-9007; Punta Uva; mains US$12-25; ☺ 5-9pm Thu-Tue) This Argentine-owned restaurant with only five tables is renowned for its rotating menu of three appetizers, five main dishes and three desserts. New offerings get chalked up on the board daily, anchored by perennial favorites such as red tuna in garlic, *bife de entraña* with chimichurri (beef in

a marinade of parsley, garlic and spices) and *dulce de leche* crepes. Reserve ahead.

La Pecora Nera ITALIAN **$$$**
(☑ 2750-0490; Playa Cocles; mains US$15-30; ☺ 5:30-10pm Tue-Sun; ☑) If you're looking to splurge on a fancy meal during your trip, do it at this romantic eatery run by Ilario Giannoni. On a lovely, candlelit patio, deftly prepared Italian seafood and pasta dishes are served alongside unusual offerings such as the delicate *carpaccio di carambola:* transparent slices of starfruit topped with shrimp, tomatoes and balsamic vinaigrette. Menu options change frequently.

WORTH A TRIP

VISITING INDIGENOUS COMMUNITIES

At least two indigenous groups occupied the territory on the Caribbean side of the country from pre-Columbian times. The Bribrí people tended to inhabit lowland areas, while the Cabécar people made their home high in the Cordillera de Talamanca. Over the last century, members of both ethnic groups have migrated to the Pacific side. But many have stayed on the coast, intermarrying with Jamaican immigrants and even working in the banana industry. Today the Bribrí tend to be more acculturated, while the Cabécar are more isolated.

The groups have distinct languages (which are preserved to some degree), though they share similar architecture, weapons and canoe style. They also share the spiritual belief that the planet – and the flora and fauna contained within it – are gifts from Sibö (God). *Taking Care of Sibö's Gifts,* by Juanita Sánchez, Gloria Mayorga and Paula Palmer, is a remarkable record of Bribrí history and available online.

Making it Happen

There are several reserves on the Caribbean slopes of the Cordillera de Talamanca, including the Talamanca Cabécar territory (which is more difficult to visit) and the Bribrí territory, where locals are more equipped to handle visitors.

The most interesting destination is **Yorkín**, in the Reserva Indígena Yorkín. Only reachable by boat, the village is situated on the Río Yorkín, bordering Panama. Immersive day, one-night and two-night tours (from $210 per person including meals, transfers and experiences) entail travel via dugout canoe followed by local demonstrations of roof thatching, the uses of medicinal plants, and basket-weaving. You can tuck into a Bribrí-style lunch and learn the chocolate-making process (eating some samples for dessert). An optional hike in the highlands is also possible. It's a rewarding experience, well worth the time and effort to get there.

Alternatively, you can do day trips (US$59) to the **territory of the Kèköldi** (a tiny group ethnically related to the Bribrí), where you'll go on a 2½-hour nature-spotting hike to the village and enjoy a traditional lunch cooked over a log fire by members of the community.

Visiting these territories independently is not recommended. Not only are many spots difficult to reach but in most cases villages do not have the infrastructure to accommodate streams of tourists. During your visit, bear in mind that these are people's private homes and work spaces, not tourist attractions.

Terraventuras (p171) in Puerto Viejo runs day tours to Bribrí (US$80 per person) that include a meeting with an Awa (a Bribrí doctor), who will demonstrate medicinal customs and do a purification ceremony. Willie's Tours (p163) in Cahuita does day, one-night and two-night trips to Yorkín and a day trip to the Kèköldi territory.

There is an extensive wine list, but you can't go wrong with the well-chosen and relatively inexpensive house wines.

ℹ Getting There & Away

Buses heading from Puerto Viejo to Manzanillo will stop at Playa Cocles, Playa Chiquita or Punta Uva on request. Alternatively, it's an easy and pleasant 30- to 40-minute slow cycle from Puerto Viejo to Punta Uva (bike hire is roughly US$10 per day). Don't cycle without strong bike lights after dark, as these roads are not lit.

Manzanillo

POP 3250

The chilled-out village of Manzanillo has long been off the beaten track, even after the paved road arrived in 2003. This little town is still a vibrant outpost of Afro-Caribbean culture and has also remained pristine, thanks to the 1985 establishment of the Refugio Nacional de Vida Silvestre Gandoca-Manzanillo, which includes the village and imposes strict regulations on regional development.

Activities are of a simple nature, *in* nature: hiking, snorkeling and kayaking reign supreme. As elsewhere, ask about riptides before heading out.

🏃 Activities

Bad Barts SNORKELING

(☑8650-2860, 2759-9012; www.badbartsmanzanillo.com; per hour bike/snorkel/kayak rental US$2/4/6; ⊗8am-5pm Tue-Sun) Near the bus stop in Manzanillo, this outfit rents snorkel and scuba gear, kayaks, boogie boards and bicycles. Hours can vary; call ahead.

🛏 Sleeping

Cabinas Manzanillo CABINA $

(☑2759-9033, 8327-3291; s/d US$35/40; P🗨) Run by the ever-helpful Sandra Castillo and Pablo Bustamante, these eight *cabinas* at Manzanillo's western edge are so clean you could eat off the tile floors. The cheery rooms have big beds, industrial-strength ceiling fans, TVs, safes and spacious bathrooms with hot water. There's also a shared kitchen. From Maxi's Restaurant, travel 300m west toward Punta Uva, then make a left onto the signposted dirt road.

Sumaqtikaq Cabins GUESTHOUSE $$

(☑2759-9146, 2261-8186, 8860-9331; www.cabinas-sumaqtikaq.com; incl breakfast cabins for 2-3

people US$60, 5 people US$80, houses for 11 people US$300; P🗨) The best option for groups, this guesthouse with indigenous art and a pretty garden has two double rooms, a room sleeping five and a two-story house sleeping 11. Facilities include shared kitchen, barbecue and laundry service. Some rooms have refrigerators, mosquito nets and hammocks. Tours to the nearby Gandoca-Manzanillo wildlife refuge (p186) can be arranged here. There's a four-night minimum stay.

Almonds & Corals Lodge BUNGALOW $$$

(☑2759-9031, 2271-3000, in USA 1-888-373-9042; www.almondsandcorals.com; ste incl breakfast US$145-245, additional person from US$20; P@🗨🛢) 🏄 Buried in the jungle, this beachfront spot is popular with honeymooners. Its 24 green palm-roofed bungalows, with netted walls, in-room safes, mini fridges and rain showers, are connected by wooden boardwalks. Accommodation features four-poster beds, Jacuzzis, and patios with hammocks from which to enjoy nature's serenade. A breakfast buffet is included; other meals can be purchased at the restaurant.

Wi-fi is available in the lobby only.

Congo Bongo BUNGALOW $$$

(☑2759-9016; www.congo-bongo.com; bungalows US$132-195, extra person US$15; P🗨) About 1km outside Manzanillo towards Punta Uva, these seven charming cottages surrounded by dense forest (formerly a cacao plantation) offer fully equipped kitchens and plenty of living space, including open-air terraces and strategically placed hammocks that are perfect for wildlife-watching. A network of trails leads through the 6 hectares of grounds to the beautiful beach. There's a two-night minimum stay.

🍴 Eating

Maxi's Restaurant CARIBBEAN $$

(☑2759-9086; mains US$7-14, lobster US$45-70; ⊗noon-10pm; 🗨🍴) Manzanillo's most famous restaurant draws a tourist crowd with large platters of grilled seafood, *pargo rojo* (whole red snapper), *ceviche*, pork and rice, steak, and pricey Caribbean-style lobster. Service can be slow, but the open-air upstairs dining area is a wonderful seaside setting for a meal and a beer with views of the beach and the street below.

It's at the end of the road into town (where buses arrive).

Cool & Calm Cafe
CARIBBEAN $$$

(mains US$12-26; ⏰11am-9pm Wed-Mon) Directly across from Manzanillo's western beachfront, this front-porch eatery plies visitors with fine Caribbean cooking – from snapper to shrimp to chicken to lobster – with a few extras like guacamole, tacos and veggie curry thrown in for good measure. Owner Andy offers Caribbean cooking classes and a 'reef-to-plate' tour where, in certain seasons, you can dive for your own lobster or fish.

Andy catches the lobster and prepares his outrageous lobster *caribeño* daily.

ℹ Getting There & Away

Buses to Puerto Limón via Puerto Viejo depart from Manzanillo at 5:30am, 6am, 10:30am, 3pm and 6pm (to Puerto Limón roughly US$5, 2½ hours; to Puerto Viejo US$1.50, 30 minutes). Buses from Puerto Limón to Manzanillo (via Puerto Viejo) depart at 5am, 7am, 8:30am, 10:30am, 12:45pm and 5:15pm.

Autotransportes Mepe also runs one direct bus daily between Manzanillo and San José (about US$13, five hours), leaving Manzanillo at 7am.

Refugio Nacional de Vida Silvestre Gandoca-Manzanillo

This little-explored **refuge** (Regama; 📞2759-9100; US$6; ⏰8am-4pm) protects nearly 70% of the southern Caribbean coast, extending from Manzanillo all the way to the Panamanian border. It encompasses 50 sq km of land plus 44 sq km of marine environment. The peaceful, pristine stretch of sandy white beach – one of the area's main attractions and the center of village life in Manzanillo – stretches from Punta Uva in the west to Punta Mona in the east. Offshore, a 5-sq-km coral reef is a teeming habitat for lobsters, sea fans and long-spined urchins.

🏃 Activities

Hiking

A coastal trail heads 5.5km east out of Manzanillo to **Punta Mona**. The first part of this path, which leads from Manzanillo to Tom Bay (about a 40-minute walk), is well trammeled and clearly marked and doesn't require a guide. Once you pass Tom Bay, however, the path gets murky and it's easy to get lost, so ask about conditions before you set out, or hire a local guide. It's a rewarding walk with amazing scenery, as well as excel-

lent (and safe) swimming and snorkeling at the end.

Another, more difficult, 9km trail leaves from just west of Manzanillo and skirts the southern edges of the Pantano Punta Mona, continuing to the small community of **Gandoca**. This trail is not commonly walked, as most people access Punta Mona and Gandoca by boat or from the park entrance at the northern edge of the refuge, which is located on the road to Sixaola. If you want to try to hike this, be sure to hire a guide.

A third trail in the reserve takes visitors through thick forest. Parts of this trail were previously dangerous or difficult to access, but now some sections are covered with a boardwalk made of wood and plastic. Again, however, it's best to use a local guide.

Snorkeling & Diving

The undersea portion of the park cradles one of the two accessible living coral reefs in the country. Comprising five types of coral, the reefs begin in about 1m of water and extend 5km offshore to a barrier reef that local fishers have long relied on and researchers have only recently discovered. This colorful undersea world is home to some 400 species of fish and crustaceans. **Punta Mona** is a popular destination for snorkeling, though it's a trek, so you may wish to hire a boat. Otherwise, you can snorkel offshore at **Manzanillo** at the eastern end of the beach; the riptide can be dangerous here, so inquire about conditions before setting out. Also check out the Coral Reef Information Center at Bad Barts (p185) in Manzanillo.

Conditions vary widely, and visibility can be adversely affected by weather changes.

Kayaking

You can explore some of the area's waterways by kayak; rental is available at Bad Barts (p185). Paddle out to the reef, and on clear days you'll be able to gaze right into the water and see marine life. If you have kids in tow, head along the coastline west or east of Manzanillo village for shorter paddles.

Dolphin-Watching

In 1997 a group of local guides in Manzanillo identified tucuxi dolphins, a little-known species previously not found in Costa Rica, and began to observe their interactions with bottlenose dolphins. A third species – the Atlantic spotted dolphin – is also common in this area. This unprecedented activity has attracted the attention of marine biologists and conservationists, who are following these animals with great interest.

For dolphin-watching trips in the reserve (from US$50 for three hours), contact Bad Barts (p185). Note that in Costa Rica it is illegal to swim with dolphins; be sure to keep a distance from the animals and refrain from touching or bothering them.

Turtle-Watching

Marine turtles – especially leatherback but also green, hawksbill and loggerhead – nest on the beaches between Punta Mona and the Río Sixaola. Leatherbacks nest from March to July, with a peak in April and May. Local conservation efforts are under way to protect these nesting grounds, as the growth of the area's human population has led to increased theft of turtle eggs.

During turtle season, no flashlights, fires or camping are allowed on the beach. All tourists must be accompanied by a local guide to minimize disturbance of the nesting turtles.

👉 Tours

You could explore the refuge on your own, but without a guide you'll likely miss out on the incredible diversity of medicinal plants, exotic birds and earthbound animals. Most guides charge from US$35 per person per trek, depending on the size of the group. Ask at Maxi's (p185) in Manzanillo.

Recommended local guides include **Florentino Grenald** (☑ 8841-2732; 4hr tours per person from US$40), who used to serve as the reserve's administrator, **Omar** (☑ 8932-0030; ⊗ 4-5hr hikes per person US$40) and **Abel Bustamante** (☑ 2759-9043).

🛏️ Sleeping & Eating

Pack some snacks for a day hike, or call ahead to Punta Mona to make reservations for lunch there. The exotic garden contains plants from all over the world, making for some truly delicious organic salads. After a hike, grab a fruit smoothie and some tasty Caribbean food at Cool & Calm Café in Manzanillo, just a short walk north of the refuge entrance.

⭐ **Punta Mona**   CABINA **$$**
(www.puntamona.org; cabinas per person incl 3 organic meals US$90; @) 🚶 Accessible via a two-hour trek or a 15-minute boat ride, this 35-hectare organic farm and retreat 5km southeast of Manzanillo is a thriving experiment in permaculture design and sus-

tainable living. More than 200 varieties of fruit and nut trees and hundreds of edible greens, roots, veggies and medicinal plants grow here. Vegetarian meals are included in the rate.

At the time of research Punta Mona was one of the largest sources of useful plants in the world, and Stephen Brooks, who set the place up, was also establishing the world's first eco-versity here. He continues to host yoga retreats and a jungle camp. To arrange accommodation and transportation, email contact@puntamona.org ahead of your visit. Day trips with lunch are also possible in this paradise setting; boat taxis cost roughly US$50.

Nature Observatorio   CAMPGROUND **$$$**
(☑ 8628-2663; www.natureobservatorio.com; adult/child US$160/100) 🚶 Located 80ft up in a tree within the Gandoca-Manzanillo wildlife refuge, this observation deck and tree house allows guests to experience life in the canopy of an old-growth forest. The open-air, two-story accommodation features hammocks and comfy beds from which monkeys, kinkajous and toucans are regularly spotted. To reach the platform, guests must climb the tree (harnesses provided).

The owner, an ardent conservationist, collects his customers in Manzanillo at 1pm each day and leads them on a 45-minute hike to the tree, which he helps them to scale on a rope ladder. Dinner and breakfast are delivered up the tree in a basket. The entire deck is only 60 sq meters and includes just two units sleeping two people each.

ℹ️ Information

An excellent photo book on the area, with commentary in Spanish and English, is *Refugio Nacional de Vida Silvestre Gandoca-Manzanillo* by Juan José Pucci, available locally and online.

Minae (☑ 2755-0302, 2759-9100; ⊗ 8am-4pm Fri & Sat) is located in the green wooden house as you enter Manzanillo; when it's open it generally has trail maps of the refuge.

ℹ️ Getting There & Away

Buses to Manzanillo drop off in front of Maxi's Restaurant (p185). From there it's about 1km to the refuge entrance. A bridge allows guests to enter the park without having to wade through the water at high tide. Another good option for accessing different areas of the park is to hire a boat. **José** (☑ 5006-3361) operates a good local water taxi.

GETTING TO PANAMA

Welcome to Costa Rica's most entertaining border crossing! An old railroad bridge spans the churning waters of the Río Sixaola, connecting Costa Rica with Panama amid a sea of agricultural plantations. Oversize buses and trucks used to ply this route – making for a surreal scene whenever one of them came clattering along the wood planks, forcing pedestrians to scatter to the edges. Today there's a parallel bridge for motor-vehicle traffic, but pedestrians still get the fun of walking across the old bridge.

From here, most travelers make for Bocas del Toro, a picturesque archipelago of jungle islands that's home to lovely beaches and endangered red frogs. It's easily accessible by regular water taxi from the docks at Almirante.

The border is open 7am to 5pm (8am to 6pm in Guabito, Panama, which is an hour ahead of Costa Rica), though one or both sides may close for lunch at around 1pm. At the entrance to the bridge, on the right-hand side, pay the US$8 Costa Rican departure tax and get your exit stamp at the Costa Rican immigration office. It's best to bring cash in case the electronic machine is not working. Once you're over the bridge, stop at Panamanian immigration to get your passport stamped and pay the US$4 entry tax. Note that in Panama you will be required to show proof of onward travel out of Panama, or another central American country, to your home country, such as a copy of your plane ticket home. To cross, you'll need a passport valid for more than six months; sometimes proof of at least US$500 in your bank account is also required, although it's not often requested at the Sixaola border. Be prepared with a copy of a recent bank statement or ATM receipt. A copy of your passport is always a good idea, too. Personal cars (not rentals) can cross here. Be aware that sometimes lines here can be long; plan your onward travel accordingly.

Guabito has no hotels or banks, but in a pinch you can exchange colones at the market across the street. From the border, half-hourly buses (about US$2, one hour) run to Terminal Piquera in Changuinola, where you can transfer to one of the frequent buses to Almirante (roughly US$2, 45 minutes) for the water taxi. Alternatively, from Guabito you can take a collective taxi (per person around US$10, one hour) straight to Almirante. From this point, hourly water taxis (per person US$6, 25 minutes) make the trip to Bocas del Toro between 6:30am and 6pm.

For a more streamlined, if slightly more expensive, trip to Bocas del Toro, take one of the daily shuttles from Cahuita or Puerto Viejo de Talamanca (it's US$33 with Caribe Shuttle, p172).

Sixaola

POP 3400

This is the end of the road – literally. Bumpy tarmac leads to an old railroad bridge over the Río Sixaola that serves as the border crossing into Panama. Like most border towns, Sixaola is hardly scenic: it's an extravaganza of dingy houses and roadside stalls selling rubber boots.

There's no good reason to stay in Sixaola, but if you get stuck, head for safe, clean **Cabinas Sanchez** (☑2754-2126; d/tr US$20/30; ✳🖂).

ⓘ Getting There & Away

The bus station is just north of the border crossing, one block east of the main drag.

Buses to San José (about US$14, six hours) run hourly from 6am to 1pm, and at 3pm, 4pm and 7pm, with a change in Puerto Limón (about US$7, three hours from Sixaola). All buses pass Bribrí and Cahuita.

There are also regular buses to Puerto Viejo (about US$3, one hour), running hourly between 6am and 7pm Monday to Saturday, every two hours on Sunday.

Northwestern Costa Rica

Best Places to Eat

➡ Café Caburé (p205)

➡ Café Liberia (p223)

➡ Taco Taco (p204)

➡ Region 5 (p223)

➡ Orchid Coffee (p204)

Best Places to Stay

➡ Casitas Tenorio B&B (p215)

➡ Capulín Cabins & Farm (p201)

➡ Celeste Mountain Lodge (p215)

➡ Hotel Belmar (p204)

➡ Casa Batsu (p201)

➡ Río Perdido (p219)

Why Go?

What did you come to Costa Rica for? To lounge on pristine beaches and ride glorious waves? To hike up volcanoes and soak in geothermal springs? To spy on birds and monkeys and get lost among ancient trees? The northwestern corner of Costa Rica packs in all this and more. Unlike any other part of the country, Guanacaste – in the far northwest – is a wide, flat expanse of grasslands and dry tropical forest, where savanna vistas are broken only by windblown trees. Further east, the Cordillera de Guanacaste rises majestically out of the plains in a line of sputtering, steaming volcanic peaks that beg exploration. Further south, higher altitudes create misty, mystical cloud forests, teeming with life. What did you come to Costa Rica for? Here it is...

When to Go

➡ Guanacaste is Costa Rica's driest province, getting very little rain from November to April, when the winds bless (and blast) Bahía Salinas.

➡ By contrast, the 'green' season is very, very green in the cloud forest.

➡ From May to November there are fewer tourists, and prices for accommodations are reduced.

➡ Humpback whales migrate up the coast in September and October, putting on a spectacular and splashy show.

➡ Other seasonal events to watch out for are the blooming of the yellow cortezas in March and the *fiestas Guanacastecas* that occur throughout the year.

Northwestern Costa Rica Highlights

❶ Monteverde (p191) Spotting the resplendent quetzal through the mist.

❷ Cloud Forest Canopy Tours (p198) Zipping and swinging through the canopy.

❸ Parque Nacional Palo Verde (p220) Checking off your bird list at Costa Rica's largest wetland sanctuary.

❹ Parque Nacional Volcán Tenorio (p216) Hiking along the Río Celeste and marveling at her cerulean-blue waters.

❺ Llanos de Cortés (p233) Cooling off with a refreshing waterfall shower and bath.

❻ Parque Nacional Rincón de la Vieja (p227) Trekking the

circuit of waterfalls, pools and volcanic vents.

❼ Playa Naranjo (p231) Surfing the legendary beach break at Witch's Rock.

❽ Bahía Salinas (p236) Satisfying your need for speed off the windiest beaches in Central America.

Parks & Reserves

Northwestern Costa Rica has a wealth of parks and reserves, from little-visited national parks to the highlight on many visitors' itineraries, Monteverde Cloud Forest.

Parque Nacional Palo Verde (p220) Stay at the research station and take a guided tour to see some of the 300-plus bird species recorded in this rich wetland.

Parque Nacional Rincón de la Vieja (p227) Peaceful, muddy isolation can be found just outside of Liberia, where bubbling thermal activity abounds.

Refugio Nacional de Vida Silvestre Bahía Junquillal (p233) A small and peaceful protected site, this refuge has a beach backed by mangrove swamp and tropical dry forest.

Reserva Biológica Bosque Nuboso Monteverde (p210) Costa Rica's most famous cloud forest, Monteverde receives a steady stream of visitors but hasn't lost its magic.

Reserva Biológica Lomas de Barbudal (p237) If you're here in March, you might be lucky enough to catch the yellow blooms of the corteza amarilla tree in this tropical dry forest reserve.

Reserva Santa Elena (p212) With fewer crowds and a higher elevation than neighboring Monteverde, this is a mistier and more mysterious place to experience the cloud forest.

Sector Santa Rosa (p230) Access legendary surf, hike through the largest stand of tropical dry forest in Central America and visit a historical battle site.

Sector Murciélago (p231) Brave the notorious roads to explore deserted beaches, or catch a boat to surf the country's most celebrated break.

ⓘ Getting There & Away

More and more visitors are flying directly into Liberia's Aeropuerto Internacional Daniel Oduber Quirós (p226), a convenient international airport that makes for quick escapes to both northwestern Costa Rica and the beaches of the Península de Nicoya. Liberia is also a major transportation center for buses traveling the Interamericana, from the border with Nicaragua to San José. Regular buses also connect the Península de Nicoya to hubs such as Santa Cruz and Nicoya and coastal points beyond.

This is a heavily touristed region, and entrepreneurs have picked up on the need for more transportation options. If you're looking for a ride that's cheaper than a rented car and more comfortable (and faster) than a public bus, you'll probably be able to find a shuttle bus. Several companies ply the most popular routes.

If you do opt to rent, consider a 4WD vehicle (or at least one with a high carriage) during the rainy season.

MONTEVERDE & AROUND

Spread out on the slopes of the Cordillera de Tilarán, this area is a sprawling chain of villages, farms and nature reserves. The biggest population center – the village of Santa Elena – runs seamlessly uphill into next-door neighbor Cerro Plano and then tiny Monteverde, which borders its namesake reserve.

The Reserva Biológica Bosque Nuboso Monteverde (p210; Monteverde Cloud Forest Reserve) is the most famous one, but there are public and private properties of all shapes and sizes – from tiny family *fincas* (farms) to the vast Bosque Eterno de los Niños (p193; Children's Eternal Rainforest) – that blanket this whole area in luscious green. As a result, there are trails to hike, birds to spot, waterfalls to swim and adventures to be had at every turn.

Monteverde & Santa Elena

POP 6750

Strung between two lovingly preserved cloud forests, this slim corridor of civilization consists of the Tico village of Santa Elena and the Quaker settlement of Monteverde, each with an eponymous cloud forest reserve. The cloud forests are premier destinations for everyone from budget backpackers to well-heeled retirees.

On a good day, the Monteverde area is a place where you can be inspired about the possibility of a world in which organic farming and alternative energy sources are the norm; on a bad day, it can feel like Disneyland in Birkenstocks. Take heart in the fact that the local community continues to fight the good fight to maintain the fragile balance between nature and commerce.

⊙ Sights

The sights in Monteverde and Santa Elena are mostly geared to bringing the wildlife a little closer, whether it's bats, butterflies, frog, snakes or flowers. These stops can be

Monteverde & Santa Elena

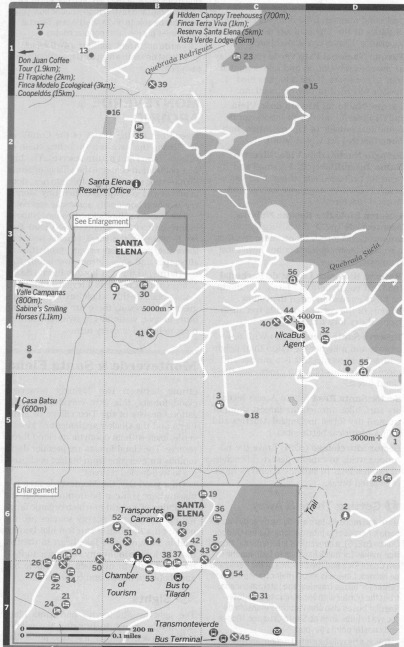

Hidden Canopy Treehouses (700m);
Finca Terra Viva (1km);
Reserva Santa Elena (5km);
Vista Verde Lodge (6km)

Quebrada Rodríguez

17

13

Don Juan Coffee
Tour (1.9km);
El Trapiche (2km);
Finca Modelo Ecological (3km);
Coopeldós (15km)

23

39

15

16

35

Santa Elena
Reserve Office

See Enlargement

SANTA
ELENA

Quebrada Sucia

56

Valle Campanas
(800m);
Sabine's Smiling
Horses (1.1km)

7

30

5000m

44

40   4000m

NicaBus
Agent

32

41

10   55

8

3

18

3000m

1

28

Enlargement

19

SANTA
ELENA

Transportes
Carranza

52

36

49

51

48

4

42

5

46   20

38 37

43

26

50

54

27

34

Chamber
of
Tourism

53

Bus to
Tilarán

31

22

24   21

Trail

2

200 m

0.1 miles

Transmonteverde
Bus Terminal

45

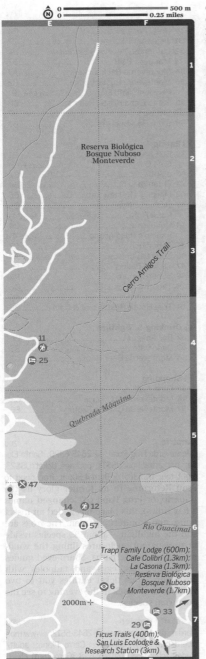

entertaining and educational, especially for children, but it's even more rewarding when you see these creatures in the wild. And you're in the wild now, so go out there and see it.

San Luis Ecolodge & Research Station
NATURE RESERVE

(www.ecolodgesanluis.com; San Luis) Formerly a tropical biology research station, this drop-dead gorgeous facility is Monteverde's best-kept secret. Administered by the University of Georgia, it integrates academia with high-quality ecotourism and education. The 62-hectare campus is set on a cinematic jade plateau with cloud forested mountains jackknifing on three sides and keyhole sea views to the west. Travelers can soak up this stunning natural beauty when they stay at the Ecolodge San Luis (p202).

Adjoining the southern reach of the Monteverde reserve (p210), much of the campus overlooks the boiling waters of the Río San Luis. Its average elevation of 1100m makes it a tad lower and warmer than Monteverde; birdwatchers have recorded some 230 species attracted by the slightly nicer weather. There's a working farm with tropical fruit orchards and a coffee harvest from November to March, and a number of trails into primary and secondary forest.

From the main road between Santa Elena and Monteverde, turn south at the Hotel Fonda Vela (p203) and head down the mountain for three steep kilometers. Don't miss the distant view of the San Luis waterfalls as you descend. Look for a signed turnoff to the left. With advance warning, the lodge can also help with transportation.

Bosque Eterno de los Niños
NATURE RESERVE

(Children's Eternal Rainforest, BEN; ☑ 2645-5305; www.acmcr.org; adult/child US$12/free, guided night hike US$22/14, transportation per person US$4; ⊙ 7:30am-5:30pm, night hike 5:30pm; ⊕)
✔ What became of the 1980s efforts of a group of Swedish schoolchildren to save the rainforest? Only this enormous 220 sq km reserve – the largest private reserve in the country. It's mostly inaccessible to tourists, with the exception of the well-marked 3.5km Sendero Bajo del Tigre (p198), which is actually a series of shorter trails. Make reservations in advance for the popular two-hour night hikes. At the entrance there's an education center for children and a fabulous vista over the reserve.

The Estación Biológica San Gerardo, reachable by a rather gnarly 2½-hour trail

NORTHWESTERN COSTA RICA MONTEVERDE & SANTA ELENA

Monteverde & Santa Elena

from Reserva Santa Elena (p212), is managed by BEN and has dorm beds for researchers and students, but you may be able to stay overnight with prior arrangements.

Monteverde Friends School CULTURAL CENTRE (www.mfschool.org; Monteverde; per person US$15; ⊙tours 8am Tue & Fri; ⊛) Spending time at this schoolhouse is a great way for children to learn about and interact with the local culture. With advance reservation, visitors can sit in on morning assembly and tour the grounds. Kids are even invited to attend a class (and recess!) with an English-speaking buddy.

Volunteers who can make a long-term commitment are invited to work with local students, providing tutoring, art projects, music lessons, technology assistance or other individualized attention.

Ranario ZOO
(Monteverde Frog Pond; ☑2645-6320; Santa Elena; per attraction US$14, package ticket US$23, night tour US$30; ⊙9am-4:30pm, frog pond to 8pm) Returning to its former glory as the Ranario, or Frog Pond (it's changed names a few times), this place has added an insect house and a butterfly garden. The frogs are still the highlight – about 25 species reside in transparent enclosures lining the winding indoor jungle paths. Sharp-eyed guides point out frogs, eggs and tadpoles with flashlights. Your ticket entitles you to two visits, so come back in the evening to see the nocturnal species.

Butterfly Garden ZOO
(Jardín de Mariposas; ☑2645-5512; www.monteverdebutterflygarden.com; Cerro Plano; adult/student/child US$15/10/5; ⊙8:30am-4pm) Head

here for everything you ever wanted to know about butterflies. There are four gardens representing different habitats; they're home to more than 40 species. Up-close observation cases allow you to witness the butterflies as they emerge from the chrysalis (if your timing is right). Other exhibits feature the industrious leafcutter ant and the ruthless tarantula hawk (actually a wasp that eats tarantulas) and lots of scorpions. Kids love this place, and knowledgeable naturalist guides truly enhance the experience.

🏃 Activities

SkyTram   CABLE CAR

(☑2479-4100, toll free USA 1-804-GOTOSKY; www.skyadventures.travel; Santa Elena; adult/student/child US$46/38/32; ⊙8am-3pm) Owned by SkyTrek (p199), SkyTram is a wheelchair-accessible gondola that floats gently over the cloud forest. On a clear day you can see from the volcanoes in the east to the Pacific in the west. Packages are available if you're also interested in the SkyTrek (canopy tour) and SkyWalk (hanging bridges).

Revive Healing Arts   MASSAGE

(☑8372-2002; www.revivehealingarts.com; Monteverde; treatments from US$60; ⊙by appointment) Owner Karen Gordon's signature offering, the Mountain Massage, is custom designed to soothe your aching muscles, no matter what adventures you've been on. She also offers Reiki, craniosacral therapy and personalized retreat programs.

Curi-Cancha Reserve   HIKING, BIRDWATCHING

(☑2645-6915, 8356-1431; www.curi-cancha.com; US$15, night tour US$18, natural history tour US$35, bird tour US$75; ⊙7am-3:30pm, guided hike 7:30am & 1:30pm) Bordering Monteverde but without the crowds, this lovely private reserve on the banks of the Río Cuecha is popular among birders. There are about 10km of well-marked trails, a hummingbird garden and a view of the continental divide. Make reservations for the guided hikes, including the early-morning bird walks and specialized three-hour natural history walks.

LOCAL KNOWLEDGE

THE TALE OF THE GOLDEN TOAD

Once upon a time in the cloud forests of Monteverde, there lived the *Bufo periglenes* (golden toad), also known as the *sapo dorado*. Because this bright orange, exotic little toad was often seen scrambling amid the Monteverde leaf litter – the only place in the world where it appeared – it became something of a Monteverde mascot. Sadly, the golden toad has not been seen since 1989 and is now believed to be extinct.

In the late 1980s, unexplained rapid declines in frog and toad populations all over the world spurred an international conference of herpetologists to address these alarming developments. Amphibians, once common, were becoming rare or had already disappeared, and the scientists were unable to agree upon a reason for the sudden demise of so many species in so many different habitats.

Several factors may be to blame for these declines, including the fact that amphibians breathe both with primitive lungs and through their perpetually moist skin, which makes them susceptible to airborne toxins. Their skin also provides little protection against UV light, which studies have shown can result in higher mortality rates to amphibian embryos and damaged DNA that in turn causes deformities. Pesticides also have been proven to cause deformities and hermaphroditism. And then there's the global issue of habitat loss. If all that didn't tell a bleak enough story, scientists have since discovered that the worldwide spread of chytridiomycosis disease (caused by the fungus *Batrachochytrium dendrobatidis*, in case you were wondering) has decimated amphibian populations everywhere.

According to the Global Amphibian Assessment, 30% of New World amphibians (1187 species) are currently threatened with extinction. In response to this dire statistic, an international coalition of zoos and wildlife conservation organizations have jointly established **Amphibian Ark** (www.amphibianark.org), an attempt to 'bank' as many species as possible in the event of further die-offs. We may never know what happened to the golden toad, but as one of the first warning signs that the ecosystem is off balance, its mysterious disappearance might have given a chance for survival – and a happy never-ending? – to other amphibian species.

Life in the Cloud Forest

To explore the Monteverde cloud forest is to arrive at the pinnacle of Costa Rica's continental divide. A blast of swirling, misty euphoria surrounds you, where lichen-draped trees soar, exotic birds gossip, and orchids and bromeliads bloom. Life is abundant, throbbing and palpable.

Two Forests, Two Ecosystems

Warm, humid trade winds from the Caribbean sweep up forested slopes to the Reserva Biológica Bosque Nuboso Monteverde, where they cool and condense into clouds that congregate over the nearby Reserva Santa Elena. The two forests are each rich in diversity and oxygen, but the slight temperature and topographical differences mean that each has its own unique ecosystem.

Cloud Flora

The most abundant life form in the cloud forest, epiphytes seem to take over the trees they are growing on, yet they are not parasites and they do not harm their hosts. These clever plants get their nutrients from the floating mist, which explains their exposed roots. Look closely, and you'll see that one tree might be covered in dozens of epiphytes. This is one of the major reasons that cloud forests can claim such biodiversity: in Monteverde it's estimated that epiphytes represent almost 30% of the flora species.

The biggest family of epiphytes is the orchids, with nearly 500 species (the greatest diversity of orchids on the planet). Most amazingly, this figure includes some 34 endemic species – those that do not exist anywhere else.

1. Walking in the Reserva Biológica Bosque Nuboso Monteverde
2. Rufous-tailed hummingbird
3. Oerstedella endressii orchid

Cloud Birds

Playing an important role in the pollination of orchids and other blooming plants, hummingbirds are among the most visible of the cloud-forest creatures. Their unique ability to fly in place, backwards and upside down allows them to drink on the fly, as it were. There are some 30 species buzzing around; check them out at Cafe Colibri, just outside the Monteverde reserve.

You'll hear the three-wattled bellbird long before you see it, as the male's distinctive song is supposedly one of the loudest bird calls on earth. As you might guess, the male has three long wattles hanging from its beak.

The most famous cloud-forest resident is the resplendent quetzal. This exotic beauty lives up to its name, and males have long plumes of jade green and electric blue. Quetzals move seasonally between elevations, but if you're in the right place at the right time, a good bird guide should be able to find one.

Quaker Connection

The Quakers were the original conservationists here. In the early 1950s, about a dozen pacifist farming families decided to leave the US so that they would not be drafted to fight in the Korean War. They settled in this remote perch and called it Monteverde (literally, 'Green Mountain'). They have been actively involved in protecting this unique environment ever since. *Walking with Wolf*, by Kay Chornook, tells the story of one of these pioneers, Wolf Guindon, who helped establish the Cloud Forest Preserve.

Cerro Amigos
HIKING

Take a hike up to the highest peak in the area (1842m) for good views of the surrounding rainforest and, on a clear day, Volcán Arenal, 20km away to the northeast. Behind Hotel Belmar (p204) in Cerro Plano, take the dirt road going downhill, then the next left. The trail ascends roughly 300m in 3km.

Note that this trail does not connect to the trails in the Monteverde reserve (p210).

Reserva Bajo del Tigre
HIKING

(✆ 2645-5200; www.acmcr.org/contenido/esta ciones-y-senderos/reserva-bajo-del-tigre; adult/ student/child US$13/11/8, night hike adult/student/ child/transportation US$23/20/14/4; ⏰ 8am-5pm, night hike 5:30pm; ⊕) This section of the Bosque Eterno de los Niños (p193) is the only bit that's really accessible to the public. It's a sweet slice of forest with a small children's center, 3.3km of walking trails and a lookout platform with views to the gulf.

🏊 Courses

Monteverde Institute
LANGUAGE

(✆ 2645-5053; www.monteverde-institute.org; Monteverde; week-long courses US$390, homestay incl meals per day US$23) This nonprofit educational institute in Monteverde offers interdisciplinary courses in Spanish, as well as more specialized programs in tropical ecology, conservation and ecotourism, among other topics. Courses are occasionally open to the public, as are volunteer opportunities in education and reforestation.

Centro Panamericano de Idiomas
LANGUAGE

(CPI; ✆ 2265-6306; www.cpi-edu.com; Cerro Plano; week-long classes US$460; ⏰ 8am-5pm) Specializes in Spanish language education, with courses geared toward families, teenagers, medical professionals and retirees. For fun: optional dance and cooking classes are included in tuition fees.

👉 Tours

There's not a lot of diversity when it comes to tours in the Monteverde/Santa Elena region. Most reserves offer guided hikes, morning bird walks and spooky night hikes. Other than that, you'll find canopy tours and coffee tours – both provide a good energy boost! Keep in mind that locals work on a commission-based system, so take all unsolicited advice with a degree of skepticism.

Horseback Riding

Do like the Ticos do and explore the countryside from the saddle of a horse. You don't have to be an expert rider; most companies (and horses) are used to beginners. There are normally several options for routes and duration, ranging from two hours to full days.

Horse Trek Monteverde
HORSE RIDING

(✆ 8379-9827; www.horsetrekmonteverde.com; Rte 606, Santa Elena; per person US$49-85; ⏰ 7am-7pm Mon-Fri, 10am-6pm Sat-Sun) Owner and guide Marvin Anchia is a Santa Elena native, a professional horse trainer and an amateur naturalist who offers an excellent, intimate horseback riding experience. Choose between two-hour rides through coffee plantations, scenic half-day rides in the cloud forest and all-day cowboy experiences. The horses are well cared for, well trained and a joy to ride. Located just west of downtown Santa Elena.

Sabine's Smiling Horses
HORSEBACK RIDING

(✆ 2645-6894, 8385-2424; www.horseback-riding -tour.com; 2hr/3hr/all-day ride per person US$45/ 65/105; ⏰ tours 9am, 1pm & 3pm) Conversant in four languages (in addition to equine), Sabine will make sure you're comfortable on your horse, whether you're a novice rider or an experienced cowboy. Her long-standing operation offers a variety of treks including a popular waterfall tour (three hours) and a magical full moon tour (monthly). And yes, the horses really do smile.

Caballeriza El Rodeo
HORSEBACK RIDING

(✆ 2645-6306, 2645-5764; elrodeo02@gmail.com; Santa Elena; per person US$40-60) Based at a local *finca*, this outfit offers tours on private trails through rainforest, coffee plantations and grasslands, with plenty of pauses to spot wildlife and admire the fantastic landscapes. The specialty is a sunset tour to a spot overlooking the Golfo de Nicoya. *¡Que hermoso!*

Canopy Tours

Wonder where the whole canopy tour craze was born? Santa Elena is the site of Costa Rica's first ziplines, today eclipsed in adrenaline by the nearly 100 imitators who have followed, some of which are right here in town. You won't be spotting any quetzals or coatis as you whoosh your way over the canopy, but if you came to Costa Rica to fly, this is the absolute best place to do it. If you want to explore the treetops without the adrenaline rush, several outfits also have systems of hanging bridges. Transportation from your lodging is included in prices.

Finca Modelo Ecologica
ADVENTURE

(✆ 2645-5581; www.familiabrenestours.com; La Cruz; treetop/canyoning/combo US$40/70/100; ⏰ treetop 8am-4pm, canyoning 8am, 11am & 2pm)

The Brenes family *finca* offers a number of unique and thrilling diversions. Their masterpiece is the two-hour canyoning tour, which descends six glorious waterfalls, the highest of which is 40m. No experience necessary, just an adventurous spirit. The treetop tour involves climbing a 40m ficus tree, using ropes and rappels to go up and down.

The *finca* is located 2km north of Santa Elena in the village of La Cruz; transportation from your hotel is included in the price.

Original Canopy Tour   ADVENTURE

(☑2645-5243; www.theoriginalcanopy.com; adult/student/child US$45/35/25; ⏰Tours 7:30am, 10:30am & 2:30pm) The storied zipline tour that started the trend. With 15 cables, a Tarzan swing and a rappel through the center of an old fig tree, it's a lot of fun. Your adrenaline rush may not be as big as at some of the other canopy tours, but you'll enjoy smaller groups and more emphasis on the natural surroundings. They combine tours (adding coffee tours or horse rides), if you need a caffeine jolt or equestrian action afterwards. Original Canopy is located way uphill near the Cloud Forest Lodge (p203), 2km off the main Santa Elena–Monteverde Rd.

Selvatura   ADVENTURE

(☑2645-5929; www.selvatura.com; canopy tour US$50, walkways US$30, each exhibit US$5-15; ⏰7:30am-4pm) One of the bigger games in town, Selvatura has 3km of cables, 18 platforms and a Tarzan swing over a stretch of incredibly beautiful primary cloud forest. In addition to the cables, it has 3km of 'Treetops Walkways' and extras including a hummingbird garden, a butterfly garden and an amphibian and reptile exhibition.

Selvatura is 6km north of Santa Elena, near the reserve. There's a booking office in town near the church.

100% Aventura   ADVENTURE

(☑2645-6388; www.aventuracanopytour.com; Rte 619, Santa Elena; canopy tour adult/child US$50/40, bridges US$35/30; ⏰tours 8am, 11am, 1pm & 3pm) Aventura boasts the longest zipline (nearly 1600m!) in Latin America. The 19 platforms are spiced up with a Tarzan swing, a 15m rappel and a Superman zipline that makes you feel as if you really are flying. It also has a network of suspension bridges, laced through secondary forest. Reservations required. You can also do ATV and horseback tours.

It's about 3km north of Santa Elena on the road to the Reserva Santa Elena (p212), but there's a booking office in town.

Extremo Canopy   ADVENTURE

(☑2645-6058; www.monteverdeextremo.com; Santa Elena; canopy tour US$53, bungee US$73, Tarzan swing US$42; ⏰8am-4pm) This place has a canopy ride that allows you to fly Superman-style through the air, the highest and most adrenaline-addled Tarzan swing in the area, and a bungee jump. One way or another, you will scream. Located in secondary forest, the views are marvelous but they herd some pretty big groups through here, so it's not exactly a nature experience.

SkyTrek   ADVENTURE

(☑2479-4100, toll free USA 1-804-GOTOSKY; www.skyadventures.travel; Santa Elena; adult/student/child SkyWalk US$39/32/27, SkyTrek US$81/67/56; ⏰7:30am-5pm) This seriously fast canopy tour, zooming over swatches of primary forest, consists of 11 platforms attached to steel towers spread out along a road. Speeds reach up to 64km/h, which is probably why SkyTrek was the first canopy tour with a real brake system. **SkyWalk** is a 2km guided tour over five suspended bridges; a night tour is also available.

You can book online or at the office in town (across from Tico y Rico restaurant and next to Neko Sushi). The park is located up near the Reserva Santa Elena (p212).

Guided Hikes

In addition to the two biggies anchoring this area at the north and south, Monteverde and Santa Elena are home to dozens of smaller private reserves and the 220 sq km Bosque Eterno de los Niños (p193). The Monteverde (p210) and Santa Elena (p212) reserves are special – very special – because they are essentially the only cloud forest reserves in the area. But if you want to immerse yourself in nature, get some exercise, spot some monkeys, admire a scenic vista or cool off in a waterfall, there are countless places to do so (most of which will be significantly less crowded than the Monteverde reserve).

Pasión Costa Rica   HIKING

(☑8304-7161, 8304-7242; www.pasioncostarica.com) Guacimal-born Marcos Mendez has an encyclopedic knowledge of Costa Rica's flora and fauna, and leads engaging tours around the area, specializing in smaller groups and customized tours. He's been a guide for more than 20 years, and you might say, the *pasión* shines through. Tour times are flexible and include transportation.

Santa Maria Night Walk   HIKING

(☑ 2645-6548; www.nightwalksantamarias.com; Santa Elena; per person US$25; ⊙ tour 5:30pm) Night walks have become so popular because 80 per cent of the cloud forest creatures are nocturnal. This one takes place on a private Santa Elena *finca* (farm) with a 10-hectare swathe of primary and secondary forest. Expert guides point out active nocturnal wildlife, ranging from snakes and spiders to sloths and kinkajous. Flashlights provided.

Valle Escondido   HIKING

(Hidden Valley; ☑ 2645-6601; www.valleescondido-preserve.com; Cerro Plano; day use US$20, night tour adult/child US$25/15; ⊙ 6am-4:30pm, night tour 5:30pm) Reserve in advance for the popular two-hour guided night tour, then come back the next day to explore the reserve on your own. Located behind Monteverde Inn in Cerro Plano, the well-marked trail winds through a deep canyon into an 11-hectare reserve, passing wonderful vistas and luscious waterfalls. It's recommended for birding and wildlife watching during the day, when it's quiet with few tourists.

Food & Drink

Café de Monteverde   FOOD & DRINK

(☑ 2645-7550; www.cafedemonteverde.com; Monteverde; tour per person US$18; ⊙ coffee tasting 7:30am-4.30pm, tours 8am & 1:30pm) 🍴 Stop by the shop in Monteverde to take a crash course in coffee and sample the delicious blends. You can also sign on for the three-hour tour on sustainable agriculture, which visits organic *fincas* implementing techniques such as composting and solar energy. Learn how coffee growing has helped shape this community and how it can improve the local environment.

El Trapiche   FOOD & DRINK

(☑ 2645-7650; www.eltrapichetour.com; Santa Elena; adult/child US$32/12; ⊙ tours 10am & 3pm Mon-Sat, 3pm Sun) Visit this picturesque family *finca* in Santa Elena, where they grow coffee, sugarcane, bananas and plantains. See the coffee process firsthand, take a ride in a traditional ox cart, and try your hand at making sugar. Lots of samples along the way, including sugarcane liquor, sugarcane toffee and – of course – delicious coffee. Kids love this one.

Caburé Chocolate Tour   FOOD & DRINK

(☑ 2645-5020; www.cabure.net; Monteverde; per person US$15; ⊙ tours 1pm & 4pm Mon-Sat) Bob, the owner of the Caburé chocolate shop in Monteverde, shares his secrets about the magical cacao pod and how to transform it into the food of the gods. There are plenty of opportunities for taste testing along the way, and you'll try your hand at making truffles.

Don Juan Coffee Tour   FOOD & DRINK

(☑ 2645-7100; www.donjuancoffeetour.com; Santa Elena; adult/child US$35/15; night tour US$40/20; ⊙ 7am-4:30pm, tours 8am, 1pm & 6pm) Don Juan's three-in-one tours cover all your favorite vices (okay, maybe not *all* your favorites, but three of the good ones). It's a pretty cursory overview of how sugarcane is harvested and processed, how cacao beans are transformed into dark, decadent chocolate, and how coffee happens, from plant to bean to cup.

🛏 Sleeping

Santa Elena and Monteverde are lined with lodgings, from fun hostels and friendly farmstays to luscious, luxurious mountain lodges. Accommodations are packed into village streets and spread out on the forested hills around town.

With many accommodations and transport options, Santa Elena appeals to budget travelers. Midrange and high-end visitors might consider Cerro Plano, Monteverde or further afield for closer interaction with nature (a vehicle – preferably 4WD – may be required).

> ### PAVING THE WAY
>
> A 1983 feature article in *National Geographic* billed the Monteverde and Santa Elena area as the place to view one of Central America's most famous birds – the resplendent quetzal. Suddenly, hordes of tourists armed with tripods and telephoto lenses started braving Monteverde's notoriously awful access roads, which came as a huge shock to its Quaker community. In an effort to stem the tourist flow, local communities lobbied to stop developers from paving the roads. It worked for a while, but eventually, the lobby to spur development bested the lobby to limit development. With the paving of the main access road – tentative first steps were being made in 2017 – this precious experiment in sustainable ecotourism will undergo a new set of trials.

🛏 Santa Elena

⭐ Casa Tranquilo HOSTEL $

(☎2645-6782; www.casatranquilohostel.com; dm/ d with bathroom/d without bathroom incl breakfast US$12/35/28; 🅿@🛜) The wonderful Tico hospitality starts first thing in the morning with homemade banana bread or pancakes. In addition to the excellent breakfast, staff lead free guided hikes, sharing their in-depth local expertise. Rooms are simple and spotless, some featuring skylights and gulf views. Colorful murals adorn the outside, so you'll know you are in the right place.

Pensión Santa Elena HOSTEL $

(☎2645-5051; www.pensionsantaelena.com; incl breakfast, d US$32-38, d without bathroom US$28, ste US$45-60; 🅿@🛜) This full-service hostel right in central Santa Elena is a perennial favorite, offering budget travelers top-notch service and *pura vida* hospitality. Each room is different, with something to suit every budget. The 'grand' rooms in the an-nex feature perks including superior beds, stone showers and iPod docks. There are also four family lofts with bunk beds. Bonus: Taco Taco (p204) is right next door!

Sleepers HOSTEL $

(☎8305-0113; www.sleeperssleepcheaperhostels. com; dm/s/d incl breakfast US$12/25/30) Next to Sloth Backpackers in central Santa Elena. Downstairs it looks like a friendly restau-rant, but it's actually a crowded communal kitchen, where happy travelers prepare and share meals. Upstairs it looks like a modern motel, but it's actually a hostel, where hap-py travelers surf the web and catch a breeze on the balcony. Rooms are spotless, with en suite bathrooms. A special rooftop 'suite' (US$35) has the best view in the place.

Camino Verde B&B B&B $

(☎2645-5641; www.hotelcaminoverde.com; incl breakfast, s & d standard US$45, deluxe US$55; 🅿🛜) This travelers' nest offers an assort-ment of spacious rooms with wood ceilings and tile floors. A new addition contains more expensive (and recommended) deluxe rooms with whitewashed walls and con-temporary furnishing. There's a sweet little restaurant and a rambling garden. Rocking chairs are scattered about the porch, offer-ing a perfect spot to soak up the scenic view.

Monteverde Backpackers HOSTEL $

(☎2645-5844; www.monteverdebackpackers.com; dm incl breakfast US$12-15; 🅿@🛜) Small and friendly, Monteverde Backpackers is part of the Costa Rica Hostel Network. The dorms are clean and comfy enough, the showers are hot, the location in Santa Elena is quiet and management is helpful. Freebies include coffee, hammocks and a sunset hike. Break-fast is DIY, so you can make 'em how you like 'em (eggs, that is). Dorms only; private rooms were done away with in terms of egalitarian-ism (or maybe business concerns).

Cabinas Eddy CABINA $

(☎2645-6635; www.cabinas-eddy.com; d US$40-60, without bathroom US$35; 🅿@🛜) This budget spot continues to get rave reviews for its amazing breakfasts, attentive service, spic-and-span rooms and common areas, and delightful manager Freddy (son of Eddy, by the way). The rooms are spotless, as is the fully equipped communal kitchen. The bal-cony is a great place to relax with a cup of free coffee and take in the view.

You'll find Eddy in the barbershop down-stairs, should you need a trim.

Cabinas & Hotel Vista al Golfo CABINA $

(☎2645-6321; www.cabinasvistaalgolfo.com; incl breakfast dm US$14, r with/without bathroom US$37/30, ste US$50; 🅿🛜) This bright, kitschy lodge is well kept, the showers are hot and the owners will make you feel right at home. On a clear day the upstairs balconies have great views of the Golfo de Nicoya. The fully wired/wi-fi common space is furnished with beanbags. The 'suite' in the blue house next door is worth the step up in price.

Capulín Cabins & Farm CABINA $$

(☎2645-6719; www.cabinascapulin.com; cabina US$60-90; 🅿🛜) Observe traditional farm life, hike the trails to spot birds and monkeys or just swing in a hammock and watch the show in the sky. There are eight comfortable cabins of varying sizes – some with kitchens and some with fantastic views to the gulf. Sirlainey and her Tico family couldn't be more generous in sharing their knowledge of the area. The farm is located just north of downtown Santa Elena.

Casa Batsu B&B $$

(☎2645-7004; www.casabatsu.org; d incl breakfast US$100; 🅿🛜) Carlos and Paula remodeled their family farmhouse, filled it with art, jazz and delicious food, and then opened their doors to share the love. Five rooms are furnished with pillow-strewn beds and striking stone showers. You'll enjoy the decadent breakfasts, for sure, but do make a reservation for dinner one night (mains US$25 to US$30), as Carlos is an amazing chef. *Batsu* is the indigenous Bri-Bri word for hummingbird.

Valle Campanas
FARMSTAY $$

(☑ 2645-5631; www.vallecampanas.com; incl breakfast, d US$84, f US$126-138; P ☎) Four humble cabins are scattered around Leo and Reina's coffee and sugar plantation. The functional cabins have shiny kitchens, wide porches with hammocks and plenty of polished wood. Trails wind around the grounds, allowing guests to observe a working farm (*finca*). It produces eggs, milk, honey and fresh fruits, all of which you'll sample in the scrumptious breakfasts.

Ecolodge San Luis
LODGE $$

(University of Georgia Costa Rica; ☑ 2645-7363; www.ecolodgesanluis.com; San Luis; dm/s/d incl meals US$60/90/180; P @ ☎) This comfortable lodge is set on a stunning 62-hectare campus in San Luis, on the mountain slopes below Monteverde. Comfortable accommodations are built into a longhouse, with soaring beamed ceilings and a common balcony overlooking a forest teeming with monkeys and migratory birds. Nourishing meals and guided hikes are also included.

Finca Terra Viva
FARMSTAY $$

(☑ 2645-5454; www.terravivacr.com; d/casita incl breakfast US$50/90; P @ ☎) 🏐 A 121-hectare working dairy *finca* surrounded by lush forest, this unique place offers guests an authentic rural experience, with an element of environmental consciousness raising. Try feeding baby cows and making cheese at the organic dairy, hike on trails through farm and forest and observe the measures the farm is taking to minimize its environmental footprint. Horseback and night tours, as well as the dairy tour, are free to guests, but also available to others for US$30. Terra Viva is about 3km north of town on the road toward Reserva Santa Elena.

Monteverde Rustic Lodge
LODGE $$

(☑ 2645-6256; www.monteverderusticlodge.com; d/tr/q incl breakfast US$75/90/125; P ☎) Funny thing about the Rustic Lodge: it's not that rustic. The furnishings play along with the theme, but remodeled rooms are spotless, comfortable and even upscale. Decorated in subtle earth tones, the 14 rooms have tile floors, floral curtains and lots of stained wood. The shared balcony overlooks a blooming garden. Small, quiet, atmospheric.

Jaguarundi Lodge
HOSTEL $$

(☑ 2645-5216; www.jaguarundilodge.com; d incl breakfast US$65; P ☎) A big change took place here in 2016, with all the dorms replaced by double rooms, and a new name out front. It's akin to a well-appointed mountain lodge but only 200m from town; you might expect the resident troupe of capuchin monkeys to accompany you to the pub next door.

Vista Verde Lodge
LODGE $$

(☑ 8380-1517, 2200-5225; www.vistaverdehotel.com; d/tr/q incl breakfast from US$77/88/99; P) 🏐 Wanna get away? Drive your 4WD 7km north of town to this remote, weatherbeaten lodge, where you'll fall asleep to the sounds of the rainforest. Wood-paneled rooms with picture windows take in views of Volcán Arenal and beyond. If it feels a little damp (as it does), head to the cozy common area to warm your feet beside the fire. Some 4km of trails run through 64 hectares of primary and secondary forest. Hike to the waterfall, which provides the hydroelectric energy that this place runs on. The lodge is located about 4km past Reserva Santa Elena and 3km past Selvatura Adventure Park.

Santa Elena Hostel Resort
HOSTEL $$

(☑ 2645-7879; www.costaricahostels.net; dm US$14, d with/without balcony US$58/52; P ☎) With fish in the koi pond and monkeys on the rooftops, this newish hostel may seem like a fan-cooled paradise. The shady grounds are strung with hammocks for sunny days, while there's a big stone fireplace for cool nights. The rooms have stained-wood walls and high sloped ceilings. It's worth paying for private balconies with sweet views. A bar, kitchen and on-site restaurant make this even more of a one-stop shop. If it seems eerily familiar to a hostel in La Fortuna, that's because the same guy owns this one, too.

Arco Iris Ecolodge
LODGE $$

(☑ 2645-5067; www.arcoirislodge.com; s/d/tr budget from US$33/44/54, standard US$70/90/100, superior US$105/120/135; P ☎) This clutch of pretty cabins is on a little hill overlooking Santa Elena and the surrounding forests. Rooms vary in size and style, but all are quite lovely, with lots of stained wood, rainforest showers and private terraces. The honeymoon cabin is a two-level dream. A system of private trails winds through the property, one to a majestic Pacific lookout.

Attentive German owner Susana sees to it that the site remains impeccable.

Hotel Claro de Luna
B&B $$

(☑ 2645-5269; www.clarodelunahotel.com; d incl breakfast US$75-111; P ☎) This graceful old mahogany gingerbread-style house in Santa Elena is surrounded by gorgeous gardens bursting with heliconias, orchids and other tropical blooms. A jacuzzi lurks amidst all that foliage, too. The rooms are simple but cheerful, with brightly painted interiors and floral quilts. Unfortunately, sound travels easily in this old house, so get a deluxe annex room if you can.

Hotel El Atardecer
LODGE **$$**

(📞 2645-5462; www.atardecerhotel.com; s/d/tr/q incl breakfast US$45/70/90/100; P 🛜) This attractive two-story wooden lodge is located away from the main drag in Santa Elena, guaranteeing a good night's rest. Surrounding a spacious courtyard restaurant, the musty, yet ample, tiled rooms have high, beamed ceilings, wood paneling and good mattresses. The selling point is the shared balcony, a magnificent place for – you guessed it – the sunset.

If there's no room at *this* inn, Rosa's daughter runs El Amanecer down the block; it's similarly named, built and priced (double/triple US$65/75).

Cloud Forest Lodge
LODGE **$$$**

(📞 2645-5058; www.cloudforestlodge.com; s/d/tr/q incl breakfast US$110/119/145/169; P @ 🛜) Sleep in the clouds – this hilltop lodge is up there, surrounded by 28 hectares of primary and secondary forest. There are trails to walk, species to check off your bird list and gulf views to marvel at. The wooden cabins are spacious and comfortable but hardly luxurious, though you'll enjoy the view from your private porch.

The Original Canopy Tour (p199) is right here at the lodge, which is about 2km from the main road, and 4km from Santa Elena. It's a pleasant walk into town, but you'll get your exercise on the way back uphill.

Hotel Poco a Poco
HOTEL **$$$**

(📞 2645-6000; www.hotelpocoapoco.com; d incl breakfast US$150-175; P @ 🛜 ⚊) ✦ There's a lot to love about Poco a Poco, of course. The restaurant is also excellent, and the contemporary architecture is striking. The whole place is family friendly, with a small playground, kiddie pool and ceramic critters peeking out in unexpected places. Rooms show off a sophisticated style, but you'll pay more for the upper-floor views.

They've earned four of five leaves in the government's sustainable tourism rating system.

🛏 Monteverde & Cerro Plano

Los Pinos Cabañas y Jardines
LODGE **$$**

(📞 2645-5252; www.lospinos.net; Cerro Plano; d standard/superior US$95/150, ste d/tr US$110/140, cabinas US$250-280; P 🛜) ✦ Fourteen freestanding *cabañas* (cabins) are scattered around the forested gardens of this 9-hectare property, which once formed part of the family *finca*. Each *cabaña* affords plenty of privacy, plus a fully equipped kitchen and small terrace. The grounds have tons of birdlife, a playground, walking trails and an organic garden. Awesome option for families. Family cabins have three rooms, while superior rooms have fireplaces and wraparound balconies. Los Pinos also garners five leaves in the sustainable tourism ratings. The *cabañas* lack some basic niceties such as storage and hammocks.

Hotel El Bosque
CABINA **$$**

(📞 2645-5158; www.bosquelodgecr.com; Monteverde; d/tr/q incl breakfast US$95/110/125; P ✳ 🛜) On the edge of the Bosque Eterno de los Niños (p193) in Monteverde, Benito's place is a pleasant surprise. Wooden duplex cabins are surrounded by tropical gardens and primary forest, with many kilometers of trails to get lost on. Wildlife abounds – keep your eyes open for agoutis, coatis, capuchin monkeys and amazing birds. Walking distance to pastries and pizza.

Mariposa B&B
B&B **$$**

(📞 2645-5013; www.mariposabb.com; Monteverde; incl breakfast s/d/tr/q US$40/65/80/90, apt d/q US$90/120; P 🛜) Just 2km from the Monteverde reserve (p210), this friendly place has nice rooms with stained-wood walls, terracotta floors, writing desks and beamed ceilings, not to mention a sweet local family looking after guests. It's nestled in the forest, with a sunny terrace for observing wildlife or just savoring a cup of local joe. The traditional Tico breakfast is a highlight.

Hotel Fonda Vela
LODGE **$$$**

(📞 2645-5125; www.fondavela.com; Monteverde; d/ste incl breakfast US$175/245; P @ 🛜 ⚊) With unique architectural styling and 14 hectares of trail-laced grounds, this long-standing lodge offers underwhelming standard rooms and gracious light-filled suites, all hung with paintings by hotel founder Paul Warren Smith. There's also a big covered pool (a rarity in these parts), two jacuzzis, flat-screen tellies and ping-pong and pool tables, making it a nice place to come home to. Located about 2km from the Monteverde reserve.

★ **Hotel Belmar** HOTEL $$$
(☎2645-5201; www.hotelbelmar.net; Cerro Plano; peninsula r US$215-235, deluxe chalets US$249-349, ste US$450-554; P@�jjj) ✦ Every room at the Belmar boasts views of forest or gulf (or both!). The gorgeous light-filled rooms are decked out with handcrafted furniture and high-thread-count linens. There are spectacular sunsets from the private balconies – the higher you go, the more spectacular they are. Other perks include yoga classes, spa services and a fabulous restaurant with those same jaw-dropping views.

Incidentally, this place is a *real* ecoresort, boasting five leaves from the Certificate of Sustainable Tourism program. Solar-heated water, biodigested energy and rainwater harvesting are just a few of the sustainable practices at the Belmar.

Trapp Family Lodge HOTEL $$$
(☎2645-5858; www.trapphotelmonteverde.com; Monteverde; incl breakfast, d US$120-135, ste US$135-155; P�jjj) ✦ Here's some contemporary luxury in the midst of the cloud forest. The 20 spacious rooms have high wooden ceilings, big bathrooms and fabulous views from picture windows overlooking gardens or cloud forest. And the Trapp family extends their renowned hospitality, promising warmth no matter what the weather.

It has four out of five leaves in the sustainable tourism rankings. You can't get much closer to the Monteverde reserve than here (it's less than 1km from the entrance). The trade-off, of course, is that it's far away from everything else. There's an elegant (but overpriced) restaurant, with a second breakfast-only nook nearly complete at the time of research.

✖ Eating

The kitchens of Santa Elena and Monteverde offer high quality but poor value. You'll be delighted by the organic ingredients, local flavors and international zest, but not by the high price tags. Even the local *sodas* (places serving counter lunches) and bakeries are more expensive than they ought to be. Santa Elena has the most budget options.

✖ Santa Elena

★ **Orchid Coffee** CAFE $
(☎2645-6850; www.orchidcoffeecr.com; mains US$8-12; ⊙7am-7pm; jj) Feeling peckish? Go straight to this lovely Santa Elena cafe,

filled with art and light. Grab a seat on the front porch and take a bite of heaven. It calls itself a coffee shop, but there's a full menu of traditional and nontraditional breakfast items, sweet and savory crepes, interesting and unusual salads and thoroughly satisfying sandwiches.

★ **Taco Taco** MEXICAN $
(☎5108-0525; www.facebook.com/tacotacomonteverde; mains US$5-8; ⊙noon-8pm; j) Quick and convenient, this *taquería* (taco stall) offers tasty Tex-Mex tacos, and burritos and quesadillas filled with shredded chicken. There's also slow-roasted short rib, roasted veggies and battered mahimahi. The only difficulty is deciding what to eat (though you really can't go wrong). Choose from two locations: this, the original deck location in front of Pensión Santa Elena (p201), is perfect for people-watching, but the new two-toned terrace restaurant next to SuperCompro is a step up in comfort.

Raulito's Pollo Asado CHICKEN $
(☎8308-0810; mains US$4-5; ⊙8am-9:30pm) Scrappy street dogs and chatty *taxistas* vie for attention at this porcelain-countered wonder. Watch as golden, crispy morsels are transferred from the spit to your plate with a heap of rice, fries, salad or *gallo pinto* (blended rice and beans). Wash it down with an icy *horchata* (rice milk and cinnamon drink) and still walk away with some beer money. Like the neighboring church, it's a local institution. It also offers cheap yet filling breakfasts.

Passi Flora VEGETARIAN $
(☎2645-6782; mains US$7-10; ⊙noon-9pm; j) Good for the body, good for the soul and good for the earth. That's what this joint strives for in its menu of vegetarian and vegan delights. It's a pretty comprehensive offering, with sandwiches, salads, pasta, rice and *rollitos* (empanadas). It's all fresh and deliciously satisfying. Look for the Buddha mosaic and you'll know you're in the right place. Appropriately, it's next to Casa Tranquilo (p201).

Sabor Tico SODA $
(☎2645-5827; www.restaurantesabortico.com; Centro Comercial; mains US$5-8; ⊙11am-10pm) Ticos and travelers alike rave about this local joint. Look for tasty twists on the standard fare, such as *olla de carne* (beef soup), *chorreadas Ticas* (fried corn cakes with sour cream) and tamales (holiday fare, typically). The *gallos*

(soft tortillas with delicious fillings of your choice) are a perfect alternative to the more filling *casados* (set meals) for lunch. The original down-home location (7am to 9pm) is opposite the soccer field.

Soda La Amistad

SODA $

(2645-6108; mains US$3-6; ⏰10am-9pm; ✈) Friendly and family run, this is a well-loved *soda* that's convenient if you're staying along this side road. You'll find typical, tasty *casados*, burgers, pasta and a list of handy translations on the menu. Herbivores will appreciate the veggie options, which include one burger and *casado*. These ladies know their stuff (and it's cheap).

Toro Tinto

STEAK $$

(2645-6252; www.facebook.com/torotinto.cr; mains $9-14; ⏰noon-10pm) This Argentinean steakhouse lures in customers with soft lighting and a cozy brick-and-wood interior. It keeps them sated with steaks that are perfectly cut and grilled to order, plus unexpected specials and delicious desserts. The wine selection is good – mostly Chilean and Argentine – but pricey. This place will warm your cloud-soaked soul.

Bon Appetit!

ITALIAN $$

(2645-5301; mains US$12-20; ⏰11am-10pm; ❄🍴) Spare surroundings and high ceilings, polite staff and big tables make this place on the outskirts of town a top spot for a post-activity meal. There's super-cheesy pizza (and cheesier jazz), but also some nice carnivorous options such as the tenderloin in red wine. Small platters of paninis, burgers and chicken fingers cater to the kiddies.

El Jardín

INTERNATIONAL $$$

(2645-5057; www.monteverdelodge.com; Monteverde Lodge; lunch US$8-14, dinner US$16-22; ⏰7am-10pm; 📶) Arguably the 'finest' dining in the area. The menu is wide ranging, always highlighting the local flavors. But these are not your typical *tipica* (traditional plates) – beef tenderloin served on a sugarcane kebab, and pan-fried trout topped with orange sauce. The setting – with windows to the trees – is lovely and the service is superb. Romantics can opt for a private table in the garden. Worth the drive in off the main road.

Tree House Restaurant & Café

CAFE $$$

(2645-5751; www.treehouse.cr; mains US$15-22; ⏰11am-10pm; 📶) It's a fine line between hokey and happy. But this restaurant – built around a half-century-old *higuerón* (fig) tree – definitely raises a smile. There's a menu of well-prepared if overpriced standards, from *ceviche* to *sopa Azteca* (Mexican tortilla soup) to burgers. The service is spot-on. It's a lively space to have a bite, linger over wine and occasionally catch live music.

Cold? Try the Chocolate Tree House, a devilish dash of coffee and chocolate-flavored liqueurs.

Morpho's Restaurant

INTERNATIONAL $$$

(2645-7373; www.morphosrestaurant.com; mains US$8-20; ⏰11am-9pm; ✈) Dine among gushing waterfalls and fluttering butterflies at this downtown restaurant. Some call it 'romantic,' others call it 'kitschy' – but nobody can dispute the varied menu, which combines local ingredients with gourmet flair. Veggies, a word of caution: the 'veggie burger' is really just an egg sandwich; there are other vegetarian options such as salads, soups and pastas. Your receipt earns a discount to the adjoining **orchid garden** (2645-5308; www.monteverdeorchidgarden.net; adult/child over 6yr/under 6yr US$12/6/free; ⏰8am-5pm).

✖ Monteverde & Cerro Plano

Quimera's

TAPAS $

(2645-7037; Cerro Plano; tapas US$7-10; ⏰11am-11pm) Come to this casual cafe for unexpected creations, such as sea bass in ginger and rum, shrimp skewers in mango sauce, and roasted eggplant with smoked cheese and sun-dried tomatoes. The place promises 'Latin-infused tapas,' but the menu is actually infused with flavors and ingredients from all over the world. Start yourself off with one of the house caipirinhas.

Stella's Bakery

BAKERY $$

(2645-5560; Monteverde; mains US$8-15; ⏰6:30am-6pm; 📶) A bakery for birders. Come in the morning for strong coffee and sweet pastries, or later for rich, warming soup, and sandwiches on homemade bread. Plates such as the huevos rancheros satisfy, especially with a heap of passion fruit cheesecake for dessert. Whenever you come, keep an eye on the bird feeder, which attracts tanagers, mot-mots and an emerald-green toucanet.

Café Caburé

CAFE $$

(2645-5020; www.caburare.net; Monteverde; lunch US$6-12, dinner US$16-20; ⏰9am-8pm Mon-Sat; 📶) This Argentine cafe above the Bat Jungle specializes in creative and delicious everything, from sandwiches on homemade bread and fresh salads, to more elaborate fare such as sea bass in almond sauce or filet mignon with *chimichurri*. Save room for dessert: the chocolate treats are high art. There's a hot chocolate, an Argentine brownie and (yes!) the cafe's Chocolate Tour (p200).

d'Sofia
FUSION $$
(⊘2645-7017; Cerro Plano; mains US$12-16; ⊕11:30am-9:30pm; 🐾) With its Nuevo Latino cuisine – a modern fusion of traditional Latin American cooking styles – d'Sofia has established itself as one of the best places in town. Think plantain-crusted sea bass, seafood chimichanga or beef tenderloin with roasted red pepper and cashew sauce. The ambience is enhanced by groovy music, picture windows, romantic candle lighting and potent cocktails.

🍷 Drinking & Nightlife

Nightlife in these parts generally involves a guided hike and nocturnal critters, but since these misty green mountains draw artists and dreamers, there's a smattering of regular cultural offerings. When there's anything going on, you'll see it heavily advertised around town. You'll see some action at the bars in Santa Elena, especially during the dry season.

Beso Cafe
CAFE
(⊘2645-6874; Santa Elena; ⊕8am-8pm) We overheard someone saying, 'This is the best cup of coffee I've had in Costa Rica.' Hard to quantify in the Monteverde region, but espressos, lattes and cappuccinos are about all they do here (plus a couple of sandwiches on offer), and they do it very well indeed.

Monteverde Beer House
BEER GARDEN
(⊘8659-2054; www.facebook.com/monteverde beerhouse; Santa Elena; ⊕10am-10pm; 🐾) It's not a brewery – contrary to the sign – but it does offer a selection of local craft beers. There's a shady deck out back and smiling servers on hand; it's a perfect atmosphere for kicking back after a day of adventures. The Middle Eastern food (mains US$6 to US$10) is hit or miss, but if you're hungry, go for the shakshuka. The Israeli owner was in the process of opening a new bar near the Tree House (p205) at the time of research.

Bar Amigos
BAR
(⊘2645-5071; www.baramigos.com; Santa Elena; ⊕noon-3am) With picture windows overlooking the mountainside, this Santa Elena mainstay evokes the atmosphere of a ski lodge. But, no, there are DJs, karaoke and billiards plus sports on the screens. This is the one consistent place in the area to let loose, so there's usually a good, rowdy mix of Ticos and tourists. The food, such as the *chifrijo* (rice and pinto beans with fried pork and capped with fresh tomato salsa and corn chips), is surprisingly good.

🔒 Shopping

★ Luna Azul
JEWELRY
(⊘2645-6638; www.facebook.com/lunaazulmon teverde; Cerro Plano; ⊕9am-6pm Mon-Sat, from 10:30am Sun) This super-cute gallery and gift shop is packed to the gills with jewelry, clothing, soaps, sculpture and macramé, among other things. Owner Stephanie's jewelry in particular is stylish and stunning, crafted from silver, shell, crystals and turquoise.

Monteverde Art House
ARTS & CRAFTS
(Casa de Arte; ⊘2645-5275; www.facebook.com/ monteverde.arthouse; Cerro Plano; ⊕9am-6pm) You'll find several rooms stuffed with colorful Costa Rican artistry here. The goods include jewelry, ceramic work, Boruca textiles and traditional handicrafts. There's a big variety of offerings, including some paintings and more contemporary work, but it's mostly at the crafts end of the arty-crafty spectrum. Great for souvenirs.

Monteverde Cheese Factory
FOOD & DRINK
(La Lechería; ⊘2645-7090; www.monteverde cheesefactory.com; Monteverde; ⊕7:30am-5pm Mon-Sat, to 4pm Sun) The Monteverde Cheese Factory was started in 1953 by Monteverde's original Quaker settlers. The factory produces everything from a creamy Gouda to a very nice sharp white cheddar, as well as other dairy products such as yogurt and, most importantly, ice cream. Don't miss the chance to sample Monte Rico, a Monteverde original. Sadly, they no longer offer tours.

Until the upswing in ecotourism, this was Monteverde's number one employer. The Monteverde Cheese Factory is the second-largest cheese producer in the country. Now owned by the Mexican giant Sigma Alimentos, the factory still uses the original name and recipes.

ℹ️ Information

EMERGENCY
Police (⊘2645-6248; Santa Elena)

INTERNET ACCESS
Nearly all hotels and hostels have wi-fi, while some accommodations also offer computers with internet access.

MEDICAL SERVICES

Consultorio Médico (☑ 2645-7778; Cerro Plano; ⊘ 24hr) Across the intersection from Hotel Heliconia.

Red Cross (☑ 2645-6128; www.cruzroja.or.cr; ⊘ 24hr) Hospital located just north of Santa Elena.

MONEY

Banks and ATMs are clustered in the downtown quadrant of Santa Elena.

Banco de Costa Rica (Cerro Plano; ⊘ 9am-4pm Mon-Fri)

Banco Nacional (Santa Elena; ⊘ 8:30am-3:45pm Mon-Fri, 9am-1pm Sat)

Banco Popular (☑ 2542-3390; Centro Comercial Plaza Monteverde, Santa Elena; ⊘ 8:45am-4:30pm Mon-Fri)

POST

Correos de Costa Rica (Santa Elena; ⊘ 8am-4:30pm Mon-Fri, to noon Sat) Across from the shopping mall.

TOURIST INFORMATION

Most hotels, hostels and guesthouses are eager to assist their guests, whether by booking tours or making transportation arrangements.

Chamber of Tourism (☑ 2645-6565; Santa Elena; ⊘ 9am-noon & 1-7pm) Operated by the local chamber of commerce, this office promotes its member hotels and tour companies; it's not necessarily an unbiased source.

Monteverde Info (www.monteverdeinfo.com) This comprehensive website is chock full of information, with listings for hotels, tours, restaurants, transportation and more.

ⓘ Getting There & Away

After local protesters took to the streets in 2013, the transportation ministry announced that it would invest the necessary US$16 million to pave the 18km road from Guacimal to Santa Elena, which is the main access route to Monteverde. At the time of research in 2017, it hadn't been completed. The other route, from Lake Arenal, remains a wonderfully wild and rocky ride; it's used by all the taxi-boat-taxi vehicles.

BUS

Most buses stop at the bus terminal across from the Centro Comercial mini-mall on the hill above downtown Santa Elena, and do not continue to Monteverde; you'll have to walk or take a taxi if that's where you plan to stay. On the trip in, keep all bags at your feet and not in the overhead bin.

Note that the bus to Tilarán does not leave from the terminal, but from downtown Santa Elena, just meters down the street from the Vitosi pharmacy. Note that buses to Puntarenas can also drop you off in Las Juntas.

If you're traveling to Managua or Grenada in Nicaragua, you can make arrangements to meet the international bus en route on the Interamericana in Lagartos with:

Monteverde Experts (☑ 2645-7263; www.monteverdeexperts.com; Rte 606; ⊘ 8am-5pm) Agent for TicaBus.

NicaBus Agent (☑ 2645-7063; www.nicabus.com.ni/en/agencies; Cerro Plano)

CAR

While most Costa Rican communities regularly request paved roads in their region, preservationists in Monteverde have done the opposite. All roads around here are shockingly rough. Even if you arrive on a newly paved road via Guacimal, you'll still want a 4WD to get to the more remote lodges and reserves.

There are three roads from the Interamericana. Coming from the south, the first well-signed turnoff is at Rancho Grande (18km north of the Puntarenas exit). The first stretch of this route (from Sardinal to Guacimal) was paved in 2011. The remaining 17km (from Guacimal to Santa Elena) was scheduled to be paved in 2016. That hasn't happened yet; at the time of research, it took about three hours to drive to San José, but that time will be reduced with the road improvements.

BUSES FROM MONTEVERDE

DESTINATION	COMPANY	COST (US$)	DURATION	FREQUENCY
Las Juntas	Transmonteverde	2	1½hr	4:20am, 3pm
Puntarenas via Las Juntas via Sardinal via Lagartos	Transmonteverde	3	3hr	4:20am, 5:30am, 6am, 3pm
Reserva Monteverde (Monteverde Cloud Forest Reserve)	local bus	1.20	30min	departs 6:15am, 7:30am, 1:20pm, 3pm; returns 6:45am, 11:30am, 2pm, 4pm
San José	Tilarán Transportes	5	5hr	6:30am, 2:30pm
Tilarán, with connection to La Fortuna	local bus	3	2½hr (7 to La Fortuna)	5am, 7am, 11:30am, 4pm

208

CHRIS GALLAGHER/GETTY IMAGES ©

ASCENT XMEDIA/GETTY IMAGES ©

1. Rainforest Wildlife
Animals in the rainforest region around
Monteverde include Hoffmans two-toed sloth.

2. Bosque Nuboso Monteverde (p210)
There are 13km of marked trails in the Monteverde
Cloud Forest.

3. Llanos de Cortés (p233)
One of most spectacular waterfalls in the country
feeds into a pool that's perfect for swimming.

4. Playa Naranjo (p231)
Surfers flock here for the legendary break at
Witch's Rock.

KRYSIA CAMPOS/GETTY IMAGES ©

A second, shorter road goes via Juntas, but it's not paved except for the first few kilometers.

If coming from the north, drivers can take the paved road from Cañas via Tilarán and then take the rough road from Tilarán to Santa Elena.

If you're coming from Arenal, consider taking the lakeside route through Tronadora and Río Chiquito, instead of through Tilarán. The roads are rougher, but the panoramas of the lake, volcano and surrounding countryside are magnificent.

There are two gas stations open for business in the area, one of which is in Cerro Plano.

TAXI-BOAT-TAXI

The fastest route between Monteverde–Santa Elena and La Fortuna is via a taxi-boat-taxi combo (US$25 to US$30, four hours, departs 8am and 2pm), which can be arranged through almost any hotel or tour operator, including **Monteverde Tours** (Desafío Adventure Company; ☑ 2645-5874; www.monteverdetours.com; ⊙ 7am-7pm Mon-Fri, 10am-6pm Sat & Sun), in either town. A 4WD minivan can pick you up at your hotel and take you to Río Chiquito, meeting a boat that crosses Laguna de Arenal, where a van on the other side continues to La Fortuna. This is increasingly becoming the primary transportation between La Fortuna and Monteverde as it's incredibly scenic, reasonably priced and saves half a day of rough travel.

TAXI

Taxis wait in front of the Chamber of Tourism (p207) next to the Catholic Church and chicken stand in Santa Elena to take travelers to the reserves (about US$10) or other out-of-town destinations.

Bosque Nuboso Monteverde

Here is a virginal forest dripping with mist, dangling with mossy vines, sprouting with ferns and bromeliads, gushing with creeks, and nurturing rivulets of evolution. It's so moving that when Quaker settlers first arrived here in the 1950s, they agreed to preserve about a third of their property to protect this watershed. The community later joined forces with environmental organizations to purchase 328 hectares adjacent to the already preserved area. This was called the **Reserva Biológica Bosque Nuboso Monteverde** (Monteverde Cloud Forest Wildlife Biological Reserve; ☑ 2645-5122; www.reservamonteverde.com; adult/student/under 6yr US$20/10/free; ⊙ 7am-4pm), which the Centro Científico Tropical (Tropical Science Center) began administering in 1975. Nowadays the reserve totals 105 sq km.

Due to its fragile environment, the reserve allows a maximum of 160 people at any given time; during the dry season this limit is usually reached by 10am. Assure your admission by making advance reservations for a spot on a tour. Otherwise, be an early bird and arrive before the gates open.

🏃 Activities

Hiking

Visitors should note that the reserve's walking trails can be muddy, even during the dry season. You're essentially walking around in a cloud, so don't bother complaining, just bring rain gear, suitable boots and a smile. Many of the trails have been stabilized with concrete blocks or wooden boards, but unpaved trails deeper in the preserve turn sloppy during the rainy season.

There are 13km of marked and maintained trails – a free map is provided with your entrance fee. The three most popular trails, suitable for day hikes, make a rough triangle (El Triángulo) to the east of the reserve entrance. The following trails make up triangle's sides:

Sendero Bosque Nuboso A popular 1.9km interpretive walk through the cloud forest that begins at the ranger station (park entrance); it's paralleled by the more open, 2km **El Camino**, a favorite of birdwatchers.

Sendero Pantanoso A 1.6km hike that traverses swamps, pine forests and the continental divide; it forms the far side of El Triángulo.

Sendero Río The 2km trail returns to the entrance, following the **Quebrada Cuecha** past a few photogenic waterfalls.

Bisecting the triangle, the gorgeous **Chomogo Trail** (1.8km) lifts hikers to 1680m, the highest point within the triangle. Other little trails crisscross the region, including the worthwhile **Sendero Brillante** (300m), with bird's-eye views of a miniature forest. Keep in mind that despite valiant efforts to contain crowd sizes, these shorter trails are among the most trafficked in the country.

The trail to the **Mirador La Ventana** (elevation 1550m) is moderately steep and leads further afield to a wooden deck overlooking the continental divide. To the west, you can see the Golfo de Nicoya and the Pacific on clear days. To the east, you can see the Peñas Blancas valley and the San Carlos plain. Even on wet, cloudy days it's magical, especially when the winds are howling and fine swirling mist washes over you in waves.

All over these woods, in hidden pockets and secluded gullies, that mist collects into rivulets that gather into threads that stream into a foaming waterfall, visible from **Sendero Cascada**. From here the pools form a gushing river, best glimpsed from **Sendero Río** or **Sendero Quebrada Cuecha**. There's a 100m suspension bridge about 1km from the ranger station on **Sendero Wilford Guindon**. Like a miniature Golden Gate suspended in the canopy, you can feel it rock and sway with each step.

There are also trails to three backcountry shelters that begin at the far corners of the triangle. Even longer trails, many of them less developed, stretch out east across the reserve and down the Peñas Blancas river valley to the lowlands north of the Cordillera de Tilarán and into the Bosque Eterno de los Niños (p193). If you have the time, these hikes are highly recommended, as few tourists venture beyond the triangle. It's important to first talk to the park service, as you will be dealing with rugged terrain; a guide is highly recommended. Note that backcountry camping and sleeping in the shelters is normally no longer allowed.

Wildlife-Watching

Monteverde is a birdwatching paradise, with the list of recorded species topping out at more than 400. The resplendent quetzal is most often spotted during the March and April nesting season, though you may get lucky any time of year. Keep your ears open for the three-wattled bellbird, a kind of cotinga that is famous for its distinctive call. If you're keen on birds, a specialized bird tour is highly recommended.

For those interested in spotting mammals, the cloud forest's limited visibility and abundance of higher primates (human beings) can make wildlife watching quite difficult. That said, there are some commonly sighted species (especially in the backcountry), including coatis, howler monkeys, capuchins, sloths, agoutis and squirrels (as in 'real' squirrel, not the squirrel monkey). Most animals avoid the main trails, so get off the beaten track.

☞ Tours

Although you can (and should) hike around the reserve on your own, a guide will provide an informative overview and enhance your experience. Make reservations at least a

day in advance for park-run tours. The English-speaking guides are trained naturalists; proceeds benefit environmental education in local schools. The reserve can also recommend excellent guides for private tours.

Birdwatching Tours BIRDWATCHING
(✆2645-5112; per person incl entry fee US$64; ⏱ tours depart 6am) These guided bird walks usually last four to five hours, checking off as many as 40 species of birds out of a possible 500. There's a three-person minimum, six-person maximum. Book in advance through the reserve office.

Natural History Tours ECOTOUR
(✆2645-5122, reservations 2645-5112; adult/student excl entry fee US$37/27; ⏱ tours depart 7:30am, 11am & 1:30pm) These tours start with an informative 10-minute orientation, followed by a 2½- to three-hour walk in the woods. You'll learn all about the characteristics of a cloud forest and identify some of its most unique flora. Your ticket is valid for the entire day; you can continue to explore on your own when the tour is over. Reservations required.

Night Tours OUTDOORS
(✆2645-5122; www.reservamonteverde.com; with/without transportation US$25/20; ⏱ tours depart 5:45pm) Two-hour night tours of the reserve offer the opportunity to observe the 70% of regional wildlife that has nocturnal habits. Frogs, bats and other night critters are increasingly active as the sun sets. Tours are by flashlight (bring your own for the best visibility). Arrange this tour in advance by at least the morning of the tour

🛏 Sleeping & Eating

La Casona LODGE $$
(✆2645-5122; www.reservamonteverde.com; r incl three meals & reserve admission per person US$93) At the entrance to the reserve, this mountain lodge is usually used by researchers and student groups, but it's open to tourists when there's room. The six plain private rooms feel rather institutional, but they're clean and comfortable – and you can't get any closer to the park. Your hard-earned cash directly contributes to protecting the cloud forest.

Cafe Colibrí CAFE $
(✆2645-7768; sandwiches US$5-6; ⏱ 8am-5pm) Just outside the reserve gates, the 'Hummingbird Cafe' is a top-notch spot to refuel after a hike in the woods. The drinks will

warm your body, but the sound of dozens of hummingbirds in the garden will delight your heart. Many say the sandwiches are just okay; come for the coffee (US$2) and *colibris* (hummingbirds). Great photo ops.

An identification board shows the nine species that you're likely to see.

❶ Information

The visitors center, adjacent to the reserve gift shop, is where you can get information and buy trail guides, maps and bird and mammal lists, as well as souvenirs and postcards. Leave your passport to rent a pair of binoculars (US$10).

The reserve is managed by the Centro Científico Tropical and supported by donations through the Friends of Monteverde Cloud Forest (www.friendsofmonteverde.org).

The annual rainfall here is about 3000mm, though parts of the reserve reportedly get twice as much. It's usually cool, with high temperatures around 18°C (64°F); wear appropriate clothing. It's important to remember that the cloud forest is, unsurprisingly, often cloudy.

❶ Getting There & Away

Public buses (☑ 8811-8902; autotransportes.carranza@yahoo.com) (US$1.20, 30 minutes) depart the Banco Nacional (p207) in Santa Elena at 6:15am, 7:30am, 1:20pm and 3pm. Buses return from the reserve at 6:45am, 11:30am, 2pm and 4pm. You can flag down the buses from anywhere on the road between Santa Elena and the reserve – inquire at your lodgings about what time they will pass by. Taxis are also available for around US$10.

The 6km walk from Santa Elena is uphill but offers lovely views – look for paths that run parallel to the road. The birdwatching is magnificent, especially in the last 2km.

INTERAMERICANA NORTE

Despite Tico speed demons and lumbering big rigs, the Interamericana offers a wide-angle view of the region. The main artery connecting San José with Managua runs through kilometers of tropical dry forest and neat roadside villages to the open Guanacaste grasslands, where savanna vistas are broken only by windblown trees. Along the way, thin, mostly earthen roads branch off and wander up the slopes of hulking volcanoes shrouded in cloud forest, skirt hidden waterfalls and meander into vast estuaries that kiss pristine bays.

❶ Getting There & Away

The 50km stretch of road between Cañas and Liberia has undergone a huge, US$200 million improvement in recent years. There are additional lanes, overpasses and on-off ramps that have made driving easier (and much faster) along this stretch. The only downside is that some formerly easy turns into towns have been complicated by the overpasses. Your destination is probably not on the Interamericana itself, but somewhere off of it. Once you leave the highway, you may wish you had a 4WD.

If you're traveling by bus, you are likely to have to break your journey (to change buses) in Cañas, Bagaces, Liberia or La Cruz.

Montes de Oro

Northeast of Puntarenas, Montes de Oro is a gold-mining district that's tucked into the slopes and valleys of the Cordillera de Tilarán. A good number of day-trippers come up from Puntarenas and other coastal towns to fly through the trees on one of the

---

DON'T MISS

RESERVA SANTA ELENA

The exquisitely misty 310-hectare **Reserva Santa Elena** (☑ 2645-7107, 2645-5390; www.reservasantaelena.org; adult/student US$14/7, guided hike US$15; ⊙ 7am-4pm) offers a completely different cloud forest experience to Monteverde. Cutting through the veiled forest, the reserve's 12km of dewy trails see much less traffic, retaining a magic that is sometimes missing at Monteverde. Open since 1992, Santa Elena was one of the first community-managed conservation projects in the country.

The reserve itself is about 6km northeast of the village of Santa Elena; the **reserve office** (Reserva Bosque Nuboso Santa Elena; ☑ 2645-5390; www.reservasantaelena.org; Colegio Técnico Profesional; ⊙ 7am-5pm Mon-Fri) is in town. The reserve has a simple restaurant, coffee shop and gift store. Note that all proceeds go toward managing the reserve as well as to environmental education programs in local schools.

LE ENSEÑADA LODGE & WILDLIFE REFUGE

La Enseñada Lodge & Wildlife Refuge (☎2289-6655; www.laensenada.net; Km 155 Interamericana, Abangaritos; s/d/tr/q US$55/65/75/89, meals US$8-18; P🐕🎧🏊) is a wonderfully remote 324-hectare working cattle ranch, salt farm and papaya orchard. It is an incredible setting for birding, horseback riding and good old-fashioned R&R. Rustic but comfortable wooden bungalows face the Golfo de Nicoya, and have private solar-heated bathrooms and patios with hammocks. There's also a restaurant, tennis courts, a romantically rickety jetty and a terrific trail network.

Containing primary and secondary forest (a rarity in this part of the country), as well as mangrove swamps at the mouth of the Río Abangares, this property has been declared a national wildlife refuge. **Boat tours** to the mangroves (per person US$102) offer the chance to glimpse dozens of bird species, caimans and crocs, while **horseback tours** (US$30) take you through the tropical dry forest.

country's biggest canopy tours. Otherwise, this area is largely off the beaten track, with few facilities catering to independent travelers; you'll need your own vehicle (a 4WD, of course) and a sense of adventure. In the district capital Miramar, you'll discover a real Tico town that's largely untouched by tourism. And if you make it all the way up to Zapotal, at 1500m above sea level, you'll have unparalleled views all the way down to the Golfo de Nicoya and a cloud forest of your very own.

🏃 Activities

Colinas Verdes Zapotal   HIKING, MOUNTAIN BIKING
(☎2639-8516, 8829-0619; www.colinasverdescr. com; Jabonal; admission to trails US$10) You'll find a little bit of magic amid the clouds at Colinas Verdes, set on 35 hectares of emerald-green hills and misty skies. Much of the property has been set aside for conservation and reforestation, but you'll find 4km of biking/hiking trails winding their way through the forest, with five hanging bridges, four short zipline cables and countless stunning vistas.

**Finca Daniel
Adventure Park**   ADVENTURE SPORTS
(☎2639-8303, 8382-3312; www.finca-daniel. com; Tajo Alto; rope obstacle course US$60, canopy tour US$99-114) Just when you thought you had arrived in a place where no tourist had gone before... there's a flag-waving, adrenaline-rushing, scream-inducing adventure park, catering to busloads of daytrippers from the coast. It offers purportedly one of the biggest canopy tours in the country, with 25 cables and 11 waterfalls (some dip-worthy). There's also a rope obstacle

course through the trees. The place is definitely fun, but the big groups may be a detractor. If you don't have your own wheels, the adventure park can bus you in from Puntarenas, Jacó, the northern Península de Nicoya, or even San José. It's located on the grounds of the Hotel Vista Golfo, about 7km north of Miramar, in Tajo Alto.

🛏 Sleeping

There are a few lovely places to stay around Miramar and Zapotal, but they are all small and this region is remote, so make sure to reserve in advance so you're not stranded.

Hotel Vista Golfo   HOTEL $$
(☎8382-3312, 2639-8303; www.finca-daniel.com; Tajo Alto; d/tr/q incl breakfast US$87/100/110, ste incl breakfast US$120-150; P❄🎧🏊) On-site at the Finca Daniel Adventure Park, this hotel is a pleasant place with a tranquil mountain setting that's perfect for getting a little fresh air. Comfortable rooms have traditional decor and private terraces, some with sweeping views of the Golfo de Nicoya. Located 7km due north of Miramar.

ℹ Getting There & Away

The town of Miramar is the capital of this district and the main population center. It's 6km north of the Interamericana on a good paved road. The small village of Zapotal is a further 16km northeast, and it's a rough road into the clouds.

There are four buses a day connecting Miramar to San José (US$4, 2½ hours). Nonetheless, this is a difficult area to navigate without your own car. Be advised that the roads here are frequently washed out during the rainy season, so a 4WD is highly recommended.

Volcán Tenorio Area

Part of the Area de Conservación Arenal (ACA), Parque Nacional Volcán Tenorio is a cool, misty and magical place highlighted by cloud forests and the icy-blue Río Celeste; the region is known locally by the river's name. The park entrance is located just north of Bijagua (pronounced 'bee-hag-gwa'); the town, which leads the way in rural community tourism, is the main base for visiting this natural wonder.

❶ Getting There & Away

About 7km north of Cañas, Hwy 6 branches off the Interamericana and heads north toward Upala, passing through the small town of Bijagua. From Bijagua, there is a graded dirt road on the right that leads 9km to the entrance of Parque Nacional Volcán Tenorio (p216). If you're coming from the east, you can also reach the park from Hwy 4, coming up from La Fortuna. If you have your own wheels, it's a doable day trip from Liberia, Cañas or La Fortuna.

If you don't have your own wheels, you can catch a bus from Liberia (US$4), San José or Upala (US$2.50) to Bijagua, then book a tour locally or catch a taxi (US$50) to the park entrance.

Bijagua

POP 5200

The only sizable town in the Tenorio sphere is Bijagua, a small farming community that's strung out along Hwy 6, halfway between the Interamericana and the bigger town of Upala. It's a hidden gem.

Bijagua is a leader in rural community tourism. It started with the Heliconias Rainforest Lodge, managed by a cooperative of local families. That spirit continues in small-scale tours that mimic – on a more charming level – the night tours and chocolate tours of more established tourism centers. Now the 'graduates' of Heliconias have founded their own businesses, and a growing entrepreneurial spirit along with a genuine down-to-earth Tico vibe make this a wonderful place to base yourself while visiting the nearby hotspots of Tenorio (p216), Palo Verde (p220), and even La Fortuna (the big one).

◉ Sights

Finca Verde Lodge FARM
(☑2466-8069, 8918-4805; www.fincaverdelodge.com/activities; day/night tour US$12/14; ⊘tours at 8am, 10am, noon, 2pm & 4pm; ℗) Sloths, frogs, snakes, butterflies and prolific birdlife inhabit the gorgeous grounds of this *finca*, worth a visit to see the methods of a working organic farm. It's located on a rather rough road a few kilometers southeast of the main highway.

🏃 Activities

Jorge Soto BIRDWATCHING
(☑8314-9784) Jorge is an independent bird guide and one of the top guys in this part of the country. He can cater trips to your needs (and life lists!). He doesn't have an office, but you can inquire for him at the Heliconias Rainforest Lodge or at Casitas Tenorio.

Bijagua Rainforest Tours OUTDOORS
(☑8998-2954, 2466-8242; www.bijaguarainforesttours.com) Marlon Brenes and his team have been working this patch of northern Costa Rica for more than a decade. Knowledgeable and efficient, they're well connected to local sustainable tourism efforts and also offer wider-ranging trips to sights including Palo Verde (p220) and La Fortuna. Their guesthouse, Casa Natural View (US$85), is just down the hill from Casitas Tenorio.

Frog's Paradise WILDLIFE WATCHING
(⊘5:30pm-dark) With a flashlight and a walking stick, you'll accompany Miguel on

DON'T MISS

HOTTEST THERMAL POOLS

Costa Rica's volcano-powered thermal pools and mud pots provide plenty of good, clean fun for beauty queens and would-be mud wrestlers.

Hot Springs Río Negro (p227) On the slopes of Volcán Rincón de la Vieja, with several pools in a jungle setting.

Río Perdido (p219) Thermal pools, hanging bridges and low-key luxury characterize this thermal canyon experience near Volcán Miravalles.

Borinquen Mountain Resort & Spa (p229) The pinnacle of indulgent dirt exists in the remote heights of Rincón de la Vieja. If mineral mud is not your thing, you can opt instead for a skin treatment of coconut, cappuccino or chocolate.

a night walk around former cattle grazing land, now a wildlife wonderland. You'll likely see some of the 20 regional frog species, and maybe owls, fruit-eating bats, sleeping birds, creeping insects and the things that eat them. Phosphorescent mushrooms too (you don't have to take them to see them!). Located on the road to Cataratas Bijagua Lodge.

Heliconias
Rainforest Lodge
BIRDWATCHING, HIKING

(Hanging Bridges; ☑ 2466-8483; per person US$17; ☺ 8am-5pm) Get a different perspective on the forest from this trail of hanging bridges. It's a beautiful spot – rife with butterflies and birdlife – and you're likely to have the trail to yourself. Located about 4km from the main road. At the time of research the bridges were closed due to inspection and safety reasons, with plans to reopen in 2018. One of the three bridges was wiped out by Hurricane Otto in 2016, so it's lost a bit of its luster.

👉 Tours

Chocolate Tree Tour
FOOD & DRINK

(☑ 2470-8061, 8309-5826; www.treechocolate. com; 1½ hr tour US$15; ☺ 9am-5pm) Gerardo Solorzano will guide you around his *finca*, which produces cacao and many other crops. But you want the chocolate, right? You'll see the entire process – cutting, fermentation, drying, roasting, husking – and end on a happy note with a cup of hot or cold chocolate, courtesy of Gerardo's partner Runia. Located 4km off Rte 6, after making the right turn just past Super Ale's *soda*, 8km north of Bijagua.

🛏 Sleeping

There's a shortage of budget options, but little Bijagua has a pretty good range of places to stay. You'll find them on the main road, Hwy 6, or nestled into the hills east or west of town.

Río Celeste Backpackers
HOSTEL $

(☑ 2466-8600; www.bijaguabackpackers.jimdo. com; Rte 6; campsite/dm/d US$8/15/35; ℗ ☎) The best budget option is this little house that has been turned into a hostel. There are two private rooms and one eight-bed dormitory; guests share two bathrooms, a kitchen and a small living area. There's camping in the yard (on the porch when it rains) and a shuttle bus to Parque Nacional Volcán Tenorio (p216; US$12 per person).

★ Casitas Tenorio B&B
B&B $$

(☑ 8439-9084, 8312-1248; www.casitastenorio. com; d incl breakfast US$80-130; ℗ ☎) ❂ This sweet family-run farm has six spare but gracious *casitas* (cottages) surrounded by wildlife. Tico/Aussie couple Donald and Pip are committed to rural community tourism. The charm of this place is experiencing life on the farm – you can milk the cows on the morning dairy tour – and exploring the fruit tree-laden grounds. Your breakfast comes straight from the chickens!

It's 2km southeast from Bijagua, on the road to Heliconias Rainforest Lodge.

Cataratas Bijagua Lodge
LODGE $$

(☑ 8937-4687; www.cataratasbijagua.com; d/tr/q incl breakfast US$70/85/100; ℗ ☎) ❂ Owners Warner and Carla have turned their family's dairy farm into a beautiful ecolodge, with six rustic cabins set on gorgeous jungle grounds with views of both Tenorio and Miravalles. The wildlife-filled grounds are ripe for exploring, with a river trail leading to a private waterfall. Located 2km west of Bijagua; look for the turnoff near the Casita del Maiz.

Warner and Carla don't speak much English, so brush up on your Spanish.

Hotel Cacao
HOTEL $$

(☑ 2466-6142; s/d/tr/q incl breakfast US$60/75/ 95/115; ℗ ✳ ☎) Set in a yellow concrete building, this motel-style place has spacious rooms with new tiles and wooden beds plus a few decorative flourishes such as hanging masks and pottery. There's plenty of deck seating with lovely views of Volcán Miravalles. On-site laundry, shared kitchen and nice hot showers. It's located 300m northwest of the main highway. There's a handy *soda* across the street.

★ Celeste Mountain Lodge
LODGE $$$

(☑ 2278-6628; www.celestemountainlodge.com; s/d/tr/q incl all meals US$165/210/250/290; ℗ ☎) ❂ Innovative and sustainable, this contemporary, open-air, hilltop lodge in the shadow of Tenorio is stunning. The 18 rooms are small but stylish, with wooden shutters that open onto immobilizing vistas. Winding through labyrinthine gardens, a trail is laid with geotextile (no more muddy shoes!), making for soundless hiking and prime birdwatching. The price includes meals at the excellent gourmet restaurant.

Hot water comes from solar power, and cooking gas is partially produced by kitchen waste. There's even an ingenious 'tropical hot bath' heated by burning salvaged wood.

The lodge is located about halfway down the new access road from Bijagua to Tenorio, and about 4km east of town.

Finca Mei Tai B&B $$$

(☎8411-7801; www.finca-meitai.com; d/tr/q incl breakfast US$100/120/140; P🅿️❄️) Set on 40 hectares of forest and pastures 3km west of Bijagua, this family *finca* is crisscrossed by walking trails and dotted with farm animals. The two guest rooms have an abundance of natural light, local hardwoods and graceful details. Eric and Cecile built their place with the intention of living well and helping others to do the same. To get here, take the turnoff across from Pizzeria Barrigon. A third guest room was being added in 2017.

Sueño Celeste B&B $$$

(☎2466-8221; www.sueno-celeste.com; Km 28, Hwy 6; d/tr/q US$114/144/174; P🅿️❄️) This cute B&B at the southern end of Bijagua has a collection of stylish bungalows with polished-concrete floors, frilly bed linens, beamed ceilings and molded-concrete rain showers, scattered around a garden plot with Volcán Tenorio views. The fastidious Belgian owners will make sure you're oriented and informed during your stay.

Co-owner Dominique paints all the cool nature-themed murals.

Tenorio Lodge LODGE $$$

(☎2466-8282; www.tenoriolodge.com; s/d/tr incl breakfast US$165/185/205; P🅿️@📶) 🍴 On a lush hilltop 1km south of Bijagua, this lodge has 12 romantic and roomy bungalows featuring orthopedic beds, stone or wood floors and floor-to-ceiling windows with amazing views of Volcán Tenorio. On the 7-hectare property you'll find a restaurant, two ponds, a heliconia garden and two hot tubs to luxuriate in after a long day of hiking.

The lodge's sustainability efforts include using solar heating for hot water, using biodegradable shampoos and soaps, watering the crops with waste water, and drying clothes naturally rather than with a dryer.

🍴 Eating

Sprinkled along Hwy 6, Bijagua has the requisite *sodas*, a pizzeria and a few other places to eat in addition to hotel restaurants. It's all pretty standard stuff, although you can experience the very beginnings of a farm-to-table movement at the Hummingbird Cafe.

Hummingbird Cafe INTERNATIONAL $$

(☎2466-8069, 8502-0326; www.fincaverdelodge.com/hummingbird-cafe; Finca Verde Lodge; mains US$8-12; ⏱7am-9:30pm; 🍴) 🍴 This family restaurant is a surprising change of pace from the Tico fare in town. The emphasis is on fresh ingredients, many of which are grown right here on the family's organic farm (p214). Specialties include vegetarian red-chili enchiladas, fresh salads and tasty pizza pies. Come early (or stay late) and take a tour of the farm. There are four comfortable cabins (including breakfast US$70 to US$110) on the grounds.

ℹ️ Getting There & Away

About 6km northwest of Cañas, a paved road branches off the Interamericana and heads north to Upala, passing between Volcán Miravalles to the west and Volcán Tenorio to the east. Smack dab in the middle of these mighty volcanoes sits Bijagua. It's about 40km north of Cañas and 27km south of Upala. There is no gas here: fill your tank before you arrive.

Buses between San José and Upala stop in Bijagua (US$8, four daily). There are also local buses (US$2, 45 minutes) making the circuit from Cañas to Upala, stopping here. There are also frequent services to Bagaces (US$3, one hour), from where you can continue to the thermal baths of Volcán Miravalles.

A relatively new road bisecting the Tenorio National Park has made driving from La Fortuna a relatively straight shot (two to 2½ hours). A bus from there requires transferring in Cañas.

Yo Viajo (www.yoviajocr.com) is a handy app for determining bus schedules here and throughout the country.

Parque Nacional Volcán Tenorio

They say that when God finished painting the sky blue, he washed his paintbrushes in the Río Celeste. The heavenly blue river and its waterfalls and lagoons – found in **Parque Nacional Volcán Tenorio** (☎2206-5369, 2466-7010; www.sinac.go.cr/ES/ac/acat/pnvt/Paginas/default.aspx; adult/child US$12/2; ⏱8am-4pm, last entry 2pm) – are among the most spectacular natural phenomena in Costa Rica, which is probably why the park is known to locals simply as Río Celeste.

Established in 1976, this magical 184 sq km national park remains a blissfully pristine rainforest teeming with wildlife. Soaring 1916m above the cloud forest is the park's namesake, Volcán Tenorio, which consists of three peaked craters: Montezuma, Tenorio I (the tallest) and Tenorio II.

Your first stop will be the Puesto El Pilón ranger station at the park entrance, which houses a small exhibit of photographs and dead animals. Pick up a free English or Spanish hiking map.

🏃 Activities

A well-signed trail begins at the ranger station parking lot (park entrance) and winds 1.5km through the rainforest until you reach an intersection. Turn left and climb down a very steep but sturdy staircase to the **Catarata de Río Celeste**, a milky-blue waterfall that cascades 30m down the rocks into a fantastically aquamarine pool.

It's 400m further to the **Mirador**, where you'll have gorgeous views of Tenorio from the double-decker wooden platform. Further on is the technicolor **Pozo Azul** (Blue Lagoon). The trail loops around the lagoon for 400m until you arrive at the confluence of rivers known as **Los Teñidores** (The Stainers). Here two small rivers – one whitish blue and one brownish yellow – mix together to create the blueberry milk of Río Celeste.

Note that swimming is strictly prohibited everywhere along this trail. The nearby hot springs were closed after some tourists were burned in 2011. Hiking to the volcano crater is also strictly prohibited.

Allow three to four hours to complete the entire hike. It's about a 7km round-trip, but parts of the trail are steep and rocky. The trail is wet and muddy year-round. Good hiking shoes or boots are a must; you can rent boots for US$6 at the park entrance. After your hike, you'll find an area to wash your footwear near the trailhead.

🛏️ Sleeping & Eating

There are some sweet places to stay along the road to the national park, ranging from friendly budget *cabinas* to swanky mountain lodges. If you really want to get away from it all, there are a few lodges north of the park in the vicinity of the village of San Miguel.

La Carolina Lodge   LODGE $$
(📞 2466-6393; www.lacarolinalodge.com; per person incl meals US$75-95; 🅿️🛜) Flanked by a roaring river and tucked into the trees on the volcano slope, this isolated lodge is also a working cattle ranch. Cabins are rustic and romantic. The river is delicious for swimming, and a wood-fired hot tub is luxurious for soaking. Room rates include guided hikes and horseback rides in the surrounding countryside.

Amazing organic meals featuring poultry and meat from the farm are cooked over an outdoor wood-burning stove.

The lodge is about 1.3km west of the charming ranching hamlet of San Miguel; turn off the highway 5km north of Bijagua and follow the signs. It's a rough road from here to the national park; don't say we didn't warn you!

Posada Cielo Roto   CABIN $$
(📞 2466-6049; www.cielorotocostarica.com; per person incl 3 meals US$75) Eight wood cabins perched on the northern slope of Volcán Tenorio offer traditional Tico living, where dinner is cooked over a wood stove and guests gather around the fireplace. Gregarious Mario goes out of his way to extend the warmest of welcomes. Rates include a guided hike to Río Celeste and a horseback riding outing on the property. Cash only.

To get here, take the turn to San Miguel that is signposted 5km north of Bijagua. The *posada* (guesthouse) is about 10km east on a sometimes brutal road.

Catarata Río Celeste Hotel   HOTEL $$
(📞 2201-0176, 8938-9927; www.cataratariaceleste.com; d/bungalow/ste US$66/84/121; 🅿️🛜) Located about 1.5km from the park entrance, this family-run property is spread out over nice landscaped grounds. There are six simple tiled rooms that share a hammock-strung terrace, as well as five more luxurious bungalows with jacuzzis, outdoor showers and volcano views. Many different tours are on offer, as well as a pleasant open-air restaurant that attracts tour groups.

Cabinas Piuri   HOTEL $$
(📞 8699-6858, 8706-0617; www.facebook.com/cabinaspiuri; s/d incl breakfast US$35/50, planetarium r US$55, ste US$80; 🅿️🛜) About 1km past the park entrance, this unusual property (Piuri is the indigenous name for the Río Celeste) is perched on a gorgeous slice beside the milky-blue Río Celeste. Accommodations vary from colorful *cabinas* with king-size beds to an egg-shaped 'planetarium.' Soak in an inviting stone dipping pool on the river banks or take this unique opportunity to swim in the magnificent river itself.

The spacious restaurant has expansive views.

Posada Río Celeste   CABINA $$
(📞 8356-0285, for English 8978-2676; www.posadarioceleste.com; d incl breakfast US$70; 🅿️) This homey property offers eight clean, rustic rooms (but with cable TV!) and hearty

home-cooked meals, all on a family farm in a rural ranching community 1km northeast of the park entrance. Two talkative parrots inhabit the blooming gardens. Staff can organize hiking, horseback riding and swimming in and out of the park. Even if you're not staying here, this is a perfect pit stop for lunch after hiking in the park. There's no menu: Wuilbert and Vilma will serve up whatever they have cooking on their stove. Portions are huge and prices are reasonable.

Rio Celeste Hideaway   HOTEL $$$

(☑2206-4000; www.riocelestehideaway.com; d & ste incl breakfast US$370-428; P🖨) Five-star elegance, about 1.5km from the park gate. Huge, 90 sq m thatched *casitas* (cottages) with wooden floors, pastel paint jobs and antique furnishings are sprinkled among the lush landscaped grounds. Beds are covered with canopies and draped in 300-thread-count sheets. Even the bathrooms are luxurious here, with soaking tubs, outdoor showers and 'his' and 'hers' basin sinks.

Restaurant Casta   COSTA RICAN $

(☑8445-7235; casados US$7-8; ⊙7am-7pm) You want a *casado* or hot chocolate to warm you up after a long walk in the park? Here's the

place, just 1km west (toward Bijagua) from the park entrance. The menu's short, but who needs to think after a day's worth of hiking?

❶ Getting There & Away

There's no bus to the national park. The closest you can get is Bijagua, from where you can book a tour at almost any hotel, or take a taxi for US$50 round trip.

The main access road is a 30km road that connects Bijagua (Hwy 6) and Guatuso (Hwy 4), indicated by a small brown sign just north of the Agro Logos hardware store. This road has been graded in recent years (and may soon be paved). It passes the national park (and many lodgings) along the way. The entrance to the national park is about 9km from Bijagua and 21km from Guatuso – not a bad day trip from La Fortuna (about a two hour or so drive).

Five kilometers north of Bijagua is a gravel road to San Miguel. The only real reason to take this goat path is if you're staying at La Carolina (p217) or Cielo Roto (p217). Turning left at the San Miguel intersection will bring you to La Carolina Lodge (1.3km). It's about 10km to Cielo Roto from the turnoff (2km past San Miguel village).

Cañas

If you're cruising north on the Interamericana, Cañas is the first town of any size in Guanacaste, Costa Rica's driest province. *Sabanero* (cowboy) culture is evident on the sweltering streets, where full-custom pickup trucks share the road with swaggering cowboys on horseback. It's a dusty, typically Latin American town, where almost everyone struts slowly and businesses shut down for lunch. It's all centered around the Parque Central, a large bull ring and the decidedly atypical **Catholic church** (cnr Calle Central & Av Central; ⊙hours vary).

Although you're better off basing yourself in livelier Liberia or the more scenic Bijagua, Cañas is a good place to organize rafting trips on the nearby Río Corobicí or for exploring Parque Nacional Palo Verde (p220).

Most visitors can accomplish everything they want to do in Cañas in just a few hours, so there's no real need to spend the night. But should you care to linger (or if you really can't drive any longer), there are some decent accommodation options. The places in town are functional but not fabulous; by contrast, **Hotel Hacienda La Pacífica** (☑2669-6050; www.pacificacr.com; d/apt incl breakfast US$90/125; P🖨), north of Cañas, is atmospheric indeed.

BUSES FROM CAÑAS

DESTINATION	COMPANY	COST (US$)	DURATION	FREQUENCY
Liberia	Reina del Campo	3	1hr	8 daily, 6am-5:40pm
San José	Empresa La Cañera	5	3½hr	8 daily, 5:30am-5pm
Tilarán	Transporte Villana	1	40min	7 daily, 5am-3:30pm
Upala	Transportes Upala	3	2hr	3 daily (en route from San José)

✱ Getting There & Away

All buses arrive and depart from **Terminal Cañas** (La Cañera; Calle Central btwn Avs 11 & 13) at the northern end of town. There are a few *sodas* (places serving counter lunches) and snack bars. You can store your bags at the desk.

Volcán Miravalles Area

Volcán Miravalles (2028m) is the highest volcano in the Cordillera de Guanacaste, and although the main crater is dormant, the geothermal activity beneath the ground has led to its development as a hot springs destination. Miravalles isn't a national park or refuge, but the volcano itself is afforded a modicum of protection by being within the Zona Protectora Miravalles.

North of Fortuna de Bagaces, government-run Proyecto Geotérmico Miravalles is an ambitious project that uses geothermal energy to produce electricity, primarily for export to Nicaragua and Panama. It also produces about 18% of Costa Rica's electricity. A few bright steel tubes from the plant snake along the flanks of the volcano, adding an eerie, alien feel to the remote landscape.

✱ Activities

Volcán Miravalles and other volcanoes are critical sources of renewable energy for Costa Rica. But the geothermal energy visitors crave comes in liquid form: most of the area's hot springs are north of the tiny village of La Fortuna de Bagaces (not to be confused with La Fortuna de Arenal).

Río Perdido   HOT SPRINGS, HIKING
(☑ 2673-3600, toll free USA 1-888-326-5070; www.rioperdido.com; San Bernardo de Bagaces; day pass adult/child US$40/30, spa treatment US$55-95) This fabulous facility, set amid an otherworldly volcanic landscape, is a wonderful place to soak in Miravalles' soothing waters. The day pass allows access to miles of hiking trails, complete with waterfalls and panoramic views, plus the thermal river and hot springs, where temperatures range from 32°C (90°F) to 46°C (115°F).

Stay the night in eco-chic bungalows (single/double US$230/275). The bungalows are contemporary and cool, with polished-concrete floors, bold patterns, lots of windows and raised terraces facing the forest. There's also swim-up bar, hanging bridges and glorious views all around.

Las Hornillas   HOT SPRINGS, HIKING
(☑ 2100-1233, 8839-9769; www.hornillas.com; La Fortuna de Bagaces; tours incl lunch US$35-55; ☺9am-5pm) On Miravalles' southern slopes, Las Hornillas has a lunar landscape, with bubbling pools and fumaroles. Hike to see the volcanic action up close, then soak in four thermal pools and fly down a 250m slide. An additional tour involves a tractor ride followed by a walk across hanging bridges through the forest to reach a series of spectacular waterfalls. Spend the night in one of the rustic cabins (per person US$55) on the property, and you can soak in the pools by the light of the silvery moon.

El Guayacán   HOT SPRINGS
(☑ 2673-0349; www.termaleselguayacan.com; La Unión; adult/child US$10/8; ☺8am-10pm) Just behind **Thermo Manía** (☑ 2673-0233; www.thermomania.net; adult/child US$12/10; ☺8am-10pm) – the road sign is not terribly obvious) – this is a family *finca* that's hissing and smoking with vents and mud pots. There are eight thermal pools and one cold pool with a waterslide. You can also take a guided tour of the fumaroles (stay on the trail!).

Yökö Termales   HOT SPRINGS
(☑ 2673-0410; www.yokotermales.com; Miravalles; adult/child US$10/8; ☺7am-10pm) Four hot springs and a larger pool with a small waterslide and waterfall, in an attractive meadow at the foot of Miravalles. The views are magnificent, but there's little shade around the pools (though one has a true 'wet' bar, jacuzzi, and sauna). The 12 canary-tinted **rooms** (including breakfast US$40 to US$125) are a decent, but not magical, sleeping option.

Termales Miravalles   HOT SPRINGS
(☑ 2673-0606; www.facebook.com/termalesmiravalles; adult/child US$7/5; ☺7:30am-10pm)

Termales Miravalles has four pools and a super waterslide, all lying along a thermal stream. There's more cement and less nature than some of the other hot springs in the area, but there is a pretty sweet volcano view. On Saturday nights, the place often hosts a dance party with a live band. Directly across the main road from Yökö (p219).

Tours

Many tour companies offer organized trips to the various hot springs, sometimes with additional activities such as hiking, horseback riding and ziplining. Packages include transportation from Bahía Salinas, Liberia or the northern Península de Nicoya.

Canyon Adventure　　　ADVENTURE
(☑ 2673-3600; www.rioperdido.com; San Bernardo de Bagaces; adult/child US$60/50) You've done canopy tours, but have you tried a *canyon* tour? This new take on a tried-and-true adventure will have you zipping from platform to platform, most of which are mounted on rocks or canyon walls. The route is challenging and fun, with five ziplines plus a series of bridges, swings and steel cables. One of Rio Perdido many attractions, Canyon Adventure also gives full access to the thermal river, hot springs and hiking trails.

Miravalles Volcano Adventure Center　　　ADVENTURE
(☑ 8719-4276; www.facebook.com/Rainforestlink; Guayabo; canopy tour adult/child US$40/30, tours US$35-90, cabins US$30) There's something for everybody at this adventure center near the base of the volcano. The centerpiece of the complex is the canopy tour, which has 12 cables and hanging bridges through fields and forest. The place also has an on-site spa, horseback riding and other adventures, including an all-day expedition to the Miravalles crater.

ⓘ Getting There & Away

Volcán Miravalles is 27km northeast of Bagaces. Head north on a paved road through the communities of Salitral and Torno, where the road splits. Take the left-hand fork to reach Guayabo, with a few *sodas* and basic *cabinas;* to the right, you'll find Fortuna de Bagaces, with easier access to the hot springs. The road reconnects north of the two towns and continues toward Upala.

There are hourly buses connecting Bagaces with Guayabo and Fortuna de Bagaces (US$1, 45 minutes). Make sure to take the bus that passes the *termales* (ask the driver); there are two routes and one bypasses them completely. There are also direct buses here from Liberia.

When returning, it's easier to go to *el cruce* (the road crossing) 1km north from Thermo Manía (p219), because all the buses back toward civilization stop there; only a few a day turn down the road that goes directly past the hot springs.

Parque Nacional Palo Verde

The 184 sq km **Parque Nacional Palo Verde** (☑ 2206-5965, 2680-5965; adult/child US$12/2, guided tours US$48; ⊙ 8am-4pm) is a wetland sanctuary in Costa Rica's driest province. It lies on the northeastern bank of the mouth of the Río Tempisque and at the head of the Golfo de Nicoya. All the major rivers in the region drain into this ancient intersection of two basins, which creates a mosaic of habitats, including mangrove swamps, marshes, grassy savannas and evergreen forests. A number of low limestone hills provide lookouts over the park, and the park's shallow, permanent lagoons are focal points for wildlife. The park derives its name from the abundant *palo verdes* (green trees), small shrubs that are green year-round. The park is contiguous in the north with the 73 sq km Refugio de Vida Silvestre Dr Rafael Lucas Rodríguez Caballero and the Reserva Biológica Lomas de Barbudal (p237).

The mosquitoes are legendary in this place. By all means, bring insect repellent!

⚘ Activities

Hiking

You can explore the park's well-maintained trails on your own or accompany an OTS (Organization for Tropical Studies) guide on his or her regular one-hour guided walk (adult/child US$30/20). Contact OTS ahead

---

FARMSTAYS

Northwestern Costa Rica is farm country. From the cattle ranches of the lowlands to the coffee plantations on the mountain slopes, much of this land has been devoted to agriculture. As the economy changes, many farming families have discovered that they can supplement their income by inviting guests home. As such, the region offers many opportunities for farmstays, where travelers can experience authentic rural life and interact closely with hardworking farmers.

of time if you'd like the guided walk, which takes place between 8am and 1pm, depending on conditions. Pick up a map at the park entrance.

From the entrance, the first trailhead you'll reach is for the **Sendero Roco**, which is a short steep climb up to a scenic viewpoint over the lagoon. On a clear day you can see the Río Tempisque to the Golfo de Nicoya. Next along, the **Sendero Mapache** traverses three distinct habitats in a short 700m. See if you can tell the difference between the deciduous lowland, limestone and evergreen forests.

Along the shore of the lagoon, the 900m **Sendero El Pizote** is prime for spotting waterbirds. And at the far end of the park, beyond the ranger station, you can hike 1400m along the **Sendero La Cantera** to reach a splendid lookout that takes in the whole area.

No matter which trail you choose, remember that it gets fiercely hot in the dry season – carry ample water, wear a sun hat and avoid hiking at midday.

Wildlife-Watching

Palo Verde has the greatest concentrations of waterfowl and shorebirds in Central America; over 300 bird species have been recorded here. Birdwatchers come to see the large flocks of herons (including rare black-crowned night herons), storks (including the endangered jabirú), spoonbills, egrets, ibises, grebes and ducks. Forest birds, including scarlet macaws, great curassows, keel-billed toucans and parrots, are also common. Frequently sighted mammals include deer, coatis, armadillos, monkeys and peccaries, as well as the largest population of jaguarundis in Costa Rica. There are also numerous reptiles in the wetlands including crocodiles that are reportedly up to 5m in length.

The dry season (December to March) is the best time to visit, as flocks of birds tend to congregate in the remaining lakes and marshes. Plus, the trees lose their leaves, allowing for clearer viewing. Mammals are occasionally seen around the watering holes. That said, the entire basin swelters during the dry season, so bring adequate sun protection. During the wet months, large portions of the area are flooded, and access may be limited. If you'd like some help spotting and identifying furred and feathered creatures, OTS offers guided bird walks and night tours.

☞ Tours

To fully appreciate the size and topography of the park, it's worth organizing a boat trip (per person US$57) down the Río Tempisque, a wide, brown, brackish river contained on either side by mangroves. Arrangements can be made through the OTS Hacienda Palo Verde Research Station.

Boat tours depart from the dock in Puerto Chamorro, on the main park road, 2km from the ranger station. If you arrive early enough, you may be able to show up and find a free spot on an outgoing boat. You can also hire a boatman from Puerto Humo, which is reachable by the 'Rosaria' bus from Nicoya. Tour operators on the Península de Nicoya and in La Fortuna bring tour groups to Palo Verde, but if you can get here, you'll save plenty of money by arranging everything yourself.

El Viejo Wetlands WILDLIFE
(Hacienda el Viejo; ☎2296-0966; www.elviejowetlands.com; cultural tour US$25, boat tour US$71; ☺7am-3pm) ✎ Bordering Parque Nacional Palo Verde, this impressive facility is operated by a successful sugarcane family that has devoted 20 sq km to a wetlands refuge. In addition to hiking, biking and boat tours (some of which enter the national park), they also do a sugarcane demonstration; you'll make 'agua de sapo' (toad water) from lime, ginger and sugarcane. Meals are served in the historic and atmospheric Casona (mansion). The main entrance is about 15km south of Filadelfia. Head southeast out of town on Calle 5 and follow the signs. El Viejo can also provide transportation from anywhere on the northern Península de Nicoya.

🛏 Sleeping & Eating

OTS Hacienda Palo Verde
Research Station LODGE $$
(☎2524-0607; www.ots.ac.cr; r incl meals per adult/child US$90/38; 🅿🛜) Run by the Organization for Tropical Studies, this station conducts tropical research and teaches graduate-level classes. But it also has rustic cabins with bunk beds and fans, which are rented out to 'natural history visitors.' The research station is on a well-signed road 8km from the park entrance. Camping is not permitted at the research station but you may inquire at the park office to see if they will allow it.

❶ Getting There & Away

The main road to the entrance, usually passable by ordinary cars year-round, begins from a signed turnoff from the Interamericana, opposite Bagaces. The 28km gravel road has tiny brown signs that direct you when the road forks. Once inside the park, another 8km brings you to the limestone hill, Cerro Guayacán (and the OTS Hacienda Palo Verde Research Station), from where there are great views; 2km further are the Palo Verde park headquarters and ranger station. You can drive through a swampy maze of roads to the Reserva Biológica Lomas de Barbudal (p237) without returning to the Interamericana, but be sure to ask rangers about road conditions.

Buses connecting Cañas and Liberia can drop you in Bagaces, opposite the turnoff to the park, but still a good distance away. If you're staying at the Palo Verde Research Station, the staff may be able to pick you up, but be sure to make advance arrangements.

You can take the 'Rosaria' bus from Nicoya to Puerto Humo, and then bargain with local boatmen to take you to Puerto Chamorro, the dock where all the tours leave, just 2km from the ranger station.

Liberia

POP 56,900

The sunny rural capital of Guanacaste has long served as a transportation hub to Nicaragua, as well as being the standard-bearer of Costa Rica's *sabanero* (cowboy) culture. Today, tourism is fast becoming a significant contributor to the economy. With an expanding international airport (p226), Liberia is a safer and more chilled-out Costa Rican gateway than San José.

Most of the historic buildings in the town center are in need of a paint job (some locals dream of it becoming a historic district like Nicaragua's Granada), though the 'White City' is pleasant, with a good range of accommodations. Still, it's largely a launch pad for exploring Parque Nacional Rincón de la Vieja (p227) and the beaches of the Península de Nicoya, rather than a destination in itself. The area may be transformed by Discovery Costa Rica, a billion-dollar, 890-hectare theme park due to be built between 2018 and 2020.

◉ Sights

The blocks around the intersection of Av Central and Calle Real contain several of Liberia's oldest houses, many dating back about 150 years. Locals harbor a long-term dream to pedestrianize Calle Real (south of the park), the historic thoroughfare into and out of the city, to replicate places like nearby Grenada in Nicaragua.

Ponderosa Adventure Park WILDLIFE RESERVE
(☑ 2105-7181; www.ponderosaadventurepark.com; tour adult/child US$50/35, 3-tour package adult/child US$115/105; ☉ 8am-5pm) Elephants, zebras, giraffes and other African animals are right at home in the dry Guanacaste heat, as you can see at this private wildlife reserve. The safari tour allows you to get up close and personal with the (sort of) wild animals. Kayaking, ziplining, horseback riding and ATVs are also on offer. The park is in El Salto, about 11km south of town on the Interamericana, halfway to Bagaces.

La Agonía CHURCH
(La Iglesia de la Ermita de Nuestro Señor de la Agonía; cnr Av Central & Calle 9; ☉ variable) With whitewashed walls and twin pillars flanking the front door, La Agonía typifies the Spanish colonial architecture that earned Liberia its 'White City' nickname. This is the city's oldest church, built in 1825. There is supposedly an art and culture exhibit inside, but it's difficult to say for sure, as the doors are usually locked tight. Check at the house next door to the church for opening hours; if you can't go in, at least check out the massive yellow iguana statue in the park.

🛏 Sleeping

Liberia is at its busiest during the dry season – reservations are strongly recommended on weekends and over Christmas, Easter and Día de Guanacaste. During the wet season, most of the midrange and top-end hotels give discounts. In town, most of the lodgings are budget and midrange options, but you'll find some high-end international chain hotels near the airport.

Hotel Liberia GUESTHOUSE $
(☑ 2666-0161; www.hotelliberiacr.com; Calle Real btwn Avs Central & 2; dm/s/d incl breakfast from US$13/32/45; 🅿 🛜) It's hard to resist the glorious shady courtyard at this century-old guesthouse, one of Liberia's best budget options. Appealing *'casona'* rooms are in the old building, where high ceilings, tile floors and wooden furniture contribute to an old-fashioned ambience. Less atmospheric (and cheaper) *'torre'* rooms and dorms are in the newer concrete building at the back of the courtyard.

Hospedaje Dodero HOSTEL $
(☑ 2665-4326, 8729-7524; www.hospedajedodero.yolasite.com; Av 11 btwn Calles 12 & 14; dm US$11, s US$17-20, d US$25-30; ❄ 🛜) This place is super clean, has super service and is close

to the bus station. All rooms have shared bathrooms; some have air-con. There's a communal outdoor kitchen overlooking a small yard filled with flowers and hung with hammocks. It's nothing fancy, but it's very friendly. Shawn, the owner, has an incredibly comprehensive bus schedule in a three-ring binder.

La Posada del Tope GUESTHOUSE $
(☑2666-3876; www.facebook.com/hotellaposadadeltope; Calle Real btwn Avs 2 & 4; d US$25; P@🛜) Rooms are in the 'casa real' (royal house) across the street from the wooden lobby. Set around an awesome garden and furnished with eclectic art and antiques, this place has a lot of personality. Rooms are basic and clean enough, and bathrooms are shared (mostly), but the price is right. The bilingual Tico owner, Denis, is a wealth of information. This is the official office for NicaBus in town, which may save you some hassle at the Liberia terminal.

Hotel Javy HOTEL $$
(☑2666-9253; www.hoteljavy.com; cnr Av 19 & Calle 19; d incl breakfast US$50; P✳🛜) Isabel is your hostess with the mostest. This charming lady goes out of her way to make sure her guests are happy, not least by preparing an enormous, delicious breakfast to send you off feeling satisfied. The rooms are light-filled and comfortable, with firm beds, incongruously formal furnishings and spotless new bathrooms. The location, 2km northeast of Parque Central, and 200m north of the IPEC, is not so convenient, particularly without a car.

🍴 Eating

Liberia has a good selection of restaurants, both in town and on the road to the airport. If you've been on the road for months and are dying for it, 'modernized' Liberia has some chain fast-food joints near the highway. If you're taking the bus, pick up some snacks for the road at the **market** (Av 7 btwn Calles 10 & 12; ⏰6am-7pm Mon-Sat, to noon Sun) next to Terminal Liberia.

Donde Pipe CAFE $
(☑2665-4343; www.dondepipe.com; cnr Calle 8 & Av 5; mains US$7-11; ⏰8am-6pm; 🛜👪) This little cafe is a local favorite, thanks to free wi-fi, strong coffee and scrumptious sweets and breakfasts. In addition to cafe fare, the menu features local specialties such as chifrijos (rice and pinto beans with fried pork, fresh tomato salsa and corn chips) and tamales,

plus fresh fruit juices. Has a children's menu. Friendly staff, air-con and a block from the bus station: need we say more?

Los Comales COSTA RICAN $
(☑2665-0105; Calle Real btwn Avs 7 & 5; dishes US$4-8; ⏰6:30am-2pm) ¡Poder Tica! This convivial and popular local spot is run by a women's collective. Come for traditional Guanacaste fare such as arroz de mais (rice with chicken and corn). Lunchtime is crowded which means slow service. There's a dozen fresh juices and batidos (fruit shakes made with milk or water) to wet your whistle.

★Region 5 COSTA RICAN $$
(☑4700-9523; cnr Av 25 de Julio & Calle 2; mains $8-22; ⏰noon-9pm) 'Costa Rican by birth, Guanacasteco, thank god!' boasts this new steakhouse, named for the province and set in the historic home of beloved Liberian doctor Enrique Briceño. Lunches feature Nicoyan treats including chorreadas (sweet corn pancakes) and tanelas (sweet empanadas). Meaty evening fare includes baby back ribs and New York steaks; tuna steak in seafood sauce is a wonderful surprise.

★Mariajuana CAFE $$
(☑2665-7217; www.facebook.com/mariajuana restaurante; cnr Calle 3 & Av 1; mains US$7-17; ⏰11:30am-11:30pm Tue-Sat, from 3pm Sun; 🛜🖶👪) It's moved across town, but its dreamcatchers, African masks and cat-themed art are still all the rage. Sip a regional Guanaca beer (made with local honey for a sweet finish) while swinging under the giant mango tree, and snack on appetizers (US$7 to US$8) or substantial steak or seafood platters. Finish off a hot Guanacaste afternoon with a 'heart-attack sundae'. On the site of the former Meson Liberiano.

Café Liberia FUSION $$
(☑2665-1660; Calle Real btwn Avs 2 & 4; mains US$9-14; ⏰9am-9pm Tue-Sat; 🛜) This beautifully restored colonial-era building has heavy wooden furniture and frescoed ceilings, creating a romantic ambience for enjoying rich coffee and gourmet fare. French chef Sebastian and his Tica wife Lijia have taken staple foods to new levels: ceviche is served with irresistible, warm fresh-baked tortilla chips. The courtyard hosts occasional live music and has a multilingual bookshelf.

Green House FUSION $$
(Casa Verde; ☑2665-5037; www.facebook.com/TheGreenHouseCR; Hwy 21; mains US$6-12; ⏰11am-9pm; 🛜🖶) When they say 'green

Liberia

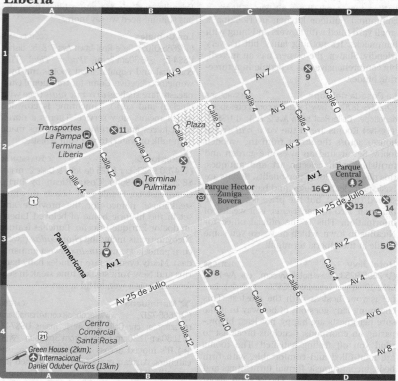

house' they mean it – this is a glass building, filled with plants. There are green-paneled windows and many veggie options on the menu. Come into the light-filled dining room for a delightful fusion of flavors, such as grilled chicken with mango salsa and excellent fish tacos. Located on the airport road, about 8km west of town.

Jauja
INTERNATIONAL **$$**

(☑ 2665-2061; www.facebook.com/jaujarestaurante; cnr Av 25 de Julio & Calle 10; mains US$10-15; ◷8am-10pm Mon-Sat; ☎🖥) This stylish indoor-outdoor bar-cafe (the name's pronounced 'How-ha') on the main drag is unusual for its upscale ambience and classy cuisine. Service is also excellent. Look for wood-fired pizza, tender grass-fed steaks, and burgers on home-baked buns. It's popular with the local professional set, as well as tourists and expats.

It thumps to an '80s soundtrack, for better or worse.

Pizza Pronto
PIZZA **$$**

(☑ 2666-2098; cnr Av 4 & Calle 1; mains US$10-18; ◷noon-3pm & 6-10pm) This very cute old-world pizzeria, where the wood is stacked next to the smoking courtyard oven, keeps it romantic and simple – just pizza, pasta and salads. The pizzas are delish, ranging from the recommended vegetarian option to the not-so-recommended taco pizza. You can choose from a list of more than 30 pizzas or create your own.

Toro Negro Steakhouse
STEAK **$$$**

(☑ 2666-2456; cnr Av Central & Calle 1; mains US$12-18; ◷11am-9:30pm Tue-Sun; ☎🖥) Located in a beautiful colonial-era building, this family-friendly restaurant has an extensive Italian-Tico menu specializing in meat dishes such as New York strip steak, filet mignon and burgers. The rustic interior is inviting, but you can't beat the outdoor balcony for people-watching and enjoying the evening breeze.

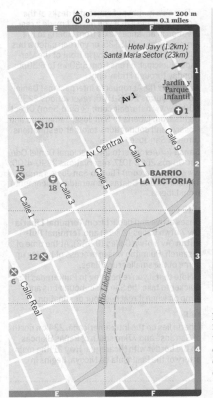

Hotel Javy (1.2km);
Santa María Sector (23km)

Av 1

Jardín y
Parque
Infantil

Av Central

Calle 9
Calle 7
Calle 5
Calle 3
Calle 1

BARRIO
LA VICTORIA

Calle Real

Río Liberia

0 ——— 200 m
0 ——— 0.1 miles

Liberia

places for a drink. There's also sports and music videos on the big screen, but the volume is usually turned down so patrons can enjoy the tranquil atmosphere. The menu offers very tasty pub grub and Tico fare (shared appetizers US$10).

Guana's SPORTS BAR
(☑2665-3022; Calle 2 btwn Avs 25 de Julio & 1; ☺11am-2am) Facing Parque Central, this open-air bar has cold beer, decent pizza and football on the big screen. The place picks up on weekends, when the party spills out into the courtyard and onto the sidewalk. Chuck back a cold Imperial and people watch to your heart's content.

Morales House BAR
(☑2665-2490; cnr Av 1 & Calle 14; ☺6pm-2am) A real Guanacaste *sabanero* hangout, this barnlike bar has bull heads on the walls, blaring *ranchera* music and American sports on TV. Bonus: thick, juicy steaks for hungry buckaroos.

For more economic but similar fare, the same owner runs the **Taqueria de la Calle** (Calle Real btwn Avs Central & 2; $3-7; ☺12:30pm-10:30pm Wed-Sun, from 2pm Tue; ⊞☎), opposite Hotel Liberia (p222), as well as **La Pastelera**, next to Cafe Liberia (p223). Many of the same chefs are employed across the three locales.

☕ Drinking & Nightlife

There is no shortage of watering holes from the main square on down to the Interamericana. It's up to you to decide if you want to drink at the sports bar, the cocktails bar, the cowboy bar or the art cafe. What kind of mood are you in?

Palermo Lounge COCKTAIL BAR
(☑2240-3325; cnr Av Central & Calle 3; ☺4pm-midnight Mon-Thu, from 10am Fri-Sun) This tropical garden, lush with greenery and waterfalls, is one of the city's most pleasant

❶ Information

MEDICAL SERVICES
Hospital Dr Enrique Baltodano Briceño
(☑2666-0011, emergencies 2666-0318; Rte 918) Behind the stadium on the northeastern outskirts of town.

NORTHWESTERN COSTA RICA LIBERIA

MONEY

Liberia probably has more banks per square meter than any other town in Costa Rica.

BAC San José (☑ 2295-9797; Centro Comercial Santa Rosa, Rte 21; ⊙ 9am-6pm Mon-Fri, to 1pm Sat)

Banco de Costa Rica (☑ 2666-2582; cnr Calle Real & Av 1; ⊙ 9am-4pm Mon-Fri)

Banco Nacional (☑ 2666-0191; Av 25 de Julio btwn Calles 6 & 8; ⊙ 8:30am-7pm Mon-Fri, 9am-3pm Sat)

Citibank (cnr Interamericana & Av 25 de Julio; ⊙ 9am-6pm Mon-Fri, to 12:30pm Sat)

POST

Post Office (Correos de Costa Rica; www. correos.go.cr; cnr Av 3 & Calle 8; ⊙ 8am-5pm Mon-Fri, until noon Sat)

❶ Getting There & Away

AIR

Located 12km west of Liberia, **Aeropuerto Internacional Daniel Oduber Quirós** (LIR; www. liberiacostaricaairport.net) serves as the country's second international airport, providing easy access to all those beautiful beaches without the hassle of San José. In January 2012 it unveiled its sleek and modern US$35 million terminal.

The majority of international flights go to the USA and Canada, though there are some regional flights on Copa Air (to Panama) and Taca (to Guatemala). Domestic flights mainly go to San José.

There's a number of car-rental desks at the airport near the exit if you haven't made a reservation in advance. Taxis from Liberia to the airport are about US$25, or you can catch a bus (US$1, 30 minutes, hourly) in front of the Mercado Municipal; it runs from 5:30am to 6:30pm, Monday through Friday only.

NatureAir (☑ Aeropuerto Internacional Daniel Oduber Quirós 2668-1106, reservations 2299-6000; www.natureair.com; ⊙ 6am-5pm) Direct flights from Liberia to San José, Tamarindo and Nosara, and connections to other destinations through San José.

Sansa (☑ Aeropuerto Internacional Daniel Oduber Quirós 2668-1017, reservations 2290-4100; www.flysansa.com) Flies to San José, Tambor, Tamarindo and Costas Esmeraldas (Nicaragua) from Liberia.

BUS

Buses arrive and depart from **Terminal Liberia** (Av 7 btwn Calles 12 & 14) and **Terminal Pulmitan** (Av 5 btwn Calles 10 & 12). At the time of research, Pulmitan was in process of buying up some of the smaller rural lines.

Note that if you're heading to Puntarenas it's quicker to take the San José–bound bus and jump off when it reaches your destination.

CAR

Liberia lies on the Interamericana, 234km north of San José and 77km south of Peñas Blancas on the border with Nicaragua. Hwy 21, the main artery of the Península de Nicoya, begins in

BUSES FROM LIBERIA

DESTINATION (COMPANY)	COST (US$)	DURATION	TERMINAL	FREQUENCY
Cañas (Reina del Campo)	2	1½hr	Liberia	half-hourly, 5:30am-5:30pm
Curubandé	2	40min	Liberia	6:40am, noon, 5pm
La Cruz/Peñas Blancas (Arrieta)	2.50	1½-2hr	Liberia	5:30am, 8:30am, 9am, 11am
Nicoya, via Filadelfia and Santa Cruz (La Pampa)	2.50	1½hr	Liberia	half-hourly, 4:30am-8:20pm
Playa Flamingo and Brasilito (La Pampa)	2	1½hr	Liberia	6am, 8am, 10am, 11am, 12:30pm, 5pm, 6pm
Playas del Coco (Pulmitan)	1.50	1hr	Pulmitan	half-hourly, 5am-11am, plus 12:30pm, 2:30pm, 6:30pm
Playa Hermosa (La Pampa)	2	1½hr	Liberia	5 daily, 7:30am-5:30pm
Playa Tamarindo (La Pampa)	2	2hr	Liberia	7 daily, 3:50am-12:30pm; hourly, 2pm-6pm
Puntarenas (Reina del Campo)	3	3hr	Liberia	9 daily, 5am-3:30pm
San José (Pulmitan)	8	4hr	Pulmitan	14 daily, 3am-10pm

Liberia and heads southwest. A dirt road leads 25km from Barrio La Victoria to the Santa María entrance of Parque Nacional Rincón de la Vieja; the partially paved road to the Las Pailas entrance begins from the Interamericana, 5km north of Liberia.

It's generally hard to find street signs here, and locals still give directions using nearby locales and distances ('100 meters, then turn left at the *pulpería*'), rather than actual street names.

There are more than a dozen car-rental agencies in Liberia, most of which have desks at the airport. Most companies will drop off your car at your hotel upon request.

Adobe (☑ 2667-0608, in USA 866-767-8651; www.adobecar.com; ◷ 8am-5pm) is one of the cheapest companies in Costa Rica. Drop-off point is next to Hotel Liberia (p222).

Parque Nacional Rincón de la Vieja

Given its proximity to Liberia – really just a hop, a skip and a few bumps away – this 141 sq km **national park** (☑ 2661-8139; ◷ 8am-3pm Tue-Sun) feels refreshingly uncrowded and remote. The name (which translates as 'old lady's nook') comes from its steamy main attraction, the active Volcán Rincón de la Vieja (1895m). The park also covers several other peaks in the same volcanic range, including the highest, Volcán Santa María (1916m). Exhaling geothermal energy, the park bubbles with multihued fumaroles, tepid springs and steaming, flatulent mud pots, as well as a young and feisty *volcancito* (small volcano). All of these can be visited on foot via well-maintained (but often steep) trails. Note the Las Pailas sector is closed on Monday.

🏃 Activities

Hiking

From the Santa María ranger station (p229), there's 12km of hiking trails which take in the hot springs. Since the 2012 eruptions, the trek to the summit of Rincón de la Vieja is no longer open to the public.

Catarata La Cangreja   HIKING
A four-hour, 5.1km (each direction) hike leads to Catarata La Cangreja, where falls drop 50m from a cliff into a small swimmable lagoon. The trail winds through forest past massive strangler figs, then to open savanna spiked with yucca on the volcano's flanks, where views stretch to the Palo Verde wetlands and the Pacific beyond.

Sendero Las Pailas   HIKING
A circular trail known as Sendero Las Pailas – about 3km in total – takes you east of Las Pailas ranger station (p229), past boiling mud pools (*las pailas*), sulfurous fumaroles and a *volcancito* (small volcano). This is the most popular (and most crowded) section of the park, as it's an easy but worthwhile trail with a lot to see. A plan to pave this trail has yet to come to fruition, but it is the easiest and flattest of all the park's pathways.

Thermal Springs

There's no better way to recover from a grueling hike than by soaking in thermal springs. Many of the springs are reported to have therapeutic properties, always a good thing if you've been hitting the *guaro cacique* (sugarcane liquor) a little too hard.

In the Sector Santa María, a trail leads 2.8km west through the 'enchanted forest,' past the lovely **Catarata Bosque Encantado** (Enchanted Forest Falls), to sulfurous hot springs. Don't soak in them for more than about half an hour (some people suggest much less) without taking a dip in the nearby cold springs, 2km away, to cool off. If you want real-deal, volcano-created thermal pools, here they are – it doesn't get more 'natural' than this.

On the fringes of the park, there are several private facilities that have thermal pools with varying temperatures: no hiking required. Many companies and hotels offer tours to these sites from Liberia.

Hot Springs Río Negro   HOT SPRINGS
(☑ 2690-2900; www.guachipelin.com; per person US$20; ◷ 9am-5pm) Set in the dry forest along the Río Negro, this magical place is managed by the Hacienda Guachipelín (p229). Ten natural, stone-crafted hot pools are accessed by a lovely wooded trail, with hanging bridges leading to pools on either side of the raging river. Pools range in temperature from 28°C (82°F) to 53°C (127°F).

About 1km from the Las Pailas ranger station (p229), turn toward Rincon de la Vieja Lodge (p229) and the Santa María sector. The hot springs will be on your right.

Simbiosis Spa   SPA
(☑ 2666-8075; www.guachipelin.com; pools US$15, 50-min treatment US$60-75; ◷ 9am-5pm) A short jaunt from the park entrance, this spa takes advantage of the volcanic activity happening right on the property. Guests can see the boiling mud pools that are the source of their mud bath; an on-site geyser occasionally puts

FLORA & FAUNA OF RINCÓN DE LA VIEJA

The park was created in 1973 to protect a vital watershed that feeds 32 rivers and streams. Its relatively remote location means that wildlife, rare elsewhere, is out in force here, with the major volcanic crater making for a rather dramatic backdrop to the scene. Volcanic activity has occurred many times since the late 1960s; the most recent eruption of steam and ash was in 2012. At the moment, the volcano is gently active and does not present any danger – ask locally for the latest news, as volcanoes do act up. Note that the crater itself is off-limits, as the 2012 eruptions have made it unsafe.

Elevations in the park range from less than 600m to 1916m, meaning visitors pass through a variety of habitats as they ascend the volcanoes, though the majority of the trees in the park are typical of those found in dry tropical forests throughout Guanacaste. The park is home to the country's highest density of Costa Rica's national flower, the increasingly rare purple orchid (Cattleya skinneri), locally known as *guaria morada*.

on a show. Four pools (two warm, two cool) and a range of massage options.

Tours

Lodges in the area can arrange tours such as horseback riding, mountain biking, guided waterfall and hot-spring hikes, rappeling, rafting and tubing on the lesser-known Río Colorado and, everyone's favorite cash burner, canopy tours. Tours are offered by Borinquen Mountain Resort, Buena Vista Lodge, Canyon de la Vieja Adventure Lodge and Hacienda Guachipelín. Transportation from Liberia may also be provided, if needed.

Canyon de la Vieja
Adventure Lodge   SPA, ADVENTURE TOUR

(☑ 2665-5912; www.canondelavieja.com; spa US$15, tours US$40-50; ⊙8am-4pm) On the bank of the crystal-blue Río Colorado, this sprawling lodge operates a full-service spa, with cool and warm pools, mud baths, massage and other treatments. The river current is strong, but the swimming hole is glorious for cooling off on a hot day (unfortunately, there's not much shade). The lodge also offers horseback riding, tubing, rafting and canopy tours.

The lodge is 8km north of Liberia. Accommodation (single/double including breakfast US$80/100) is also available.

Sleeping & Eating

There is a rustic cafe near the park entrance to Las Pailas that will serve you a sandwich or sell you a bottle of water. It's not much, so you're better off coming prepared with a picnic and plenty of water. Otherwise, your eating options are mostly restricted to the hotels. There are a few *sodas* in Curubandé, if you want to change it up.

El Sol Verde   CAMPGROUND $

(☑ 2665-5357; www.elsolverde.com; campsite US$10, tent houses US$29, d/q US$52/71; ℗ 🛜)
🌿 The feisty German couple here offer three Spanish-tiled, wood-walled rooms. Alternatively, bed down in the camping area, where there are a few furnished tent houses, a shared outdoor kitchen, solar-heated showers and plenty of space to pitch your own tent. The mural-painted terrace is a lovely place to relax. Located in Curubandé village. You'll find hiking, swimming and wildlife in the immediate vicinity.

Casa Rural Aroma de Campo   HOTEL $$

(☑ 2665-0008, reservations 7010-5776; www.aromadecampo.com; s/d/tr/q incl breakfast US$58/81/110/128, bungalow incl breakfast US$116; ℗ 🛜 ✖) Near the village of Curubandé, this serene, epiphyte-hung, hammock-strung oasis has six rooms with polished hardwood floors, open bathrooms, colorful wall art, mosquito nets and a classy rural sensibility. Scattered around the property, an additional six prefab bungalows have bold colors and glass walls for better immersion in the forested setting. Delicious meals are served family-style in the courtyard. Warning: the pet parrot is an early riser.

Buena Vista Lodge   LODGE $$

(☑ 2690-1414; www.buenavistalodgecr.com; d incl breakfast US$70-100; ℗ 🛜 ✖) 🌿 Part cattle ranch, part adventure lodge, this expansive place is set on 809 hectares in the park's western sector. On the grounds are three waterfalls, thermal pools, a canopy tour, hanging bridges and a thrilling 400m mountain waterslide. Choose between rustic stained-wood rooms and more private log cabins with glorious views. This lodge caters to package tourists big time.

Accessible via the village of Cañas Dulces. The resort's sustainable practices include composting, environmental education classes and using methane gas for cooking and to run the laundry's dryers.

Rinconcito Lodge

LODGE $$

(☑ 2666-2764, 2200-0074; www.rinconcitolodge. com; San Jorge; lodge s/d US$34/47, standard s/d US$52/74, superior d US$78; [P][☎]) Just 3km from the Santa María sector of the park, this affordable option has attractive, rustic cabins that are surrounded by some of the prettiest pastoral scenery imaginable. The cheaper rooms are tiny, but they are clean and fresh. The lodge also offers horseback riding and ziplining tours. Located in San Jorge on Rte 918, near El Tanque.

Rincón de la Vieja Lodge

LODGE $$

(☑ 2200-0238; s/d incl breakfast from US$60/70; [P][@][≋]) ⟋ Closest to the Las Pailas entrance, this hacienda is on 400 hectares of protected land in breezy horse country. In addition to the 49 rustic rooms, there is a small pond, a family-style **restaurant** and a canopy tour. Staff members are utterly charming.

Rancho Curubandé Lodge

LODGE $$

(☑ 2665-0375; www.rancho-curubande.com; s/d/ tr incl breakfast US$62/74/85; [P][✳][☎]) Set on a working *finca* (farm), this is a pleasant, family-run place. Leopauldina keeps 16 spotless and simple rooms with beamed ceilings and a wide common front porch lit by tasteful wrought-iron chandeliers. Located on the road to Las Pailas, about 600m from the Interamericana.

Borinquen Mountain Resort & Spa

RESORT $$$

(☑ 2690-1900; www.borinquenresort.com; d incl breakfast US$220-365; [P][✳][☎][≋]) The area's most luxurious resort is located on the western flank of the park. It features nicely appointed bungalows with private decks and jaw-dropping mountain views. Hot springs, mud baths and natural saunas are surrounded by greenery. A treatment at the elegant **Anáhuac Spa** (9am to 6pm) – suspended over the steaming jungle – is the icing on this decadent mud pie.

The resort is accessible via the village of Cañas Dulces. It's 15km past the village on the main road to the entrance, and then another 3km from the entrance to the resort.

All the expected adventure tours are on offer here.

Hacienda Guachipelín

HOTEL $$$

(☑ 2666-8075; www.guachipelin.com; s/d/ tr/q incl breakfast US$84/102/132/152; [P][✳][☎][≋]) This appealing 19th-century working cattle ranch is set on 12 sq km of primary and secondary forest. The 54 rooms are spacious and comfortable with traditional wood furniture and wide, welcoming verandas. All rooms enjoy lovely views of the volcano and surrounding grounds. You'll appreciate the welcome drink at check-in. It's 10km from the park entrance. Be warned that the onsite 'adventure center' makes this place feel a little like a vacation factory, catering largely to package tourists who descend for organized horse tours, in-house canopy tours and guided hikes in the national park.

ℹ️ Information

The two main entrances to the park each have their own ranger station, where you sign in, pay admission and get free maps. Most visitors enter through **Las Pailas ranger station** (☑ 2666-5051; www.acguanacaste.ac.cr; adult/6-12yr/ under 5yr US$15/5/free; ☺ 8am-4pm Tue-Sun, no entry after 3pm) on the western flank, where most of the trails begin. The **Santa María ranger station** (☑ 2666-5051; www.acguanacaste. ac.cr; adult/6-12yr/under 5yr US$15/5/free; ☺ 7am-4pm, no entry after 3pm), to the east, is in the Hacienda Santa María, a 19th-century *rancho* that was reputedly once owned by US President Lyndon Johnson. This is your access point to the sulfurous springs.

ℹ️ Getting There & Away

The Las Pailas sector is accessible via a good 20km road that begins at a signed turnoff from the Interamericana, 5km north of Liberia. It's paved for the first part of the drive past Curubandé. If you're not staying at the Hacienda Guachipelín, you'll have to pay (US$1.50 per person) to drive on its private road, which takes you to the park entrance.

The Santa María ranger station, in the east, is accessible via a rougher gravel road beginning at Barrio La Victoria in Liberia. Head east on Av 11, go around the stadium and continue north on Rte 918 for about 20km to the park entrance.

While both roads are passable by regular cars throughout the dry season, a 4WD is required during the rainy season and is highly recommended at all other times. To travel between the two sectors you needn't double back to Liberia: one kilometer from the Las Pailas park entrance is the turn toward Rincón de la Vieja Lodge, Río Negro hot springs (p227) and the Sector Santa María.

There's no public transportation to the park entrances, but a Transbasa Rte 523 bus travels

CURUBANDA & THE VOLCANO

According to Costa Rican indigenous folk legend, a princess named Curubanda fell in love with the chief of a rival tribe, Mixcoac. When her father, Curubande (pay close attention to the names!) learned of the Romeo-and-Juliet-in-Costa-Rica relationship, he threw his proposed son-in-law into the volcano. Soon thereafter, Curubanda had a son. To allow him to be close to his father, she threw *him* into the volcano. The Greeks, apparently, don't hold a monopoly on family tragedy.

For the rest of her life, sorrowful Curubanda lived in the shadow of the volcano, becoming a powerful *curandero* (witch). Learning the secrets of forest medicine, many locals sought her out for her curative powers, saying 'I'm going to look for *la vieja* (the old lady).' And so the volcano is known today.

from Liberia to Curubandé three times daily in each direction (US$2, 35 minutes, 6:40am, noon, 5pm). Any hotel in Liberia can arrange transport to the park for around US$20 per person. Otherwise, you can hire a 4WD taxi from Liberia for about US$40 to Las Pailas, or US$65 to Santa María, each way.

The road to Cañas Dulces and beyond, toward Buena Vista Lodge (p228) and Borinquen Mountain Resort & Spa (p229), is well signed about 11.5km north of Liberia, where it intersects with the Interamericana. Note that there is no access to the park from this side, so you'll have to go all the way back to the Interamericana and enter through Las Pailas.

Sector Santa Rosa

Established in 1971 as a national park, the **Sector Santa Rosa** (2666-5051; www. acguanacaste.ac.cr; adult/child US$15/5, surfing or snorkeling surcharge US$12; 8am-4pm) is now a part of the much larger Area de Conservación Guanacaste (ACG). This sprawling area was established to protect the largest remaining stand of tropical dry forest in Central America. With its primordial acacia thorn trees and tall jaragua grass, this rare landscape resembles the African savanna, though closer inspection reveals more American species of plants, including cacti and bromeliads.

Aside from the startlingly dry landscape, Santa Rosa has some legendary surf breaks, important nesting beaches for several species of sea turtle, and deep historical gravitas. Difficult access means that most of the Santa Rosa sector is fairly empty, though it can get reasonably busy on weekends in the dry season, when Ticos flock to the park in search of their often hard-to-find history.

Sights

Santa Rosa was the site of game-changing battles from three different eras, ranking it among the country's most significant historical sites. This history is commemorated with a museum and a monument. Santa Rosa also contains an important nesting site for olive ridley turtles and famous surf breaks.

Monument de los Heroes VIEWPOINT, MONUMENT (incl in park admission) Climb up the steep staircase behind La Casona to reach a lookout point with a stunning view of three volcanoes. The monument itself was built to honor the heroes of the two important battles that took place in this vicinity – the defeat of William Walker's *filibusteros* in 1856 and the repelling of a separate Nicaraguan invasion in 1919.

Playa Nancite BEACH
Playa Nancite is a critical nesting site for olive ridley turtles. This species is known for its *arribada* (mass arrival), when hundreds (or thousands) of nesting turtles arrive at once to deposit their eggs on the beach. This phenomenon occurs about once a month (usually during a new moon) between August and December. Nancite is a restricted area; no tourist visits were allowed at the time of research.

La Casona MUSEUM, HISTORIC BUILDING
(2666-5051; www.acguanacaste.ac.cr/1997/ecod esarrollo/ecoturismo/museosantarosaing.html; incl in park admission; 8-11:30am & 1-4pm) La Casona is the main edifice of the old Hacienda Santa Rosa. The battle of 1856 was fought around this building. There are wonderful displays detailing (in English and Spanish) the old gold-rush route, William Walker's evil imperial plans and the 14-minute battle breakdown. There are also exhibits on the region's natural history. La Casona is located near the park headquarters (both are about 7km from the park entrance).

The original building was burned down in 2001 by poachers who were involved in another war, this one with park rangers. The rebuilt building has smoke alarms. Two hiking trails leave from behind the museum.

🏃 Activities

Hiking

Several hiking trails originate near the park headquarters (7km from the park entrance), including a gentle hike to the **Mirador Valle Naranjo**, with spectacular views of Playa Naranjo. From the southern end of Playa Naranjo there are two hiking trails: **Sendero Carbonal** is a 5km trail that swings inland along the mangroves and past Laguna El Limbo, where the crocs hang out; **Sendero Aceituno** parallels Playa Naranjo for 13km and terminates near the estuary across from Witch's Rock.

The main road is lined with short trails to small waterfalls and other photogenic natural wonders.

Surfing

The majority of travelers are here for one reason only: the chance to surf the near-perfect, world-class beach break at Playa Naranjo, **Witch's Rock** (Roca Bruja). This break is famous for its fast, hollow 3m rights. There are also fun lefts when it isn't pumping. Near **Playa Portrero Grande**, you'll find the best right in all of Costa Rica, the famous surf break Ollie's Point. It offers a nice, long ride, especially with a southern swell. The breaks can get busy in the dry season, but in the wet months from July through December you'll often have the beach to yourself.

⭐ Ollie's Point
SURFING

Surfers make pilgrimages to this isolated beach, near Playa Portrero Grande, to find the best right in all of Costa Rica. This famous surf break offers a nice, long ride, especially with a southern swell. The bottom here is a mix of sand and rocks, and the year-round offshore is perfect for tight turns and slow closes. Ollie's Point is only accessible by boat from Playas del Coco or Tamarindo. Or you can do as Patrick and Wingnut did in *Endless Summer II* and crash-land your chartered plane on the beach (ahem, not actually recommended). Shortboarding is preferred.

Playa Naranjo
SURFING

(surfing surcharge US$12) A spectacular beach in the southernmost part of the Santa Rosa sector (p230), Playa Naranjo attracts wave riders who come to surf the legendary beach break at **Witch's Rock** (Roca Bruja), famous for its 3m curls (not recommended for beginners). Be careful of rocks near the river mouth and crocodiles near the estuary, a rich feeding ground during tide changes.

The beach is stunning, with a sweet, rounded boulder-strewn point to the north and shark-fin headlands to the south. Even further south, Nicoya and Papagayo peninsular silhouettes reach out in a dramatic attempt to outdo each other.

NORTHWESTERN COSTA RICA SECTOR SANTA ROSA

WORTH A TRIP

SECTOR MURCIÉLAGO

Encompassing the wild northern coastline of the Península Santa Elena, Sector Murciélago (Bat Sector) is where you'll find the isolated white-sand beach of **Playa Blanca** and the trailhead for the **Poza el General** watering hole, which attracts birds and animals year-round.

Sector Murciélago is not accessible from the Santa Rosa sector: to get to the northern Sector Murciélago, you'll need to turn off the Interamericana near the police checkpoint that is 10km north of Santa Rosa. After 8km, bear left at the village of Cuajiniquíl. Continue on the gravel road for another 9km, passing such historic sights as the former hacienda of the late Nicaraguan dictator Anastasio Somoza (it's currently a training ground for the Costa Rican police) and the airstrip that was used by Lieutenant Colonel Oliver North to 'secretly' smuggle goods to the Nicaraguan Contras in the 1980s. Continue straight until you cross a river, then hang a right and keep going straight over two more rivers until you reach the village of Murciélago and the park entrance.

Continue on a dirt road to the remote bays and beaches of El Hachal (5km), Bahía Santa Elena (8km) and Bahía Playa Blanca (17km). A 4WD is a must, and even then the road may be impassable in the wet season. Also, signage is nonexistent. Have fun!

The sector's Ollie's Point, named in jest after Oliver North, is one of the country's best surf breaks, and can reached by boat from Tamarindo.

Playa Naranjo is 18km from the park entrance and 11km from the Santa Rosa research station. The road from the station to the beach is notoriously bad; it's impassable except in the driest months, and even then requires a 4WD. Call ahead regarding road conditions. There's a campground with pit toilets but no potable water, so be sure to bring your own.

Wildlife-Watching

The wildlife in Santa Rosa is both varied and prolific, especially during the dry season, when trees lose their leaves and animals congregate around the remaining water sources. More than 250 bird species have been recorded here, including the raucous white-throated magpie jay, unmistakable with its long crest of manically curled feathers. The forests contain parrots and parakeets, trogons and tanagers; as you head down to the coast you'll be rewarded by sightings of various coastal birds.

Dozens of bat species have been identified in Santa Rosa. Other mammals you'll have a reasonable chance of seeing include deer, coatis, peccaries, armadillos, coyotes, raccoons, three kinds of monkeys and a variety of other species – about 115 in all. There are also many thousands of insect species, including about 4000 moths and butterflies (bring insect repellent).

Reptiles include lizards, iguanas, snakes, crocodiles and four species of sea turtle. The olive ridley sea turtle is the most numerous, and during the July to December nesting season tens of thousands of turtles make their nests on Santa Rosa's beaches, especially Playa Nancite (p230). From August to December, *arribada* (mass arrival) takes place about once a month and lasts for four days. During September and October especially, it's sometimes possible to see as many as 8000 of these 40kg turtles on the beach at the same time. Playa Nancite is strictly protected and entry is restricted.

🛏 Sleeping

The Santa Rosa research station (Centro de Investigación del Bosque Tropical Seco; ☑ 2666-5051; www.acguanacaste.ac.cr/biodesarrollo/centro-de-investigacion-y-estaciones-biologicas/centro-de-investigacion-del-bosque-tropical-seco; dm US$15) is usually occupied by visiting researchers. There's a shady developed campground (per person US$19) nearby, with picnic benches, grills, flushing toilets and cold-water showers. Playa Naranjo (p231) also has pit toilets and showers but no potable water – bring your own, and don't expect complete solitude: everyone shares one sandy flat basin, only moderately sheltered from gusty winds by thin trees. Bring extra water, just in case.

SANTA ROSA IN HISTORY

This stretch of coast is famous among Ticos as a national stronghold. Costa Rica has been invaded three times, and the enemy has always surrendered in Santa Rosa.

The best known of these incidents is the Battle of Santa Rosa, which took place on March 20, 1856, when Costa Rica was invaded by the soon-to-be-self-declared president of Nicaragua, an uppity American named William Walker. Walker was the head of a group of foreign pirates and adventurers known as the 'Filibusters' that had already seized Baja and southwest Nicaragua and were attempting to gain control over all of Central America. In a brilliant display of military prowess, Costa Rican president Juan Rafael Mora Porras managed to assemble a ragtag group of fighters and surround Walker's army in the main building of the old Hacienda Santa Rosa, known as La Casona. The battle was over in just 14 minutes, and Walker was forever driven from Costa Rican soil.

Santa Rosa was also the site of battles between Costa Rican troops and invading forces from Nicaragua in the 20th century. The first – in 1919 – was a somewhat honorable attempt to overthrow the Costa Rican dictator General Federico Tinoco. Then, in 1955, Nicaraguan dictator Anastasio Somoza led a failed coup d'état. Today you can still see Somoza's abandoned tank, which lies in a ditch beside the road just beyond the entrance to the park.

The area's military history didn't end with Somoza. In the 1980s, US Marine lieutenant-colonel Oliver North illegally sold weapons to Iran and used the profits to fund the Nicaraguan Contras during the Sandinistas-Contra war. The troops' staging area was just north of Santa Rosa at Playa Potrero Grande (near the famous surf break now known as Ollie's Point).

Santa Elena Lodge LODGE $$

(📞 2679-1038; www.santaelenalodge.com; Cuajiniquíl; s/d US$55/85; 🅿️❄️📶) Retired fisherman Manuel offers a fine deal in the quaint village of Cuajiniquíl (Kwah-hee-nee-kil). The eight-room house is convenient to Santa Rosa and Murciélago parks and nearby beaches. The lovely cedar woods used to remodel the old home give it a solid feel, while details such as the book exchange make you feel right at home.

❶ Getting There & Away

Access to the Sector Santa Rosa park entrance is on the western side of the Interamericana, 35km north of Liberia and 45km south of the Nicaragua border. The well-signed main park entrance can be reached by public transportation: take any bus between Liberia and the Nicaraguan border and ask the driver to let you off at the park entrance. Rangers can help you catch a return bus. You can also arrange private transportation from the hotels in Liberia for about US$20 to US$30 per person round trip.

From the entrance it's another 7km to park headquarters, where you'll also find the museum (p230) and the campgrounds. This office administers the Area de Conservación Guanacaste (ACG).

From this complex, a very rough track leads down to Playa Naranjo (p231), 11km away. Even during the dry season this road is only passable with a high-clearance 4WD, and you must sign an eerie waiver at the park entrance stating that you willingly assume all liability for driving here. The park also requires that you be completely self-sufficient should you choose to undertake the trip, which means bringing all your own water and knowing how to do your own car repairs. During the rainy months (May to November) the road is open to hikers and horses but closed to all vehicles. If you want to surf here, it's infinitely easier to gain access to the beach by hiring a boat from Playas del Coco or Tamarindo further south.

Refugio Nacional de Vida Silvestre Bahía Junquillal

Overlooking the Bahía Junquillal, just north of the Sector Murciélago, this 505-hectare **wildlife refuge** (📞 2666-5051; www.acguanacaste.ac.cr; US$15; ⏰ 7am-5pm) is part of the vast Area de Conservación Guanacaste (ACG). The quiet bay and beautiful protected beach offer gentle swimming and snorkeling opportunities, making this a popular destination for Tico families on weekends

LLANOS DE CORTÉS

If you have time to visit only one waterfall in Costa Rica, make it **Llanos de Cortés** (admission by donation, parking US$4; ⏰ 8am-5pm; 🅿️). Scramble down a short, steep trail to reach the spectacular 12m-high, 15m-wide waterfall, which you'll hear before you see. The falls drop into a tranquil pond with a white sandy beach that's perfect for swimming and sunbathing. Go 'backstage' and relax on the rocks behind the waterfall curtain, or shower beneath its lukewarm waters.

and holidays. On a clear day, you'll see Volcán Orosí in the distance.

Two short **trails** (totaling 1.7km) hug the coast, traversing dry tropical forest. They lead to a marine bird lookout in one direction and to the mangroves in the other. Keep your eye out for pelicans and frigate birds, as well as capuchin monkeys, coatis and other scavengers.

There is a campground (per person US$19) near the ranger station, which is a few hundred meters past the park entrance. Very popular among domestic tourists, it's outfitted with brick grills and picnic tables at every site. There are pit latrines. If you don't care to camp, the nearest accommodations are 7km north, in Bahía Salinas.

On weekends, there may be vendors near the beach selling *ceviche* (seafood marinated in lemon or lime juice, garlic and seasonings), grilled meat and cold drinks. Otherwise, there are several seafood *sodas* (places serving counter lunches) in the nearby village of Cuajiniquíl.

The Refugio Nacional de Vida Silvestre Bahía Junquillal is administered from the ACG park headquarters at Santa Rosa (p230). The ranger station here is in telephone and radio contact with Santa Rosa.

❶ Getting There & Away

From the Interamericana, turn off at the police checkpoint, following the signs about 8km to Cuajiniquíl. Don't go into Cuajiniquíl: just before you reach the village, turn right, remaining on the paved road to continue 4km to the park entrance. You'll know you're getting close when that glorious cobalt bay appears from out of nowhere on your left.

If you're coming from Bahía Salinas, take the paved road that heads south from El Soley. It hugs the coast, depositing you at the park in a mere 7km.

La Cruz

POP 11,100 (DISTRICT)

La Cruz is the closest town to the Peñas Blancas border crossing with Nicaragua, and is the principal gateway to Bahía Salinas, Costa Rica's premier kitesurfing destination. La Cruz itself is a fairly sleepy provincial town set on a mountaintop plateau, with lots of Tico charm and magical views of an epic, windswept bay. El Mirador or the neighboring bar are required stops to stretch your legs and widen your worldview.

◉ Sights

El Mirador Centro Turistico   VIEWPOINT
(☑2679-9058; www.facebook.com/Elmiradorlacruz; ◷7am-4pm) **FREE** Don't cruise through La Cruz without stopping at this oddly shaped 'tourist and cultural center' on the western edge of town. You might stumble across an exhibit or a concert, but the main attraction is the jaw-dropping 180-degree view of Bahía Salinas. You can also peek into Nicaragua from here. The **cafe** at the back is a fine lunch stop. Note that opening hours can be inconsistent. It's operated by the local tourism board.

☞ Tours

Hacienda El Cenizaro   ADVENTURE
(☑8367-1692; www.haciendaelcenizaro.com; Rte 935; tours from US$99; ◷8am-5pm) On the road to Bahía Salinas, this attractive hacienda sits back from the road, overlooking its farmland spotted with bulls. It's an atmospheric location to hop on a horse or an ATV. Horseback tours traverse the tropical dry forest, but ATVs carry you to new heights for splendid bay views. They share their trails with Bike House (p237).

The ranch is about 3.5km downhill from the El Mirador Centro Turistico on Rte 935.

Spider Monkey Canopy Tour   ADVENTURE
(☑8357-4983, 8316-9824; spidermonkeytours@hotmail.com; tour US$45; ◷8am-4pm) On the road to Bahía Salinas you'll find the requisite canopy tour, with 11 cables and a Tarzan swing. Get a new perspective on the tropical dry forest! If there's no staff around, check at the restaurant down the road, Hacienda Quebrada de Agua.

🛏 Sleeping & Eating

For an atmospheric meal, stop by El Mirador Centro Turistico, where you can have lunch with a view over the jewel-toned Bahía Salinas (opening hours can be spotty, though). Otherwise, there's a handful of conspicuous places on the Interamericana. Better yet,

---

LAS FIESTAS DE GUANACASTE

Guanacastecos love their horses almost as much as they love their fiestas. And what better way to get the best of both worlds than with a *tope* (horse parade)? In addition to the *tope*, these traditional holiday fiestas are a mix of Western rodeo and country fair, complete with cattle auctions, food stalls, music, dancing, drinking and, of course, bull riding. (In Costa Rica the bulls are never killed, so watching the berserk helmetless, bareback bucking-bronco action is usually gore-free.) Even better than watching the bull riding is the aftermath, when the local drunks and young machos jump into the ring to act as volunteer rodeo clowns.

Though the bull riding usually draws the biggest crowds, the main event is the *tope* itself, where you can see the high-stepping gait of the *sabanero*'s (cowboy's) horse; this demands endurance and skill from both horse and rider.

Topes are also a great place to catch the region's traditional dance, known as the *punto guanacasteco*. The women wear long flowing skirts meant to resemble traditional handcrafted, hand-painted oxcart wheels. The old-fashioned courtship dance is frequently interrupted by young men, who shout rhyming verses to try to win over a love interest. The dance and accompanying music are fast paced, full of passion and fun to watch.

Topes usually occur on Costa Rican civic holidays, though you can bet on finding big parties during Semana Santa (the week before Easter), the week between Christmas and New Year, and on July 25, the anniversary of Guanacaste's annexation.

GETTING TO NICARAGUA

Crossing the border into Nicaragua at Peñas Blancas is a highly variable experience, sometimes taking a half hour or less, sometimes taking many hours. Here's what you need to know:

➡ Peñas Blancas is a busy border crossing (open 6am to midnight), which can be a major hassle at peak times. Avoid crossing the border shortly before closing time and in the days leading up to major holidays.

➡ Make sure you have at least six months' validity on your passport. If your passport is about to expire, you will be denied entry into Nicaragua.

➡ Car rental companies in Costa Rica won't allow you to take the vehicle out of the country. Leave your car in one of the nearby guarded parking areas (assuming you're coming back, of course). Don't leave any valuables in the car.

➡ Costa Rica charges a US$7 land exit fee, payable by credit or debit card.

➡ The border posts are about 1km apart. If you're on an international bus (TicaBus), you'll get a lift between posts. Otherwise, you'll have to hoof it. Hordes of generally useless touts will offer to 'guide' you through the simple crossing – let them carry your luggage if you like, but agree on a fee beforehand.

➡ Entering and leaving Nicaragua costs US$12, which must be paid in US dollars. You'll also be charged US$2 to enter the state of Rivas.

➡ You may be asked to show a proof of exit, such as a return bus ticket or a flight reservation out of Nicaragua.

➡ There are no banks at the border, but there are plenty of money changers hanging around. Rates will be not be to your advantage, obviously.

There's a fairly fabulous duty-free shop waiting for you in Sapoá, the Nicaraguan equivalent of Peñas Blancas. Relax with your purchases on the 45-minute bus ride to Rivas (departing every 45 minutes or so). Rivas is a quiet transport hub, though its well-preserved 17th-century center is worth exploring. If you're good at bargaining (and you will have to bargain hard), there are taxis waiting on the Nicaraguan side of the border to whisk you to Rivas (US$30).

wait until you drive down into Bahia Salinas for a more relaxed meal.

Hotel La Mirada   HOTEL $

(☎ 2679-9702; www.hotellamirada.com; Av 1; d US$45-65; P❋☎) This is the town's spiffiest spot. Family owned and lovingly cared for, rooms are spacious and clean, with high, beamed ceilings and loft sleeping spaces. The biggest rooms have kitchenettes and air-con. Despite the name, there's no view to speak of. It's just off the Interamericana, 100 meters north and east of the Banco Nacional de Costa Rica.

Hotel Amalia Inn   INN $

(☎ 2679-9618; Calle Central near Av 2; s/d with fan US$25/35, s/d with air-con US$40/50; P❋☎⚓) This yellow stucco house on a cliff isn't a bad place to spend the night. Its eight homey rooms are furnished rather randomly and have attractive brick floors and wooden ceilings. Walls in the meandering house are hung with modernist paintings by Amalia's late husband, Lester Bounds. The shared terracotta terraces have stupendous bay views.

Amalia's granddaughter Elka is now the lady of the house; short of offering meals she'll make you feel right at home. There are big ceiling fans if you don't pay extra for the air-con.

Hotel Casa del Viento   HOTEL $$

(☎ 2679-8060; r US$30-95; P☎⚓) With a lovely mosaic-bottomed pool (now with a filter!) and breezy **restaurant** at the top of the hill in town, this is a great place for a beer in the evenings. Fan-cooled rooms are crowded and sort of clean; those on the 2nd level have more light and outstanding views. There's a new common kitchen and monkey-viewing platform out back.

It's across the street from the El Mirador Centro Turistico.

Drinking & Nightlife

Mirador Punta Descartes COCKTAIL BAR
(☑ 2679-9015; www.lacruzhotel.com; Calle Central near Av Central; ⊙ 11am-11pm) Don't come for the food, but do come for the drinks and spectacular view over the bay in an easy chair. Whether you're watching a fiery sunset or a slashing lightning storm, it's a memorable experience, particularly with a tequila sunrise (sunset?) in hand.

ℹ️ Information

Change money in town to avoid the high rates at the border.

Banco Nacional (☑ 2212-2000; ⊙ 8:30am-3:45pm Mon-Fri) At the junction of the short road into the town center.

Banco Popular (☑ 2681-4600; ⊙ 8:45am-4:30pm Mon-Fri, 8:15-11:30am Sat) In the town center, just south of the Catholic church.

Cruz Roja (☑ 2528-0177, emergency 2679-9146; ⊙ office 7:30am-5pm Mon-Fri, emergency 24 hrs) A small clinic just north of the town center on the road towards the border.

ℹ️ Getting There & Away

The bus station is located on the western edge of town, just north of the road to Bahía Salinas near Hotel Casa del Viento (p235). A **Transportes Deldú counter** (☑ 2223-7011; www.facebook.com/transportedeldu; Rte 935; ⊙ 7:30am-12:30pm & 1:30-6pm) down the street from the terminal sells tickets and stores luggage. Transportes Deldú services run only to the Peñas Blancas border with Nicaragua; to catch a TransNica bus through to Managua, you'll need to flag down a bus on the Interamericana.

The following services depart from La Cruz.

Peñas Blancas US$1, 45 minutes, 10 departures almost hourly from 5am to 5:30pm.

Playa Jobo US$2, 30 minutes, departs four times daily from 8:30am to 5:30pm from the bus terminal.

San José via Liberia US$7, five hours, departs hourly from 5am to 7pm.

Bahía Salinas

Welcome to the kitesurfing capital of Costa Rica, where giddy riders shred beneath magnificent rainbows that arch over a wide bay that extends all the way to Nicaragua. The destination has a deconstructed nature – communities congregate on empty beaches clumped with tropical forests that are home to howler monkey tribes and linked by dirt roads. The result is a pleasingly *tranquilo*, rural vibe.

Bahía Salinas is a stunning, under-the-radar destination even if you don't ride wind. But not for long. The glorious sands of Playa Jobo are no longer deserted after the opening of a gigantic, 400-room five-star resort. The road heading south is already partially paved and more development will certainly follow, for better and for worse.

🏃 Activities

If wind isn't your thing, head around the point to Playa Jobo – a perfect, 300m-wide horseshoe bay with calm water – or Playa Rajada, on the southernmost arm of Salinas. Rajada is ruggedly gorgeous and sheltered enough to be almost placid. In September and October, humpback whales often congregate here.

Boating

Boats can be rented in the village of El Jobo or at one of the local resorts to visit Isla Bolaños, a seabird refuge home to the brown pelican (visits are restricted to April through November to avoid disturbing nesting seabirds). Ask around about fishing and diving trips to Isla Despense, Isla Caballo and Isla Murcielago, with its resident bull sharks.

Kitesurfing

Bahía Salinas is an internationally known mecca for kitesurfers between November and March, when the wind howls fairly consistently. The shape of the hills surrounding the bay funnels the winds into a predictable pattern (though it can be gusty, ranging between 20 and 40 knots), and the sandy, protected beaches make this a great place for both beginners and experienced riders.

It's important to remember that there are inherent dangers to kiting (namely the risk of losing a limb – yikes!), so seek professional instruction if you're not experienced. The Professional Air Sports Association (PASA) and the International Kiteboarding Organization (IKO) have set standards for beginner instruction. You'll need to take a nine-hour certification course to rent gear and safely go out on your own.

The road follows the curve of the bay to the consistently windy beaches of Playa Papaturro and Playa Copal. Copal is an incredibly wide, beige beach backed by scrubby manzanillo trees with views across the sea all the way to Nicaragua. It does get

RESERVA BIOLÓGICA LOMAS DE BARBUDAL

Forming a cohesive unit with Palo Verde, the 26 sq km **Reserva Biológica Lomas de Barbudal** (☎2659-9194, 2257-2239; adult/child US$12/2; ⊙7am-4pm) is a tropical dry forest reserve that's famous for its huge diversity of resident bees. If that doesn't make you want to come here, maybe the troops of white-faced capuchin monkeys will be more appealing.

In any case, Lomas de Barbudal is an accessible option for off-the-beaten-track independent hiking. A small **visitors center** (Visitors Center; ☎2686-4967; ⊙9am-4pm) has maps and other information. You can explore the reserve on four different hiking trails; Sendero La Catarata (waterfall trail) rewards with an amazing cascade that merits a dip.

The turnoff to Lomas de Barbudal from the Interamericana is 14km southeast of Liberia and 12km northwest of Bagaces. From here it's 7km to the entrance of the reserve on a rough unpaved road. Some steep sections may require 4WD in the rainy season.

incredibly windy here; though picturesque, this is not the place for beachcombing.

The turnoff to Papaturro is clearly marked. Playa Copal has two access roads. The first is through the farmland behind Plaza Copal; it's a public road, but you must close the gate behind you so the animals don't get out. The second is more clearly marked – follow the signs to KiteHouse.

Kiteboarding Costa Rica
KITESURFING

(☎8370-4894; www.kiteboardingcostarica.com; Playa Copal; lessons per hr US$45-65; ⊙Nov-May) This highly regarded kitesurfing school operates out of the KiteHouse (p238) at the western end of Playa Copal. IKO-certified instructors speak Spanish, French and English. If you've already got your certification and are confident about your abilities, you can also just rent equipment here. If you feel like something different, they'll take you out on the bay in a sailboat.

Kitesurf School 2000
KITESURFING

(☎8826-5221, 2676-1042; www.bluedreamhotel.com; Playa Papaturro; lessons per hr US$35-45; ⊙8am-8pm) Make reservations in advance to take lessons or rent gear at the area's original kite shop (IKO certified). Formerly known as Kitesurf 2000, it's located at the Blue Dream Hotel (p237), 250m from Papaturro. Lessons are available in Spanish, English and Italian. Cash only.

Mountain Biking

It's not just kitesurfers who can get their kicks in Bahía Salinas – this is also mountain biking territory. Explore back roads, beaches and the single-track cross-country

area at Hacienda El Cenizaro (p234), also a great horseback riding destination.

🛏 Sleeping & Eating

Bike House
B&B $

(☎8704-7486; www.thebikehousecostarica.com; cabina incl breakfast US$40; ☎) This friendly B&B caters to travelers who prefer their adventure with two wheels on the ground. Accommodations are simple and sweet, with a shady common porch with hammocks. Owner Carole prepares delicious food using organic local ingredients. She can also help make arrangements for kitesurfing if you want to give it a try.

Carole leads a variety of half-day (US$80), full-day, and even eight-day (US$1900) cycling trips in the area. A week-long, all-female camp combines biking, yoga and surfing.

The Bike House is about 200m west of the Tempatal school. Plans were underway for new paths to open up in 2018.

Blue Dream Hotel
HOTEL $

(☎8826-5221, 2676-1042; www.bluedreamhotel.com; Playa Papaturro; dm US$17, standard s/d US$35/45, bungalow s/d US$52/58, ste s/d/tr US$65/67/77; P❄@☎) This friendly hotel offers marvelous views over Playa Papaturro from every room on its terraced hillside. Lodgings range from simple and comfortable rooms with Spanish tiles to more spacious chalet-style suites with private balconies. All have access to a hammock-strung garden. The Italian chef serves a hearty breakfast and amazing old-country fare.

There's a guitar on hand and a funny blue-eyed dog. Kitesurf School 2000 is located here.

★ KiteHouse
GUESTHOUSE $$

(☎ 2676-1045, 8370-4894; www.kiteboardingcos tarica.com; Playa Copal; dm US$20-25, cabina US$55-70, villa from US$90; ☺ Nov-May; ❋ 🖤 🎏) This excellent operation has taken over the western end of Playa Copal, with kiteboarding lessons, rentals, a wide range of accommodations and a hilltop **restaurant** (6pm to 9pm Tuesday to Sunday). Every sleeping option – from dorm room to villa – has a terrific view of the beach. The rooms also have kitchenettes; there are few other places to eat.

El Fogon de Juanita
SODA $

(Playa Copal; mains US$8-10; ☺ 8am-9pm; 🎏) The former Blue Dream (p237) chef has opened her own place down the road, to rave reviews. Specializing in pastas (lasagna is a fave) and pizzas, Juana also conjures up a flavorful *arroz* (rice dish) or two. For tips on riding the waves, her son Mauricio, a kiteboarding instructor, is often just a shout away.

❶ Getting There & Away

BUS

Buses (US$2) make the 30-minute run between the La Cruz bus terminal and the village of Jobo four times a day in either direction. A taxi to the beaches costs about US$20.

CAR

From La Cruz, the road is paved at first, but gravel for the last 9km. It leads down from the lookout point in La Cruz past the small coastal fishing community of Puerto Soley, at the eastern end of Playa Papaturro.

If you're driving from the south, there's a paved route to El Soley. Instead of driving all the way to La Cruz, turn off the Interamericana near the police checkpoint, following signs to Cuajiniquíl. After about 8km, just before the village, bear right toward Junquillal (don't go into the village). The paved road follows the coast about 12km north to El Soley, from where you'll pick up the gravel road from La Cruz.

Arenal & Northern Lowlands

Best Places to Eat

➡ Restaurant Don Rufino (p252)

➡ Kappa Sushi (p251)

➡ La Ventanita (p259)

➡ Gingerbread Hotel & Restaurant (p263)

➡ La Gavilana Herbs & Art (p259)

Best Wildlife-Watching

➡ Arenal Natura (p242)

➡ Refugio Nacional de Vida Silvestre Caño Negro (p267)

➡ Chilamate Rainforest Eco Retreat (p280)

➡ Estación Biológica La Selva (p282)

➡ Frog's Heaven (p283)

Why Go?

You know about the region's main attraction: that now-dormant volcano, surrounded by old lava fields, bubbling hot springs and a stunning lake. Venture further onto the wild rivers and into the tropical jungle of the northern lowlands and you will discover real-life Costa Rica, where agricultural commerce and ecological conservation converge as a work in green progress. Stretching from the borderlands of Nicaragua south to the Cordillera de Tilarán, *fincas* (farms) of banana, sugarcane and pineapple roll across humid plains. Community tourism lives and breathes here, creating added revenue for a historically farm-based economy. You can spot a macaw in the wild, paddle into roaring rapids and cruise inky lagoons, all with lifelong resident guides, then nest in lodges that double as private rainforest reserves. When the tourist hordes get you down, make your way here for a refreshing blast of rural realism and an invigorating dose of wild beauty.

When to Go

➡ There's no dry season in the northern lowlands: the lush jungles surrounding the rivers in the region, such as the Río Frío and the Río Sarapiquí, receive rainfall at almost any time of year.

➡ There is a less-wet season, though, from January to April, when there's lower rainfall.

➡ Because there's so much rain, you can run the rivers any time of year, but they flow faster from July to December.

➡ Wildlife also abounds year-round, but skies will be clearer and trails less muddy from January to April.

➡ Fun *sabanero* (cowboy) street festivals take place in La Fortuna in February and in Ciudad Quesada (San Carlos) in April.

Arenal & Northern Lowlands Highlights

❶ Parque Nacional Volcán Arenal (p254) Taking in striking views of the volcano's cloud-ringed cone.

❷ Eco Termales Hot Springs (p243) Soothing your weary muscles in volcano-heated pools in La Fortuna.

❸ El Castillo (p255) Marvelling at sweeping lake or volcano views from your perch in this charming village.

❹ Proyecto Asis (p275) Getting up close and personal with orphaned or injured wild animals.

❺ Venado Caves (p267) Getting down and dirty while exploring the underworld.

❻ Refugio Nacional de Vida Silvestre Caño Negro (p267) Exploring the lagoons, counting caimans and spying on spoonbills.

❼ Boca Tapada (p275) Falling asleep to the forest symphony of cicadas, frogs and birds in this remote corner of the country.

❽ Río Sarapiquí (p278) Getting thrills and chills while riding the rapids.

❾ Wildlife-Watching (p280) Spotting howlers, sloths, peccaries and all manner of birdlife while exploring the grounds of your ecolodge.

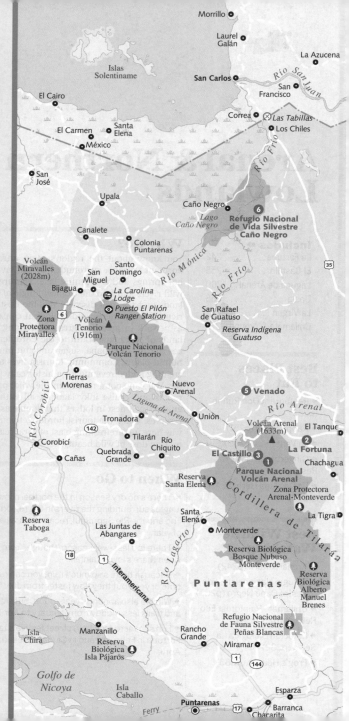

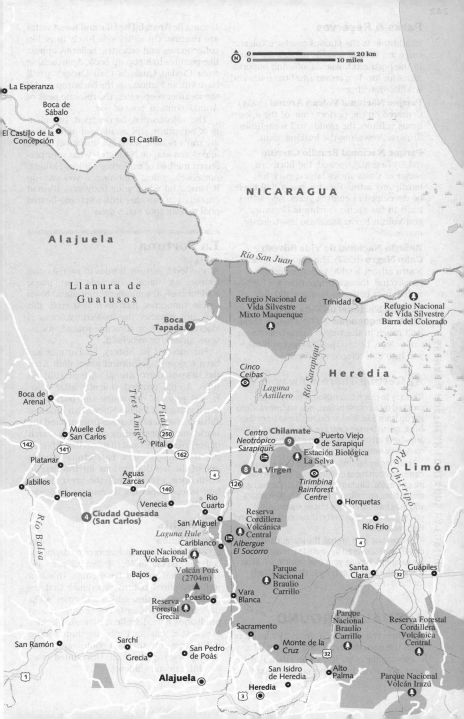

Parks & Reserves

In addition to the famous must-see volcano, there are several notable refuges and parks in the northern lowlands, offering opportunities for low-key, crowd-free boat tours and wildlife-watching.

Parque Nacional Volcán Arenal (p254) Centered on the perfect cone of the eponymous volcano, the clouds will sometimes disperse, revealing the hulking giant.

Parque Nacional Braulio Carrillo (p279) Recently opened, the northern sector of Costa Rica's largest park has hardly any infrastructure, but it will likely be developed in coming years. Accessible trails in the Sector Quebrada Gonzalez and Volcan Barva areas are less-touristy marvels.

Refugio Nacional de Vida Silvestre Caño Negro (p267) The lagoons of Caño Negro attract a wide variety of birds year-round, though prime time for bird-watchers is between January and July.

Refugio Nacional de Vida Silvestre Mixto Maquenque (p275) Though there isn't much in the way of infrastructure at this refuge, Boca Tapada lodges can take you into this remote rainforest.

ℹ Getting There & Away

It's easy to reach this region, which is criss-crossed by a couple of fast, new highways. Coming up from San José or driving down from the Nicaraguan border near Los Chiles, you can be anywhere in the region within a few hours if you have your own vehicle.

Traveling by bus may take a bit longer, but you can still reach most destinations without too much hassle. Ciudad Quesada (San Carlos) is a major transportation hub for the region where you may have to change buses, especially if you're journeying between the Arenal region and the Lowlands.

By contrast with Arenal, the lowlands are still largely undiscovered by tourists (though this is changing). Having your own vehicle will allow you greater ease in getting to its appealingly far-flung reaches.

ARENAL & AROUND

Whether you approach from the west or from the east, the drive into the Arenal area is spectacular. Coming from Tilarán in the west, the road hugs the northern bank of Laguna de Arenal. The lake and forest vistas are riveting. On either side lovely inns, hip coffeehouses and eccentric galleries appear like pictures in a pop-up book. Approaching from Ciudad Quesada (San Carlos), you'll have Volcán Platanar as the backdrop, and if the weather cooperates, the resolute peak of Arenal looms in front of you.

The volcano may be dormant, but plenty of adventure still awaits you here. There are trails to hike, waterfalls to rappel down, and sloths to spot. No matter what your preferred method of exploring – hiking, biking, horseback riding, ziplining – you can do it here. And when your body says it's had enough, you can ease into a volcano-heated pool to soak your aches away.

La Fortuna

POP 15,400

At eye level, you see hordes of tourists and tour-selling touts, postcards and pizza: evidence of a somnolent mountain town whose innocence has been shattered. But look up: whether the majestic volcano is cloud-shrouded or sunshine-soaked, it's always something to behold.

For most of its history, La Fortuna has been a sleepy agricultural town, 6km from the base of Cerro Arenal (Arenal Hill). In 1968, Arenal erupted violently after nearly 400 years of dormancy and buried the small villages of Pueblo Nuevo, San Luís and Tabacón. Suddenly, tourists from around the world started descending en masse in search of fiery night skies and that inevitable blurry photo of creeping lava. La Fortuna remains one of the top destinations for travelers in Costa Rica, even though the great mountain stopped spewing its molten discharge in 2010.

◉ Sights

Arenal Natura   PARK
(☑ 2479-1616; www.arenalnatura.com; day/night/bird tour US$35/44/49; ⊙ 8am-5:30pm; ⌘) Located 6km west of La Fortuna, this is a well-manicured nature experience that includes frogs, turtles, snakes and crocs, all in their appointed places. The birdlife is also prodigious here. Excellent naturalist guides ensure that you don't miss anything hiding in the trees, and there's a photography tour to help you capture it all. Discounted rates for children and students.

Mirador El Silencio
NATURE RESERVE

(☑ 2479-9900; www.miradorelsilencio.com; US$6)
🅿 Set on 22 hectares, this private reserve about 11km west of La Fortuna is a mix of primary and secondary forest, filled with life, from vibrant blue morpho butterflies to three species of monkeys, plus a wide variety of plant life. Four trails are marked with informative signs, not to mention a couple of fabulous lookouts.

Ecocentro Danaus
NATURE RESERVE

(☑ 2479-7019; www.ecocentrodanaus.com; with/without guide US$18/12, guided night tour US$35; ☺7:30am-5pm, night tour 5:30pm; 🅿) 🅿 This center, 4km east of town, has a well-developed trail system that's good for birding, as well as for spotting mammals such as sloths, coatis and howler monkeys. The admission fee also includes a visit to a butterfly garden, a ranarium featuring poison-dart frogs, and a small lake containing caiman and turtles. Reserve in advance for the excellent night tour.

You can walk part of the way, but eventually the sidewalk ends. In other words, it's much safer to take a taxi or your own car.

Catarata Río Fortuna
WATERFALL

(www.cataratariofortuna.com; Diagonal 301; US$15; ☺8am-5pm; 🅿) You can glimpse the sparkling 70m ribbon of clear water that pours through a sheer canyon of dark volcanic rock arrayed in bromeliads and ferns with minimal sweat equity. But it's worth the climb down and out to see it from the jungle floor. Though it's dangerous to dive beneath the thundering falls, a series of perfect swimming holes with spectacular views tile the canyon in aquamarine. Early arrival means you might beat the crowds: the parking lot fills quickly.

The waterfall is located at the end of the main road (301) going uphill from La Fortuna.

🏃 Activities

Hot Springs

Beneath La Fortuna the lava is still curdling and heating countless bubbling springs. There are free, natural hot springs in the area that any local can point you toward (ask about 'El Chollín'). If you're after a more comfortable experience, consider one of the area's resorts.

★ Eco Termales Hot Springs
HOT SPRINGS

(☑ 2479-8787; www.ecotermalesfortuna.cr; Via 142; with/without meal US$57/37; ☺10am, 1pm & 5pm; 🅿) 🅿 Everything from the natural circulation systems in the pools to the soft lighting is understated, luxurious and romantic at this gated, reservations-only complex about 4.5km northwest of town. Lush greenery surrounds the walking paths that cut through these gorgeous grounds. Only 150 visitors are admitted at a time, to maintain the ambience of serenity and seclusion.

Cocktails – served while you soak – come highly recommended (at an additional cost). The add-on lunch is a traditional Tico offering (rice/beans/meat) and includes dessert and coffee.

Paradise Hot Springs
HOT SPRINGS

(www.paradisehotspringscr.com; Via 142; adult/child US$28/16; ☺11am-9pm) This low-key place has one lovely, large pool with a waterfall and several smaller, secluded pools, surrounded by lush vegetation and tropical blooms. The pools vary in temperature (up to 40°C/104°F), some with hydromassage. Paradise is much simpler than the other larger spring settings, but there are fewer people, and your experience is bound to be more relaxing and romantic.

Lockers, towels and nonalcoholic drinks are included with admission. There's a restaurant if you want to eat or drink something more potent. Paradise can be found about 7km uphill (west) of downtown La Fortuna.

Springs Resort & Spa
HOT SPRINGS

(☑ in USA 954-727-8333, 2401-3313; www.thespringscostarica.com; 2-day admission US$65; ☺8am-10pm; 🅿) If you're looking for a luxurious hot-spring experience (even Will Smith stayed here while filming a movie), the Springs features 28 free-form pools with varying temperatures, volcano views, landscaped gardens, waterfalls and swim-up bars, including a jungle bar with a waterslide. The whole scene is human-made, yet lovely. The rough 3km road from La Fortuna was being paved during research.

Bigger packages including activities like tubing and horseback riding, as well as the Springs, start at $150. The resort rooms definitely come at Hollywood prices.

Baldi Hot Springs
HOT SPRINGS

(☑ 2479-9917; www.baldihotsprings.cr; with/without buffet US$57/35; ☺9am-10pm; 🅿) Big

enough so that there's something for everyone, Baldi, about 4.5km northwest of town, has 25 thermal pools ranging in temperature from 32°C (90°F) to a scalding 67°C (153°F). There are waterfalls and soaking pools for chill-seekers and 'Xtreme' slides for thrill-seekers, plus a good-size children's play area. At night, the thumping music and swim-up bars attract a young party crowd, but drinks are pricey.

Tabacón Hot Springs　　　　HOT SPRINGS

(📞 2519-1999; www.tabacon.com; day pass incl lunch & dinner adult/child US$115/40; ⊙10am-

10pm) 🍃 Some say it's cheesy and some say it's fun (we say it's both.) Broad-leaf palms, rare orchids and other florid tropical blooms part to reveal a 40°C (104°F) waterfall pouring over a fake cliff, concealing constructed caves complete with camouflaged cup holders. Lounged across each well-placed stone-like substance are overheated tourists of various shapes and sizes, relaxing.

The spa, 14km west of La Fortuna, is on the site of a 1975 volcanic eruption that killed one local. The former village of Tabacón was destroyed in the 1968 eruption, when 78 people were killed. Don't sweat it:

La Fortuna

the volcano is once again dormant. For now. Note that an absolutely free hot spot on the river is located just 50m south of this property, much to the consternation of Tabacón.

Hiking

Although it's no longer active, Volcán Arenal is the big draw here. There is a well-marked trail system within the park, and several private reserves on its outskirts. Waterfalls, lava flows and crater lakes are all worthy destinations, which you can reach without a guide.

📚 Courses

★**Costa Rica Cooking** COOKING
(📞 2479-1569; www.costaricacooking.com; per person US$125) Scott's 3½-hour cooking classes focuses on Costa Rican food with a modern twist, starting with a Tico mojito. Recipes include *ceviche*, *patacones* (fried green plantains) and other Costa Rican staples sourced from local and sometimes organic ingredients. Menus vary but always involves three courses, and you can enjoy a great view while you cook. Farm-to-Table and food presentation classes are also available, as are vegetarian and vegan options. Located inside Gecko's Waterfall Grill (p251), just before the La Fortuna waterfall. Scott also runs the **dog rescue center** (📞 2479-1569; www.crdogrescue.com; US$25 donation) next door.

🧭 Tours

Tour companies run rampant here, each seeking their piece of 'fortune'. Commissions are big business, so shop around before you

book. And keep in mind that you can actually do many of the activities on offer on your own – or by booking directly with the service provider. Tour companies offer many packages that combine activities (canopy tour, guided hike, horseback riding etc) with a dip in the hot springs. Make sure you understand exactly what's included, especially admission fees to parks and springs.

Tour operators also offer a slew of pricey tours to distant destinations, such as Caño Negro, Río Celeste and Venado Caves. If you're short of time, this is a fine option, though you'll save yourself a ton of money (and probably have a much better experience) if you actually go to the place and organize a tour upon arrival.

★**Don Olivo Chocolate Tour** TOURS
(📞 6110-3556, 2469-1371; www.facebook.com/tourdechocolatedonolivo; Via 142; tour US$25; ⊙ 8am, 10am, 1pm & 3pm; ⊛) Let Don Olivo or his son show you around their family *finca*, showing off their sugar cane, oranges and – of course – cocoa plants. The process of turning this funny fruit into the decadent treat that we all know and love is truly fascinating. Bonus: lots of taste-testing along the way.

It's located about 5km east of town on the main road, Via 142, just before the town of Tanque.

Alberto's Horse Tours HORSEBACK RIDING
(📞 2479-7711, 2479-9043; www.facebook.com/albertoshorses; Ruta 702; per person US$85; ⊙ 8:30am-1:30pm) Alberto and his son lead

popular horseback-riding trips to the Catarata de la Fortuna. It's a three- or four-hour trip, but you'll spend about an hour off your horse, when you hike down to the falls for a swim or a photo op. Beautiful setting, beautiful horses. Cash only. You'll find Alberto on Ruta 702, about 2km south of town.

Red Lava Tours
HIKING

(✆ 2479-8004; www.redlavatouristservicecenter. com; 2-Volcano Extreme Hike US$75, Volcano Valley Hike US$70) The fact that they label themselves as a 'touristic service company' means they're not just interested in selling you a tour. This helpful bunch, next to the bus terminal, offers some unique alternatives to the standard area tours (like a 'two-volcano' extreme hike, with cocktails and a mud facial at the end), and seem to have great fun doing so.

Bike Arenal
CYCLING

(✆ 2479-9020, 2479-7150; www.bikearenal.com; cnr Ruta 702 & Av 319A; rental per day/week US$25/150, half-/full-day tour US$85/135; ⊙ 7am-6pm) This outfit offers a variety of bike tours for all levels of rider, including a popular ride around the lake and a half-day ride to El Castillo. You can also do versions of these rides on your own. Make advance arrangements for rental and an English-speaking bike mechanic will bring the bicycle to you.

On the road south out of town (702).

PureTrek Canyoning
CANYONING

(✆ 2479-1313, US toll free 1-866-569-5723; www. puretrekcanyoning.com; 4hr incl transportation & lunch US$101; ⊙ 7am-10pm; ▣) ✿ The reputable PureTrek leads guided rappels down three waterfalls, one of which is 50m high. Also included: rock climbing and 'monkey drop,' which is actually a zipline with a rappel at the end of it. High marks for attention to safety and high-quality gear. It gets some big groups, but it does a good job keeping things moving.

Check-in at PureTrek headquarters, located in a tree house 6km west of town. Combo trips including ATV, pedalboard, and farm-to-table food options are available.

Arenal Mundo Aventura
ADVENTURE TOUR, HIKING

(✆ 2479-9762; www.arenalmundoaventura. com; adult/child canopy tours US$69/52, hiking US$53/37, Maleku cultural experience $35/19; ⊙ 8am-1:30pm; ▣) An all-in-one adventure park, this place offers various guided hikes, rappelling and horseback riding, as well as

a canopy tour. It also hosts performances of indigenous Maleku dance and song. It is 2km south of La Fortuna, on the road to Chachagua.

Desafío Adventure Company
ADVENTURE

(✆ 2479-0020; www.desafiocostarica.com; Calle 2; tours from US$75; ⊙ 6:30am-9pm) Desafío is a tour agency that has the widest range of tours in Fortuna – everything from paddling trips on the Río Balsa, horse-riding treks to Volcán Arenal, adventure tours rappelling down waterfalls, and mountain-bike expeditions. It can also arrange your transfer to Monteverde by boat or bike.

Nature Tours

Arenal Oasis
BIRD-WATCHING, NIGHT WALK

(✆ 2479-9526; www.arenaloasis.com; night/bird walks US$40/55; ⊙ bird walk 6am, night tour 5:45pm) The Rojas Bonilla family has created this wild frog sanctuary, home to some 35 species of croaking critters. The frogs are just the beginning of this night walk, which continues into the rainforest to see what other nocturnal animals await. If you're more of a morning person, it also does a bird-watching tour. Reservations recommended. Located 3km from La Fortuna's center; hotel pick-up costs US$10.

This is part of the Arenal Oasis (p249) hotel, located just southwest of town on the way to the waterfall.

Aventuras Arenal
TOURS

(✆ 2479-9133; www.aventurasarenal.com; Via 142; kayaking US$60, hiking from US$65, horse riding US$60-75; ⊙ 7am-8pm) Around for over 25 years, this outfit organizes a variety of local day tours on bike, boat and horseback. It also does trips further afield, including to Caño Negro and Río Celeste.

Jacamar Naturalist Tours
HIKING, ADVENTURE TOUR

(✆ 2479-9767; www.arenaltours.com; Parque Central, Via 142; bird-watching $68; ⊙ 7am-9pm) Recommended for its variety of naturalist hikes, including Volcán Arenal, waterfall and hanging bridges. Customers rave about the guides' flexibility and attentiveness.

Canopy Tours

Arenal Paraíso Canopy Tours
CANOPY TOUR

(✆ 2479-1100; www.arenalparaiso.com; Via 142; tours US$50; ⊙ 8am-5pm; ▣) A dozen cables zip across the canyon of the Río Arenal, giving a unique perspective on two waterfalls, as well as the rainforest canopy. Also includes admission to the resort's swimming pool and 13 thermal pools, which are hidden among the rocks and greenery on the hillside.

The resort and canopy tours are located on Via 142, uphill and west of La Fortuna town.

Athica Canopy CANOPY TOUR
(Arenal Canopy Adventure; ☑2479-1405; www.are nalcanopy.com/arenal-canopy-english/athica-cano py-tour; Via 142; canopy tour adult/child US$55/45, canopy/horseback combo US$75/68; ☺8am, 10:30am, 1pm & 3pm) This canopy tour is set up to give you a new perspective on Volcán Arenal and the surrounding conservation area. There are 10 cables and 14 platforms, as well as the ever-popular Tarzan swing. It's also possible to add on a two-hour horseback riding trip.

Canopy Los Cañones CANOPY TOUR
(☑2479-1047; www.hotelloslagos.com; US$55) 🌶
Located at the Hotel Los Lagos, the Canopy Los Cañones has 12 cables over the rainforest, ranging from 50m to 500m long. The price includes admission to a frog farm, crocodile farm, butterfly farm, hot springs, natural pools and waterslides, all on the hotel grounds. The hotel is located about 6km west of La Fortuna, just off Via 142.

Ecoglide CANOPY TOUR
(☑2479-7120; www.arenalecoglide.com; adult/child US$75; ☺canopy tours at 8am, 10am, 1pm & 3pm; 👶) Ecoglide is the biggest canopy game in town, featuring 13 cables, 15 platforms and a 'Tarzan' swing. The dual-cable safety system provides extra security and peace of mind. Located off Via 142, about 5km west (uphill) from La Fortuna.

Kayaking, Canoeing & Rafting
La Fortuna is not a river-running hub like you'll find in other parts of the country, but there are a few companies offering canoeing and kayaking in the area. If you wish to go white-water rafting, tour companies do take groups from La Fortuna to run the Sarapiquí and other distant rivers. Some offer the option to get dropped afterwards in San José or on the Caribbean coast – a good way to have some fun on a travel day.

Wave Rafting RAFTING
(☑2479-7262; www.waveexpeditions.com; cnr Calle 472 & Av 331; river trips US$70-100; ☺6am-9pm) Wave Expeditions runs the wild Ríos Toro and Sarapiquí, as well as the mellower

Balsa, in both rafts and tubes. There's also hiking, horseback riding, caving, canyoning and tortilla making on offer, through second-party tour companies.

Canoa Aventura CANOEING
(☑2479-8200; www.canoa-aventura.com; Via 142; canoe/kayak trip US$57; ☺6:30am-9:30pm) 🌶 This long-standing family-run company specializes in canoe and float trips (leisurely trips aimed at observation and relaxation) led by bilingual naturalist guides. Most are geared toward wildlife- and bird-watching. Canoa is the sister company of the Maquenque Lodge (p276) in Boca Tapada and can arrange an overnight stay there.

Aguas Bravas RAFTING, KAYAKING
(☑2479-7645; www.aguasbravascr.com; rafting US$80-100; ☺7am-7pm) The rafting and ziplining trips take place on the Río Sarapiquí so it's not exactly in the area, but they can pick you up at your hotel in La Fortuna.

Note that its office is in Sarapiquí, not in La Fortuna; from La Fortuna, call or book online.

🛏 Sleeping

🛏 La Fortuna
There are loads of places to stay in town. In fact, the tourist infrastructure has overflowed out of town, so that now there are lodges strung out along the roads heading south and west. With Parque Nacional Volcán Arenal at their doorstep, many of these places on the outskirts have hiking trails, hot springs and volcano views right on the property, but restaurants and other facilities are limited.

Sleeping Indian Guesthouse GUESTHOUSE $
(☑8446-9149, 2479-8431; sleepingindianguest house@gmail.com; Av 331, near Calle 442; d incl breakfast US$45; 🔊) Named for the nearby mountain formation (indio dormido), this delightful second-story guesthouse's five sweet fan-cooled rooms have lofty ceilings, tile floors, colorful paint jobs and big windows. The spacious common area includes a fully equipped kitchen, balconies with volcano views, and a homey living room well stocked with books and games. Manager Heidy's artwork graces many of its walls.

Earplugs are provided to the noise-sensitive; breakfast is served at the Lava Lounge (p252).

Gringo Pete's
HOSTEL **$**

(Calle 460 A; dm/private US$6/8; 🛜) 'Quiet, clean and cheap,' said one guest, and the prices are indeed pretty sweet. Groovy red couches, books and a chess set populate the common area; the kitchen is ample and clean. Set off in a quieter space a few blocks from the town center, Pete's mantra is 'bed and breakfast: you make both.' This is definitely old-school hosteling.

Pete's is the purple house with the amusing signage at the end of the block. They have a second location two blocks west of the bus station.

Hostel Backpackers La Fortuna
HOSTEL **$**

(📞 2479-9129; www.hostelbackpackerslafortuna. com; Calle 474; dm/s/d/tr/q US$15/53/58/72/84; P❄@🛜☲) The rooms at this rather grown up hostel are done in whites and beiges, and the courtyard is lush, lovely and strung with hammocks. Guests are invited to go down the street to the sister property, Arenal Hostel Resort, to join the party (swimming pool, bar) and then to return here for quiet, comfort and good night's sleep.

This should not be confused with Arenal Backpackers Resort, up the hill a bit out of town, which is a different (and cooler) beast altogether.

Arenal Backpackers Resort
HOSTEL **$**

(📞 2479-7000; www.arenalbackpackersresort.com; Via 142; dm US$14-18, tents s/d US$35/40, r s/d US$55/80; P❄@🛜☲) The original hostel resort in La Fortuna, this self-proclaimed 'five-star hostel' with volcano views is pretty cushy. Sleep on orthopedic mattresses and take hot showers in your en suite bathroom (even in the dorms). A step up from the dorms are the raised tents, which have double beds and electricity (but no proper walls, so you'll hear your neighbors loud and clear).

The main attraction is the landscaped pool with swim-up bar, where backpackers spend lazy days lounging with a cold beer. You'll be in a traveler's party bubble here. Not that there's anything wrong with that.

La Fortuna Suites
GUESTHOUSE **$**

(📞 8328-7447; www.lafortunasuites.com; Av 331A; d/ste incl breakfast from US$45/75; P❄🛜) Here's a chance to luxuriate in some high-end amenities (Apple TV and Netflix, for example) at budget prices. We're talking high-thread-count sheets and memory-foam mattresses, custom-made furniture and flat-screen TVs, gourmet breakfast on the balcony and killer views. Despite all these perks, guests agree that the thing that makes this place special is the hospitality shown by the hosts.

Located 300m west of Parque Central, behind La Choza Inn. If you can, get the suite with terrace access.

Arenal Hostel Resort
HOSTEL **$$**

(📞 2479-9222; www.arenalhostelresort.com; Via 142; dm/s/d/tr/q US$17/50/60/80/90; P❄🛜☲) 🍴 A combination of hostel and resort, this sprawling place is arranged around a landscaped garden, complete with hammocks, small pool, party-place bar and volcano view. All rooms are clean, spacious and air-conditioned, with en suite bathrooms. A word of warning: a recurring complaint is that reservations were 'lost' or clients were 'bumped' to Hostel Backpackers La Fortuna.

There's a number of places with very similar names in town, which causes confusion for customers and taxi drivers alike. To add to the confusion, the same company also advertises the Arenal Hostel Resort Tower, featuring private rooms but no dorm option.

La Choza Inn
INN **$$**

(📞 2479-9361, 2479-9091; www.lachozainnhos tel.com; Av 331; incl breakfast, dm US$10-15, s/d US$35/50; P❄@🛜) With all the budget 'resorts' in town, it's refreshing to find a charming, old-fashioned, family-run inn, where facilities are basic but the staff is always accommodating. Take your pick from the dark, palm-wood dorms or the attractive doubles boasting volcanic views from the balcony. A clean common kitchen and one-time free transport to Tabacón hot springs are other perks.

Air-con is US$10 extra.

Selina La Fortuna
HOSTEL **$$**

(📞 800-1022-463; www.selina.com/la-fortuna; dm/tent US16/50, d US$65-80; P❄🛜☲) The big-gun Central American hostel's arrival in La Fortuna is a game-changer, offering everything from shared dorms to luxurious tents to high-end hotel rooms, with amenities like a swimming pool, bar and small movie theater/chill-out room. The super-friendly staff make this a welcome option for the weary budget traveler.

No bracelet needed to enter, as is de ri-gueur in hostel culture.

Hotel Monte Real
HOTEL **$$**

(📞 2479-9357; www.monterealhotel.com; Av 325, btwn Calles 464 & 466; incl breakfast, r US$92, ste US$102-115; P ❄ 🔊 ⛷) A smart, modern property on the edge of the Río Burio. This location combines the convenience of town with the nature and rusticity of the forest – meaning lovely gardens and wildlife on your doorstep. Spacious rooms have Spanish-tile floors, stained-wood ceilings and sliding glass doors, some with private balcony. Ask Angel, the gardener, where all the cool animals are.

Downtown Inn BOUTIQUE HOTEL **$$**
(✆4000-2027; www.fortunadowntowninn.com; Main Square, Via 142; d incl breakfast US$100; P ❄ 🔊 ⛷) The old Bromelia Hotel, right off the main square, has been re-imagined and features two dozen smart rooms, most with terraces overlooking the pool, furnished with posh rocking chairs. You might not want a room facing the square, however, although the windows seem well insulated. A quality addition to Fortuna's lodging options. Car parking is 100m away.

Hotel Arenal Rabfer HOTEL **$$**
(✆2479-9187; www.arenalrabfer.com; Calle 468; s/d/tr/q incl breakfast US$75/85/100/115; P ❄ 🔊 ⛷) Arguably the most architecturally appealing of the downtown options, with a striking shingled 2nd floor. Set up around a pebbled pool area and shady palm garden, the rooms are spacious with high slanted ceilings and crisp white paint. Located on a quiet side street, two blocks from the action. Refurbishment was apparently imminent at the time of research.

🛏 West of La Fortuna

The road to the Arenal turnoff is lined with places to stay, ranging from quaint *cabinas* to luxurious lodges. Most of the area's high-end accommodations are located along this stretch. It's not particularly convenient if you don't have your own transportation.

⭐**Roca Negra del Arenal** GUESTHOUSE **$$**
(✆2479-9237; www.hotelrocanegradelarenal.com; d/q US$80/110, breakfast US$7; P ❄ 🔊 ⛷) What makes this gem of a guesthouse so special? It's the paradisiacal setting, 2km from town. The luscious tiled pool and Jacuzzi are surrounded with tropical gardens that are bursting with blooms and buzzing with bees and birds, from parrots to peacocks. The spacious rooms have stained-wood accents, huge tile bathrooms and semiprivate terraces facing the garden (complete with rockers).

Plenty of feathered and furry friends roam the grounds. Along with the ever-charming owner, they make for quite a welcome party. If you came for R&R in exotic environs, look no further.

Arenal Oasis BUNGALOW **$$**
(✆2479-9526, 2479-8472; www.arenaloasis.com; d incl breakfast US$88; P 🔊) 🐾 Located only 3.5km from the center of La Fortuna but still surrounded by vegetation and wildlife, this place is truly an oasis. The accommodations are in dark but cozy log-cabin bungalows, with private porches facing the rainforest. It's a family-run operation that truly lends a personal touch.

Arenal Oasis is located to the west of town, 1km south of the main road; turn off at the cemetery. This is the site of a popular night frog-watching tour, too. A larger 'villa' accommodates families. Three new cabins will be added in January 2018.

Hotel Campo Verde BUNGALOW **$$**
(✆2479-1080; www.hotelcampoverde.com; d/tr/q incl breakfast from US$100/120/140; P 🔊) An absolutely darling family-owned property, 9km west of town. Canary-yellow wooden bungalows have vaulted beamed ceilings, two queen beds, lovely drapes and chandeliers, and a sweet tiled patio blessed with two waiting rockers. Book the wooden bungalows furthest from the road at the foot of the mountain, where the views are unbeatable and connect to 2km of trails.

Spring for a luxe (king bed/Jacuzzi) for $10 more.

Erupciones Inn B&B B&B **$$**
(✆2479-1400; www.erupcionesinn.com; d incl breakfast US$70-80; P ❄ 🔊) You can admire Arenal from every single colorful *cabina* at this riverside property 11km from La Fortuna (even while brushing your teeth!): take it in from a seat on your private patio. The cheaper *cabinas* are a bit plain, while the more expensive ones are bigger and more polished. Overall, service is sweet. And did we mention the views?

Nayara Hotel, Spa & Gardens HOTEL **$$$**
(✆2479-1600; www.arenalnayara.com; r/ste incl breakfast US$320/440; P ❄ @ 🔊 ⛷) This intimate and indulgent hotel, 6km west of town, has amassed a slew of awards for its Asian-inspired architecture, minimalist decor and richly romantic setting. The 50 rooms have exquisite furnishings and bedding, dark woods, high-tech gadgetry,

outdoor showers and private outdoor Jacuzzis where you can soak up views of Volcán Arenal. Exquisite.

Guests over the age of 16 can access all the amenities at the new, even fancier, Nayara Springs next door, a separate complex owned by the same company.

El Silencio del Campo
LODGE $$$

(☑2479-7055; www.hotelsilenciodelcampo.com; d/tr/q incl breakfast US$247/277/307; P❋☏☲) This lovely lodge about 4km west of town has 23 stand-alone cabins that are luxurious without being showy. The property's pièce de résistance, though, is the hot spring – for guests only – with half a dozen decadent pools in a range of temperatures. Guests can also experience life on a working farm and feast on fresh eggs for breakfast.

Arenal Volcano Inn
INN $$$

(☑2479-1122, in USA 1-315-215-0460; www.arenalvolcanoinn.com; incl breakfast s/d from US$132/145, deluxe US$154/168, ste US$218/232; P❋☏☲) Resembling an upper-middle-class enclave, about 6km northwest of La Fortuna, this appealing lodging has sidewalks winding through perfectly manicured lawns, connecting the red-tile-roof bungalows and swimming pool. The bungalows open to private terraces that face the mighty mountain. Inside, clean, white walls and linens are complemented by dark stained wood trimmings, with all the amenities you'd expect.

🛏 South of La Fortuna

Just a few kilometers south of town, a partially paved road trundles to the base of Cerro Chato, and hotels now dot either side of it. Even further flung is the village of Chachagua, 12km south along the road to San Ramón. Crisscrossed by local rivers, this authentic, agrarian, market *pueblo* is an antidote to the touristy brouhaha of La Fortuna.

Rancho Cerro Azul
BUNGALOW $$

(☑2479-7360; www.ranchocerroazul.com; d/tr/q US$90/105/120; P❋☏) Eight cute, shingled cabins face the parking lot but back up to the forest, with private porches overlooking the trees. A 200m trail leads to the rushing river, with the volcano beyond. The cabins have woody interiors and stylish details. Think: simple, natural, beautiful, comfortable (but with cable television). The superi-

or and deluxe cabins are roomier and have king beds.

Located on the road to La Fortuna Waterfall, just before Down to Earth Coffee.

Catarata Eco-Lodge
LODGE $$

(☑2479-9522; www.cataratalodge.com; s/d/tr/q incl breakfast US$80/85/100/115; P❋☏☲) ✈ Set at the base of Cerro Chato and surrounded by forest, this place is ideal if you want to get away from it all (but not too far away, as you're still just 4km from town). The digs are decent little Spanish-tile and wood rooms, with hammocks strung on the terrace. The restaurant is also recommended.

Villas Josipek
CABINA $$

(☑2430-5252; www.costaricavillasjosipek.com; Ruta 702; d/tr US$85/125; P❋☏☲) Just north of Chachagua village, these immaculate, simple wooden cabins with full kitchens and volcano views are surrounded by private rainforest trails that penetrate the Bosque Eterno de Los Niños. Ask your hosts, Jorge and Sioni, to point out the sly sloth that sometimes inhabits the Guarumu tree near the lobby. A rather rustic 'spa' was under construction during research.

Within the grounds, you can take an 800m stroll through the Jardín Botánico Josipek, home to rose gardens, rainforest and medicinal plants, as well as a contemplative labyrinth and a giant plastic brontosaurus. Villas Josipek is about 10km south of La Fortuna proper.

★ Finca Luna Nueva
LODGE $$$

(☑2468-4006; www.fincalunanuevalodge.com; San Isidro; s/d/tr incl breakfast US$95/105/120; @☏☲) ✈ Bordering the Children's Eternal Rainforest, this special place started as a spice farm then blossomed into an ecolodge. It's a pretty impressive amalgam of sustainability and luxury, featuring lovely *casas* built from reclaimed wood, an ozonated swimming pool, solar-heated Jacuzzi, a huge medicinal plant garden and an amazing restaurant, supplied by the onsite organic farm.

Located about 17km south of La Fortuna, in the village of San Isidro.

Chachagua Rainforest Ecolodge
LODGE $$$

(☑2468-1020; www.chachaguarainforesthotel.com; d/bungalow incl breakfast US$180/215; P⟳❋☏☲) Situated on a private reserve that abuts the Bosque Eterno de Los Niños, and comprising a working orchard, cattle ranch and fish farm, plus humid rainforest, this a naturalist's dream. Explore on hiking trails or on horseback. The rooms are nice but arguably overpriced, while the stylish, spacious bungalows – some with air-con and Jacuzzis – are gorgeous.

To get here, drive 11km south of La Fortuna. On the southern side of Chachagua, fork right off the main road and follow the signs on a 2km dirt track that may require a 4WD in the rainy season.

Green Lagoon HOTEL $$$
(☑2479-7700; www.greenlagoon.net; d US$124) Perched high above the Río Fortuna Catarata, this 'well-being resort' is great for birders and froggers, er, frog-lovers – especially with the resident naturalist on hand to point out specimens. The rooms are fairly plain, but comfortable. The 'wellness' comes in with spa services, garden, a yoga space, and vegetarian restaurant. Spring for a superior with a balcony if you can.

At the waterfall parking lot, turn right up the unpaved drive.

Casa Luna Hotel & Spa HOTEL $$$
(☑2479-7368; www.casalunahotel.com; s/d/ste incl breakfast US$145/155/260; P❈ 🐾❄) The snazziest joint on this rustic road (heading toward the famed waterfall), this walled-off complex initially seems like a gated community. But, once inside, you'll see that the landscaped gardens and adobe-style lodgings are lovely. Wooden doors open into 36 elegant, split-level duplexes with private patios, as well as four deluxe rooms and two junior suites.

There's a full menu of spa treatments, and attentive service.

✕ Eating

Unless you're eating exclusively at *sodas,* you'll find the restaurants in La Fortuna to be more expensive than in other parts of the country. But there are some excellent, innovative kitchens, including a few that are part of the farm-to-table movement. The restaurants are mostly clustered in town, but there are also places to eat on the road heading west.

Soda Mima SODA $
(Off Via 142; ☺6am-8pm Mon-Sat, to noon Sun) Nothing fancy from afar, the love radiates outward from Don Alvaro's kitchen to warm your belly and your heart. Cheap, delicious *casados* (set meals) and gallo pintos are standard fare, but add some marinated peppers from the big jar if you dare. Customer artwork in various languages adorns the walls, the most fitting of which reads: 'Don Alvaro Rocks.'

In the parking lot behind Cafeto Chill Out and the big chicken restaurant.

Gecko's Waterfall Grill INTERNATIONAL $
(☑2479-1569; www.geckoscostarica.com; mains US$6-7; ☺11am-5pm) Good cheap eats (quesadillas, breakfast burritos), rich smoothies and artisanal beers are the payoff at this cafe, located just before the big waterfall. Treat yourself to a breakfast burrito – you walked all the way, didn't you?

La Muerta FAST FOOD $
(Fast Food; ☑2479-1407; Calle 472; mains US$6-10; ☺11am-10pm) A slightly healthier take on fast food, this small stand features a lineup of Latin American favorites like *tacos al pastor* (shredded pork), *choripan* (sausage sandwich), and *patacones* (fried green plantains), as well as burritos and hamburgers, and a bit of bouncy reggae with your *batido* (fruit shake). If you dare, go for the El Miedo ('the fear') hot sauce.

Situated 50m south of Alamo car rental, next to the Chifa Familia Feliz.

Rainforest Café CAFE $
(☑2479-7239; Calle 468; mains US$7-10; ☺7am-10pm; 🐾📶) We know it's bad form to start with dessert, but the irresistible sweets at this popular spot are beautiful to behold and delicious to devour. The savory menu features tasty burritos, *casados*, sandwiches etc. There's also a full menu of coffees, including some tempting specialty drinks (such as Mono Loco: coffee, banana, milk, chocolate and cinnamon).

There's a dash of urban-coffeehouse atmosphere here, and it's popular with cool Costa Rican kids with plastic to-go cups.

Soda Viquez SODA $
(☑2479-7133; cnr Calle 468 & Av 325; mains US$5-10; ☺8am-10pm; 📶) Travelers adore the 'local flavor' that's served up at Soda Viquez (in all senses of the expression). It's a super-friendly spot, offering tasty *típico* (traditional dishes), especially *casados*, rice dishes and fresh fruit *batidos*. Prices are reasonable and portions ample.

Kappa Sushi SUSHI $
(Calle 468, btwn Av 331 & Av 333; sushi & rolls US$6-12; ☺noon-10pm; 📶) When you're surrounded by mountains and cattle farms, who's thinking of sushi? Well, you should. The fish

is fresh (you're not *that* far from the ocean) and the preparations innovative. The dragon roll (shrimp tempura, avocado and eel sauce) is a favorite. Enjoy the view of Arenal (or is it Fuji?) while you feast on raw fish – or go for the veg options.

'Kappa' isn't a Japanese word at all, but a combination of the owners' names, Kattya and Pablo.

Anch'io Ristorante & Pizzeria   ITALIAN $$
(☎ 2479-7024; Via 142; mains US$10-18; ⊙ noon-10pm; P 🛜 🛏) If you have a hankering for pizza, you can't do better than Anch'io, where the crust is crispy thin, the toppings are plentiful and the pie is cooked in a wood-fired oven. Start yourself off with a traditional antipasto. Accompany it with cold beer or a bottle of red. Add super service and pleasant patio seating, and you've got yourself a winner.

The large tables lend to a good group/family atmosphere.

Orgánico Fortuna   VEGETARIAN $$
(☎ 8572-2115; www.organicofortuna.com; Calle 466; mains US$10-15; ⊙ 11am-9pm) A lovely little family operation that preaches better living through better eating, and the proof is in the pudding (or maybe the falafel). Delicious locally sourced ingredients are prepared with care. Smoothies, coffee with almond milk, and even some gluten-free bread and other options. If you're there long enough, you may even overhear a violin lesson in the back room.

There are inspirational quotations on the wall such as 'Let food be your medicine.'

Café Mediterraneo   ITALIAN $$
(☎ 2479-7497; Ruta 702; mains US$10-15; ⊙ 11:30am-10pm) This delightful osteria is worth the jaunt out of town, cooking up homemade pasta and pizza like the Arenal: bacon, egg, ham, mushroom and basil. Customers rave about the personable service and decadent desserts like Nutella on pizza dough. Strangely, they also offer Texas-bred Angus beef, while a herd of highly affronted Tico cattle stare from across the road.

Located just after Bike Arenal and before El Establo bar, on the road out of the town center.

Chifa La Familia Feliz   FUSION $$
(☎ 8469-6327; Calle 472; mains US$8-12; ⊙ 11am-10pm; 🛜 🛏 🛏) If you're looking for a change of taste – a *real* change from *casados* and pizza – check this out. *Chifa* means 'Chi-

nese food' in Peruvian-Spanish. So what we have here is Peruvian Chinese food, which is something special indeed. The chef goes out of his way to welcome and satisfy all comers.

Lava Lounge   INTERNATIONAL $$
(☎ 2479-7365; www.lavaloungecostarica.com; Via 142; mains US$8-15, specials US$22-24; ⊙ 7am-10:30pm; P 🛜 🛏) This hip, open-air restaurant is a relief when you just can't abide another *casado*. There is pizza and pasta, wraps and salads, and loads of vegetarian options. Service can be variable during peak hours, but the picnic tables and *palapa* (thatched) roof create a cool, rustic vibe. Add colorful cocktails and occasional live music, and the place is pretty irresistible.

Restaurant Don Rufino   INTERNATIONAL $$$
(☎ 2479-9997; www.donrufino.com; cnr Via 142 & Calle 466; mains US$16-40; ⊙ 11am-11pm) The vibe is trendy at this indoor-outdoor grill. The highlight is the perfectly prepared grilled meats: the New York Steak with mushrooms is to die for. If you're cutting back, go for Grandma's BBQ chicken (with chocolate, wrapped in a banana leaf) or the chef's special tuna (seasoned with ginger oil, served with rice noodles, tamarind sauce and cashew nuts).

🍷 Drinking & Nightlife

La Fortuna Pub   PUB
(www.facebook.com/lafortunapub; Via 142; ⊙ 2pm-midnight Sun-Thu, to 1am Fri-Sat) A new joint just uphill from the town center, these guys are all about Tico artisanal beers, offering a dozen different home-country bottled *cervezas*. They also brew their own beer in small batches that disappear quickly, so watch their Facebook page for the next arrival. A standard pub food menu satisfies, while weekend live music and Sunday's open mic add to the buzz.

Down to Earth   COFFEE
(☎ 2479-8568; www.godowntoearth.org; Diagonal 301; tour US$25; ⊙ 8am-8pm) On the road up to La Fortuna Waterfall, this place is all about the coffee, which is brewed from single-origin beans from the owner's farm in the Dota Tarrazu Valley. There's no food here, just coffee – smooth, strong and revitalizing. Matias explains the 'biology of good taste' for coffee cognoscenti and novice alike.

The coffee tour is not necessarily for children, but there *is* the Rainforest Chocolate tour right next door.

El Establo
BAR

(☑ 2479-7675; Ruta 702; ⊙ 5pm-2am Wed-Sat) La Fortuna's raucous *sendero* bar with an attached disco fronts the bull ring and attracts an ever-enthusiastic local following. The age demographic here ranges from 18 to 88. That's almost always a good thing. And the beer's cheap, too!

On the road south out of town, just after Cafe Mediterraneo.

🛍 Shopping

Hecho A Mano
ARTS & CRAFTS

(Handmade Art Shop; ☑ 8611-0018; www.facebook. com/handmadeartshop; Calle 468; ⊙ 9am-9pm Mon-Fri, from 10am Sat & Sun) There's no shortage of souvenirs for sale in La Fortuna, but this unique shop is something special, carrying an excellent selection of arts and crafts by local and national artists. You'll find representative pieces from Costa Rica's many subcultures, including Boruca masks, rasta handicrafts, lots of macrame and some lovely handmade jewelry.

Neptune's House of Hammocks
HOMEWARES

(☑ 2479-8269; Diagonal 301; hammocks US$40-50; ⊙ 8am-6pm) On the road to La Catarata de la Fortuna, Daniel been watching the tourist traffic come and go for over a decade while he weaves his magic hammocks. Take a breather and test one out.

ℹ Information

MEDICAL SERVICES

Centro Medico Sanar (☑ 2479-9420; cnr Calle 464 & Av 331; ⊙ 8am-8:30pm) Medical consultation, ambulance services and pharmacy.

MONEY

Line up to get some colones (or dollars) at banks all around town.

BAC San José (cnr Av 331 & Calle 466; ⊙ 9am-6pm Mon-Fri, to 1pm Sat)

Banco de Costa Rica (Via 142; ⊙ 9am-4pm Mon-Fri)

Banco Nacional (cnr Calle 468 & Av 331; ⊙ 8:30am-3:45pm Mon-Fri)

Banco Popular (☑ 2479-9422; cnr Via 142 & Calle 460A; ⊙ 8:45am-4:30pm Mon-Fri, 8:15-11:30am Sat)

POST

Correos de Costa Rica (Av 331; ⊙ 8am-5:30pm Mon-Fri, 7:30am-noon Sat) Located northeast of the Parque Central.

ℹ Getting There & Away

BUS

The **bus terminal** (Av 325) is on the river road. Keep an eye on your bags as this is a busy transit center.

For San José, an alternative is to take the bus to Ciudad Quesada, from where there are frequent departures to San José. However, you'll pay more doing so.

To reach Monteverde/Santa Elena (US$4, six to eight hours), take the early bus to Tilarán, where you'll have to wait a few hours for the onward bus to Santa Elena.

A great and friendly source of bus information for the entire country is Red Lava Tours, located right next to the terminal. Co-owner Sonia is known to locals as the Google of La Fortuna.

BUSES FROM LA FORTUNA

DESTINATION	COMPANY	COST (US$)	DURATION	FREQUENCY
Ciudad Quesada (San Carlos)	Auto-Transportes San José–San Carlos	2	1hr	20 daily, 4:30am-7pm
San José	Auto-Transportes San José–San Carlos	5	4hr	12:45pm, 2:45pm
San Ramon via Chachagua		2	2hr	5:30am, 9am, 1pm, 4pm
Tilarán, with connection to Monteverde	Auto-Transportes Tilarán, departs from the Parque Central	3	3½hr	7:30am, 12:30pm, 5pm

TAXI-BOAT-TAXI

The fastest route between Monteverde-Santa Elena and La Fortuna is the taxi-boat-taxi combo (formerly known as jeep-boat-jeep, which sounds sexy but it was the same thing). It is actually a minivan with the requisite yellow 'turismo' tattoo, which takes you to Laguna de Arenal, meeting a boat that crosses the lake, where a 4WD van on the other side continues to Monteverde. It's a terrific transportation option that can be arranged through almost any hotel or tour operator in La Fortuna or Monteverde (US$25 to US$35, four hours).

This is now the first transportation choice for many between La Fortuna and Monteverde as it's incredibly scenic and reasonably priced.

❶ Getting Around

BICYCLE

Biking is a reasonable option to get around town and reach some of the top tourist attractions. The challenging 7km ride from town to La Catarata is a classic. Make advance arrangement to rent a bike from Bike Arenal (p246) and they'll drop it off at your hotel.

CAR

La Fortuna is easy to access by public transportation, but nearby attractions such as the hot springs, Parque Nacional Volcán Arenal and Laguna de Arenal demand internal combustion (or a tour operator). If you're thinking of doing a day trip to Río Celeste, Caño Negro or Venada Caves, you might also consider renting a car for the day.

Adobe Rent a Car (☑ 2479-7202; www.adobe car.com; Av 325; ☺ 8am-5pm)

Alamo (☑ 2479-9090; www.alamocostarica. com; cnr Via 142 & Calle 472; ☺ 7:30am-5:30pm)

Parque Nacional Volcán Arenal

For most of modern history, Volcán Arenal was just another dormant volcano surrounded by fertile farmland. But for about 42 years – from its destructive explosion in 1968 until its sudden subsiding in 2010 – the volcano was an ever-active and awe-striking natural wonder, producing menacing ash columns, massive explosions and streams of glowing molten rock almost daily.

The fiery views are gone for now, but **Arenal** (☑ 2461-8499; adult/child US$15/5; ☺ 8am-4pm, last entrance 2:30pm) is still a worthy destination, thanks to the dense forest covering her lower slopes and foothills, and her picture-perfect conical shape up top (often shrouded in clouds, but still). The Parque Nacional Volcán Arenal is part of the Area de Conservación Arenal, which protects most of the Cordillera de Tilarán. This area is rugged and varied, rich with wildlife and laced with trails.

🏃 Activities

Hiking

From the ranger station (which has trail maps available), you can hike the **Sendero Los Heliconias**, a 1km circular track that passes by the site of the 1968 lava flow. A 1.5km-long path branches off this trail and leads to an overlook. The **Sendero Las Coladas** also branches off the Heliconias trail and wraps around the volcano for 2km past the 1993 lava flow before connecting with the **Sendero Los Tucanes**, which extends for another 3km through the tropical rainforest at the base of the volcano. To return to the parking area, you'll have to turn back – you'll get good views of the summit on the way.

From the park headquarters (not the ranger station) is the 1.3km **Sendero Los Miradores**, which leads down to the shores of the volcanic lake and provides a good angle for volcano viewing. Also from park headquarters, the **Old Lava Flow Trail** is an interesting and strenuous lower elevation trail following the flow of the massive 1992 eruption. The 4km round trip takes two hours to complete. If you want to keep hiking, combine it with the **Sendero El Ceibo**, a scenic 1.8km trail through secondary forest.

There are additional trails departing from Arenal Observatory Lodge and on a nearby private reserve.

Waterfall Trail   HIKING
(www.arenalobservatorylodge.com; Arenal Observatory Lodge; day pass per person US$10) This scenic hike departing from Arenal Observatory Lodge is an easy, 2km round-trip hike to a 12m waterfall. The terrain starts out flat then descends into a grotto where you'll find a thundering gusher of a waterfall. You'll feel the mist long before you see its majesty.

Arenal 1968   HIKING
(☑ 2462-1212; www.arenal1968.com; El Castillo–La Fortuna; trails US$12, mountain bike park US$12; ☺ 7am-10pm) This private network of trails along the original 1968 lava flow is right next to the park entrance. There's a *mirador* (lookout) that on a clear day offers a

picture-perfect volcano view. It's located 1.2km from the highway turnoff to the park, just before the ranger station.

The 16km of mountain bike trails, separate from the lava hiking trails, lets you see the park in a different way.

☞ Tours

In addition to hiking, it's also possible to explore the park on horseback, mountain bike or ATV.

Arenal Wilberth Stables   HORSEBACK RIDING
(☑ 2479-7522; www.arenalwilberthstable.com; per person 1/2hr US$40/65; ☺ 7:30am, 11am & 2:30pm) Two-hour horseback-riding tours depart from these stables at the foot of Arenal. The ride takes in forest and farmland, as well as lake and volcano views. The stables are opposite the entrance to the national park, but there's an office in La Fortuna, next to Arenal Hostel Resort (p248).

Original ATV   ADVENTURE
(☑ 2479-7522; www.originalarenalatv.com; rental per hr US$60-90, tour per person US$100-130; ☺ 7:30am, 11am, & 2:30pm) This wild 2½-hour ATV ride takes place on a private farm near the national park, with volcano views all around. Along the way, you can cool off (and clean off) with a dip in the river. It's located across from the park entrance, but they also have an office in La Fortuna, at the Arenal Hostel Resort. Tour price includes transportation from your hotel.

🛏 Sleeping

Arenal Observatory Lodge   LODGE $$$
(☑ 2479-1070, reservations 2290-7011; arenalobservatorylodge.com; d/tr/q without bathroom US$100/$115/130, with bathroom from US$140/155/185; [P] ❄ @ 🛜 🏊) High on the Arenal slopes, this sprawling lodge is the only accommodation in the national park. Rooms range from La Casona's rustic doubles with shared bathrooms and views from the porch, to junior suites with king-size beds, local art and huge picture windows framing the volcano. The rooms (paper-thin walls) could stand a bit of improvement, as could the night-time lighting.

There's a decent international restaurant on the grounds (just as well as there's obviously nowhere else to eat in the area). There's also a small museum, with exhibits on the history, volcanology and hydrology of Arenal. Rates include access to the swimming pool and hiking trails, as well as a free guided walk each morning.

ℹ Information

The **ranger station** (☑ 2461-8499; ☺ 8am-4pm) is on the western side of the volcano. The complex housing the station includes an information center and parking lot. From here, trails lead 3.4km toward the volcano.

ℹ Getting There & Away

To get to the ranger station by car, head west from La Fortuna for 15km, then turn left at the 'Parque Nacional' sign and take the 2km good dirt road to the entrance on the left side of the road. You can also take an 8am bus toward Tilarán (tell the driver to drop you off at the park) and catch the 2pm bus back to La Fortuna.

If you are heading to Arenal Observatory Lodge, continue driving on the dirt road. About 3km past the ranger station you will come to a small one-lane bridge and parking area. After crossing the bridge you'll reach a fork in the road; left goes to Arenal Observatory Lodge and right goes to the village of El Castillo. Turn left and continue 2.6km to reach the lodge. This steep, hard-packed gravel and partially paved road is fine for most vehicles, but a 4WD is recommended.

A taxi from La Fortuna to either the lodge or El Castillo will cost about US$30.

El Castillo

POP 300

Just an hour around the bend from La Fortuna, the tiny mountain village of El Castillo is a beautiful, bucolic, and bumpy alternative, if you don't mind the somewhat treacherous roads. This picturesque locale, created as a relocation zone after the great eruption of 1968, has easy access to Parque Nacional Volcán Arenal and amazing, up-close views of the looming mountain – with little of the tourist madness of its bigger neighbor.

There is a tight-knit expat community here, some of whom have opened appealing lodges and top-notch restaurants. There are hiking trails and swimming holes. There are even a few worthy attractions – a butterfly house and an eco-zoo. The only thing El Castillo doesn't have is a sidewalk. And maybe that's a good thing.

⊙ Sights

Arenal EcoZoo   ZOO
(El Serpentario; ☑ 2479-1059; www.arenaleco zoo.com; La Fortuna–El Castillo road; adult/child

Around La Fortuna

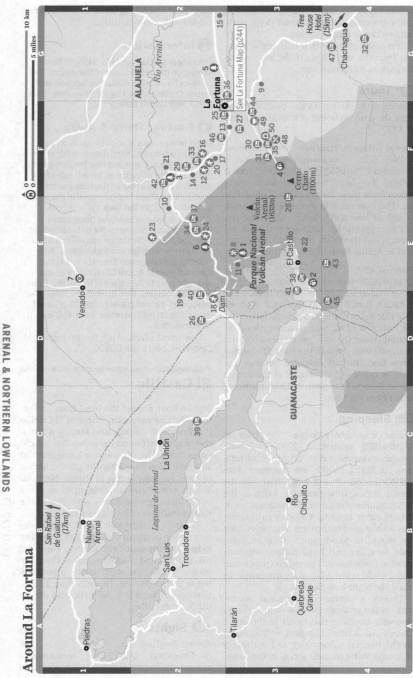

See La Fortuna Map (p244)

Tree House Hotel (15km)

San Rafael de Guatuso (17km)

ARENAL & NORTHERN LOWLANDS

Around La Fortuna

US$15/12, with guide US$23/16; ⊙8am-7pm) This snake house offers a hands-on animal experience, as in, handling and milking a venomous snake. It is also home to a red-tailed boa (one of the largest snakes in the world), as well as frogs, amphibious lizards, iguanas, turtles, scorpions, tarantulas and butterflies. Ask about feeding time if you want to see snakes devouring bugs, frogs and even other snakes. Located on the main road uphill from the lake, which connects to La Fortuna.

El Castillo-Arenal
Butterfly Conservatory   WILDLIFE RESERVE
(☑2479-1149; www.butterflyconservatory.org; El Castillo–La Fortuna road; adult/student US$15/11; ⊙8am-4pm) More than just a butterfly conservatory (although it has one of the largest butterfly exhibitions in Costa Rica). Altogether there are six domed habitats, a ranarium, an insect museum, a medicinal herb garden, and an hour's worth of trails through a botanic garden and along the river. The birding is also excellent here, and there are wonderful volcano views. The conservatory is located on the main road uphill from the lake, which connects to La Fortuna.

🕿 Tours

La Gavilana   TOURS
(☑2479-1747, 8433-7902; www.gavilana.com; El Castillo–La Fortuna road; waterfall tour US$90, base camp day tour $99, Big Forest hike US$159) The adventurous folk at La Gavilana Herbs & Art offer a Big Forest trail hike between El Castillo and San Gerardo (near Santa Elena). Traversing old-growth forests and raging

rivers, hikers overnight at the rustic Rancho Maximo. Dinner and breakfast are provided. The office is on the main road uphill from the lake, which connects to La Fortuna.

La Gavilana offers a few additional adventures, including a base camp day tour and one-day waterfall tour; foodies might want to try the fermentation workshop, a pickler's delight.

Sky Adventures
CANOPY TOUR

(☎ 2479-4100; www.skyadventures.travel; adult/ child Sky Walk US$39/27, Sky Tram US$46/32, Sky River Drift US$72/57, Sky Limit US$81/56, Sky Trek US$81/56; ☺ 7:30am-4pm) El Castillo's entry in the canopy-tour category has ziplines (Sky Trek), a floating gondola (Sky Tram) and a series of hanging bridges (Sky Walk). It's safe and well run, and visitors tend to leave smiling. A unique combo, Sky River Drift combines a zipline with tree-climbing and river tubing, while Sky Limit combines ziplining with rappel and other high-altitude challenges.

There's also mountain biking on the property. Sky Adventures is located uphill from the lake and the El Castillo–La Fortuna road, just past the Arenal Tropical Gardens.

Rancho Adventure Tours
ADVENTURE

(☎ 8302-7318; www.ranchomargot.com; farm tour US$35, other tours US$55) Rancho Margot offers a good selection of guided tours, including horseback riding on the southern side of Laguna de Arenal, kayaking on the lake, and touring the ranch itself to learn about the workings of a sustainable farm. The activities are free to guests of the Rancho. Located where the El Castillo–La Fortuna road intersects with Rancho Margot Rd.

🛏 Sleeping

For a tiny place, El Castillo has an impressive range of accommodations, from funky budget lodgings to charming B&Bs to expansive ecolodges. You'll find them clustered in the village, up on the hillside, and strung out along the lake shore. If you've got your tent, you can pitch it for free on the lakefront (take the dirt track just across from the church) and enjoy the best views in town.

Essence Arenal
HOTEL $

(☎ 2479-1131; www.essencearenal.com; d with/ without bathroom US$48/35, additional person $12, tents US$30-48; P@ল̃≋) 🍴 Perched on a 22-hectare hilltop with incredible volcano and lake views, this 'boutique hostel' is the best cheap sleep in the region. Bed down in a basic but clean room or a fancy tent, done up with plush bedding and wood furnishings (some have terraces and Jacuzzis for $10 extra). It's an eclectic, positive-energy place, offering group hikes, yoga classes and good vibes.

Guests participate in the loving preparation of vegetarian meals (with ingredients sourced from its own organic farm) that will delight even the most hardcore carnivore; the restaurant is open 7am to 8pm. To get here, turn left towards the Butterfly Conservatory and continue 1km uphill to the hostel.

Cabinas Los Tucanes
HOTEL $$

(☎ 2479-1076; www.arenalcabinaslostucanes.com; El Castillo–La Fortuna road; d/tr/q US$55/65/80, breakfast US$5; ল̃) Here you'll find huge, bright, spotless and spacious rooms, with plain decor but fabulous vistas from the picture windows, situated uphill from the lake. The top-floor rooms catch a nice breeze off the terrace; you'll pay extra for the view but it's money well spent. Fanny and Licho take care of this place, and they'll take care of you too.

Hummingbird Nest
B&B $$

(Nido del Colibrí; ☎ 8835-8711, 2479-1174; www. hummingbirdnestbb.com; d/tr/q incl breakfast US$85/95/100; P❊ল̃) At the entrance to town, a small, steep path leads to this charming B&B, owned by a former flight attendant and world traveler who found a small slice of paradise to call her own. Her quaint complex has two guest rooms and a garden full of hummingbirds (hence the name). Soak the night away in a huge garden Jacuzzi.

In high season, an extra house below the B&B is available to rent.

★ Rancho Margot
RESORT, LODGE $$$

(☎ 8302-7318; www.ranchomargot.org; cnr El Castillo-La Fortuna road & Rancho Margot road; incl meals dm per person US$80, bungalow s/d US$175/250; Pল̃≋) 🍴 Part resort lodge, part organic farm, Rancho Margot is 61 hectares of cinematic loveliness, set along the rushing Río Caño Negro and surrounded by rainforested mountains. There are comfortable dorm-style bunkhouse accommodations but, if your budget allows, spring for a beautiful teak-furnished bungalow, blessed with views of hulking mountains, weeping jungle and a placid lake.

Prices include a two-hour guided tour of the farm and daily yoga classes. Hiking trails and (free) hot springs are at hand. Prices are more attractive the longer you stay. Located where the El Castillo-La Fortuna road meets Rancho Margot Rd.

Majestic Lodge
GUESTHOUSE $$$

(📲 8703-1561, 2479-1085; www.majesticlodgecostarica.com; El Fósforo–El Castillo road; r US$130; 🅿️ ❄️ 🛜 🏊) This lovely boutique lodge has a prime perch overlooking Laguna de Arenal. It's easy to hang out all day, enjoying the view from the covered deck or soaking in the gorgeous stone swimming pool (and Jacuzzi). The plush lodge rooms have beautiful handcrafted wooden furniture and exquisite tiled bathrooms, while 'Pie in the Sky' *cabinas* also have fully equipped kitchens.

There are varying discounts depending on how many rooms you rent, and how long you stay. Just ask Walter; he also runs the onsite Howlers Bar and is building another property in 'downtown' Castillo.

The lodge is on the main El Fósforo–El Castillo road that parallels the lakefront.

Nepenthe
B&B $$$

(📲 8892-5501; www.nepenthe-costarica.com; d incl breakfast US$115; 🅿️ ❄️ 🛜 🏊) South of El Castillo, the highlight here is the spectacular, spring-fed infinity pool overlooking Laguna de Arenal. Lodge-like cabins are simple, tiled numbers with colorful artisanal accents, set in a gentle arc of a ranch-style building. Hammocks on the patio allow you to take it all in. Incredible views, but you may need a four-wheel drive to reach it – seriously.

The aptly named Phoenix restaurant on site is in its fourth incarnation. Some cabins come with fully equipped kitchens. A separate house is available for up to 12 persons.

🍴 Eating & Drinking

Your eating options are pretty limited in El Castillo, but there are some good ones – enough to keep you fed for a couple of days. In addition to the few places in the village, some lodgings on the outskirts have recommended restaurants. Of course, there are more choices in La Fortuna, but you'll have to traverse 9km of dust, ruts and stones: not the easiest way to digest a meal.

★ La Ventanita
CAFE $

(📲 2479-1735; El Castillo–La Fortuna road; mains US$3-5; ⏰ 11am-9pm; 🍴) *La Ventanita* is the 'little window' where you place your order. Soon enough, you'll be devouring the best *chifrijo* (rice and pinto beans with fried pork, capped with fresh tomato salsa and corn chips) that you've ever had, along with a nutritious and delicious *batido*. It's typical food with a twist – pulled pork and bacon burritos, for example.

California expat Kelly is a wealth of information about the area, so ask away. It's on the main El Castillo–La Fortuna road.

La Gavilana Herbs & Art
BAKERY $

(📲 8533-7902; www.facebook.com/gavilanacr; snacks US$2-6; ⏰ 8am-5pm Mon-Fri, 9am-2pm Sat) Meet Tomas and Hannah. He's Czech and makes the hot sauce and vinegar; she's American and bakes the cookies and breads. Their place, southwest of El Castillo, is decked with paintings (Hannah), while the grounds contain a food forest (Thomas), filled with medicinal herbs and fruit trees. The whole place is filled with love, beauty and creativity. Reservations requested.

Fusion Grill
FUSION $$

(📲 2479-1949; www.fusiongrillrestaurant.com; El Castillo–La Fortuna road; mains US$8-15; ⏰ 7am-10pm) Set in an open-air dining room with an incredible vista of the volcano, Fusion Grill shows off a little swank (at least, more than other restaurants in El Castillo). Chef Adrian Ramirez whips up a mean *parillada mixta* (mixed grill), but your favorite part of the meal might be the specialty desserts like pineapple or banana *flambé*.

The restaurant is uphill from the lake on the El Castillo–La Fortuna road.

Howlers Bar & Grill
BAR

(📲 2479-1785; www.facebook.com/howlersbarandgrill; ⏰ 11:30am-8:30pm Tue-Sun) This lakefront bar is a fun choice for a night out drinking in El Castillo. (Good thing, as it's your only choice.) The American-style pub grub is excellent, as is the cold draught beer. It's a popular place for the expat community to congregate, guaranteeing an upbeat, *pura vida* vibe. Part of the Majestic Lodge property.

🛈 Getting There & Away

El Castillo is located 8km past the entrance to Parque Nacional Volcán Arenal. It's a rough gravel road, and it gets a bit worse once you get to the village.

There is no public transportation, but a private **shuttle bus** (☑ 8887-9141; Calle 472) runs from the Super Christian in La Fortuna (one hour, US$9) at 7:30am, 12:30pm and 5:30pm. The bus departs Rancho Margot (p258) at 6am, 10am and 4pm, returning from La Fortuna at 6am, 10am and 4pm. Contact the father and son drivers Arturo and Luis at 8887-9141, whose van will be either white, grey or green. This bus also will drop you at the entrance to the national park for US$4.

Laguna de Arenal

About 18km west of La Fortuna you'll arrive at a 750m-long causeway across the dam that created Laguna de Arenal, the largest lake in the country at 88 sq km. Arenal and Tronadora were submerged during its 1979 creation, but the lake now supplies valuable water to Guanacaste, sport fish like rainbow bass, and hydroelectricity for the region. High winds also produce power with the aid of huge steel windmills, though windsurfers and kitesurfers frequently steal a breeze or two.

Circling the lake is one of the premier road trips in Costa Rica. The road is lined with odd and elegant businesses; strong winds and high elevations give the lake a temperate feel and the scenic views of lakeside forests and Volcán Arenal are about as romantic as they come.

🏃 Activities

Laguna de Arenal offers scores of secluded bays and coves to explore as well as a forested island. You'll usually find a kayak concession set up on the dam's western end, but take care because when the wind kicks in it can be a nightmare to make it back. This is also a popular route for cycling (inquire at Bike Arenal, p246), and the area has a few other attractions.

Mistico Hanging Bridges　　　CANOPY TOUR
(Puentes Colgantes de Arenal; ☑ 2479-8282; www.misticopark.com; adult/child US$24/free, tours US$36-47; ⏲ 7:30am-4:30pm, tours 6am, 9am & 2pm) Unlike the fly-by view you'll get on a zipline canopy tour, a walk along these hanging bridges allows you to explore the rainforest and canopy from six suspended bridges and 10 traditional bridges at a more natural and peaceful pace. All are accessible from a single 3km trail that winds through a tunnel and skirts a waterfall.

The longest swaying bridge is 97m long and the highest is 25m above the ground. Reservations are required for guided bird-watching tours or informative naturalist tours. The Tilarán bus can drop you off at the entrance, but it's a 3km climb from the bus stop. There are also loads of tours from La Fortuna, and you can book directly at Mistico's office, 25m north of Banco Nacional.

Fishing Lake Arenal　　　FISHING
(Marc El Belga; ☑ 8389-2989; www.fishinglakearenalcr.com; Arenal Lake Dam Dock; half-/full-day tours US$225/350) Marc, aka 'Marc el Belga' ('the Belgian') sits in a lawn chair outside his car near the jeep-boat-jeep drop-off near the dam. For more than two decades he's been helping visitors find the big ones in the depths of Arenal: rainbow bass, machaca, and the delicious gaupote. It's hard to miss him.

Arenal Kayaks　　　KAYAKING
(☑ 2694-4336; www.arenalkayaks.com; 2hr tour US$35) Two-hour guided paddle on Laguna de Arenal, including wildlife-watching and swim stops. Hotel pick-up included.

Represa Arenal

Forget for a moment that there are always ecological issues associated with dams and revel in the fact that this one created a rather magnificent lake (it took a village, or two, in the exchange). In the absence of wind, the glassy surface of Represa Arenal (Arenal Dam) reflects the volcano and the surrounding mountains teeming with cloud forest. Crowds congregate to admire the view and snap photos. Unfortunately, there's no convenient place to stop, so you'll often encounter a minor traffic jam, especially at the dam's western end.

🛏 Sleeping

Lost Iguana　　　RESORT $$$
(☑ toll-free in USA 800-479-1557, 2479-1557; www.lostiguanacr.com; r/ste/casita incl breakfast US$265/295/535; P❋@🛜🛁) This stylish and splashy resort, just 1.5km from the dam, is set among lush rainforest and rushing streams with glorious views at every turn. Luxurious rooms have private balconies looking out on Arenal, beds with Egyptian

cotton sheets, a terracotta wet bar and an invaluable sense of peace and privacy.

Upgrade to a suite for a Jacuzzi or outdoor rain shower. Also on the grounds: a romantic restaurant, a gorgeous bi-level pool with swim-up bar, and the well-equipped Golden Gecko Spa.

Arenal Lodge LODGE $$$
(☑ 2479-1881; www.arenallodge.com; incl breakfast d standard/superior US$115/120, f US$150, junior ste US$165; P✳🛜🚻) Arenal Lodge is at the top of a steep 2.5km ascent, though the entire lodge is awash with views of Arenal and the surrounding cloud forest. Standard rooms are just that, but the spacious junior suites are tiled and have wicker furniture and a picture window or balcony with volcano views.

The grounds are crisscrossed by hiking trails, and the lodge also has a Jacuzzi, billiards room, restaurant and private stables. Just off Ruta 142.

❶ Getting There & Away

The Represa Arenal (Arenal Dam) is about 18km west of La Fortuna. It's an easy drive if you have your own vehicle. If not, there are plenty of tour operators (or taxis) who will bring you to this corner of the region. You can also wait for the bus to Tilarán, which runs twice a day.

Nuevo Arenal

POP 2600

Although steeped in aging *extranjero cultura* (expat culture), this two-horse town still feels very Tico (albeit with a German-Swiss twist). A rest stop for travelers heading to Tilarán and points beyond, it's certainly a pleasant (and cheap) place to spend the night. The tiny downtown also has a gas station, two banks, a supermarket and a bus stop near the park. It even has a rickety old *plaza del toros* (bullring).

In case you were wondering what happened to old Arenal, it's about 27m below the surface of Laguna de Arenal. In order to create a large enough reservoir for the dam, the Costa Rican government had to make certain, er, sacrifices, which ultimately resulted in the forced relocation of 3500 people. Today the humble residents of Nuevo Arenal don't seem to be fazed by history, especially since they now own premium lakeside property.

🛏 Sleeping

There are a few budget options right in town, in addition to the expat-owned properties that line the lake.

Aurora Inn HOTEL $
(☑ 2694-4245; r US$24; P@🛜) You'd never know it from the street, but these rooms are rather sweet, spotless and spacious wood cabin-like constructions with lovely lake views and vaulted beamed ceilings. Located on the eastern side of the square, across from the sports field, it's one of the only budget options on Laguna de Arenal. The attached restaurant does decent pizza.

★ La Ceiba Tree Lodge LODGE $$
(☑ 8313-1475, 2692-8050; www.ceibalodge.com; s/d/tr/q from US$65/90/115/135; P✳🛜) About 22km west of the dam, this lovely, laid-back lodge overlooks a magnificent 54m ceiba tree. Eight spacious, Spanish-tile rooms are hung with original paintings and fronted by Maya-inspired carved doors. Each room has rustic artifacts, polished-wood ceilings and vast views of Laguna de Arenal. The tropical gardens and spacious terrace make this mountaintop spot a tranquil retreat.

Three 'comfort rooms' with queen beds and nicer bathrooms cost $30 extra. Owner Dirk founded one of Costa Rica's first beer gardens, the Maya Lounge, in San Jose, before heading to the countryside of Arenal.

Agua Inn B&B $$
(☑ 2694-4218; www.aguainn.com; Ruta 142; d incl breakfast US$80; P🛜🚻) The sound of the rushing river will lull you to sleep at this intimate B&B on the banks of the Río Cote. This gorgeous property is designed for total relaxation, with a jungle-shaded pool and a private lake trail. Four simple rooms feature soothing tones and plush linens, with a shared balcony providing a lovely view over the property.

Lucky Bug B&B B&B $$
(☑ 2694-4515; www.luckybugcr.net; d/ste incl breakfast from US$100/125; P🛜🚻) Set on a rainforest lagoon, 3km west of Nuevo Arenal, the five blissfully isolated bungalows at the Lucky Bug feature works and decorative details by local artisans. Here are blond-wood floors, wrought-iron butterflies, hand-painted geckos, mosaic washbasins and end tables. Each room is unique and captivating. There's a rainforest trail in the grounds and kayaks for use on the lagoon.

There is also an onsite Caballo Negro Restaurant featuring hearty German fare, and the fabulously quirky Lucky Bug Gallery. Should you fall in love with a painting of a bug or something bigger, they can ship it for you.

La Mansion INN $$$
([✒]2692-8018; www.lamansionarenal.com; d/ste incl breakfast from US$205/225; [P][⚡][✵]) About 15.5km west of the dam, the cottages, pool and restaurant at La Mansion enjoy amazing lake views. The large split-level rooms feature king-size beds, private terraces and mural-painted walls. The fabulous infinity lap pool is surrounded by a relaxing patio and an ornamental garden featuring Chorotega pottery. Or jump in the Jacuzzi to wind down. Lovely all around.

With a bar shaped like the bow of a ship, onsite restaurant Le Bistro is a romantic spot for lunch or dinner, with panoramic views from the dining room and outdoor patio. It has a substantial menu of well-prepared European food. There's quite a show at sunset.

Villa Decary B&B $$$
([✒]2694-4330, in US or Canada 1-800-556-0505; www.villadecary.com; r US$125, casitas US$160-180; [P][✵][⚡]) This country inn 2km east of Nuevo Arenal is an all-round winner, offering epic views and unparalleled hospitality. Rooms feature bright serape bedspreads and original artwork, and boast balconies with vistas of the woodland below and the lake beyond. *Casitas* (sleeping four) have kitchenettes. Birds and botany are why the owners came here, and you'll see a lot of both.

Decary also boasts one of the best collections of palm trees in Costa Rica, which explains why it's named for a French botanist who discovered a new species of palm. It's situated 24.5km west of the dam.

✕ Eating

Nuevo Arenal is a surprising little foodie Shangri-la, with enough eating options to keep you out of the kitchen for at least a week. In addition to the charming (and quite delicious) places in town, you'll also find one of the country's top-rated restaurants in a charming and disarming gingerbread house on the lake shore.

Tinajas Arenal CAFE $$
([✒]8926-3365, 2694-4667; www.tinajasarenal.com; mains US$9-17; [⊙]9am-9:30pm; [⚡][✒][⚡]) [✐] With glorious sunsets and a dock for boat access, this is a hidden gem. The chef – who works in tandem with his talented mom – has created a menu of traditional favorites and new surprises, using fresh seafood and organic ingredients grown right here. At the southern end of Nuevo Arenal, turn off the main road and follow the signs.

Sample the refreshing cocktail *a la casa, limon hierba* (lemonade with mint).

Los Platillos Voladores ITALIAN $$
([✒]2694-5005; www.facebook.com/losplatillosvoladores; mains US$6-14; [⊙]11:30am-7:30pm) The plates really do fly out of this carry-out joint right in the center of Nuevo Arenal, which gets raves for its homemade pasta, roast chicken and fresh salads. It's mostly Italian – the eggplant Parmesan is delectable – but the rotating menu features a variety of fish, chicken and meat dishes. Enjoy the views of the lake from the patio.

Moya's Place CAFE, PIZZA $$
([✒]2694-4001; Ruta 142; mains US$8-12; [⊙]11am-9pm) Murals, masks and other indigenous-inspired art adorn the walls at this friendly cafe. Take your pick from the delicious sandwiches, well-stuffed wraps and burritos, and tasty thin-crust pizza. This place is a sort of local gathering spot, where Ticos and expats alike gather to eat, drink and laugh. The food is good and the beer is cold.

Las Delicias SODA $$
([✒]8320-7102; mains US$5-12; [⊙]7am-9pm; [⚡]) A cheap and cheerful *soda* near the top of the hill as you approach town, with ample wooden-table seating. It does Western-style breakfasts, pasta dishes, quesadillas and grilled steaks on the cheap, but it's known for its *casados*.

Tom's Pan BAKERY $$
(Original German Bakery; [✒]2694-4547; Ruta 142; mains US$9-16; [⊙]8am-4:30pm Mon-Sat; [P][⚡]) Better known as the 'German bakery,' thanks to the signs that litter the lake road, this landmark is a famous rest stop for road-trippers heading to/from Tilarán. Its breads, strudels and cakes are all homemade, and it also has German sausages, sandwiches and beer. Surprisingly pricey for the setting.

★**Gingerbread
Hotel & Restaurant**   INTERNATIONAL **$$$**
(☑ 2694-0039, 8351-7815; www.gingerbreadarenal.
com; Ruta 142; mains US$25-40; ⏰ 5-9pm Tue-Sat;
🅿) Don't miss the chance to eat at one of
the best restaurants in northwestern Costa
Rica, right on the lake. The larger-than-life,
New York–trained Israeli chef turns out
transcendent meals from the freshest local
ingredients. Favorites include mushrooms
smothered in gravy, blackened tuna salad
and enormous, juicy burgers. It's big food
that goes down well. Cash only, reservations
recommended.

If you want to sleep where you eat, book
one of the sweet boutique rooms upstairs,
each showcasing fabulous murals and other
artwork by local creatives.

ⓘ Getting There & Away

Nuevo Arenal is 27km west of the dam, or an
hour's drive from La Fortuna. There's not much
public transportation in these parts, except the
twice-daily bus that runs between La Fortuna
and Tilarán.

West End of Laguna de Arenal

The hamlet of Piedras anchors the western
end of Laguna de Arenal. It's more of an in-
tersection than a town, but it has attracted a
group of expats who appreciate the spectac-
ular lakefront scenery and the proximity to
Tilarán. This is also where most of the wind-
surfing goes down.

🛏 Sleeping

There's plenty of good karma at this end of
the lake, where you can stay in one of two
uplifting yoga lodges.

★**Living Forest**   B&B **$$**
(☑ 8708-8822, 7031-3239; www.lakearenalretreats.
com; d with bathroom US$70, dm/d/tr/q without
bathroom US$35/55/75/85; 🅿🛜🐾) Interior
designer, massage therapist, yogi and free
spirit: Johanna Harmala has combined
these traits to create this inviting, inspiring retreat on the banks of the Río Sabalito, about 15km west of Nuevo Arenal. The
jewel-toned rooms are furnished with attractive walnut beds, with shared or private
access to beautiful open-air stone bathrooms. Minimum two-night stay; rates for
longer stays negotiable.

WINDSURFING

Consistent winds blow across northwestern Costa Rica, and this consisten-
cy attracts wind riders. Laguna de
Arenal is rated one of the best windsurfing spots in the world, and kitesurfers
sail here too. From late November to
April, **Tico Wind** (☑ 8383-2694, 2692-
2002; www.ticowind.com; SUP/kitesurf/
windsurf rental per day US$20/90/99,
windsurfing lessons per hr US$50; ⏰ Nov-
Apr) sets up camp on the lake shore
and offers lessons in both. It has state-
of-the-art boards and sails, with equipment to suit varied wind conditions. The
launch is located 15km west of Nuevo
Arenal. The entrance is by the big, white
chain-link fence with 'ICE' painted on it.
Follow the dirt road 1km to the shore. It
gets a little chilly on Laguna de Arenal,
but rentals usually include wetsuits, as
well as harnesses and helmets.

There's a swimming hole, as well as yoga
and spa services, and a variety of feel-good
workshops throughout the year.

Mystica Lodge   LODGE **$$$**
(☑ 2692-1001; www.mysticacostarica.com; incl
breakfast d US$110-160, villa US$195; ⏰ noon-
9pm; 🅿@🛜) Here's an invitation to relax
and reconnect – with nature, your body and
your breath. Comfortable, colorful rooms
have Spanish-tile floors, woven bedspreads,
wooden accents and an inviting front porch
with volcano views. Yoga and meditation
classes are held in a gorgeous sheltered
hardwood yoga space overlooking a gur-
gling creek, and there's a tree house healing
center for Reiki and massage.

The organic garden supplies many of the
ingredients for breakfast and dinner.

✕ Eating & Drinking

There are only a few restaurants strung out
along the western end of Lagua de Arenal,
but they are varied and delicious. You'll have
no problem finding a lunch stop to please
everyone in the car.

Equus Bar-Restaurant   BARBECUE **$$**
(☑ 8389-2669; mains US$6-14; ⏰ 11am-midnight)
Follow your nose to this authentic stone-
built tavern, 14.5km west of Nuevo Arenal,

where the meat is cooked in an open fire pit, producing decadent, delicious aromas. Take a seat at a wooden-slab picnic table and dig in. A local favorite, this place has been run by the same family for more than a quarter of a century.

If you needed another reason to stop, Equus turns into a live-music venue/disco at night featuring music from ranchero to reggae.

Café y Macadamia CAFE $$
(☑2692-2000; www.facebook.com/pages/Café -Y-Macadamia-Costa-Rica/790381744426077; pastries & coffee US$2-4, mains US$6-13; ⊙8am-8pm; P🛜) We should start by acknowledging that $4 is a lot for a muffin, BUT these banana macadamia nut muffins are irresistible, especially when accompanied by a cup of Costa Rica coffee and a spectacular view over Laguna de Arenal. About 20.5km west of Nuevo Arenal, this is a perfect pit stop during your drive around the lake.

Lake Arenal Hotel & Brewery BREWERY
(☑2695-5050; www.lakearenalhotel.com; just off Ruta 142; ⊙11am-9pm; 🛜🍴) If you like beer, the only hotel (that we're aware of) that has a microbrewery onsite, mixing up the hops and barley to bring you delicious and unusual beers, such as the LAB chili lager and piña blonde. Drink it while feeling the lake breezes and admiring the views at the top-floor restaurant, serving standard pub grub.

The hotel itself has 21 rooms (single/ double including breakfast from US$75/95, dorms US$25) with rustic bohemian charm,

THE SCENIC ROUTE

If you're driving between Arenal and Monteverde, consider taking the scenic route through Tronadora and Río Chiquito instead of driving through Tilarán. The distance is a bit longer and the roads are a bit rougher, but the marvelous vistas are well worth it. Look for the turnoff to Río Chiquito about 1km east of Tronadora. Note: if you go this route, there are no gas stations between Nuevo Arenal and Santa Elena, and the gas gets guzzled on the rough mountain roads. Make sure you fill up when you can.

featuring textured paint jobs and interesting artworks. You'll pay more for lake views and private patios. The hotel and brewery are located just off Route 142, before you reach the village of Tejona.

🛈 Getting There & Away

There's not much public transportation in these parts, except the twice-daily bus that runs between La Fortuna and Tilarán. Pledras is where you can get off the bus to reach the destinations around here, but you'll need a taxi from there to travel out to them.

San Luis & Tronadora

San Luis and Tronadora are the tiny twin communities on the southern side of Laguna de Arenal. They are the last outposts of civilization before the landscape gets swallowed by eternal rainforest (the Children's Eternal Rainforest, to be exact) further south and east. (The 'old' Tronadora did in fact get swallowed up by Arenal's waters when the dam was built.) A small contingent of travelers trickles through here – mostly windsurfers and wanderers – but this wild and windy corner of the lake feels blissfully undiscovered.

🛏 Sleeping & Eating

Monte Terras B&B $$
(☑2693-1349; www.monteterras.com; d incl breakfast US$80; P🛜) Set amid a blooming, bird-filled garden in Tronadora, here you'll find a handful of comfy *cabinas,* each with high ceilings, polished concrete floors, colorful paint jobs and tropical artwork. Dutch owners Kees and Griselda go out of their way to make sure their guests are content. Be warned that this place is crazy windy from December to March.

Brisas Del Lago SODA $$
(☑2695-3363; San Luis; mains US$6-11; ⊙11am-10pm Tue-Sat, from 1pm Sun; P🛜) If you don't mind a little detour, here is your lunch stop between Monteverde and Arenal. Simple Tico fare is done with panache at this dressed-up *soda.* They marinate chicken breasts in their own BBQ sauce, skewer Thai-style shrimp and slather up teriyaki chicken. The garlic fish is sensational. Just past the Catholic church in the community of San Luis.

ℹ Getting There & Away

On the southern side of Laguna de Arenal, the main lake road (Ruta 142) takes a sharp turn south to head toward Tilarán. If you take the northbound road instead, it quickly turns to gravel and descends into San Luis and, 3km further, Tronadora.

Tilarán

POP 8700

Near the southwestern end of Laguna de Arenal, the small town of Tilarán has a laid-back, middle-class charm thanks to its long-running status as a regional ranching center. Nowadays, it's also the main commercial center for the growing community of expats that resides along the shores of Laguna de Arenal.

Most visitors, however, are just passing through, traveling between La Fortuna and Monteverde. Because it's situated on the slopes of the Cordillera de Tilarán, this little hub is a somewhat cooler alternative (in climate and atmosphere) than the towns along the Interamericana.

Waiting here for the next bus? Enjoy an ice cream under the spaceship-like peach-colored structure in the main plaza while ogling the modernistic church, which rivals the beauty in nearby Cañas.

◉ Sights

★ Viento Fresco   WATERFALL

(☑ 2695-3434; www.vientofresco.net; Ruta 145, Campos del Oro; adult/child US$15/10, horseback tour US$55/45; ☉ 7:30am-5pm; ⊞) Driving between Monteverde and Arenal, there is no good excuse for skipping this stop. Viento Fresco is a series of five cascades, including the spectacular Arco Iris (Rainbow Falls), which drops 75m into a refreshing shallow pool that's perfect for swimming. The 1.3km of trails are well maintained, but there are no crowds or commercialism to mar the natural beauty of this place. You'll probably have the falls to yourself, especially if you go early in the day.

Add on a horseback riding tour or grab lunch at the restaurant to support this family-run operation. It's located 11km south of Tilarán on the road to Santa Elena.

✻ Festivals & Events

Vuelta al Lago Arenal   SPORTS

(www.vueltaallagoarenal.com; ☉ Mar) They say that it's virtually impossible to circumnavi-gate the lake. But *they* have never participated in the Vuelta al Lago Arenal, an annual event in March, when some 4000 cyclists do just that. It takes two days – one off-road and one on – to complete the 148km route. Most participants camp along the route.

Transportation of camping equipment is provided but participants are responsible for their own provisions.

🛏 Sleeping & Eating

Right in the center of town, you'll find a few restaurants catering to the drive-through traffic between La Fortuna and Monteverde. Cheaper meals can be found in the *mercado* (market) beside the bus terminal, or pop into the supermarket across from the park.

Hotel Wilson Tilarán   HOTEL $

(☑ 2695-5043; Calle 2; s/d without bathroom US$14/22, with bathroom US$20/26; ℗) As cheap as they come, rooms are tiny and cleanish. If you can get one of the rooms toward the back, this is a decent budget choice on the western side of Parque Central – and just a half block from the bus terminal. There's an appealing retro bar, Encuentro, on the street front.

Typical no-frills Wilson hotel, but with flat-screen TVs.

Hotel Cielo Azul   HOTEL $$

(☑ 2695-4000; www.cieloazulresort.com; d incl breakfast US$75; ℗ 🛜 ≋) Situated 500m before town, when coming from Nuevo Arenal, this hillside property has 12 rooms with tiled floors, whitewashed walls and new bathrooms. There's a good-size pool with a waterslide and a pretty spectacular vista. A convenient jumping-off point for activities on the lake or on the volcano.

Hotel Guadalupe   HOTEL $$

(☑ 2695-5943; www.hotelguadalupe.co.cr; Av 4, near Calle 1; s/d incl breakfast US$42/60; ℗ ❄ 🛜 ≋) This modern hotel attracts traveling business types, who make themselves at home in simple rooms, which are dressed up with jewel tones and tiled floors. Service is friendly and efficient. There is a decent restaurant onsite, as well as a swimming pool, kids' pool and hot tub. Bigger family rooms are available, but only some rooms have air-con.

ℹ Getting There & Away

Tilarán is 24km east of the Interamericana at Cañas, and 75km east of La Fortuna via the

BUSES FROM TILARÁN

DESTINATION	COMPANY	COST (US$)	DURATION	FREQUENCY
Cañas	Transporte Villana	1	30min	15 daily, 5am-7:45pm (8 Sun)
San José	Pulmitan	7	4hr	5am, 7am, 9:30am & 2pm daily; 5pm Sat & Sun only
Santa Elena/ Monteverde	TransMonteverde	3	2½hr	7am, 4pm

paved but winding lake road. The route from Tilarán to Santa Elena and Monteverde is paved for the first stretch, but then it becomes steep, rocky and rough. Just drive carefully on the bumpy bits.

BUS

Buses arrive and depart from the terminal half a block west of Parque Central. Be aware that Sunday afternoon buses to San José can sell out as much as a day in advance. There is no longer direct bus service to La Fortuna or Puntarenas.

NORTHERN LOWLANDS

In the far reaches of the northern lowlands, the vast, steamy stretches of pineapple and banana plantations intermingle with rainforest, wetlands and undisturbed wildness. Once a hotbed for Contras and *contrabandistas*, this sector is crisscrossed by swift highways, well-trafficked by trucks laden with fresh-picked fruit and hefty cattle on their way to market. Most travelers cruise right through, heading to the Caribbean coast or Nicaragua. But those who venture off the highway and brave the bumpy roads will be rewarded. The waterways along the Nicaraguan border provide habitats for an enormous diversity of bird life. Keep your eyes peeled, and you may even spot the rare great green macaw, which is making a comeback in these parts.

Upala

POP 6100

Just 9km south of the Nicaraguan border in the northwestern corner of the northern lowlands, Upala is a small *ranchero* town with a bustling market and plenty of tasty *sodas*. This low-lying town was hit heavily in November 2016 by Hurricane Otto, which caused at least nine deaths. Most visitors are Costa Rican business people who come to negotiate for a few dozen calves or a truckload of grain. It's a somewhat convenient

public-transit stopover between the Volcán Tenorio area and the Caño Negro, but there's no reason to linger. (One positive effect of the hurricane has been the construction of a new bus terminal outside of town.)

🛏 Sleeping & Eating

Cabinas Maleku   CABINA $
(☑ 2470-0142; Av 3; d with/without air-con US$36/32; P ❋ ☎) Wrapping around a gravel parking lot, set just off the main plaza, these cute and comfortable *cabinas* are blessed with mosaic-tile patios decorated with hand-painted Sarchí-style wooden chairs and plenty of potted plants. It's a cheerful cheapie, for sure. There's an attached *soda* too.

Hotel Wilson Aeropuerto   HOTEL $$
(☑ 2470-3636; www.facebook.com/hotelwilson upala; d incl breakfast US$50; P ❋ ☎ ☎) One of the nicer Wilson properties, this is a business motel-style facility with a popular bar and restaurant and a big Jacuzzi-fed swimming pool. The 63 rooms are plain but clean, with mostly wood furniture and linoleum floors, plus other appreciated amenities. You'll need a car to reach this location, or a lot of derring-do if you're walking the 1.5km from town along the highway.

Rancho Don Horacio   COSTA RICAN $
(☑ 2470-3222; Av 7; mains US$6-9; ☺11am-11pm) If you need a place to rest your weary feet while awaiting the next bus (the terminal's just 300m away) you can't do much better than Horacio's. The decorations, as they are, consist of soccer paraphernalia and Elvis bric-a-brac. The menu leans on Rio Zapote fish and Upala beef. Fun, lively family join with televised *futbol* on every wall.

❶ Getting There & Away

From Upala, the well-maintained, paved Hwy 6 runs south via Bijagua, intersecting with the Interamericana just north of Cañas. Hwy 4, also paved, runs in a more southeasterly direction to Muelle de San Carlos (near La Fortuna). A rough, unpaved road, usually passable to all cars, skirts the Refugio Nacional de Vida Silvestre Caño Negro on the way to Los Chiles, the former official border crossing with Nicaragua.

Confusingly, there are two bus terminals – the new one built after Hurricane Otto is 2016 lies 1.5 km from the center and the other is near the main square. Most buses go through both, and also stop on the main plaza. Taxis congregate here too. **Transportes Upala** (📞 2221-3318; cnr Hwy 6 & Hwy 4) has 12 daily buses to Ciudad Quesada (San Carlos; US$2, two hours, 3:30am to 6pm), and three daily services to San José (US$4, five hours, 4:30am, 5:15am and 9:30am), via Bijagua and Cañas. Thrice-daily buses go to Caño Negro (US$2, two hours, 4am, 11:30am and 4pm). Some of the San Carlos buses pass through Guatuso.

Refuge Nacional de Vida Silvestre Caño Negro

Part of the Área de Conservación Arenal–Huetar Norte, this remote, 102-sq-km **refuge** (📞 2471-1309; www.ligambiente.com; adult/child US$5/1; ⊗ 8am-4pm) has long lured anglers seeking that elusive 18kg snook, and birders hoping to glimpse rare waterfowl. During the dry season water levels drop, concentrating the birds (and fish) in photogenically (or tasty) close quarters. From January to March, avian density is world class.

The Río Frío is a table-flat, swampy expanse of marsh and lagoon that is similar in appearance, if not size, to other famous wetlands such as the Florida Everglades or the Mekong Delta. North of town, it's a slender river that carves looming forest. During the wet season, the river breaks its banks to form one immense 800-hectare lake. By April it has almost completely disappeared – until the May rains begin. This cycle has

proceeded without fail for millennia, and the small fishing communities around the its edges adapt to each seasonal nuance.

🏃 Activities

Caño Negro is regarded among birders as one of the premier destinations in Central America. During the dry season, the sheer density of birds in the park is astounding, but the variety of species is also impressive. At last count, more than 300 species of bird live here at least part of the year. In the winter months, there are huge congregations of migratory ducks, as well as six species of kingfisher, herons, cormorants, three types of egret, ibises, rails, anhingas, roseate spoonbills, toucans and storks. The refuge is also the only reliable site in Costa Rica for olivaceous cormorants, Nicaraguan grackles and lesser yellow-headed vultures.

Conspicuous reptiles include the spectacled caiman, green iguana and striped basilisk. Howler monkeys, white-faced capuchins and two-toed sloths are common. Despite incursions from poachers, pumas, jaguars and tapirs have been recorded here in surprising numbers.

Caño Negro is also home to an abundance of river turtles, which were historically an important part of the Maleku diet. Prior to a hunt, the Maleku would appease the turtle god, Javara, by fasting and abstaining from sex. If the hunt was successful, the Maleku would later celebrate by feasting on smoked turtle meat and consuming large quantities of *chicha,* a spirit derived from maize. And, well, they probably had some sex too.

Mosquitoes in Caño Negro are damn near prehistoric. Bring bug spray or suffer the consequences.

WORTH A TRIP

VENADO CAVES

Four kilometers south of Venado (Spanish for 'deer') along a good dirt road, the **Venado Caves** (Cavernas de Venado; 📞 2478-8008, 8653-2086; www.cavernasdelvenadocr.com; adult/child US$28, photographer US$20; ⊗ 8am-3pm, last admission 2pm) are an adventurous excursion into an eight-chamber limestone labyrinth that extends for almost 3km. A bilingual guide leads small groups on two-hour tours through the darkness, squeezing through narrow passes, pointing out the most interesting rock formations while dodging bats and bugs. You'll be provided with rubber boots, headlamps and helmets, plus a shower afterwards. You'll definitely want to bring a change of clothes.

Any tour operator in La Fortuna can arrange this trip for you. If you're driving yourself, the caves are well signed from Hwy 4. Otherwise, Cabinas Los Almendros (p273) offers transportation from San Rafael de Guatuso. Cash only if paying at the caves.

JOHN COLETTI/GETTY IMAGES ©

ESDELVAL/GETTY IMAGES ©

GUIZIOU FRANCK/GETTY IMAGES ©

3

**1. Parque Nacional
Volcán Arenal (p254)**
Trails and walkways thread through
the park.

**2. Tabacón Hot Springs
(p244)**
La Fortuna has a range of thermal
springs; this one was built on the
site of a 1974 volcanic eruption.

**3. Catarata Río Fortuna
(p243)**
A sparkling 70m of water pours
through to the jungle floor.

4. Volcán Arenal (p254)
Dense forest covers the foothills of
the volcano, which was still active
in 2010.

Tours

Hiring a local guide is quick, easy and full of advantages – you'll pay less, you'll be supporting the local economy, and you'll have more privacy when you're out on the water. If you're spending the night in the area, your lodge can make arrangements for a tour. Otherwise, there are a few local outfits with an office (or at least a sign) in the village center.

Sportfishing trips can also be arranged through the lodges. Be sure to inquire about obtaining a seasonal fishing licence, which is normally required. (Bring your passport.)

Chambita's Tours   BIRDWATCHING
(☑ 8412-3269; www.facebook.com/chambita.romero; half-/full-day birding tour 2 people US$80/140) Barnaby Romero Hernandez, known locally as 'Chambita', is a rising star in the naturalist community, well-respected for his vast birding knowledge. He also leads fishing trips on the river. He doesn't have a fixed office but can be reached by phone or his Facebook page.

Pantanal Tour   BOATING
(www.facebook.com/pantanal.toursa; Caño Negro; tours US$35-66) Marlon Castro and Juan Ríos can take you in their boat for sportfishing or ecological tours of the lagoon. They also lead horseback riding trips and kayaking outings. Their office, not always staffed, is on the main plaza of Caño Negro.

Paraíso Tropical   BOATING
(☑ 2471-1621, 8823-4026; per person kayak/horse/boat tours US$10/30/50; ☺ 8am-4pm) Visit Joel and Rosi Sandoval Bardos at their office in town. Joel does a variety of nature tours around the refuge, including a two-hour boat tour of the lagoon (up to four people). Joel guided a trip on the Río Frío in 2014 that bagged a world-record 14.5kg tropical gar. The office is on the main square of the town.

Sleeping & Eating

Caño Negro is a small village, so all the lodges have easy access to the lagoon.

Kingfisher Lodge   CABINA $
(☑ 2471-1116; www.kingfisherlodgecr.com; r US$40-60; P ☺ ✳) Located about 400m from the village center, these rustic *cabinas* surround a well-kept lawn; all have heavy wood furniture and hammock-strung porches (only some have air-con). Your host, Don Antonio,

is the big-gun refuge guide and boat captain in town. The reception is located 400m to the east, in a house at the opposite end of the main town square.

Hotel de Campo Caño Negro   LODGE $$
(☑ 2471-1012; www.hoteldecampo.com; s & d incl breakfast US$95; P ✳ ☺ ✉) Set in an orchard of mango and citrus trees next to the 'Chapel' lagoon, this friendly hotel is a fisher's and bird-watcher's paradise. After angling for tarpons or spying on spoonbills, relax in the ceramic-tiled *casitas,* decked with vaulted beamed ceilings and tasteful bedding. The stylish restaurant (7:30am to 9:30pm) serves top-notch Italian and seafood.

Boats, guides, kayaks, and fishing equipment are all available for hire. Owner Mauro will proudly lead you around his tropical 'botanical garden' of more than 100 tree species.

★ **Caño Negro Natural Lodge**   LODGE $$$
(☑ 2471-1426; www.canonegrolodge.com; d incl breakfast US$145; P ✳ ☺ ✉) ✆ Perched on land that becomes a virtual island in the Río Frío during the rainy season, this lodge is surprisingly upscale. Well-appointed rooms have sliding glass doors, wooden and wrought-iron furnishings, and tiny terraces facing the garden. Relax in the pool or Jacuzzi or stroll the leafy grounds. Just off the main road before Caño Negro's main plaza.

Staff can make arrangements for boat tours of the lagoon. There's a lovely patio restaurant serving freshly prepared meals and a friendly bartender who will bend your ear as you bend your elbow. Lunch and dinner are extra, but worth the price.

Buses will stop at the 'front door.' If you are driving on Ruta 35 towards Los Chiles, exit the highway 8 km before Los Chiles when you see the signs for the lodge.

ⓘ Information

Visitors to the park should stop at the ranger station to pay their admission fee. It's located on the western edge of the village, near the Kingfisher Lodge, but is not always attended. Note that there are no banks or gas stations in town.

ⓘ Getting There & Away

Thanks to improved roads, tour operators are able to offer relatively inexpensive trips to Caño Negro from all over the country. However, you don't need them to explore the river. It's much more intriguing and rewarding to rent some

THE WEEPING FOREST

Extensive deforestation of the Caño Negro area began in the 1970s in response to increased population density and the subsequent need for more farmland. Although logging was allowed to proceed in the area for almost 20 years, the government took action in 1991 with the creation of the Refugio Nacional de Vida Silvestre Caño Negro. Since its creation, Caño Negro has served as a safe habitat for the region's aquatic and terrestrial birds, and has acted as a refuge for numerous migratory birds.

However, illegal logging and poaching have continued around the perimeter of the park, and wildlife has suffered. In the last two decades, one-time residents of the park including ocelots, manatees, sharks and macaws have vanished. Tarpon and caiman populations are decreasing, and fewer migratory birds are returning to the park each year. Additionally, anglers are reporting record lows in both the size and number of their catches.

Satellite images show that the lake is shrinking each year, and that water levels in the Río Frío are dropping rapidly. It's difficult to say with certainty what is causing these changes, though the farms surrounding Caño Negro require extensive irrigation, and sugarcane is nearly 10 times as water-intensive as wheat.

Locals are extremely worried about the stability of the park, as entire communities are dependent on fishing and tourism for their survival. In response to the growing need to regulate development in the region, residents have formed a number of organizations aimed at controlling development in the northern lowlands. If you want to support the Caño Negro community, book your tour in town and spend your tourist dollar locally.

wheels (or hop on a bus), navigate the rutted road into the rural flatlands and hire a local guide from Caño Negro village. It's also a lot cheaper, and it puts money directly into the hands of locals, thus encouraging communities in the area to protect wildlife.

The village of Caño Negro and the entrance to the park lie on the rough road connecting Upala and Los Chiles, Ruta 138, which is passable to all cars during the dry season. However, this road is frequently washed out during the rainy season, when a 4WD is required.

During the rainy season and much of the dry season, you can also catch a boat to and from Los Chiles, but this is only by private reservation (at Paraíso Tropical in Caño Negro, or at the dock in Los Chiles), for $200.

In addition, the following bus routes serve Caño Negro village:

Los Chiles (US$2, one hour) Departing Los Chiles at 5am and 2pm; departing Caño Negro at 6:30am, 1pm and 6pm.

Upala (US$2.50, 2½ hours) Departing Upala at 4am, 11:30am and 4pm; departing Caño Negro at 6:30am, 1pm and 3pm.

Los Chiles

POP 9900

Seventy kilometers north of Muelle on a smooth, paved road through the sugarcane, and just 6km south of the Nicaraguan border, lies the sweltering farming and fishing town of Los Chiles. Arranged with dilapidated grace around a ragged soccer field and along the unmanicured banks of the leisurely Río Frío, the humid lowland village was originally settled by merchants and fisherfolk who worked on the nearby Río San Juan, much of which forms the border. Amazingly, for Costa Rica, there are street signs on every corner of this *pueblito*.

In the 1980s, American-trained Contras were a presence in town as part of the United States' subversive military actions against Nicaragua's Sandinista government.

With the opening of the new border crossing at Las Tablillas, travelers to and from Nicaragua are no longer obligated to pass through Los Chiles, but it remains an enjoyable water route to Caño Negro.

Tours

Los Chiles is a convenient base to organize boat trips to Caño Negro. Inquire at Restaurante Heliconia (p272) about these trips. Otherwise just head to the dock, where you can hire boat captains to take you up the lovely, chocolatey Río Frío during the dry season and all the way into Lago Caño Negro during the rainy season.

Three- to four-hour trips cost anywhere from US$50 to US$100 for a small group, depending on the size and type of boat. If possible, make arrangements a day in advance and get an early start in the morning: the earlier out, the more you'll see.

Sleeping & Eating

With the new border crossing at Las Tablillas, it's usually possible to cruise right by Los Chiles without spending the night. If that doesn't work for you, you'll find a limited selection of hotels in town.

Hotel y Cabinas Carolina CABINA$
(☎ 2471-1151; Av 2A, near Calle 5; r from US$30; P❋❄🛜) Not your typical border-town accommodations. This friendly, family-run option gets good reviews for attentive staff, spotless rooms and above-average local food. It's near the main highway, just a few blocks south of the bus station. However, there is no attendant on Sundays, so you'll have to phone to see a room.

Restaurante Heliconia COSTA RICAN$
(☎ 8307-8585, 2471-2096; Av Central (Av 0), near Av 6; mains US$6-10; ⊙ 6am-10pm) Across from the immigration office and next to Hotel Wilson Tulipán, this is a decent option for lunch or a smoothie. It also provides information on tours and transportation; ask Mayra about boat trips to Caño Negro or taxi rides to the border.

ℹ Information

Banco Nacional (☎ 2212-2000; Av 1, btwn Calles 0 (Calle Central) & 1; ⊙ 8:30am-3:45pm Mon-Fri) Close to the central park and soccer field, changes cash and traveler's checks and has a 24-hour ATM.
Cruz Roja (Red Cross; ☎ 2471-1037, 2471-2025; cnr Calle 2 & Av 1; ⊙ 24hr) Located at the northwestern corner of the plaza.

ℹ Getting There & Away

BOAT
The boat docks are located about 1km west of the bus terminal. With the opening of the land border at Las Tablillas, this river border is pretty sleepy. If you do arrange a boat across the border, before hopping on you need to stop at the **immigration office** (Migración; ☎ 2471-1233; Av Central (Av 0), btwn Calle 4 & Calle 6; ⊙ 8am-6pm), across the street from Hotel Wilson Tulipán.

BUS
All buses arrive and leave from the **terminal** (Av 1, near Calle 5) behind Soda Pamela, near the intersection of Hwy 35. **Chilsaca** (☎ 2460-1886; www.chilsaca.com; Plaza San Carlos) has 16 daily buses to Ciudad Quesada (US$2.25, two hours) from 4:30am to 6pm; you can transfer here for La Fortuna. Autotransportes San Carlos has two daily buses to San José (US$6, five hours), departing at 5am and 3pm. There are

---

ℹ GETTING TO NICARAGUA

If you're heading north to Nicaragua, be thankful for the 2015 construction of the Puente Santa Fe, a bridge that crosses the Río San Juan just north of the Nicaraguan border. As a result, there is now a border crossing at Las Tablillas, 6km north of Los Chiles.

➡ The border crossing at Las Tablillas (open 8am to 4pm) now handles a good amount of the Costa Rican–Nicaraguan traffic, so you might encounter some lines depending on when you decide to cross.

➡ Hourly buses connect Los Chiles and Las Tablillas (US$1, 10 minutes). Or, get the bus directly from San José or Ciudad Quesada (San Carlos). These buses run daily.

➡ You will have to pay a Costa Rica land exit fee of US$7 at immigration, payable by credit or debit card only (no cash).

➡ After walking across the border, you'll go through Nicaraguan immigration. The entrance fee is US$12, payable in US dollars or córdobas.

➡ After exiting immigration, you can catch a boat up the river or hop on a bus or a *collectivo* to San Carlos (US$2.20, 30 minutes).

If you are entering Costa Rica from Nicaragua, you can take an hourly bus to Los Chiles or Ciudad Quesada or catch the direct bus to San José, which departs at 2:30pm.

If you want to get to/from Nicaragua the old-fashioned way, you can still go to the immigration office in Los Chiles and then catch a boat up the river, but you'll have to arrange this privately with one of the boat captains (no regular service operates). You'll avoid the Costa Rica land exit fee, but you'll still have to pay US$12 to enter Nicaragua. It's actually a more enjoyable trip than the land crossing, but it takes some time.

also three departures to Caño Negro (US$4, 40 minutes) at 5am, noon and 4:30pm. Timetables are subject to change, so always check ahead.

CAR

You're likely to get here via Hwy 35 from Muelle. Skid marks and reptilian roadkill do break up the beautiful monotony of orange groves, sage-blue pineapple fields and dense sugarcane plantations. More scenic is the road running for 50km from Upala, through Caño Negro, another recently paved option.

San Rafael de Guatuso

POP 8600

The main population center of this agricultural area, San Rafael de Guatuso is a small town without too much to offer travelers – except its central location off Highway 4. The humble town is a decent base for exploring the fantastic Venado Caves to the south and is nearly equidistant to the blue waters of Río Celeste and the Parque Nacional Volcán Tenorio to the west, Arenal to the south and Caño Negro to the north. The area is also home to the few remaining indigenous Maleku, who reside in *palenques* (indigenous settlements) near here.

Sleeping & Eating

Cabinas Los Almendros CABINA $
(📞8887-0495; cabinaslosalmendros@gmail.com; Av 12, near Av 10; s/d/tr incl breakfast US$35/40/50; 🅿❋🛜) A cute family-run motel with well-maintained rooms, painting of recent vintage, lovely bedding and cute curtains. Each room is named after a different jungle beast or bird, complete with hand-carved wooden sculpture. Set on the edge of town behind the Banco Nacional, this is easily the best choice in the area.

The folk at Los Almendros offer transportation and tours to the Maleku reservation, Venado Caves and Río Celeste (Parque Nacional Volcán Tenorio).

Soda La Suyapa SODA $
(Hwy 4, near Calle 1A; mains US$4-8; ☉6am-8pm) Recommended by locals as the best *soda* in this humble town, La Suyapa offers a fresh take on the traditional. *Casados* come with noodles and potato salad unless you request otherwise. *Bebidas* include options like fresh-pressed carrot juice and fresh-squeezed lemonade. There are also burgers and excellent fried chicken. Located right off the highway.

Getting There & Away

Guatuso lies on Hwy 4, midway between Upala and Muelle de San Carlos (about 40km from each). Buses leave frequently for Ciudad Quesada, where you can connect to La Fortuna. There is also one daily bus to Tilarán (three hours, 7:30pm) via Nuevo Arenal, and three daily buses to San José (five hours, 8am, 11:30am and 3pm).

From Guatuso, a newly graded dirt road (plans to pave it are in the works) covers the 21km to the entrance of Parque Nacional Volcán Tenorio and onward to Bijagua. It's a relatively smooth ride with stunning views.

Muelle de San Carlos

POP 4900

This small crossroads village – locally called Muelle – was once an important dock (hence the name) as it's the most inland spot from which the Río San Carlos is navigable. These days it is sugarcane country and serves as a rest stop for truckers and travelers. It's also only 27km east of La Fortuna. If you have your own wheels, Muelle makes a quaint, quiet base for visiting Arenal and environs.

Sights

Centro Turistico Las Iguanas BRIDGE
(Iguana Bridge; 📞2462-1107) This bridge is a popular spot for tourists en route from La Fortuna to Caño Negro. Countless iguanas hang out in the bamboo and trees above the river, providing some great photo ops. Walk across the bridge to see how many you can count – but watch your step! The bridge is 1.8km north of the main intersection in Muelle, where Ruta 35 takes a sharp turn to cross the river.

Sleeping & Eating

Turismo Rural de Juanilama AGRITURISMO $
(Comunidad Agroecológica Juanilama; www.turismo ruraljuanilama.org; Juanilama, off Hwy 35; per person US$35, tours US$15-20) Seven kilometres north of Santa Rosa de Pocosol, off Hwy 35, is this unique opportunity to be part of rural life. This cooperative, female-driven effort took root 15 years ago and now involves 90 local families. You stay in one of the comfortable and modern family homes: you may even end up watching Tico *novelas* (soap operas) over breakfast.

While here, you can take a hike in their 19-hectare reserve, learn about their crops and various home remedies, and make a bit of sugar-cane water. Options include a tour of the dairy, a cooking class, and a walk to the waterfalls. You can also volunteer at the local school.

Tilajari Resort Hotel
RESORT $$$

(☑ 2462-1212; www.tilajari.com; d incl breakfast from US$110; P⊖❋@🛜🏊) This country club turned luxury resort has landscaped grounds overlooking the Río San Carlos and comfortable, well-appointed rooms. Amenities include racquetball and tennis courts, restaurant, pool, sauna, spa and butterfly garden, plus access to the neighboring 400-hectare private rainforest reserve with several trails. The resort is 800m west of the intersection at Muelle, on the road to Ciudad Quesada.

The facilities are a bit dated but the place offers good value for the price.

Subasta Ganadera Sancarleña
STEAK $$

(☑ 2462-1000; www.subastasganaderascr.com; Muelle de San Carlos; mains US$4-12; ⊙bar & restaurant 10am-11pm) Overlooking a bull pen, this place is bustling with hungry *campesinos* (farmers). It has an expansive menu of local dishes, and is a great spot for a cold beer. Come for lunch on Tuesday or Thursday to see the cattle auction. It's 100m north of the gas station in Muelle San Carlos.

ⓘ Getting There & Away

A 24-hour gas station lies at the main intersection of Hwy 4 (which connects Ciudad Quesada and Upala) and Hwy 35 (running from San José to Los Chiles). Buses pass through en route to all of those destinations.

Ciudad Quesada (San Carlos)

The official name of this small city is Ciudad Quesada (sometimes abbreviated to 'Quesada'), but all the locals know it as San Carlos, and local buses often list San Carlos as the destination. We'd like to think the 'cheesy' name stems from its position as the country's number one dairy supplier, but it might just have been someone's name.

It's long been a bustling ranching and agricultural center, known for its *talabaterías* (saddle shops). Although San Carlos is surrounded by pastoral countryside, the city has developed into the commercial center of the region – it's gritty and quite congested. Fortunately, there's no real reason to enter the city, except to change buses.

🏃 Activities

Ciudad Quesada is not exactly a destination in itself. But if you're driving this way, why not stop for a soak? Popular with Tico families, the thermal pools here are an affordable and pleasant alternative to the overdone, overpopulated springs in La Fortuna. The hot springs and resorts are located about 8km east of town, heading toward Aguas Zarcas.

El Tucano Resort
HOT SPRINGS

(☑ 2460-6000; www.hoteltucano.com; Ruta 140, La Marina de San Carlos; US$20; 🏊) A posh but aging resort, set amid gorgeous primary forest. The thermal springs feed three pools of varying temperatures – perfect for soaking away your ills. The spring-fed river that streams through the property creates warm, delightful rapids. It's 'family friendly' and the pools are open late, in case you plan on a restful night.

The spacious, colonial-style rooms (doubles US$120 to US$135, suites US$145 to US$200) enjoy forest views from the terrace.

Termales del Bosque
HOT SPRINGS

(☑ 2460-4740; www.termalesdelbosque.com; Ruta 140; adult/child US$12/6; ⊙8am-10pm) Luxury here is low-key, with therapeutic

BUSES FROM CIUDAD QUESADA

DESTINATION	COMPANY	COST (US$)	DURATION	FREQUENCY
La Fortuna	Transpisa	2	1½-2hr	16 daily, 4:30am-10:10pm
Los Chiles	Chilsaca	2	2hr	14 daily, 4:15am-7:30pm; direct bus 3pm
Puerto Viejo de Sarapiquí	Transportes Linaco	4	2hr	8 daily, 4:40am- 6:30pm
San José	Autotransportes San José-San Carlos	3	2½hr	hourly 4am-6pm; direct buses 6:40am & 6:15pm
Upala	Transportes Upala/ Transpisa	4	3hr	9 daily, 4:25am-10:10pm

soaking available in seven natural hot- and warm-water springs. The stone pools are surrounded by lush greenery and built into the riverbank, in a forested valley populated by morpho butterflies. About 10km east of Ciudad Quesada on Ruta 140.

Just down the road from El Tucano, for comparison's sake.

🛏 Sleeping & Eating

Apart from the plethora of chain restaurants, you'll find a few decent local *sodas* near the park. The restaurants at the resort are also good (albeit more expensive) options.

Tree Houses Hotel   HOTEL **$$$**
(✆2475-6507; www.treehouseshotelcostarica.com; Ruta 141, Florencia de Santa Clara; d incl breakfast US$113-199, extra person US$15; P✳️🛜) Fulfil your childhood fantasy with a couple of nights in an awesome treetop hideout. With solid wood construction and big windows facing the rainforest, the comfortable cabins have all the ground-level amenities you would expect (including air-con), plus fabulous wrap-around porches that bring you even closer to the birds and monkeys. About 17km northwest of Ciudad Quesada (San Carlos).

Rates include a guided hike in the surrounding 36-hectare forest preserve. Assuming you have your own vehicle, it's within striking distance of the activities around Arenal, but removed from the hullabaloo. It's 300m north of the cemetery in Santa Clara. Two-night minimum stay required.

ℹ Getting There & Away

Terminal Quesada is about 1km from the town center. Taxis (US$1) and a twice-hourly bus (US$0.50) make regular runs between town and the terminal, or you can walk if you don't mind hauling your luggage uphill.

Boca Tapada Area

Here's an off-the-beaten-track destination for adventurous souls. The rocky roads and lack of signage (even less than usual) could mean a few unintended detours, but it's worth the effort for a glimpse into an ecological extravaganza. On the roads that pass pineapple fields and packing plants, your fellow travelers will be commuting *campesinos* (agricultural workers) going about their day-to-day business. And at the end of the

PROYECTO ASIS

Proyecto Asis (✆2475-9121; www.institutoasis.com; adult/child US$31/18, incl volunteering US$54/31; ⊗tours 8:30am & 1pm) is an animal rescue center. It's a volunteer project. It's Spanish classes. This community-based organization is doing a lot of good, and you can help. The introductory experience is a 1½-hour tour of the wildlife rescue center, but it's worth springing for the three-hour 'volunteering' experience, which includes hands-on interaction with the animals. It's pricey, but the cause is worthy.

Asis also offers homestays in the local community. It's located about 20km west of Ciudad Quesada, past the village of Florencia. Reserve at least a day in advance.

road, you'll be rewarded with a luxuriant bit of rainforest replete with the songs of frogs and rare birds, and an inkling of the symbiosis that can happen when humans make the effort. Local lodges offer tours into the **Refugio Nacional de Vida Silvestre Mixto Maquenque**.

🛏 Sleeping

Mi Pedacito de Cielo   LODGE **$$**
(✆8308-9595, 7177-0708; www.pedacitodecielo.com; s/d/tr incl breakfast US$65/75/85; P🛜) 🌿 Perched above the Río San Carlos, 'my little piece of heaven' is a rustic retreat, with 14 wooden bungalows offering river and rainforest views. Swing in the hammock-chair and listen to the rainforest come alive. Super friendly service and don Mario's excellent home-cooked meals are perks. Situated 33km north of Pital, just off the main road.

There are hiking trails in the attached 300-hectare reserve. Three plush-er rooms with all the modern trappings like air-con are located 2km away from the lodge proper, next to beautiful Laguna Vicripalma (named for Mario's children). It's walking or driving distance to dinner, but right at the foot of the reserve.

Laguna del Lagarto Lodge   LODGE **$$**
(✆2289-8163, 7216-4190; www.lagarto-lodge-costa-rica.com; s/d/tr US$65/85/95, meals US$8-15; P🛜) 🌿 Surrounded by virgin rainforest, this outpost is legendary among birders.

The basic screened rooms here share large, hammock-strung verandas. It's not fancy, but it's wild and lovely, with feeders and fruit attracting toucans, tanagers and more. The lodge is about 35km north of Pital on the main road, which is quite bumpy.

There are 16km of trails, and canoes to explore the surrounding lagoons, where caimans dwell and Jesus Christ lizards make tracks across the water's surface.

★ **Maquenque Eco-Lodge** LODGE $$$
(☑ 2479-7785; www.maquenqueecolodge.com; s/d/tr incl breakfast from US$105/130/155; P 🎧 🛜 ⛱) 🦜 Set on 80 glorious, bird-filled hectares, 14 unique bungalows overlook a lagoon and tropical garden, while additional tree houses are perched in the nearby rainforest. The place is a birders' (and photographers') paradise, with countless species flocking to feeders and fruit trees in the grounds. To get here, you'll have to cross the San Carlos River in one of their boats.

In addition to birds, encountering a roving band of coatimundis might make your day, too. Prices include a guided morning rainforest hike, a student-led tour of a local school and use of canoes on the lagoon, as well as the opportunity to support sustainable tourism by planting a tree in the rainforest (by request). Be sure to arrange your boat crossing ahead of time

ℹ Getting There & Away

Getting to Boca Tapada is an adventure in itself. The nearest town of note is Pital, north of Aguas Zarcas. About 2km north of Pital, take a right at the fork (after the bus stop) and follow the signs. It's a slow, rough 40km, but worth it.

Buses reach Boca Tapada on a two-hour trip from Pital, departing Pital at 9:30am and 4:30pm. Leaving Boca Tapada, the buses to Pital depart at 5:30am and 12:30pm (the early bus goes past the lodges, for the later one you'll have to hoof it into town). You can reach Pital on frequent buses from Ciudad Quesada (US$2, 1½ hours) or four daily buses from San José (US$4, four hours).

The lodges can also arrange transfers from La Fortuna or San José.

SARAPIQUÍ VALLEY

This flat, steaming stretch of *finca*-dotted lowlands was once part of the United Fruit Company's vast banana holdings. Harvests were carried from the plantations down to Puerto Viejo de Sarapiquí, where they were shipped downriver on boats destined for North America. In 1880 a railway connected rural Costa Rica with the port of Puerto Limón, and Puerto Viejo de Sarapiquí became a backwater. Although it's never managed to recover its former glory as a transport route, the river again shot to prominence as one of the premier destinations in the country for kayakers and rafters. With the Parque Nacional Braulio Carrillo as its backyard, this is also one of the best regions for wildlife-watching, especially considering how easy it is to get here.

San Miguel

POP 2300

Coming from San José or Alajuela, Hwy 126 curves up the slopes of the Cordillera Central, leaving behind the urban bustle and passing Volcán Poás before descending again into pastureland. This is *campesino* country, where the plodding hoofbeat of cattle is about the speed of life, as the hard-to-spot rural speed bumps will remind you, if you take those curves too quickly. You're off the beaten track now, and if you're self-driving, you may as well linger, because there are few Costa Rican corners quite this beautiful and unheralded.

⌖ Tours

Mi Cafecito FOOD & DRINK
(☑ 2476-0215; www.micafecitocoffeetour.com; tour US$24; ⊙ 8am-5pm) About 5km south of San Miguel, in the foothills of Volcán Poas, Mi Cafecito makes for the perfect coffee break if you're heading to/from the Sarapiquí Valley. Including more than 200 small farmers, this co-op shows off the whole process of growing, harvesting and roasting coffee beans, especially using organic farming practices. The walk through the farm also yields expansive views of the gorgeous Sarapiquí Valley.

Even if you don't want to take a tour, there is a big shady cafe where you can get a cup o' joe (and food too). A package tour includes lunch.

🛏 Sleeping & Eating

The best lunch stop near San Miguel is 5km south of town at Mi Cafecito. In town, there is at least one *soda* that promises breakfast, as well as bird-watching, tourist information, *cabañas* and clean bathrooms.

★ **Albergue El Socorro** FARMSTAY $$

(📞8820-2160; www.albergueelsocorrosarapiqui.com; per person incl meals US$75; 🅿@) Albergue El Socorro is a small family *finca*, located 1000m above sea level, on a plateau surrounded by a magnificent knife's edge of green mountains, tucked between the looming Cerro Congo and Volcan Poas. There are three cozy A-framed cabins, from where guests can explore trails through the rainforest, discover waterfalls, swim in rivers or help on the dairy farm.

The owner was born and raised here, but in 2009 a massive earthquake struck the area, destroying the road to San Miguel along with his home and dairy. This wonderful family rebuilt the ranch from scratch and incorporated a tourism component, which provides a rare opportunity to slow down and experience authentic rural Tico living. This is the real *pura vida*. From San Miguel, turn off Hwy 126 east onto Calle a El Socorro, just before the cemetery if you're headed north, and then head south.

❶ Getting There & Away

From Ciudad Quesada (San Carlos), Hwy 140 heads east for about 40km before terminating sharply when it runs into Hwy 126. This intersection – in the hills of the Cordillera Central – is where San Miguel is. You can't miss the sharp turn as the two highways merge and continue north for 12km toward La Virgen. If you're coming from La Virgen, it's about 15km south of downtown.

La Virgen

POP 2250

Tucked into the densely jungled shores of the wild and scenic Río Sarapiquí, La Virgen was one of the small towns that prospered during the heyday of the banana trade. Although United Fruit has long since shipped out, the town remains dependent on its nearby pineapple fields. And it still lives by that river.

For over a decade, La Virgen was the premier kayaking and rafting destination in Costa Rica. Dedicated groups of hardcore paddlers spent happy weeks running the Río Sarapiquí. But a tremendous 2009 earthquake and landslide altered the course of the river and flattened La Virgen's tourist economy. Some businesses folded, others relocated to La Fortuna, and a few held on. Now, independent kayakers are starting to

come back and there are a couple of river outfitters offering exhilarating trips on the Class II–IV waters of the Río Sarapiquí.

◉ Sights

Dave & Dave's Nature Park WILDLIFE RESERVE, BIRD-WATCHING

(📞2761-0801; www.sarapiquieco-observatory.com; US$40; ⊙7am-5pm) Father and son Dave and Dave greet all comers to this 4.5-hectare reserve on the Río Sarapiquí, 200m north of the cemetery. You don't have to be a birder to get great glimpses or photos from the two viewing platforms, with feeders attracting toucans, trogans, tanagers and 10 species of hummingbird. Follow a self-guided trail system that winds through secondary forest all the way down to the river. A welcome bonus is the free coffee.

Snake Garden ZOO

(📞2761-1059; www.snakegardencr.com; adult/child US$15/10, night tour US$30/24; ⊙9am-5pm) Get face to face with 50 species of reptiles and amphibians, including poison-dart frogs, rattlesnakes, crocs and turtles. The star attraction is a gigantic 80kg Burmese python. Make reservations for the night tour, which shows off many species of frogs you won't see during the day. It's 200m north of the cemetery.

🛏 Sleeping

There are cheap digs in town, or consider staying in one of the more interesting lodges on the road to Puerto Viejo.

Tirimbina Rainforest Center & Lodge LODGE $$

(📞2761-0333, 215 2761-0055; www.tirimbina.org; incl breakfast, dm US$62, d US$90-110, day pass US$17; 🅿❄@🛜) Situated 2km from La Virgen, this is a working environmental research and education center. The spacious accommodations are located at the lodge or at a more remote field station; dorms with shared bathrooms as well as doubles are on offer. Tirimbina reserve has over 5km of trails; tours include bird-watching, frog and bat tours, night walks and a recommended chocolate tour.

The 345-hectare private reserve is connected to the nearby Sarapiquís Rainforest Lodge (p278) by two long suspension bridges. The island between has been closed, unfortunately.

RUNNING THE SARAPIQUÍ

The Río Sarapiquí isn't as wild as the white water on the Río Pacuare near Turrialba, but it will get your heart racing. Even better, the dense jungle that hugs the riverbank is lush and primitive, with chances to glimpse wildlife from your raft.

You can run the Sarapiquí year-round, but December offers the biggest water. The rest of the year, the river fluctuates with rainfall. The bottom line is: if it's been raining, the river will be at its best. Where once there were nearly a dozen outfitters in La Virgen, now there are just a handful. Two of them are actually based in Chilamate and one is in Puerto Viejo – but all ride the same rapids, offering roughly the same Class II–IV options at similar prices.

Aguas Bravas (☎2761-1645; www.aguasbravascr.com; rafting trips US$75, safari float US$65; ◷9am-5:30pm) This well-established rafting outfit has set up shop along the Río Sarapiquí (complete with onsite hostel). Aguas Bravas has two tours on offer: take a gentle safari float to spot birds, iguanas, caimans and other wildlife, or sign up to splash through 14km of 'extreme rapids' on the San Miguel section of the river. Both include a spot of lunch.

Aventuras del Sarapiquí (☎2766-6768; www.sarapiqui.com; river trips US$60-95) This highly recommended outfitter offers land, air and water adventures. In addition to white-water rafting (both Class II and III/IV trips), you can also fly through the air on a 12-cable canopy tour. Or, stay down to earth with horseback riding, mountain biking or good old-fashioned hiking. Situated just off the highway. For the Class IV rapids, a minimum of four experienced people are required.

Sarapiquí Outdoor Center (☎2761-1123; www.costaricaraft.com; 2/4hr rafting trip US$65/90, guided kayak trips from US$90) David Duarte is the local paddling authority. In addition to its rafting excursions, SOC offers kayak rental, lessons and clinics. Indie paddlers should check in for up-to-date river information. If you need somewhere to sleep before you hit the water, you can crash in the simple rooms or camp in one of the available, all-inclusive tents – no equipment necessary. Located about 18km southwest of Sarapiquí, off Hwy 126.

Green Rivers (☎2766-6265, 2766-5274; www.costaricagreenrive.wixsite.com/sarapiquiraft ing; tours US$60-80; ☻) Operating out of Posada Andrea Cristina B&B (p281), this outfit is run by the ever-amiable Kevín Martínez and his wife, Evelyn. They offer a wide variety of rafting and kayaking tours, from family-friendly floats to adrenaline-pumping, rapid-surfing rides. They also know their nature, so they do natural history and bird tours, too.

Tropical Duckies (☎8760-3787, 2766-0095; www.tropicalduckies.com; off Hwy 126; adults/children US$56/50; ◷departs 9am & 1pm) Highly recommended for beginners and families, this outfit does tours and instruction in inflatable kayaks, which allow for a fun paddle even when the river is low. Paddle on flat moving water or Class III rapids (or somewhere in between). Reserve ahead.

Hacienda Pozo Azul BUNGALOW $$
(☎2438-2616, 2761-1360; www.haciendapozoa
zul.com; d/tr/q incl breakfast US$85/99/124;
P@☗) ✐ Near the southern end of La Virgen, Pozo Azul features stylish 'tent suites' scattered on the edge of the tree line, all on raised polished-wood platforms and dressed with plush bedding and mosquito nets. At night, the frogs and wildlife sing you to sleep as raindrops patter on the canvas roof.

Pozo Azul also has a bar-restaurant near the highway with a lovely riverside veranda, though it caters mostly to big tour groups.

Sarapiquís Rainforest Lodge LODGE $$$
(☎2761-1415; www.sarapiquis.com; d with/without breakfast US$110/85; P☺❄@☒) ✐ About 2km north of La Virgen, this ecolodge offers bat-proof lighting and an education in pre-Columbian culture and environmental conservation. Modeled after a 15th-century pre-Columbian village, the *palenque*-style thatched-roof buildings each contain a clutch of sparse but spacious rooms, with huge solar-heated bathroom and shared circular balconies. The restaurant incorporates ingredients used in indigenous cuisine.

✕ Eating & Drinking

El Chante SODA $

(☑ 2761-0032; www.facebook.com/restauranteel
chante; mains US$6-10; ⊙ 11am-11pm) This La
Virgen favorite has welcoming service and
the food is tasty and filling. The place is popular (and it has televisions) so it can get loud
in the evenings. About 800m south of 'downtown' La Virgen, on the highway.

Restaurante Mar y Tierra COSTA RICAN $

(☑ 8434-2832; mains US$8-10; ⊙ 8am-10pm)
You can't miss this roadside restaurant, set
in an A-frame in the middle of town. The
seafood and steak restaurant is popular with
both locals and travelers. Try the *arroz Mar
y Tierra*, a Tico take on surf and turf.

Bar & Cabinas El Río BAR

(☑ 2761-0138; ⊙ noon-10pm) At the southern
end of town, turn off the main road and
make your way down to this atmospheric
riverside hangout, set on rough-hewn stilts
high above the river. Locals congregate on
the upper deck to sip cold beers and nosh on
filling Tico fare.

From here, you can stumble right into
your bed if you stay in one of the A-frame
bungalows (with fan/air-con US$15/20) near
the road.

❶ Getting There & Away

La Virgen lies on Hwy 126, about 8km north of
San Miguel and 17km west of Puerto Viejo de
Sarapiquí. It's a paved but curvy route (especially heading south, where the road starts to climb
into the mountains). Buses ply this route from
San José via San Miguel to Puerto Viejo, stopping in La Virgen along the way. Local buses run
hourly between La Virgen and Puerto Viejo de
Sarapiquí (US$1, 30 minutes) from 6am to 8pm.

In the fall of 2017 the new Vuelta Kooper Chilamate Hwy, aka Hwy 4, opened west of here,
connecting the Sarapiquí Valley to Muelle and
beyond, and cutting the trip to La Fortuna in half.

Chilamate & Around

The narrow, paved Hwy 4 runs for about
15km between La Virgen and Puerto Viejo,
connecting a few farming villages such as
the don't-blink-or-you'll-miss-it hamlet of
Chilamate. On the northern side, the road
is lined with small businesses, prosperous
family *fincas* and acres upon acres of picturesque pineapple plantations. On the southern side is the wild Río Sarapiquí, providing
a dramatic landscape for a handful of excellent ecolodges.

Beyond the river, these lodges are surrounded by their own private reserves of primary and secondary forest, crisscrossed by
hiking trails, which are begging for exploration. And beyond that, the landscape merg-
es seamlessly into the unexplored northern
reaches of **Parque Nacional Braulio Carrillo**. Technically, travelers cannot access the
park from here, but nothing stops the wildlife – an enormous diversity of birdlife and
even mammals like monkeys, kinkajous and
peccaries – from sneaking out and spying on
unsuspecting passers-by.

The whole region – from La Virgen to
Puerto Viejo – is defined by the Río Sarapiquí. Several of the river-running companies have set up shop east of town.

☞ Tours

While agriculture remains the primary
money-maker in the region, many folks recognize that tourism also has a role to play
in the local economy. And it doesn't have to
be an either/or. Entrepreneurial local farmers have started supplementing their agricultural activities with farm tours, allowing

ARENAL & NORTHERN LOWLANDS CHILAMATE & AROUND

WORTH A TRIP

CINCO CEIBAS

In the huge, 1100-hectare Finca Pangola there is a swathe of dense, green primary rainforest, home to some of the oldest and largest trees in all of Costa Rica. This is **Cinco
Ceibas** (☑ 2476-0606; www.cincoceibas.com; full-day tour incl lunch US$125). And yes, there
are five glorious ceiba trees that you see, as you walk 1.2km along the raised wooden
boardwalk through the jungle. The stroll is paired with horseback riding, kayaking or an
ox-cart ride, plus lunch, for a carefully choreographed adventure.

Cinco Ceibas offers transportation for day-trippers from San José or La Fortuna. If you
have your own wheels, it's a one-hour drive on mostly gravel roads from La Virgen. From
the highway north of town, take the turn off to Pueblo Nuevo.

visitors a view into Tico rural lifestyles, sustainable farming practices, and the ins and outs of producing delicious food.

Costa Rica Best Chocolate FOOD & DRINK
(☑ 8501-7951, 8816-3729; adult/child US$30/20; ☺ tours 8am, 10am, 1pm & 3pm) Where does chocolate come from? This local Chilamate family can answer that question for you, starting with the cacao plants growing on their farm. The two-hour demonstration covers the whole chocolate-making process, with plenty of tasting along the way. Choose from four (chocolate) bars at the end of the tour. About 5km west of downtown Sarapiquí, on the main highway.

Organic Paradise Tour FOOD & DRINK
(☑ 2761-0706; www.organicparadisetour.com; adult/child US$$35/14; ☺ 8am, 10am, 1pm & 3pm) Take a bumpy ride on a tractor-drawn carriage and learn everything you ever wanted to know about pineapples (and peppers). The two-hour tour focuses on the production process and what it means to be organic, but it also offers real insight into Costa Rican farm culture, as well as practical tips like how to choose your pineapple at the supermarket.

The tour is educational and surprisingly entertaining. And, of course, you get to sample the goods. Located 1km from the Chilamate school and 4km north of the main highway – follow the signs for 'Tour de Piña.'

🛏 Sleeping & Eating

This scenic stretch of Hwy 126 and Hwy 4 is home to a few excellent ecolodges. Good news for budget travelers: you don't have to stay at them to take advantage of their private trails and other interesting attractions.

Isla del Río HOSTEL $
(☑ 2766-6525; www.aguasbravascr.com; dm US$12, r with/without bathroom US$40/35, breakfast US$6; ℗ 🛜) After riding the rapids, you can hunker down at this riverside hostel, operated by Aguas Bravas (p278). It's a clean, basic set-up with solid wooden beds, clean bathrooms and hearty breakfasts. There are trails for exploring, as well as an outdoor hangout area where you can lounge in a hammock, listen to the rushing river and recall your rafting adventure.

On the main highway about 6km west of Sarapiquí.

★ Chilamate Rainforest Eco Retreat LODGE $$$
(☑ 2766-6949; www.chilamaterainforest.com; incl breakfast dm US$30-35, s/d/tr/q US$90/110/130/155; ℗ 🛜) ⏀ Family-run and family-friendly, this is an inviting and innovative retreat, where owners Davis and Meghan are dedicated to protecting the environment and investing in community. Built on 20 hectares of secondary forest, the solar-powered cabins are basic but full of character, with hand-crafted furniture and natural air cooling. Located just off the main highway, about 5km west of Sarapiquí.

The restaurant serves incredible breakfast and dinner buffets, using local, organic ingredients. Covered, flat walkways allow you to move between buildings in the complex without ever getting wet (after all, this is the rainforest!). Behind the cabins, 6km of paths wind through the jungle, where you're likely to spot sloths, monkeys, toucans, frogs, snakes and more. And when you can't take the heat, head to the nearby river swimming hole, complete with Tarzan swing from the bridge.

Selva Verde Lodge LODGE $$$
(☑ in USA & Canada 800-451-7111, 2761-1800; www.selvaverde.com; incl breakfast s/d US$120/140, bungalow s/d US$140/170; ℗ ✳ 🛜 🏊) This former *finca* in Chilamate is now an elegant lodge protecting 200 hectares of rainforest. Choose to stay at the river lodge, elevated above the forest floor, or in a private bungalow, tucked away in the nearby trees. Rooms have shiny wooden floors, solar-heated showers and wide verandas with forest views. On the main highway about 6km west of Sarapiquí.

There are three walking trails through the grounds and into the premontane tropical wet forest, as well as medicinal and butterfly gardens, various boat tours on the Río Sarapiquí and an onsite Italian kitchen.

La Quinta de Sarapiquí Lodge LODGE $$$
(☑ 2761-1052; www.laquintasarapiqui.com; d/tr/q incl breakfast US$110/125/140; ℗ ✳ 🛜 🏊) ⏀ At this family-run lodge on the banks of the Río Sardinal, covered paths crisscross the landscaped garden, connecting thatched-roof, hammock-strung rooms. You can swim in the pretty saltwater pool or in the nearby river swimming hole; observe the creatures in the frog house, caimen nursery and butterfly garden; or hike the trails through secondary forest.

Even if you're not staying here, you can get a day pass (US$12) to explore the animal exhibits and hiking trails.

Rancho Magallanes
COSTA RICAN $

(☏2766-5606; chicken US$5-12; ⏰10am-10pm) Rancho Magallanes is a sweet roadside restaurant with a wood-burning brick oven where they roast whole chickens and serve them quite simply with tortillas and banana salsa. You can dine with the truckers by the roadside or in the more upscale riverside dining area, painted with colorful jungle scenes.

ℹ Getting There & Away

Any bus between La Virgen and Puerto Viejo de Sarapiquí can drop you off at the entrances to the ecolodges along Hwy 4, while a taxi from La Virgen will cost from US$8 to US$10.

Puerto Viejo de Sarapiquí

POP 9600

At the scenic confluence of the Ríos Puerto Viejo and Sarapiquí, this was once the most important port in Costa Rica. Boats laden with fruit, coffee and other commercial exports plied the Sarapiquí as far as the Nicaraguan border, then turned east on the Río San Juan to the sea.

Today it is simply a gritty but pleasant palm-shaded market town. The town has made concessions to the new economy, with the local polytechnic high school offering students advanced tourism, ecology and agriculture degrees. The school even has its own reserve, laced with trails. Visitors, meanwhile, can choose from any number of activities in the surrounding area, such as bird-watching, rafting, kayaking, boating and hiking.

Every April, the locals celebrate the victory over William Walker and his invading *yanqui filibusteros*, who were defeated near here in the Battle of Sardinal in 1856.

☞ Tours

Oasis Nature Tours
BOATING

(☏2766-6108, 2766-6260, 8816-6462; www.oasis naturetours.com; full-day tour incl transportation from San José per person US$85-100, safari boat tour per person US$35) This is just one of several guides that runs boat tours on the local rivers. Also offers ziplining, rafting and other guided adventures. Right next to the bus terminal, down the alley in a blue house.

Anhinga Tours
BOATING

(☏8346-1220, 2766-5858; www.anhinga.jimdo. com; Av 7; tours per person US$25) This local guide takes travelers out to explore the Río Sarapiquí and its tributaries. Located on the east–west road at the end of town leading to the river.

🛏 Sleeping

This stretch of jungle boasts quite a range of accommodations, from budget bunks in town designed for local long-term plantation workers to several excellent lodges on the outskirts.

Cabinas Laura
CABINA $

(☏2766-6316; s/d US$25/30; 🅿✳@🛜) Located on the road to the pier, behind Banco Nacional, this place is quiet and cheap. The 22 rooms are simple but spotless, with shiny tiles, wooden furnishings and cable TV.

Posada Andrea Cristina B&B
B&B $$

(☏2766-6265; www.posadaandreacristina.wix site.com/andreacristina; d incl breakfast US$64; 🅿🛜) On the edge of town and at the edge of the forest, this charming B&B is a rough-around-the-edges gem. The grounds are swarming with birds, not to mention the frogs that populate the pond. Quaint cabins all have high, beamed ceilings, colorful paint jobs and private terraces. There's also a funky tree house, built around a thriving Inga tree.

Your delightful host, Alex Martínez, is also a birding guide, and bakes a mean loaf of bread.

Hotel Gavilán
HOTEL $$

(☏2234-9507; www.gavilanlodge.com; d/tr/q from US$70/85/100; 🅿✳🛜) Sitting on a 100-hectare reserve just across the Sarapiquí from 'downtown', this former cattle *hacienda* is a bird-watching haven, with 5km of private trails on the grounds. The tired but cozy rooms have pastel paint jobs and wide porches, some of which have river views. Management is quite charming, offering private boat tours and bird walks upon request.

Hotel Ara Ambigua
HOTEL $$

(☏2766-7101; www.hotelaraambigua.com; s/d/ tr/q incl breakfast from US$95/95/112/128; 🅿✳🛜) About 1km west of Puerto Viejo, this countryside retreat (named for the great green macaw) offers oddly formal but well-equipped rooms, set on gorgeous grounds. There are birds buzzing in the luscious, blooming gardens, poison-dart frogs in the

ARENAL & NORTHERN LOWLANDS PUERTO VIEJO DE SARAPIQUÍ

ranario (frog pond) and caimans in the small lake.

Even if you're not staying here, the onsite restaurant, La Casona, is an excellent place to grab lunch and spy on your feathered friends.

✖ Eating

Most of the lodgings in and around Puerto Viejo have onsite restaurants or provide meals. Otherwise, there are several *sodas* in Puerto Viejo de Sarapiquí and a supermarket at the western end of town. A couple of interesting restaurants are along the highway between Puerto Viejo and La Virgen (not your typical *sodas*), and the Hotel El Bambú restaurant has some nice choices.

Congo Jack's BBQ   AMERICAN $
(☑8447-6684; Calle 1, near Av 3; mains US$6-10; ⊙11am-9pm) Here's a clean, tiny box of a restaurant that seems to have borrowed its gleaming white tiles from the clinic next door. It's borrowed its menu, certainly, from North America, with BBQ pulled-pork sandwiches and other 'fast food,' all claiming to be not fried. Except the french fries, of course.

Restaurante y Pizzeria La Casona   PIZZA $$
(☑2766-7101; www.hotelaraambigua.com; meals US$8-16; ⊙8am-10pm; 🔊🌐) The restaurant at Hotel Ara Ambigua (p281) is particularly recommended for its oven-baked pizza and traditional, homemade cuisine served in an open-air *rancho* (small house). If you're looking for something beyond the pizza/*casado* routine, try the tangy Frida Kahlo chicken. The deck offers a sweet view of the gardens, where birds flutter by as you enjoy your meal.

ℹ Information

Banco de Costa Rica (Calle Central; ⊙9am-4pm Mon-Fri) At the entrance to the town.
Banco Nacional (☑2766-5658; Av 7; ⊙8:45am-4:30pm Mon-Fri) Near the dock.
Cruz Roja (☑administration 2764-2424, emergency 2766-6212; Av 4) Provides medical care.

ℹ Getting There & Away

The **bus terminal** (Calle Central; ⊙5am-7pm) is right across from the park, near Hotel El Bambú. Local buses run hourly between La Virgen and Puerto Viejo de Sarapiquí (US$1, 30 minutes) from 5am to 8pm.

Ciudad Quesada (Transportes Linaco) US$3, two hours, departs eight times daily from 4:40am to 6:30pm.
Guápiles (Transportes Guapileños) US$2, one hour, departs 10 times daily from 5:30am to 5pm.
Rio Frio 16 departures daily from 6am to 7pm.
San José (Autotransportes Sarapiquí and Empresarios Guapileños) US$2.50, two hours, departs 5am, 5:15am, 5:30am, 7am, 8am, 9:30am, 11am, 1:30pm, 3pm, 4:30pm and 5:30pm.

Estación Biológica La Selva

Not to be confused with Selva Verde Lodge in Chilamate, Estación Biológica La Selva is a working biological research station equipped with laboratories, experimental plots, a herbarium and an extensive library. The station is usually teeming with scientists and students researching the nearby private reserve.

The area protected by La Selva is 16 sq km of premontane wet tropical rainforest, much of which is undisturbed. It's bordered to the south by the 476-sq-km Parque Nacional Braulio Carrillo, creating a protected area large enough to support a great diversity of life. More than 886 bird species have been recorded here, as well as 120 mammal species (including 70 species of bat and five species of big cat), 1850 species of vascular plant (especially from the orchid, philodendron, coffee and legume families) and thousands of insect species – with 500 types of ant alone.

☞ Tours

OTS La Selva Research Station   HIKING
(☑2766-6565, in USA 919-684-5774; www.three paths.co.cr; guided hike US$35, bird-watching US$50; ⊙guided hike 8am & 1:30pm, bird-watching hike 5:45am) Reservations are required for three-hour guided hikes with a bilingual naturalist guide. You'll head across the hanging bridge and into 57km of well-developed jungle trails, some of which are wheelchair accessible. Unguided hiking is forbidden, although you'll be allowed to wander a bit after your guided tour. You should also make reservations for the popular guided bird-watching hikes.

Sleeping

OTS La Selva Research Station LODGE $$
(2766-6565; www.threepaths.co.cr; per person incl meals US$90-95; P) Rooms are equipped with twin beds, private bathrooms, fans and balconies overlooking the forest. Prices include meals and two daily guided hikes.

Getting There & Away

Public buses between Puerto Viejo and Río Frío/Horquetas can drop you off along the highway, which is 1km from the entrance to La Selva. Alternatively, catch a taxi from Puerto Viejo, which is about 4km away.

Horquetas & Around

South of Puerto Viejo de Sarapiquí, plantations line Hwy 4 and sprawl all the way to the marshes and mangroves of the Caribbean coast. To the west, the rugged hills of the Cordillera Central mark the northeastern boundary of Parque Nacional Braulio Carrillo. Most travelers on this scenic stretch of highway are either heading to the Caribbean coast or to the Central Valley. However, some are pulling off the road to visit one of the area's unique off-the-beaten-track destinations, like the world-class botanical garden at Heliconia Island or the backyard frog habitats at Frog's Heaven.

Sights

Heliconia Island GARDENS
(2764-5220; www.heliconiaisland.com; self-guided/guided tours US$10/18, d/q from US$82/104; 8am-5pm; P) Drive down a rugged road, walk across the bridge and enter a masterpiece of landscape architecture that is home to more than 80 varieties of heliconias, tropical flowers, plants and trees. The 2-hectare island overlooking the Río Puerto Viejo is also a refuge for 228 species of bird, including a spectacled owl who returns every year to raise her family. There are resident howler monkeys, river otters, sloths, and a few friendly dogs that will greet you upon arrival.

Dutch owners Henk and Carolien offer guided tours to show off the most memorable plants, including rare hybrids of heliconia found only on the island. They also own swatches of secondary forest on either side of the garden, which offers a wild forest buffer and attracts wildlife. The admission fee is waived for overnight guests, who stay in immaculate raised cabins with stone floors and breezy balconies. Heliconia Island is about 5km north of Horquetas.

Frog's Heaven GARDENS
(Cielo de Ranas; 2764-2724, 8891-8589; www.frogsheaven.org; adult/child US$25/12; 8am-8pm;) The frogs hop free in this lovely tropical garden, which provides a perfect habitat for more than 28 species. On guided tours you're likely to see old favorites like the red-eyed tree frog and poison-dart frogs, as well as some lesser-known exotic amphibians, such as the translucent glass frog and the wrinkly Mexican tree frog. Come for the twilight tour to see a whole different frog world.

This place is also excellent for birding and – occasionally – spotting other creatures too. Reserve at least a day ahead. Located in Horquetas, diagonal from the church.

Sleeping

The tricky thing about the lodges in Horquetas is that they're not exactly in Horquetas. They use this address because it is the nearest vestige of civilization – but these lodges are out there. Some of them are *way* out there. Make reservations and follow instructions on how to get there. And don't forget your sense of adventure (and humor), because you're going to need it.

Yatama Ecolodge LODGE $$
(7015-1121; www.yatamaecolodge.com; per person incl 3 meals US$80) Are you willing to forgo some creature comforts for the chance to commune with the rainforest? At Yatama, you'll sleep in primitive wooden cabins with intermittent solar-fed electricity. You'll slog through the mud to glimpse frogs, birds and bugs. You'll eat satisfying food. You'll skip showers in favor of river swims. And you'll revel in the vibrancy of the forest.

Staff pick you up in Horquetas to make the treacherous, 45-minute drive up to this primitive lodge on the edge of the Parque Nacional Braulio Carrillo. Bring insect repellent, rubber boots and an adventurous spirit.

Rara Avis CABINA $$
(2764-1111, 2200-4238; www.rara-avis.com; lodge per person incl meals and hikes US$89) When they say remote, they mean remote. This private reserve, 13 sq km of high-altitude tropical rainforest, is accessible only to guests who

make the three-hour tractor ride up a steep, muddy hill. Accommodations are rustic: there's no electricity, though the kerosene lamps and starry skies are unforgettable. Prices include all meals, transportation from Horquetas and two guided hikes per day.

The private reserve borders the eastern edge of Parque Nacional Braulio Carrillo and has no real dry season. Bird-watching here is excellent, with more than 350 documented species, while mammals including monkeys, coatis, anteaters and pacas are often seen. Since getting here is time-consuming and difficult, a two-night stay is recommended. You can also arrange to travel on horseback instead of by tractor ($35 per person), but you'll have to hike the last 3km yourself. Pickup is from Calle Fernandez in Horquetas.

Sueño Azul Resort RESORT $$$
(☏ 2764-1000; www.suenoazulresort.com; d US$120-150, extra person US$20; P ❄ ☎ ☞ ☲) Sueño Azul has a stunning perch at the confluence of the Ríos Sarapiquí and San Rafael. The vast property has hiking trails, a suspension bridge, a canopy tour and a waterfall, as well as a stable of gorgeous horses. The facility itself is looking worse for wear, but rooms are comfortable enough, with log beds and river views.

The restaurant, unfortunately, is overpriced and uninspiring – which is a shame, as there are no other options in the vicinity. From Horquetas, follow the signs over the suspension bridge to the property entrance, from where it's another 1.4km (with another precarious bridge crossing) to the resort itself.

❶ Getting There & Away

About 12 smoothly paved kilometers from Puerto Viejo de Sarapiquí is the village of Horquetas, around which you'll find the turnoffs for Frog's Heaven, Heliconia Island and the other resorts. From Horquetas it's another 15km to Hwy 32, which connects San José to the Caribbean coast and bisects Parque Nacional Braulio Carrillo on the way to San José.

Península de Nicoya

Most Beautiful Beaches

➡ Playa Conchal (p297)

➡ Playa Junquillal (p309)

➡ Playa Carrillo (p325)

➡ Playa San Miguel (p327)

➡ Playa Cocolito (p335)

Best Places to Stay

➡ Hotel Quinta Esencia (p297)

➡ Villa Mango B&B (p314)

➡ Costa Rica Yoga Spa (p315)

➡ Camp Supertramp (p322)

➡ Canaima Chill House (p331)

➡ Mar Y Sol Ecotel (p343)

Why Go?

Maybe you've come to the Península de Nicoya to sample the sapphire waters that peel left and right, curling into perfect barrels up and down the coast. Or perhaps you just want to hunker down on a pristine patch of sand and soak up some sun. By day, you might ramble down rugged roads, fording rivers and navigating ridges with massive coastal views. By night, you can spy on nesting sea turtles or take a midnight dip in the luxuriant Pacific. In between adventures, you'll find no shortage of boutique bunks, tasty kitchens and indulgent spas to shelter and nourish body and soul. Whether you come for the thrills or just to chill, the Nicoya peninsula delivers. You'll find that the days (or weeks, or months) drift away on ocean breezes, disappearing all too quickly.

When to Go

➡ Accommodation rates are lower from May to November. Prices rise significantly during holiday weeks (Christmas, New Year and Easter).

➡ Peak rainfalls through September and October mean the peninsula is at its most lush; the air isn't nearly as dusty, rivers swell, whales are migrating and prices are cheap.

Península de Nicoya Highlights

1 **Playas del Coco** (p288) Diving down deep to spy on sea turtles, manta rays and bull sharks.

2 **Nosara** (p313) Catching morning swells and relishing afternoon asanas.

3 **Refugio Nacional de Fauna Silvestre Ostional** (p317) Marveling at Mother Nature's ways during *arribada*, the mass arrival of nesting olive ridley turtles.

4 **Playa Carrillo** (p325) Sitting beneath the palms and watching a spectacular sunset.

5 **LocosCocos** (p328) Devouring delectable *ceviche* and ice-cold *cerveza* on postcard-perfect Playa San Miguel.

6 **Mal País and Santa Teresa** (p328) Surfing luscious breaks and feasting on farm-fresh cooking.

7 **Refugio Nacional de Vida Silvestre Curú** (p343) Kayaking and swimming in the bioluminescent waters.

8 **Reserva Natural Absoluta Cabo Blanco** (p334) Hiking to a wilderness beach at the tip of the peninsula.

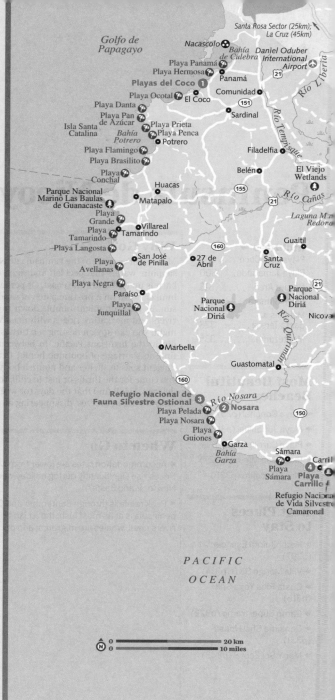

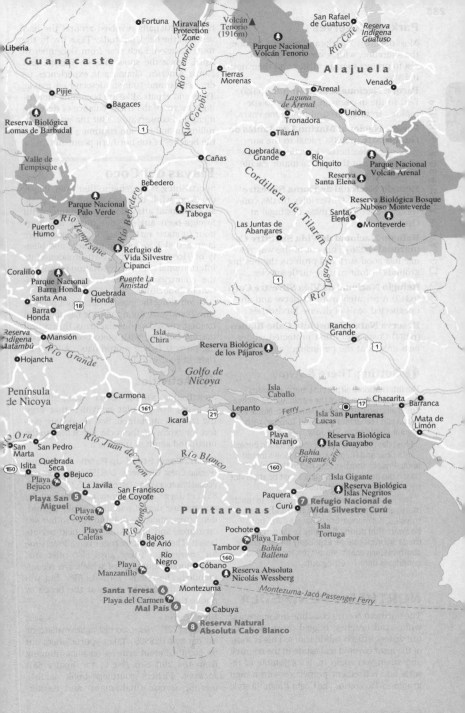

Parks & Reserves

Most of Nicoya's parks and reserves lie along the shoreline, with several stretching out to sea to protect marine turtles and their nesting sites.

Parque Nacional Barra Honda (p312) Best in the dry season; you can go spelunking in underground limestone caves.

Parque Nacional Marino Las Baulas de Guanacaste (p298) Crucial to the survival of the leatherback turtle, this park protects one of the turtle's major Pacific nesting sites.

Refugio Nacional de Fauna Silvestre Ostional (p317) Olive ridley turtles converge in *arribadas* (mass nestings) at Ostional.

Refugio Nacional de Vida Silvestre Camaronal (p326) This out-of-the-way refuge has good surf and protects the nesting grounds of four marine-turtle species.

Refugio Nacional de Vida Silvestre Curú (p343) A privately owned reserve and an unexpected oasis of diverse landscapes.

Reserva Natural Absoluta Cabo Blanco (p334) Costa Rica's first protected wilderness area is at the peninsula's cape.

❶ Getting There & Away

The international airport in Liberia provides easy access to much of the Península de Nicoya. Small airstrips also serve Tamarindo, Nosara, Punta Islita (charters only) and Tambor, with regular flights from San José.

Most destinations are served by public buses; Santa Cruz and Nicoya are the region's inland hubs. Private shuttles also run to the major beach destinations (including a fast boat service between Jacó and Montezuma).

You'll probably want your own vehicle to reach more remote places. To drive the roads less traveled, it's mandatory to have a 4WD, but be aware that during the rainy season many roads are impassable, especially on the remote southwestern coast. Always ask locally about conditions before setting out.

NORTHERN PENINSULA

The northern Nicoya coastline in a snapshot: white-sand beaches, rugged green hills, azure waters, stucco subdivisions. This is some of the most coveted real estate in the country, and when you zoom in, it's a jumble of resorts and retirement properties with a high gringo-to-Tico ratio. The Costa Rican lifestyle here traditionally revolved around the harvest and the herd, but today Ticos live by the tourist season. Each year from December to April, when the snow falls on Europe and North America, Guanacaste experiences its dry season and tourists descend en masse. Ticos and expats alike are becoming increasingly aware of the tricky balance of development and conservation. But the waves keep rolling in and the sun continues to smile on the beaches of the northern peninsula.

Playas del Coco

Sportfishing is the engine that built Playas del Coco, while deep-sea diving has become an additional attraction. You'll mingle with foreign-born anglers and divers at happy hour (it starts rather early). That said, there is an actual Tico community here and plenty of Tico tourists. The town broadened its international sporting reputation by hosting the country's first-ever Ironman competition in June 2017.

Stroll along the grassy beachfront plaza at sunset and gaze upon the wide bay sheltered by long, rugged peninsular arms, the natural marina bobbing with motorboats and fishing *pangas* (small motorboats). All will be right in your world.

🏃 Activities

Sportfishing, sailing, scuba diving and sea kayaking are popular activities that keep the troops entertained. Sea kayaks are perfect for exploring the rocky headlands to the north and south of the beach.

Pacific Coast Stand-Up Paddle WATER SPORTS (Pacific Coast Discovery; ☏ 8359-5118; www.paci ficcoastsuptours.com; lessons US$35, tours US$65-85) Let Jorge and his crew take you out for an amazing day of paddling, exploring hidden coves, spotting dolphins and other sea creatures, and picnicking on a near-private beach. The three-hour tour even allows time for snorkeling. These guys also offer surf and snorkel tours, all of which are recommended. There is no formal office, but you can find these folks down at the beach or phone them beforehand.

Blue Marlin FISHING (☏ 2670-2222; www.sportfishingbluemarlin.com; half-day from US$500) Takes sportsfishers out on eight different cruises, on boats ranging from the 28ft *Sea Fox* to the luxury 55ft *Jackpot*. Fishers routinely hook sailfish, marlin, *dorado* (mahi-mahi) and roosterfish. This company practices catch and release with all species.

🛏 Sleeping

When it comes to lodgings in Playas del Coco, the emphasis seems to be on quantity rather than quality. There are loads of places to stay, but many of them are uninspiring. Fortunately, things have perked up a bit in recent years, with some newer hostels and a couple of unique high-end (though not too expensive) options.

Garden House at M&M   HOSTEL **$**
(☑ 2670-0273; gardenhouse@hotelmym.com; La Chorrera; dm $20-25, d incl breakfast $60; ❄ 🤶 🍴) There are plenty of budget *cabinas* (cabins) in Coco but this is the only proper hostel. After many changes in name and management, the property is now known as the Garden House – operated by the good folks behind Hotel M&M. There are two dorm rooms, a handful of privates and a sweet swimming pool, all within striking distance of the beach.

Villa del Sol   HOTEL **$$**
(☑ 2670-0085, in Canada 514-400-9101; www.villadelsol.com; La Chorrera; d incl breakfast US$65-85, apt US$85-105; 🅿 ❄ @ 🤶 🍴) About 1km

north of the town center, this leafy, tranquil property attracts monkeys, iguanas and a good variety of birdlife, in addition to happy travelers lounging on hammocks. The main building has stylish rooms with sunset-view balconies. In the back building, studio apartments (sleeping four) offer excellent value. Walk to the beach in five minutes.

Hotel M&M   HOTEL **$$**
(☑ 2670-1212; www.hotelmym.com; s/d/tr incl breakfast US$40/55/75; 🅿 🤶) A romantic beachfront hacienda with a wooden balcony overlooking the boardwalk. Fan-cooled rooms have ceramic tiled floors, beamed ceilings and cold-water showers. This simple place is one of the only beachfront properties in Coco. And if the beach is not your thing, you can take a dip in the pool at sister property Garden House. Strangely, although M&M is slightly more expensive than the Garden House, it doesn't have air-con, whereas its sister hostel does – if that matters in your decision-making process.

Pato Loco Inn   GUESTHOUSE **$$**
(☑ 2670-0145; www.patolocoinn.com; d/tr/q incl breakfast US$58/68/78; 🅿 ❄ @ 🤶 🍴 🍴) Coloradan Mary Cox and parrot Simon offer a warm welcome to Coco Beach, with a wide

---

DEEP DIVES

The northern peninsula is one of the best and most easily accessible dive destinations in the country, though visibility varies greatly (9m to 15m, and sometimes up to 20m). Typical dive sites include the following:

➡ Volcanic rock pinnacles near the coast

➡ Isla Santa Catalina (about 20km to the southwest)

➡ Isla Murciélago (40km to the northwest, near the tip of Península Santa Elena)

There is no colorful hard coral such as you would see at a reef, but the sites make up for it with abundant marine life. Plenty of turtles and pelagics meander through, including mantas, sharks and whales. You'll be lost in huge schools of smaller tropical fish. These waters are sometimes home to humpback whales, who can be heard underwater during calving season (January to March) and seen during migration season (June and July).

Isla Santa Catalina and Isla Murciélago both host migrant manta rays from December to late April, and Murciélago is also known for its regular sightings of resident bull sharks. Divers also head to Narizones, which is a good deep dive (about 27m), while Punta Gorda is an easy descent for inexperienced divers.

Costa Rica Dive Center (☑ 2670-0308; www.summer-salt.com; Las Chorreras; 2-tank dives from US$80) This friendly Swiss-run dive shop (formerly known as Summer Salt) has professional, bilingual staff. Snorkelers are also welcome on the dive boats. Follow the sign to Summer Salt.

Rich Coast Diving (☑ 2670-0176; www.richcoastdiving.com; 2-tank dives from US$85, Open Water courses US$550; ⏰ 7:30am-6pm) This Dutch outfit is one of the largest dive operations in Coco. They offer the regular range of local dives (good for spotting sharks, rays and schools of fish) as well as more expensive trips to the Islas Catalinas and Murciélagos. CDC certified.

range of rooms, a friendly bar and the best American breakfast in town (think biscuits and gravy). Most rooms feature stenciling or thematic murals, hand-painted by Mary herself. Stop by for Monday or Friday happy hour to shoot the breeze with expats.

Hotel Chantel
BOUTIQUE HOTEL $$$

(2670-0389; www.hotelchantel.com; d incl breakfast US$69-89, ste US$115-200; P✳☎✉🐾) Perched on a cliff overlooking the coast, this intimate hotel is a step up from other local lodgings. Eleven rooms feature tasteful wood and wicker furniture, contemporary artwork and private terraces with stunning vistas of Playas del Coco. The elegant infinity pool and the breezy rooftop restaurant Lookout share the same panoramic view. It's a short drive from town: just south of Flor de Itabo, head west off the main road and follow the signs.

Rancho Armadillo
HOTEL $$$

(8336-9645, 2670-0108; www.ranchoarmadillo.com; d incl breakfast standard US$204, deluxe US$244-278; P✳☎✉) Near the entrance to town, this private estate is on a hillside about 600m off the main road (mostly paved), with ocean views to remind you where you are. It's set on 25 acres with plenty of wildlife, and the seven rooms are decorated with individually crafted furniture, hand-woven tapestries and local artwork. Self-catering gourmands will appreciate the professional kitchen.

Hotel La Puerta del Sol
HOTEL $$$

(2670-0195; www.lapuertadelsolcostarica.com; d/ste incl breakfast US$124/178; P✳☎✉) Alessandro's unpretentiously luxurious Mediterranean-inspired hotel is a short walk from the town and the beach, but a world away from the traffic and the noise. There are two large suites and eight huge pastel-colored rooms, with polished brick and concrete floors, king-sized beds and private terraces. The grounds are lush with blooming tropical flowers surrounding a glorious pool.

✗ Eating

Coco's main drag is lined with places to eat, but it's hard to distinguish one from another on this noisy, crowded street. Our favorite places are on the beach (of course) or tucked away in the quieter corners of town. Not surprisingly, it excels at seafood.

Heladeria & Pasteleria
Dolce Amaro
ICE CREAM $

(7025-2216; Plaza de Nino; ice cream US$3-5, pastries US$3-4; ☉8am-noon & 3-9pm Tue-Sat,

from 9:30am Sun; ✳🐾) Charming north Italian couple Elena and Francisco, from the hills of Venezia, offer a mind-boggling combination of homemade ice cream (18 flavors at last count) and killer pastries such as the *chocolatosa* (super chocolate). All the ice-cream making and espresso equipment comes from the old country. It's behind Panaderia Tutu.

Tuanis Bowls
SUSHI $

(Plaza del Coco; dishes US$8-9; ☉9am-8pm) A fresh face on the Coco scene, this laid-back shack offers a select few (simply delish) items such as acai bowls featuring the Brazilian wonder-fruit in a variety of mixtures (add cacao chips or chia), and tuna *poke* bowls which taste like the fish just leapt from the nearby waves. From the Tico slang for 'cool' – Tuanis really is.

Lookout
SEAFOOD $$

(8755-7246; www.thelookoutcoco.com; oysters US$2-3, small plates US$6-15; ☉4-10pm Wed-Sun; ☎🐾) So many things to love about the Lookout: sustainably harvested Pacific oysters, locally brewed craft beers, and a small but intriguing menu of snacks, *ceviches* and sandwiches. And then there's the view, taking in the Golfo de Papagayo and the Cordillera de Guanacaste in the distance. Service, however, can be slow. Located on the top floor of the Hotel Chantel.

La Dolce Vita
ITALIAN $$

(2670-1384; www.ladolcevitacostarica.com; La Chorrera; mains US$15-20; ☉noon-10pm; 🐾) Set in the Pueblito Sur open-air mall/food court about 500m north of the main drag, this is the local expat choice for oven-fresh pizza in Playas del Coco. The setting brings to mind suburban USA, but you can't argue with the tuna or octopus carpaccio. It also serves a range of pastas, distinctive seafood dishes and traditional grills.

Citron
FUSION $$$

(2670-0942; www.citroncoco.com; appetizers US$10, mains US$15-24; ☉5:30-10pm Mon-Sat) The contemporary menu features fresh ingredients and innovative preparations, including enticing specials from the wok (such as sea bass poached with scallions, soy sauce and sesame oil). Save room for a decadent Mediterranean dessert like *panna cotta*. Despite the shopping-mall setting, you can dine in the sophisticated, minimalist dining room or on an open-air deck, surrounded by pochote trees. It sometimes stays open later in high season.

Restaurante Donde
Claudio y Gloria   SEAFOOD $$$

(✍ 2670-1514; www.dondeclaudioygloria.com; La Chorrera; breakfast US$5-10, lunch US$10-20, mains US$14-24; ☺ 7am-9pm; ☺) Founded by Playas del Coco pioneers Claudio and Gloria Rojas, this casual, beachfront seafood restaurant has been a local landmark since 1955. The setting is perfect – breakfast, lunch or dinner – for watching beach goings on. Food is consistently good (though pricey). Service can be slow, but you're in no hurry, right? Owner Javier rents a few rooms at the property next door.

🍷 Drinking & Nightlife

Bamboo   BAR

(✍ 2670-0711; www.facebook.com/elcocobeach; appetizers US$5-10, mains US$8-16, pizzas US$16-28; ☺ 11am-11pm; ☺) The former Tiki Coco offers a front-row seat for the ongoing beach-volleyball action or, even better, a killer sunset. This open-air beach bar offers beach-accented gastropub fare, ice-cold beers and hand-crafted cocktails, not to mention service with a smile. Happy-hour specials nightly from 3pm to 9pm.

Zi Lounge   CLUB

(✍ 2670-1978; www.zilounge.com; ☺ 11am-2:30am; ☺) This is a pretty snazzy nightspot for a beer-drinking fishing port, but it suffers from an identity crisis – with a food menu that spans the globe, plus hookahs, sports on the TVs, nightly DJs and occasional live music. Still, people seem to be having a good time. Plus, you have to love an eight-hour happy hour (11am to 7pm).

ⓘ Information

Police (✍ 2670-0258) Southeast of the plaza by the beach.

ⓘ Getting There & Away

It's easy to get to Playas del Coco, which is located 25km from the Liberia airport; the journey takes only an hour or so by bus.

San José buses arrive and depart from the main terminal, about 100m south of Pato Loco Inn (p289). Buses for Liberia, Filadelfia and, very rarely, Playa Panama, stop next to the red awning and benches opposite the Hard Rock Cafe.

Liberia US$2, one hour, departs hourly from 5am to 11pm.

San José Pulmitan US$10, five hours, departs 4am, 8am and 2pm.

Playa Hermosa

Playa Hermosa (Beautiful Beach) is a lovely, wide and languid sheltered bay, framed by headlands and sprinkled with coconut palms and olive trees. Although it's only 5.5km (by road) north of Playas del Coco, and development is springing up rapidly along this entire coastline, Hermosa feels more remote.

🏃 Activities

North Pacific Tours   FISHING

(✍ 8398-8129; www.northpacifictours.com; fishing trips from US$400, surfing trips from US$300) This fish and surf operation knows where to find the biggest fish and the biggest breaks. Captain Mauricio and first mate Daniel will take you on their 26ft fishing boat, *Don Manual,* for coastal fishing, snorkeling and/or surfing. Split-charters available. Trips vary in length from half to full days.

BA Divers   DIVING

(✍ 2672-0032; www.badivers.cr; Rte 159; 2-tank dives from US$120; ☺ 7am-5pm) BA's very experienced and efficient crew will take you out on the *Legend* to hit the local dive sites around Playa Hermosa. Longer trips to the Bat Islands are also on offer. Located on the main road at the southern end of town, next to Restaurante Plaza del Mar.

🛏 Sleeping

Congo's Hostel & Camping   HOSTEL $

(✍ 2672-1168; www.congoshostel.com; campsites US$9, dm incl breakfast US$12-15; 🅿 ✳ ☺) This decent, friendly budget option is on the second beach-access road, just one block from the beach. It's a ramshackle but relaxed place, offering hammocks, secure parking (US$2) and an open-air communal kitchen. The four-bed dorm rooms have metal beds with worn mattresses and a bathroom. Breakfast is coffee and tortillas.

La Gaviota Tropical   HOTEL $$$

(✍ 2672-0011; www.lagaviotatropical.com; r/ste/master ste US$150/170/290; 🅿 ✳ ✳ ☷) It's ingenious: a vertical hotel. All five huge suites (fully equipped and impeccably decorated) face the sea. Cool off in the small but spectacular infinity pool on the top floor. Downstairs, you can enjoy an excellent meal at **Roberto's restaurant** (mains US$15-20; ☺ 11am-10pm; ☺) or walk a few steps to the sand.

Bosque del Mar   HOTEL $$$

(✍ 2672-0046; www.bosquedelmar.com; d/tr/q US$225/282/339; 🅿 ✳ @ ☺ ☷) ✐ Perched on the sand at the southern end of the beach, this lovely all-suite hotel offers a stunning location. Guests relish the gorgeous gardens, private terraces and contemporary design elements. Pay more for beachfront suites, which allow you to enjoy ocean views while soaking in your own open-air hot tub. Get here via the first beach-access road.

Hotel El Velero HOTEL $$$
(☑2672-0036, 2672-1017; www.costaricahotel.net; d US$140; P✴✿✾) Just steps from the beach, this resort hotel has 22 spacious rooms decorated with woodwork, bamboo beds with colorful bedspreads, wicker ceiling fans and granite washbasins. Ask for a seafront room on the 2nd floor for maximum views.

Eating

Ginger MEDITERRANEAN $$
(☑2672-0041; www.gingercostarica.com; tapas US$6-13; ⊙5-10pm Tue-Sun; ☑) On the east side of the main road, you'll see this stunner cantilevered into the trees. This is not the restaurant you would expect to find in an unassuming beach village. The chic ambience complements a gourmet list of Asian- and Mediterranean-inspired tapas, fresh-fruit cocktails and a decent wine list. Reservations recommended for dinner during busy seasons.

La Casita del Marisco SEAFOOD $$
(☑2672-0226; ceviches & soups US$8-10, mains US$10-15; ⊙noon-10pm) A rather hidden, unassuming gem near the end of town, this place has Ticos and gringos alike raving about the soups, *ceviches* and all things fishy. And you've got a great view of the famous Monkey Head rock in the bay: what could be better? Go the whole hog and treat yourself to a lobster. It's located across from Las Brisas condominiums.

A more visible version of this restaurant exists in Playas del Coco, too.

Aqua Sport COSTA RICAN $$
(☑2672-0151; www.facebook.com/aquasportcr; mains US$10-20; ⊙10am-10pm; ☎) This colorful, fun beach bar is an excellent place to pass an evening feasting on burgers or fish tacos and swilling beers. Or sample the Peruvian specialties, such as *lomo saltado* (salted pork), *diabla* shrimp (spicy with tomato sauce) and of course *ceviche*. Take a seat in the giant green rocking chair and chill.

❶ Getting There & Away

BUS
Buses to Liberia and San José depart from the main road on the northern end of the beach and make a stop in Sardinal.
Liberia La Pampa (Map p224; ☑2665-7530, 2686-7245; www.transporteslapampa.com); US$2, 1¼ hours, departs eight times from 5am to 7pm.
San José Tralapa (p98; US$11, six hours, departs 5am.

CAR
Coming from Liberia, you'll drive west for 14km, crossing the steel bridge and entering the village of Comunidad. Before the Do-It Center, turn right and drive another 1.6km. Turn left at the sign for Playa Panamá. Continue 11km and turn left onto the road that will take you into Hermosa. The entire route is paved, albeit winding.

If you have some time, it's worth exploring the beaches along the Golfo de Papagayo. Playa Panamá is right in the middle of the gulf with mangroves on one side, and a placid bay that feels almost like a lake. In between are the rustic Playa Bonita and Playa Buena.

Playa Ocotal

There is not much of a town here – just a few vacation rentals and an attractive resort. That's one reason it feels like a rustic outpost amid the condo-mania of the northern peninsula. The beach is gray and wooded, populated by mischievous magpie-jays, while the picturesque northernmost corner is dotted with small, brightly painted fishing boats rocking on the tide as wide-winged brown pelicans glide around them, and kids cavort on the sand. The water is warm and placid, and you can snorkel around the rocks at the southern end.

Playa Ocotal is about 4km southwest of Playas del Coco by paved road and it's worth a trip simply to eat at Father Rooster.

🏃 Activities

Rocket Frog Divers DIVING
(☑2670-1589; www.scuba-dive-costa-rica.com; 2-tank dives US$85-165, depending on location; ⊙8am-6pm) An awesome upstart dive shop on the Los Almendros property which hits 22 local dive sites and motors out to the Islas Catalinas to dive with mantas. The 36ft, purpose-designed *Pacific Express* promises to make it to distant dive sites in half the time of other vessels.

Diamante Eco Adventure Park ADVENTURE
(☑2105-5200, toll-free international 1-800 464 5554; www.diamanteecoadventurepark.com; Playa Matapalo; adult/child packages from US$42/34; ☺8:30am-4:30pm) Here's an attempt to fit all of Costa Rica into one adventure park. This park offers almost every activity in the book, including all-terrain vehicle (ATV) tours, fishing, hiking, biking, horseback riding, kayaking, snorkeling, scuba diving, stand-up paddling, surfing and ziplining. There's also an animal sanctuary and a botanical garden. And if you need a rest after your adventures, a hammock-strung beach.

🛏 Sleeping & Eating

Los Almendros de Ocotal APARTMENT $$
(☑2670-1560; www.losalmendrosrentals.com; studio/apt/villa US$82/180/237; P✳@🛜🌊) Perched on the hillside just above the beach, these studios and apartments are a great option for divers, beach bums and self-caterers. Studios (no beach view, unfortunately) sleep two, apartments sleep four and villas sleep six. Fancier units have a private pool and terrace, and there are Jacuzzis downstairs at the foot of the beach.

Villa Casa Blanca GUESTHOUSE $$$
(☑2670-0518; http://boutiquehotelsguanacaste. typepad.com; d/ste US$110/125; P✳🛜🌊) This gracious stucco mansion houses a friendly B&B. The property is charming in an artistic Old World way, with plenty of eclectic art, a two-tiered swimming pool and a wide porch offering glorious ocean views. The rooms are a little tired, but adequate. It's a five-minute walk down to the beach, or you can take a bike from the lobby.

Father Rooster Bar & Grill PUB FOOD $$
(☑2670-1246; www.fatherrooster.com; mains US$10-20; ☺11am-10pm; 🛜) This colorful gastropub by the sea serves up tasty sandwiches and US pub fare, as well as top-notch (though expensive) cocktails. Try the Tica Linda, a wicked mix of Cacique, juice and grenadine. You can't beat the location, whether you sit in the rockers on the shaded terrace or at tables under the palms, sunk into the sand. *Pura vida!*

❶ Getting There & Away

There are hourly buses between Liberia and Playas del Coco, some of which continue on to Ocotal. Otherwise, it's not too long a walk from Coco, which is around 4km away by road; a taxi from Coco should cost under US$10.

Bahía Potrero

Although they're lined up in a row, Playas Danta, Pan de Azúcar, Potrero, Flamingo, Brasilito and Conchal have little in common. The beaches range from gray sand to white sand to crushed seashells, with a wide variety of development along the way. It's gratifying to know that even here – along this busy strip of coastline – it's still possible to find a pretty *playa* (beach) without another soul on it.

Coming from the north, it's tempting to take the road from Sardinal to Potrero. Keep in mind there's a reason why locals call this route the 'Monkey Trail.' The first 8km of gravel road leading to the small town of Nuevo Colón is fine, but the second half is pretty brutal, and should only be tackled in dry season with a 4WD. The Monkey Trail begins 5km west of El Coco; turn right at the Castrol Oil sign and follow the signs for Congo Trail Canopy Tour. At the 'T' intersection in Nuevo Colón, turn left, bear left at the fork and continue for 5km until you reach Congo Trail Canopy. From there, it's a hair-raising 6km drive to Bahía Potrero.

To avoid the rough roads, return to the main peninsular highway from El Coco, then head south through Filadelfia and on to Belén (a distance of 18km), from where a paved road heads 25km west to Huacas. Take the road leading north until you hit the ocean in Brasilito. If you turn right and head north, you'll pass Playa Flamingo and Bahía Potrero before reaching Playa Pan de Azúcar. If you make a left instead and head south, you will end up at Playa Conchal.

Potrero

Several beaches – largely undeveloped – are strung along this low-key bay. Playa Prieta is a gorgeous black-sand beach, with crystal-blue waters and lush green vegetation, making for a colorful landscape indeed. The small cove is ideal for swimming, sunbathing and strolling. To the south, the gorgeous white-sand beach at Playa Penca curves around another little cove, where stand-up paddleboarders ply the sheltered turquoise bay toward gleaming offshore islets. Further south is the more developed 'town' beach, Playa Potrero.

There's a small fishing *pueblo* (village) at Potrero, just beyond the northern end of the eponymous beach. This is where the bus line ends, so these beaches won't see the weekend rush found at Brasilito. It's a nice walk (at low tide) from Flamingo along the beach.

Golfo de
Papagayo

○ Liberia

Playa Pan de
Azúcar ○

○ Playa
Junquillal

PACIFIC
OCEAN

Golfo de
Nicoya

○ Playa
Carrillo

○ Playa
San Miguel

Reserva Natural
Absoluta Cabo Blanco

RCHOI/GETTY IMAGES ©

Undiscovered Nicoya

1 WEEK

When it comes to beautiful beaches, Península de Nicoya is blessed richly indeed. Development here is uneven, which means there are plenty of hidden nooks, secluded coves and pristine paradises that remain unexploited.

Of course, you can't just take a direct flight to paradise; you have to work for it. In Costa Rica, that usually means switching to 4WD, driving over some brutally bumpy roads, and perhaps fording a river or two. (Note: this itinerary is not recommended during the rainy season.)

Starting from **Liberia**, your first destination is **Playa Pan de Azúcar** (p298), accessible via the infamous Monkey Trail. It's a rough ride but you won't care once you reach this jigsaw of rugged cliffs and clandestine coves. The only place to sleep is the Hotel Sugar Beach (p298) – a sweet choice.

Heading south, you'll pass through resort towns like Playa Flamingo (p296) and fishing villages like Playa Brasilito (p297). The main road detours inland, so you can buzz right by Tamarindo. It's not until you reach **Playa Junquillal** (p309) that you'll start to feel you're really out there. And you are. Unless the surf's up, this stunning wilderness beach is often deserted.

Keep moving south, skipping Nosara and Sámara, but stopping at **Playa Carrillo** (p325), a white-sand beauty, framed by granite and backed by towering palms. Locals descend from the village to watch the sunset. You should join them.

The area between Carrillo and Santa Teresa remains one of the peninsula's most isolated and wonderful stretches of coastline. Tackle the rugged roads and you'll be rewarded with miles of abandoned beaches backed by forest-covered hills. Our favorite is **Playa San Miguel** (p327), at once desolate and divine. Don't miss sundowners at LocosCocos (p328).

Your final stop is the **Reserva Natural Absoluta Cabo Blanco** (p334), a nature reserve that covers the entire tip of Península de Nicoya. Here, the evergreen forests and wilderness beaches are mostly empty of visitors – a perfect ending to your tour of Undiscovered Nicoya.

JODIE ELLENOR/ALAMY STOCK PHOTO ©

Top: Playa Carillo (p325)
Bottom: Halloween crab, Reserva Natural Absoluta Cabo Blanco (p334)

🛏 Sleeping & Eating

Pitaya Lodge
HOTEL $$

(📞2654-4145; www.pitayalodge.com; d/q incl breakfast US$75/95; 🅿❄🛜🏊) Oddly situated on the main drag north of Potrero, this little place (named for the popular dragon fruit) is set up like a roadside motel – a strip of rooms facing the pool, facing the road. That said, it has a boutique feel, with batik fabrics adorning earth-toned walls. It's a 15-minute walk to Playa Penca.

Bahía del Sol
BOUTIQUE HOTEL $$$

(📞2654-4671; www.bahiadelsolhotel.com; d/ste incl breakfast from US$220/316, 4-person ste US$468; 🅿❄@🛜🏊) With a prime beachfront location at Playa Potrero, this luxurious spot gets high marks for four-star laid-back elegance. Large, tropically themed rooms surround a pool with a swim-up bar and a garden with hammocks and day beds. Out front, the lawn leads to the upscale hotel restaurant, Nasu, and a beach peppered with *palapas* (shelters with thatched, palm-leaf roofs and open sides). Recently added 'deluxe superior' rooms fall between a standard and a suite, with an in-room Jacuzzi (US$280).

The Shack
AMERICAN $

(La Choza; 📞2654-6038; www.facebook.com/TheShackCR; breakfast US$6-7; ⏰8am-2:30pm; 🅿🛜) Set beneath a stilted tin roof twirling with ceiling fans, this fabulous diner is Potrero's favorite spot to grab a bite. It focuses on inexpensive yet filling brunches such as breakfast burritos, various egg specials and oatmeal bowls. And the Bostonian owner says the homemade bagels are coming back!

Beach House
BAR

(📞2654-6203; www.beachhousecr.com; ⏰11am-10pm; 🛜🎶) It's hard to resist this colorful shack on the beach offering cold fruity cocktails and glorious sunset views. You'd expect seafood and pub fare, but there's also live music and a playroom for kids. The 'you hook it, we cook it' special is on offer for fishing folk at a US$6 surcharge.

ⓘ Getting There & Away

Departing Potrero, buses begin their route on the southeast corner of the soccer field. All buses go via Flamingo.

San José Tralapa (p98); US$10, six hours, departs 2:45am, 9am and 2pm.

Santa Cruz Transportes Folklórica (www.transportesfolklorica.com); US$3, two hours, departs eight times per day from 6am to 9:40pm.

Playa Flamingo

Any time a once-pristine slice of paradise sprouts McMansions and condos and gets stitched up with a network of roads, there is a tendency to point fingers and raise hell about what was and what now is. And, yes, at Flamingo it does feel like the developers won. But that does not change the fact that this sugary, postcard-worthy white-sand and shell beach is glorious. Kissed by a serene blue sea with the rugged keys of the Catalinas floating off in the distance, it attracts a local Tico scene along with package tourists. Nose the air if you must, but admire the ocean in front of you, not the developments behind. Budget options and small-scale or independent lodgings of any sort are nonexistent. If you want to visit the beach but save a few bucks, consider staying in nearby Brasilito.

🍴 Eating

La Cuchara Verde
VEGETARIAN $$

(📞8811-0222; mains US$8-12; ⏰8am-3:30pm Mon-Fri; 🛜🎶) ✈ 'Positive food' is promised at this good-vibes vegetarian cafe. Burgers, sandwiches, pastries and egg dishes will sate your animal-free appetite. Pair your meal with an organic iced tea or a fresh-fruit smoothie.

Angelina's
SEAFOOD $$$

(📞2654-4839; www.angelinasplayaflamingo.com; pizza US$16-19, mains US$16-29; ⏰11:30am-10pm) Relatively formal for Costa Rica, Angelina's offers fine dining in a breezy, open-air setting, upstairs at the Plaza mini-mall. Innovative seafood preparations feature tropical fruits and local flavors. Frugal travelers can feast on pizzas with unique toppings or delectable pasta dishes, washed down with Costa Rican craft beers.

ⓘ Getting There & Away

Buses depart from the traffic circle near the town entrance and travel via Brasilito. Some also head north into Potrero and then turn around. Schedules change often, so ask locally about departure times as well as the best place on the road to wait for the bus.

Liberia La Pampa (p292); US$3, two hours, departs 5am, 10:30am, 12:30pm and 3:40pm.

San José Tralapa (p98); US$13, six hours, departs 9am and 2pm.

Santa Cruz Transportes Folklórica (📞2680-3161; www.transportesfolklorica.com; cnr Calle 7 & Av 3); US$3, 1½ hours, departs 12 times per day from 6am to 10pm.

Playa Brasilito

Unlike the other touristy towns along this stretch, Brasilito feels like an authentic *pueblo,* complete with a town square, a beachfront soccer pitch, a pink-washed *iglesia* (church) and a friendly Tico community. All of which makes up for the beach, which has much better neighbors on either side. Fortunately, it's just a short stroll along the sea to sugary Conchal.

🛏 Sleeping

★Hotel Quinta Esencia B&B $$
(✆2654-5455; www.hotel-quintaesencia.net; d incl breakfast $75; ▣❄🛜🌊) An artistic vibe pervades this chilled-out lodging, built around the trees on the northern edge of Brasilito. The comfortable guest rooms feature driftwood, bamboo and neutral tones, accented by ribbons of color. Co-owner Stephanie is an artist, and you'll see her work scattered about the premises. There's a lot of love (and a few cute cats) here. It's up a somewhat rough, muddy road.

Diversion Tropical CABINA $$
(✆2654-5519; www.diversiontropical.com; s/d/tr US$49/55/61; ▣❄🛜🌊) Next to Papaya (p297), this is an outstanding deal in a busy roadside location. Tiled rooms are clean but cramped, with those upstairs giving a glimpse of the ocean. Guests have free use of snorkel gear, while kayaks are available for rental. Communal facilities (aka the 'Fun Zone') include an outdoor kitchen and grill, a book exchange, board games and darts. Under new ownership, added perks include memory-foam mattresses.

Hotel Brasilito HOTEL $$
(✆2654-4237; www.brasilito.com; dm US$74-94, s/d US$64/95; ▣❄🛜) On the beach side of the plaza, this basic hotel offers simple, clean rooms with wood floors and ceiling fans, lined up along a wide balcony. Sea-view rooms cost a little more, but are worth the splurge. Otherwise, the patio's hammocks are ideal for soaking up the sunset. Budget rooms (no air-con) are also available. There are 10 different price categories for rooms, from budget singles to family options.

Conchal Hotel HOTEL $$$
(✆2654-9125; www.conchalcr.com; d incl breakfast US$106-123; ▣❄@🛜🌊) This bougainvillea- and palm-dappled lodge is a sweet retreat. Spacious rooms are fitted with unique design touches, such as beamed ceilings and wrought-iron furniture. Enjoy the lovely gardens while lounging poolside or from the privacy of your patio. A simple but scrumptious continental breakfast is served at the Papaya Restaurant, which is also recommended for other meals.

🍴 Eating

Camarón Dorado SEAFOOD $$
(Golden Shrimp; ✆2654-4028; cnr of Plaza Deportes; set meals US$9, children's plates US$7-9, fish platters US$14-28; ⊙noon-10pm) Conveniently located on the corner where the main square meets the beach, just before Don Brasilito's, this local favorite has been serving up fresh seafood for years (although the shrimp really aren't golden). The sign says it all: lunch and dinner on the beach – what could be better?

The Spot INTERNATIONAL $$
(✆2654-5463; www.facebook.com/thespotbrasilito; tapas US$6-8, mains US$12-14; ⊙7am-9pm Tue-Sun; 🛜🌊) Downstairs from the Hotel Brasilito, this restaurant occupying a fresh, open-air patio serves a wide range of international fare, from French *petit déjeuner* (breakfast) to Mediterranean tapas and American burgers. Tropical decor and ocean views promise a pleasant experience.

Papaya Restaurant SEAFOOD $$$
(✆2654-9125; www.conchalcr.com; mains US$16-20; ⊙8:30am-6:30pm Thu-Tue; 🛜🌊) Vegetarians and seafood lovers, rejoice! For the former, there are all-day breakfasts, power salads and falafel wraps. For the latter, there are seafood salads, fresh grilled fish and jumbo shrimp. Come during the day for big burritos and flatbread sandwiches, or come at night for fancier fare – and (sometimes) live music. The restaurant is in the Conchal Hotel.

ℹ Getting There & Away

All buses to/from Playa Flamingo and Potrero (US$3) travel through Brasilito (originating in Liberia, Santa Cruz or San José). There are three daily buses to San José. Buy tickets in advance at the **Tralapa Agencia** (✆2221-7202; ⊙8am-6pm Mon & Wed-Sat, to 3pm Sun, closed noon-1pm) at the north end of Brasilito, across from the sports field (the bus stops here, too).

Playa Conchal

Just 1km south of Brasilito is Playa Conchal, a gorgeous stretch of palm-backed sea and sand. Conchal rates among Costa Rica's most beautiful beaches. The name comes from

DON'T MISS

PLAYA PAN DE AZÚCAR

Although buses stop at Potrero, travelers with their own ride can continue 3km north on a paved road to 'Sugar-Bread Beach,' named for the strip of sugary white sand that's protected at both ends by rocky headlands. This is one of the most scenic stretches of road in all of northern Costa Rica, as dry rugged cliffs sheer down into aquamarine coves sheltered by offshore islets. The ocean here is calm, clear and perfect for snorkeling. The remote location – and the lack of cheap accommodations – create an atmosphere of total seclusion.

Perched on its own little piece of paradise, **Hotel Sugar Beach** (☎2654-4242; www.sugar-beach.com; d/ste incl breakfast from US$158/280; P※@☎☎) ✈ is the only accommodation on this *playa*. If it's out of your budget (or full), there are more options in nearby Bahía Potrero.

The drive from Potrero to Playa Pan de Azúcar is one of the most scenic stretches of paved road in all of northern Costa Rica. (This is a rarity in Costa Rica: a totally remote, perfectly private, drop-dead gorgeous 'secret spot' that doesn't require a 4WD.)

the billions of *conchas* (shells) that wash up on the beach, and are gradually crushed into coarse sand. The shallows drift from an intense turquoise to sea-foam green deeper out – a rarity on the Pacific coast. If you have snorkeling gear, this is the place to use it.

The beach is often packed with locals, tourists and countless vendors, but on weekdays during low season, Playa Conchal is pure paradise. The further south you stroll, the wider, sweeter and more spectacular the beach becomes.

You can walk to Conchal from Brasilito depending on the tide and the amount of rain (the gully between the two beaches may flood, but local dudes with off-road vehicles will ferry you across, for a price).

Playa Grande

Playa Grande is a wide, gorgeous beach, famous among conservationists and surfers alike. By day, offshore winds create steep and powerful waves. By night, an ancient cycle continues, as leatherback sea turtles bearing clutches of eggs follow the ocean currents back to their birthplace. The beach stretches from the Tamarindo estuary, around a dome rock – with tide pools and superb surf fishing – and on to equally grand Playa Ventanas. Even confident swimmers should obey riptide signs, as people have drowned here.

Since 1991 Playa Grande has been part of the Parque Nacional Marino Las Baulas de Guanacaste, protecting one of the world's most important leatherback nesting areas. At night it's only possible to visit the beach on a guided tour.

You'll notice many 'For Sale' signs bordering the park, and the inevitable whine of the chainsaw, which gives one pause for thought as to which way this community is going.

◉ Sights

Parque Nacional Marino Las Baulas de Guanacaste PARK
(☎2653-0470; adult/child US$12/2, turtle tours incl park admission US$35; ☉8am-noon & 1-5pm, tours 6pm-2am) Las Baulas national marine park encompasses the entire beach at Playa Grande, as well as the adjacent land and 220 sq km of ocean. This is one of the world's most important nesting areas for the critically endangered *baula* (leatherback turtle). In the evenings from October to March, rangers lead tours to witness the turtles' amazing cycle of life. Canoe tours explore the mangroves, home to caimans and crocodiles, as well as numerous bird species such as the roseate spoonbill.

🏃 Activities

Surfing

Surfing is the main motivation for coming to Playa Grande, and it is indeed spectacular. There are two main beach breaks – one at either end of the beach - especially at high tide in the early morning. Unfortunately, when the surf's up the breaks get crowded, so chat up some locals to learn their secrets.

Playa Grande Surf Camp SURFING
(☎2653-1074; www.playagrandesurfcamp.com; board rental per day US$20, 2hr lessons US$40) In addition to board rental and surf lessons, this outfit also offers surf packages which include accommodations, and can arrange transpor-

tation to the best breaks on the peninsula. It's in the southern part of Playa Grande.

Frijoles Locos Surf & Spa SURFING
(2652-9235; www.frijoleslocos.com; boards per hour US$5-25, 1½hr lessons from US$30; 9am-6pm) An all-purpose surf shop where you can rent surfboards and sign up for lessons. Afterwards, recover with a deep-tissue massage or another spa treatment. This place also rents just about everything you need to guarantee a great day at the beach, including bikes, snorkel gear, boogie boards and paddleboards, and shade tents. Enjoy!

Wildlife-Watching
Playa Grande is a wilderness beach, nearly surrounded by mangrove swamps. Protected by the Tamarindo Wildlife Sanctuary (in addition to the Las Baulas national park), this place is teeming with wildlife – and not only turtles. Local guides lead canoe expeditions in the Tamarindo estuary, where you can spot crocs, monkeys, anteaters and *pizotes* (coatis), not to mention a stunning variety of birds.

Black Turtle Tours WILDLIFE
(8534-8664; Hotel Las Tortugas; canoe tour per person US$30, turtle tour per person US$25) Paddle a canoe through the saltwater jungle that dominates the Tamarindo Wildlife Sanctuary, at the southern end of Playa Grande. This maze of mangroves – including five different species – is home to a spectacular array of flora and fauna. Your guide, Jhonathan, will help you spot it.

🛏 Sleeping

Lodgings are located at the two ends of Playa Grande. At the northern end, you'll find the heart of the village, with Hotel Las Tortugas (p300), the main beach entrance, the ranger station and the bulk of facilities. At the southern end, a handful of guesthouses have opened up in the Palm Beach Estates development, where there's another beach-access point. Further south is Hotel Bula Bula and the boats to Tamarindo.

Playa Grande Surf Camp CABINA $
(2653-1074; www.pgsc.com; dm US$25, d US$45-50; P☀☎☲) Aside from offering boards, lessons and trips, the surf camp is also a great budget-accommodations option. Three cute, thatched, A-frame *cabinas* have private porches and hammocks, just steps from the beach. There are also two breezy elevated *cabinas* that sleep two. Surf pack-

ages available. A recently opened smart cafe downstairs and an outdoor shared kitchen up the ante here.

★ La Marejada Hotel BOUTIQUE HOTEL $$
(2653-0594, in USA & Canada 800-559-3415; www.hotelswell.com; r US$90; ☀☎☲) Hidden behind a bamboo fence, this stylish nest is a gem. The eight elegantly understated rooms have stone-tile floors, rattan and wooden furnishings, and queen beds. There's not a lot of space here, but it's lovingly cared for and generously shared. Surf lessons and massage services are offered onsite, not to mention an excellent restaurant.

Indra Inn GUESTHOUSE $$
(www.indrainn.com; r US$72; P☀☎) It's not too fancy at Indra Inn, but it doesn't have to be. The grounds are blooming with fruit trees and hung with hammocks. Rooms are freshly updated (the old bar has recently been converted into four rooms) and simply decorated. Owners Matt, Natalia and Dante are charming hosts. Other perks include irresistible breakfasts, daily yoga classes and good vibes.

BP Surf Hostel CABINA $$
(8879-5643; bpsurf@gmail.com; r US$75; P☀☎☲) We know a bargain when we see one, and we see one here. Four spacious *cabinas* feature spotless tile floors and bathrooms, well-stocked kitchens and shiny stained-wood furnishings. They're lined up in a row, facing a small swimming pool and shady bar. Everything you need in one convenient, comfortable package.

Hotel Cantarana INN $$$
(2653-0486; www.hotel-cantarana.com; Palm Beach Estates; s/d US$120/135; P☀☎☲) This is a lovely, intimate inn nestled into the semi-gated Palm Beach Estates. Spacious and luxurious rooms each have a private terrace overlooking the glittering pool and gorgeous gardens. A highlight is the restaurant, set on the 2nd-floor terrace amid the treetops. Open for breakfast and dinner, the kitchen creates tasty concoctions from local ingredients.

Hotel Bula Bula HOTEL $$$
(2653-0975; www.hotelbulabula.com; r incl breakfast US$141; P☀☎☲) At the southern end of town, Hotel Bula Bula has decked out its rooms with king-size beds, tropical paint jobs and whimsical local art. The grounds are gorgeous and the front porch is well equipped with rattan rockers. Most importantly: cocktails. The Great Waltini's

hardwood bar puts out some seriously potent drinks, including rum yummies, margaritas and the mysterious Siberian. Monday Mexican Nights crank up the fiesta a notch or two.

Hotel Las Tortugas
HOTEL $$$

(☑ 2653-0423; www.lastortugashotel.com; d economy/standard US$160/180, apt US$250; P ❋ ☎ ❄) ✐ Local hero and granddad of Playa Grande, Louis Wilson was instrumental in the designation of the national park. Abutting the beach, his hotel is carefully designed to keep ambient light away from the turtle-nesting area. Rooms are modest, but they're only about 15 steps from the waves. Apartments (500m inland) offer more space and amenities, including kitchenettes and private porches.

✖ Eating & Drinking

Taco Star
MEXICAN $

(tacos US$3; ☺ 9am-6pm Tue-Sun) Three words: beachfront taco stand. Hefty beef and veggie tacos and fresh fruit *batidos* (shakes) will sustain you for a full day of sun and surf. Can't beat it.

Cafe Del Pueblo
ITALIAN $$$

(☑ 2653-2315; mains US$10-22; ☺ 5-10pm Mon-Sat) Just east of town, this open-air Italian restaurant is a gem. Thin-crust pizzas get good reviews, and regulars rave about the innovative seafood preparations, tender steaks and homemade pasta dishes. Dine under the stars on the patio. Reservations recommended on weekends.

Kike's Place
BEER GARDEN

(☑ 2653-0834; ☺ noon-10pm) For nightlife on the northern end of Playa Grande, Kike's is the only game in town. Order the local catch of the day from the blackboard until 10pm, or hang out playing pool and watching odd (and old) movies under the array of international flags above the bar. A bit more Tico flavor than your hotel bar, for sure.

ⓘ Information

Playa Grande Clinic (☑ 2653-2767, 24hr emergency 8827-7774; www.facebook.com/pgclinic; ☺ Mon-Fri) If you get rolled too hard in the surf and need a doctor, find this clinic next to Kike's Place.

ⓘ Getting There & Away

The Santa Cruz bus (516) to and from the coastal towns stops at Playa Grande twice daily, at 7am and 3pm, but the road is paved so it's also an easy drive.

Alternatively, catch a boat across the estuary from Tamarindo to the southern end of Grande (around US$2 per person, from 7am to 4pm). From Playa Grande arrange your boat to Tamarindo at Hotel Bula Bula (p299) or just pop up on the beach – the boatmen will see you. Note: three tourists have been attacked and one surfer lost his lower leg to a croc in the estuary – take the boat and don't try crossing on the cheap.

Playa Tamarindo
POP 6400

If Patrick and Wingnut from the 1994 surfing movie *Endless Summer II* surfed a time machine to present-day Tamarindo, they'd fall off their boards. A quarter century of hedonism has transformed the once-dusty burg into 'Tamagringo', whose perennial status as Costa Rica's top surf and party destination has made it the first and last stop for legions of tourists.

Despite its party-town reputation, Tamarindo offers more than just drinking and surfing. It forms part of Parque Nacional Marino Las Baulas de Guanacaste, and the beach retains an allure for kids and adults alike. Foodies will find some of the best restaurants in the country. There's a thriving market on Saturday mornings and fierce competition has kept lodging prices reasonably low. Its central location makes it a great base for exploring the northern peninsula.

🏃 Activities

Costa Rica Stand-Up Paddle Adventures
ADVENTURE SPORTS

(☑ 8780-1774; www.costaricasupadventures.com; board rental from US$30, lessons/tours US$85/155) Yoga classes on the ocean: here's your chance to do sun salutations on a stand-up paddleboard. If you prefer more traditional SUP activities – say, paddling – you can do that too. Lessons take place right on the beach at Nogui's, while tours go out to ride the surf or explore the flat waters of the estuaries.

Ser Om Shanti Yoga Studio
YOGA

(☑ 8591-6236; www.seryogastudio.com; Plaza Tamarindo, 2nd floor; classes from US$15) There's a full schedule of daily hatha and Vinyasa yoga classes, as well as Pilates and restorative yoga. It all takes place in a bright, airy studio on the top floor of Plaza Tamarindo.

E-Bike Costa Rica
MOUNTAIN BIKING

(☑ 8458-7963; www.ebikecostarica.com; rental per day/week US$40/200; ☺ 8am-6pm) Well, some days you don't feel like pedaling. No problem! You can hire electric bikes and skateboards here that operate with a few flicks of the wrist, and travel up to 70km on one battery charge. Don't forget the helmet, though.

Located below Om Shanti yoga studio, and next to El Niño Parque.

Surfing

Like a gift from the surf gods, Tamarindo is often at its best when neighboring Playa Grande is flat. The most popular wave is a medium-sized right that breaks directly in front of the Tamarindo Diria hotel. The waters here are full of virgin surfers learning to pop up. There is also a good left that's fed by the river mouth, though be advised that crocodiles are occasionally sighted here, particularly when the tide is rising (which is, coincidentally, the best time to surf). There can be head-high waves in front of the rocks near El Be. More advanced surfers will appreciate the bigger, faster and less crowded waves at neighboring beaches: Playa Langosta, on the other side of the point; Playas Avellanas, Negra and Junquillal to the south; and Playa Grande to the north.

There are countless surf schools offering lessons and board rental in Tamarindo. Surf lessons hover at around US$45 for 1½ to two hours, and most operators will let you keep the board for a few hours beyond that to practice.

★ **Iguana Surf**   SURFING

(☑ 2653-0613; www.iguanasurf.net; board rental per day US$20, group/semiprivate/private lessons US$45/65/80; ☺ 8am-6pm) Iguana Surf has been giving lessons for some 25 years, so they probably know what they're doing. Excellent for couples, families or anyone really. The two-hour lesson includes a rash guard and locker, in addition to the surfboard. After your lesson, all gear is half-price.

Learn Improve Surf Company   SURFING

(☑ 8316-0509; www.learnimprovesurfcompany.com; lessons per person US$70) Edgar Sanchez wants to teach you how to surf. This upstart company excels at offering instruction for all ages and abilities. It also takes more advanced wave riders on surf tours to Playa Avellanas and Playa Grande.

Matos Surf Shop   SURFING

(☑ 2653-0845; www.matossurfshop.com; Sunrise Commercial Center; board rental per day US$10; ☺ 8am-7pm) In addition to giving lessons and renting boards, this place also offers surf photography and video (in case you wanted to star in your own version of *Endless Summer*). Tamarindo's cheapest rates for board rental and sales. There is another outlet in Playa Grande.

Kelly's Surf Shop   SURFING

(☑ 2653-1355; www.kellysurfshop.com; board rental per day/week US$20/120, group/semiprivate/private lessons US$50/65/90; ☺ 9am-6pm) One of the best surf shops in the area, Kelly's has a terrific selection of newish boards that it rents by the day or week. Premium boards cost a bit more. Staff are super informative, with lessons, advice and other recommendations to get you out on the waves. You can also rent bikes here.

Blue Trailz   SURFING

(☑ 2653-1705; www.bluetrailz.com; board rental per day US$15, group/semiprivate/private surf lessons US$45/60/80; ☺ 7am-7pm) Blue Trailz offers surf lessons, board rental and other more comprehensive surf packages. The experienced and amiable surf instructors come highly recommended. Good discounts are possible if you book ahead online. There's a hostel (p303) at the back, if you're inclined to stay after your lesson.

Witch's Rock Surf Camp   SURFING

(☑ 2653-1262; www.witchsrocksurfcamp.com; weeklong package from US$868; ☺ 6am-10pm) 🏄 Weeklong packages include lessons, board rental and a place to stay on the beach. Excursions to Witch's Rock and Ollie's Point are also available. *Endless Summer* surf legend Robert August shapes boards here.

Diving

Tamarindo is a surf town. But that doesn't mean there's nothing to see below the waves. Enticing dive sites in the vicinity include the nearby Cabo Velas and the Islas Catalinas.

Freedive Costa Rica   DIVING

(☑ 8353-1290; www.freedivecostarica.com; Plaza Conchal; free diving US$35-55, snorkeling US$55, spearfishing US$145; ☺ 9:30am-5:30pm) Owner Gauthier Ghilain claims free diving is 'the most natural, intimate and pure form of communion with the underwater world.' It requires no bulky gear and minimal training. He promises a safe and super-fun environment in which to learn how to explore the deep blue sea in new ways.

Tamarindo Diving   DIVING

(☑ 8583-5873; www.tamarindodiving.net; 2-tank dives US$110) It's called Tamarindo Diving, although trips actually depart from Playa

Playa Tamarindo

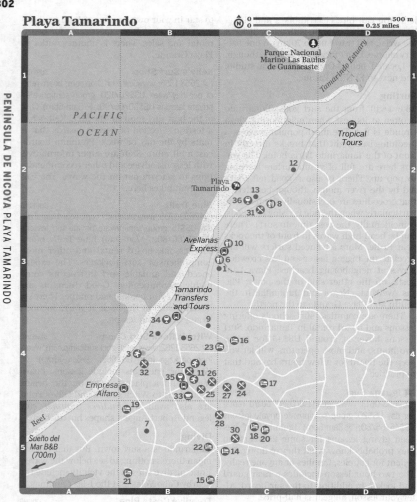

Flamingo and head out to the Islas Catalinas. (It's a trade-off: you'll spend more time on the road but less time on the boat motoring to your destination.) Turtles, dolphins and whales are often spotted from the boat, while eagle rays, sharks and manta rays are lurking below the surface.

⇨ Tours

There are tour agencies all around town, offering surf lessons of course, but also boat tours, canopy tours, snorkeling trips, ATV rentals, sea kayaking and stand-up paddling. Bike and board rental is also easy to find.

⎮ Sleeping

Tamarindo is packed with lodging options in all price ranges, including all manner of hostels, guesthouses and high-end resorts. The center can feel a bit oppressive, with crowded streets and nonstop heat, but it's not that hard to escape the hullabaloo by staying on the south side of town. Things quieten down pretty quickly when you leave the main drag. We list high-season rates; prices drop significantly during other times of year.

Tamarindo Backpackers HOSTEL $
(☎ 2653-1720; www.tamarindobackpackershos tel.com; dm US$15, d with/without bathroom

Playa Tamarindo

US$50/40; P❋@🖥🏊) This attractive yellow hacienda has a great vibe that welcomes all comers. Private rooms (mostly with shared bathroom) are excellent value, with Spanish-tiled floors, mural-painted walls, beamed ceilings and flat-screen TVs. The dorms are quite clean but otherwise unspectacular. Outside, hammocks are strung in the tropical gardens and around a small pool. It's a five-minute walk to the beach.

Located just uphill from the Mini Pura Vida Hostel (*not* Pura Vida Hostel!)

La Botella de Leche　　　　HOSTEL $
(📞2653-0189; www.labotelladeleche.com; dm US$13-15, d US$50; P❋@🖥) With a relaxed vibe, this congenial spot – aka 'the Bottle of Milk' – is recommended for its warm and attentive management, plus air-conditioned rooms and dormitories. Stenciled walls pretty up the otherwise plain rooms. Facilities include a shared kitchen, surfboard racks, hammocks and a TV lounge.

Pura Vida Hostel　　　　HOSTEL $
(📞2653-2464; dm US$18-20, d with/without bathroom US$60/50; ❋@🖥) Inside this leafy compound are dorms and private rooms accented by trippy murals and mirrored mosaics. The vibe is friendly and super chill, especially in the common *rancho*, furnished with hammocks and rocking chairs. They sometimes organize open-mic nights, live music and fire shows in keeping with the *rockero*-themed

murals in the rooms. Free bikes and boards are available too. (This is not the Mini Pura Vida Hostel, the name of which is the result of an unpleasant business breakup.)

Blue Trailz Hostel　　　　HOSTEL $
(📞2653-1705; dm/r US$15/69; ❋@🖥) Across the street from the beach, this immaculate and intimate hostel is popular among the surfer set. Budget travelers appreciate the clean, cool dorms (with air-con) as well as the attentive service from the staff. Guests get reduced rates on boards, bikes, lessons and tours at the Blue Trailz (p301) surf shop out front. Sweet.

Hotel Mahayana　　　　HOTEL $$
(📞2653-1154; www.hotelmahayana.com; d US$65; P❋🖥) The Mahayana is a sweet retreat, away from the hustle and bustle of the main drag. Spotless, citrus-painted rooms are fitted with high ceilings, big windows and private terraces (with hammocks). The courtyard contains a small, cool pool and an outdoor kitchen, which is at your disposal.

Villas Macondo　　　　HOTEL $$
(📞2653-0812; www.villasmacondo.com; s/d/tr US$50/60/70, with air-con US$75/87/97, apt US$125-170; P❋@🖥🏊) Although it's only 200m from the beach, this establishment is an oasis of serenity in an otherwise frenzied town – it's also one of the best deals around. Beautiful modern villas with private

TAMARINDO'S LANGUAGE SCHOOLS

Use your vacation time wisely by learning Spanish. There are several language schools in Tamarindo, all of which offer weeklong intensive courses at various levels. Packages usually include 'homestay' accommodations with a Tico family. Here's a Tamarindo special: 'Spanish & Surf' packages that include language classes, surf lessons, accommodations and board rentals.

Coastal Spanish Institute (☑2653-2673; www.coastalspanish.com; per week from US$525) This Spanish school is located right on the beach in downtown Tamarindo (which may make it more difficult to concentrate on your grammar and vocabulary). It specializes in weekly surf and Spanish packages, which include 20 hours of Spanish classes and six hours of surf instruction, as well as board rental.

Instituto de Wayra (☑2653-0359; www.spanish-wayra.co.cr; per week from US$320; ⊙7am-5:30pm Mon-Fri, 10am-4pm Sun) A Spanish program that offers small class sizes and an immersive experience. The school recommends (and arranges) homestays so students have more opportunities to polish up their language skills.

hammocks and patios surround a solar-heated pool and tropical garden. Larger apartments are equipped with kitchens; ideal for families. Extra credit for naming it after Garcia-Marquez's fictional town.

Harry's El Escondite GUESTHOUSE $$
(☑8842-3419; www.esconditetamarindo.com; d/tr US$80/100; ❋🗧☒) Four attractive *cabinas* – with full kitchens and private patios – are arranged around a tropical garden with hammocks and a small swimming pool. Upstairs, guests share an open-air kitchen and sundeck. Free use of surfboards and bikes makes Harry a hero.

★ Beach Bungalows B&B $$$
(☑8800-0011; www.tamarindobeachbungalows.com; d incl breakfast US$214; ℗🗧☒) 🖉 Shaded by palms, these two-story teak bungalows feel like a luxurious retreat. In each bungalow, the upstairs is a rich yet rustic sleeping area, while the downstairs is an open-air poolside chill-out lounge. Guests enjoy a decadent breakfast, as well as free use of bikes, a gas grill and a common kitchen. Not exactly on the beach, but why quibble?

Ocho Artisan Bungalows BOUTIQUE HOTEL $$$
(☑8365-9666; www.ochoartisanbungalows.com; bungalow/casita $240/350; ℗❋🗧) A slice of paradise just a block off the main drag. Meander through the jungle-like grounds' inlaid wooden paths to any of seven bungalows (plus one *casita*) with pristine patios, or trundle over to the outdoor bar overlooking the beach. The stately and roomy habitations, comfortable for up to four, shine with newness; even the *mosquiteros* (mosquito nets) look fancy.

Tamarindo Bay Boutique Hotel BOUTIQUE HOTEL $$$
(☑2653-2692; www.tamarindobayhotel.com; d incl breakfast from US$125; ℗❋🗧☒) Here's a romantic getaway for grown-ups only, where contemporary design goes hand in hand with environmental consciousness. Slick modern rooms have king-size beds and rainforest showers. Bikes, snorkel gear and boogie boards are at your disposal. But our favorite feature is the swimming pool, complete with multicolored LED lighting and recycled plastic decking. The open-air breakfast terrace is a treat, too.

Hotel Luamey BOUTIQUE HOTEL $$$
(☑2653-1510; www.hotelluamey.com; d from US$150; ℗❋🗧☒) Simply exquisite, this boutique hotel is an oasis of serenity and beauty in the midst of Tamarindo chaos. Spacious *cabaña* suites are decorated in soothing earth tones, with dark wood furnishings, stone showers and private patios (where breakfast is served). Service is very accommodating. Yoga and surf classes offered.

Sueño del Mar B&B B&B $$$
(☑2653-0284; www.sueno-del-mar.com; d US$237, casitas US$277-367; ℗❋@🗧☒) This exquisite B&B on Playa Langosta is set in a stunning faux-dobe Spanish-style *posada*. The rooms have four-poster beds, artfully placed crafts and open-air garden showers, while the romantic honeymoon suite has a wraparound window with sea views.

There's private beach access beyond the pool and tropical garden, and a priceless, pervasive atmosphere of seclusion and beauty. No children allowed.

✖ Eating

★ **La Bodega** BREAKFAST, SANDWICHES $
(☎8395-6184; www.labodegatamarindo.com; Nahua Hotel; mains US$6-8; ⏰7am-3pm Mon-Sat; 🐕🍴♿) This delightful shop and cafe specializes in unique combinations of ingredients, focusing on whatever is fresh, local and organic. For breakfast, it does amazing things with eggs, while lunch is a daily changing menu of sandwiches and salads. Any time of day, you can't go wrong with its banana bread or lemon scones and a cup of fresh brewed java.

★ **Green Papaya** MEXICAN $
(☎2652-0863; www.facebook.com/Gr33nPapaya; mains US$5-10; ⏰11am-9pm Tue-Sun; ❄🐕🍴♿) Swing on up to the bar for a breakfast burrito or pull up a tree-stump stool to sample the fantastic fare. The mahi-mahi tacos are perfection in a tortilla, while non-meat-eaters will appreciate the multiple veggie options including enchiladas in creamy chipotle sauce. You'll go loco for the Chocolate Lovers dessert. Everything is funky, fresh and friendly – don't miss it.

Surf Shack BURGERS $
(☎2653-2346; www.facebook.com/surfshacktamarindo; mains US$5-10; ⏰11am-9pm Fri-Wed; 🐕) If you are craving a big bad burger, Surf Shack has you covered, with a good selection of patties, thick-cut onion rings and irresistible milkshakes. Tin-can walls and surfboard decor create a laid-back vibe, enhanced by the drinks coming from the bar. It's steps from the beach; the sea breeze is the perfect accompaniment to anything you order.

Nordico Coffee House CAFE $
(www.nordicocoffee.com; Plaza Tamarindo; US$5-8; ⏰7am-4pm Mon-Fri, 8am-3pm Sat) A Danish-Guatemalan couple have created this clean, well-lit place to eat and people-watch, towering above Tamarindo Plaza. The blue-and-white tiled walls, decorated with whale themes, shine brightly, and hip young staff are attentive. Smoothies, sandwiches and salads, sheltered from the sun in air-con coolness. Next to Ser Om Yoga Studio (p300).

Falafel Bar LEBANESE $
(☎2653-1268; www.facebook.com/tamarindofalafelbar; mains US$5-10; ⏰7am-10pm Wed-Mon; 🍴) When you get tired of *casados*, head to this Middle Eastern cafe for all the faves: shawarma, falafel, tabbouleh, hummus and kebabs. The pita bread is made fresh daily. Fresh juice and coffee in the morning; a real 'bar' at night.

Sprout INTERNATIONAL $$
(☎2653-2374; mains US$13-15; ⏰11am-10pm Mon-Sat; 🐕🍴♿) Sprout specializes in – wait for it – healthy food. Here, 'healthy' is a code word for fresh, nutritious and delicious, with a menu featuring giant salad bowls, veggie wraps and straight-out-of-the-surf seafood (including amazing fish tacos). Wash it down with a glass of organic wine or a 'Green Day' *batido* (spinach and mango flavor) and you'll be feeling fine.

Utopia FRENCH $$
(☎2275-4375, 7073-3584; ⏰5:30-10pm) Hervé is out to impress with dishes including creamy chicken vol au vent, *moules marinière* (mussels in white wine) and a passel of veggie dishes. But the pastry chef saves his best for last, with unholy black-and-white mousse and other delectables. Thursday is Latin night, with salsa and merengue dancing. It's next to Pura Vida Hostel (p303).

La Baula PIZZA $$
(☎2653-1450; www.facebook.com/PizzeriaLaBaula; mains US$12-16; ⏰5:30-10:30pm; 🍴♿) The best pie in Tamarindo, by some accounts. This casual open-air restaurant has 28 different pizzas with a wide variety of toppings, as well as salads. It's also one of the most family-friendly restaurants in town, with a playground to keep the kids entertained. The open-air, woodsy setting requires insect repellent.

Seasons by Shlomy MEDITERRANEAN $$$
(☎8368-6983; www.seasonstamarindo.com; Hotel Arco Iris; small plates US$8-12, mains US$18-20; ⏰6-10pm Mon-Sat; 🍴) Don't leave town without eating here. Israeli chef Shlomy offers a short list of carefully selected and perfectly prepared dishes. Depending on the availability of ingredients, you might start with grilled octopus or a lobster-leek terrine. Follow up with seared tuna in a honey and chili marinade or filet mignon in red-wine sauce. Perfection on a plate. Understated yet elegant, this mostly open-air restaurant also has some indoor seating and romantic poolside tables, and now offers a children's menu too. Reservations are recommended.

Dragonfly Bar & Grill ASIAN $$$
(☎2653-1506; www.dragonflybarandgrill.com; mains US$18-22; ⏰5:30-10pm Wed-Mon; 🅿🐕🍴) Beloved for its refined menu and its upscale tiki-bar atmosphere, this open-air dining room has twinkling lights and lanterns. The eclectic menu leans Asian, but fuses international elements. Go for the goodness-filled

Buddha Bowl or the fiery Thai beef served on glass noodles. Desserts such as *tres leches* (three-milk pudding) are also divine.

🍸 Drinking & Nightlife

The main drag in Tamarindo has the festive feel of spring break, with well-oiled patrons spilling out onto the beach, drinks in hand. Almost every hour is happy hour, all around you. If you're not sure where to start, go for sundowners at any bar on the beachfront strip – if you can wait that long.

★ Cafe Tico
CAFE

(📞 8861-7732; www.facebook.com/cafeticotamarindo; ⏰ 7am-3pm Mon-Sat, to 1pm Sun; 📶) Walk in. Take a deep breath. Smell the magic brewing? On the wall it says, 'good days start with coffee.' Sip it on the shady patio while snacking on a homemade pastry. *Pura vida*.

Sharky's
SPORTS BAR

(📞 8729-8274; www.sharkysbars.com; ⏰ 6pm-2am) If you want to catch the big game, look no further than Sharky's. Besides nine screens showing sports, there are burgers, wings and lots of beer. There's a nightly lineup of fun and games, including karaoke night on Tuesday and ladies' night on Saturday. The motto is '*un zarpe mas?*' (one last drink?). Get ready to get your drink on.

El Be!
BAR

(📞 2653-2637; ⏰ 10am-10pm) Formerly Le Beach Club, this place has changed languages (and added an exclamation point!) but the cool vibe remains the same. Lounge on beach beds or hammocks and listen to the DJ's sounds. Happy hour (4pm to 7pm) features drink specials, live jazz music and fabulous sunsets. It's not a bad option for food if you're feeling peckish.

ℹ️ TAMARINDO'S DRUG PROBLEM

Like a few other Tico beach towns with a young surfer crowd, Tamarindo has a bit of a nocturnal drug culture, a by-product of the country's place as a way station on the South America–North America trade route. The casual stroller will be approached with offers for drugs (and sometimes women) after the sun goes down. It's an annoyance at best; it's still illegal if you get caught with drugs, and in recent years more violence along the beaches has occurred relating to San José–based gangs moving in.

Volcano Brewing Company
BEER GARDEN

(www.volcanobrewingcompany.com; ⏰ 11am-10pm) Beer on the beach is never a bad thing, and when it's Tico home brew, even better. The 10 varieties of *cerveza* are a bit pricey, but consider the location. Stare into the Pacific over your plastic cup of Gato Malo (Bad Cat) stout – and you can order from El Vaquero restaurant next door. It's right next to Witch's Rock Surf Camp (p301).

ℹ️ Information

BAC San José (Plaza Conchal; ⏰ 9am-6pm Mon-Fri, to 1pm Sat)

Backwash Laundry (⏰ 8am-8pm Mon-Sat) Get your filthy unmentionables washed, dried and folded.

Banco de Costa Rica (Plaza Conchal; ⏰ 24hr) Twenty-four hour ATM.

Coastal Emergency Medical Service (📞 2653-1974, emergency 8835-8074; ⏰ 24hr)

ℹ️ Getting There & Away

Surfers and other beach party people flock to Tamarindo by air, bus and car. If you choose your lodgings wisely, there's no need for a car, as you can walk to the beach and book tours of other outings in the area.

AIR

The airstrip is 3km north of town; a hotel bus is usually on hand to pick up arriving passengers. During high season, **Sansa** (📞 2290-4100; www.flysansa.com; Tamarindo Airport) has three daily flights to and from San José (one way US$140), as does Nature Air (one way US$124). Nature Air has two flights from Liberia. If you book early or go for the promotional fares, you can get pretty good discounts on these prices.

BUS

The **Empresa Alfaro** (📞 2653-0268, 2222-2666; ⏰ 7:30am-5:30pm Mon-Sat, 9am-3:30pm Sun) office is near the beach, while other buses depart from the bus stop in front of Pacific Park.

Private shuttle buses offer a faster (albeit more expensive) option. **Tamarindo Shuttle** (📞 2653-0505; www.tamarindotransfersandtours.com; Centro Comercial Galerías del Mar) provides comfortable and convenient transfers from Tamarindo to destinations around the country, including both airports. **Tropical Tours** (📞 2640-0811, 2640-1900; www.tropicaltourshuttles.com) has daily shuttles that connect Tamarindo to San José, as well as to several destinations in the southern part of the Nicoya peninsula.

CAR & TAXI

By car from Liberia, take Hwy 21 to Belén, then Hwy 155 via Huacas to Tamarindo. A taxi costs about US$50 to or from Liberia.

BUSES FROM TAMARINDO

DESTINATION	COMPANY	PRICE (US$)	DURATION	DEPARTURES
Liberia	La Pampa	3	2½hhr	12 times per day 3:30am-6pm
San José	Alfaro	11	5½hr	3am & 5:30am
San José	Tralapa	11	5½hr	7am
Santa Cruz	Tralapa	2	1½hr	6am, 8:30am & noon

Amazingly, there's no gas station here. For that, you'll have to drive 15 paved kilometers to Huacas, hang a right and go up the hill. The gas station is 4km ahead, on the right.

❶ Getting Around

Here's a great service. **Avellanas Express** (one way/return US$6/12; ☺8am-5pm) runs a surf shuttle to area beaches. There are two different 'lines' from Tamarindo: the Blue Line goes back and forth to Playa Conchal; and the Green Line goes south to Avellanas and Negra. Based at Neptuno Surf Shop.

Playas Avellanas & Negra

These popular surfing beaches have some of the best, most consistent waves in the area, made famous in the surf classic *Endless Summer II*. The killer waves have led to one section being nicknamed 'Little Hawaii.'

Playa Avellanas is an absolutely stunning pristine sweep of pale golden sand. Backed by mangroves in the center and with two gentle hillsides on either end, it has plenty of room for surfers and sunbathers to have an intimate experience even when there are lots of heads in town.

Playa Negra is also undeniably romantic. Though the sand is a bit darker and the beach is broken up by rocky outcrops, gorgeous dusty back roads link tide pools of expat shredders who picked this place to exist (and surf) peacefully. Though there isn't much local soul here, the beach itself is a beaut.

🏃 Activities

The waves at Playa Avellanas are decent for beginners and intermediate surfers. Little Hawaii is the powerful and open-faced right featured in *Endless Summer II*, while the beach break barrels at low tide. Still, advanced surfers get bored here, so they go to Playa Negra, which is blessed by a world-class right that barrels. Further south is (hush hush) Playa Tortuga, an epic break for advanced surfers only. The waves are best between April and November, but start getting good in March.

Avellanas Surf School　　　　SURFING
(☎2653-1531; www.avellanas-surf-school.com; board rental per day US$20, lessons adult/child US$70/60; ☺8am-5pm) Mauricio Ortega is a local guy who loves to surf and wants to share his expertise and lifestyle with anyone who cares to partake. He and his wife Dialan run this highly rated surf school, and rent out a handful of cabins and villas close to the waves. Located next to Lola's (p309).

Playa Negra SUP Wave Riders　　SURFING
(☎8702-7894, 2652-9420; www.playanegrasup waveriders.com; lessons US$65-85, tours US$50-70) In less than two hours, you'll learn how to stand up and paddle, either by touring the flats of the local estuary or by heading out on the open ocean waves. If you already know what you're doing, rental boards are also available. ASI certified.

🛏 Sleeping

There's not really a village here – just a series of surf-oriented lodgings strung out along the road that connects the two beaches. That said, there's a nice range of sleeping options, from hippy surf camps to more sophisticated guesthouses and villas. If you prefer to sleep out under the stars, you'll find a few places to string a hammock or pitch a tent at the southern end of Playa Avellanas.

Casa Surf　　　　　　GUESTHOUSE $
(☎2652-9075; www.casa-surf.com; Playa Avellanas; dm per person US$15; ℗) 🏄 Casa Surf looks tropically terrific, with bamboo exterior and palm thatch roof. Inside, you'll find simple, clean rooms – brightly painted and fastidiously kept – with shared access to a bathroom and a kitchen. The upstairs hammock deck is an enticing place to spend an afternoon (or night). Also available: bike rental, book exchange and community guitar.

The casa offers an excellent-value surf, sleep and eat option (US$30), which includes two meals daily and surfboard rental.

NO-STRAW CHALLENGE

A Canadian boy living in Avellanas, Max Machum, was inspired to try to eliminate plastic drinking straws from restaurants when he heard the Leatherback Project's director describe how he had to remove a straw from a turtle's nose to save its life. His ambitious idea was picked up by Lola's on the Beach (p309), which invested in biodegradable, environmentally friendly straws, and by other local restaurants.

There's a national conversation in Costa Rica about how to eliminate plastics entirely – and it got its start here. You can spread the word and also specifically ask not to be given a straw when ordering drinks. More information is available on the 'No Straw Challenge' Facebook site.

Kon Tiki
HOSTEL **$**

(☑ 2652-9117; www.kontikiplayanegra.com; Playa Negra; r per person US$20; [P][🔊]) Along the road from Avellanas, this low-key and inviting place has a rambling collection of colorful cabins on stilts. In the middle of it all is a rickety pavilion where guests swing in hammocks and devour pizza and other affordable fare. Bathroom facilities are shared. It's popular with surfers and howler monkeys.

Peace Retreat
B&B **$$**

(www.peaceretreat.ca; Playa Negra; s/d US$80/100, without bathroom US$60/75; [P][🔊][🌊]) Sweet screened teak cabins are sprinkled around the jungly grounds, while additional rooms are perched above the central Casa Yoga. This is a place for relaxing and detoxing, rejuvenating and rejoicing. Morning yoga classes are open to the community. 'Retreat' packages are also available.

Las Avellanas Villas
APARTMENT **$$**

(☑ 2652-9212; www.lasavellanasvillas.com; Playa Avellanas; d/tr/q US$90/100/110, air-con supplement US$10; [P][❄][🔊]) Thoughtfully designed, these five stunning *casitas* are oases of tranquillity and balance, with private teak terraces, polished concrete floors, indoor greenery, open-air showers and large windows streaming with natural light. For practical matters, there are surfboard racks and hammocks (of course). Full kitchens make this option perfect for families or groups. The grounds are about 800m from the beach.

Café Playa Negra
GUESTHOUSE **$$**

(☑ 2652-9351; www.cafeplayanegra.com; Playa Negra; s/d/tr/q incl breakfast US$55/75/90/120; [P][❄][@][🔊][🌊]) These stylish, minimalist digs upstairs from the cafe have polished concrete floors and elevated beds, dressed with colorful bedspreads and other artistic touches. There's a groovy shared deck with comfy hammock chairs and an inviting swimming pool. The downstairs cafe, open all day, is worth a stop no matter where you are sleeping. Sample delectable sandwiches and super-fresh seafood.

Playa Negra Surf Lodge
CABINA **$$**

(☑ 2652-9270; www.playanegrasurflodge.com; Playa Negra; s/d/tr/q US$55/65/75/85, studio US$80, all incl breakfast; [❄][🔊][🌊]) The quaint *cabinas* here are set around a gorgeous tropical garden teeming with hummingbirds, butterflies and parakeets. Simple rooms have freshly painted walls and a few artistic details. Guests also have access to a shared terrace and plenty of hammocks. Don't skip out on lunch at the onsite Jalapeño Eatery & Market. Studios have private kitchens.

Hotel Mauna Loa
BUNGALOW **$$**

(☑ 2652-9012; www.hotelmaunaloa.com; Playa Avellanas; d/tr/q from US$90/120/140, kitchen-use supplement US$20-30; [P][❄][🔊][🌊]) This hip spot offers a straight shot to the beach. Paths lead from the gorgeous pool area through a lush garden to attractive podlike bungalows. Look for open-air showers and swaying hammocks outdoors, and pastel-brushed walls and comfy orthopedic beds indoors. Prepare meals in the communal kitchen or eat at the onsite Italian restaurant. It's closed from June to September.

✗ Eating

A legendary beach cafe that's named after a pig: that's the main eating destination in these surfer outposts. There are also some low-key markets and one renowned restaurant worth the trip into Negra.

Jalapeño Eatery & Market
MEXICAN **$**

(☑ 2652-9270; www.playanegrasurflodge.com Playa Negra; mains US$7-10; ⊙ 8am-4pm Mon-Sat) There's something special about this glorified taco bar. Ingredients are all organically produced or locally sourced. Tortillas are hand-rolled; hot sauce and other condiments are homemade; chickens and eggs come from the neighbor's farm. Even the fish is usually speared by the chef/owner. (So don't complain if it takes longer than you expected.)

Lola's on the Beach CAFE $$
(www.facebook.com/playaavellana; Playa Avellanas; mains US$6-12; ⊙11am-5pm Tue-Sun; P ⊛) Hang out at this stylish beach cafe while waiting for the waves. Slanted wood chairs are planted in the sand beneath thatched umbrellas. A tree-stump bar overlooks an open kitchen, where the beachy cuisine is tops. Kudos for their determined efforts to recycle cooking oils and not use any plastics (you'll get a groovy paper straw, if you ask).

In case you're wondering, Lola was an enormous and lovable pig, aka the 'Queen of Avellanas.' She has since passed, but her legacy lives on in 'little' Lolita!

Villa Deevena FUSION $$$
(☑2653-2328; www.villadeevena.com; Playa Negra; mains US$19-33; ⊙7am-10pm; P ⊛ ⊛) Foodies drive from all over Guanacaste to sample the fare at this hidden gem. It's worth the search for this otherworldly restaurant, the brainchild of chef Patrick Jamon (let the jokes begin: *jamon* means 'ham' in Spanish). Start with a fresh-fruit cocktail while you peruse the masterful menu: perfect preparations of seafood, slow-roasted meats and one-of-a-kind desserts. Reservations recommended.

The property also offers simple but elegant luxury at its minimalist two- to four-person bungalows (double occupancy US$124). Swish accommodations – decorated with hardwood and soothing tones – surround the glittering saltwater pool.

❶ Getting There & Away

BUS
There is no public transportation between Tamarindo and these beaches, though surf camps often organize trips. You can also catch a ride on the Avellanas Express (p307), which departs Tamarindo at 10am, 2pm and 5pm, with the first two shuttles going all the way to Playa Negra. To return to Tamarindo, the shuttle departs from Playa Negra at 11am and 3pm, and from Avellanas at 11:15am, 3:15pm and 6pm.

CAR
From Tamarindo, drive 5km inland to the village of Villareal, and turn right on to the dirt road. This road becomes progressively worse as you get further from Tamarindo and it usually requires a 4WD. If you're not coming from Tam-

arindo, drive west from Santa Cruz on the paved highway, through 27 de Abril to Paraíso, then follow the signs to the beach of your choice. As always, do not leave valuables in your car, especially at the beaches.

Playa Junquillal

Hard to pronounce and almost as difficult to find, Junquillal (say 'hoon-kee-yal') is a 2km-wide gray-sand wilderness beach that's absolutely stunning and mostly deserted. To the south, a dome boulder crumbles into a jutting rock reef and beyond that is a vast, 200-hectare estuary carved by the Río Nanda Mojo. To the north is a narrow rise of bluffs sprouting clumps of palm trees. Sunsets are downright surreal, with blinding golds, molten oranges and shocking pinks. The sea does swirl with fierce rip currents, however, and when it gets big, surfers descend from Negra. Even when the surf isn't high, it's dangerous out there. Don't let kids or even intermediate swimmers venture out alone.

With far more Ticos than tourists, Junquillal has an inviting authenticity unique in the northern peninsula. The nearest town is 4km inland at Paraíso.

🛏 Sleeping

El Castillo Divertido HOTEL $
(☑8351-5162, 2658-8428; www.castillodivertido.com; s US$20-30, d US$30-50; P ⊛) This colorful castle, decked out with crenellated walls and carved masks, is just 100m from the beach, offering panoramic views from its rooftop bar. Take advantage of the one-of-a-kind kayaking tours through the Río Nanda Moja and surrounding mangroves. On Friday nights, all guests are invited to partake of cold drinks and delicious grilled meat at a weekly sunset BBQ.

TURTLES

Olive ridley turtles nest in Junquillal from July to November, with a peak in numbers from August to October, but in smaller numbers than at the refuges; Junquillal is also an important nesting site for leatherbacks. Though the area is not officially protected, conservation groups such as **Asociacion Vida Verdiazul** (☑2658-7251; www.verdiazulcr.org; roundabout, Beach Rd) have teamed up with local communities to protect the nesting sites and eliminate poaching.

PENÍNSULA DE NICOYA PLAYA JUNQUILLAL

GUAITIL

An interesting excursion from Santa Cruz, Guaitil is a small potter community, where attractive ceramics are made from local clays, using earthy reds, creams and blacks in pre-Columbian Chorotega style. Ceramics are sold outside the potters' houses and also in San Vicente, 2km beyond Guaitil. If you ask, you can watch part of the potting process, and residents will be happy to give you a few lessons for a small fee. You might also find traditional foods, such as corn tamales and *rosquillos* (cheese rings), here.

★ **Mundo Milo Ecolodge**　　　BUNGALOW $$
(☏2658-7010; www.mundomilo.com; d incl breakfast US$67-77; P✿🖥️🐾) 🐾 Attention to detail is paramount at this unique ecolodge. Choose between three fan-cooled (or low-electric aircon), skylit bungalows, surrounded by lush vegetation and styled after a different world region (Africa, Mexico, Persia). The pool is an artful arc overlooking tropical woodland, with monkeys howling, birds chanting and waves crashing in the distance. Lieke, your hostess, is also a wonderful cook.

ℹ️ Getting There & Away

BUS

Buses depart from Junquillal to Santa Cruz (US$3, 1½ hours) at 6am, 9am, 12:30pm and 4:30pm; you can catch the bus anywhere along the main road. Buses from Santa Cruz to Junquillal depart from the Mercado Municipal at 5am, 10am, 2:30pm and 5:30pm.

CAR

If you're driving, it's about 16km by paved road from Santa Cruz to 27 de Abril, and another smooth 17km into town.

From Junquillal, it's possible to drive 35km south to Nosara via the legendary surf spot of Marbella. However, this is a very rough dirt road for 4WD only and it may be impassable in the rainy season. There are no gas stations on the coastal road and little traffic, so ask locally before setting out. It's easier to reach beaches south of Junquillal from Nicoya.

Santa Cruz

POP 12,300

A stop in Santa Cruz, a *sabanero* (cowboy) town typical of inland Nicoya, provides some local flavor missing from foreign-dominated beach towns. Unfortunately, there aren't any attention-worthy sights, so most travelers' experience of Santa Cruz consists of changing buses. However, the town is an important regional administrative center, and a good base for visiting Guaitil. At certain times of the year you can also witness the Guanacaste bull-riding tradition in the city's bullring. In Costa Rica, the bull is never killed, but brave (or foolhardy!) citizens take their chances dodging them.

In 1993, about three central city blocks burned to the ground in a devastating fire. An important landmark is the vacant-lot-looking field known as Plaza de Los Mangos, which was once a large grassy square with mango trees. Soon after the fire, the attractive and shady Parque Bernabela Ramos opened 400m south of Plaza de Los Mangos.

🛏️ Sleeping

Hotel La Pampa　　　HOTEL $
(☏2680-0586; Av 5 btwn Calles 2 & Central; s/d from US$36/40; P✿🖥️🐾) A good budget option, this peach-tinted hotel is 50m west of the Plaza de Los Mangos. It isn't all that inspiring from the outside, but the rooms are clean and modern, providing a decent place to lay your head.

La Calle de Alcalá　　　HOTEL $$
(☏2680-1515, 2680-0000; www.hotellacallede alcala.com; Av 7 btwn Calles 1 & 3; s/d/ste US$58/77/140; P✿🖥️🐾) With its stucco arches and landscaped garden around a pool, this hotel gets points for design. Carved wooden doors open into small tiled rooms with rattan furnishings. It's one block due east of the bus terminal; a convenient stopover option.

ℹ️ Getting There & Away

Santa Cruz is 57km from Liberia and 25km south of Filadelfia on the main peninsular highway. A paved road leads 16km west to 27 de Abril, from where dirt roads continue to Playa Tamarindo, Playa Junquillal and other beaches. There's a gas station off the main intersection with the highway.

CENTRAL PENINSULA

Nicoya

POP 16,100

A hub between the beaches and ranches, the big cities and *pueblitos,* Nicoya (23km south of Santa Cruz) offers a blast of Tico time.

Truckers, road-trippers and locals converge around a grid, packed with commerce and crowned with a gorgeous *iglesia* (church) that makes the leafy Parque Central worth a loiter. That said, there's no reason to linger longer than you need to. Nicoya is not fabulous. Just real.

One theory has it that Nicoya was named after an indigenous Chorotega chief, Nicoa, who welcomed Spanish conquistador Gil González de Ávila in 1523 (a gesture he regretted). A second theory is that it derives from the Nahuatl words *necoc iāuh*, meaning 'on both sides is water(s),' describing the town's location between two rivers. Regardless, following Avila's arrival, the Chorotega were wiped out by the colonists, though many Nicoyans still proudly claim their indigenous heritage.

🛌 Sleeping & Eating

Mundiplaza Hotel HOTEL **$**
(☎2685-3535; Calle 3; s/d US$30/40; ❄ 🛜) Located right in the center of Nicoya, this is a perfectly pleasant place to spend the night. With colorful paint jobs (a few could use some touching up) and tile bathrooms, it's relatively clean and well maintained. The shared balcony has striking views to the Nicoya hills, though the road noise can be excessive.

Hotel Curime Resort HOTEL **$**
(☎2685-5238; d from US$40; 🅿❄🛜🏊) This unexpected nature resort is a surprise in gritty Nicoya, though there's little reason to overnight here. The lodgings are in run-down but pleasant bungalows, scattered about 3.5 acres of unkempt grounds. The place has an Olympic-sized pool and other underwhelming sporting facilities. Located about 1km southeast of Nicoya proper, just off Ruta 150.

Cafe Daniela SODA **$**
(☎2686-6148; www.facebook.com/cafedaniela; Calle 3; mains US$6-10; ⊙7am-9pm Mon-Sat; ✍) A popular *soda* (cheap lunch counter) serving appetizing *comida típica* (typical local food) such as *gallo pinto* (stir-fry of rice and beans) in the morning, and fish, beef, chicken and veggie *casados* (set meals) later on. All served in bright tiled environs.

❶ Information

Banco de Costa Rica (Calle Central; ⊙8:30am-3pm Mon-Fri)

Banco Popular (Calle 3; ⊙9am-4:30pm Mon-Fri, 8:15-11:30am Sat) Also has a 24-hour ATM at Hospital La Anexión.

THE NICOYA DIET

Minnesota-born author Dan Buettner has garnered attention in recent years with his study of the earth's 'blue zones': areas where people tend to live longer and healthier lives than anywhere else. He's written three books on the subject, including *The Blue Zones Solution: Eating and Living Like the World's Healthiest People* (2015). Among these long-lived groups are the residents of Costa Rica's Nicoya peninsula. Buettner has broken the Blue Zone lifestyle into nine key components, diet only comprising a part of it. Also crucial to longevity, he claims, are exercise, faith, community and friendship.

But the diet is significant, and in the traditional Nicoyan intake, which includes yams, squash, bananas and beans, carbohydrates may make up as much as 68% of a Nicoyan's daily calories. Buettner points out that the 'three sisters' of traditional Central American agriculture – beans, corn and squash – are alive and well in Tico cooking today. Factor in that Nicoyans, before preparing their customary tortillas, soak their corn kernels in lime, extracting more calcium and amino acids from the corn – and that means the staple morning platter, the *gallo pinto* of rice, beans, cheese, guacamole and tortilla (sometimes with egg) is an amazingly well-rounded meal.

Among the top 'longevity foods' of Nicoya, according to Buettner, are the maize *nixtamal* (cornmeal soaked in lime), *ayote* (squash), papaya, yams, black beans, bananas and *pejivalle* (peach palms, pronounced 'pay-hee-vall-yay'). You can find freshly roasted *pejivalle* along many roadside stands – Costa Ricans like to eat them salted or with a dollop of mayonnaise. As a genetic blueprint, Nicoyans also have a strong dose of indigenous Chorotega blood, mixed with that of freed African slaves and Spaniards, and get a high dose of Vitamin D on this torrid, sunny peninsula, the waters of which have the highest calcium content in the country.

Nicoya: live long and prosper.

BUSES FROM NICOYA

DESTINATION	COMPANY	COST (US$)	DURATION	DEPARTURES
Liberia	Transportes La Pampa	2.60	2hr	every 30-60min, 7am-8:30pm
Playa Nosara	Empresa Traroc	3	2hr	4:45am, 10am, 12:30pm, 3:30pm & 5:30pm Mon-Sat. No early bus Sun
Sámara & Playa Carrillo	Empresa Traroc	3.60	1½hr	10 daily, 6am-8pm
San José	Empresa Alfaro	7.50	5hr	5 daily

Hospital La Anexión (☑ 2685-8400; ⊘ 24hr) The peninsula's main hospital is on the north side of Nicoya.

❶ Getting There & Away

Most buses arrive at and depart from the **bus terminal** (Calle 5) southeast of Parque Central.

Parque Nacional Barra Honda

Parque Nacional Barra Honda is situated about halfway between Nicoya and the mouth of the Río Tempisque. The main attraction of this inland park is a massive underground system of caverns composed of soft limestone, carved by rainfall and erosion over a period of about 70 million years. Speleologists have discovered more than 40 caverns, some reaching as far as 200m deep, though to date only 19 have been fully explored. There have also been discoveries of pre-Columbian remains dating to 300 BC.

In addition to the caverns, there's a plethora of wildlife around. More than 80 bird species have been sighted, as well as large bat populations, anteaters and armadillos.

◉ Sights

Parque Nacional Barra Honda Caverns　　　　　　　CAVE
(☑ 2659-1551; adult/child US$12/2, guided tour incl park admission US$29; ⊘ trails 8am-4pm, caverns to 1pm) This 23-sq-km national park protects a system of some 40 caverns. The only cave with regular public access is the 41m-deep La Terciopelo, which has incredible speleothems (calcite figures that rise and fall in the cave's interior). It's quite the underground art museum. Stalagmites, stalactites and a host of beautiful formations have evocative names such as fried eggs, organ, soda straws, flowers and shark's teeth. Call the ranger station one day in advance to arrange the four-hour guided tour.

🏃 Activities

While **wildlife-watching** underground in the park's caverns, you'll have the chance to see such fun-loving creatures as bats, albino salamanders, blind fish and a variety of squiggly invertebrates. On the surface, howler and white-faced monkeys, armadillos, *pizotes* (coatis), kinkajous and white-tailed deer are regularly spotted, as are striped hog-nosed skunks and anteaters.

The Barra Honda hills have a few well-marked **hiking** trails through deciduous, dry tropical forest. Before or after visiting the cave, you can hike 3.5km to the top of Cerro Barra Honda, which has a *mirador* (lookout point) with a view of Río Tempisque and Golfo de Nicoya. You won't need a guide to hike the trails.

❶ Getting There & Away

To reach Barra Honda by public transportation, take a bus from Nicoya to Santa Ana (US$3.50, twice daily except Sunday), which will get you within striking distance (about 1km away). Alternatively, take a taxi from Nicoya for about US$20 round trip. You can arrange for your driver to pick you up at a specified time.

If you have your own vehicle, take the peninsular highway south out of Nicoya toward Mansión and make a left on the access road leading to Puente La Amistad. From here, continue another 1.5km and make a left on the signed road to Barra Honda. The dirt road will take you to the village of Barra Honda then wind to the left for another 6km, passing Santa Ana, before ending at the national-park gate. The road is clearly marked, and there are several signs along the way indicating the direction of the park. After the village of Barra Honda, the road is unpaved, but in good condition.

If you are coming to the park from Puente La Amistad, you will see the access road to Barra Honda signed about 16km after leaving the bridge.

Nosara Area

Nosara is a cocktail of international surf culture, stunning backroad topography, expat mayhem and yoga bliss. Here, three stunning beaches are stitched together by a network of swerving, rutted roads that meander over coastal hills and kiss the coast just west of the small village of Nosara. Inland are remnant pockets of luxuriant vegetation that attract birds and other wildlife. The area has seen little logging, partly because of the nearby wildlife refuge, but a newly paved access road (in process at the time of research) will likely lead to more development and visitors.

The area is spread out, so your own wheels are a plus. Eight kilometers inland, Nosara is where you'll find gas, as well as the airport. Most accommodations and restaurants are in Playa Pelada and Playa Guiones. Many unidentified little roads make it hard to navigate: for a handy map visit the website of Nosara Travel (p317).

◉ Sights

Playa Garza   BEACH
From the south, the first beach you'll hit is Playa Garza, still a sleepy Tico fishing village with an arc of pale brown sand, and headlands on either side of the rippling bay. Fishing boats bob offshore and there's a point break to the north side. There are a few *cabinas* and *sodas* here, lots of sand space, and precious few tourists.

Playa Guiones   BEACH
Playa Guiones is quite simply a sip of raw nectar: a wide, generous arc of marbled sand, with a few pebbles and shells mixed in, excellent beach breaks and plenty of space. It's an easygoing place for surfers, surf dogs and surf babies – you might just see unattended strollers lodged in the wet sand at low tide. This is Nosara's most developed beach.

Playa Pelada   BEACH
North of Guiones, Playa Pelada is rough and rugged, and less endowed with surfers and luxury (perhaps a luxury in itself). Things feel both spookier and more profound in Pelada. This beach lacks surf, so it's wonderful for children. It also has sheared-away boulders tumbling into a foaming sea, two alluring beachside restaurants and a fishing-village intimacy that Guiones lacks.

Refuge for Wildlife   ANIMAL SANCTUARY
(☑2682-5049, 8708-2601; www.refugeforwildlife. com; Nosara; per person US$50; ☉by appoint-

ment) Make an appointment to visit this animal rescue center. Brenda Bombard is an incurable animal lover who has devoted two decades to caring for injured and abandoned howler monkeys. Two-hour tours are highly educational, sharing information about the habits of howler monkeys and the center's efforts to rescue and release them (with an impressive 85% success rate). Volunteer opportunities available. As the refuge isn't open to the public without an appointment, they will contact you with directions once your appointment is made.

Sibu Sanctuary   ZOO
(☑8413-8889; www.sibusanctuary.org; US$65; ☉tours 10:30am) Reservations are absolutely required to visit this wildlife sanctuary, set on 50 glorious acres of jungle and garden. The sanctuary is dedicated to rescuing, rehabilitating and eventually releasing howler monkeys who have been injured or abandoned. The educational visits include some time with the primates, as well as a guided tour of the grounds. The fee supports the good work of this private center.

Sibu Sanctuary is located in the village of Santa María, due west of Nosara village.

Reserva Biológica Nosara   NATURE RESERVE
(☑2682-0035; www.lagartalodge.com; US$10, private tour US$25; ☉8am-4pm, guided tours 6:30am & 3pm) The private 35-hectare reserve behind Lagarta Lodge (p315) has trails leading through a mangrove wetland down to the river and beach. Stop in the Lagarta lobby to pick up a map of a two-hour self-guided tour. This is a great spot for birding, reptile-spotting and other wildlife-watching. Boat tours of the mangroves are also available. Access is free to Lagarta guests.

⚹ Activities

Playa Ponies   HORSEBACK RIDING
(☑2682-5096; www.playaponies.org; Playa Pelada; 1hr/2hr/half-day tours US$40/55/100; ⊕) Carrie and Neno want to take you riding on jungly trails and windswept beaches, with special routes designed for families with children. From the 'five corners' of Pelada, head north 500m on Hwy 160, than turn left. Alternatively, they can meet you at the Mobil station.

Tica Massage   SPA
(☑2682-0096; www.ticamassage.com; Playa Guiones; massages US$40-100; ☉9am-5pm) After a hard day of surfing, treat yourself to a spa treatment at Tica Massage, in the Heart of Guiones Wellness Center. Services cater

especially to surfers; or opt for a foot massage, a face massage or an invigorating 'Sea Glow' massage.

Miss Sky
TOURS

(☑2682-0969; www.missskycanopytour.com; Nosara; adult/child 5-12yr US$75/50; ⊙tours 8am & 1:30pm) Miss Sky's ziplines run from mountainside to mountainside above a pristine private reserve. If you can keep your eyes open, you'll be rewarded with glorious views of forest, sea and sky.

Surfing

Safari Surf
SURFING

(☑2682-0113, from US or Canada 866-433-3355; www.safarisurfschool.com; Olas Verdes Hotel, Playa Guiones; 1-week packages from US$1580; ⊙7am-6pm) This all-inclusive surf school offers one-week packages, complete with lodging, meals, surf lessons and gear, as well as some extra activities (depending on the package). Different packages cater to budget travelers and women, in addition to the 'signature' Tortuga package. The quality of surf instruction is universally praised.

Coconut Harry's
SURFING

(☑2682-0574; www.coconutharrys.com; Playa Guiones; board rental per day US$15-20, lessons adult/child US$55/45; ⊙8am-5pm) At the main intersection in Guiones, this popular surf shop offers top-notch private lessons, as well as board rental and stand-up paddleboard rental. Conveniently, there's a second location near the main break at Playa Guiones.

Juan Surfo's Surf Shop
SURFING

(☑2682-1081; www.surfocostarica.com; Playa Guiones; board rental per day US$15-20, lessons per hour US$45; ⊙8am-6pm) Juan Surfo is a highly recommended Tico surf teacher who gives lessons at Playa Guiones. His shop offers the regular rentals, transportation and surf tours, as well as some rooms for rental at the nearby Surf Lodge. Located on the northern loop road, 200m from the beach.

Yoga

Pilates Nosara
YOGA

(☑8663-7354; www.pilatesnosara.com; Playa Guiones; per person from US$15; ⊙8am-2pm) Now located in a beautiful studio at Bodhi Tree (p315), this school offers Pilates mat and reformer classes (six daily during the high season), as well as teacher training and retreats. Turn off from the first Guiones access road.

Nosara Wellness
YOGA

(☑2682-0360; www.nosarawellness.com; Playa Pelada; classes US$14, private sessions from US$60) This wellness center in Pelada offers everything from massage and acupuncture to pilates and yoga. If that's all too mainstream for you, sign up for a session of aerial yoga, which promises to 'realign you from the compression of gravity.' Located just off the main road (Ruta 160) connecting Nosara to Play Pelada and northern points.

🛏 Sleeping

The main access roads to Playa Guiones are lined with hostels, hotels, guesthouses and more. Some of the Playa Pelada options are up in the hills, away from the beach. Prices outside of high season can be 20% lower or better, as in much of the country.

★ 4 You Hostal
HOSTEL $

(☑2682-1316; www.4youhostal.com; Playa Guiones; dm/s/d/bungalow US$20/34/44/60; P ❄ �🛜) A fantastic hostel close to the Guiones action. The high-end minimalist design makes this evolutionary flophouse (read: dorm) feel luxurious. Within the dorm are three pods that have walls that don't quite reach the soaring ceiling, allowing for extra privacy. Decked out with Balinese furniture and plenty of hammocks, not to mention a spotless community kitchen and rooftop terrace. Located on the north beach-access road, just before it intersects with Ruta 160, the main Nosara-Pelada road.

Nosara Beach Hostel
HOSTEL $

(☑2682-0238; www.facebook.com/nosara-beach-hostel; Playa Guiones; dm/d/d with air-con US$20/65/80; ❄🛜) 🅿 Lounge in a hammock on the breezy porch, overlooking the iguana-filled gardens, just steps from the surf. You have a stone shower to wash away the sand and a comfy wooden bunk to crash on. There's a big communal kitchen, a spacious TV room and – bonus – foosball. The vibe is super chill.

★ Villa Mango B&B
B&B $$

(☑2682-1168; www.villamangocr.com; Playa Pelada; s/d/tr/q incl breakfast US$84/96/113/130, air-con US$10; P ❄ 🛜 🏊) At this B&B in the trees set high on a hillside with views of both bays, you can't help but relax. The seven spacious rooms have a Mediterranean flair, with gorgeous views and rustic stone and wood details. Lounge on the luxurious terrace, swim in the saltwater pool or take a short stroll down to the isolated stretch of beach.

The owner, Agnes, is delightful. Reserve in advance during high season.

Bodhi Tree
HOTEL $$

([phone]2682-0256; www.bodhitreeyogaresort.com; Playa Guiones; dm from US$97; [P][*][@][*]) Set on a lush hillside, this yoga resort is traversed by a gurgling river, complete with waterfall. The setting is gorgeous and serene – perfect for reconnecting with your breath, your body and the nature around you. The most affordable accommodations are simple, offering comfortable beds and ample storage space, as well as shared bathrooms with stone sinks and open-air showers. Yoga classes are held in a magnificent open-air studio with 360 degrees of canopy views. All rates include one daily class. Free electric shuttles and bikes to town, and the popular juice bar and restaurant are open to nonguests.

Green Sanctuary
GUESTHOUSE $$

([phone]8320-9822; www.hotelgreensanctuary.com; Playa Guiones; d/tr incl breakfast US$95/111; [*][@][*]) It's a 700m hike to the beach, but that's the only complaint about this spot in the woods. A stone path winds through the trees, connecting units made from old cargo containers; each has a private terrace, complete with hammock, and is surprisingly private. Take the southernmost access road from the beach and head all the way up the hill.

★ Costa Rica Yoga Spa
LODGE $$$

([phone]in USA 888-533-6461, 2682-0192; www.costaricayogaspa.com; Nosara; dm from US$165, additional person US$149, ste from US$279; [P][@]) 🖋 This gorgeous mountaintop retreat takes care of all of the details, providing delightful accommodations, gourmet vegetarian meals (included), yoga classes and transportation to the beach. The most affordable lodging is in shared rooms – with two bunkbeds, they offer less privacy, but still feature teak furniture, polished concrete floors and balconies with rewarding views. About 5km north of Nosara village. Take a *tuk-tuk* to get here if you don't have your own wheels.

Lagarta Lodge
LODGE $$$

([phone]2682-0035; www.lagartalodge.com; Playa Pelada; ste US$390-499; [P][*][@][*]) 🖋 Completely transformed by a recent renovation, 'the Lizard' now offers 26 stunning suites overlooking the ocean and rivers, at the northern end of Pelada. The balcony restaurant is worth a visit just for the spectacular sea and sunset views. One night here might cost what your plane ticket did, but you'll never forget it, either. The owners make an effort to contribute to local community education, and the onsite art gallery is dedicated to the indigenous Maleku people. The adjacent Reserva Biologica Nosara (p313) is free for guests to wander, and the onsite spa and restaurant ensconce you further in the lap of luxury.

Living Hotel & Spa
BOUTIQUE HOTEL $$$

([phone]2682-5201; www.livinghotelnosara.com; Playa Guiones; d incl breakfast with/without bathroom US$165/95; [P][*][@][@][*]) Relax amid the simplicity and serenity of this tropical paradise. Pristine white rooms have tile floors, shiny wood ceilings and pretty stenciled walls. Tropical gardens surround the sparkling swimming pool, with plenty of communal space in the thatch-roof *rancho*. Located on the north beach access road.

Refresh your palate with a fresh-squeezed juice or some other healthy treat from Jasmine's Cafe (p316); refresh your mind and muscles with something from the full menu of spa treatments.

L'Acqua Viva Hotel & Spa
HOTEL $$$

([phone]2682-1087, in Canada 1-877-216-0181, toll-free in USA 1-888-273-1977; www.lacquaviva.com; r US$180, ste US$270-300; [P][*][@][*]) One of the most luxurious resorts in the central peninsula. Inside and out, the property is stunning, with water, wood and bamboo features throughout. The 36 contemporary rooms are decorated in minimalist style with all the five-star amenities you'd expect. Yet we do have one complaint: in a no-man's land between Guiones and Pelada, it's too far from the beach.

It's 100m south of the turnoff to Pelada.

Nosara Suites
HOTEL $$$

([phone]2682-0087, 2682-1036; www.nosarasuites.com; Playa Guiones; d US$130-150; [P][*][@][*]) Clearly the designer was given free rein in these six swish suites, which feature glass-floored lofts, floating staircases and plenty of original artwork. Also enjoy the king-size beds and rain showers. It's set upstairs from Cafe de Paris, a local landmark. Unfortunately, the location on the main road is sometimes noisy.

✖ Eating

Robin's Cafe & Ice Cream
CAFE $

([phone]2682-0617; www.robinsicecream.com; Playa Guiones; mains US$6-8, ice cream US$2-4; ⊙8am-5pm Mon-Sat, 10am-4pm Sun; [@]🖋) Perfectly suited to Nosara's health-conscious yogis and surfers. You'll see Robin working the kitchen, preparing a welcome menu of sweet and savory crepes, tempting wraps, and sandwiches on homemade, whole-wheat focaccias. If you must indulge your sweet tooth (trust us, you must), the ice cream is sublime. On the road to the beach in 'downtown' Nosara.

Seekretspot
GELATO $

(☑ 2682-1325; Playa Pelada; ice cream US$3-6; ⊙hours vary; ☏) The secret is out: come to this sweet shack for an authentic gelato or *sorbetto*, made with love by Stefano and Frederica. For local flavor, go for coffee or coconut. If you need a pick-me-up, there are also fresh-brewed espresso drinks. Perfectly situated on your way back to Nosara from Playa Pelada, with a second location in Guiones, in case you miss the first.

Rosi's Soda Tica
SODA $

(☑ 2682-0728; Playa Guiones; mains US$3-6; ⊙8am-3pm Mon-Sat) Now with two prominent locations, this is the favorite *soda* in Guiones and it's a damn good one. It's a perfect spot for breakfast, whether it's banana pancakes or huevos rancheros. At lunchtime, Rosi keeps it real with *casados* (set menus) and the like. It takes time, but you can't rush perfection. The 'downtown' location is on the main drag.

Jasmine's Cafe
VEGETARIAN $

(Living Hotel; mains US$7-12; ⊙7am-4pm; ☝) Plant-based nutritional yumminess in a cool little shack next to Living Hotel (p315), and you might even get a banjo serenade from the juicer. Noodle salads, veggie *patacones* (fried green plantains) and a couple of different veggie burgers round out the food menu while drinks like the Free Green (kale, cacao nibs, almond milk) will power you through your Nosara day.

Burgers & Beers
BURGERS $$

(Peje; ☑ 2682-5558; www.facebook.com/burgersandbeerscr; Playa Guiones; mains US$14-16; ⊙noon-10pm; ☏☝) Take your pick from six burgers and you'll get a plump, juicy patty of goodness, served on a fresh bun with big french-fry wedges. There's also a veggie burger and fish of the day, as well as a dozen craft beers on tap. Located on the north beach-access road.

El Chivo
MEXICAN $$

(☑ 2682-0887; www.elchivo.co; Playa Pelada; mains US$12-20; ⊙11am-10pm) A groovy roadside joint in the middle of the Pelada wilderness. Tacos are a favorite – try the house specialty, the buttery chipotle-lime shrimp version. Like any upstanding Mexican place, bargain Taco Tuesday is mandatory.

But there's also chimichurri-style steak and gut-busting 'wet' burritos (with cheese/sour cream) and a long list of tequilas and local beers, set among skull-and-wrestling-mask decor.

Al Chile
MEXICAN $$

(Main St, Playa Guiones; mains US$12-14; ⊙11am-10pm) Fresh ingredients, friendly staff and amazing Tico-Mex served under the inviting shade of a *palapa*. A taco combo platter allows you to sample three different varieties, and spice lovers *must* try the homemade five-chili salsa. Zingy hibiscus-and-ginger *frescas* are on tap (add a dash of vodka if you like), and you can finish with a churro or caramelized banana. It's part of the Sunset Shack hotel.

Beach Dog Café
CAFE $$

(☑ 2682-1293; www.facebook.com/beachdogcafe; Playa Guiones; lunch mains US$6-10, dinner mains US$12-15; ⊙8am-10pm Mon-Sat, to 4pm Sun; ☏☏☝) Just steps from the beach, this groovy cafe, cojoined with a hostel of the same name, serves decadent and delicious food. Try banana-bread French toast for breakfast, or uber-popular fish tacos for lunch. Dinner is served every night but Sunday, and it occasionally hosts live music and shows movies on the beach.

Next to Coconut Harry's beach location.

La Luna
INTERNATIONAL $$$

(☑ 2682-0122; Playa Pelada; dishes US$16-25; ⊙7am-10pm) Located on the beach, this trendy restaurant-bar has cushy couches right on the sand, perfect for sunset drinks. The interior is equally appealing, with soaring ceilings, a gorgeous hardwood bar and walls adorned with work by local artists. Asian and Mediterranean flourishes round out the eclectic menu, and the views (and cocktails) are intoxicating. Call ahead for reservations.

This will be your first sign of civilization if you've walked the beach from Playa Guiones and meandered up the footpath to Pelada.

Marlin Bill's
SEAFOOD $$$

(☑ 2682-0458; Playa Guiones; meals US$15-25, burgers US$7-15; ⊙11am-10pm Mon-Sat, to 3pm Sun) Across the main road from 'downtown' Guiones, this old-timers' restaurant has views all the way to the ocean. The casual, open-air patio is a perfect place to feast on grilled tuna, *ceviche* and other fresh seafood. Bill is famous for his burgers, and Sunday brunch includes an awesome eggs Benedict.

🍷 Drinking & Nightlife

Hear live music and get your groove on at the bar at **Kaya Sol** (Playa Guiones). The Beach Dog Café also has live music some evenings. Head to **Bar Olga** (Playa Pelada) after dark for drinking and dancing.

ℹ Information

Banco Popular (☎2682-0267, 2682-0011; Playa Guiones; ⏰9am-4:30pm Mon-Fri, 8:15-11:30am Sat)

Nosara Travel (☎2682-0300; www.nosara travel.com; Nosara; ⏰9am-3pm Mon-Fri) Download a decent Nosara map from its website.

NosaraNet & Frog Pad (☎2682-4039; www.thefrogpad.com; Villa Tortuga, Playa Guiones; ⏰9am-7pm Mon-Sat, 10am-6pm Sun; 🖥) An all-purpose stop for information, supplies and communication. Dave can answer any question. You can also buy some reading material, rent a movie (or bike or surfboard) and surf the net.

Police (☎2682-0317; Nosara) Next to the Red Cross and post office on the southeast corner of the soccer field in Nosara village center.

Tourist Police (☎2632-0311; Plaza Guiones, Playa Guiones) On the main Guiones road at Plaza Guiones.

ℹ Getting There & Away

You can get here by airplane or bus, and there are many accommodations options close to the beach; so you don't really need your own vehicle in Nosara. That said, it's a sprawling area so you'll appreciate a car if you intend to explore the environs.

AIR

NatureAir (p96) has two daily flights to and from San José for about US$149 one way. It offers discounts based on the weight of your luggage.

BUS

Local buses depart from the *pulpería* (corner grocery store) by the soccer field. Traroc buses depart for Nicoya (US$3.60, two hours) at 5am, 7am, noon and 3pm. To get to Sámara, take any bus out of Nosara and ask the driver to drop you off at *'la bomba de Sámara'* (Sámara gas station). From there, flag down one of the buses traveling from Nicoya to Sámara.

CAR

From Nicoya, a paved road leads toward Playa Sámara. About 5km before Sámara, turn onto a windy, bumpy (and, in the dry season, dusty) dirt road to Nosara village (4WD recommended). This road was being paved at the time of research, so cross your fingers, folks. It's also possible (in the dry season) to drive north to Ostional, Junquillal and Paraíso, though you'll have to ford a few rivers. Ask around before trying this in the rainy season, when Río Nosara becomes impassable.

There are two gas stations in Nosara village, and a couple of rental car agencies in the area:

Economy Rent a Car (☎2299-2000; www.economyrentacar.com; Playa Guiones; ⏰8am-6pm)

National (☎2242-7878; www.natcar.com; Playa Guiones; ⏰8am-5pm)

Refugio Nacional de Fauna Silvestre Ostional

This 248-hectare coastal **refuge** (☎2683-0400; www.areasyparques.com/areasprotegidas/ostional; adult/child US$12/2, turtle tours incl admission US$20) extends from Punta India in the north to Playa Guiones in the south, and includes the beaches of Playa Nosara and Playa Ostional. It was created in 1992 to protect the *arribadas* (mass nestings of the olive ridley sea turtles), which occur from from July to December (peaking in September and October). Ostional is one of two main nesting grounds for this turtle in Costa Rica, along with Playa Nancite in Parque Nacional Santa Rosa.

Outside of *arribada*, Ostional is usually deserted. But there is 5km of unbroken beach here, sprinkled with driftwood and swaying coconut palms. It's an ideal spot for surfing and sunbathing, birding and beachcombing.

🏃 Activities

Surfing

Surfers catch some good lefts and rights here just after low tide. Otherwise, this stretch of sea is notorious for strong currents and isn't suitable for swimming (unless you're green and have flippers).

Wildlife-Watching

Ostional is rife with sea creatures, even in addition to the turtles. Rocky Punta India at the northwestern end of the refuge has tide pools that abound with marine life, such as sea anemones, urchins and starfish. Along the beach, thousands of almost transparent ghost crabs go about their business, as do the bright-red Sally Lightfoot crabs.

The sparse vegetation behind the beach consists mainly of deciduous trees and is home to iguanas, crabs, howler monkeys, *pizotes* (coatis) and birds. Near the southeastern edge of the refuge is a small mangrove swamp where there is good birdwatching.

Surfing the Peninsula

For decades, surfers have descended to this rugged peninsula in search of the perfect wave. Now the spectacular coastline is dotted by enticing beach towns with good vibrations and epic surf. You can surf almost anywhere along the coast, but here are a few of our favorite spots.

Playa Grande

Playa Grande is across the river and a world away from tourist-jammed Tamarindo. It doubles as a national park that protects leatherback turtle nesting grounds, which means the wide, rambling beach is damn near pristine. The wave shapes up beautifully with head-high sets year-round. The village has a little hub at either end of the beach, where you'll find a handful of tasty kitchens and comfy inns catering to the visiting surfers. However, marked and numbered build-ing plots suggest that development may change things quickly.

Playas Avellanas & Negra

South of Tamarindo, you'll find two of the most celebrated surf spots on the peninsula, though the nearby villages still retain an appealing atmosphere of rustic-ity and remoteness. Playa Avellanas is an understated yet elegant place to nest, within reach of white-sand beaches and a break that's kind to beginners. Nearby, the surf swells big and gnarly at Playa Negra, breaking on beautiful dark sand. To dodge the crowds, seek out the still-hidden waves tucked between all the big names.

Nosara

Within striking distance of three different beach breaks, Nosara offers consistent surf and a welcome cloud of hippie-chic

JONATHAN GREGSON/LONELY PLANET ©

KRYSSIA CAMPOS/GETTY IMAGES ©

IAN MCDONNELL/GETTY IMAGES ©

1. Nosara (p313)
2. Playa Tamarindo (p300)
3. Guanacaste province

comfort. The town is a maze of rough dirt roads, backed by lush rainforest – although it is growing and changing rapidly (the long-promised paved road into town is underway, folks). Here, yoga studios and spa treatments are the antidote for your surf-sore body.

Mal País & Santa Teresa

At the southern end of the peninsula, Mal País and Santa Teresa are favored by young, hip and sexy surfers from around the world. The beach is long and the swell is consistent, which means you can generally find your own space – particularly if you drive to the far northern beaches. There's a wonderful farm-to-table movement happening here, so you'll be well fed throughout your stay.

SURF CAMPS

In addition to room and board, most all-inclusive surf camps include equipment and daily instruction, as well as some nonsurf tours and other activities. Camps may cater to beginners, budget travelers, families, women, yogis and more. Places that specialize in all-inclusive surf camps include the following:

➡ **Malpaís Surf Camp** (p331), Mal País
➡ **Peaks & Swells Surf Camp** (p339), Montezuma
➡ **Safari Surf** (p314), Nosara
➡ **Casa Surf** (p307), Playa Avellanas
➡ **Witch's Rock Surf Camp** (p301), Tamarindo
➡ **Blue Trailz** (p301), Tamarindo
➡ **Playa Grande Surf Camp** (p298), Playa Grande

THE PARK'S TURTLES

The olive ridley is one of the smallest species of sea turtle, typically weighing around 45kg. Although they are endangered, there are a few beaches in the world where ridleys nest in large groups that can number in the thousands. Scientists believe that this behavior is an attempt to overwhelm predators.

Prior to the creation of the park, coastal residents used to harvest and sell eggs indiscriminately (raw turtle eggs increase sexual vigor, or so they say). In recent years, however, an imaginative conservation plan has been put into place. Residents of Ostional are allowed to harvest eggs from the first laying, as these eggs are often trampled by subsequent waves of nesting turtles anyway (you can gulp down an eye-opening turtle-egg-and-hot-sauce shot at the local *mercado:* you'll see a sign advertising this on the main north–south road through town). By allowing this limited harvesting, the community maintains its economic livelihood, and the villagers in turn act as park rangers to prevent poachers from infringing on their enterprise.

Tours

Mass arrivals of nesting turtles occur every three or four weeks during the rainy season (usually on dark nights preceding a new moon) and last about four nights. It's possible to see turtles in lesser numbers almost any night during nesting season. In the dry season a fitting consolation prize is the small number of leatherback and green turtles that also nest here. Many tour operators in the region offer tours to Ostional during nesting season, or you can arrange with local guides to visit independently.

Minae
WILDLIFE

(☏2682-0400; ⊙8am-4pm Mon-Sat) The government agency that controls wildlife, Minae can help larger groups organize turtle-watching, because each guide is only allowed to bring 10 people on the beach at one time. They're located in a light-green building behind the cemetery, right on the beach. Authorized guides can be identified by the government-issued carnet, and a T-shirt with the proper logo.

Sleeping & Eating

Most turtle tourists come on tours or drive themselves from Nosara or Sámara; but there are a few simple guesthouses in town for those who care to spend the night (and avoid driving on the treacherous road in the dark). North of the village, there are a few fancier accommodations options.

Ostional Turtle Lodge
LODGE $

(☏2682-0131; www.ostionalturtlelodge.com; s/d/tr/q from US$26/40/56/70, air-con US$6; P❋ 🛜) A great guesthouse with only five simple rooms equipped with the basics, as well as a more spacious and stylish chalet. Guests spend most of their time in the exquisite community *rancho* on the communal patio's sofas and easy chairs, backed by mangroves, overlooking pastureland and within earshot of the sea. Just off of Route 160, this is the first lodging you'll encounter coming from the south and Nosara.

Luna Azul
HOTEL $$$

(☏2682-1400; www.hotellunaazul.com; d incl breakfast US$192; P❋🛜▣) This elegant hotel is a surprise, with its spacious bungalows and inviting infinity pool. From the outdoor showers to the private terraces, this is a place for relaxing – and perhaps eyeing a monkey or a bird or two. There is a fine onsite restaurant with the same chef for the past decade. About 4km north of Ostional village. The owner, Rolf, a retired Swiss biologist, is helpful in arranging turtle tours and other excursions.

Las Tortugas Pizzeria
COSTA RICAN $

(☏2682-0627; mains US$5-7; ⊙8am-9pm) About the only place to eat in town besides the *soda*, this roadhouse restaurant has a nice lunch and drinks menu and serves massive, delicious breakfasts and cocktails throughout the day. Don't come for the pizzas, despite the name – the other food's much better. The perfect place to while away the hours, waiting for a bus or a turtle tour.

Treetops Inn
INTERNATIONAL $$$

(☏2682-1335; www.costaricatreetopsinn.com; San Juanillo; lunch/dinner per person US$32/62; ⊙lunch 11am-2pm, dinner by reservation) Jack and Karen Hunter are renowned for their decadent five-course candlelit dinners (reserve one day in advance), potent piña coladas, fresh-picked mango margaritas, and their engaging storytelling. The prix-fixe meals feature the best of local ingredients, especially seafood and tropical fruit. It all takes place on a shaded deck with marvelous views of the forest canopy and the ocean beyond. The couple also rents out two rooms – one that is actually in the treetops, and another bungalow on the beach. Located about 8km north of Ostional in the village of San Juanillo. Cash only.

❶ Getting There & Away

Ostional village is about 8km northwest of Nosara village. During the dry months there is one daily bus from Santa Cruz (two hours), departing Ostional at 5am and returning from Santa Cruz at 12:30pm. From Nosara, there are buses to Ostional at 5am, 7:15am and 3:30pm (30 minutes, US$1) and return buses at 2:30pm and 6pm. Note that at any time of the year the road can get washed out by rain.

If you're driving, you'll need a 4WD, as the journey requires at least one river crossing. Ask locally about conditions before setting out. From the main road joining Nosara beach and village, head north and cross the bridge over the Río Nosara. After 2km, you'll reach a T-junction. Take the left fork (which is signed) and continue about 6km north to Ostional.

Beyond Ostional, the dirt road continues on to San Juanillo and Marbella before arriving in Paraíso, northeast of Junquillal. Again, inquire locally before attempting this drive, and don't be afraid to use your 4WD.

Playa Sámara
POP 4150

Is Sámara the black hole of happiness? That's what more than one expat has said after stopping here on vacation and never leaving. On the surface it's just a laid-back beach town with barefoot, three-star appeal. The crescent-shaped strip of pale-gray sand spans two rocky headlands, where the sea is calm and beautiful. It's not spectacular, just safe, mellow, reasonably developed, easily navigable on foot and accessible by public transportation. Not surprisingly, it's popular with vacationing Ticos, foreign families and backpackers, a somewhat rare, happy mix of visitors and locals. But be careful, the longer you stay the less you'll want to leave.

If you've got some extra time and a 4WD, explore the hidden beaches north of Sámara, such as Playas Barrigona and Buenavista.

🏃 Activities

No matter what you like to do at the beach, you can probably do it at Playa Sámara. Ex-

pert surfers might get bored by Sámara's inconsistent waves, but beginners will have a blast. Otherwise, there's hiking, horseback riding and sea kayaking, as well as snorkeling out around Isla la Chora. Take a break from the beach to explore the forested hillsides on foot or by zipline. Samara is not far from the turtle tours up the coast in Ostional, or just to the south on the coast at Playa Camaronal.

Pato Surf School　SURFING
(☑8761-4638; www.patossurfingsamara.com; board rental per day US$15, lessons US$35-45; ☺8am-5pm) Pato offers inexpensive and quality board rental, as well as beginner surf instruction, on the beach at the southwest end of town. The instructors are top-notch. Pay for a lesson and get free board rental for five days. Also on offer: stand-up paddle rental and lessons; kayak rental and tours; snorkel gear; and beach massages. What else do you want?

C&C Surf School　SURFING
(☑8817-2203, 8599-1874; www.facebook.com/CC-Surf-School-241875342489270; board rentals per day US$15, lessons group/private US$45/60; ☺8am-8pm) A great choice at the south end of the bach, offering lessons for individuals, pairs and small groups. Especially recommended for beginners. Owner Adolfo Gómez is a champion longboarder who has represented Costa Rica in the Central American Surfing Games. It's down at the south end of the beach behind Casa Valeria.

Guana Bike　MOUNTAIN BIKING
(Samara on Wheels; ☑8730-7981; www.guanabike.isamara.co; per day US$10; ☺8am-6pm Mon-Sat) It's easier to navigate Sámara's narrow streets on a bike than a car, for sure. And at this price, why not? This family-run local business will get you the wheels you need to cruise the mean streets of Guanacaste for a day, a week, or a month. Next to Coco's restaurant/bar.

Sámara Trails　HIKING
(Samara Adventure Company; ☑2656-0920; www.samaratrails.com; adult/child US$40/30; ☺6:30am & 2:30pm, with reservation) This hike departs from the office across from Wingnuts, then follows a 6km route through a mango plantation and into the Werner Sauter Biological Reserve, located in the hills above Sámara. In 2½ hours, your naturalist guide covers the history of the area and the ecology of the dry tropical forest. The office in town is on the main road.

Wingnuts
CANOPY TOUR

(2656-0153; www.wingnutscanopy.com; adult/child US$60/45; ⊙tours 8am, 9am, noon & 1pm) One entrepreneurial family found a way to preserve their beautiful, wild patch of dry tropical forest: by setting up a small-scale canopy tour. Family-owned and professionally run, this 10-platform operation is unique for its personal approach, as groups max out at 10 people. The price includes transportation from your hotel in Sámara.

Flying Crocodile
SCENIC FLIGHTS

(2656-8048; www.flying-crocodile.com; per person 20min/30min/60min US$110/150/230) About 6km north of Sámara in Playa Buenavista, the Flying Crocodile offers ultralight flights over the nearby beaches and mangroves. Onsite there is also a pretty cool hotel, set on jungly grounds and populated by wildlife.

Leo Tours
ADVENTURE

(8995-6820; www.leotourssamara.com; kayak-snorkel per person US$40) Leo has kayaks, fishing rods, snorkel gear and even a boat. That means he'll take you out for any kind of water fun you crave, from sea kayaking to sportfishing. A favorite tour is kayaking out to Isla la Chora, where you can snorkel around the island. Find him on the beach 50m northeast of Gusto.

Courses

Centro de Idiomas Intercultura
LANGUAGE

(2656-3000; www.interculturacostarica.com; courses per week with/without homestay US$470/315) Centro de Idiomas Intercultura is right on the beach, which makes for a pleasant – if not always productive – place to study. Language courses can be arranged with or without a family homestay. Courses for kids are also available.

Sleeping

In town, it's nearly impossible to be more than two blocks from the beach. Many hotels, hostels and charming guesthouses are clustered in the small rectangular grid that borders the sand. If you prefer to be further away from the action, there are some real gems west of town. Generally, budget options greet you with a brisk cold morning shower, while midrange and top-end facilities have hot water.

★ Camp Supertramp
HOSTEL $

(2656-0373; www.campsupertramp.com; Camino Buena Vista; campsites per person US$8, dm US$15) Something truly unique's going down here, 2km east of town. The list of things to love is long: Thomas (the owner), Subwoofer (the dog), the jungle shower, the fire pit, the 1971 VW bus, the table-tennis table and the volleyball court. Both the multilevel Monkey Room and Deluxe Dorm have new beds. The vibe here is fun-filled and super chill.

El Cactus Hostel
HOSTEL $

(2656-3224; www.samarabackpacker.com; dm US$16, d US$35-62; ⊛⊠) Brightly painted in citrus colors, El Cactus is a great option for Sámara's backpacker set, especially those who prefer serenity over revelry. Fresh rooms have wooden furniture, clean linens and hot-water showers. Hammocks hang around a small pool, and a fully fitted kitchen is also available. Located on a side street in the center of town, 100m from the beach.

Casa Paraiso
GUESTHOUSE $

(2656-0741; scodinzolo@libero.it; dm/d US$15/60; ⊛) A lovely little guesthouse tucked in behind Ahora Sí. Four simple rooms and a shared dorm are brushed in deep blues and inviting pastels, with thematic murals, high ceilings and comfy beds. Ceiling fans will keep you cool while hot-water showers will warm you up. Hostess Sylvia will overwhelm you with her charm, and there's Italian cooking at the restaurant.

Sámara Palm Lodge
GUESTHOUSE $$

(2656-1169; www.samarapalmlodge.com; d US$70-80; ⓟ⊛⊛⊠) An inviting little Swiss-owned lodge on the edge of town. Eight spotless rooms feature tropical decor, with stained wood furniture, tile floors and bold colorful artwork. They face a lush garden and enticing swimming pool. Just over the bridge, a little west of town but just a five-minute walk to the beach.

La Mansion B&B
B&B $$

(Bed and Best Breakfast; 2265-0165; www.samarainfocenter.com/accommodations/b-bs/la-mansion-b-b; s US$40, d US$50-80, ste US$150; ⓟ⊛⊛) This whitewashed concrete hacienda, twirling with fans and bursting with colorful knickknacks, is on a quiet street. There's loads of charm: rooms are spacious and bright, and ex-Arizonian hostess Marlene McCauley is proud of her huge and delicious breakfast repasts. Her artwork adorns the walls and you can even buy one of her cute bird-themed postcards. Air-con is extra.

Tico Adventure Lodge
LODGE $$

(2656-0628; www.ticoadventurelodge.com; tw/d/q/apt US$59/74/90/160; ⓟ⊛⊛⊠) The US owners are proud of the fact that they built this lodge without cutting down a single tree, and they have every reason to be – it's pretty sharp. Nine double rooms and several larger apartments are surrounded by lush vegetation and old-growth trees. There's an outdoor kitchen and cookout area for communal use, a Jacuzzi, and a yoga/spa area.

Casa del Mar   HOTEL **$$**
(☑2656-0264; www.casadelmarsamara.net; s/d/tr US$90/90/110, without bathroom US$40/55/70; **P**✳︎🛜💲) 𝄢 Surrounding a big mango tree and a tiny swimming pool are 17 rooms with whitewashed stucco walls and tile floors. The rooms that share a bathroom are a steal. The beach, where the hotel provides chairs and towels for its guests, is right across the street. The French- and English-speaking staff are friendly and attentive. At the main Sámara intersection.

★**LazDivaz**   B&B **$$$**
(☑2656-0295; www.lazdivaz.com; d US$113-124; **P**🛜) They call it a B&C. No breakfast, just coffee. These three darling *casitas* are perched in the sand, about 400m east of the village center. The lodgings are simply decorated, but immaculately clean and exceedingly comfortable. Your main entertainment here will be swinging in a hammock and watching the sea and sky. *Pura vida.*

Las Ranas   LODGE **$$$**
(☑2656-0609; www.lodgelasranas.com; d/tr US$125/142; **P**✳︎🛜💲) A sharp stucco lodge with a king's location. We're talking nearly 180 degrees of ocean vistas from the restaurant, pool and upper rooms. And those rooms are gorgeous, with canopy beds, granite-tile floors, balconies, and soaring beamed ceilings – one even has a kitchenette. It's a few kilometers west of town, so you'll need wheels.

This place is worth the trip as the leafy grounds are alive with birdlife and other animals. Spotted here: a stunning pair of western tanagers.

Sámara Tree House Inn   BUNGALOW **$$$**
(☑2656-0733; www.samaratreehouse.com; d incl breakfast US$110-170; **P**✳︎🛜💲) These six stilted tree houses for grown-ups are so appealing that you might not want to leave. Fully equipped kitchens have pots and pans hanging from driftwood racks, huge windows welcome light and breezes, and hammocks hang underneath. The pricier units face the beach. You can't get much closer than this to the ocean without getting on a surfboard.

El Pequeño Gecko Verde   BUNGALOW **$$$**
(☑2656-1176; www.gecko-verde.com; d US$120-165, q US$240; **P**✳︎🛜💲) A hidden slice of heaven. Contemporary and classy, these bungalows have beds dressed in plush linens, artisanal carvings on the walls, private terraces with hammocks and outdoor dining areas, and outdoor stone showers. Onsite amenities include a saltwater swimming pool with waterfall, lush gardens and a fabulous open-air restaurant and bar. Located several kilometers west of town.

✖ Eating

★**Lo Que Hay**   MEXICAN **$**
(☑2656-0811; www.loquehaybeachbar.com; tacos US$2, mains US$8-12; ⊗7am-11pm) This rocking beachside *taquería* and pub offers six delectable taco fillings: fish, chorizo, chicken, beef, pork or veggie. The grilled avocados stuffed with *pico de gallo* are great. Even without tacos, a good time will be had as the bar crowd drinks into the wee small hours.

Luv Burger   VEGETARIAN, BURGERS **$**
(☑2656-3348; www.luvburger.com; mains US$5-8; ⊗8am-5pm; 🖉) Moved to the beachfront from its former mini-mall locale, it's all veggie, all the time, from vegan pancakes for breakfast to guilt-free ice cream for dessert – even burgers and sandwiches are meat-free. Coffee drinks are made only with soy or almond milk.

Roots Bakery   BAKERY **$**
(☑8924-2770; www.facebook.com/rootsbakerycafe EnSamara; items US$3-5; ⊗7am-4pm Mon-Sat, to noon Sun; 🛜) The carrot cake is really good, and the spinach quiche is better. But the cinnamon buns are otherworldly – so rich, gooey, sweet and chewy that you might have to do penance after you eat one. Required eating. Roots is on the main drag, opposite the turnoff to Carrillo. Like many places to eat in Sámara, it's cash only.

Fiesta Crêp'   FRENCH **$**
(mains US$4-6; ⊗8am-8pm Thu-Tue) Salty or sweet? The savory crepes are good, the sweet ones even better, and during the day hummingbirds zoom in and out of the garden patio. If the banana-chocolate or passion-fruit-cream offerings aren't quite enough, there's a list of cocktails and French wines, and the expat owners are eager to pour them. On the town's main north–south drag.

Ahora Sí   VEGETARIAN **$**
(☑2656-0741; www.ahorasi.isamara.co; mains US$5-11; ⊗8am-10pm; **P**🛜🖉) Sylvia of

Bergamo runs this vegetarian restaurant and all-natural cocktail bar, and the fish joint next door. Expect smoothies with coconut milk, gnocchi with chive or smoked cheese, soy burgers, and imported Italian pasta. All served on a lovingly decorated tiled patio where the chairbacks are shaped into musical notes and the menus contain inspirational quotes. Good vibes, good food. It's about one block from the beach in the southeast corner of town.

Sámara Organics –
Mercado Organico MARKET $$
(☑2656-3046; www.samaraorganics.com; smoothies & juices US$4-5; ☺7am-8pm) It's not cheap, but self-caterers (and anybody with a dietary restriction) will appreciate this cafe and market, well-stocked with organic produce and delicious prepared foods. Come get your healthy food fix, and enjoy the small seating area for a chat or read. On the main beach road, parallel to the water.

Casa Esmeralda SODA $$
(☑2656-0489; www.facebook.com/casaesmeralda .samara; mains US$9-20; ☺7am-10pm) A favorite with locals, this is a dressed-up *soda* with tablecloths, faux-adobe walls and excellent food. The menu ranges from the expected (*arroz con pollo* – chicken with rice) to the exotic (Italian octopus appetizer), all of which is fantastic. Be prepared to wait when it gets busy. About a block from the beach at the southeast end of town. It has rooms to rent upstairs.

El Lagarto BARBECUE $$
(☑2656-0750; mains US$11-25; ☺3-11pm; ☏) Grilled meats are the big draw at this alfresco restaurant, studded with old trees and walking distance to the waves. Watching the chefs work their magic on the giant wood-fired oven is part of the fun. The Surf & Turf is highly recommended, as are the cocktails.

Locanda PIZZA $$
(Locanda Hotel & Pizzeria; ☑2656-0036; www.lo candasamarabeach.com; mains US$12-16; ☺7am-11pm) Ask anyone in Sámara where the best pizza in town is and they'll point you here, at the southern corner of the beach. The thin-crust slices disappear as quickly as the sun over the horizon. Enjoy the two-for-one drink specials – maybe a Pink Lady or a Down Under Fizz – while the waves wash over your mind.

La Dolce Vita ITALIAN $$
(☑2656-3371; www.facebook.com/ladolcevita.sa mara; US$8-15; ☺5-10pm) Life is sweet when you're sitting under a giant *palapa* on the sand, drinking a smoothie and watching the surfers. This is a popular spot for pizza and sundowners, thanks to affable Italian owners and a prime beachfront locale.

Life is even sweeter when your bed is just a few meters away. The interior-facing guest rooms have bamboo furniture and jewel-painted walls.

🍸 Drinking & Nightlife

Flying Taco BAR
(El Taco Volador; ☑8409-5376; ☺11am-2am; ☏) A laid-back, Tex-Mex beach bar near the soccer field. It's open for lunch – and the grub is recommended – but it's more fun to come at night, when you can also sing karaoke, play poker and drink margaritas. The Wednesday open-mic 'Taco Jam' fills the bar with musical talent of varying levels, having a blast. But don't forget the tacos. It's just down the street from the main north–south drag.

Microbar MICROBREWERY
(☺5pm-midnight) Not an inch of space is wasted in this smart little bar on the main road, which serves up 21 Costa Rican microbrews plus infused 'beertails' like the Terremoto (dark rum and dark beer) and the Apocatopia (vanilla, bourbon, light ale). You get a serving of popcorn with every drink. The head-bobbing electronica throbs, and your head might tomorrow, too.

Media Luna COCKTAIL BAR
(Tapas y Vino; ☑8416-1852; www.facebook.com/ Media-Luna; ☺6pm-2am) Art deco artistic touches with a Latin backbeat on the main drag. A full complement of tapas and specialty drinks like the Guaro Sour keep you smiling while you're immersed at the dartboard, pool table, or in the super-popular Latin Dance Night (Thursday) when the room gets packed and the DJ keeps it lively till the wee hours.

🛍 Shopping

Sámara has a more creative vibe than most beach towns on the peninsula. You'll find a handful of galleries selling hand-crafted jewelry and exquisite items, as well as vendors hawking their wares at stands along the main road, and at your beachside restaurant tables.

Cocotales JEWELRY
(☑8807-7056; ☺8am-8pm) Carlos Caicedo travels around South America to procure gorgeous semiprecious stones, which he

crafts into fine jewelry right here in the back of his shop, on the main north–south road. There are also plenty of clever creations from recycled materials. But his most unique and eye-catching pieces are crafted from cocoa beans (grown locally, of course).

ℹ Information

Banco Costa Rica (⊘9am-4pm Mon-Fri, ATM 24hr) Just off the main road, across from the soccer field.

Banco Nacional (☑2656-0086; ⊘9am-5pm Mon-Fri) Located next to the church.

La Vida Verde (Green Life; ☑2656-1051; greenlife@samarabeach.com; per kg US$3; ⊘8am-6pm Mon-Sat) Drop your dirty duds off at this laundry, 75m west of Banco Nacional. Or call ahead for pickup and delivery.

Post office (⊘8am-noon & 1:15-5:30pm Mon-Fri) Located in the same building as the police station, on the main road where it meets the beach.

Samara Beach (www.samarabeach.com) Surf this excellent website to get the skinny on Sámara, including a decent tourist map of the village and beach.

Samara Info Center (☑2656-2424; www. samarainfocenter.com; ⊘8am-6pm) Located in front of Lo Que Hay, the Info Center is run by the amiable Brenda and Christopher. It's basically a tour consolidator, but they can help with accommodations, restaurant recommendations, transportation and simply answering questions about Sámara and Carrillo. And it books tours.

ℹ Getting There & Away

Playa Sámara lies about 35km southwest of Nicoya on a paved road. The nearby Carrillo airstrip is now closed; the nearest charter flight one could book would be for Nosara.

Traroc buses go to Nicoya (US$3.60, one hour) 10 times a day from 5:30am to 7pm. Heading in the opposite direction, these same buses go to Playa Carrillo. Coming into town from other parts of the peninsula you'll need to disembark at the gas station (la bomba) and hitch your way into town. Hitching is never entirely safe, and we don't recommend it. Travellers who hitch should understand that they are taking a small but potentially serious risk.

Playa Carrillo

POP 1800

About 4km southeast of Sámara, Carrillo is a wide, crescent-shaped beach with clean white sand, cracked granite headlands and a jungle backdrop. On weekends and holidays, the palm-fringed boulevard is lined with cars and the beach crowded with Tico families. At other times, it's practically deserted. The little town is on a hillside above the beach and attracts a trickle of sunbathers and surfers working their way down the coast. Interesting and pretty tidal pools form at high tide at the southern end of the beach near town.

🎣 Activities

Kingfisher Sportfishing FISHING (☑8358-9561, 2656-0091; www.costaricabillfishing.com; half-day excursions from US$900) A well-known local outfit offering deep-sea fishing on board the *Kingfisher*. Captain Rick and his crew provide top-notch service. Packages include accommodations at the luxurious Villa Oasis. The boat picks you up at the southern end of Playa Carrillo, where the boats are moored. .

Carrillo Tours TOURS (☑2656-0543; www.carrillotours.com; ⊘8am-7pm) On the road up the hill, next to a mini *mercado*, Carrillo Tours organizes turtle tours, snorkeling, kayaking, horseback riding and trips to Palo Verde. There's an office in Sámara as well, which is more extensive and reliably open – it's on the main road.

🛏 Sleeping & Eating

La Posada B&B $$ (☑2656-3131; www.laposada.co.cr; d incl breakfast US$60-75; P❄🛜) High on the hill with sweeping panoramas of the trees and the sea, this B&B makes a sweet retreat. Simple rooms have wood and wicker furniture and tropical flourishes. It's worth the extra US$10 for an ocean-view room, but the communal terrace will give you a similarly awesome visual experience. Twice-weekly yoga classes are held on the terrace. Larger room available for families.

La Tropicale BUNGALOW $$ (☑2656-0159, 8884-9471; www.latropicaleguesthouse.com; d/q incl breakfast US$60/140; P❄🛜⛱) Across from La Selva wildlife reserve is this fun, funky, fabulous inn that has ramshackle charm and plenty of hip touches. A stony path winds around the sparkling swimming pool and through mango, papaya and coconut trees. Stand-alone bungalows are draped with bold linens, lit with funky light fixtures and hung with original art. Owner Arnaud has stepped it up a notch with the onsite Chez Nous restaurant, featuring French and seafood specialties.

Hideaway Hotel
BOUTIQUE HOTEL $$$

(☑ 2656-1145; www.thehideawayplayasamara.com; d/tr/q incl breakfast US$110/145/180, penthouse US$349-499; P❋🖥❄) Midway between Carrillo and Sámara, this attractive white-washed place is noteworthy for its super service and intimate atmosphere. A dozen spacious tiled suites all overlook the pleasant pool and blooming gardens. The airy restaurant is excellent. There is a small beach at the end of the road; alternatively, Playa Carrillo is a 15-minute walk. A separate 'penthouse' houses six to eight guests.

❶ Getting There & Away

The airstrip in Carillo is now closed, even to charter services. Buses operated by **Traroc** (☑ 2685-5352; www.traroc.com) originate in Estrada, just east of here. From Carrillo, the buses go to Sámara, then continue on to Nicoya (US$3.60, 90 minutes, 10 daily). The fare to Sámara is 60¢ for a 20-minute ride.

Islita Area

The coast southeast of Playa Carrillo remains one of the peninsula's most isolated and wonderful stretches of coastline, mainly because much of it is inaccessible and lacking in accommodations. But if you're willing to tackle rugged roads or venture down the coastline in a sea kayak (or possibly on foot), you'll be rewarded with abandoned beaches backed by pristine wilderness and rugged hills.

Islita is a pretty little town centered on a church and a soccer field, spruced up by artwork. The place looks unexpectedly prosperous, thanks to the efforts of the Hotel Punta Islita, which channels funding into the local community.

There are a few small breaks in front of the hotel, where you'll find a gorgeous cove punctuated with that evocative wave-thrashed boulder that is Punta Islita. At high tide the beach narrows, but at low tide it is wide, and as romantic as those vistas from above.

◉ Sights

Ara Project
ZOO

(☑ 8351-7849; www.thearaproject.org; admission by donation US$20; ⊙4-5pm) A local NGO that is dedicated to the conservation of Costa Rica's two species of macaw: the great green macaw and the scarlet macaw. The group rehabilitates injured or rescued birds and eventually reintroduces them into the wild.

From the lookout point, you can watch scarlet macaws return to their roost. It's quite a sight.There is an informative visitor center with lots of information about the organization. The easiest way to get here is to arrange transport with Ara in advance.It is possible to walk here, taking the dirt trail near the Hotel Punta Islita, in 20 to 30 minutes.

Refugio Nacional de Vida Silvestre Camaronal
WILDLIFE RESERVE

(Playa Camaronal; ☑ 2659-8375; www.fundecodes.org/refugio-nacional-de-vida-silvestre-camaronal; US$6; ⊙8am-6pm) A good beach and point break, this charcoal gray stretch north of Punta Islita is strewn with driftwood and sheltered by two headlands. This beach also happens to be a protected nesting site for leatherback, olive ridley, hawksbill and black turtles, hence its protected status. Hotel Punta Islita offers turtle tours to Camaronal, as do tour operators in Sámara and Carrillo.

Playa Corzalito
BEACH

About 4km south of Punta Islita, Playa Corzalito is backed by mangrove swamps, offering plenty of opportunities to spot birds and other wildlife.

Playa Bejuco
BEACH

South of Punta Islita, Playa Bejuco is backed by mangrove swamps, offering excellent wildlife-watching opportunities.

Museo Islita
MUSEUM

(☑ 2656-2039; www.museoislita.org; ⊙8am-4pm Mon-Sat) FREE Facing the soccer field, this little museum, sponsored by the Hotel Punta Islita, is an imaginative contemporary art house. It's basically a studio and gallery, featuring artwork and handicrafts by local artists. Pick up a map for the **Arte Contemporáneo al Aire Libre**, which includes mosaics, carvings and paintings that adorn everything from houses to tree trunks around the village.

🛏 Sleeping & Eating

Hotel Punta Islita
RESORT $$$

(☑ 2231-6122; www.hotelpuntaislita.com; d incl breakfast US$280; P❋@❄) ✎ This hilltop hotel has 54 fully equipped rooms with staggering ocean views. (If you spring for a suite, you'll enjoy this view from a private outdoor Jacuzzi.) The infinity pool and surrounding grounds are stunning. The amenities onsite do not stop, including a full-service spa, a beach club with a sunken pool bar and lounges on a rolling lawn.

This luxury resort serves as an example of how to ethically operate a hotel. In addition to implementing sustainability measures and organizing community arts projects, it has sponsored the construction of various public buildings, including the local art gallery, elementary school and village church (which hosts many destination weddings, so that was a win-win).

Pacifico COSTA RICAN $$$
(☑2661-4044; Hotel Punta Islita; mains US$14-28; ⊙7am-10pm; ℗🛜) The restaurant at the Hotel Punta Islita showcases Tico flavors with the freshest seafood, local meats and poultry, and organic produce. A superlative ocean view complements the beautiful food presentations.

❶ Getting There & Away

There's no public transportation to Punta Islita. In any case, you'll probably want your own vehicle to explore the coastline, preferably a 4WD.

There's a permanent bridge over the Río Ora, so the 10km journey between Puerto Carrillo and Punta Islita ist a lot easier than it once was. South of the bridge, the road condition is less reliable; proceed with caution during the rainy season.

Commercial flights have stopped here, but you can charter a flight from San Jose for about US$150.

Playas San Miguel & Coyote

Two of the most gorgeous – yet least visited – beaches in Costa Rica are on this stretch of the peninsula, just south of Bejuca. Playa San Miguel is a stunning, desolate beach buffeted by a hulking granite headland and backed by elegant coconut palms. There are a couple of restaurants spread out on the beach, but not much more. Playa Coyote, to the south, is likewise a wilderness beach, but at high tide much of the fine, silver-gray sand gets swallowed up. Both beaches serve as nesting grounds for olive ridley turtles.

A number of in-the-know foreigners have settled in the area and opened accommodations and restaurants near the shoreline. If you're looking for a proper village, La Javilla is located 2km inland from Playa San Miguel; further south, San Francisco de Coyote is 4km inland from Playa Coyote. Get here before this slice of 'old' Costa Rica becomes the 'new' Costa Rica.

🏃 Activities

You can surf crowd-free beach breaks off San Miguel, particularly when the tide is rising. At Coyote there is an offshore reef that can be surfed at high tide. When swimming, you are advised to take precautions as the surf can pick up, and there are not many people in the area to help you in an emergency. If you have your own sea kayak, these beaches (as well as nearby Islita) are perfect for coastal exploration.

Mike's Jungle Butterfly Farm GARDENS
(☑8719-1703; www.facebook.com/junglebutterfly farm; Nandayure, Pueblo Nuevo; tours adult/child US$25/12; ⊙9am-3pm Mon-Sat) Mike's beautiful 47-acre mountainside property, 10 minutes north of San Miguel, includes walking trails and a butterfly *rancho*. In addition to the butterflies, you might spot howler monkeys, agoutis and iguanas. He also has colonies of wild bees; you can buy their honey in the gift shop. Book ahead for a tour. Turn west at the Catholic Church/sports field in Nadayure.

Turtle Trax VOLUNTEERING
(www.turtle-trax.com; San Francisco) Turtle Trax collaborates with environmental watchdog CREMA (Rescue Center for Endangered Marine Species; cremacr.org) to offer opportunities to visiting volunteers who want to help monitor the turtle beaches in the area. Tasks include patrolling the beach, recording data, collecting eggs, maintaining the hatcheries and releasing the newly hatched *tortuguitas* (baby turtles). The organization also offers one-day and longer environmental tours. Located 100m south of the school in San Francisco de Coyote.

Turtle Trax can organize affordable (rustic) housing and transportation for volunteers. Other opportunities include working in the local schools and collecting trash on the beach.

🛏 Sleeping

There's a smattering of unique and lovely lodgings spread out along this coast, though they are few and far between. Alternatively, both villages have *cabinas* that are acceptable options in which to pass a night. You can camp on either beach if you're self-sufficient, but there are no services.

Laguna Mar BOUTIQUE HOTEL $$
(☑2655-8181, in USA 704-851-8181; www.lagu namarhotel.com; Javilla; s US$46, d incl breakfast

US$74-93; [P][✳][🛜][❄]) In the center of unassuming La Javilla (2km from the beach), this semi-swanky hotel is incongruous with the setting, but still lovely. Rooms are simple but sophisticated, with high-thread-count linens and flat-screen TVs, set around a sublime three-in-one swimming pool. A bargain 'surfer' room on offer for that lucky solo traveler. Extra props for the excellent European restaurant. It's just off the main road.

Cristal Azul
B&B $$$

([✓]2655-8135; www.cristalazulhotel.com; d from US$255; [P][🛜][❄]) Spectacular panoramas surround you at this hilltop retreat, where the four *cabinas* feature floor-to-ceiling windows, open-air showers and super-comfortable beds. It's worth the treacherous journey to spend a few days swinging in a hammock or lounging around the infinity pool (which really does seem to go on forever). Eager to share their little piece of paradise, your hosts are delightful. A 4WD, and a half-day's patience, is required to drive here. Two-night minimum stay.

Casa Caletas
BOUTIQUE HOTEL $$$

([✓]2655-1271; www.casacaletas.com; Punta Coyote; s/d/tri/ste US$96/120/145/155; [P][✳][🛜][❄]) Sitting pretty on a bank of the Río Coyote, this gorgeous property is at once blessedly intimate and blissfully isolated. Rooms are gorgeously decorated with heavy wood furniture and folksy art. A walking trail leads to the beach.

Take the road from San Francisco de Coyote toward Mal País and follow the signs for the hotel. If driving from Playa Naranjo (the Puntarenas Ferry) take the road toward Jicaral; at the main plaza in San Francisco de Coyote, turn left.

All the rooms have private terraces with views to the ocean. Taking advantage of the same panorama, the infinity pool lives up to its name.

✖ Eating

★ LocosCocos
SEAFOOD $$

(www.locoscocos.com; Playa San Miguel; mains US$5-12; ⊙11am-sunset Tue-Sun; [🌶]) Best. Beach. Bar. And that's saying something in Costa Rica. On an amazing, nearly deserted stretch of beach, Henner serves up his secret-family-recipe *ceviche* out of an old shipping container. Ice cold beers cap off this near-perfect experience. Also, if you time it right, you might get to see an amazing show in the sky (aka sunset).

It's 1km downhill from the Cristal Azul boutique hotel (it has the same owners).

Pizza Tree
PIZZA $$

([✓]2655-8063; pizzas US$9-12; ⊙noon-10pm; [P][✓]) If there is anything more fun than eating pizza in a tree house, we're not sure what it is. Take a seat at the top of this ramshackle, Seuss-like structure and feast on thin-crust pizzas and focaccia from the wood-fired brick oven. The owner is Italian but the concept is purely Tico. Situated 2km northeast of San Miguel beach.

El Barco
INTERNATIONAL $$

([✓]2655-1003; www.el-barco-costarica.com; mains US$12-16; ⊙11:30am-9pm Wed-Mon; [🛜][✓]) It looks like a boat, but it's actually a building, facing a sweet slice of sand on Playa Coyote (close to the 'T' intersection at the beach). Hokey, perhaps, but there's nothing gimmicky about the delicious and nutritious creations coming out of the kitchen. Fresh salads, hearty sandwiches and more substantial pasta and rice dishes will keep you sated.

❶ Getting There & Away

You can reach these beach towns by bus, but they are rather remote with minimal facilities, so you may feel stranded if you don't have your own vehicle. If your plans are limited to lounging on a deserted beach, you should be OK.

Transportes Arsa ([✓]2650-0179; www.transportesarsa.com) has two daily buses from San José that take about four hours to reach the beach (optimistically). The buses depart San José at 6am and 3:30pm. Return buses leave Bejuco at 2am, 3:45am and 1pm, passing through San Miguel and Coyote a half-hour or an hour later. This service is sketchy in the rainy season and the trip may take longer if road conditions are bad.

SOUTHERN PENINSULA

Mal País & Santa Teresa
POP 2500 (COMBINED)

Santa Teresa didn't even have electricity until the mid-1990s. Then one major landowner died and his property was subdivided, and the landscape north of the Playa El Carmen intersection changed forever. These days, you'll need to balance the annoyance of the omnipresent ATVs kicking up dust with the restaurants serving gob-smackingly delicious food and the yoga dens with transformational ocean views.

It's still a wonderful surfing town, though no longer a secret one, and there are plenty of great places to eat and a modicum of nightlife. The entire area unfurls along one bumpy coastal road that rambles south from Santa Teresa through Playa El Carmen and terminates in the relaxed, sleepy fishing hamlet of Mal País.

◉ Sights

Playa Hermosa
BEACH

Somewhere north of town, Playa Santa Teresa ends and Playa Hermosa starts. This gorgeous beach deserves its *hermosa* (beautiful) moniker and then some. It's wide and flat and spectacular at low tide. The beach nearly disappears at high tide. Somewhere between low and high is surf tide, when you can ride the wide beach break left or right from center. You can surf the point break (at the north end of the beach) at any time.

Playa Santa Teresa
BEACH

Playa Santa Teresa is a long, stunning beach that's famous for its fast and powerful beach break. The surf is pretty consistent and can be surfed at virtually any time of day. At the north end of the beach, Roca Mar – aka Suck Rock – is an awesome point break and a local favorite. The break La Lora is named for the nightclub that marks the turnoff from the main road, which is how you find it.

Playa El Carmen
BEACH

Playa El Carmen, downhill from the main T intersection coming into town, is a good beach break that can be surfed anytime. The beach is wide and sandy and curls into successive coves, so it makes good beachcombing and swimming terrain too.

Playa Manzanillo
BEACH

About 8km north of the Playa El Carmen intersection, past Playa Hermosa, Playa Manzanillo is a combination of sand and rock that's best surfed when the tide is rising and there's an offshore wind.

🏃 Activities

Surfing is the raison d'être for most visits to Santa Teresa and Mal País, and perhaps for the town itself. Most travelers want to do little else, except maybe stretch their muscles with a little yoga. That said, it's a gorgeous, pristine coastline: horseback riding or fishing trips can be easily arranged, as well as a fun-filled ziplining jaunt.

Freedom Ride SUP
WATER SPORTS

(☑ 2640-0939, 8737-8781; www.sup-costarica.com; Mal País; rental half-/full day US$25/40, lessons per person US$50; ⏰ 9am-6pm) A stand-up paddle place with sharp management and excellent safety and instruction techniques. Andy offers lessons for first-timers and rentals for old-timers, as well as tours that are entertaining for anyone. Located near the fishing pier in Mal País.

Canopy Mal País
ADVENTURE SPORTS

(☑ 2640-0360; www.canopymalpais.com; US$50; ⏰ 9am-3pm) You don't think of ziplining when you come to a surf town? You should. Just south of Mal País, Carlos and crew provide one of the most entertaining experiences around, joking so much you'll forget your fear of heights on the 11 cables, including one that stretches 500m across the jungle below. And the last cable is a surfboard ride!

Certified to work with disabled persons and children. The onsite cafe, Mariolita's, makes some nice, fresh food and drinks.

Surfing

The long, flat beach stretches for many kilometers along this southwestern coast of the peninsula. The entire area is saturated with surf shops. This is a good place to pick up an inexpensive board, which you can probably sell later. Most of the local shops also do rentals and repairs; chat them up to find out about their secret surf spots.

Kina Surf Shop
SURFING

(☑ 2640-0627; www.kinasurfcr.com; Santa Teresa; lessons per person US$60, board rentals per day US$12-20; ⏰ 9am-5pm) A terrific, efficient surf shop near the break in Santa Teresa. Kina claims to have the best selection of rental boards in the area, with 60-something quality boards available. The 90-minute lessons for beginner, intermediate and advanced surfers also come highly recommended. We expect owner Eric may never return to the cold Atlantic waters of New Jersey.

Around 300m north of the soccer field in Villas Solar, a small shopping complex.

Nalu Surf School
SURFING

(☑ 2649-0391, 8358-4436; www.nalusurfschool. com; Santa Teresa; board rental per day US$10-20, group/private lessons US$50/65) Located 300m north of the Playa El Carmen intersection (next to Ronny's Supermarket), this surf school is recommended for its fun and professional approach to instruction. Lessons usually take place at Playa El Carmen, but these guys will also transport you to other breaks in the area. The shop has a good selection of boards for rental and purchase.

Pura Vida Adventures SURFING
(☑ in USA 1-415-465-2162; www.puravidaadventures.com; Playa El Carmen; weekly rates from US$2795) An excellent women-only retreat in Playa El Carmen that combines surfing and yoga in weeklong experiences that also include all meals. It's on the beach side of the main north–south road, just north of Calle Buenos Aires.

Yoga

Many surfers know that yoga is the perfect antidote to their sore flippers. Several studios in the area offer drop-in classes.

Casa Zen YOGA
(☑ 2640-0523; www.zencostarica.com; Santa Teresa; classes per person US$9) Three daily classes take place in a lovely second-story, open-air studio, surrounded by trees. Most of the classes are a hatha-inspired Vinyasa flow, but there's also cardio fit and other styles. Yoga by candlelight is a sublime way to transition from day to night. Multiclass packages are available. Located behind the Plaza Royal.

Yoga Studio at Nautilus YOGA
(☑ 2640-0991; www.hotelnautiluscostarica.com; Santa Teresa; group/private classes US$14/60; ☺ 9am & 6pm) What's not to love about rooftop yoga? Twice-daily classes are held on the deck at the Nautilus Boutique Hotel, offering lovely views over the village. It offers Vinyasa flow and kundalini, power and restorative yoga. Look for the Nautilus or Canaima Chill House signs.

Horizon Yoga Hotel YOGA
(☑ 2640-0524; www.horizon-yogahotel.com; Calle Buenos Aires, Santa Teresa; classes per person US$15) Offers two classes daily, in a serene environment overlooking the ocean. As with other schools, weekly and other passes are available. About 100m north of Supermarket Ronny, turn off the main road and drive 50m up the hill.

🛏 **Sleeping**

Frank's Place is the landmark that occupies the main corner at Playa El Carmen. Stretching to the north, Santa Teresa is a dusty hamlet that's crammed with guesthouses, cafes and surf shops ('uncontrolled development' is a phrase which comes to

mind.) Stretching to the south, Mal País is more sparsely developed and more densely forested, offering a quieter, old-school hippie atmosphere.

Don Jon's BUNGALOW $
(☑ 2640-0700; www.donjonsonline.com; Santa Teresa; dm/bungalows & tree houses/apt US$20/70/120; P ✳ 🛜) Just 100m from the surf, this is the perfect base for anybody looking to 'relax to the max.' Rustic teak bungalows are creatively decorated, while attractive Spanish-tiled dorms have high-beamed ceilings and plenty of hammocks in the garden. An amazing treehouse structure not only has an appealing room, but also hosts yoga classes. It's 150m past the soccer field. Not all rooms have air-con.

The restaurant knows its audience, serving filling breakfasts, giant burritos, delicious fish tacos and strong drinks.

Casa Zen GUESTHOUSE $
(☑ 2640-0523; www.zencostarica.com; Santa Teresa; dm/d/tr/q incl breakfast US$15/35/42/50; P 🛜) This lovely Asian-inspired guesthouse is decked out in celestial murals and Buddha sculptures. The colorful but basic rooms share bathrooms and two fully equipped kitchens. Some guests have complained that the thin walls and passing traffic detract from the Zen atmosphere; we would argue that the noise is just an opportunity to practice more Zen. On the beach access road.

Just down the alley from Casa Zen is our favorite swimming beach in the area. With white and powdery sand, it's protected by rock reefs on both sides. Lovely hangout spot.

Camping Elimar CAMPGROUND $
(☑ 8357-9819; Mal País; per person US$6) Set on a stunning slice of rocky coastline is this humble family-run campground where a pebble beach rolls on to a rock reef that becomes tide pools. There's ample shade and flat ground where you can pitch your tent, as well as a shared, fully equipped kitchen, showers, bathrooms and electricity. Just off the main north–south road.

⭐ **Casa Pampa** GUESTHOUSE $$
(☑ 8576-0231; www.casapampa.com; Santa Teresa; r US$35, ste US$75-85; P ✳ 🛜) 🗭 Possibly the best deal in all of Santa Teresa. The location is super convenient – surrounded by an overflowing garden, on a quiet road, yet still close to town and the beach. The modest surf chalet has six spick-and-span rooms

with kitchenettes and an outdoor lounge area. Rinse off in the refreshing outdoor shower on your return from the waves.

All rooms have air-con but you'll pay more to use it. Casa Pampa has also taken some initiative in community composting and recycling programs.

Hotel Meli Melo
HOTEL $$

(☑2640-0575; www.hotelmelimelo.com; Santa Teresa; d/tr/q US$60/75/90, apt US$90-120; P✳🛜) A cheerful B&B, smack dab in the center of town and close to the main surf break. Clean, colorful rooms have all standard amenities, plus a private terrace, a common kitchen, tropical gardens and an outdoor shower. Everyone gets a shelf in the communal fridge and access to free bikes. Meli takes great pride in her hotel and it shows.

A new fully equipped apartment with a kitchen is also available. Just over 2km north of the main T intersection on the north–south beach road.

Pachamama
HOTEL $$

(☑2640-0195; www.pacha-malpais.com; Mal País; surf camp rooms US$25, bungalows US$65-75, houses US$160; P🛜) This sweet property offers tremendous value, especially in its quaint faux-adobe bungalows, each with a kitchenette and shady front porch. There's also a two-bedroom house with a romantic wooden loft. Wildlife abounds in the tropical garden. About 1.5km from the T intersection dividing Santa Teresa and Mal País.

Mal País veteran Franz continues to improve the place – surf camp rooms and a BBQ pit were the newest additions at time of research.

Historic footnote: members of the Red Hot Chili Peppers used to attend the now-defunct jam session here.

Malpaís Surf Camp & Resort
LODGE $$

(☑2640-0031; www.malpaissurfcamp.com; Mal País; campsite per person US$15, dm US$17, d with/without bathroom US$73/40, villa from US$108; P✳@🛜🏊) There are comfortable, private *cabañas* and more luxurious digs, but the best deal at this surfers' lodge is the open-air *rancho*, with a tin roof and pebble floors, which you can share with three other surfers. Explore the landscaped tropical grounds, swim in the luscious pool, grab a cold beer in the open-air lounge and soak up the good vibes.

One villa has air-con and TV. South of the T junction.

Star Mountain
LODGE $$

(☑2640-0101; www.starmountaineco.com; Mal País; s/d/tr US$69/85/95, casitas US$159-169; P🛜🏊) 🌿 Set on a 90-hectare private reserve, replete with birds, butterflies and monkeys, Star Mountain is a true escape back to nature. The lodge has four spacious guest rooms, a wide porch with hammocks and rockers, a yoga studio and a glorious pool. It's 2km from the beach in Mal País; turn off the main road at Mary's Restaurant.

Three kilometers of trails traverse the grounds, which you can explore on foot or on horseback.

Funky Monkey Lodge
BUNGALOW $$

(☑2640-0272; www.funkymonkeylodge.com; Santa Teresa; d US$96-102, apt US$136-195; P✳🛜🏊) Located about 100m up a side road off the main drag, this funky lodge has sweet, rustic bungalows built out of bamboo. Each has an open-air shower, balcony with hammock and access to a communal kitchen. Also: table tennis, pool and board games... good times!

Funky Monkey's restaurant turns out some amazing things (eg banana pancakes for breakfast). No matter where you are staying, be sure to stop by on a Wednesday or Saturday night for super sushi.

★Canaima Chill House
BOUTIQUE HOTEL $$$

(☑2640-0410; www.hotel-canaima-chill-house.com; Santa Teresa; d/q US$100/130; P🛜🏊) A 'chill house' is an apt descriptor for this eight-room boutique eco-chic hotel, set in the jungle. Super-stylish suites have breezy indoor-outdoor living areas, well-equipped kitchens, awesome hanging bamboo beds and loads of natural materials (such as stone grotto showers).

Located 400m uphill from the sign for Nautilus Hotel. It can be walked, but you may want a taxi.

Guests share the Jacuzzi and plunge pool, and commune in the sunken pillow lounge.

Hotel Moana
BOUTIQUE HOTEL $$$

(☑2640-0230, toll-free in USA 888-865-8032; www.moanacostarica.com; Mal País; r standard/deluxe US$110/145, ste US$245-275, all incl breakfast; P✳🛜🏊) A simply stunning boutique property etched into the wooded hillside above Mal País. Standard rooms are all-wood garden cottages, decked out with African art. Make the climb to the junior suites for 180-degree views of the coast. There are wood floors throughout, rain showers inside and outside, and sliding glass doors. The top-shelf Papaya Lounge shares that stunning perch.

Atrapasueños
Dreamcatcher Hotel
BOUTIQUE HOTEL $$$

(☏2640-0080; www.dreamcatcherhotel.com; Santa Teresa; d incl breakfast US$140-170, apt US$250; P❋🕸🖥) This family-owned place, steps from the beach, offers the intimacy of a B&B and the luxury of a boutique hotel. With a balcony or terrace overlooking lush gardens, the rooms have hardwood floors, exotic art and tapestries, and big glass sliding doors. A lovely mosaic pool is surrounded by a sun terrace with an outdoor shower.

Florblanca
VILLA $$$

(☏2640-0232; www.florblanca.com; Santa Teresa; villas incl breakfast from US$400; P❋🕸🖥) 🏊 Truly in a class of their own, these romantic villas are scattered around 3hectares of land next to a pristine white-sand beach. Indoor-outdoor spaces are flooded with natural light, and are replete with design details such as open-air bathrooms and sunken indoor-outdoor living areas. Perks include complimentary yoga, bikes and surfboards. An isolated location, 4km north of the intersection. The sensational restaurant Nectar is also highly recommended. The hotel has scored 4 out of 5 'leaves' in the national eco-sustainability rating, and endeavors to benefit the local community.

✖ Eating

Zwart Cafe
CAFE $

(☏2640-0011; Santa Teresa; mains US$4-8; ☺7am-5pm; 🕸) *Zwart* means 'black' in Dutch, but this shabby-chic, artist-owned gallery and cafe is all white (or mostly, damn dust!). You'll love the surf-inspired Technicolor canvases, the lively outdoor patio and the breakfasts, including chocolate chip pancakes. At lunch it's all about the burritos. About 2km north of the T intersection, on the right if you're heading north. There's a dynamite used bookstore here too.

Mafra's Bakery
BAKERY $

(mall at entrance to Playa El Carmen; pastries & bread US$2-4; ☺8am-7pm Mon-Sat) Not the biggest bakery in Playa El Carmen, but longtime residents swear by this Italian *panadería* in the first mall you see as you come into town. Francheska and company whip up a mean *bombolini*, so scrumptious you'll be licking the cream off your fingers afterward.

And, a bunch of good focaccia and pizza-like items too. *Buono appetito!*

Burger Rancho
BURGERS $$

(☏2640-0583; www.facebook.com/BurgerRancho; Santa Teresa; mains US$10-12; ☺11am-10pm; 🥗) Get your burger on at this open-air *rancho* across from the soccer field. Check the blackboard for daily changing specials, including veggie choices like a portobello mushroom burger, fish options like a Hawaiian tuna burger, and other interesting burgers such as a chorizo one. There's other food too, but why would you want to do that? Cash only.

Restaurante & Pizzeria
Playa Carmen
PIZZA $$

(☏2640-0110; www.restaurantepizzeriaplayacarmen.com; Playa El Carmen; mains US$10-23; ☺9am-10pm) The location right on the *playa* is hard to beat, and the list of *ceviche* and cooked fish shows it's more than just a pizzeria. It's a popular spot for sundowners, thanks to the happy-hour specials (two-for-one drinks) and the amazing show that takes place in the sky. Come hobnob with the locals and enjoy.

★ Koji's
JAPANESE $$$

(☏2640-0815; www.santa-teresa.com/kojis; Playa Hermosa; sushi US$5-10; ☺5:30-9:30pm Tue-Sat) Koji Hyodo's sushi shack is a twinkling beacon of fresh, raw excellence. The atmosphere and service are superior, of course, but his food is a higher truth. The grilled octopus is barely fried and sprinkled with sea salt, and there's a sweet crunch to his lobster sashimi, sliced tracing-paper thin and sprinkled with fresh ginger. Uphill from the main road.

Bajo El Arbol
TAPAS $$$

(Playa El Carmen; mains US$15-18; ☺6-10pm) If you can't afford a flight to Spain, just sit down 'Beneath the Tree.' Basque chef Julio whips up extraordinary *escalivada* (eggplant and pepper dish), and the *pulpo a la gallega* (octopus), topped with crunchy sea salt, is so damned good it ought to be illegal. Add a half bottle of Spanish wine, and you'll be smiling till the next morning.

There's also a convenient four-room guesthouse attached. Just 200m north of the T intersection, in Playa El Carmen.

Papaya Lounge
INTERNATIONAL $$$

(☏2640-0230; www.moanacostarica.com; Hotel Moana, Mal País; tapas US$6-15; ☺7:30-10am Tue, 7:30-10am & 5-9pm Wed-Mon) The top-shelf restaurant at the Hotel Moana (p331) is on a stunning perch and has jaw-dropping views and Latin-inspired tapas. The emphasis on local ingredients results in delights such as beef braised in chili and coffee, and seafood skewers in habanero-and-passion-fruit glaze. If you're wondering how much to order, two tapas per person should do the trick.

Mary's Restaurant FUSION $$$
(☑2640-0153; www.maryscostarica.com; Mal País; mains US$10-22; ☺5:30-10pm Thu-Tue) At the far end of Mal País village, this unassuming, open-air restaurant has a polished concrete floor, wood oven, pool table and blackboard menu. It offers delicious wood-fired pizzas, homemade bacon and sausages, grilled seafood and fresh produce straight from the farm. It's all fabulous. Its secret? Using only fresh, organic ingredients from local farms and fishers.

A boutique home and yurt are available to rent, in case you don't want to leave for a couple of days.

Brisas Del Mar SEAFOOD $$$
(☑2640-0941; Playa El Carmen; mains US$15-22; ☺8-10pm Mon-Sat; P) It's worth the steep climb for the sensational views and fancy-looking seafood at the poolside patio restaurant at the Hotel Buenos Aires. Begin with a specialty cocktail as you peruse the day's menu written on the blackboard. Look for fresh *fruits de mer* prepared with international influences; it's almost always fantastic. Cash only.

🍷 Drinking

It's no mystery where the party is going on: Thursdays at Kika, Sundays at Roca Mar and any night of the week – around sunset – at Pizzeria Playa Carmen. **Nativos** (☑2640-0356; www.facebook.com/NativoSportsBar; Playa El Carmen; ☺11:30am-11pm), a Tico-owned sports bar, is smack-dab in the middle of things.

Roca Mar BAR
(☑2640-0250; Santa Teresa; ☺noon-9pm; 📶) Tucked away at the Blue Surf Sanctuary hotel at the northern end of town, this is pretty perfect beach lounge attracts a local expat crowd. Beanbags are stuck in the sand, and hammocks are slung in the trees – all perfectly positioned for sunset. There's an official Sunset Party on Sunday evenings – a family-friendly event with live music and fire dancers.

Kika LIVE MUSIC
(☑2640-0408; www.facebook.com/kika.santateresa; Santa Teresa; ☺5pm-2am) This Argentine-owned restaurant is a popular spot for dinner and drinks by candlelight (Grandma's pork gets rave reviews). But things really pick up after dark on Thursday, when a local punk-rock-ska cover band takes the stage, attracting a lively crowd for drinking and dancing.

ℹ Information

Banco de Costa Rica (☑2211-1111; Playa El Carmen; ☺9am-4pm Mon-Fri) has a 24-hour ATM. Directly across the street at the Centro Comercial Playa El Carmen you'll find a branch of **Banco Nacional** (☑2640-0598; Playa El Carmen; ☺1-7pm Mon-Fri) with an ATM. They'll occasionally run out of cash, so stock up before the weekend.

Malpaisnet (www.malpais.net) A useful website with lots of local information, including a handy map of the area.

ℹ Getting There & Away

BUS
All buses begin and end at Ginger Café, 100m south of Cuesta Arriba hostel, but you can flag the bus down anywhere along the road in Santa Teresa. At Frank's Place, the buses turn left and head inland toward Cóbano.

A direct bus to San José via the Paquera ferry departs at 7:30am and 3:30pm (US$13, six hours). Local buses to Cóbano (US$2, 45 minutes) depart at 7am and noon.

Tropical Tours (☑2640 1900, Whatsapp 8890 9197; www.tropicaltourshuttles.com), with its main office right next to Frank's Place, offers reliable shuttle service around the peninsula and as far as Liberia and the Nicaragua border.

CAR
Consider renting a car if you want to check out some of the more distant breaks. The closest gas station is 2km up the Cóbano road from Playa El Carmen.

Alamo (☑2242-7733; www.alamocostarica.com; Playa El Carmen; ☺8am-5pm) Located at Frank's Place.

Budget (☑2640-0500; www.budget.co.cr; Centro Comercial, Playa El Carmen; ☺8am-6pm Mon-Sat, to 4pm Sun) Next to Banco Nacional.

ℹ Getting Around

Santa Teresa and Mal País are dirt-road types of towns: during the dry season, life gets extremely dusty. The preponderance of ATVs stirs up more grit (and the ire of locals) so consider using a

WORTH A TRIP

RESERVA NATURAL ABSOLUTA CABO BLANCO

Just 11km south of Montezuma is Costa Rica's oldest protected wilderness area. **Cabo Blanco** (☎2642-0093; adult/child US$12/2; ⊙8am-4pm Wed-Sun) comprises 12 sq km of land and 17 sq km of surrounding ocean, and includes the entire southern tip of the Península de Nicoya. The moist microclimate on the tip of the peninsula fosters the growth of evergreen forests, which are unique when compared with the dry tropical forests typical of Nicoya. The park also encompasses a number of pristine white-sand beaches and offshore islands that are favored nesting areas for various bird species.

Cabo Blanco is called an 'absolute' nature reserve because visitors were originally not permitted (prior to the late 1980s). Even though the name hasn't changed, a limited number of trails have been opened to visitors, but the reserve remains closed on Monday and Tuesday to minimize environmental impact.

The **ranger station** (☎2642-0093; ⊙8am-4pm Wed-Sun) is 2km south of Cabuya at the entrance to the park; trail maps are available here.

Buses (US$1.50, 45 minutes) depart from the park entrance for Montezuma at 7am, 9am, 11am and 3pm, passing through Cabuya about 15 minutes later. A taxi from Montezuma to the park costs about US$10 to US$15 (US$10 to Cabuya itself, an extra US$5 to the reserve).

bicycle to get around town, so you're not contributing to the problem. If you must drive, please go slowly. Taxis between Mal País, Playa El Carmen and Santa Teresa range from US$4 to US$8.

Cabuya

POP 200

This tiny, bucolic village unfurls along a rugged dirt road about 7km south of Montezuma. Populated by a tight-knit community of Ticos and expats, it is a hidden gem with easy access to the Cabo Blanco reserve, ideal for those looking to chill. Don't miss the amazing **Cabuya ficus tree**, which is reportedly the largest strangler fig in Costa Rica, measuring 40m high and 22m in diameter.

The beach here is rocky and not great for swimming or surfing. But you're a short walk from **Playa los Cedros**, a great surf spot that is halfway between Montezuma and Cabuya. Alternatively, at low tide you can walk across the natural bridge to **Isla Cabuya**, which has a small sandy beach and good snorkeling spots, as well as an evocative island cemetery. Keep an eye on the tides or you'll have to swim back.

🛏 Sleeping & Eating

El Ancla De Oro　　　　　　　CABINA $
(☎2642-0369; www.hotelelancladeoro.com; s/d US$20/30, cabinas US$35-70; P🐕) This rustic outpost gets mixed reviews from readers. But it seems to be a decent option for budget travelers who want to experience life in the

treetops. The best accommodations are secluded stand-alone 'jungalows,' where you just may spot howler and white-faced monkeys from bed (it's rumored that they're in charge of the cleaning). Located on the road to Montezuma.

Howler Monkey Hotel　　　　　HOTEL $$
(☎2642-0303; www.howlermonkeyhotel.com; s/d/tr/q US$80/100/110/120; P🐕❄) Follow the signs down the side road to these large rustic A-frame bungalows with kitchenettes (useful as eating options are limited). The place is right on a slice of very quiet, rocky beach. The friendly owners are a wealth of information, and also offer bikes and kayaks. It's called Howler Monkey Hotel for a reason: expect a wake-up call.

Hotel Celaje　　　　　　　　CABINA $$$
(Piratas del Celaje; ☎2642-0374; www.celaje. com; s/d/tr/q incl breakfast US$87/102/118/134; P🐕❄) This sweet spot is a collection of spacious, stained-wood A-frame bungalows set on a sublime palm-dappled slice of shore. The grounds are decorated with artistic touches, like coconut lamps and seashell mobiles. The place is right on a beautiful beach, which is not great for swimming due to rocks, but the pool is glorious.

A nice walk at low tide is from here to the Isla Cabuya cemetery.

Café Coyote　　　　　　　　PIZZA $
(☎2642-0354; www.cabuyacr.com/cafe-coyote; mains US$5-11, pizzas US$14-18; ⊙8am-10pm; 🐕) Jenny can help you with just about anything,

from calling a taxi to organizing an adventure outing, pouring you a cold *cerveza* or making you a tasty pizza (her specialty). She also offers delicious breakfasts and other meals to sate your appetite at any time of day. Pick hubby Wilfredo's brain on local birding over a pizza. They also rent a funky converted trailer and apartment (US$25 to US$50) with a kitchenette. It's just after the intersection where the Cabuya road turns right toward Mal Pais.

Panadería Cabuya   CAFE $
(📱 2642-1184; www.facebook.com/panaderiacafeteria.cabuya; mains US$7-20; ⏰ 6:30am-8pm Mon & Wed-Sat, to 6pm Sun; 🌐) A local landmark on the main road from Cabuya to Reserva Cabo Blanco. Set on a tropical patio, this inviting cafe serves up a stellar menu including fresh bread, pastries and strong coffee for breakfast, as well as soups and sandwiches for later. If you have a thing for tall, dark and handsome, you should meet the chocolate cake.

❶ Getting There & Away

Driving from Montezuma, it's a straight shot 7km down the coast to the village of Cabuya. Minibuses make this run – en route to Cabo Blanco – four times a day in either direction.

If you find Café Coyote you have found the road to Mal País, which is about 7km due west on the stunningly scenic Star Mountain Rd (passable only during the dry season). Make sure you have a 4WD, especially during the rainy season, as these roads are rugged and there is at least one river crossing.

Montezuma

POP 7500

Montezuma is an endearing beach town that demands you abandon the car to stroll, swim and (if you can stroll a little further) surf. The warm and wild ocean and that remnant, ever-audible jungle have helped this rocky nook cultivate an inviting, boho vibe. Typical tourist offerings such as canopy tours do a brisk trade here, but you'll also bump up against Montezuma's internationally inflected, artsy-rootsy beach culture in yoga classes, volunteer corps, veggie-friendly dining rooms and neo-Rastas hawking handcrafted jewelry and uplifting herbs. No wonder locals lovingly call this town 'Montefuma.'

It's not perfect. The accommodations are not a great value, and the places to eat can be that way too (though there are some absolute gems). But in this barefoot *pueblo,* which unfurls along several kilometers of rugged coastline, you're never far from the rhythm and sound of the sea, and that is a beautiful thing.

◉ Sights

Picture-perfect white-sand beaches are strung along the coast, separated by small rocky headlands, offering great beachcombing and ideal tide-pool contemplation. Unfortunately, there are strong riptides, so inquire locally before going for a swim.

★ **Montezuma Waterfalls**   WATERFALL
(parking US$2) A 40-minute river hike leads to a waterfall with a delicious swimming hole. Further along, a second set of falls offers a good 10m leap into deep water. Reach the 'diving platform' from the trail: do not try to scale the slippery rocks! Daring souls can test their Tarzan skills on the rope that swings over a third set. A lot of travelers enjoy these thrills but a few of them have died, so do it at your own risk.

To get to the parking area, head south from town and you'll see it just past Hotel La Cascada; once parked, take the trail to the right just after the bridge. You'll want proper hiking footwear. There are official rangers/guards (in official vests/hats) who work the trail and can offer the best advice, free of charge, on the safest routes to take, particularly during rainy season. Families with children or elderly members may want to enter via Sun Trails (p339), which has easy access but charges US$4 parking.

Playa Cocolito   BEACH
Here's your chance to see a waterfall crashing down a cliff, straight onto the rocks and into the ocean. El Chorro Waterfall is the pièce de résistance of Playa Cocolito, which is itself pretty irresistible.

It's a hot, two-hour, 12km hike from Montezuma: leave at sunrise to spot plenty of wildlife along the way. Alternatively, this is a popular destination for horseback riding. In any case, be sure to bring water and snacks as there are no facilities here.

The waters here are a dreamy, iridescent azure, with pink rocky cliffs creating two inviting swimming areas. It's far enough from the action that you are likely to have the place to yourself.

LMSPENCER/SHUTTERSTOCK ©

RON LEVINE/GETTY IMAGES ©

3

1. Montezuma Waterfalls (p335)
A river hike leads to waterfalls and swimming holes.

2. Playa Sámara (p321)
A mellow beach village and surf favorite.

3. Turtles (p320)
Turtle hatchlings find their way to the ocean in Reserva Nacional de Fauna Silvestre Ostional.

4. Montezuma tours (p339)
Ziplining, snorkeling and horseback riding are all on offer.

Montezuma

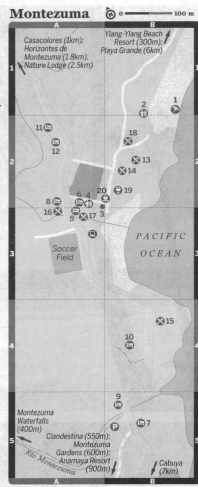

Montezuma

◎ Sights
1 Playa Montezuma B1

✪ Activities, Courses & Tours
Montezuma Yoga .... (see 10)
2 Peaks & Swells Surf Camp B1
3 Sun Trails A2
4 Young Vision Surf School A2
Zuma Tours .... (see 3)

🛏 Sleeping
5 Downtown Montezuma Hostel A3
6 El Sano Banano A2
7 Hotel Amor de Mar B5
8 Hotel El Jardín A2
9 Hotel La Cascada B5
10 Hotel Los Mangos B4
11 Luna Llena A2
12 Luz en el Cielo A2

✕ Eating
13 Cocolores B2
14 Orgánico B2
15 Playa de los Artistas B4
16 Puggo's A3
17 Soda El Balcón del Mar A3
18 The Bakery B2

⚇ Drinking & Nightlife
19 Chico's Bar B2

ⓘ Transport
Montezuma Expeditions .... (see 4)
20 Zuma Tours B2

Playa Montezuma   BEACH
The best beach close to town is just to the
north, where the sand is powdery and sheltered from big swells. This is your glorious
sun-soaked crash pad. The water's shade of
teal is immediately nourishing, the temperature is perfect and fish are abundant. At the
north end of the beach, look for the trail that
leads to a cove known as Piedra Colorada.
A small waterfall forms a freshwater pool,
which is a perfect swimming spot.

🏃 Activities

Young Vision Surf School   SURFING
(☎ 8669-6835; www.youngvisionsurf.com; 2hr
lessons US$45) Manny and Alvaro get rave
reviews for their knowledge, enthusiasm
and patience with new surfers of all ages.
Daily lessons take place on Playa Grande,
with no more than three people in the class.
Surfboard, rash guard and fresh fruit are included. They also offer weeklong camps spe-

Playa Grande   BEACH
About 7km north of town, Playa Grande is
the best surf beach in the area. It's a 3km-
plus stretch of waves and sand, which never
gets too crowded as it requires a 30-minute
hike to get here. But what a hike it is, wan-
dering along between the turquoise waters
of the Pacific and the lush greenery of the
Montezuma Biological Reserve.

Playa Grande is sometimes a destination
for topless or nude sunbathers. This is not
the cultural norm in Costa Rica, so please
be discreet if you're trying to get rid of your
tan lines.

cifically for families, surfer chicks and yogis. Inquire at Sano Banano (p340) for details.

Peaks & Swells Surf Camp SURFING
(2642-0067; www.surfcamppeaksnswells.com; 7-day camp per person US$2950; 🖳) Weeklong camps that are geared to women, families and mountain bikers. If one of these is you, here's a chance to learn how to surf, following systematic methods of instruction. Located on the beach, just north of 'downtown' Montezuma.

Montezuma Yoga YOGA
(8704-1632, 2642-1311; www.montezumayoga. com; per person US$14; ⊙8:30am Mon-Fri, 6pm Tue, Wed, Sat & Sun) Anusara-inspired instruction, which pairs Iyengar alignment principles with a Vinyasa flow, is available in a gorgeous studio kissed by ocean breezes, sheltered by a peaked tin roof and serenaded by the sounds of nature. The Sunday-night candlelight class is a close-to-heaven experience. On the grounds of Hotel Los Mangos (p340).

👉 Tours

Tour operators around town rent everything from bodyboards to bikes. They can also arrange speed-boat transfers to Jacó and private shuttle transfers to other places.

The most popular tour is a boat trip to Isla Tortuga (p345), which costs around US$60 including lunch, fruit, drinks and snorkeling gear. Although the island is certainly beautiful (the *most* beautiful in Costa Rica, by many accounts), travelers complain that the outing feels like a tourist circus, especially during high season when the entire island is full of boat tours.

Also popular are guided hikes in Cabo Blanco and horseback riding to Playa Cocolito.

Sun Trails TOURS
(Montezuma Waterfall Canopy Tour; 2642-0808; www.montezumatraveladventures.com; tours US$45; ⊙9am, 1pm & 3pm) Tour company Sun Trails operates a 1½-hour canopy tour. After you've flown down eight ziplines, you'll hike down – rather than up – to the waterfalls. Bring your swimsuit, so you can jump off the rocks and cool off. Park at the canopy entrance (US$4) for quick access to the falls via a suspension bridge. This company has opened a spotless new lodge on the other side of the swinging bridge, Sun Trails Hotel, with the latest amenities.

Zuma Tours TOURS
(2642-0024; www.zumatours.net; Tortuga snorkeling US$60, canopy tours US$45-50; ⊙7am-9pm) Makes arrangements for transportation and tours of all sorts: snorkeling trips to Isla Tortuga, horseback riding in Cabo Blanco and more. Located on the main downhill east–west street, towards the water.

🛏️ Sleeping

Montezuma is a town distinguished by poor-value lodging, so it makes sense to book in advance. Note that some hotels have a three-night minimum during holiday weeks. There's a sprinkling of guesthouses and boutique hotels north of Montezuma, off the road to Cóbano, some of which are highly recommended, but all of which are only suitable if you have wheels.

⭐**Luz en el Cielo** HOSTEL, B&B $
(2642-0030; www.luzenelcielo.com; dm US$18-28, d/q US$90/136, all incl breakfast; 🅿🛜) In the heart of the jungle but two minutes from town, this homey hostel and B&B is an inviting retreat. Crowded dorm rooms are super clean with sturdy wood furniture and lockers, while the 'luxury' dorms are more spacious, with private balconies and en suite bathrooms. The treetop *cabinas* are also wonderful. Amazing breakfasts from Organico (p341), enticing hammocks and super-friendly staff.

Luna Llena HOSTEL $
(2642-0390; www.lunallenahotel.com; dm US$15, s/d US$55/65, without bathroom US$28/38; 🅿🛜) On the northern edge of town on a hilltop overlooking the bay, this budget option is absolutely delightful and truly unique. The rooms are simple but stylish, colorful and clean; most have balconies. There is one massive kitchen, a BBQ grill and a breezy communal lounge with rattan chair-swings and stunning ocean views. Wildlife abounds in the surrounding trees.

Free daily onsite yoga classes May to December at 4pm.

Downtown Montezuma Hostel HOSTEL $
(8516-6921; www.dtmontezuma.com; dm US$14, d with/without bathroom US$45/35; 🛜) This funky little two-story hostel has art on all the walls, a clean communal kitchen and plenty of hammocks for your swinging pleasure. Rates all include all-you-can drink coffee and make-your-own pancakes for breakfast. The rooms – four-bed dorms and

private doubles – are nothing special, but guests love the fun, friendly vibe. Quiet time after 11pm is strictly enforced.

Located just where the main road meets the town proper, close to the T intersection.

Hotel Los Mangos   HOTEL $

(☑2642-0076; www.hotellosmangos.com; r with/without bathroom US$75/35, bungalows US$90; P ☀ 🖥 🛋) Scattered across mango-dotted gardens, this whimsical hotel has plain, painted-wood rooms in the main building and attractive (though dark) octagonal bungalows offering more privacy. Monkeys populate the mango trees and yoga classes (p339) are held in the gorgeous, ocean-view yoga pavilion, next to a pool with an accompanying Jacuzzi. On the road south of town on the way to the waterfall.

Horizontes de Montezuma   GUESTHOUSE $$

(☑8403-6838; www.facebook.com/hotelhorizontes demontezuma; d US$85; P ☀ 🖥 🛋) This gem is situated about 2km north (and uphill) from Montezuma, in a colonial-style building surrounded by spectacular blooming gardens. Rooms are crisp, clean and impeccable, with a few fine stylistic touches, including very chic bathrooms. Private verandas yield glorious views of the forest canopy. The hosts go above and beyond to make sure their guests are supremely satisfied.

Hotel La Cascada   HOTEL $$

(☑2642-0057; www.lacascadamontezuma.com; s & d incl breakfast US$60, air-con US$10; P ☀ 🖥) At the mouth of the river, en route to the waterfalls, this classic Montezuma hotel has 15 simple wooden rooms with flowy curtains and crisp white sheets. A huge 2nd-floor terrace faces the ocean and has hammocks perfect for swinging, snoozing or spying on the local troop of howlers (monkeys, not drunks). Owner Itza runs a clean, family-oriented operation.

The onsite restaurant, b.bar, is the perfect place to recover from your waterfall hike with a smoothie or by partnering a Costa Rican craft ale with a burger and yucca fries.

Hotel El Jardín   CABINA $$

(Cabinas El Jardín; ☑2642-0074; www.hotelel jardin.com; d US$85-105, casas US$130-135; P ☀ @ 🖥 🛋) This hillside hotel has 16 stained-wood cabinas, some with stone bathrooms, wide balconies and ocean views. The grounds are landscaped with tropical flowers and lush palms. The centerpiece is surely the bilevel swimming pool, complete

with whirlpool and waterfall, making this place quite a nice little three-star resort. Right at the entrance to town, where Ruta 624 hits 'downtown.'

El Sano Banano   HOTEL $$

(☑2642-0523; www.elsanobanano.com; s/d/tr/q US$80/86/108/130; P ☀ 🖥) A well-run hotel in the center of town. Although its many businesses take up an entire city block, it has just 12 prim and comfortable rooms with whimsical paint jobs. Many rooms do not have windows, but the walls are adorned with trees, flowers and ocean views.

Guests may use the Ylang Ylang Resort pool for free.

The attached restaurant has appetizing baked goods and an inviting terrace on the main drag. It's also worth showing up in the evening when the restaurant shows nightly films in the garden out back.

Anamaya Resort   RESORT $$$

(☑2642-1289; www.anamaya.com; per week incl 3 meals from US$1125; P ☀ 🛋) Billed as a 'mind, body, and soul retreat,' Anamaya's perch, high above Montezuma, is pretty damn special. With ocean panoramas and weeping jungle on all sides, this environment is certainly dramatic enough to spark enlightenment, if only for a heartbeat. The yoga space floats off the main house and has that insane aforementioned view, as does the adjacent infinity pool.

Yoga classes, surf lessons and lots of other activities are available as 'retreat add-ons'. Monthlong teacher training happens here, too. Located on a side road just past the waterfalls.

Casacolores   BUNGALOW $$$

(☑2642-0283; www.casacolores.com; 1-/2-bedroom casas US$101/158; P ☀ 🖥 🛋) Nine bright houses (each painted and named for a color of the rainbow) are fully equipped with kitchens and big porches with hammocks. They're set amid blooming tropical gardens, with a stone-rimmed swimming pool onsite. The location is sort of a no-man's land (a 20-minute uphill hike from town) but there's plenty of wildlife wandering around these jungly grounds.

Ylang-Ylang Beach Resort   RESORT $$$

(☑in USA 888-795-8494, 2642-0402; www.ylang ylangresort.com; tents/r/bungalows incl breakfast & dinner US$200/250/333; ☀ 🖥 🛋) Walk 15 minutes north along the beach to this lush four-star property, complete with beautifully appointed rooms and bungalows, and a palm-fringed swimming pool, yoga center, gourmet organic restaurant and spa. The decor is lovely and tropical, with tile floors, stenciled walls and colorful tapestries. All accommodations have outdoor terraces facing the glorious sea.

Does that say US$200 for a tent? Yes, it does. It's actually a tent *cabin*, with a wooden floor, private bathroom and king-size bed, but still, it's a tent.

Hotel Amor de Mar B&B $$$

(☑2642-0262; www.amordemar.com; d with/without ocean view from US$150/102, villas US$282-305; P🖅) A lovely B&B just south of town with nine unique rooms, replete with exquisite touches like timber-framed mirrors, organic lanterns, and rocking chairs on a terrace. Then there's the palm-dappled lawn that rolls out to the tide pools and the Pacific beyond, and a tented massage table. It's gorgeous to look at, although the back rooms get some road noise.

The breakfast (US$5 to US$7) includes home-made challah and linseed breads and jams by owner Ori.

🍴 Eating & Drinking

Montezuma is experiencing the same food revolution that is taking place on other parts of the peninsula. Local ingredients are meeting international chefs, with magnificent results. Montezuma is also good for traditional Tico fare, often with oceanside service. Most of the restaurants are clustered along the beach.

The Bakery COSTA RICAN $

(Restaurante y Panadería; ⊙6am-10pm) A gentle feeling permeates this no-frills Tico family operation on the beach road, adorned with Hindu tapestries and a mural of the nearby beach. It's cheap, too, and you'll love the refreshing *batidos* (fruit shakes), as well as the filling *casados* and *arrozes* (rice dishes). Early risers go for the homemade pancakes or French toast. The menu's scrawled in ballpoint ink on a pink sheet of paper. Formerly known as Kalibó.

Soda El Balcón del Mar SEAFOOD $

(www.facebook.com/sodaelbalcondelmar; mains US$8-12; ⊙7am-midnight) Hang out below the Tico-themed red-white-and-blue Chinese lanterns on the balcony overlooking the beach, watch flocks of pelicans drift by and kiss the afternoon goodbye. Lip-smacking appetizers include mussels and clams, and you can get a whole-fish catch of the day if that's your thing. Some wait for the grill to heat up, though, for a healthy rack of BBQ ribs. Located across from the taxi stand.

★Clandestina LATIN AMERICAN $$

(Cocina Hispanoamericana; ☑8315-8003; www.facebook.com/clandestinamontezuma; mains US$8-12; ⊙noon-9pm Tue-Sat; 🖅) The secret is out. The hottest restaurant in Montezuma is this awesome, artistic place in the trees at the butterfly gardens. Look for innovative takes on Central American standards, such as daily changing taco specials and delectable chicken mole enchiladas. Vegetarians are joyfully accommodated with yam and lentil cakes or *chilles rellenos* (stuffed peppers). Try the Butterfly Beer, brewed onsite.

Tierra y Fuego ITALIAN $$

(☑2642-1593; mains US$8-15; ⊙5-10pm; P🖅) Take a taxi up to this gem in the hills above Montezuma – fittingly in the Delicias neighborhood. This Italian outpost seems straight out of the Tuscan countryside, complete with brick ovens, and chickens roasting over the fire. The menu is mostly pizza and pasta, but the flavors are divine – not surprising given the ingredients are all imported or grown onsite.

Cocolores INTERNATIONAL $$

(☑2642-0348; mains US$9-22; ⊙5-10pm Tue-Sun) Set on a beachside terrace lit with lanterns, Cocolores is one of Montezuma's top spots for an upscale dinner. The wide-ranging menu includes curries, pasta, fajitas and steaks, all prepared and served with careful attention to delicious details. Prices aren't cheap but it's worth it.

Puggo's MIDDLE EASTERN $$

(☑8705-1077, 2642-0325; Ruta 624; mains US$10-20; ⊙5-11pm) A locally beloved restaurant decorated like a bedouin tent, Puggo's specializes in Middle Eastern cuisine, including falafel, hummus, kebabs and aromatic fish, which are dressed in imported spices and herbs and roasted whole. Cap it off with a strong cup of Turkish coffee. It now shares space with a sushi restaurant, Natsu, if that floats your boat instead. Located just before the soccer field, heading south of town.

Orgánico VEGETARIAN $$

(☑2642-1322; www.organicocostarica.com; mains US$8-12; ⊙8am-10pm; 🖅) When they say 'pure food made with love,' they mean it –

this healthy cafe turns out vegetarian and vegan dishes such as spicy Thai burgers, smoothies named for icons like Marley and Hendrix (try the Purple Haze) and more (as well as meaty options too). The avocado ice cream is something everyone should try. There's live music almost nightly, including a wildly popular open mic on Monday nights. It's opposite the church square, on the road leading north to the beach

★ **Playa de los Artistas** INTERNATIONAL $$$
(☑ 2642-0920; www.montezumabeach.com/playa-de-los-artistas; mains US$9-18; ⏱ 4:30-8:30pm Tue-Fri, from noon Sat) Most romantic dinner ever. If you're lucky, you'll snag one of the tree-trunk tables under the palms. The international menu with Mediterranean influences changes daily, though you can always count on fresh seafood roasted in the wood oven. The service is flawless, the cooking is innovative and the setting is downright dreamy. Cash only (back to reality) so bring lots. Located just past the soccer field, on the beach side of the road leading to the waterfall.

Chico's Bar BAR
(⏱ 11am-2am) When it comes to nightlife, Chico's is the main game in town, which means that everybody – old, young, Ticos, tourists, rowdy, dowdy – ends up here eventually, especially on Thursday night, which is reggae night. Snag a table on the back patio for a lovely view of the beach and beyond. On the main road parallel to the beach.

ℹ Information

The only ATM in town is a BCR *cajero automático* located across from Chico's Bar, and it sometimes runs out of cash in a town where many restaurants insist upon it. The nearest full-service bank is in Cóbano, which is just down the road and also has a few more ATMs. For money exchange, tour operators in town will take US dollars, euros or traveler's checks.

Right next to the bus stop, **El Parque** (☑ 2642-0164; ⏱ 7am-8pm) is a central place to get your laundry done. There are a few other low-cost *lavandarias* along this same road.

ℹ Getting There & Around

BOAT
Zuma Tours (p339) operates a fast water shuttle connecting Montezuma to Jacó in an hour. At US$40 or so, it's not cheap, but it'll save you a day's worth of travel. From Montezuma, boats depart at 8:30am daily, and the price includes van transfer from the beach to the Jacó bus terminal. From Jacó, the departure to Montezuma is at 11am. During the high season, it may run an additional shuttle, departing Montezuma at 1:30pm and departing Jacó at 3pm. Book in advance from any tour operator. Also, dress appropriately; you will get wet.

BUS
Buses depart Montezuma from the sandy lot on the beach, across from the soccer field. Buy tickets directly from the driver. To get to Mal País and Santa Teresa, go to Cóbano and change buses. The Paquera bus can drop you at the entrance to Refugio Nacional de Vida Silvestre Curú.

Montezuma Expeditions (☑ 2430-6541; www.montezumaexpeditions.com; US$40-70) and Tropical Tours (p333) operate daily private shuttles to San José, La Fortuna, Monteverde, Jacó, Manuel Antonio, Dominical, Tamarindo, Sámara and Liberia.

CAR
Although the road from Paquera to Cóbano is paved, the stretch between Cóbano and Montezuma is not, and it can be brutal. During the rainy season you may need a 4WD. In the village itself, parking can be a problem, though it's easy enough to walk everywhere.

Playas Pochote & Tambor

POP 13,250

These two mangrove-backed, gray-sand beaches are protected by Bahía Ballena, the largest bay on the southeastern peninsula, and are surrounded by small fishing communities. In the past 15 years, the area has slowly developed as a resort destination, but

BUSES FROM MONTEZUMA

DESTINATION	PRICE (US$)	DURATION	DEPARTURES
Cabo Blanco via Cabuya	1.50	45min	8 buses 5:30am-8pm
Cóbano	2	1hr	8:15am, 10:15am, 12:15pm & 4:15pm
Paquera, via Cóbano	3	2hr	3:45am, 6am, 10am, noon, 2pm & 4pm
San José	14	5hr	7:30am & 3:30pm

for the most part, Pochote and Tambor are mellow, authentic Tico beaches, providing plenty of opportunities for hiking, swimming, kayaking and even whale-watching.

The beaches begin 14km south of Paquera, at the mangrove-shrouded, fishing *pueblo* of Pochote, and stretch for about 8km southwest to Tambor. The two villages are divided by the narrow estuary of the Río Pánica.

It should also be said that there is one rather conspicuous all-inclusive megaresort in the Tambor area – Hotel Barceló Playa Tambor (its garish entrance looks like the UN). The huge place has a convention center and golf course, but once you're in the *pueblo*, you won't even know it's there.

Both beaches are safe for swimming and kayaking, and there are occasional whale sightings in the bay. Pochote and Tambor also have easy access to the Refugio Nacional de Vida Silvestre Curú and all that it has to offer.

🛏 Sleeping

⭐ **Mar y Sol Ecotel**   GUESTHOUSE $
(☑ in USA 1-720-432-9551, 8335-5300, 2683-1065; www.marysolecotel.com; d/q US$69/89; P ✳ 🛜) The location seems odd – stuck on a side road with no beach in sight – but the attentive owners and art-filled premises make it an excellent budget option. Eight rooms have been thoughtfully decked out with custom furniture and mural-painted walls. Aircon and hot water are available on request. The beach is actually only 400m away, you just can't see it.

Cabinas Cristina   CABINAS $
(☑ 2683-0028; r US$30-62; P 🛜) Just 50m from the beach, and across from Tambor's rather romantically ramshackle Victorian church, this old standby has simple and spotless rooms, and a small but tasty homestyle restaurant. The owners are warm and welcoming and offer valuable travel tips. Room prices vary with size and amenities (ie you'll pay more for air-con). One large unit has a full kitchen.

Tambor Tropical   BOUTIQUE HOTEL $$$
(☑ 2365-2872; www.tambortropical.com; ste incl breakfast US$170-230; P ✳ 🛜 🏊) Romantically set on the beach amid a palm-fringed garden, Tambor Tropical is a lovely boutique hotel with stunning architecture. The 12 roomy, hexagonal suites all have dark wood interiors, full kitchens and private verandas, most with sunrise views. The place is a boon

for birders: nearly 300 species have been spotted around the property, including some raucous scarlet macaws.

Hotel Costa Coral   BOUTIQUE HOTEL $$$
(☑ 2683-0207; www.hotelcostacoral.com; s/d/tr/q US$95/110/120/140; P ✳ 🛜 🏊) A major price shift has made this charming hotel in the center of Tambor more of a bargain. Nine classy rooms surround a gorgeous garden that is bursting with blooms. Recommended restaurant and spa onsite. The glorious beach is a mere five-minute walk away. On the downside, locals question the hotel's inconsistent opening hours.

ℹ Getting There & Around

The airport is just north of the entrance to Hotel Barceló Playa Tambor. Hotels will arrange pickup at the airport for an extra fee. Between them, Sansa (p96) and NatureAir (p96) have up to a dozen daily flights to and from San José (one way US$115 to US$134).

There's a **Budget** (☑ 2436-2085; www.budget.co.cr; Ruta 160; ⊗ 8am-6pm Mon-Sat, to 4pm Sun) car-rental place 4km from the Tambor airport. It has a free shuttle to and from the 'terminal.' If you're not renting wheels, you can hop on one of the Paquera–Montezuma buses passing through here.

Refugio Nacional de Vida Silvestre Curú

Situated at the eastern end of the peninsula and only 6km south of Paquera, the tiny, 84-hectare **Refugio Nacional de Vida Silvestre Curú** (☑ 2641-0100; www.curuwildliferefuge.com; adult/child US$12/6; ⊗ 7am-3pm) holds a great variety of landscapes, including dry tropical forest, semideciduous forest and five types of mangrove swamp. The rugged coastline is also home to a series of secluded coves and white-sand beaches that are perfect for snorkeling and swimming, while hiking trails traverse varied but beautiful landscapes.

🏃 Activities

Visitors have access to 17 well-marked, easy to moderate trails, through the various landscapes. Or, join a variety of tours: horseback riding on the beach, kayaking through the estuary, snorkeling around the coves, or hiking with a naturalist guide. Local fauna includes iguanas, deer, three types of monkey, agoutis and *pacas*, plus three species of wildcat. Crabs, lobsters, chitons (mollusks), shellfish, sea turtles and other marine creatures can be found on the beaches and in the tide pools. Birdwatchers have recorded more than 232 avian species.

Turismo Curú TOURS
(2641-0004; www.curutourism.com; snorkeling US$40, bioluminescence tour US$55; 8am-9pm) Anything that you might want to do at Curú wildlife refuge, Luis can make it happen. A boat trip to Tortuga includes snorkeling at Islas Mortreros and a beach BBQ. The most unique offering is the evening Bioluminescence Tour, kayaking to beautiful Quesera beach and swimming/snorkeling in the luminescent waters. The office is right on the beach.

Sleeping

Refugio Nacional de Vida Silvestre Curú Cabinas CABINA $
(2641-0100; www.curuwildliferefuge.com; r per person US$30) There are six rustic *cabinas* on the grounds of the wildlife reserve. The accommodations are bare and the showers are cold, but they are beautifully situated about 50m from the waves. Also, you'll be in good company (white-faced capuchin monkeys, primarily). Your reserve fee is included in the cost of the room. Advance arrangements required. Meals are US$10.

Getting There & Away

The entrance to the refuge is clearly signed on the paved road between Paquera and Tambor (about 6km from Paquera). Alternatively, the Paquera–Montezuma bus passes this way and will drop you at the park entrance upon request.

Paquera
POP 7900

The tiny village of Paquera is about 12km by road from Playa Naranjo and 4km from the Paquera ferry terminal. Paquera is not much of a destination in its own right, but it can be a useful base for a few days of exploring Refugio Nacional de Vida Silvestre Curú and the offshore islands. Short of that, you might want to spend a night here if you arrive on a late ferry from Puntarenas – instead of tackling those challenging roads in the dark.

WHO WAS KARL HOFFMANN?

It's a common cry among local birders in places like Curú when they spot the attractive red-and-yellow-headed woodpecker *Melanerpes hoffmanni*: 'oh, that's a Hoffmann's!' But who was this Hoffmann?

Karl Hoffmann is one of many *extranjeros* (foreigners) to play a role in Costa Rica's history, but even among 19th-century adventurers, his is a unique story. Born in Stettin, Prussia in 1823, Hoffmann obtained his medical degree from the University of Berlin at age 23. At university he met Alexander von Frantzius, with whom he would travel to Costa Rica in December 1853. They shared a passion for medicine and natural history.

Hoffmann worked as a doctor, naturally, but also sold spirits from his home to make ends meet, as well as being the editor of a German newspaper. But his name lives on, literally, in his work as a naturalist: he collected and sent more than 1,000 plant and animal specimens to Berlin, and 22 Costa Rican plants and 16 animals now bear his surname, among them orchids, sloths and that woodpecker.

Hoffmann's exploits went even beyond the realm of naturalist: when William Walker's infamous filibusters invaded Costa Rica in 1856, he was called upon as chief surgeon of the young nation's military, and served bravely and intelligently in the famed victory at Santa Rosa, and later under more difficult circumstances trying to combat not Walker's rifles, but an invisible killer, cholera.

Hoffmann was rewarded with a pension from the Costa Rican nation, though he didn't live long enough to enjoy it. In 1859, he and his wife resettled in Puntarenas, but Amelia died of typhoid soon after. Hoffmann's own death, at the young age of 35, followed shortly after his wife's. He is remembered fondly by his second country for his medical, scientific and humanitarian endeavors. He was buried in his lieutenant's uniform and, seven decades later, in May 1929, he was reinterred with full military honors in San Jose's national cemetery, his ashes buried in an urn between the twin banners of Germany and Costa Rica, with thousands of citizens, contemporary president Cleto Gonzalez Viquez, and the Costa Rican cabinet in attendance.

🛏 Sleeping

While there are some budget *cabinas* right in town, there's nothing to be gained by staying there. You're better off staying on the outskirts (or in the hills, if you can afford it), for a more peaceful setting.

Mapi's Cabins   CABINA $
(☑ 2641-1133; www.costarica4vacation.com; r US$40; ❋ 🕏 🌊) Mapi's is a comfortable stop. Your room price includes a decent bed, cool air-con and warm showers. Bonus: fill up on mangoes and other tropical fruits grown onsite. This is a popular stop for humming-birds, so bring your camera. It's is located just north of town, along the road to the ferry.

Hotel Vista Las Islas   HOTEL $$$
(Eco Boutique Hotel; ☑ 2641-0722, 2641-0817; www.hotelvistalasislas.com; d US$192; 🅿 ❋ 🕏 🌊) As implied by the name, the amazing pano-ramic view of the islands is the selling point here. It really is spectacular, and you can enjoy it from your private balcony, from the restaurant or from the magnificent infinity pool. It's a short walk (15min) to Playa Órga-nos, where you can swim, surf or stand-up paddle.

❶ Getting There & Away

All transportation is geared to the arrival and de-parture of the Puntarenas ferry. If either the bus or the ferry is running late, the other will wait.

BOAT

Ferry Naviera Tambor (☑ 2661-2084; www. navieratambor.com; adult/child/bicycle/ motorcycle/car US $1.65/1/4/7/23) leaves daily at 5:30am, 9am, 11am, 2pm, 5pm and 8pm. The trip to Puntarenas takes about an hour. Buy a ticket at the window, reboard your car and then drive on to the ferry; you can't buy a ticket on board. Show up at least an hour early on holidays and busy weekends. The terminal contains a *soda* where you can grab a bite while waiting for the boat.

BUS

Buses meet arriving passengers at the ferry terminal and take them to Paquera, Tambor and Montezuma. They can be crowded, so try to get off the ferry fast to secure a seat. Most travelers take the bus from the terminal directly to Mon-tezuma (US$3, two hours). Many taxi drivers will tell you the bus won't come, but this isn't true. There are no northbound buses.

Islands Near Bahía Gigante

The waters in and around the isolated Bahía Gigante, 9km southeast of Playa Naranjo, are studded with rocky islets and deserted islands. Isla San Lucas is tucked into the Golfo de Nicoya, while lovely Islas Gigante and Tortuga hang off the southeastern cor-ner of the peninsula. These idyllic outposts are popular destinations for sportfishers and sea kayakers, scuba divers and snorkel-ers, who relish the fantasy of exploring some uncharted desert isle.

☞ Tours

In addition to party cruises departing from Jacó, tour operators in Jacó and Montezu-ma offer smaller-scale excursions to these islands, especially Isla Tortuga. Hotels in Tambor can also make the arrangements.

Turismo Curú offers a half-day boat trip to Isla Tortuga, which is only 3km from the wildlife refuge. This unique tour makes an effort to avoid the crowds by visiting in the morning (when other boats are still en route) and hitting lesser-known spots.

Hotel Vista Las Islas has the advantage of proximity to Tortuga. Its all-day tour in-cludes snorkeling and lunch, as well as kay-aking or horseback riding. The hotel also offers day trips to Isla San Lucas.

Isla Tortuga

Isla Tortuga is actually two uninhabited islands, just offshore from Refugio Nacion-al de Vida Silvestre Curú. This stunner – a quintessential tropical paradise – is widely regarded as the most beautiful island in Cos-ta Rica. The pure white sand feels like baby powder; gargantuan coconut palms tower overhead; and clear turquoise waters lap up on the shores. Snorkelers usually enjoy good visibility and a wide variety of sea life, although there is no reef here. Jet Skis and kayaks are sometimes on offer, depending on your tour.

Unfortunately, Tortuga receives heavy boat traffic from tour operators from Mon-tezuma and Jacó, and the crowds quickly detract from the magic of this place. If pos-sible, avoid weekends and holidays. Even better, avoid high season.

Isla San Lucas

The largest island in Bahía Gigante (just over 600 hectares) is about 5km off the coast from Playa Naranjo. From a distance, it seems like a beautiful desert island, but the 'Island of Unspeakable Horrors' has a 400-year history as one of the most notorious prisons in Latin America. In 2001 the island was declared a national park. Visitors can expect to learn about the island's checkered history and explore the 100-year-old remains of the prison. Most tours also allow time to hike the trails and relax on the island's sandy shores.

Isla San Lucas was first used by Spanish conquistadors as a detention center for local tribes in the 16th century. Later, the Costa Rican government used the island to detain political prisoners until 1992. Writer José León Sánchez wrote about his experiences as a prisoner in his book *La Isla de Hombres Solos* (Island of the Lonely Men). Sánchez spent 30 years in this jail for a crime he didn't commit; he was later absolved of the crime.

Nowadays, visitors can explore the remains of the prison and church and bear witness to the island's history of suffering and redemption.

Playa Naranjo

POP 200

This tiny village next to the ferry terminal is nothing more than a few *sodas* and small hotels that cater to travelers either waiting for the ferry or arriving from Puntarenas. There isn't any reason to hang around.

ⓘ Getting There & Away

All transportation is geared to the arrival and departure of the Puntarenas ferry, so don't worry – if one is running late, the other will wait.

BOAT

The **Coonatramar ferry** (☎ 2661-1069; www. coonatramar.com; adult/child/bicycle/motorcycle/car US$2/1/4/6/18) to Puntarenas departs daily at 8am, 12:30pm, 4:30pm and 8:30pm, and can accommodate both cars and passengers. The trip takes 1½ hours. If traveling by car, get out and buy a ticket at the window, get back in your car and then drive on to the ferry. You cannot buy a ticket on board. Show up at least an hour early on holidays and busy weekends, as you'll be competing with a whole lot of other drivers to make it on.

BUS

Buses meet the arriving ferry and take passengers on to Jicaral, for travel on to the more northerly parts of the peninsula. If you're headed to Montezuma or Mal País, take the other ferry from Puntarenas to Paquera.

CAR

If you are driving yourself, it's unlikely that you'll need to pass this way. Heading north, you'll be better off driving over the Puente de la Amistad to the peninsula instead of taking the ferry. And heading to Mal País or Montezuma, you should take the Puntarenas–Paquera ferry. That said, Ruta 21 is a mostly paved road that connects Playa Naranjo to Nicoya (via Jicaral). It is also possible to get to Paquera (and further to Mal País or Montezuma) via a scenic, rugged and steep but passable road over three inland ridges with magical vistas of Bahía Gigante. A 4WD is recommended, especially in the rainy season when there might be rivers to cross.

Central Pacific Coast

Best Places to Eat

➡ Exotica (p404)

➡ Z Gastro Bar (p375)

➡ Graffiti (p365)

➡ Sabor Español (p400)

➡ Ylang-Ylang (p404)

➡ Kapi Kapi Restaurant (p381)

Best Places to Stay

➡ El Castillo (p403)

➡ Villas Jacquelina (p374)

➡ Rafiki Safari Lodge (p388)

➡ Danyasa Yoga Retreat (p394)

➡ Cascada Verde (p399)

➡ Makanda by the Sea (p379)

Why Go?

Stretching from the rough-and-ready port of Puntarenas to the tiny town of Uvita, the central Pacific coast is home to wet and dry tropical forests, sun-drenched beaches and a healthy dose of wildlife. On shore, national parks protect endangered squirrel monkeys and scarlet macaws, while offshore waters nurture migrating whales and pods of dolphins.

With so much biodiversity packed into a small geographic area, it's no wonder the region is often thought of as Costa Rica in miniature. Given its close proximity to San José, and its well-developed system of paved roads, this part of the country is a favorite weekend getaway for domestic and international travelers.

While threats of unregulated growth are real, particularly with a new, $3.5-billion international airport approved for construction in Orotina, it's also important to see the bigger picture, namely the stunning nature that first put the central Pacific coast on the map.

When to Go

➡ Rains fall heavily from April to November, making this the best time to hit the waves in Playa Hermosa and Jacó.

➡ Whale watching in Uvita is at its best from December to March and again from July to November.

➡ Festival fans will want to visit when music and art gatherings light up Jacó and Uvita in January and February.

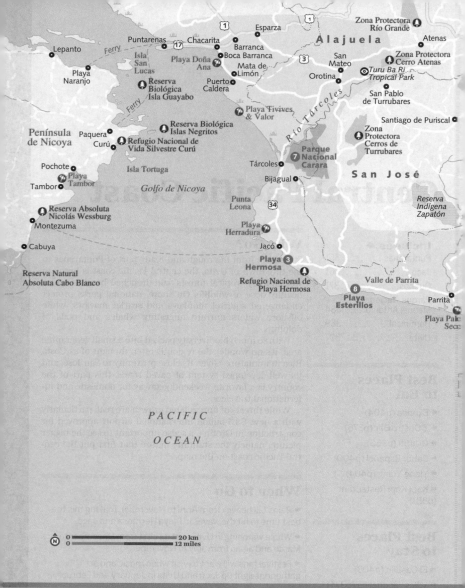

Central Pacific Coast Highlights

1 Parque Nacional Manuel Antonio (p384) Spying on playful monkeys and slow-moving sloths, adventuring in the rainforest and catching some sun at the beach.

2 Dominical (p389) Surfing by day, raging by night, with spiritual yoga and festival interludes.

3 Playa Hermosa (p368) Surfing some of the country's best beach breaks – or watching the pros.

4 Parque Nacional Marino Ballena (p401) Scanning the horizon for pods of breaching humpback whales from a

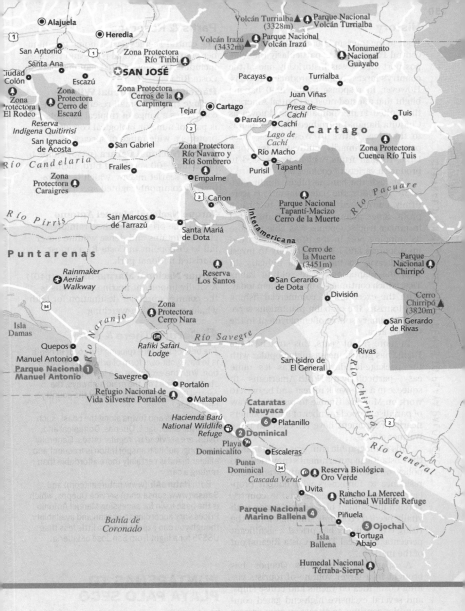

Alajuela ○ ①

① 1

San Antonio

Santa Ana

Heredia ○

① 1

Ciudad Colón ○

Escazú ○

Zona Protectora El Rodeo ①

Zona Protectora Cerro de Escazú ①

Reserva Indígena Quitirrisí

San Ignacio de Acosta ○

San Gabriel ○

Zona Protectora Cerro de la Carpintera ①

Tejar ○

Volcán Turrialba ▲ (3328m)

Parque Nacional Volcán Turrialba ▲

Volcán Irazú ▲ (3432m)

Parque Nacional Volcán Irazú ▲

Monumento Nacional Guayabo ①

Zona Protectora Río Tiribí ①

✪ **SAN JOSÉ**

Pacayas ○

Turrialba ○

Juan Viñas ○

Tuis ○

Cartago

Presa de Cachí

② **Cartago** ●

Paraíso ○

Cachí ○

Lago de Cachí

Río Macho ○

Zona Protectora Río Navarro y Río Sombrero ①

Zona Protectora Cuenca Río Tuis ①

Río Pacuare

Frailes ○

Zona Protectora Caraigres ①

Empalme ○

② Cañón ○

San Marcos de Tarrazú ○

Santa María de Dota ○

Parque Nacional Tapantí-Macizo Cerro de la Muerte ①

Purisil ○

Tapantí ○

Río Candelaria

Río Pirris

Puntarenas

Rainmaker Aerial Walkway

Interamericana

Cerro de la Muerte ▲ (3451m)

Parque Nacional Chirripó ①

Reserva Los Santos ①

San Gerardo de Dota ○

División ○

Cerro Chirripó ▲ (3820m)

34

Isla Damas

Zona Protectora Cerro Nara ①

Río Naranjo

Río Savegre

San Gerardo de Rivas ○

Rafiki Safari Lodge

Quepos ○

Manuel Antonio ○

Parque Nacional Manuel Antonio ①

Rivas ○

Savegre ○

Portalón ○

San Isidro de El General ○

Río Chirripó

2

Refugio Nacional de Vida Silvestre Portalón ①

Matapalo ○

Cataratas Nauyaca

⑥ Platanillo ○

Río General

Hacienda Barú National Wildlife Refuge ①

② **Dominical**

⑦

Playa Dominicalito

Escaleras ○

Punta Dominical

34

Cascada Verde

Reserva Biológica Oro Verde ① ①

Bahía de Coronado

Uvita ○

Rancho La Merced National Wildlife Refuge ①

Parque Nacional Marino Ballena ④

Piñuela ○

⑤ Ojochal ○

Isla Ballena

Tortuga Abajo ○

Humedal Nacional Térraba-Sierpe ①

History

Prior to the tourism boom in Costa Rica, the central Pacific coast – particularly the Quepos port area – was historically one of the country's largest banana-producing regions. However, in response to the 1940 banana blight that affected most of Central America, the United Fruit Company (also known as Chiquita Banana) introduced African palms to the area. Native to West Africa, these palms are primarily cultivated for their large, reddish fruits, which are pressed to produce a variety of cooking oils.

Although the banana blight finally ended in the 1960s, the palm plantations were firmly entrenched and starting to turn a profit. Since palm oil is easily transported in tanker trucks, Quepos was able to close its shipping port in the 1970s, which freed up resources and allowed the city to invest more heavily in the palm-oil industry. In 1995 the plantations were sold to Palma Tica, which continues to operate them today. With the exception of commercial fishing and tourism, the oil-palm plantations serve as the primary source of employment in the Quepos area.

In more recent years, this stretch of the Pacific has grown increasingly popular with the package-holiday crowd, as it's quite easy – particularly for North Americans – to squeeze in a one-week retreat and be back to work on Monday. Unable to resist the draw of paradise, a good number of baby boomers nearing retirement have relocated to these warmer climes.

This demographic shift was facilitated by the Costa Rican government's (now defunct) policy of offering tax incentives and legal residence to foreigners who bought property or started businesses in the country. Foreign investment blessed this region with vitally needed economic stimuli, though the rising cost of living has priced a significant percentage of local Ticos (Costa Ricans) out of the market.

A sparkling marina at Quepos has brought in a larger volume of tourists visiting Costa Rica on yachts and cruise ships, and several exclusive high-end gated communities continue to attract an even greater number of wealthy immigrants. Things have changed quickly along this stretch of coastline, though it's difficult to imagine that the authenticity of the coastal fishing villages, agricultural plantations and protected areas could ever be totally lost.

Parks & Reserves

The central Pacific coast is home to a number of excellent national parks and reserves, including the most visited national park in Costa Rica.

Hacienda Barú National Wildlife Refuge (p389) A small reserve that encompasses a range of tropical habitats and is part of a major biological corridor that protects a wide range of species.

Parque Nacional Carara (p356) Home to more than 400 species of bird, including the rare scarlet macaw, which is, amazingly, a commonly sighted species in the park.

Parque Nacional Manuel Antonio (p384) The pristine beaches, rainforest-clad mountains and dense wildlife never fail to disappoint in Costa Rica's most touristed national park.

Parque Nacional Marino Ballena (p401) A vitally important marine park; this is the country's premier destination for both whale- and dolphin-watching.

❶ Getting There & Away

The best option for exploring the coast in depth is to have your own form of private transportation. With the exception of a few odd unpaved stretches of dirt off the main highways, the central Pacific coast has some of the country's best roads.

Major cities and towns along the coast, such as Puntarenas, Jacó, Quepos, Dominical and Uvita, are serviced by regular buses. Generally speaking, public transportation is frequent and efficient, and is certainly more affordable than renting a car.

Both **NatureAir** (www.natureair.com) and **Sansa** (www.sansa.com) service Quepos, which is the base town for accessing Manuel Antonio. Prices vary according to season and availability, though you can expect to pay a little less than US$75 for a flight from San José or Liberia.

PUNTARENAS TO PLAYA PALO SECO

The northern reaches of the central Pacific coast extend from the maritime port of Puntarenas, a historic shipping hub that has fallen on harder times, toward the bustling town of Quepos, which is also the main access point for Parque Nacional Manuel Antonio. In between are vast swaths of forested hillsides and wilderness beaches, which together protect large concentrations of remarkable wildlife, including some very impressive crocodiles.

However, the local spotlight is fixed firmly on the surfing town of Jacó, which plays host to a colorful cast of characters, and its upmarket satellite – Playa Herradura, the yachtie haven. If the waves in Jacó are not challenging enough, nearby Playa Hermosa throws down the gauntlet with some of the most powerful waves on the Pacific coast.

Puntarenas

POP 34,100

As the closest coastal town to San José, Puntarenas was once Costa Rica's prosperous, coffee-exporting gateway to the Pacific, and a popular escape for landlocked Ticos. Some still come here on weekends, but during the week the activity along the oceanfront promenade slows to a languid pace – all the better to enjoy the beachfront *sodas* (inexpensive eateries) and busy market.

And while the polluted waters, seedy streets and slow decay will likely shape a traveler's first impression of Puntarenas, the city's ferry terminal is a convenient way to connect to the pristine beaches of southern Nicoya, and Puntarenas is also the jumping-off point for the almost-mystical Isla del Coco.

Travelers mainly pass through here en route to somewhere else; but if you stay overnight, you'll feel the vibe of a genuine working Tico town and find a couple of attractions.

⊙ Sights

Casa Fait   ARCHITECTURE
(Av 3 & Calle 3) Quite possibly the most beautiful building in Puntarenas, Casa Fait is a 1920s flight of fancy by Italian immigrant Alberto Fait Rocchi. It has a curious mix of coastal and Victorian influences, along with a touch of art nouveau.

Palacio Municipal   ARCHITECTURE
(Av 3 & Calle 9) Built in place of the previous Municipal Palace that burned down, this rather unusual 1970s structure with jutting upper floors, designed by architect Jorge Bertheau, is definitely the most unusual building in town. Beautiful or hideous? You decide!

Parque Marino del Pacífico   AQUARIUM
(☑ 2661-5272; www.parquemarino.org; adult/child under 12yr US$5/2.75; ⊙ 9am-4:30pm Tue-Sun;

ℙ 🚗) This marine park is popular with families and has an aquarium that showcases manta rays, nurse sharks, Nemo (we mean clown fish) and other creatures from the Pacific. The park sits on the site of the old train station and has a tiny splash pool for kids, a snack bar, a gift shop and an information center.

Paseo de los Turistas   WATERFRONT
(Tourists' Promenade) This beachside, pedestrian boulevard stretches along the southern edge of town. Cruise ships make visits to the eastern end of the road, and a variety of souvenir stalls and casual restaurants known as *kioscos* are there to greet passengers. Their specialty is the Churchill (see p352). On weekends, this is the place to knock back beers.

Casa de la Cultura   GALLERY
(☑ 2661-1394; Av Central btwn Calles 3 & 5; ⊙ 9am-8pm Mon-Fri, from 8am Sat & Sun) **FREE** Casa de la Cultura has an art gallery with occasional exhibits as well as a performance space offering seasonal cultural events. Outside there's a pedestrian passageway with contemporary sculptures.

Museo Histórico Marino de la Ciudad de Puntarenas   MUSEUM
(☑ 2661-5036, 2256-4139; Av Central btwn Calles 3 & 5; ⊙ 9:45am-noon & 1-5:15pm Tue-Sun) **FREE** This dusty museum describes the once-proud history of Puntarenas through audiovisual presentations, old photographs and artifacts. At the time of research it was closed for an indefinite period.

⌲ Tours

Calypso Cruises   BOATING
(☑ 2256-2727; www.calypsocruises.com; Av 3 on Victoria Park; day trips adult/student/child under 7yr US$145/135/80) This long-established, top-class catamaran, complete with two Jacuzzis and an underwater viewing window, makes day trips to Tortuga's brilliant white beaches, mostly catering to Puntarenas cruise-ship crowds. There are also kayaking, sportfishing and diving trips, many of which come with a picnic lunch, fresh fruit, snacks and booze.

✲ Festivals & Events

Fiesta de La Virgen del Mar   RELIGIOUS
(Festival of the Virgin of the Sea; ☑ 2661-0387; ⊙ Jul) Puntarenas celebrates the Fiesta de La Virgen del Mar on the Saturday closest to July 16. Lavishly decorated fishing boats

LOCAL KNOWLEDGE

THE CHURCHILL

As you wander the Paseo de Los Turistas (p351), you will inevitably encounter signs advertising something called a Churchill. This is in fact the official snack for Puntarenas, and each shop and restaurant has its own way of making one, but generally the ingredients include: shaved ice, fruit, syrup and condensed and powdered milk. If you are thinking that a Churchill sounds pretty gross, you are on the right track.

We inform you of the Churchill not to imply that you ingest one, but instead to tell the interesting story behind how this unhealthy and frankly inedible product has been the standard treat of Puntarenas for more than six decades. According to legend, the refreshment was born in the 1940s when a storekeeper called Joaquín Aguilar Esquivel realized he wanted to eat something sweet, milky and delicious. Back then, ice cream was not available in hot Puntarenas, and milk wouldn't keep, so Aguilar worked around that by requesting the aforementioned items. He ordered this same repulsive snack so many times that eventually restaurant owners standardized it, and named it after the guy they believed Esquivel resembled: Winston Churchill.

The Churchill is an institution in Puntarenas, and there is even a 'Churchill Coloso' (colossal Churchill) with scoops of ice cream and the works, which is available at **Kiosco Mar de Plata** (Churchill Coloso US$5). Maybe if you and a travel buddy make some kind of bet, the loser has to take down an entire Churchill Coloso?

and yachts sail around the harbor, seeking protection from the Virgin for another year at sea. There are also boat races, a carnival, and plenty of food, drinking and dancing.

🛏 Sleeping

There's no shortage of accommodations in Puntarenas, though a slew of the very cheapest ones ones cater to the clientele that want to pay by the hour. Also, high humidity and lots of rain makes even the most upscale options muggy, so make sure there's a fan.

Hotel Cabezas HOTEL $
(☑2661-1045; Av 1 btwn Calles 2 & 4; r with/without bathroom US$30/24, with air-con & bathroom US$40; ❄🕙) This no-nonsense budget option is an excellent choice. Get buzzed in and head up the stairs to the pastel-painted rooms with functional overhead fans and screened windows, which means you'll sleep deeply without needing air-con. Although you certainly shouldn't leave your valuables strewn about, this cheapie is safe, secure and surprisingly quiet.

Hotel La Punta HOTEL $$
(☑2661-0696; www.hotellapunta.net; cnr Av 1 & Calle 35; r weekday/weekend US$50/70; P❄🕙🏊) For early-morning ferry departures, Hotel La Punta is an appealing choice. Conveniently located one block from the dock, its 12 rooms are arranged around a landscaped courtyard and small pool. Comfortable accommodations feature terracotta floors, cable TV and fridge. The nicest option in Puntarenas proper.

Double Tree Resort by Hilton Central Pacific RESORT $$$
(☑800-555-5555, 2663-0808; www.doubletree centralpacific.com; all-inclusive package per person from US$283, child under 12yr US$55; P❄🕙🏊) This all-inclusive, family-friendly resort comes with its own arsenal of amenities, from enormously curvaceous swimming pool, immense offerings of water sports and around-the-clock entertainment to the spa and a plethora of tours. While there are certainly nicer beaches down the coastline, there is excellent value to be had here, especially if you book in advance online. Around 30km from Puntarenas.

🍴 Eating

The freshest, cheapest food is available in the stands and *sodas* near the Central Market. This is also the stomping ground of a motley mix of sailors, drunks and prostitutes, but the scene is raffish rather than dangerous – during the day, at least. More restaurants are along the Paseo de los Turistas between Calles Central and 3.

Self-caterers can head to the **MegaSuper supermarket** (☑2661-5301; Calle 1 btwn Avs 1 & 3; ⊙8am-9pm) or the Central Market, where you can find cut-to-order tuna steaks for a pittance.

Marisquería El Kaite Blanco SEAFOOD $

(☑2661-5566; Av 1 btwn Calles 17 & 19; dishes US$7-12; ☺11am-9pm Tue-Sun) On the north side of town, this rambling restaurant is popular with locals, and serves good seafood and a variety of tasty *bocas* (appetizers). We're partial to the spicy clams, but some locals argue that the ones next door at Marisquería El Kaite Negro are tastier.

La Casona COSTA RICAN $

(☑2661-1626; cnr Av 1 & Calle 9; casados US$6-12; ☺10am-9pm Mon-Sat) This lemon-yellow house is an incredibly popular lunch spot, attracting countless locals who jam onto the shaded, greenery-laden deck across from Parque Mora y Cañas. Portions of grilled fish are heaped, and soups are served in bathtub-sized bowls – bring your appetite.

★ El Shrimp Shack SEAFOOD $$

(☑2661-0585; www.elshrimpshack.com; Av 3 btwn Calles 3 & 7; meals US$8-19; ☺11am-3:30pm; 🛜) Offering the most upscale dining in Puntarenas, El Shrimp Shack's silly name belies a gracious interior – wood-paneled walls, marble-topped tables, antique light sconces and a stunning stained-glass ceiling, all within a century-old house with harbor views. Shrimp dishes feature prominently, though other options include burgers and excellent *ceviche*. Old-school service. Delicious pineapple and mint smoothie.

🍷 Drinking & Nightlife

★ Isla Coco's Bar & Grill BAR

(☑8876-9355, 4700-3142; ☺6-11pm Tue-Fri, noon-midnight Sat, noon-9pm Sun) This new social hub has it all: a tiki bar, bountiful seafood, a tour desk, live music and even a sushi hut.

Capitán Moreno's CLUB

(☑2661-6888; cnr Paseo de los Turistas & Calle 13; ☺11am-6pm Mon-Fri, 10am-8pm Sat & Sun) A time-honored spot for shaking some booty, with a huge dance floor right on the beach. Popular with a younger Tico crowd.

El Oasis del Pacífico CLUB

(☑2661-6368; cnr Paseo de los Turistas & Calle 5; ☺9am-10pm Sun-Thu, to 1am Fri & Sat) A popular spot with a lengthy bar and a warehouse-sized dance floor. We hope you enjoy reggaetón.

ℹ Orientation

Situated at the end of a sandy peninsula (8km long but only 100m to 600m wide), Puntarenas is just 110km west of San José by paved highway. The city has 60 calles (streets) running north to south, but only five avenidas (avenues) running west to east at its widest point. The southerly promenade, where you'll find the cruise-ship pier and some restaurants, is called the Paseo de los Turistas. As in all of Costa Rica, street names are largely irrelevant, and landmarks are used for orientation.

ℹ Information

The major banks along Av 3, to the west of the market, exchange money and are equipped with 24-hour ATMs. There's also a Banco de Costa Rica (BCR) ATM opposite the pier on Paseo de los Turistas.

Puntarenas Tourism Office (Catup; Cámara de Turismo de Puntarenas; ☑2661-2980; Paseo de los Turistas; ☺8am-5pm Mon-Fri; 🛜) Opposite the pier on the 2nd floor of Plaza del Pacífico. It closes for lunch.

ℹ Getting There & Away

BOAT

Car and passenger ferries bound for Paquera and Playa Naranjo depart several times a day from the **northwestern dock** (Av 3 btwn Calles 31 & 33). If you are driving and will be taking the car ferry, arrive at the dock early to get in line. The vehicle section tends to fill up quickly and you may not make it on. In addition, make sure that you have purchased your ticket from the walk-up ticket window before driving onto the ferry. You will not be admitted onto the boat if you don't already have a ticket.

Schedules change seasonally and can be affected by inclement weather. Check with the ferry office by the dock for any changes. Many hotels in town also have up-to-date schedules posted.

BUSES FROM PUNTARENAS

DESTINATION	COST (US$)	DURATION	FREQUENCY
Jacó	2.72	1½hr	6:50am, 8:50am, 2:20pm, 4pm, 6:30pm
Quepos	4.39	3hr	12 daily 4:30am-3:30pm
San José	4.70	2½hr	hourly 4am-9pm
Monteverde	2.72	3hr	8am, 1:15pm, 1:30pm, 2:15pm

NATURE PICTURE LIBRARY/ALAMY STOCK PHOTO ©

1. Tent-making bats, Hacienda Barú National Wildlife Refuge (p389) **2.** Humpback whale breaching, Parque Nacional Marino Ballena (p401) **3.** Tanager (p495) **4.** Catarata Manantial de Agua Viva (p358)

CLAUDE HUOT/SHUTTERSTOCK ©

Reserves of the Central Pacific Coast

Costa Rica's best road trip follows the Costanera Sur, along a string of fantastic natural parks. Replete with wet and dry tropical forests and long beaches, these parks are alive with brightly colored birds, curious monkeys and a veritable army of iguanas – all of which show off the country's stunning biodiversity.

Rancho La Merced National Wildlife Refuge (p397) Surrounding Parque Nacional Marino Ballena on the southern part of the central Pacific coast, this former cattle ranch has excellent horse trails, primary and secondary forest, and miles of mangrove channels.

Parque Nacional Marino Ballena (p401) It's appropriate that this lovely, increasingly touristed national park has a sandbar shaped like a whale's tail; from the beaches it's possible to spot the migrating giants as they swim near shore.

Hacienda Barú National Wildlife Refuge (p389) Excellent trails and naturalist-led hikes make this the best birdwatching spot on the central Pacific coast. And just in case spotting rare tropical birds doesn't thrill you, there's also a zipline.

Catarata Manantial de Agua Viva (p358) With macaws overhead, this picture-perfect jungle waterfall drops 183m from one swimming pool to the next. It's best during the rainy season, when the flows are full.

Coonatramar (☎2661-1069; www.coonatramar.com; adult/child/bike/car US$2/1.10/4/18) has daily departures to Playa Naranjo (for transfer to Nicoya and points west) at 6:30am, 10am, 2:30pm and 7pm.

Naviera Tambor (☎2661-2084; www.navieratambor.com; adult/child/bike/car US$1.60/1/4.40/23) has daily departures to Paquera (for transfer to Montezuma and Mal País) at 5am, 9am, 11am, 2pm, 5pm and 8:30pm.

BUS

Buses for San José depart from the large navy-blue building on the north corner of Calle 2 and Paseo de los Turistas. Book your ticket ahead of time on holidays and weekends. Buses for other destinations leave from across the street, on the beach side of the Paseo.

❶ Getting Around

Buses marked 'Ferry' run up Av Central and go to the ferry terminal, 1.5km from downtown. The taxi fare from the San José bus terminal in Puntarenas to the northwestern ferry terminal is about US$3.

Buses for the port of Caldera (also going past Playa Doña Ana and Mata de Limón) leave from the market about every hour and head out of town along Av Central.

Around Puntarenas

The road heading south from Puntarenas skirts the coastline, and a few kilometers out of town you'll start to see the forested peaks of the Cordillera de Tilarán in the distance. Just as the port city fades into the distance, the water gets cleaner, the air crisper and the vegetation more lush. At this point, you should take a deep breath and heave a sigh of relief – the Pacific coastline gets a whole lot more beautiful as you head further south, with beaches, surfing opportunities and mangroves aplenty.

◉ Sights & Activities

South of Puntarenas you'll find good waves (for experienced surfers only) and birdwatching opportunities in the coastal mangroves.

Playa Doña Ana   BEACH

(entry US$3, parking US$2) The pair of beaches known as Playa Doña Ana are relatively undeveloped and have an isolated and unhurried feel. Surfers can find some decent breaks here, though, like Playa San Isidro, they are more popular for Tico beachcombers on day trips from Puntarenas, especially during weekends in high season. There are snack bars, picnic shelters and changing areas, and supervised swimming areas.

Playa San Isidro   BEACH

About 8km south of Puntarenas is Playa San Isidro, the first 'real' beach on the central Pacific coast. It's popular with beachcombers from Puntarenas.

Boca Barranca   SURFING

About 12km south of Puntarenas is, according to some, the third-longest left-hand surf break in the world. Conditions here are best at low tide, and it is possible to surf here year-round. However, be advised that there isn't much in the way of services out here, so be sure that you're confident in the water and seek local advice before hitting the break.

Mata de Limón   BIRDWATCHING

Around 20km south of Puntarenas is Mata de Limón, a picturesque little hamlet situated on a mangrove lagoon, locally famous for its birdwatching. If you arrive during low tide, you'll see flocks of feathered creatures descending on the lagoon to scrounge for tasty morsels. Mata de Limón is divided by a river, with the lagoon and most facilities on the south side.

❶ Getting There & Away

Buses heading for the Caldera port depart hourly from the market in Puntarenas, and can easily drop you off at any of the spots along the highway. If you're driving, the break at Boca Barranca is located near the bridge on the Costanera Sur (South Coastal Hwy), while the entrance to Playa Doña Ana is a little further south (look for a sign that says 'Paradero Turístico Doña Ana'). The turnoff for Mata de Limón is located about 5.5km south of Playa Doña Ana.

Parque Nacional Carara

Situated at the mouth of the Río Tárcoles, this 52-sq-km **park** (US$10; ◷7am-4pm Dec-Apr, 8am-4pm May-Nov) is only 50km southeast of Puntarenas by road or about 90km west of San José via the Orotina highway. Straddling the transition between the dry forests of Costa Rica's northwest and the sodden rainforests of the southern Pacific lowlands, this national park is a biological melting pot of the two. Acacias intermingle with strangler figs, and cacti with deciduous kapok trees, creating heterogeneity of habitats with a blend of wildlife to match, including the scarlet macaw and Costa Rica's largest crocodiles.

The park's four trails can easily be explored in half a day; come early to maximize wildlife sightings.

◉ Sights

Crocodile Bridge   WILDLIFE RESERVE

If you're driving from Puntarenas or San José, pull over by the Río Tárcoles bridge, also known as Crocodile Bridge. It's a top tourist attraction in the area, as the sandbanks below regularly feature a couple dozen massive, basking crocodiles. They're visible year-round, but the best time for seeing them is during low tide in the dry season.

Crocodiles this large are rare in Costa Rica as they've been hunted vigorously for their leather. However, the crocs are tolerated here as they are the main attractions of wildlife tours that depart from Tárcoles. Note that if your tour guide feeds the crocs, this is illegal and potentially dangerous, as it leads to the crocs losing their fear of humans and equating their presence with food.

🏃 Activities

Wildlife-Watching

Dominated by open secondary forest with patches of dense, mature forest and wetlands, Carara offers superb birdwatching. More than 400 species of bird inhabit the reserve, though your chances of spotting rarer species will be greatly enhanced with the help of an experienced guide. Commonly sighted species include orange-billed sparrows, five kinds of trogon, crimson-fronted parakeets, blue-headed parrots, golden-naped woodpeckers, rose-throated becards, gray-headed tanagers, red-capped manikins, rufous-tailed jacamars and royal flycatchers.

The most exciting birds for many visitors to see, especially in June or July when chicks may be present, are the brilliantly patterned scarlet macaws, rare birds that are nonetheless commonly seen in the Parque Nacional Carara. The scarlet macaw's distinctive call echoes loudly through the canopy, usually moments before a pair appears against the blue sky. If you're having problems spotting them, it may help to inquire at the ranger station, which keeps tabs on where nesting pairs are located.

Birds aside, the trails at Carara are home to several mammal species, including red brockets, white-tailed deer, collared peccaries, monkeys, sloths and agoutis. The national park is also home to one of Costa Rica's largest populations of tayras, weasel-like animals that scurry along the forest floor. And, although most travelers aren't too keen to stumble upon an American crocodile, some truly monstrous specimens can be viewed from a safe distance at the nearby Crocodile Bridge. According to the park rangers, the best chance of spotting wildlife is at 7am, when the park opens.

Hiking

Some 600m south of the Crocodile Bridge on the left-hand side is a locked gate leading to the **Sendero Laguna Meándrica**. This trail penetrates deep into the reserve and passes through open secondary forest and patches of dense mature forest and wetlands. About 4km from the entrance is Laguna Meándrica, which has large populations of heron, smoothbill and kingfisher. If you continue past the lagoon, you'll have a good chance of spotting mammals and the occasional crocodile, though you will have to turn back to

---

SCARLET MACAWS

With a shocking bright-red body, blue-and-yellow wings, a long, red tail and a white face, the scarlet macaw (*Ara macao*) is one of the most visually arresting birds in the neotropical rainforest. It also mates for life and can live up to 75 years. Flying across the forest canopy in pairs, uttering their loud, grating squawks – there are few birds in Costa Rica with such character, presence and beauty.

Prior to the 1960s the scarlet macaw was distributed across much of Costa Rica, though trapping, poaching, habitat destruction and increased use of pesticides devastated the population. By the 1990s the distribution was reduced to two isolated pockets: the Península de Osa and Parque Nacional Carara.

Fortunately, these charismatic creatures are thriving in large colonies at both locales, and sightings are virtually guaranteed if you have the time and patience to spare. Furthermore, despite this fragmentation, the International Union for the Conservation of Nature continues to evaluate the species as 'Least Concern,' which bodes well for the future of this truly emblematic rainforest denizen.

exit. Note that this trail closes in September and October due to occasional flooding.

Another 2km south of the trailhead is the Carara ranger station, where there are bathrooms. There are two short trail loops within the park that pass through the sultry semi-gloom of the rainforest, characteristic of most of the park. They are accessed via the short, paved, wheelchair-accessible **interpretative trail**, also known as the Universal Trail, that begins at the ranger station. The first, **Sendero Las Aráceas**, is 1.2km long and links up with the second, **Sendero Quebrada Bonita** (another 1.5km). Sendero Quebrada Bonita is your best bet for seeing wildlife such as agoutis and ample birdlife, as it's furthest from the main road.

Guides can be hired at the ranger station for US$25 per person (two-person minimum, and deals available for groups) for a two-hour hike. One particularly knowledgeable guide is **Victor Mora Chaves** (☑ 8723-3008; www.victourscostarica.com), who specializes in birding and photography.

❶ Information

Carara ranger station (⊙ 7am-4pm Dec-Apr, 8am-4pm May-Nov) Info on the park and hiring guides; 3km south of Río Tárcoles.

DANGERS & ANNOYANCES

Heavy tourist traffic along the Pacific coast has also been a draw for petty theft in the area. In years past, vehicles parked at the Laguna Meándrica trailhead were sometimes broken into. There are now guards on duty, but it is still safer to leave your car by the Carara ranger station and walk along the Costanera Sur for 2km north or 1km south. Alternatively, park beside Restaurante Los Cocodrilos (remember to tip the parking attendants on your return).

❶ Getting There & Away

Any bus traveling between Puntarenas and Jacó can leave you at the park entrance. You can also catch buses headed north or south in front of Restaurante Los Cocodrilos. This may be a bit problematic on weekends, when buses are full, so go midweek if you are relying on a bus ride. If you're driving, the entrance to Carara is right on the Costanera and is clearly marked.

Tárcoles & Around

POP 3100

The small, unassuming town of Tárcoles is little more than a few rows of houses strung along a series of dirt roads that parallel the ocean. As you'd imagine, this tiny, dusty Tico

town isn't much of a tourist draw, though the surrounding area is perfect for fans of the superlative, especially if you're interested in seeing what's claimed to be the country's tallest waterfall and some of its biggest crocodiles. With the 2017 announcement that a new, US$3.5-billion international airport will be constructed in nearby Orotina, you can bet that Tárcoles won't stay unassuming for long, though.

◉ Sights

★**Catarata Manantial de Agua Viva**   WATERFALL
(☑ 2275-6242, 8831-2980; US$20; ⊙ 7am-5pm) This 200m-high waterfall is claimed to be the highest in the country. From the entrance, it's a steep 3km (45-minute) hike down into the valley; at the bottom, the river continues through a series of natural swimming holes. The falls are most dramatic at their fullest, during the rainy season, though the serene rainforest setting is beautiful any time of year. A 5km dirt road past Hotel Villa Lapas leads to the primary entrance to the falls. Keep an eye out for brightly colored poison-dart frogs as well as the occasional pair of scarlet macaws.

Pura Vida Gardens & Waterfalls   GARDENS
(☑ 2645-1001, 8352-9419; www.puravidagarden. com; adult/child under 12yr US$20/10; ⊙ 7:30am-4pm Mon-Sat) Just before the village of Bijagual, this private botanical garden offers great vistas of Manantial de Agua Viva cascading down the side of a cliff, and there are some pleasant hiking trails where you might see nesting toucans and other wildlife. The onsite restaurant caters to the Adventure Dining (www.adventurediningcostarica. com) crowds. Dining is by reservation only, starting at 4:30pm.

☞ Tours

This area is known for crocodile-watching tours, and travelers anywhere near this part of the coast will be bombarded with advertisements and flyers for them. Although it will be hard for adrenaline junkies to resist, some of these tours have a dubious impact on the natural habitat of the magnificent animals who lurk in the mudflats of the Río Tárcoles. Although they are definitely a spectacle to behold, it's frustrating to watch the crocodiles being hand-fed by some of the tour guides; it's illegal to feed wildlife in Costa Rica. If you do visit the crocodiles on a tour, ask a lot of questions and do your part to encourage responsible interaction with the animals. Tours usually cost US$35 per person for two hours.

Jungle Crocodile Safari (☑2637-0656; www.junglecrocodilesafari.com; per person US$35; ☉ tours 8:30am, 10:30am, 1:30pm, 3:30pm) is one of the better companies with an office in Tárcoles, while **Crocodile Man Tour** (☑2637-0771, 2637-0426; www.crocodilemantour.com; adult/child US$35/25, under 5yr free; ☉ 8am-4pm) is the most famous (mainly for the irresponsible feeding practices, which have since ceased). The tours leave from town or you can arrange to be picked up at your hotel.

🛏 Sleeping

Hotel Villa Lapas   RESORT $$
(☑2637-0232; www.villalapas.com; all-inclusive per person from US$127; P❄️🏠🛜🏊) 🏖 Located on a private reserve comprising both secondary rainforest and tropical gardens, this resort offers rooms housed in an attractive Spanish colonial–style lodge. Guests can unwind in relative comfort in between guided hikes along the on-site trail network, birdwatching trips, canopy tours and soaks in two pools. Geared toward a birding crowd, the pace here is slow and low-key.

Alongside the Río Tarcolito, the hotel grounds include a wedding chapel.

Eden Retreat Center   SPA HOTEL $$$
(☑8718-5258; www.edenretreatcenter.com; r incl breakfast from US$190) Expat doctor and supercool woman Randi Raymond runs this new, six-room retreat center where guests can relax into a health-focused vacation involving organic local meals, yoga, meditation, vitamin IV therapy, nutrition counseling, colonics and more. Views of the sea and jungle are stunning, and the rooms are bright, plush and spacious.

The hotel is located just before Pura Vida Gardens and Waterfalls, 6km from Tárcoles.

❶ Getting There & Away

Any bus between Puntarenas and Jacó can leave you at the entrance to Tárcoles. If you're driving, the entrance to the town is right on the Costanera Sur and is clearly marked. Local buses between Orotina and Bijagual can drop you off at the entrance to the Parque Nacional Carara.

Playa Herradura

Until the mid-1990s, Playa Herradura was a rural, palm-sheltered beach of grayish-black sand that was popular mainly with campers and local fishers. In the late 1990s, however, Herradura was thrown into the spotlight having been used as the stage for the Ridley Scott movie *1492: Conquest of Paradise*. Rapid development ensued, resulting in the construction of one of the most high-profile marinas in the country, the Los Sueños marina.

Playa Herradura represents one possible future for the central Pacific coast. Sprawling complexes of condos, fancy hotels and high-rise apartments are slowly encircling the bay and snaking up the mountainside, while the marina features rows of luxury yachts and sportfishing vessels. The southern half of the beach, at the end of the Playa Herradura road, however, is a world apart from the landscaped grounds traversed by golf buggies: it remains stubbornly local, with picnicking Ticos and bars with pounding music.

🏃 Activities

SupHerr   WATER SPORTS
(☑2637-6032; www.supherr.com; 2hr SUP rental US$30, 1/2hr kayak US$20/30) Offers watersport rentals, including kayaks, boogie boards and the increasingly popular stand-up paddleboards, on Playa Herradura. Also does lessons and tours.

🛏 Sleeping

You have to pay to play in Playa Herradura, so consider moving further down the coast to Jacó if you're not prepared to bunk down in the top-end price bracket.

★ Zephyr Palace   BOUTIQUE HOTEL $$$
(☑2637-3000; www.zephyrpalace.com; ste US$412-1808; P❄️@🛜🏊) On the same property as the elegant Villa Caletas, its over-the-top sibling takes the decadence to another level of luxury. At this marble palace, seven individually decorated themed suites that wouldn't look out of place in Las Vegas evoke the splendor of ancient Rome, pharaonic Egypt and Asia. Three-night minimum. The turnoff is signposted just north of Playa Herradura.

★ Hotel Villa Caletas   BOUTIQUE HOTEL $$$
(☑2630-3000; www.hotelvillacaletas.com; r US$226-505, ste US$412; P❄️🏠🏊) 🏖 Although the views of the Pacific are amazing, what makes this bluff-top hotel truly unique is its architectural fusion, incorporating elements as varied as tropical Victorian, Hellenistic and French colonial. The ultra-exclusive accommodations are located on the tiny headland

of Punta Leona, perched high on a dramatic hillside at the end of a serpentine driveway just north of Playa Herradura.

Each room is arranged amid the tropical foliage of the terraced property, affording a singular sense of privacy and isolation. The room interiors are tastefully decorated with art and antiques, with windows looking onto spectacular views. There is also a French-influenced restaurant, several semi-private infinity pools, and a private 1km trail leading down the hillside to the beach.

**Los Sueños Marriott
Ocean & Golf Resort**   RESORT $$$
(☑ 2630-9000; www.marriott.com/sjols; r US$345-494, ste US$890; P ❂ ❄ @ ☎ ❂) With golf course behind and marina in front, this sprawling 201-room resort at Playa Herradura embodies the upscale comfort envisioned for the development, all wrapped up in a hacienda-style aesthetic. Interconnected pools meander through the landscaped property, while creature comforts include iPod docks and windows that catch the ocean breezes. Service can be erratic, though, and room wi-fi isn't free.

🍴 Eating

The 'local' side of the beach features informal dip-your-feet-in-the-sand eateries, while the Marina Village plays host to more upmarket dining establishments aimed squarely at a gringo clientele.

Dolce Vita   CAFE $
(☑ 2630-4050; cakes from US$3; ⊙ 6am-5pm; ❄ ☎) Good coffee, quiches, proper bagels and outstanding gelato are found inside this little cafe right on the marina. More recently, the menu expanded to include breakfast and a bunch of Costa Rican and Italian favorites,

---

DON'T MISS

PUNTA LEONA

Punta Leona is a closely held secret, with 'close' being the key word. Behind a couple of easy-to-miss entrances and long, winding driveways, its serene beaches – Playa Mantas and Playa Blanca – are the first a traveler can visit when headed from San José down the central Pacific coast, just an hour's drive from the capital.

The turnoff for Playa Mantas, where the public has access, is a right just after the small restaurant called Soda Nimar onto an unmarked dirt road, a 12-minute drive south of the Crocodile Bridge (p357). On the 10-minute ride down this road, security guards may take your license plate number and ask your destination. The guards are working for **Punta Leona Hotel & Club** (☑ 2630-1001; www.hotelpuntaleona.com; from US$109), a sprawling complex with a country-club vibe, a couple of restaurants, exclusive parking and beach access. Some beachgoers have memberships, and a day pass costs a whopping US$85, but there's no need to pay this, because all beaches in Costa Rica are public by law.

At the end of the entry road, you can park for US$4, grab a swim in the tranquil, azure Playa Mantas, and then set off on foot to the south, over some rocks, to your true destination – majestic Playa Blanca. At low tide, the flat rocks on the far end of the point are easy to traverse. At hide tide those will be submerged, but you should not attempt to swim over them (waves will bash you against the rocks). The best plan is to time the trip so that you can get to and from Playa Blancas when the tide is as low as possible. The reward for your efforts is a massive cove featuring soft, white sand, bathtub-calm water and swaying coconut palms. Scarlet macaws will soar overhead in couples, and you can explore a network of tide pools for fish, crabs and even octopus.

This proximate stretch of paradise is something of a local family affair, particularly on holidays. You'll want to arrive early to ensure a parking spot, and consider stopping on the way in or out at **Chanchitos** (☑ 2637-0000; Costanera Sur; mains US$7-16; ⊙ 11am-11pm), a restaurant just a bit north of the public entrance to Punta Leona (and just beside a separate entrance for club members and those with day passes). It serves up the tastiest seafood enchiladas we've ever tried. All-inclusive enthusiasts may also appreciate Punta Leona's other stay, **Hotel Arenas** (☑ 2529-0505; www.hotelarenasenpuntaleona.com; per person all-inclusive US$116; ❂), which offers a nice pool and entertainment to make sure everybody's having fun.

including a house lasagna, paninis and *ceviche*. The new Italian restaurant next door, Lanterna, is under the same ownership and gets packed in high season.

La Puesta del Sol   COSTA RICAN $
(☑ 2637-8003; mains from US$6; ☺ 11am-11pm; ℗) Right on the 'local' side of the beach, this lively eatery and bar shelters those to whom manicured golf courts are anathema. The menu is all about *casados* (set meals) and *ceviches* and the sunset goes well with your beer.

Bambú   SUSHI $$
(☑ 2630-4333; www.lsrestaurants.com; Marina Village; mains from US$9; ☺ 11am-10pm; ✳ ☎) On the waterfront overlooking the rows of gleaming yachts, this spot serves an appropriate selection of Poseidon's subjects. We're particularly partial to the spicy tuna and the 'pimpin' shrimp' roll, which comes with avocado, tempura shrimp, volcano sauce and a bunch of other things. Hits the spot when paired with an Asahi beer.

Jimmy T's Provisions   SUPERMARKET $$
(☑ 2637-8636; www.jimmytsprovisions.com; Los Sueños Marina; ☺ 6:30am-7pm) For those looking to self-cater in style, Jimmy T's is a dream come true. His small store on the docks of the Los Sueños marina caters mostly to the yachting set, but it's stacked floor to ceiling with organic, imported and rare-in-Costa Rica delicacies. Italian cheeses, grass-fed meat, Asian foods – it's a dream come true for self-caterers with *mucho* cash.

❶ Getting There & Away

There are frequent local buses (US$2, 20 minutes) connecting Playa Herradura to Jacó. If you're driving, the Herradura turnoff is on the Costanera Sur, about 6km after the Costanera Sur leaves the edge of the ocean and heads inland. From here, a paved road leads 3km west to Playa Herradura.

Jacó

POP 9500

Few places in Costa Rica generate such divergent opinions as Jacó. Partying surfers, North American retirees and international developers laud it for its devil-may-care atmosphere, bustling streets and booming real-estate opportunities. Observant ecotourists, marginalized Ticos and loyalists of the 'old Costa Rica' absolutely despise the place for the *exact* same reasons.

Jacó was the first town on the central Pacific coast to explode with tourist development and it remains a major draw for backpackers, surfers, snowbirds and city-weary *josefinos* (inhabitants of San José). Although working-class Tico neighborhoods are nearby, open-air trinket shops and tour operators line the tacky main drag which, at night, is given over to a safe but somewhat seedy mix of binge-drinking students, surfers and scantily clad ladies of negotiable affection.

While Jacó's lackadaisical charm is not for everyone, the surfing is excellent, and the restaurants and bars are great, particularly those lining classy Jacó Walk.

◎ Sights

★ **Jacó Walk**   SQUARE
This dainty new square, to which most of the towns' best restaurants have recently relocated, is adorned in multicolored bricks, potted plants and pretty lights. The restaurants all offer outdoor seating and the whole thing feels very family-friendly, with fountains, bike racks and even a children's playground. If you're guessing there's also a craft brewery, you're right.

🏃 Activities

Surfing

Although the rainy season is considered best for Pacific-coast surfing, Jacó is blessed with consistent year-round breaks. Even though more advanced surfers head further south to Playa Hermosa, the waves at Jacó are strong, steady and a lot of fun for intermediate surfers. Jacó is also a great place to learn to surf or start a surf trip as many places offer lessons and it's easy to buy and sell boards here.

If you're looking to rent a board for the day, shop around as the better places will do 24 hours for US$15 to US$20.

Tortuga Surf Camp   SURFING
(☑ 2463-3348; www.tortugasurfcamp.com; 2hr private surfing lesson incl equipment from US$50; ☺ 8am-5pm) Regardless of your age or ability, this is one of the top places in Jacó to learn to surf or improve your technique. Michael and his crew are very patient and encouraging. Lessons should be booked at least 24 hours in advance.

Vista Guapa Surf Camp   SURFING
(☑ 2643-0244; www.vistaguapa.com) Vista Guapa Surf Camp is ideal for beginners and

Jacó Center

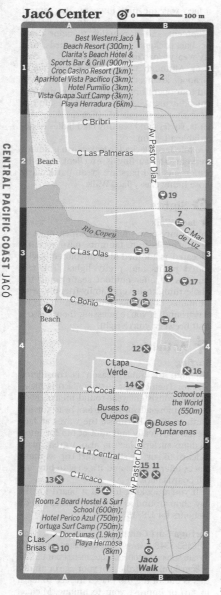

Carton Surf Shop   SURFING
(☑ 2643-3762; www.cartonsurfboards.com; Calle Madrigal; per day US$20; ☺ 8:30am-6pm) A good place to rent boards, run by the friendly Villalobos brothers, near the beach at the southern end of the main drag on Calle Madrigal.

Swimming

Jacó is generally safe for swimming, though you should avoid the areas near the estuaries, which are polluted. Be advised that the waves can get crowded with beginner surfers who don't always know how to control their boards, so keep your wits about you and stay out of their way. Riptides occasionally occur, especially when the surf gets big, so inquire about local conditions and keep an eye out for red flags marking the paths of rips.

Hiking

Mt Miros   HIKING
A worthwhile pastime that few tourists are aware of is following the trail up Mt Miros,

intermediates, with YOLO board rentals and stand-up paddleboarding (SUP) classes also offered. Weekly rates including full board start at around US$1150. Check the website for directions.

which winds through primary and secondary rainforest and offers spectacular views of Jacó and Playa Hermosa. The viewpoint is several kilometers uphill. Note that the trailhead is unmarked, so ask a local to point it out to you.

Courses

School of the World
LANGUAGE
(2643-2462; www.schooloftheworld.org; 1-/4-week package from US$355/1136) This popular school and cultural-studies center offers classes in Spanish, surfing, yoga, art, GoPro and photography (choose your ideal combo). The impressive building and activities center also houses a cafe and art gallery. On-site lodgings and homestays can be arranged, either in shared or private rooms.

Tours

Tour companies offer a huge array of activities in and around Jacó, from surfing (there are numerous surfing schools) and sea kayaking to horseback riding, canopy tours, all-terrain vehicle (ATV) tours and more extreme canyoning and waterfall-jumping adventures.

Virtually every shop, hotel and restaurant in town books tours, as Jacó operates on a lucrative commission-based system. As you'd imagine, it's hard to know who is greasing whose palms and who is running tours. Still, you shouldn't book anything from touts on the streets, and if an offer from a vendor seems too good to be true, then most likely it is. Talk to your lodgings and fellow travelers for recommendations, and it's usually better to go for companies that specialize in one (or a small handful) of activities rather than a catch-all operator that claims they can arrange everything under the sun.

Kayak Jacó
KAYAKING
(2643-1233; www.kayakjaco.com; tours from US$75; 7:30am-8pm) This reliable, responsible company facilitates kayaking and sea-canoeing trips that include snorkeling excursions to tropical islands, in a wide variety of customized day and multiday trips. Though it does have a presence at Playa Agujas, 250m east of the beach, it's best to phone or email in advance.

Discovery Horseback Tours HORSEBACK RIDING
(8838-7550; www.horseridecostarica.com; rides from US$85) Nearby beach and rainforest rides are available through this highly rec-

ommended outfit, run by an expat couple who offer an extremely high level of service and professionalism and who clearly take excellent care of their horses.

Costa Rica Waterfall Tours
ADVENTURE
(2643-1834; www.costaricawaterfalltours.com; Av Pastor Díaz; tours US$79-149; 9am-5pm) This experienced, safety-conscious operator arranges some of the most adrenaline-charged excursions in town, from tamer waterfall rappelling to extreme canyoneering and cliff jumping.

Vista Los Sueños
Rainforest Tours
ADVENTURE
(2637-6020, in USA 321-220-9631; www.canopyvistalossuenos.com; tours per person from US$95, 4-person minimum; hourly tours 8am-3pm) The longest ziplines in the area belong to Vista Los Sueños, which offers 12 cables accessed by tractor cart through the lush hillside. It also arranges recommended horse-riding and waterfall tour combos and ATV adventures, though the latter is not hugely ecofriendly.

Festivals & Events

Jungle Jam
MUSIC
(www.junglejam.com; Mar) This four-day mid-March music festival brings together rock, reggae, funk and soul artists. Past participants have included Steel Pulse, Perro Bravo, Thicker Than Thieves and Paul Damon.

Sleeping

There's a wide spread of places to lay your head in Jacó, from concrete-block dives to spendy upscale resorts, in some areas all scattered over just a few blocks.

The center of town, with its many bars and discos, means that noise may be a factor. The far northern and southern ends of town have more relaxed and quieter accommodations.

★ Room 2 Board Hostel
& Surf School
HOSTEL $
(2643-4949, in USA 323-315-0012; www.room2board.com; dm/r from US$16/65; P ※ @ 🎧 🏊) Now *this* is a hostel. On the newer side, spacious and professionally run, it has a buzzy onsite cafe, dedicated staff who arrange tours and surfing lessons, and various configurations of rooms spread over three floors. Roof-terrace hammocks catch the breeze, dorms come with excellent mattresses, solar-heated rain showers and

lockers, and there are yoga classes and movie screenings.

Rooms without bathroom are slightly pricier because they come with air-con; en suite rooms come with fan only.

Several rooms have family-friendly furniture configurations, and foot lights help guests find their way at night.

Buddha House
GUESTHOUSE $

(☑2643-3615; www.hostelbuddhahouse.com; Av Pastor Díaz; dm from US$12, r with fan & without bathroom from US$25, with air-con & without bathroom from US$40, with bathroom & air-con from US$50; P❄☕📶) Bold colors and modern art create an artistic atmosphere at this 'boutique hostel,' where the best private rooms are spacious suites. The communal areas include a breezy patio, a spotless kitchen and even a small pool, and the staff are lovely. What's less lovely is the noise: the hostel is next to a bar that parties late into the night.

Hotel de Haan
HOSTEL $

(☑2643-1795, 8879-3332; www.facebook.com/hoteldehaancr/; Calle Bohío; dm US$15, r from US$65; P@☕📶) This lively outpost is popular with backpackers and surfers on a budget. Basic private rooms have hot-water bathrooms and are tidy but dark. The open-air kitchen overlooks the pool area, and is a great place to meet and hang out with fellow travelers, which some guests do late into the night.

Beds on Bohio
HOSTEL $

(☑2643-5251; Calle Bohío; dm/r from US$12/45; ❄☕) This hostel is steps from the beach and totally chill, with surfers hanging around in a courtyard strung with hammocks, and there's cheap surfboard rental and a decent restaurant onsite. But the rooms are spartan, the kitchen and shared bathrooms of dubious cleanliness and these guys like to party late into the night. Boon or bane? You decide!

Camping El Hicaco
CAMPGROUND $

(☑8338-1647; Calle Hicaco; campsite per person US$8; P) The only proper campground in town: there are picnic tables under the trees, bathrooms and a lockup for gear, though its proximity to the bars and clubs means you might not get much shut-eye. Don't leave valuables in your tent as theft is a big problem here. Showers are free for those camping; US$2 for anyone else.

ApartHotel Vista Pacífico
HOTEL $$

(☑2643-3261; www.vistapacifico.com; r/apt incl breakfast from US$82/110; P❄☕📶) Located on the crest of a hill just north of Jacó (off Bulevar), this gem of a hotel is run by a warm young Canadian couple. Homey, comfortable rooms and suites with kitchen facilities come in a variety of configurations. Its favorable elevation offers not only panoramic views of the coastline and valley but also blessedly cool breezes.

Kids 12 and under stay free; child-friendly tours can be organized. French, English and Spanish are all spoken, and airport transport is available for a fee.

Hotel Perico Azul
HOTEL $$

(☑2643-1341; www.hotelpericoazuljaco.com; r/studio US$60/75; P❄☕📶) Tucked away off a quiet side street, this small hotel is difficult to fault. The rooms and apartments are light and spotless, with bright splashes of color, there's a small pool to relax around, staff go out of their way to make you feel welcome, and owner Mike runs the recommended Tortuga Surf Camp (p361); surfing packages can be arranged.

Note that this hotel is adults only.

Posada Jacó
HOTEL $$

(☑2643-1951; www.posadajaco.com; Calle Bohio; ste from US$85; P❄☕📶) Surprisingly quiet given it's only steps from Jacó's main drag, this tiny creekside hotel has a well-kept garden and pool area with a communal BBQ. Suites are the best deal here, complete with kitchenettes and terraces in low-key, friendly environs.

Hotel Mar de Luz
HOTEL $$

(☑2643-3000; www.mardeluz.com; Calle Mar de Luz; d/q/apt incl breakfast US$96/138/200; P❄☕📶) This adorable little hotel with Dutch-inspired murals of windmills and tulips has tidy and attractive air-conditioned rooms (outfitted with fridges, microwaves and coffee makers) and stone-walled villas that are perfect for families. The friendly owner (who speaks Dutch, Spanish, English, German and Italian) offers two swimming pools, several BBQ grills and plenty of useful information.

The owner is also extremely committed to fighting drugs and prostitution in Jacó, and is at the forefront of an admirable campaign to clean up the city.

Hotel Poseidon HOTEL **$$**

(☑ 2643-1642; www.hotel-poseidon.com; Calle Bohío; d incl breakfast from US$65; ✳@🛜🏊) It's hard to miss the huge Grecian wooden carvings that adorn the exterior of this small hotel. On the inside, tidy rooms are accented with stylish furniture and mosaic tiles (though the furniture looks weathered) and include amenities like fridges. There's also a pool with swim-up bar, a decent restaurant and a sports bar.

Selina Jacó HOSTEL **$$**

(☑ 8304 2994; www.selina.com/jaco; dm $16, d from US$72) Part of the Selina hostel empire, this latest edition was only just opening during our visit, and was understandably a bit disorganized. The beachfront spot had promise, though, and backpackers had already begun to descend for its chilled-out pool deck, cinema, and surf and SUP lessons. The yummy buffet breakfast costs US$5.

★ Croc Casino Resort RESORT **$$$**

(☑ 2643-1180; www.crocscasinoresort.com; r from US$209; ✳🛜🏊) On the tranquil northern end of Jacó, this crocodile-themed resort is surprisingly elegant. Sleek towers, an immaculate casino and sprawling pools underline the opulence, while a hip cafe and unique foodie tours lend a bit of culture. There are also two decent restaurants, and a crocodile habitat with two rescued inhabitants – Paco and Lola.

★ Hotel Pumilio BOUTIQUE HOTEL **$$$**

(☑ 2643-5678; www.hotelpumilio.com; r incl breakfast from US$150; P✳🛜🏊) In a wonderfully peaceful location along an unpaved road 2.5km north of Jacó, this intimate hotel caters to travelers who want to do their own thing yet repose in style. Luxurious rooms come with comfy beds, rain showers and outdoor kitchenettes. The waterfall-fed pool and spa are surrounded by lush greenery. There are rental bikes for pedaling down to Jacó.

DoceLunas HOTEL **$$$**

(☑ 2643-2195; www.docelunas.com; Costanera Sur; r incl breakfast US$140-225; P♿✳🛜🏊) Situated in the foothills across the highway, 'Twelve Moons' is a heavenly mountain retreat consisting of only 20 rooms sheltered in a pristine landscape of tropical rainforest. Each teak-accented room is uniquely decorated with original artwork, and the luxurious bathrooms feature double sinks and

bathtubs. Yoga classes, offered regularly, are free with room rates.

There's a full spa and a free-form, waterfall-fed pool. The open-air restaurant serves everything from marlin *ceviche* to vegan delicacies. To reach the hotel, make a left off the Costanera just after the third signed entrance for Playa Jacó.

Best Western Jacó Beach Resort HOTEL **$$$**

(☑ 2643-1000; www.bestwesternjacobeach.com; Av Pastor Díaz btwn Bulevar & Calle Ancha; r from US$168; P✳🛜🏊) The Best Western remains a solid choice for its all-inclusive resort packages. Rooms are predictably bland but comfortable and well maintained, while the pools, beach access, myriad resort activities and bounteous meals more than make up for the slightly dated accommodations. It pays to check for internet specials. Service can be inconsistent.

✖ Eating

Aside from the Quepos and Manuel Antonio area, this city proudly boasts the most diverse and delicious offerings of international cuisine on the central Pacific coast. While the vast majority of eateries cater primarily to Western palates, there are still a few local spots that have managed to remain in business.

★ Side Street Bistro FUSION **$**

(☑ 2643-2724; www.facebook.com/SideStreetBistro/; Jacó Walk; sandwiches US$6-10; ⏱11am-4pm Mon-Sat, from 10am Sun) Recently relocated to the fabulous new Jacó Walk, this place bills itself as a food truck *sin ruedas* (without wheels). The small, often-changing menu includes creative sandwiches with roasted portobello mushrooms, tuna steak and coffee-and-cacao-rubbed tenderloin. Wash them down with local booze from next door's Puddlefish (p367), Jacó's first craft brewery. Brunch highlights include chicken and waffles and the breakfast burrito.

★ Graffiti INTERNATIONAL **$$**

(☑ 2643-1708; www.facebook.com/graffiticr/; Jacó Walk; mains US$10-31; ⏱5-10pm; 🛜🍴) With shiny new digs, this long-standing favorite has upped its aesthetic appeal while retaining what first made it great: creative dishes prepared with fresh, local ingredients. Tried-and-true favorites include cacao-and-coffee-encrusted filet mignon and a macadamia- or pretzel-encrusted daily catch. Save room for decadent cheesecake and wash it all down with a yummy cocktail (cucumber-basil martini is our fave).

Reservations are highly recommended.

Juanita's
MEXICAN $$

(2643-4110; Jacó Walk; mains US$7-16; 5-11pm Mon-Fri, from 1pm Sat, from 4pm Sun;) From the same restaurateurs behind Green Room, this new Mexican place in Jacó Walk wins for its innovative, fresh dishes and cocktails but also for adorable interior design and super-friendly staff. Nightly specials include things like pork chops topped with a jalapeño-passionfruit glaze with grilled vegetables and a yucca puree. Lots of good vegetarian options, and the guacamole is divine.

Amancio's
ITALIAN $$

(2643-2373; pizza from US$8, mains US$9-22; 10am-10pm Thu-Tue) If you've got somebody to impress in Jacó, this luscious Italian spot will do the trick. The pizza's delish, the salads are super-fresh and the off-menu seafood pasta dish, which comes with juicy lobster, is pure homemade goodness.

Tsunami Sushi
JAPANESE $$

(2643-1635; Jacó Walk; meals US$11-30; noon-10pm Sun-Tue & Thu, to 11pm Wed, Fri & Sat;) Reservations are recommended at this sleek and popular sushi spot, which over the years has expanded from the central Pacific coast to open three more locations in and around the capital. We're particularly partial to its spicy lobster rolls and cucumber martinis. Play your cards right and various specials throughout the week can save you serious colones. Otherwise, it's super-pricey.

Green Room
FUSION $$

(2643-4425; www.facebook.com/Green-Room-Cafe-325667240786166/; Calle Cocal; mains US$9-20; 9am-midnight;) With an emphasis on creativity and fresh ingredients (these guys work with local organic farms), Green Room serves imaginative fare such as sweet-potato-crusted mahi mahi, seared tuna with tamarind glaze and ribs with passionfruit BBQ sauce, along with a supporting cast of salads, melts, wraps and burgers. Thirty local craft brews are on tap, and there's live music every night.

Kids eat free on Sunday and have their own menu.

TacoBar
INTERNATIONAL $$

(2643-0222; www.tacobar.info; Calle Lapa Verde; meals US$7-15; 7am-10pm Tue-Sun;) A one-stop shop for grilled fish, salads and smoothies. Get your mint lemonade in the gargantuan 1L size or your greens at the salad bar featuring more than 20 kinds of exotic and leafy components. And, of course, there's the obligatory fish taco, which may be one of the planet's greatest food combinations. The *ceviche* is a letdown, though.

Caliche's Wishbone
INTERNATIONAL $$

(2643-3406; Av Pastor Díaz; meals US$9-19; noon-10pm Thu-Tue;) Overseen by the charming Caliche, this has been a Jacó favorite for years and years. The eclectic, Mexican-inspired menu includes pitas, blackened tuna sashimi, pan-seared sea bass, and fish and shrimp tacos, though its justifiable fame comes from the fact that everything is quite simply fresh, delicious and good value. It's south of Calle Bohío.

★ Lemon Zest
FUSION $$$

(2643-2591; www.lemonzestjaco.com; Av Pastor Díaz; mains US$15-37; 5:30-10pm;) Chef Richard Lemon (a former instructor at Le Cordon Bleu Miami) wins many accolades for one of Jacó's swishest and most imaginative menus. The roster of upscale standards – 'cold feet' duck, buffalo lobster bits and an award-winning lobster Francaise – is carried out with due sophistication, accompanied by a well-matched wine list. An excellent splurge.

El Hicaco
SEAFOOD $$$

(2643-3226; www.elhicaco.com; Calle Hicaco; mains US$20-40; 11am-10pm) This oceanside spot brims with casual elegance and is regarded as one of the finer dining experiences in Jacó. Although the menu is entirely dependent on seasonal offerings, both from the land and the sea, the specialty of the house is seafood, prepared with a variety of sauces highlighted by Costa Rica's tropical produce. Service can be glacially slow.

Wednesday night in high season is lobster night, which means all-you-can-eat *langosta* for US$70. There's also live music on weekends year-round and other nights during high season.

🍸 Drinking & Nightlife

Jacó isn't the cultural capital of Costa Rica; it's where people go to get hammered and party the night away. There are numerous raging bars and dance clubs that cater to good-times-seeking expats and travelers, but choose your venues carefully, as prostitution figures prominently.

★ PuddleFish Brewery
CRAFT BEER

(☎ 2643-1659; ⏱ 5-10pm Mon-Thu, to midnight Fri & Sat, 10am-10pm Sun) From the same culinary gurus who brought Graffiti (p365) and Side Street Bistro (p365) to Jacó, this new microbrewery stationed in the glitzy new plaza Jacó Walk is the city's first. On tap are several of PuddleFish's own brews, including Punky Monkey and Lights Out Chocolate Coffee Stout, and the craft cocktails (ie the jalapeño ginger margarita) are outstanding.

A small but tasty food menu makes for delicious pairings.

Beer House
BREWERY

(☎ 8582-3773; ⏱ 5pm-midnight Mon-Sat) Tucked back into a nondescript plaza, this quaint little watering hole features 10 craft beers on tap and gourmet burgers. It's a welcome alternative to some of the grimier nightlife options around town, and when there's no live music, funk and rock'n'roll blare from a record player.

Manhattan Lounge
LOUNGE

(☎ 8704-9570; ⏱ 6am-2am; 🛜) An upscale addition to both the coffee shop and nightlife scenes of Jacó, this new lounge offers cold-brew coffee by day and Manhattans by night. Blown-up photographs of cityscapes festoon the walls, and there's outdoor seating on the front patio. Expect hip-hop music and Latin beats.

Monkey Bar
CLUB

(☎ 8329-2304; Av Pastor Díaz; ⏱ 9pm-2:30am Tue-Sun) Attracting a young crowd of locals and visitors, Monkey Bar pumps with good times, reggaetón and pheromones. There's also a big VIP lounge in the back, with bottle service and oftentimes a special DJ.

Clarita's Beach Hotel & Sports Bar & Grill
SPORTS BAR

(☎ 2643-2615; www.claritashotel.com; ⏱ 8am-10pm) Catch the game on the big screen, day-drink with an older gringo crowd (the beers are ice-cold but the mixed drinks are not very strong), and enjoy live Tico-style music played by local oldsters.

ⓘ Information

There's no independent tourist information office, though several tour offices will give information. Look for the free monthly *Jacó's Guide* or the quarterly *Info Jaco*.

DANGERS & ANNOYANCES

Aside from occasional petty crime such as pick-pocketing and breaking into cars, Jacó is not a dangerous place. But keep the following in mind:

➠ The high concentration of wealthy foreigners and comparatively poor Ticos has resulted in a thriving sex and drugs industry. The local council has cleaned things up in recent years, but not entirely.

➠ Jacó is the epicenter of Costa Rica's prostitution scene. Travelers who wish to explore this dark corner of Costa Rican nightlife should consider the health and safety risks and negative social impacts.

➠ Locals warn against walking alone on the beach at night due to muggings.

ⓘ Getting There & Away

AIR

NatureAir and **Alfa Romeo Aero Taxi** (☎ 2735-5353, 8632-8150; www.alfaromeoair.com) offer charter flights. Prices are dependent on the number of passengers, so it's best to try to organize a larger group if you're considering this option.

BOAT

The jet-boat transfer service that connects Jacó to Montezuma is, far and away, the most efficient way to get between the central Pacific coast and the Península de Nicoya. The journey across the Golfo de Nicoya only takes about an hour (compared to about seven hours overland), though at US$40 it's definitely not cheap. (For US$10 you can bring a bicycle or surfboard.) The bonus? Sometimes travelers see dolphins along the ride. Several boats leave daily from Playa Herradura, 2km north of town. Reservations are required and the most consistent departures are with **Zuma Tours** (☎ 2642-0024/50; www.zumatours.net) at 10am. It's a beach landing, so wear the right shoes.

BUS

Gray Line, Easy Ride and Monkey Ride run shared shuttles from Jacó to popular destinations such as San José (from US$45), Manuel Antonio (from US$35), Dominical/Uvita (from US$45), Sierpe (from US$60), Puerto Jiménez (US$79) and Monteverde (from US$59). Easy Ride also offers direct shuttles to Granada, Nicaragua (8:45am, US$99).

Buses for San José stop at the Plaza Jacó mall, north of the center. The bus stops for other destinations are opposite the Más x Menos supermarket (Av Pastor Díaz): stand at the bus stop in front of the supermarket if you're headed north; stand at the bus stop across the street if you're headed south. Buses originate in Puntarenas or Quepos, so consult your lodgings about the latest schedule and get to the stop early.

Puntarenas US$2.72, 1½ hours, 12 daily between 6am and 7:30pm

Quepos US$2.72, 1½ hours, 12 daily between 6am and 7pm

San José US$5.45, 2½ hours, eight daily between 6am and 7pm

ⓘ Getting Around

Getting around in Jacó is easy on foot; strolling the length of town in flip-flops takes about 20 minutes.

BICYCLE

Several places around town rent out bicycles, mopeds and scooters. Bikes can usually be rented for about US$5 an hour or US$10 to US$15 per day, though prices change depending on the season. Mopeds and small scooters cost from US$30 to US$50 per day (many places ask for a cash or credit-card deposit of about US$200).

CAR

There are several rental agencies in town, so shop around for the best rates.

Budget (☑ 2436-2082; Av Pastor Díaz, near Calle Bohío; ⊙ 8am-5pm Mon-Sat, to 4pm Sun) International car-hire company.

Economy (☑ 2643-1719; Av Pastor Díaz; ⊙ 8am-6pm) South of Calle Ancha.

Playa Hermosa

Regarded as one of the most consistent and powerful breaks in the whole country, Hermosa serves up serious surf that commands the utmost respect. You really need to know what you're doing in these parts – huge waves and strong riptides are unforgiving,

and countless surfboards here have wound up broken and strewn about on the shoreline. Unless you're a hardcore surfer, it's best to stick to gentler breaks near Jacó, but there's nothing to stop you from coming up here and watching the action.

Several places on the Pacific coast are named 'Beautiful Beach' in Spanish, and this 10km-long strip of gray sand is hardly the loveliest of the lot. Billed as an upscale alternative to Jacó, minus the hookers and the traffic, Hermosa hasn't quite avoided development, with condos popping up along the beach like mushrooms. Still, for now, it is very much a slow-paced beach village.

⃗ Activities

Surfing

Most of the surfing action takes place at the northern reaches, where there are no fewer than six clearly defined beach breaks. These have tons of power and break very near the shore, particularly in the rainy season between May and August. Conditions are highly variable, but you can expect the maximum height to top out around high tide. Swell size is largely dependent on unseen factors such as current and offshore weather patterns, but when it gets big, you'll know. At times like these, you really shouldn't be paddling out unless you have some serious experience under your belt. Playa Hermosa is not for beginners, and even intermediate surfers can get chewed up and spat out here. To watch and appreciate, park at the small road by the Backyard Hotel and wander out to the beach.

SAVING THE SQUIRREL MONKEY

With its expressive eyes and luxuriant coat, the *mono tití* (Central American squirrel monkey) is a favorite among Costa Rica's four monkey species. It is also in danger of extinction, as there are only roughly 1500 of these animals left in Manuel Antonio, one of its last remaining native habitats.

Overdevelopment is one of the animal's greatest threats. To remedy this problem, a conservation project known as the **Titi Conservation Alliance** (www.monotiti.org; ☑ 2777-2306) is taking bold measures to prevent further decline. This coalition of organizations is helping to create a sustainable wildlife corridor between Parque Nacional Manuel Antonio and the Zona Protectora Cerro Nara in the northeast.

To achieve this aim, it is reforesting the Río Naranjo, a key waterway linking the two locations. More than 65,000 trees have already been planted along 8km of the Naranjo. This not only has the effect of extending the monkeys' habitat but also provides a protected area for other wildlife to enjoy. Scientists at the Universidad Nacional de Costa Rica have mapped and selected sites for reforestation, and business owners in the area as well as private donations support the project financially.

Yoga

Vida Asana School of Yoga YOGA

(☎ 8483-7603, in USA 201-603-3602; www.vidaas ana.com) This hillside retreat offers packages combining yoga, surfing, healthy organic meals and permaculture workshops. Reservations for 'weekend recharge retreats' are highly recommended, and prices are dependent on the size of your party, the season and the extent of instruction. The accommodations are charming and set amid lush jungle. Signposted along the road from the south end of town, Calle Hermosa.

Festivals & Events

National Surfing Championship SPORTS

If you don't think you can hack it with the aspiring pros, you might want to give the surf on this beach a miss. However, consider stopping by in late July or late August, when local pro surfers descend for the annual national surf competition. Dates vary, though the event is heavily advertised around the country, especially in neighboring Jacó.

Sleeping

Most accommodations in Playa Hermosa are clustered along a few hundred meters of highway and the beach road paralleling it, which basically comprise the village. Rates vary wildly depending on season and demand, and they're often negotiable.

Hotel Brisa del Mar CABINA $

(☎ 2643-7076, 8816-2294; cabinasbrisadelmar@ hotmail.com; s/d/tr US$37/40/45; P ❄ 🛜 ⛱) A classic no-frills surfers' crash pad popular with Ticos, this spot has basic rooms with air-con, private hot shower and cable TV, as well as a communal kitchen where you can self-cater. If the surf is looking too small (or too big!), you can pass the time at the pool.

★ Tortuga del Mar LODGE $$

(☎ 2643-7132; www.tortugadelmar.net; r US$75-95; P ❄ @ 🛜 ⛱) This newer lodge is sheltered amid shady grounds, and has just nine rooms housed in a two-story building, presided over by helpful Lilly and her husband Till. Tropical modern is the style, with lofty ceilings constructed from hardwoods, catching every gust of the Pacific breezes. The best bit? The wooden deck out front to watch the surfing action. The larger studios are spacious and even feature mini kitchenettes that make self-catering a real possibility within this price bracket.

Marea Brava RESORT $$$

(☎ 2643-7111; www.mareabravacostarica.com; r/ penthouse US$120/330; P ❄ 🛜 ⛱) Tucked away into the northernmost corner of Hermosa's beachfront road, this creeper-clad hotel is one of the more characterful places in the village. The rooms are spacious and comfortable, but you can hang out by the two pools even if you're not a guest (day pass US$14) and it's right on the waterfront. Very popular with weekending Ticos.

Sandpiper Hotel HOTEL $$$

(☎ 2643-7042; www.sandpipercostarica.com; r US$90-145; P ❄ 🛜 ⛱) A central waterfront location with hammocks strung up so that guests can watch the surfing action in comfort, a little pool with a miniature waterfall, and comfortable rooms with full kitchens make this an excellent choice. It's hard not to make friends with Greg the owner and the grounds are full of iguanas and other local wildlife.

Backyard Hotel HOTEL $$$

(☎ 2643-7011; www.backyardhotel.com; r/ste incl breakfast from US$150/260; P ❄ @ 🛜 ⛱) Right next door to Playa Hermosa's perennially popular Backyard Bar – upside or downside? Your call! – Backyard Hotel entices young, moneyed surfers with tiled rooms that are enticingly cushy for little Hermosa. Rooms have private terraces, most of which have beach or jungle views. On Fridays and Saturdays there are surf competitions out front and the bar throws loud parties.

Eating

The few eateries in Hermosa cater to a surfer clientele and are quite good.

★ Vida Hermosa COSTA RICAN $

(☎ 2643-6215; www.facebook.com/VidaHermosa PlayaHermosa; mains US$4-12; ⏰ 7am-10pm) This new restaurant is the talk of Playa Hermosa for its friendly staff, sweet surf view, and, most of all, its outrageously delicious cuisine. The chef cut his teeth over at Tsunami Sushi, but with a new place of his own he's thriving (and throwing sushi nights on Friday and Saturday).

At breakfast, the hearty surfer's burrito is ideal fuel for Hemosa's gigantic waves, and the coffee's great too.

There are a couple of charming, tidy rooms available for US$100 per night.

Backyard Bar   INTERNATIONAL $
(☑ 2643-7011; mains US$5-12; ⊘ 7am-11pm; 🛜)
Backyard Bar's expansive menu serves the
usual surfer fare (tacos, pizza, burritos),
but none of it is likely to set your taste buds
alight. As the town's de facto nightspot, the
Backyard Bar occasionally hosts live music,
has a nightly happy hour and a local surf
contest every Friday and Saturday from 4pm
until sunset (first, second and third place
share the winnings: US$300).

❶ Getting There & Away

Located only 5km south of Jacó, Playa Hermosa
can be accessed by any bus heading south from
Jacó. Frequent buses running up and down the
Costanera Sur can easily pick you up, though
determined surfers can always hail a taxi (with
surf racks) or hitchhike.

Playa Esterillos

Only 15 minutes south of Jacó but *mundos*
(worlds) away, Playa Esterillos lures those
who simply want to catch some surf, sun and
scenery (sans scene), as there isn't much else
to do along this miles-long expanse of beach.
Playa Esterillos is signed off the highway in
several sections: Esterillos Oeste (West),
Centro (Central) and Este (East). Esterillos
Oeste has a mini-supermarket, a couple of
sodas, a tiny tour office and a Tico-village
vibe absent in Jacó, while Esterillos Este has
more of a resort feel, with upscale accommodations and a string of holiday homes along
the beachfront.

🛌 Sleeping

Cheaper accommodations, popular with
Ticos, are found in Esterillos Oeste, while
Esterillos Este caters to a more upmarket
clientele.

Hotel La Dolce Vita   HOTEL $$
(☑ 2778-7015; www.hotel-ladolcevita.biz; Ester-
illos Oeste; s/d incl breakfast from US$62/89;
P ❄ 🛜 ☒) The intimate Hotel La Dolce Vita
is just meters away from the beach. The
pool may be small, but you can fall asleep
lulled by the sound of the waves, and in the
morning have your breakfast served on your
private terrace at a time of your choosing.
The almond trees by the hotel attract scarlet
macaws.

★ Alma del Pacífico   RESORT $$$
(☑ 2778-7070; www.almadelpacifico.com; Esterillos
Este; bungalow/villa from US$345/463; P ❄ 🛜 ☒)

Each individually designed villa at this remarkable resort encompasses intriguing
design elements, including wooden-lattice
ceilings, sheer walls of glass framing private
gardens, concrete-poured furniture done up
with custom leatherwork, and impossibly
intricate mosaic tile work. There is also an
onsite restaurant specializing in gourmet
and organic healthy fare, and an immaculate palm-fringed infinity pool that faces the
crashing surf.

Encantada Ocean Cottages   COTTAGE $$$
(☑ 2778-7048;   www.facebook.com/encantadacr;
Esterillos Este; cottage/villa from US$153/192;
❄ 🛜 ☒) With verdant grounds and a collec-
tion of Dutch-looking cottages surrounding
a relaxing pool by the sea, Encantada is a
sanctuary. Solidifying the wellness angle, the
owners recently constructed an oceanfront
yoga deck, and classes are held at 10am daily
for guests and whoever else wanders up.

Cottages come with mini-fridges, and
there are also a couple of villas (one is ocean-
front!) with full kitchens.

Hotel Pelicano   HOTEL $$$
(☑ 2778-8105; www.pelicanbeachcostarica.com;
Esterillos Este; r/ste from US$99/170; P ⊝ ❄
🛜 ☒ ☒) The long-standing beachside Hotel
Pelicano hits a sweet spot: it's affordable,
safe, homey and on a dreamy stretch of
the Pacific. The rooms are a bit rustic but
open to balconies overlooking a small pool.
Guests can take in magnificent sunsets, go
surfing or splash around in the waves, and
the onsite restaurant is one of the best in the
area. The hotel often hosts school groups
and offers a variety of tours suitable for older children.

🍴 Eating

Besides a couple of *sodas,* Esterillos
Oeste features one excellent restaurant. A
long-abandoned shopping plaza, **Esterillos
Towncenter** (☑ 4701-9883, 6245-0700; http://
esterillostowncenter.com/EN/), has recently
sprung back to life, and now contains several interesting restaurants and shops.

★ Los Almendros   INTERNATIONAL $$
(☑ 2778-7322; Esterillos Oeste; mains from US$8;
⊘ 4-9pm Mon-Sat) Around 50m west of the
soccer field in Esterillos Oeste, an expat
has decided to take a global theme and run
with it a few miles. The results? Delectable
Jamaican jerk, Caribbean-style curry, whole
red snapper with homemade salsa, pad thai,

PLAYA PALO SECO & AROUND

Playa Palo Seco (aka Isla Palo Seco) is a quiet, unhurried black-sand beach that's off the beaten track and located near mangrove swamps with good opportunities for birdwatching. Just south of the Río Parrita, a 6km dirt road connects the eastern edge of Parrita to the beach. Another popular excursion is to visit Isla Damas, which is actually the tip of a mangrove peninsula that becomes an island at high tide. Most people arrive here on package tours from Jacó or Quepos, though you can hire a boat to take you to and from the island.

The only places to stay are a couple of secluded upmarket options off Playa Palo Seco.

Beso del Viento (☑ 2779-9674; www.besodelviento.com; incl breakfast r with/without air-con from US$118/99; P ❈ 🖀 ☲) It's worth making a detour to stay at this lovely adult-only B&B, located across the road from an isolated beach. Charming wood-floored rooms are comfortably outfitted and decorated with an elegant eye for detail, with tiled bathrooms and immaculate linens. Your lovely hosts serve superb French meals and can arrange tours for guests.

Clandestino Beach Resort (☑ 2779-8806; www.clandestinobeachresort.com; US$240-300; ❈ 🖀 ☲) Sandwiched between a mangrove-lined canal and a jungle-fringed, chocolate-sand beach, this is one secluded stretch of paradise. Twelve comfortable private bungalows are strewn around a large, open-air restaurant with a thatched roof and lots of homey-tropical touches, hand-selected by the friendly expat owner who claims to have visited every beach in Costa Rica before choosing to build her paradise here.

Parrita is about 40km south of Jacó, and can be reached on any bus heading south from there. After Parrita, the coastal road dips inland through more palm-oil plantations on the way to Quepos. A taxi from Parrita to Playa Palo Seco costs around US$10.

black-bean soup and more. The dishes are beautifully executed, the atmosphere convivial and the service sweet. Worth traveling for.

❶ Getting There & Around

While buses connecting Jacó with Quepos can drop you off at the access roads into Playa Esterillos, getting there and around is easiest with your own set of wheels.

PARQUE NACIONAL MANUEL ANTONIO & AROUND

As visitors arrive at this small outcrop of land jutting into the Pacific, the air becomes heavy with humidity, scented with thick vegetation and alive with the calls of birds and monkeys, making it suddenly apparent that *this* is the tropics. The reason to come here is Parque Nacional Manuel Antonio, one of the most picturesque bits of tropical coast in Costa Rica. If you get bored of cooing at the baby monkeys scurrying in the canopy and scanning for birds and sloths, the turquoise waves and perfect sand provide endless entertainment. However, as it's one of the country's most popular national parks, little Quepos, the once-sleepy fishing and banana village on the park's perimeter, has ballooned with this tourism-based economy, and the road from Quepos to the park is overdeveloped. Despite this, the rainforested hills and the blissful beaches make the park a stunning destination worthy of the tourist hype.

Quepos

POP 21,950

Located just 7km from the entrance to Manuel Antonio, the small, busy town of Quepos serves as the gateway to the national park, as well as a convenient port of call for travelers in need of goods and services. Although the Manuel Antonio area was rapidly and irreversibly transformed following the ecotourism boom, Quepos has largely retained an authentic Tico feel.

While many visitors to the Manuel Antonio area prefer to stay outside Quepos, accommodations in town are generally very good value, and there's a decent restaurant scene that belies the town's small size.

Quepos is also gridded with easy-to-walk streets, which provide the opportunity to interact with the friendly locals.

🏃 Activities

Note that the beaches in Quepos are polluted and not recommended for swimming. Go over the hill to Manuel Antonio instead, where some of the dreamiest waters in Costa Rica await.

Diving

The dive sites are still being developed in the Quepos and Manuel Antonio area, and some of the diving outfits take customers as far as Isla del Caño. Sites are away from the contaminated beaches, so water pollution is not a problem when diving.

Oceans Unlimited   DIVING
(🖵 2519-9544; www.scubadivingcostarica.com; 2-tank dive US$109) ⬤ This shop takes its diving very seriously, and runs most of its excursions out to Isla Larga and Isla del Caño, which is south in Bahía Drake (connected via a two-hour bus trip). It also has a range of specialized PADI certifications, and regular environmental-awareness projects that make it stand out from the pack.

Quepos

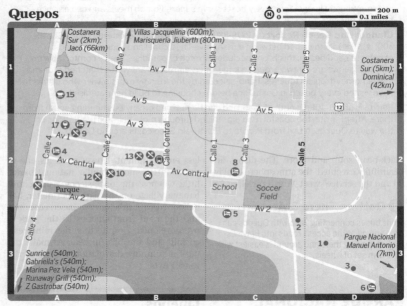

Quepos

Sportfishing

Sportfishing is big here, and offshore ventures are best from December to April, when sailfish are being hooked. By and large this is a high-dollar activity and you can expect to pay upwards of US$900 to hire a boat for the day. If you want to shop around a bit, visit the office of Marina Pez Vela (p376), 500m south of the town center.

Quepos Sailfishing Charters   FISHING
(2777-2025, in USA 800-388-9957; www.quepos fishing.com) This Quepos-based outfitter gets good reviews from sportfishers and offers charters on a fleet of variously sized boats, whether you're after sailfish, marlin, dorado or wahoo. Rates vary significantly depending on season, number of people and size of boat. It also offers packages that include accommodations and transfers.

👉 Tours

There are numerous reputable tour operators in the Quepos area, who specialize in everything from white-water rafting on nearby rivers and mangrove kayaking to paddleboarding tours and waterfall tours of the Pacific coast.

★ Paddle 9   ADVENTURE
(2777-7436; www.paddle9sup.com; tours US$60-150) These newer kids on the block are a passionate, safety-conscious team who've introduced SUP (stand-up paddleboarding) to Quepos and who delight in showing visitors around the Pacific coast. Apart from its two-hour mangrove or ocean paddleboarding tours, its most popular outing is a eight-hour journey involving paddleboarding, lunch at a tilapia farm and swimming in various waterfalls.

Unique Tours   ADVENTURE
(8844-0900, 2777-1119; www.costaricaunique tours.com) This established local operator organizes entertaining rafting tours of the Río Savegre, ocean and mangrove kayaking outings and more. But what makes it unique is that it's the only operator to offer a trip to a hidden, remote hot spring, as well as coastal hikes to Parque Nacional Manuel Antonio. Prices vary depending on group size.

H2O Adventures   ADVENTURE
(Ríos Tropicales; 2777-4092; www.h2ocr.com) The venerable Costa Rican rafting company Ríos Tropicales has a hugely popular franchise in Quepos called H2O Adventures, which organizes rafting outings on

RAINMAKER AERIAL WALKWAY

Rainmaker is a privately owned rainforest that offered the first **aerial walkway** (2779-5661, 8588-2586, 8960-3836; www.rainmakercostarica.org; entry US$20, guided tours US$30-35) through the forest canopy in Central America. Although its star has faded a bit, the place is still regarded as one of the region's best, and in 2014 a popular craft brewery, Perro Vida, opened inside the visitors center. (Tastings must be done after the aerial walkway, obviously.)

the Naranjo, El Chorro and Savegre rivers, as well as kayaking and tubing outings. Rates start at US$70 for rapids Classes II through IV.

Titi Canopy Tours   ADVENTURE
(2777-3130; www.titicanopytour.com; Costanera Sur; day/night tours US$80/100; ⏰ tours 7:30am, 11am, 2:30pm, 6pm) Offering ziplining, rappelling and Tarzan swinging adventures during the day and night, this outfit has friendly, professional guides and a convenient location just outside of central Quepos (150m south of the hospital). Rates include drinks, snacks and local transportation, and in some cases there's a minimum number of guests required (ask about this in advance).

Iguana Tours   ADVENTURE
(2777-2052; www.iguanatours.com; ⏰ 6:30am-9pm) 🖋 With tours that leave for destinations all over the central Pacific coast, this adventure-travel shop offers reputable river rafting, sea kayaking, horseback riding, mangrove tours and dolphin-watching excursions. It's no fly-by-night operation – it's been around since '89 – and has a proven commitment to ecotourism principles.

Planet Dolphin Cruises   WILDLIFE
(2777-1647, in the USA 800-943-9161; www.planet dolphin.com; morning/afternoon trip US$75/85) Planet Dolphin offers dolphin- and whale-watching tours. The cruises include refreshments (including vodka and *guaro*, a sugarcane liquor), lunch, snorkeling and transfers to your hotel, and depart from Marina Pez Vela. Some customers have complained in the past of misinformation about dolphins and unprofessional behavior by the catamaran crew.

🛏 Sleeping

Staying in Quepos offers a cheaper alternative to the sky-high prices at many lodges on the road to Manuel Antonio. It can also be more convenient, as all the banks, supermarkets and bus stops are in Quepos. Reservations are recommended during high-season weekends and holidays.

★ Villas Jacquelina   GUESTHOUSE $
(☏ 8345-1516; www.villasjacquelina.com; Calle 2; r US$35-70; P❄@🛜🏊) By far the best budget option in town, this large, rambling building offers various configurations of rooms, the newest and most popular of which is a 3rd-story, open-air terrace called the 'Birds Nest.' The place is run by the indomitable Steve, a transplant with energy to spare and tons of local knowledge, who can help arrange tours. There are large hangout spaces with hammocks, and good breakfasts, and a vibe of friendly camaraderie prevails. Several rooms are geared toward families with kids, furniture-wise, and there's a child-friendly pool.

Hotel Papa's Papalotes   HOTEL $
(☏ 2777-3774; www.papaspapalotes.com; Av 2; s with/without air-con US$45/35, d with/without air-con US$55/45; ❄🛜) A decent budget choice in central Quepos, with private rooms a better bargain than at some nearby hostels. The decor won't make your social-media posts, but the place is clean and secure. If you opt for fan-only, you'll be woken up by the dawn chorus of traffic passing along the street; pack earplugs.

Pura Vida Hostel   HOSTEL $
(☏ 2777-7775; www.puravidahostelmanuelantonio.com; dm US$10-15, r per person US$15-30, all incl breakfast; ❄@🛜) From the rainbow-hued facade to the interior murals, this place is nothing if not colorful. The rooms have tropical-colored walls, bright linens, tile floors and lockers. Big, shared balconies overlook the jungle-covered hills, where you're likely to spot squirrel monkeys passing through. It's on the southern edge of town on the road to Manuel Antonio.

Wide Mouth Frog Backpackers   HOSTEL $
(☏ 2777-2798; www.widemouthfrog.org; Apartado 256; dm US$13, r with/without bathroom from US$50/30; P❄@🛜🏊) Secure and cozy, this backpacker outpost has spacious doubles, clean shared bathrooms, a well-equipped kitchen and a large, open-air dining area that encourages socializing. There's also a TV lounge with a free DVD library and a couple of lazy dogs padding around. Cons? Some staff members won't win congeniality prizes, the cheaper private rooms are cell-like and wi-fi is patchy.

Serenity   BOUTIQUE HOTEL $$
(☏ 2777-0572; www.serenityhotelcostarica.com; Av 3; s/d incl breakfast from US$85/95; P❄🛜🏊) This intimate boutique hotel is a welcome part of the Quepos scene, and is easily the best midrange option in town. The white-washed walls, blue trim and aromatherapy offer a slice of breezy Mediterranean calm. In the rooms, guests enjoy crisp white linens, cable and a mini-fridge. Rooms upstairs get much better light but some windows face the corridor. New owners took over and renovated in 2017.

Hotel Villa Romántica   HOTEL $$
(☏ 2777-0037; www.villaromantica.com; Av 4; s/d incl breakfast from US$69/98; P❄@🛜🏊) A short walk southeast from the town center brings you to this peaceful garden oasis; rooms are dimly lit but comfortable enough, though the towels are threadbare and renovation is badly needed. If you're looking for a compromise between the convenience of staying in Quepos and the intimate proximity to nature found in Manuel Antonio, this is a passable choice.

Best Western Hotel Kamuk   HOTEL $$
(☏ 2777-0379, 2777-0811; www.kamuk.co.cr; cnr Av Central & Calle 4; r incl breakfast US$96-170; P❄❄🛜🏊) The Hotel Kamuk is all Costa Rican – from the bones of its historic building to the colonial decorative elements. Some rooms are tiny and not all pass the sniff test, but have modern conveniences, plus there's a pool and open-air restaurant. Rooms near the casino are noisy.

🍴 Eating

One benefit of staying in Quepos proper is the accessibility of a wide range of dining opportunities, and there are also a couple of good markets.

★ Marisquería Jiuberth   SEAFOOD $
(☏ 2777-1292; mains from US$7; ⏰ 11am-10pm) Run by a hardworking fisherman's family, this institution with brightly tiled floors serves the best seafood in town, yet is practically unknown to visitors because it's tucked away. Whether you have the catch of the day or the satisfying fish soup, the portions are

generous and the service attentive. Follow unpaved Calle 2 out of town. Cash only.

★ Brooklyn Bakery
BAKERY $

(Av 3; bagels US$1.50, mains US$5-8; ☻6am-3pm Mon-Sat; ☎📶) Real New York–style bagels and lox (a real rarity in Costa Rica)! Rye bread! Iced coffee! This adorable little bakery bakes its fresh wares every morning, as well as serving light bites and amazing salads throughout the day and specials at lunchtime, such as delicious Italian meatball sandwiches.

L'Angolo
DELI $

(☑8887-9538, 2777-7865; Calle 2; sandwiches US$5-7; ☻11am-10pm Mon-Sat) This deli makes excellent sandwiches with imported Italian meats and cheeses, served with a side of ill grace from the grumpy waiter, but perfect for toting on excursions to Manuel Antonio.

Soda Come Bien
CAFETERIA $

(☑2777-2550; Av 1, Mercado Central; mains US$3.50-8; ☻6am-5pm Mon-Sat, to 11am Sun) The daily rotation of delicious cafeteria options might include fish in tomato sauce, *olla de carne* (beef soup with rice) or chicken soup, but everything is fresh, the women behind the counter are friendly and the burly portions are a dream come true for hungry shoestringers. Or, pick up a fresh *empanada* before or after a long bus ride.

Farmers Market
MARKET $

(Calle 4; ☻4pm Fri-noon Sat) Self-caterers should check out the farmers market near the waterfront, where you can buy directly from farmers, fisherfolk, bakers and other food producers.

Mercado Central
MARKET $

(Central Market; Av 1; meals from US$4; ☻hours vary) The Mercado Central is packed with produce vendors and good *sodas* too numerous to list, so follow your nose and the locals.

★ Z Gastro Bar
FUSION $$

(☑2777-6948; Marina Pez Vela; mains US$15-25; ☻7am-10pm; ℗📶) Bright, open to the breeze from all sides and with colorful cushions strewn on its comfy couches, this is a terrific spot for lingering with a coffee and dessert, or over a meal of dorado *ceviche* in coconut milk, an octopus burger or delicious homemade pasta with mussels. The arty presentation matches the terrific flavors and the service is excellent.

Sunrice
SUSHI $$

(☑2519-9955; www.sunricerestaurant.com; sushi rolls US$9-12, mains US$9; ☻noon-9pm Tue-Sun) A newcomer to the Marina Pez Vela, this Latin-influenced sushi and sake bar fills its rolls with fresh tropical produce and local seafood bits. The spicy tuna over crispy rice cakes is a big hit, along with the tuna, avocado and mango poke bowl and the *omusubi* (Japanese rice balls). Dishes tend to be on the smaller side.

Runaway Grill
AMERICAN $$

(☑2519-9095; Marina Pez Vela; mains US$12-25; ☻11am-10pm; ℗✳📶) An all-round crowd pleaser, Runaway Grill's menu spans steaks, wraps, salads, tacos, burgers, sandwiches and more. Portions are sizable and come with a sea view, the mint lemonades are refreshing and enormous, and the service is friendly (though they struggle sometimes when the place is packed).

Escalofrío
ITALIAN $$

(☑2777-1902; Av Central; mains US$10-22; ☻2:30-10:30pm Tue-Sun; ✳📶) Gelato lovers should make a point of stopping here, to choose from more than 20 flavors of the heavenly stuff. This spacious alfresco restaurant may also be the only game in town on Sunday night during slow season, a godsend especially if you enjoy thin-crust wood-fired pizza.

★ Gabriella's
SEAFOOD $$$

(☑2519-9300; Marina Pez Vela; mains US$25-35; ☻4-10pm; ℗✳📶) A contender for the region's best restaurant, Gabriella's does many things well. The veranda catches the sunset, the service is attentive, but the food is the real star, with a great emphasis on fresh fish and mouthwatering steak. We're particularly big fans of the seared tuna with chipotle sauce and the spicy sausage and shrimp pasta. In a word: terrific.

🎭 Drinking & Entertainment

The nightlife in Quepos has a good blend of locals and travelers, and it's cheaper than what you'll find in the Manuel Antonio area. If you are looking for something a bit more sophisticated, however, it's easy enough to jump in a taxi. Keep in mind that the action won't start warming up until around 10pm.

Café Milagro
CAFE

(☑2777-1707; www.cafemilagro.com; Calle 4; ☻9am-5pm Mon-Sat) Café Milagro sources its coffee beans from all over Costa Rica and produces a variety of estate, single-origin and blended roasts to suit any coffee fiend's palate, with 1% of its profits going to environmental causes via international nonprofit 1% for the Planet. Unlike its other, bigger branch en route to Manuel Antonio, this has takeout coffee only (US$3.50 to US$7).

Cuban Republik Disco Lounge CLUB
(☑ 8345-9922; cover charge Fri & Sat US$2-4; ⊙ 10pm-2:30am Thu-Sat) Cuban Republik hosts the most reliable party in central Quepos, and it has various drinks specials. The DJs get loud late into the night and women get in for free before midnight on Friday night. It's a nice, mixed Tico and gringo scene.

El Gran Escape BAR
(☑ 2777-7850; Av 3; ⊙ 11am-10pm Sun-Thu, till late Fri & Sat; ☎) This long-standing pub is famous for all the fishing hats draped from the ceiling. It offers excellent fresh seafood, sports on the big screen and delicious (though pricey) burgers. Prompt bar staff too.

Dos Locos BAR
(☑ 2777-1526; Av Central; ⊙ 7am-11pm Mon-Sat, 11am-7pm Sun) This popular pseudo-Mexican restaurant is the regular watering hole for the local expat community, and serves as a venue for live music on Wednesdays and Saturdays. Opening onto the central cross streets of town, its fun for people-watching (and cheap Imperials). There's an English-language trivia night every Thursday. Added bonus: breakfast is served all day.

Casino CASINO
If you feel like putting your cash on the line, there's a small casino at the Best Western Hotel Kamuk, but the scene gets a bit seedy.

ⓘ Orientation

Downtown Quepos is a small checkerboard of dusty streets that are lined with a mix of local- and tourist-oriented shops, businesses, markets, restaurants and cafes. The town loses its well-ordered shape as it expands outward, but the sprawl is kept relatively in check by the mountains to the east and the water to the west.

South of the town center is the **Marina Pez Vela** (☑ 2774-9000; www.marinapezvela.com); its marine slips opened to much fanfare in 2010, and it now features some of the best restaurants in town.

ⓘ Information

Look out for *Quepolandia*, a free English-language monthly magazine that can be found at many of the town's businesses.

DANGERS & ANNOYANCES
➙ Theft can be a problem, and the usual commonsense precautions apply: lock valuables in a hotel safe and never leave anything in a car.
➙ When leaving bars late at night, walk in a group or take a taxi. Women should keep in mind that the town's bars attract rowdy crowds of plantation workers on weekends.

ⓘ Getting There & Away

AIR
Both NatureAir (p350) and Sansa (p350) service Quepos. Prices vary according to season and availability, though you can pay a little less than US$75 for a flight from San José or Liberia. Flights are packed in the high season, so book (and pay) for your ticket well ahead of time and reconfirm often. The airport is 5km out of town, and taxis make the trip for US$8.

There's also a US$3 entry/exit fee at the airport.

BUS
Scheduled private shuttles, operated by Gray Line, Easy Ride and Monkey Ride, run between Quepos/Manuel Antonio and popular destinations such as Jacó (US$35), Monteverde (US$59), Puerto Jiménez (US$79), San José (US$50) and Uvita (US$35).

All buses arrive at and depart from the busy, chaotic main terminal in the center of town. If you're coming and going in the high season, buy tickets for San José in advance at the **Tracopa**

BUSES FROM QUEPOS

DESTINATION	COST (US$)	DURATION	FREQUENCY
Jacó	3	1½hr	12 daily 4:30am-6pm
Puntarenas	5	3hr	12 daily 4:30am-5:30pm
San Isidro de El General, via Dominical	5	3hr	5am, 11:30am, 3:30pm, 8pm
San José	9	3½hr	9 direct daily 4am-5pm
Uvita, via Dominical	4	2hr	6am, 9:30am, 2:30pm, 5:30pm

ticket office (☑ 2777-0263; ⊙ 6am-6pm) at the bus terminal; *colectivo* (shared taxi) fares to San José are slightly cheaper and take two hours longer.

Buses between Quepos and Manuel Antonio (US$0.55) depart roughly every 30 minutes from the main terminal between 7am and 7pm, and less frequently after 7:30pm.

TAXI

Colectivo taxis run between Quepos and Manuel Antonio (US$1 for a short hop). A private taxi will cost a few thousand colones. Catch one at the **taxi stand** (Av Central) south of the market. The trip between Quepos and the park should cost about US$15.

ℹ️ Getting Around

A number of international car-rental companies, such as **Budget** (☑ 2774-0140; www.budget. co.cr; Quepos Airport; ⊙ 8am-5pm Mon-Sat, to 4pm Sun), operate in Quepos; reserve ahead and reconfirm to guarantee availability.

Quepos to Manuel Antonio

From the Quepos waterfront, the steep, narrow winding road swings uphill and inland for 7km before reaching the beaches of Manuel Antonio village and the entrance to the national park. This route passes over a number of hills awash with picturesque views of jungle-y slopes leading down to the palm-fringed coastline.

This area is home to some of Costa Rica's finest hotels and restaurants, and while shoestringers and budget travelers are catered for, this is one part of the country where those with deep pockets can bed down and dine out in the lap of luxury.

Watch out for local drivers careening around the bends at high velocities, and exercise caution and drive and walk with care, especially at night. Driving to Quepos from Manuel Antonio at around 6pm to 7pm means condemning yourself to sitting in practically immovable traffic.

👁 Sights

La Playita   BEACH
At the far western end of Playa Espadilla, beyond a rocky headland (wear sandals), this former nude beach remains one of Costa Rica's most famous gay beaches and a particular draw for young men. It's inaccessible around high tide, so time your walk. Also, don't be fooled – you do not need to pay to use the beach, as it's outside the park.

Manuel Antonio Nature Park & Wildlife Refuge   WILDLIFE RESERVE
(☑2777-0850; adult/child US$15/8; ⊙8am-4pm; 🚹) This private rainforest preserve and butterfly garden breeds about three dozen species of butterfly – a delicate population compared to the menagerie of lizards, reptiles and frogs that inspire gleeful squeals from the little ones. A jungle night tour (5:30pm to 7:30pm, US$39/29 per adult/child) showcases the colorful local frogs and their songs, while day tours (US$15/8 per adult/child) introduce you either to the fluttering or the slithering denizens (or both; joint tickets US$25).

🏃 Activities

Manuel Antonio Surf School   SURFING
(MASS; ☑ 2777-4842, 2777-1955; www.manuel antoniosurfschool.com; group lesson US$65-95) MASS offers friendly, safe and fun small-group lessons daily, lasting for three hours and with a three-to-one student-instructor ratio. Find its stand about 500m up the Manuel Antonio road south of Quepos.

Cala Spa   SPA
(☑ 2777-0777, ext 220; www.sicomono.com; Hotel Sí Como No; treatments US$70-140; ⊙10am-7pm) If you're sunburned and sore from exploring Manuel Antonio – even better if you're not – the Cala Spa offers aloe body wraps, citrus salt scrubs and various types of massage to restore body and spirit. Open daily by appointment only.

🍽 Courses

Mamá Cacao   FOOD
(☑8383-5910; thechocolatemakingworkshipma@ gmail.com; US$35-45 per person, depending on group size) Manuel Antonio chocolate-maker Mamá Cacao runs this traveling, chocolate-making workshop using beans she's gathered up from local farms. The workshop lasts two hours, during which guests prepare their own vegan and dairy truffles, sample homemade chocolates and discuss the history and nutritional value of cacao. Minimum of two people.

👉 Tours

Amigos del Río   ADVENTURE
(☑2777-0082; www.adradventurepark.com; tours US$135) Pack all of your canopy-tour jungle fantasies into one day on Amigos del Río's '10-in-One Adventure,' featuring ziplining, a Tarzan swing, rappelling down a waterfall

GAY MANUEL ANTONIO

For jet-setting gay and lesbian travelers the world over, Manuel Antonio has a reputation as something of a dream destination. Homosexuality has been decriminalized in Costa Rica since the 1970s – a rarity in all-too-often machismo-fueled, conservative Central America – and a well-established gay scene blossomed in Manuel Antonio soon after. It's not hard to understand why.

Not only is the area stunningly beautiful but it has also long attracted liberal-minded individuals, creating a burgeoning artist community and a sophisticated restaurant scene. Check out www.gaymanuelantonio.com for a full list of gay and gay-friendly accommodations, events, restaurants and bars.

During daylight hours, the epicenter of gay Manuel Antonio is the famous La Playita (p377), a beach with a long history of nude sunbathing for gay men. Alas, the days when you could sun in the buff are gone, but the end of La Playita is still widely regarded as a playful pickup scene for gay men.

and more. The seven-hour adventure tour includes a free transfer from the Quepos and Manuel Antonio area as well as breakfast and lunch. Amigos del Río is also a reliable outfit for white-water-rafting trips.

Tico Loco Adventures OUTDOORS
(☎2777-0010; www.ticolocoadventures.com; Selina Hostel; waterfall party tour US$110, minimum 4 people) Based in the Selina Hostel, this tour company offers outdoor adventures that double as parties. The waterfall party tour involves a hike to majestic falls with a cooler of drinks, and is quite popular with the hostel clientele.

Sleeping

The Quepos–Manuel Antonio road is skewed toward ultra-top-end hotels, but plenty of noteworthy midrange and budget options are hidden along the way. Low-season rates can be 40% lower than high-season rates. Reservations are a must for busy weekends and holidays.

Hostel Plinio and Bed & Breakfast HOSTEL $
(☎2777-6123; dm/d from US$14/60; ❄📶🏊) Attuned to backpacker needs, Hostel Plinio ticks most boxes: a convenient location near Quepos, a large pool and ample common areas with hammocks and sofas for socializing, an efficient tour desk and superior doubles with jungle views for couples wanting more privacy. The drawbacks? The roadside location means some rooms are noisy, and the wi-fi doesn't reach everywhere.

Backpackers Manuel Antonio HOSTEL $
(☎2777-2507; www.backpackersmanuelantonio.com; dm/d incl breakfast from US$16/39; P❄@📶🏊) This locally owned hostel has a very sociable vibe and a good location – relatively near the entrance of the park and walking distance from a good grocery store. The dorms are clean and secure (if small), and there's a grill and pool out back for socializing. Larger rooms, with a bunk and double bed, are good for groups of friends.

Vista Serena Hostel HOSTEL $
(☎2777-5162; www.vistaserena.com; dm US$11-18, bungalows with/without air-con US$60/50; P@📶) Perched scenically on a quiet hillside, this memorable hostel allows backpackers to enjoy spectacular ocean sunsets from a hammock-filled terrace and strum the communal guitar. Accommodations range from spartan econo-dorms to plusher dorms to bungalows for those who want a bit more privacy. The super-friendly owner Sonia and her staff are commendable for their efforts in assisting countless travelers.

In the morning, tea, coffee, toast and jam are complimentary.

★**Selena Manuel Antonio** HOSTEL $$
(www.selina.com/manuel-antonio/; dm US$20-25, r US$75-159; 🏊) Part of the Selina empire, which includes dozens of hostels recently opened across Central America, this one is already a legend. The dorms and private rooms are scattered among rainforested cliffs in elegant white buildings livened up with rotating art exhibits, and the bar has become the area's best nightlife spot, with frequent live music from some of the hottest local talent. Two pools. Sweet views. Killer breakfast buffet.

Didi's B&B B&B $$
(☎2777-0069; www.didiscr.com; s/d incl breakfast US$58/67; ❄📶🏊) Run by Italian Ezio, Didi's is the pick of the guesthouse lot, with

four appealing rooms with TVs encroached on by the surrounding jungle. Opting for a fan-only makes the rate even more reasonable. Three-course Italian dinners (US$25) can be prepared on request using whatever Ezio has picked up at the market.

Hotel Mimos
HOTEL $$

(☎2777-0054; www.mimoshotel.com; d/ste from US$96/220; P❋@🛜🏊) Run by kind and attentive staff, this whitewashed and wood-trimmed hotel has clean, terracotta-tiled, spacious rooms. The property is connected by lovely stone paths, bringing guests to two palm-fringed swimming pools and a hot tub (though the water is not kept hot).

Hotel Tres Banderas
HOTEL $$

(☎2777-1871; www.hoteltresbanderas.com; d/bungalow/ste incl breakfast US$90/113/135; P❋🛜🏊) This welcoming roadside inn offers 11 standard doubles, two bungalows, three suites and an apartment. They are spacious affairs with imported tiles and local woods and, while some could use a bit of air, all come with jungle-facing terraces furnished with leather rocking chairs. Good for wildlife sightings.

Dinner is often prepared on an outdoor grill and guests congregate to dine together around the deep central pool, which lends a communal flourish to the property.

Hotel Mono Azul
HOTEL $$

(☎2777-2572; www.hotelmonoazul.com; r US$85-112, child under 12yr free; P❋@🛜🏊) The Mono Azul is decent value and a good family option. Nestled in a tropical garden and decorated throughout in a rainforest theme, rooms are arranged around two pools. New owners took over in December 2014 and were still revamping the place at the time of research, adding new flat screens, air-con units and murals. We love the bamboo memory-foam pillows.

★ Gaia Hotel & Reserve
BOUTIQUE HOTEL $$$

(☎2777-9797, in USA 800-226-2515; www.gaiahr.com; r from US$435; P❋🛜🏊) This luxurious pile comprises studios, terrace suites and three-story villas and offers nature tours within its expansive grounds – a former wildlife rehabilitation center where scarlet macaws are being reintroduced through a hotel program. The restaurant – one of the best in the region – makes the most of fresh produce. Escapism and relaxation are greatly aided by the cascading pools and the spa treatments. Adults only.

Bonus: you get a 20-minute spa treatment complimentary with the room.

★ Makanda by the Sea
VILLA $$$

(☎2777-0442; www.makanda.com; studio/villa incl breakfast from US$446/548; P❋🛜🏊) A 2017 face-lift has elevated this already spectacular property to a veritable Shangri-La, featuring uniquely glamorous design elements, beautifully textured surfaces and hangout spaces that simply drip with style. Makanda comprises six villas, four studios, a suite, and a smattering of new ocean-view hotel rooms, all perched in a stellar bluff-top location with an unmatched air of intimacy and privacy.

Villa 6 (with a private pool) will take your breath away, and Villa 1 has an entire wall open to the rainforest and the ocean. The other villas and studios are air-conditioned and enclosed, though they draw upon the same Eastern-infused design schemes.

The grounds are also home to two saltwater infinity pools, two Jacuzzis, a sushi bar and a sun terrace, all offering superb views out to sea. If somehow you're still not impressed, you can access a private beach by taking either a golf cart or a few hundred steps down the side of the mountain – bliss! Note that guests must be 16 or older.

★ Arenas del Mar
BOUTIQUE HOTEL $$$

(☎2777-2777; www.arenasdelmar.com; r incl breakfast US$542-1074; P❋🛜🏊) 🌿 This visually arresting hotel and resort complex is consistently shortlisted among Costa Rica's finest upscale hotels. The rooms are designed to incorporate the beauty of the natural landscape, to great effect, especially when you're staring down the coastline from the lofty heights of your sumptuous digs. The top-tier accommodations feature ocean-view Jacuzzis.

Boons include wildlife roaming the property, expertly prepared vegetarian dishes and seafood, and the sustainability tour.

★ Hotel Villa Roca
BOUTIQUE HOTEL $$$

(☎2777-1349; www.villaroca.com; r/apt incl breakfast from $125/175; P❋🛜🏊) This gay-owned, intimate hotel caters to many of Manuel Antonio's gay travelers; it's particularly popular with men. The upstairs rooms are breezier. All guests and visitors must be 18 years or older. You can sun your buns around the beautiful, clothing-optional, 24-hour pool and hot tubs, where you may be joined by a couple of resident iguanas.

★ Hotel Sí Como No
HOTEL $$$

(☑ 2777-0777; www.sicomono.com; r US$275-450, child under 6yr free; P ❄ 🔊 🏊) ✈ This flawlessly designed hotel is an example of how to build an ecofriendly resort. The rooms are accented by rich woods and bold splashes of tropical colors, and come with sweeping balconies. The hotel has two pools (one for kids, one for adults only, both with swim-up bars), two Jacuzzis, a health spa and two excellent restaurants.

Sustainable construction and practices include energy-efficient air-con units, recycling water for landscaping use and solar-powered water heaters. No surprise, then, that Sí Como No is one of a few dozen hotels in the country to have been awarded five out of five leaves by the government-run Certified Sustainable Tourism (CST) campaign.

Hotel Costa Verde
HOTEL $$$

(☑ 2777-0584; www.costaverde.com; efficiency units/studios from US$153/182, Boeing 727 home US$565, cockpit cottage US$276; P ❄ @ 🔊 🏊) This collection of rooms and studios occupies a verdant setting frequented by troops of monkeys. Efficiency units incorporating teak trim and furnishings face the encroaching forest, while more expensive studios have full ocean views. FYI: the cheapest units are near the road! The most coveted accommodations are inside a decommissioned Boeing 727 fuselage and a newly built cockpit cottage.

The 727, which juts out of the jungle in the most surreal way, has two bedrooms with three queen-sized beds, two bathrooms, a kitchenette and a private terrace. The new cockpit cottage is accessed by a suspension bridge and sleeps two, with panoramic ocean views and a bathroom open to the jungle. (It's popular with honeymooners.)

The owners of Costa Verde are also the masterminds behind several eateries along the road to Manuel Antonio, including El Avión bar (also fashioned from a retired fuselage).

Hotel La Mariposa
BOUTIQUE HOTEL $$$

(☑ 2777-0355, in USA 800-572-6440; www.lamariposa.com; r/ste from US$194/334; P ❄ 🔊 🏊) This hotel was the area's first luxury accommodations option, so unsurprisingly it snatched up the best view of the coastline. More than 50 pristine rooms of various sizes are elegantly decorated with hand-carved furniture, but the service can be erratic, the property is dated and a number of guests have complained about the food.

This hotel was listed in the book *1000 Places to See Before You Die*, principally for the world-class views from every corner.

🍴 Eating

The road to Manuel Antonio plays host to some of the best restaurants in the area, and many hotels along this road also have good restaurants open to the public. As with sleeping venues, eating and drinking establishments along this stretch are skewed toward the upmarket. Reservations are recommended on weekends and holidays and during the busy dry season.

Falafel Bar
MEDITERRANEAN $

(☑ 2777-4135; mains US$5-9; ⏱ 11am-9:30pm Tue-Sun; 🔊 ✈) Adding to the diversity of cuisine to be found along the road, this falafel spot dishes up authentic Israeli favorites. You'll also find plenty of vegetarian options, including couscous, fresh salads, stuffed grape leaves, fab fruit smoothies and even french fries for the picky little ones.

Sancho's
MEXICAN $

(☑ 2777-0340; tacos from US$3; ⏱ 11:30am-10pm; 🔊) A great view from the open-air terrace, potent house margaritas, excellent fish tacos and humongous *chile verde* (green chili) burritos are just some of the draws at this friendly expat-run joint. A place to knock back a few beers with friends in a convivial, chilled-out atmosphere, rather than woo your date.

★ Café Milagro
FUSION $$

(☑ 2777-2272; www.cafemilagro.com; mains from US$7; ⏱ 7am-9pm) This is a fine stop for fancy coffee drinks, and even better for decadent breakfasts (banana pancakes with macadamia nuts), sandwiches (mango mahi mahi wrap) and sophisticated interpretations of Tico fare for dinner (Creole pork tenderloin). The patio itself is a lovely setting surrounded by tropical gardens; you can also order your sandwich packed for a picnic in the park.

La Luna
INTERNATIONAL $$

(☑ 2777-9797; www.gaiahr.com; Gaia Hotel; mains US$8-24; ⏱ 6am-11pm; 🔊 ✈) Unpretentious and friendly, La Luna makes a lovely spot for a special-occasion dinner, with a spectacular backdrop of jungle and ocean. An international menu offers everything from spicy tuna and mango tacos to mahi mahi *ceviche* to lobster tails, with a Tico-style twist – such as grouper baked *en papillote* (in paper), with plantain puree and coconut milk. Separate vegetarian and vegan menu available.

Agua Azul INTERNATIONAL $$

(✆2777-5280; www.cafeaguaazul.com; meals US$10-25; ☺11am-10pm Thu-Tue; 🛜) Perched on the 2nd floor with uninterrupted ocean views, Agua Azul is a killer lunch spot on this stretch of road – perfect for early-morning park visitors who are heading back to their hotel. The breezy, unpretentious open-air restaurant, renowned for its 'big-ass burger,' also serves up the likes of fajitas, *panko*-crusted tuna and a tasty fish salad.

Claro Que Sí SEAFOOD $$

(✆2777-0777; Hotel Sí Como No; meals US$9-22; ☺noon-10pm; 🛜👶) 🍃 A casual, family-friendly restaurant that passes on pretension without sacrificing quality, Claro Que Sí proudly serves organic and locally sourced food items that are in line with the philosophy of its parent hotel, Sí Como No. Guilt-free meats and fish are expertly complemented with fresh produce, resulting in flavorful dishes typical of both the Pacific and Caribbean coasts. There's a separate kids' menu.

Barba Roja SEAFOOD $$

(✆2777-0331; www.barbarojarestaurant.com; meals US$9-22; ☺11:30am-9pm Tue-Sun) A Manuel Antonio area institution, the Barba Roja is both a lively bar and a seafood-and-steak spot with a respectable sushi menu and weekly specials (Friday is smoked-rib and blues night). The terrace affords fantastic ocean views, best enjoyed with a local Libertas y La Segua craft brew (pints are US$6) or Mexican-style *michelada* (a spicy beer drink). Drinks are two-for-one every day, 4pm to 6pm.

★ Kapi Kapi Restaurant FUSION $$$

(✆2777-5049; www.restaurantekapikapi.com; meals US$16-40; ☺3-10pm; ❄🛜👶) While there is some stiff competition for the title of best restaurant in the area, this Californian creation certainly raises the bar. The menu at Kapi Kapi (a traditional greeting of the indigenous Maleku) spans the globe from America to Asia. Pan-Asian-style seafood features prominently; the macadamia-nut-crusted-mahi mahi, lobster ravioli and sugarcane-skewered prawns are all standouts.

South American wines and Costa Rican coffees complete this globetrotting culinary extravaganza. True to its name, Kapi Kapi welcomes diners with soft lights, earthy tones and soothing natural decor, which perfectly frame the dense forest lying just beyond the perimeter. There's also a separate kids' menu.

🍺 Drinking & Entertainment

Karma Lounge GAY & LESBIAN

(✆2777-7230; www.facebook.com/karmaloungema; ☺7pm-2:30am Tue-Sun) Popular mingling spot for local gay guys and visitors who want to hang out with them.

El Avión BAR

(✆2777-3378; www.costaverde.com; ☺noon-10pm; 🛜) Constructed around a 1954 Fairchild C-123 plane, allegedly purchased by the US government in the '80s for the Nicaraguan Contras but never used, this striking bar-restaurant is a great spot for a beer and stellar sunset-watching. Skip the food, though, and double-check the check, as complaints have been made about inaccuracies.

In 2000 the enterprising owners of El Avión purchased the plane for the surprisingly reasonable sum of US$3000 (it never made it out of its hangar in San José because of the Iran-Contra scandal that embroiled Oliver North and his cohorts), and proceeded to cart it piece by piece to Manuel Antonio. It now sits on the side of the main road, where it looks as if it had crash-landed into the side of the hill.

CENTRAL PACIFIC COAST QUEPOS TO MANUEL ANTONIO

ℹ GOT KIDS?

The Quepos to Manuel Antonio stretch of road is home to the lion's share of accommodations and restaurants in these parts, but it's worth pointing out that many of the high-end boutique hotels and upscale eateries are not always very welcoming to babies and young children, so check your accommodations' policy.

If you find yourself walking along the narrow, winding road (there is no shoulder), keep a close eye on your children at all times.

Manuel Antonio Area

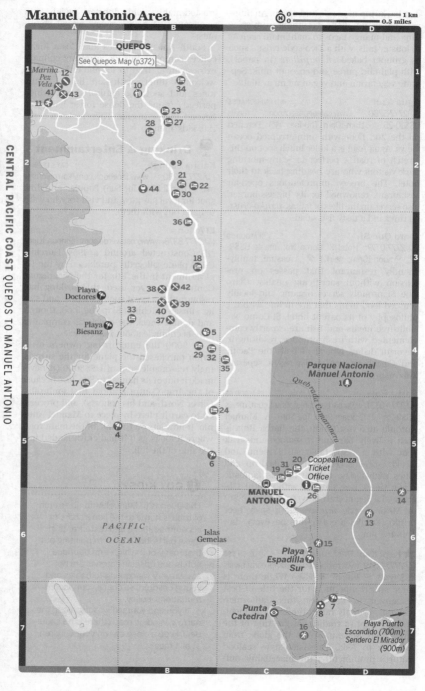

N 0 — 1 km
0 — 0.5 miles

QUEPOS
See Quepos Map (p372)

Marina Pez Vela

Playa Doctores

Playa Biesanz

Parque Nacional Manuel Antonio

Quebrada Camaronera

PACIFIC OCEAN

Islas Gemelas

Coopealianza Ticket Office

MANUEL ANTONIO

Playa Espadilla Sur

Punta Catedral

Playa Puerto Escondido (700m); Sendero El Mirador (900m)

Ronny's Place BAR
(☏ 2777-5120; www.ronnysplace.com; ⊙ noon-10pm) The insane views at Ronny's Place, of two pristine bays and jungle on all sides, make it worth a detour for a drink and a tasty meal. While plenty of places along this stretch of road boast similar views, the off-the-beaten-path location makes it feel like a secret find. Look for the well-marked dirt road off the main drag.

Sí Como No Cinema CINEMA
(☏ 2777-0777; www.sicomono.com; Hotel Sí Como No; tickets US$7; ⊙ 8pm) This 45-seat theater shows a fun rotation of popular American movies and cartoons for kids. Admission is free if you spend US$10 at the hotel's restaurant or bar.

❶ Getting There & Away

Every 30 minutes or so local buses and shared taxis connect Quepos with Manuel Antonio (20 minutes). The public bus from Quepos will let you off anywhere along the road.

A word of caution: driver visibility is limited along parts of the narrow, steep and winding road, particularly during low-light and foul-weather conditions.

Manuel Antonio Village

As you travel the road between Quepos and Parque Nacional Manuel Antonio, the din from roaring buses, packs of tourists and locals hunting foreign dollars becomes increasingly loud, reaching its somewhat chaotic, climax at Manuel Antonio village. Hordes descend on this tiny oceanside village at the entrance to the country's most visited national park. Don't show up all bright-eyed and bushy-tailed, expecting deserted beaches and untouched tropical paradise. Higher primates tend to be the most frequently sighted species, especially during

Manuel Antonio Area

the congested dry season, when tour groups arrive en masse.

But come here in low season or on a Monday (when the park is closed), and you'll find a tranquil little village with waves sedately lapping at the white sand. And, when troops of monkeys climb down from the forest canopy to the tropical sands, you can get up close and personal with some marvelous wildlife.

🏃 Activities

Body boards and kayaks can be rented all along the beach at Playa Espadilla. White-water rafting and sea kayaking are also popular in this area.

🛏 Sleeping

The village of Manuel Antonio is the closest base for exploring the national park, though the selection of sleeping options is more varied in Quepos or on the Quepos–Manuel Antonio stretch of road. Furthermore, the area is completely overrun with foreigners.

Backpackers Paradise
Costa Linda   HOSTEL $
(☑ 2777-0304; r per person from US$12; P ❋ @ 🛜) Calling this backpacker pad a paradise is stretching the truth like a rubber band, but you can't beat the price when you can amble out to the beach or the national park in five minutes. While the staff are a bit harried, and the shared bathrooms could be cleaner, the cocktail and beer prices are easy on the wallet.

Hotel Vela Bar   HOTEL $$$
(☑ 2777-0413; www.velabar.com; r US$150-170 ste US$190; P ❋ @ 🛜 ❄) This attractive little hotel offers light, bright, spacious and contemporary rooms and suites, set around an oval pool and overlooking lush gardens. Its rooms have been upgraded, and the price tag and the comfort are worth it, considering that you can stroll over to the park entrance in two minutes.

Hotel La Posada   BUNGALOW $$$
(☑ 2777-1446; www.laposadajungle.com; bungalows incl breakfast US$110-135, apt US$185-235; P ❋ 🛜 ❄) These secluded jungle bungalows and fully equipped apartments (sleeping four to six guests) all come with kitchenette, TV with DVD player, safe and terrace, and are clustered around a small pool. But the real beauty of staying here is the location right next to the park – from your lodgings

you'll see squirrel monkeys and other wildlife crisscrossing the trees and rooftops.

Cabinas & Hotel Playa Espadilla   HOTEL $$$
(☑ cabinas 2777-2113, hotel 2777-0903; www.espadilla.com; cabina/r from US$127/200; P ❋ 🛜 ❄) Two favorably located properties in one: the hotel is centered on a smallish swimming pool and tennis courts, and the more affordable *cabinas* across the road are slightly closer to the beach. While the accommodations are fairly bland for the price, and the hot water could be more consistent, you do have extremely convenient park and beach access from here.

ℹ Getting There & Away

BUS
The bus stop in Manuel Antonio is at the end of the road into the village that runs along the beach. Buses depart Manuel Antonio beach direct for San José (US$9, 3½ hours) nine times daily between 4am and 5pm. Buy tickets well in advance at the Quepos bus terminal (p376).

Buses for destinations other than San José leave from the main terminal in Quepos.

Local buses (US$0.55, 20 minutes, every 30 minutes) and shared taxis connect Manuel Antonio village with Quepos.

CAR & MOTORCYCLE
Driving the winding 7km road between Quepos and Manuel Antonio village on any day but Monday means spending time in traffic jams and potentially exorbitant parking fees.

Parque Nacional Manuel Antonio

A place of swaying palms and playful monkeys, sparkling blue water and a riot of tropical birds, **Parque Nacional Manuel Antonio** (☑ 2777-8551; park entrance US$16; ☺ 7am-3:30pm Tue-Sun) is the country's smallest and most popular national park. It became a protected area in 1972, preserving it from being razed to make room for a coastal development project. It's a truly lovely place; the clearly marked trail system winds through rainforest-backed white-sand beaches and rocky headlands, the wildlife (iguanas, sloths, monkeys) is plentiful, and the views across the bay to the pristine outer islands are gorgeous.

The downside? Crowds. Visitors are confined to around 6.8 sq km of the park (the rest is set aside for ranger patrols battling poaching) and the place gets packed when

MONKEY BUSINESS

There are a number of stands on the beach that cater to hungry tourists, though everything is exorbitantly overpriced and of dubious quality. Plus, all the food scraps have negatively impacted the monkey population. Before you offer a monkey your scraps, consider the following risks to their health:

➡ Monkeys are susceptible to bacteria transmitted from human hands.

➡ Irregular feeding will lead to aggressive behavior as well as create a dangerous dependency (picnickers in Manuel Antonio suffer downright intimidating mobs of them sometimes).

➡ Bananas are not their preferred food, and can cause serious digestive problems.

➡ Increased exposure to humans facilitates illegal poaching as well as attacks from dogs.

It goes without saying: don't feed the monkeys. And, if you do happen to come across someone doing so, take the initiative and ask them politely to stop.

midmorning tour buses roll in. Get here early (7am) and head for the furthest reaches of the park for a bit of tranquillity and the best chances to spot wildlife.

⊙ Sights

There are five beautiful beaches – three within the park and two just outside the entrance. The beaches are often numbered – most people call Playa Espadilla (outside the park) '1st beach,' Playa Espadilla Sur '2nd beach,' Playa Manuel Antonio '3rd beach,' Playa Puerto Escondido '4th beach' and Playa Playitas (outside the park) '5th beach.' Some people begin counting at Espadilla Sur, which is the first beach in the park, so it can be a bit confusing trying to figure out which beach people may be talking about. Regardless, they're all equally pristine, and provide sunbathing opportunities; check conditions with the rangers to see which ones are safe for swimming.

Rangers indefinitely closed Playa Puerto Escondido to visitors in 2017, but it can still be viewed from a lookout.

★ **Punta Catedral**   AREA
Geography fun fact: this isthmus, which is the centerpiece of the park, is called a *tombolo* and was formed by the accumulation of sand between the mainland and the peninsula beyond, which was once an island. At its end, the isthmus widens into a rocky peninsula, with thick forest in the middle, encircled by Sendero Punta Catedral. There are good views of the Pacific Ocean and various rocky islets – nesting sites for brown boobies and pelicans.

★ **Playa Espadilla Sur**   BEACH
The exposed Playa Espadilla Sur is to the north of Punta Catedral and swimming here can be dangerous. The beach is a half-hour hike from the park entrance.

Playa Manuel Antonio   BEACH
With its turquoise waters, this lovely beach fronts a deep bay, sheltered by the Punta Catedral on the west side and a promontory on the east. This is the best beach for swimming, but it also gets the most crowded with picnicking families, so get here early.

Playa Espadilla   BEACH
This wide stretch of white sand is found just outside the park entrance, in front of Manuel Antonio village.

Turtle Trap   ARCHAEOLOGICAL SITE
At the western end of Playa Manuel Antonio you can see a semicircle of rocks at low tide. Archaeologists believe that these were arranged by pre-Columbian indigenous people to function as a turtle trap. (Turtles would swim in during high tide, but when they tried to swim out after the tide started receding, they'd be trapped by the wall.)

Playa Puerto Escondido   BEACH
Visitors may visit a lookout over this gorgeous horseshoe-shaped beach, but the access point via the Sendero Puerto Escondido was closed indefinitely in 2017.

🏃 Activities

The average daily temperature is 27°C (80°F) and average annual rainfall is 3875mm. The dry season is not entirely dry, merely less wet, so you should be prepared for rain (although it can also be dry for days on end). Make sure you carry plenty of drinking water, sun protection and insect repellent.

Hiking

★ Sendero Punta Catedral   HIKING
This 1.4km loop takes in the whole of Punta Catedral, passing through dense vegetation and with glorious views of the Pacific and the offshore islands. The blink-and-you'll-miss-it 200m Sendero La Tampa cuts across part of the loop.

Sendero El Mirador   HIKING
Heading inland and into the forest from the east side of Playa Manuel Antonio, this 1.3km trail climbs to a lookout on a bluff overlooking Puerto Escondido and Punta Serrucho beyond – a stunning vista. Rangers limit the number of hikers on this trail to 45.

Sendero El Perezoso   HIKING
The main trail (1.3km) that connects the park entrance with the other trails is paved and wheelchair accessible. A new trail was added in 2015, its boardwalk parallel to the road; it provides a quieter alternative to the crowds along the main stretch. Here you'll find numerous tour groups trying to spot birds and sloths through their guides' telescopes.

A bit of eavesdropping on the numerous guides along this stretch will provide solo shoestring travelers an informal lesson on the many birds, sloths and monkeys along the way.

Sendero Principal   HIKING
The longest trail in the park, the 2.2km Sendero Principal fringes Playa Espadilla Sur in Manuel Antonio village.

Sendero La Catarata   HIKING
This 900m trail branches off the main Sendero El Perezoso and leads to an appealing little waterfall.

Wildlife-Watching

Even though visitors are funneled along the main access road, you should have no problem seeing animals here, even as you line up at the gate. White-faced capuchins are very used to people, and normally troops feed and interact within a short distance of visitors; they can be encountered anywhere along the main access road and around Playa Manuel Antonio. The capuchins are the worst culprits for snatching bags, so watch your stuff.

You'll probably also hear mantled howler monkeys soon after sunrise. Like capuchins, they can be seen virtually anywhere inside the park and even along the road to Quepos – watch for them crossing the monkey bridges that were erected by local conservation groups.

Coatis can be seen darting across various paths and can get aggressive on the beach if you're eating. Three-toed and two-toed sloths are also common in the park. Guides are extremely helpful in spotting sloths, as they tend not to move around all that much.

WHY IS THE PARK SO CROWDED?

Although the number of visitors to Parque Nacional Manuel Antonio was previously restricted to 800 per day, the park service in 2017 made an adjustment to allow 800 people in the park at any given time. A line often forms at the entrance, following a one-in-one-out policy, and wait times can stretch up to 30 minutes. The park now ends up hosting about 2000 visitors each day.

The increased tourist traffic has taken its toll on the park's wildlife, as animals are frequently driven away or – worse still – taught to scavenge for tourist handouts. And while the new policy might not sit well with conservationists, there's a reason behind it. In Costa Rica, entrance fees to national parks are funneled into a communal pot and redistributed equally to all national parks, many of which are very remote, infrequently visited and home to abundant wildlife. Without the big bucks coming in from places like Parque Nacional Manuel Antonio, the park service couldn't afford to pay rangers to protect these further-flung, less touristy parks from threats such as poaching, mining and logging.

The closure of one of the park system's top tourist draws, Parque Nacional Volcán Poás, has only exacerbated the situation. Poás was badly damaged in a series of volcanic eruptions in April 2017, and gas and vapor eruptions continued at the time of research. The park remains closed indefinitely, and the park service must scramble to make up for those lost admission fees.

However, the movements of the park's star animal and Central America's rarest primate, namely the Central American squirrel monkey, are far less predictable. These adorable monkeys are more retiring than capuchins, and though they are occasionally seen near the park entrance in the early morning, they usually melt into the forest well before opening time. With luck, however, a troop could be encountered during a morning's walk, and they often reappear in beachside trees and on the fringes of Manuel Antonio village in the early evening.

Offshore, keep your eyes peeled for pantropical spotted and bottlenose dolphins, as well as humpback whales passing by on their regular migration routes. Other possibilities include orcas (killer whales), false killers and rough-toothed dolphins.

Big lizards are also a featured sighting at Manuel Antonio – it's hard to miss the large ctenosaurs and green iguanas that bask along the beach at Playa Manuel Antonio and in the vegetation behind Playa Espadilla Sur. To spot the well-camouflaged basilisk, listen for the rustle of leaves along the edges of the trails, especially near the lagoon.

Manuel Antonio is not usually on the serious birdwatchers' trail of Costa Rica, though the list of birds here is respectable. The usual suspects include the blue-gray and palm tanagers, great-tailed grackles, bananaquits, blue dacnises and at least 15 species of hummingbird. Among the regional endemics you should look out for are the fiery-billed aracaris, black-hooded antshrikes, Baird's trogons, black-bellied whistling ducks, yellow-crowned night herons, brown pelicans, magnificent frigate birds, brown boobies, spotted sandpipers, green herons and ringed kingfishers.

⟲ Tours

Hiring a wildlife guide costs US$15 to US$20 per person (two-person minimum) for a two-hour tour. In the past, the only guides allowed in the park were members of Aguila (a local association governed by the park service), and recognized guides from tour agencies or hotels. However, these days the guys wearing Aguila shirts tend to be parking touts, and uncertified guides hang around by the park entrance, essentially charging tourists money for the privilege of looking through their telescope.

To make sure you find someone who is able to spot animals and birds and explain their role in the park ecosystem, opt for recommended guides such as **Lenny Montenegro** (🖉 8875-0437), or else ask to see the guide's Costa Rican Tourism Board (ICT) license to ascertain that they're the real deal.

We can testify to the fact that hiring a good guide dramatically improves your chances of wildlife sightings and lets you see animals and birds that you most likely would not have spotted by yourself.

ⓘ Information

The park **ticket office** (🖉 2777-6208; www. coopealianza.fi.cr; park entrance US$16; ☉7am-3:30pm) is located in Manuel Antonio village, a few hundred meters before the park entrance. The ranger station is just before Playa Manuel Antonio.

DANGERS & ANNOYANCES

Watch out for the manzanillo tree (*Hippomane mancinella*) – it has poisonous fruits that look like little crab apples, and the sap exuded by the bark and leaves is toxic, causing the skin to itch and burn. Warning signs are prominently displayed beside examples of this tree near the park entrance.

ⓘ Getting There & Away

BUS

The entrance and exit to Parque Nacional Manuel Antonio lies in Manuel Antonio village, connected to Quepos by frequent daily buses (20 minutes, every 30 minutes). Direct buses also depart for San José (US$9, 3½ hours) nine times daily between 4am and 5pm, some stopping in Quepos, some not.

CAR

Note that the road to Manuel Antonio is very narrow and congested, so it's suggested that you leave your car at your hotel and take an early-morning bus to the park entrance instead, then simply walk in.

QUEPOS TO UVITA

South of Quepos, the well-trodden central Pacific tourist trail begins to taper off, evoking the feel of the Costa Rica of yesteryear – surf shacks and empty beaches, roadside *ceviche* vendors and a little more space. Intrepid travelers can have their pick of any number of deserted beaches and great surf spots. The region is also home to the great bulk of Costa Rica's African-palm-oil industry, which should be immediately obvious

RAFIKI SAFARI LODGE

In a prime spot right by the Río Savegre, the expat owners of **Rafiki Safari Lodge** (☑8368-9944, 8419-6832; www.rafikisafari.com; r incl all meals from US$336; P @ 🛜 ⛵) have combined all the comforts of a hotel with the splendor of a jungle safari, with 10 luxury tents equipped with beds, bathroom, hot water, private porch and hydroelectric power. There's a spring-fed pool with a waterslide, and ample opportunities for horseback riding, birdwatching, hiking and white-water rafting.

All units are screened in, which allows you to see and hear the rainforest without actually having creepy-crawlies in your bed.

The owners are also masters on the *braai* (South African for BBQ), so you know that you'll eat well alongside other guests in the *rancho*-style restaurant. This place makes for a great three-day stay; it's too remote to warrant the transport for only one night, but guests exhaust all the activities on offer after three days.

The entrance to the lodge is located about 15km south of Quepos on Hwy 34, and the turnoff is just south of a bridge. From here, a 4WD dirt road parallels the Río Savegre and leads 16km inland, past the towns of Silencio and Santo Domingo, to the lodge. However, if you don't have private transportation, the lodge can arrange all of your transfers with advanced reservations.

after the few dozen kilometers of endless plantations lining the sides of the Costanera.

Known as the Costa Ballena, the beauteous length of coastline between Dominical and Ojochal focuses on three things: surfing (Dominical), whale-watching (Uvita) and gourmet cuisine (Ojochal). For the time being, the area largely retains an easygoing, unjaded allure despite the growing numbers discovering its appeal.

Matapalo

Off the Quepos–Dominical stretch of highway, Matapalo has been off most travelers' radar screens, though without good reason, as this vast, palm-fringed, gray-sand beach has some truly awesome surf. With two river-mouth breaks generating some wicked waves, Matapalo is recommended for intermediate to advanced surfers who are comfortable dealing with rapidly changing conditions, though there's usually a local lifeguard on duty.

Matapalo is not the best beach for swimming as the transient rips here are about as notorious as they come, but it's perfect for sunbathing and watching the action.

🛌 Sleeping

The accommodations are spread along the beach, with a couple of options along the access road that links the main village with the beach.

★ **Charlie's Jungle House**　　GUESTHOUSE **$$**
(☑2787-5005, 8544-3144; www.charliesjunglehouse.com; campsites per person US$10, r US$60-125; P ❄ 🛜 ⛵) Run by the effusive Charlie, this guesthouse halfway along the beach road has eight spacious, jungle-themed and colorful rooms, the largest with kitchenettes. Campers have access to a full bathroom and a common, shaded space to relax, while the onsite Jungle Cafe serves wholesome meals. Charlie is hugely knowledgeable about Matapalo, and arranges waterfall hikes, horseback rides and surf lessons.

Dreamy Contentment　　BUNGALOW **$$**
(☑2787-5223; www.dreamycontentment.com; bungalow/villa from US$105/452; P ❄ 🛜) By the beach, this Spanish-colonial property with impressive woodworking and towering trees throughout offers bungalows equipped with functional kitchenettes, the cheapest geared toward backpacking couples. The real star attraction is the villa, which has the kitchen of your dreams, a beachfront veranda and a princely bathroom complete with hot tub.

Guava Lodge　　LODGE **$$**
(☑2787-5176; www.guavalodge.com; r from US$85; 🛜) A newer collection of five tidy, wooden *cabinas* in the center of town, with an attached restaurant that's excellent (but only open in high season). Cash only.

Rafiki Beach Camp　　CABINA **$$$**
(☑2787-5014; www.rafikibeach.com; tent incl breakfast US$135; ❄ 🛜 ⛵) Near the end of

the beach road you'll find these friendly and laid-back luxury safari-style beachfront tents – all with electricity, tiled bathroom with hot shower and ocean views. There's a pool overlooking the ocean, adjacent to a *rancho* with a communal kitchen. Many guests stay here in conjunction with Rafiki Safari Lodge packages, kayaking down to Matapalo.

✕ Eating

Most accommodations offer meals. There's also the excellent **Langosta Feliz** (☑2777-5214; mains US$7-25; ⊙11am-9:30pm) restaurant across the highway from the entrance to Matapalo.

ⓘ Getting There & Away

Buses between Quepos and Dominical can drop you off at the turnoff to the village; from there it's a couple of kilometers to this off-the-beaten-track beach.

There are a few buses daily that arrive in the village proper from the north and then continue on to Dominical (US$1, 20 minutes) or Uvita (US$1.25, 45 minutes), and others that arrive in Matapalo from the south and continue to Quepos (US$2, one hour) and San José (US$8.68, four hours). The stop is in front of the village *pulpería* (convenience store), and you can ask about bus times there.

Hacienda Barú National Wildlife Refuge

Located on the Pacific coast 3km northeast of Dominical on the road to Quepos, this **wildlife refuge** (☑2787-0003; www.haciendabaru.com; US$8; ⊙7am-7pm) forms a key link in a major biological corridor called the Path of the Tapir, and is thought to have been inhabited by a large population of indigenous people. It comprises around 330 hectares of private and state-owned land that has been protected from hunting since 1976. The range of tropical habitats here include pristine beaches, riverbanks, mangrove estuaries, wetlands, primary and secondary forests, tree plantations and pastures.

This diversity of habitat plus its key position in the Path of the Tapir account for the multitude of species that have been identified in Hacienda Barú. These include 351 birds, 69 mammals, 94 reptiles and amphibians, 87 butterflies and 158 trees. Ecological tourism provides this wildlife refuge with its only source of funds, meaning money spent here helps conserve tropical rainforest.

☞ Tours

There is an impressive number of guided tours on offer. You can experience the rainforest canopy in two ways – tree climbing or a zipline course called 'Flight of the Toucan.' In addition to the canopy activities, Hacienda Barú offers birdwatching tours, hiking tours, and an overnight camping tour in the tropical rainforest. Hacienda Barú's naturalist guides come from local communities and have lived near the rainforest all of their lives. Even if you don't stop here for the sights, the onsite store carries an excellent selection of specialist titles for birdwatchers.

🛏 Sleeping

Hacienda Barú Lodge   LODGE $$
(☑2787-0003; r incl breakfast $107; P ☎) Hacienda Barú Lodge consists of six fan-cooled, two-bedroom cabins located 350m from Barú beach. Accommodations are basic, worn and a bit buggy; the upside is that guests staying here receive free admission to the refuge.

ⓘ Getting There & Away

BUS
The Quepos–Dominical–San Isidro de El General bus stops outside the hacienda entrance. The San Isidro de El General–Dominical–Uvita bus will drop you off at the Río Barú bridge, 2km from the hacienda office.

CAR
If you're driving, the El Ceibo gas station, 50m north of the Hacienda Barú Lodge, is the only one for a good distance in any direction.

TAXI
A taxi from Dominical costs about US$7.

Dominical

For as long as anybody could remember (which wasn't very long in Dominical), this was a lazy little town that drew a motley crew of surfers, backpackers and affable do-nothings, a place where a traveler could wander the dusty roads, surfboard tucked under an arm, balancing the day's activities between wave riding and hammock hang time.

Those days aren't entirely gone, but in 2015 a bunch of paver stones laid along the beach became the town's first real road. And as an increasing population of expats and gringos began to hunker down, some more sophisticated (though decidedly ecofriendly) businesses began to sprout. Now, the sheer volume of cars, bicycles and pedestrians on the main street, particularly around the time of neighboring Uvita's hippie festival Envision (p398) and in the high season, is staggering. Rainier months remain as languidly 'old Costa Rica' as ever.

◉ Sights

★ Cataratas Nauyaca WATERFALL
(☑2787-0541/2; www.cataratasnauyaca.com; horseback tour US$70, pick-up tour US$28, hike admission US$8; ⊙7am-5pm Mon-Sat 8am-4pm Sun) This center, owned and operated by a Costa Rican family, is home to the coast's most impressive waterfalls, which cascade through a protected reserve of both primary and secondary forest. The family runs horseback-riding tours and tours by pick-up truck to the falls (reservations required; Dominical pickup available), where visitors can swim in the inviting natural pools.

Alternatively, you can hike to the falls in an hour or two if you're in decent shape. Or you can hike from the office of Baru Waterfall Tours, a second entrance located just south of the town of Las Tumbas.

★ Alturas Wildlife Sanctuary NATURE RESERVE
(☑2200-5440; www.alturaswildlifesanctuary.org; minimum donation adult/under 12yr US$25/15;

⊙tours 9am, 11am, 1pm & 3pm Tue-Sun) Around 1.5km east and uphill from Dominical, this wildlife sanctuary takes in injured and orphaned animals as well as illegal pets, its mission being to rehabilitate those that can be and reintroduce them to the wild, and look after those that cannot. During the 60- to 90-minute tour you're introduced to its residents: a macaw missing an eye, monkeys that were caged since infancy, Bubba the famous coati and more. Entertaining, educational and a terrific cause.

Baru Waterfall Tours WATERFALL
(☑8767-2090; Las Tumbas; US$7; ⊙7am-4pm) A second option for accessing Cataratas Nauyaca, the hike from this alternative entrance only takes 25 minutes.

Parque Reptilandia ZOO
(☑8308-8855, 2787-0343; www.crreptiles.com; adult/child US$12/6; ⊙9am-4:30pm; P ☁) Seven kilometers up the Dominical–San Isidro road, this reptile haven is the closest thing humans have to Jurassic Park. It's got everything from crocodiles to turtles and snakes to poison-dart frogs, and our favorite is the viper section, where you can see Costa Rica's deadliest creatures, such as the fer-de-lance, pit viper and the black-headed bushmaster. Friday is feeding day, with live mice introduced into snake enclosures, which your kids may or may not love. Don't miss the the Komodo dragon.

SURF DOMINICAL

Dominical owes its fame to its seriously sick point and beach breaks, though surf conditions here are variable. There is a great opportunity to learn surfing in the white-water beach breaks, but beware of getting in too deep, as you can really get trashed out here if you don't know what you're doing. If you're just getting started, stay in the white water or make for the nearby Playa Dominicalito, which is a bit tamer.

Sunset Surf (☑8917-3143; www.sunsetsurfdominical.com; Mavi Surf Hotel; all-inclusive packages per week from US$1575; ⊙8am-4:30pm) Operated by Dylan Park, who grew up surfing the waves of Hawaii and Costa Rica, Sunset offers a variety of packages (including one for women only, and day lessons). It has a three-to-one student-instructor ratio and Park is an excellent teacher. Organic, all-natural sunblock is provided and 1% of proceeds go toward 'the planet.' Housed within Mavi Surf Hotel (p394).

Costa Rica Surf Camp (☑8812-3625, 2787-0393; www.crsurfschool.com; Hotel DiuWak; all-inclusive packages per week US$1145) This fantastic, locally owned surf school prides itself on a two-to-one student-teacher ratio, with teachers who have CPR and water-safety training and years of experience. The amiable owner, Cesar Valverde, runs a friendly, warm-hearted program. Rainy-season surf packages start at $1067 per person but get cheaper with more people involved.

OVERNIGHT AT THE WATERFALL

Waterfall hikes are a dime a dozen in Costa Rica, and most include a familiar itinerary: hike, swim, eat lunch, maybe rappel, head home. Over at family-owned **Pacific Journeys** (2266-1717; www.pacificjourneyscr.com; Las Tumbas; tour per person from US$158) tour company, based out of the tiny town of Las Tumbas, there's something better on offer.

The bilingual, experienced guides at Pacific Journeys lead people up to the top of 600ft Diamante Falls, one of the highest, most jaw-droppingly beautiful cascades in the country. To get there, travelers scale hundreds of stairs up through the company's private reserve, amid lush primary forest and past a botanical garden. Upon arrival (which takes about three hours and is moderately difficult), the group unpacks and selects mats within an open-air cavern behind the waterfall – where everybody sleeps for the night. Yep, this waterfall doubles as a hotel, and actually there are three massive waterfalls visible from the campsite.

Candles and solar-powered lights illuminate the paths and the kind and knowledgeable guides prepare yummy vegetarian meals in an open-air kitchen. The place is decidedly rustic; still, it features flush toilets and picnic benches and is protected from the elements – what else do you really need? Rappelling excursions and hikes to nearby swimming holes and cliff-jumping sites get the adrenalin pumping to the point few will mind the cold, waterfall-fed showers. Those who do can warm up with hot tea the guides prepare from spices picked from the botanical garden.

Activities

★ Airborne Arts   CIRCUS

(8302-4241; www.airbornearts.com) Ever felt like learning the flying trapeze in the middle of the Costa Rican countryside, with a view of a 100m waterfall? Do it with world-renowned acrobat couple Jonathon Conant and Christine Van Loo, who have constructed a circus-themed paradise south of the remote town of Las Tumbas. It's the perfect escape for those looking to learn how to fly.

Packages with trapeze classes, aerial silks and partner acrobatics courses are all available, and the restaurant's veggies come from the couple's onsite garden. Waterfall hikes abound in the area, as do friendly locals.

Hawk Adventures   PARAGLIDING

(8951-2710; www.paraglidedominical.com; per person US$125; 8am-6pm) A recommended tandem paragliding operation based out of Dominical, with both beach and mountain takeoffs.

Danyasa Yoga Arts School   YOGA

(2787-0229; www.danyasa.com; classes incl mat US$16; shop 9:30am-8pm) This lovely Dominical yoga studio offers a variety of classes for all levels, including unique dance-yoga-flow hybrid styles and even ecstatic moon dance. The studio also serves as a center for retreats of all kinds.

Dominical Surf Adventures   RAFTING, SURFING

(2787-0431; www.dominicalsurfadventures.com; 8am-5pm Mon-Sat, 9am-3pm Sun) A bit of an adventurer's one-stop shop, where visitors can book white-water-rafting trips, kayaking, snorkeling and dive trips and surf lessons (from US$50) from an office on the main drag. Rafting trips start at US$90 (for runs on the Class II and III Guabo) and include a more challenging run on the Río Coto Brus' Class IV rapids.

Pineapple Tours   KAYAKING

(8362-7655, 8873-3283; www.pineapplekayaktours.com; tours US$20-75) Run by a friendly young couple, Pineapple Tours runs kayaking and stand-up paddleboarding (SUP) trips to local caves, rivers and mangrove forests. Find its office next to the police station in Dominical. It also rents SUP gear, surfboards, kayaks, beach chairs and umbrellas.

Courses

Adventure Education Center   LANGUAGE

(8866-6042, 2787-0023; www.adventurespanishschool.com; classes 9am-1:30pm) This school runs one-week Spanish-language programs, costing from US$280 to US$325 without accommodations, depending on the number of hours. Private lessons are available, as are discounts for longer periods of study. Various lodging options are available, from homestays to hotels.

LMSPENCER/SHUTTERSTOCK ©

1. Jacó (p361)
This party town also has consistent year-round surf breaks.

2. Crested Caracara
This member of the hawk family can be spotted at national parks around the country.

3. Parque Nacional Manuel Antonio (p384)
Inland trails, beaches and wildlife-watching are the highlights here.

4. Playa Hermosa (p368)
A beach village with huge waves.

🛏 Sleeping

Dominical proper is home to the majority of the area's budget accommodations, while midrange and top-end places are popping up on the outskirts of town. Although most of the year Dominical has a laid-back vibe, the place goes bananas over the holidays, when Ticos flock to the coast, and around Envision time. Travelers on shoestrings can camp on the beach.

Cool Vibes Hostel HOSTEL $

(☑ 8353-6428; www.hosteldominical.com; dm/r from US$13/38; P@🖙🌊) On the road at the southern end of town, this two-story sanctuary features a relaxing lounge, communal kitchen and attractive (but occasionally malfunctioning) plunge pool lined with potted plants. Tile-floored rooms are spacious and clean, with solid beds and bamboo furniture. Cash only; air-con costs more.

Tropical Sands Dominical Eco Inn HOTEL $

(☑ 2787-0200; www.tropicalsandsdominical.com; d with/without air-con US$70/50; P🌊🖙) A lovely, secure hotel option hidden among lush foliage on the southern end of town, this place offers newly updated rooms with tile floors, wide-plank ceilings and small porches strung with hammocks. The grounds are beautiful and the new expat owners (who speak Spanish, French and English) lovingly maintain them. It's just steps from the beach, too.

Posada del Sol HOTEL $

(☑ 2787-0085; d from US$40; P🖙) There are only five rooms at this charming, secure, tidy little place on the main drag; no advance reservations are taken. There are basic comforts – hammocks outside each room, a sink to rinse out your salty beach gear and a clothesline for drying. Single travelers should check out the tiny place in the back. Located 30m south of the school.

★ Danyasa Yoga Retreat GUESTHOUSE $$

(☑ 2787-0229; www.danyasa.com; s/d/ste US$52/83/98; 🌊🖙🌊) 🏊 To visualize Danyasa, imagine eight refurbished cargo containers set amid tranquil greenery, each turned into a snug room or grander suite, with shared outdoor bamboo showers and a guest kitchen. Now imagine water features in the shape of Buddha's head, a relaxing new pool, yoga and dance classes designed to unleash your Inner Goddess and align chakras, and you're there.

Alma de Hatillo B&B $$

(☑ 8850-9034; www.cabinasalma.com; r from US$85; P🌊@🖙) Consisting of immaculate cabins clustered beneath the fruit trees in the village of Hatillo, 6km west of Dominical, this friendly B&B is run by the charming expat Sabina. Boons? Fresh produce from the property for breakfast and the owner's innate helpfulness. Banes? The location near the highway detracts from the tranquillity of the yoga classes in the open-air studio.

Hotel y Restaurante Roca Verde HOTEL $$

(☑ 2787-0036; www.rocaverde.net; r US$125-145; P🌊@🖙🌊) Overlooking the beach about 1km south of town, this hotel has common spaces with tile mosaics, festive murals and rock inlays. The 10 tropical-themed rooms are comfortable and have terracotta-tile floors and pretty handpainted flora and fauna decorating the walls. The real action takes place in the festive open-air bar and pool, and decent restaurant.

★ Mavi Surf Hotel BOUTIQUE HOTEL $$$

(☑ 2787-0429; www.mavi-surf.com; r incl breakfast US$146; P⊖🌊🖙🌊) At the top end of the surfer market, this delightful lime-green hotel is run by a friendly family of four. It's a two-minute walk to the beach, but far enough from the 'doof doof doof' of main-street bars. There are surfing racks by each spacious, air-con room and bamboo partitions offering some privacy on the breezy terrace. Excellent breakfast.

Costa Paraíso BOUTIQUE HOTEL $$$

(☑ 2787-0025; www.costa-paraiso.com; d US$158-169; P🌊🖙🌊🌊) In a prime spot overlooking a rocky cove in Playa Dominicalito, this snug hideaway with Costa Rica's steepest driveway lives up to its name. Each of the five rooms is beautifully appointed in a modern tropical style, with tile floors, wood beams and windows oriented to catch ocean breezes and views. The in-house restaurant is hit or miss.

All but two rooms have kitchenettes. Keep an eye out for the tiny sign on the ocean side, 2km south of Dominical – it's a sharp turn that goes steeply downhill.

Villas Alturas VILLA $$$

(☑ 2200-5440; www.villasalturas.com; 1-/2-bedroom villa incl breakfast US$172/249; P🌊🖙🌊) Just down the mountain from the eponymous wildlife sanctuary (p390), this posh collection of villas boasts panoramic views of the Pacific and a dramatic entryway over a newly built fishpond. The relaxing terrace comes complete with pool, bar and restaurant, and self-caterers will appreciate the full kitchens in the well-kept, stylish units.

Cascadas Farallas LODGE $$$
(☑8882-7687, in USA 888-986-0086; www.water fallvillas.com; ste/villa from US$186/339; P ❋ ☎) This spiritual retreat, 6km from Dominical along the San Isidro road, is located beside a series of cascading waterfalls. Balinese-style suites and villas are decked out from floor to ceiling with Asian art, and all have balconies facing the waterfalls. Regular yoga and meditation sessions are balanced with exclusively vegan cuisine. This eco-retreat has no TV and no wi-fi.

✖ Eating

The restaurant scene in Dominical is varied and of a high standard, catering mostly to foreign guests and including many international options. Self-caterers will appreciate the fabulous new health-food store **Mama Toucan's** (⊙9:30am-6:30pm; ☑).

★**Cafe Mono Congo** CAFE $
(www.cafemonocongo.com; mains US$4-9; ⊙6:30am-7pm; ☎☑) Perch on a swing at the bar or at a riverside table to enjoy the best espresso in town, hands down. This open-air cafe also dishes up tasty, simple breakfasts like *gallo pinto* and *huevos rancheros* and (largely veggie) lunches, using organic local produce. Find it at the junction of the road into town and the main drag – couldn't be simpler.

Café de Ensueños CAFE $
(meals US$5-9; ⊙7:30am-8pm) Run by a lovely local family, this cafe is tucked away at the end of the southern spur road. Organic coffee drinks, fresh juices and hearty breakfasts are served alfresco under a covered terrace – an excellent spot for a quiet morning. Extra hungry? Go for the gut-busting Special Breakfast or the Pancake Tropical, which comes with eggs, bacon and fruit.

Del Mar Taco Shop TACOS $
(☑8428-9050; tacos US$4; ⊙11:30am-9pm) On the approach to the beach, an expat cooks up some of the Pacific coast's best tacos in this casual surfer hangout. We prefer the fish tacos to the shrimp, which can vary in size. Also delicious are the daily Hawaiian BBQ specials and chunky burritos, and the guacamole is superb. On Taco Tuesday (April to November) tacos cost just US$2.

El Pescado Loco SEAFOOD $
(mains US$8-9; ⊙11:45am-7:30pm) This little open-air shack has only a handful of menu items, but when it comes to fish tacos with chipotle sauce and chunky guacamole, well, a taco doesn't get much better than this. The onion rings and fish and chips are nothing to sneeze at, either. Our only quibble: how about real cutlery instead of disposable?

Soda Nanyoa COSTA RICAN $
(☑2787-0013; mains US$2-8; ⊙6am-midnight; ☎) In a town that caters to gringo appetites with inflated price tags, Nanyoa is a gratifying find: an authentic, moderately priced, better-than-most Costa Rican *soda*. The big *gallo pinto* breakfasts and fresh-squeezed juice are ideal after a morning session on the waves. Beer and wine are available as well.

★**Phat Noodle** THAI $$
(☑2787-0017; mains US$10-15; ⊙11:30am-9pm Tue-Sun, 5-9pm Mon; ☑) Newish in town, this expat-owned Thai restaurant and bar serves up piping-hot bowls of rice and noodles, along with spicy margaritas, all from the inside of a converted school bus. Skilfully prepared menu items range from shrimp and crab rangoon to Thai coconut *ceviche* to green curry, and there are a great many vegan and gluten-free options as well.

Charter COSTA RICAN $$
(☑2787-0172; 1.5km north of Dominical; mains US$6-18) This Costa Rican restaurant serves excellent *comida típica* (regional specialities), but is better known for the old, hollowed-out Allegro airplane parked beside it, which supposedly is being converted into a cocktail bar (or at least that's what staff members have been claiming for years). The steaks are particularly juicy, and the penne pasta with vodka sauce is killer.

Dominical Sushi SUSHI $$
(☑8826-7946; www.dominicalsushi.com; mains US$8-13; ⊙1-10pm Sun-Thu, 1-5pm Fri, 5-10pm Sat,) In an open-air setting overlooking the Río Barú, this beachfront sushi place takes advantage of the fresh tuna and other fish caught daily in Dominical. We're big fans of its tuna sashimi and *unagi* and rainbow rolls and the menu is complemented by a selection of Japanese beers and sake.

Maracutú   VEGETARIAN, INTERNATIONAL $$
(☑ 2787-0091; www.maracatucostarica.com; meals US$10-18; ☻noon-9pm, extended hours for bar; ☎☑) This mellow, reggae-spouting 'natural restaurant' hits a lovely high note in Dominical. It serves mostly vegetarian and vegan dishes that span the globe, from falafel and burritos to pad thai and curries, with pescatarian-friendly fish tacos and wasabi tuna thrown in for good measure. The food is made from organic and locally sourced produce where possible.

Maracutú also hosts lots of live music and DJs; Wednesday night is ladies' night and the place gets packed.

🍺 Drinking & Nightlife

★ **Fuego Brew Co.**   CRAFT BEER
(☑ 8992-9559; www.fuegobrew.com; craft beer US$4-6; ☻11:30am-10:30pm) Glowing electric purple from the center of Dominical, this sleek new establishment is the town's first craft brewery and a place to sip guanabana-flavored Hefeweizen all day long. The bartenders are super nice and the bar snacks are tasty, especially the seared tuna. Upstairs is the glistening hardwood bar and restaurant, downstairs are a seven-barrel brewing system and tasting room.

Tortilla Flats   BAR
(☑ 2787-0033; ☻8am-10pm) The beachfront Tortilla Flats is the de facto place for surfers to enjoy sunset beers after a day in the water (skip the food, though). Its open-air atmosphere and easy vibes reflect the clientele, with surf videos on continuous loop, but continents may drift before you get served.

ℹ Orientation

The Costanera Sur bypasses the town entirely; the entrance to the village is immediately past the Río Barú bridge. There's an unpaved main road through the village, where many of the services are found, and a newly paved beach road parallel to the ocean. About 100m south of the intersection is a southern spur road with some more accommodations and a cafe.

ℹ Information

Dominical Information Center (☑ 2787-0454; www.dominicalinformation.com; ☻9:30am-5pm), on the main strip, near the entrance to Dominical, is a tourist info center with useful maps of town and bus timetables for the entire region. Bus-ticket, shuttle and tour booking services available.

The closest bank is in Uvita.

DANGERS & ANNOYANCES

➡ Waves, currents and riptides in Dominical are very strong, and there have been drownings in the past. Watch for red flags (which mark riptides), follow the instructions of posted signs and swim at beaches that are patrolled by lifeguards. If you're smart, the beach is no problem, but people do die here every year.

➡ Dominical attracts a heavy-duty party crowd, which in turn has led to a burgeoning drug problem.

ℹ Getting There & Away

BUS

Gray Line, Easy Ride and Monkey Ride offer private and shared shuttle services to popular destinations such as Jacó, San José, Monteverde, Tamarindo and Sierpe; Easy Ride has direct services to Granada, Nicaragua.

Buses pick up and drop off passengers along the main road in Dominical.

TAXI

Taxis to Uvita cost US$10 to US$20, while the ride to Quepos costs US$60 and to Manuel Antonio it's US$70. Cars accommodate up to five people, and can be hailed easily in town from the main road.

Escaleras

Escaleras, a small community scattered around a steep and narrow dirt loop road that branches off the Costanera, is famed for its sweeping views of the coastline. If you want to make it up here, you're going to need a 4WD to navigate one of the country's most notoriously difficult roads. Needless to say, the locals weren't kidding when they

BUSES FROM DOMINICAL

DESTINATION	COST (US$)	DURATION	FREQUENCY (DAILY)
Palmar	2	1½hr	4:45am, 8am, 11am, 12:30pm, 4pm
Quepos	5.75	1hr	5:30am, 8:30am, 11:30am, 1pm, 5pm
San José	10.25	4½hr	5:30am, 1pm
Uvita	1	20min	4:45am, 7:30am, 10:30am, 12:30pm, 4pm, 5:30pm

named the place *escaleras* (staircase). Aside from the scenic views, travelers primarily brave the road to relax in a mountain retreat that's still close enough to the action in Dominical and Uvita.

🛏 Sleeping & Eating

There's a scattering of isolated villas and B&Bs along the rough road that scales the hillside, though several have closed in recent years.

La Tierra Divina   B&B **$$**
(📋8501-8644; www.latierradivina.com; cabins US$80-99; P ❋ 🛜) This B&B consists of three unusual round cabins with fans, conical roofs and one with an ocean view, surrounded by encroaching jungle; howler monkeys drop by for an occasional visit. Owners Becky and Troy are very helpful.

The turnoff is 3km south of Dominical: first left through Dominicalito, then first right after the soccer field and 3km up the dirt road.

Pacific Edge   CABINA **$$**
(📋2200-5428, 8935-7905; www.pacificedge.info; cabin/bungalow from US$70/100; P ❋ 🛜 ⛱) Pacific Edge is located on a different access road that's 1.2km south of the first entrance to Escaleras. The owners are a worldly couple who delight in showing guests their slice of paradise. Four cabins are perched on a knife-edge ridge about 200m above sea level, while larger, fully equipped bungalows accommodate up to six. 4WD only.

Those interested in indigenous culture will find an excellent selection of Boruca masks here. No children under 13 are accepted and guests must arrive before dark.

Bar Jolly Roger   AMERICAN **$**
(📋8706-8438; 10 wings US$10; ⏲noon-10pm) If you have a hankering for delicious chicken wings, Bar Jolly Roger offers 24 varieties, in addition to burgers, pizzas, cold beers and good margaritas and other cocktails. This friendly expat outpost is up the southern entrance to Escaleras and has live music Monday through Friday from 5:30pm. Look for the smiley-face Jolly Roger sign.

❶ Getting There & Away

The first entrance to Escaleras is 4km south of the San Isidro de El General turnoff before Dominical, and the second is 4.5km past the first one. Both are on the left-hand side of the road and poorly signed.

Uvita
POP 2000

Just 17km south of Dominical, this growing village consists of some dirt roads lined with farms, guesthouses and shops, a cluster of strip malls by the main Costanera Sur entrance, and a scattering of hotels in the jungle-covered hills above. Uvita has retained its gentle pace of life during the low season, but otherwise has become quite a popular and buzzing travel destination thanks to its increasingly sought-after main attraction, Parque Nacional Marino Ballena (p401). The marine reserve has become famous for its migrating pods of humpback whales and its virtually abandoned wilderness beaches, but there are also good waterfalls nearby.

Two of the country's most important tourist events happen yearly in Uvita: an increasingly popular Whale and Dolphin Festival celebrating the arrival of the humpbacks, and the country's biggest hippie gathering, the Envision Festival (essentially a small-scale Burning Man at the beach).

◉ Sights

★**Cascada Verde**   WATERFALL
(US$2; ⏲8am-4pm) Around 2.5km inland and uphill (toward the Cascada Verde hostel), this waterfall plunges into an inviting deep pool, perfect for a refreshing dip. The best part? The waterfall also acts as an exhilarating natural waterslide with a 1.8m drop at the end; take the path to the top, lie down, cross your arms and let gravity take care of the rest!

Farmers Market   MARKET
(📋8680-9752; ⏲8am-1pm Sat) Held a short distance from the main entrance to Uvita, along the unpaved road, this sweet little farmers market on Saturdays is a good place to mingle with locals and longtime expats, and purchase psychedelic jewelry, locally grown fruit and vegetables, honey and home-cooked foods.

Rancho La Merced
National Wildlife Refuge   NATURE RESERVE
(📋2743-8032, 8861-5147; www.rancholamerced. com; tours US$35-50, self-guided walk US$6; ⏲7:30am-5:30pm) A few kilometers before Uvita, opposite the turnoff to Oro Verde, is this 506-hectare national wildlife refuge (and former cattle ranch), with primary and secondary forests and mangroves lining

the Río Morete. Here you can go on guided nature hikes and birdwatching walks, horseback-ride to Punta Uvita or opt for the 'cowboy experience,' which involves cattle roping, herding cows and riding around with real cowboys.

You can also stay at La Merced in a 1940s farmhouse, which can accommodate up to 10 people in double rooms of various sizes (doubles US$85).

Reserva Biológica Oro Verde NATURE RESERVE
(☑ 8843-8833) A few kilometers before Uvita you'll see a signed turnoff to the left on a rough dirt road (4WD only) that leads 3.5km up the hill to this private reserve on the farm of the Duarte family, who have lived in the area for more than three decades. Two-thirds of the 150-hectare property is rainforest, and there are guided hikes (US$35), occasional night tours (US$30) and 6am birdwatching walks (US$30). Reserve in advance through Uvita Information Center (p401).

🏃 Activities

Whale-Watching

Whale-watching is a huge attraction here, with humpback whales visiting the waters surrounding Parque Nacional Marino Ballena twice a year (December to April and July to November).

Bahía Aventuras ADVENTURE
(☑ 2743-8362, 8846-6576; www.bahiaaventuras. com) A well-regarded tour operator in Uvita, Bahía Aventuras has tours running the gamut, including a combo of snorkeling and whale-watching (US$90) in the Marino Ballena National Park, snorkeling around Isla del Caño in Bahía Drake (US$140), and hiking, spanning the Costa Ballena to Corcovado (US$145).

Surfing

Surfers passing through the area tend to push on to more extreme destinations further north or south, though there are occasionally some swells at **Playa Hermosa** (not to be confused with the one south of Jacó) to the north and **Playa Colonia** to the south. However, if you're a beginner, this can be a good place to practice.

Diving

⭐ **Mad About Diving** DIVING
(☑ 2743-8019; www.madaboutdivingcr.com) This friendly, safe and professional diving operator offers dives in the Parque Nacional Marino Ballena and full-day scuba excursions to Isla del Caño in Bahía Drake (US$170). Two-tank dives from US$100.

☞ Tours

⭐ **Rancho DiAndrew** OUTDOORS
(☑ 8475-1287; http://ranchodiandrew.com; tours from US$65) Fun tour operator specializing in surf retreats and nature tours, the most popular of which involves navigating a hidden gorge, plunging off a cliff and feasting on BBQ by the river. The *rancho* is perched in a patch of jungle near the town of San Josecito, and features open-air cabins and houses (from US$85/96 single/double per night). Sweet views.

Uvita Adventure Tour KAYAKING, MOUNTAIN BIKING
(☑ 8918-5681, 2743-8008; www.uvitadventure tours.com; mountain-biking/kayaking tour from US$45/75) Run by young, enthusiastic owner Victor, this small tour company offers highly recommended tours, including exhilarating mountain-biking adventures, kayaking through the mangroves and snorkeling at the marine park. At the time of research, Victor was considering adding electric-bike tours.

🎉 Festivals & Events

Envision Festival ART, MUSIC
(www.envisionfestival.com; ☉ late Feb) Four days of spoken word, music, yoga, performance art, permaculture, dreadlocks and DJs happen in Uvita in late February for the 'Costa Rican Burning Man' festival. Attendees set up camp in a jungle setting near the beach in Uvita where you might spot thousands of naked hippies.

Whale and Dolphin Festival FAIR
(www.festivaldeballenasydelfines.com; US$32; ☉ Sep-Oct) Tens of thousands descend on Uvita for this two-weekend oceanic extravaganza celebrating the arrival of humpback whales, which give birth in Costa Rican waters. Visitors take boat tours to view the marine mammals and also hang out at the nearby national marine park, where low tide reveals a sandbar in the shape of a giant whale's tail.

There are also cultural events, concerts, parades, performances and lectures.

🛏 Sleeping

The main entrance to Uvita leads inland, east of the highway, where you'll find a number of eating and sleeping options. More guesthouses, *sodas* and local businesses are west of the highway, along the bumpy dirt roads that surround the edges of the park. The high-end hotels line dirt roads up the mountain.

★ Cascada Verde
HOSTEL $

(📋 2743-8191, 8422-6504; www.cascadaverde.eu; dm/s/d from US$11/22/34; 🅿 @ 🛜) 🏄 If you're looking for a quiet retreat in the jungle, this hostel, run by a young expat couple, is for you. About 2km uphill from Uvita, it features jaw-dropping jungle views from the dining terrace, a large communal kitchen, plenty of indoor and outdoor spaces for relaxing, appealingly designed rooms with bamboo partitions, and a waterfall a short walk away.

Because of the open architecture style, be aware that there's very little noise privacy – but you'll also hear the jungle symphony surrounding you.

Rooms can be configured to accommodate kids and child-friendly tours can be organized.

Flutterby House
HOSTEL $

(📋 2743-8221, 8341-1730; www.flutterbyhouse. com; campsite US$10, dm US$14-18, d US$40-120; 🅿 @ 🛜) 🏄 Is it possible to fall in love with a hostel? If so, the ramshackle collection of colorful *Swiss Family Robinson*-style tree houses and dorms has beguiled us. The place is run by a pair of expat sisters, and the clientele here tends to be of the barefoot, surfing variety. The bar is a social hub.

Flutterby also rents out boards and bikes, sells beer for a pittance, and has a tidy, open-air communal kitchen as well as a restaurant (which offers many vegan and vegetarian options). It employs downright visionary sustainability practices; single-use plastics are banned.

Great location a short stroll from Marino Ballena's beaches; it's near the south entrance gate of the park. Follow the signs from the Costanera Sur.

Tucan Hotel
HOSTEL $

(📋 2743-8140; www.tucanhotel.com; campsite/hammock/dm US$12/12/15, d from US$33; 🅿 ✱ @ 🛜) Located 100m inland from the main highway, this cheapie is popular with international travelers of all ages. The rooms are arranged around a semi-open communal area, and there are also simple tents and hammocks, as well as a house in the trees. Bonuses include a shared kitchen, daily movies at 4pm, an Italian restaurant and a convivial atmosphere.

La Ballena Roja
GUESTHOUSE $$

(📋 8411-1852; www.laballenarojauvita.com; US$36-48) A couple hundred meters from the national park, this rustic, brightly colored guesthouse contains just a few simple rooms, a little restaurant, a cozy, book-filled common area and surfboards for rent. The lovely expat owner Tracey serves up delicious breakfasts every day, and on Wednesday through Sunday (noon to 8pm) she offers the best thin-crust pizza in town.

Cabinas Los Laureles
CABINA $$

(📋 2743-8008, 2743-8235; www.cabinasloslaureles .com; s/d from US$32/45; 🅿 @ 🛜) Set up on a forested property with a short trail running through it, this 14-room spot slightly uphill from the Costanera Sur offers authentic Costa Rican hospitality. Of the friendly Tico family that runs the place, son Victor, who runs Uvita Adventures Tour (p398), is trilingual and conscientious about referring guests to other locally run businesses. The restaurant (p400) serves delicious meals.

Finca Bavaria
BOUTIQUE HOTEL $$

(📋 8355-4465; www.finca-bavaria.de; Interamericana Km 167; s/d from US$75/90; 🅿 🛜 ✱) This expat-run inn comprises a handful of appealing rooms with wooden accents, bamboo furniture, romantic mosquito-net-draped beds and the best breakfast along the coast (US$10). The grounds are lined with walkways and hemmed by jungle, though you can take in sweeping views of the ocean from the hilltop pool. Look for the signed dirt road at Km 167.

★ Oxygen Jungle Villas
VILLA $$$

(📋 8322-4773; www.oxygenjunglevillas.com; US$249-299) Oxygen Jungle Villas has 12 mountaintop cabins constructed almost entirely of glass. The translucent and sumptuous digs allow guests to feel like part of the rainforest even from a plush, four-poster king bed, and the sundeck's infinity pool and alfresco restaurant are ideal for enjoying a tropical cocktail.

The abundant Balinese statutes and postcard-perfect view of Bahía Ballena certainly don't hurt, either, and the property features waterfall trails and an upstairs spa. Service is impeccable.

Hotel Cristal Ballena
BOUTIQUE HOTEL $$$

(☑ 2786-5354; www.cristal-ballena.com; Costanera Sur; r US$225-295; P✱❄☲) ✎ About 7km south of Uvita, surrounded by 12 hectares of private nature reserve and with sweet views of the coast from its hillside location, this boutique hotel is one of the top birding hotels in Costa Rica, with knowledgeable guides arranging birdwatching excursions. An excellent restaurant, light, bright rooms, vast, gorgeous suites and a tranquil ambience complete the picture.

Two nature trails (800m and 2km) run across the property, where you're very likely to spot some wildlife during early-morning rambles, as well as some of the 250 bird species resident in the surrounding tropical lowland forest. The gift store sells colorful Boruca masks of excellent quality.

Bungalows Ballena
BUNGALOW $$$

(☑ 2743-8543, 8309-9631; www.bungalowsballena.com; apt/bungalow US$125/250; P❄☲) These fully outfitted apartments and stand-alone bungalows are popular with Tico families and large groups. All have kitchens, wi-fi and satellite TV. The place is outfitted for kids – there's a playground and a big, welcoming pool in the shape of a whale's tail. Find it 300m north of the park's main entrance.

✖ Eating

The more upmarket accommodations have their own restaurants. There are also several *sodas* and a clutch of good restaurants in the main village and along the nearby stretch of Costanera Sur. Best pizza in town is at La Ballena Roja (p399).

★ Bar y Restaurante Los Laureles
COSTA RICAN $

(☑ 2743-8008; mains US$8-12; ☺11am-8:30pm Mon-Sat) Adorable family-run restaurant serving mainly Costa Rican and Tex-Mex cuisine, with innovative favorites such as avocado hummus and nacho *patacones* (fried green plantains cut in thin pieces), and staples like chicken wings, chili fries and quesadillas. The margaritas are killer, the service is top-notch and the open-air setting, amid tropical foliage, is super *tranquilo*.

Sibu Cafe
CAFE $

(☑ 8308-6604, 2743-8674; coffee US$2-5; ☺7am-9pm Mon-Sat, from 9am Sun; ✱❄☲) Serving the best coffee for miles around, this little cafe hides in the strip-mall part of Uvita. Latte art, chunky brownies and homemade lemon pie are all on the menu. Want something more substantial? The hardworking couple here also make excellent salads, thin-and-crispy pizza pie, veggie juice and fruit smoothies. They recently started selling their own craft beer, Sibu Russian Imperial Stout.

★ Sabor Español
SPANISH $$

(☑ 8768-9160, 2743-8312; mains US$8-22; ☺6-9:30pm Tue-Sun; ❄) Having had a successful run in Monteverde, charming Spanish couple Heri and Montse realized that they wanted to live by the ocean – to Uvita's good fortune. Thus, their sublime gazpacho, paella, *tortilla española* (Spanish omelet) and other Spanish specialties can now be savored with sangria in a lovely *rancho* setting, at the end of a dirt road in Playa Uvita.

Baker Bean
PIZZA, CAFE $$

(☑ 2743-8990; mains US$7-18; ☺6am-9pm Mon-Thu, to 10pm Fri-Sun; ✱❄☲) Just north of the main entrance to Uvita on the Costanera Sur, this oddly named joint is half pizzeria, half cafe. Locals and expats descend for good, strong morning coffee, filled bagels and Argentinean-style empanadas (ideal for picnicking), while in the restaurant half, the chef serves up ample pizzas, some topped with imported ingredients.

☕ Drinking & Nightlife

Roadshack Deli
BAR

(☑ 8304-6792; ☺11am-7pm Mon-Sat) Around 50m down the main Uvita road from the highway turnoff, this open-air, ramshackle spot is a gathering place for offbeat customers craving wraps, braised pork and other sandwiches (we like the Mother Clucker) and imaginative salads. Wash it all down with homemade craft beer or kombucha. This is an informal community center, too, with frequent live music and revelry.

ⓘ Orientation

The area off the main highway is referred to locally as Uvita, while the area next to the beach is called Playa Uvita and Playa Bahía Uvita (the southern end of the beach). The beach area is reached through two parallel roads that are roughly 500m apart – they make a C-shape connecting back to the road. The first entrance is just south of the bridge over the Río Uvita and the second entrance is in the center of town. At low tide you can walk out along Punta Uvita, but ask about conditions locally before heading out so that the rising water doesn't cut you off.

❶ Information

Uvita Information Center (☎ 8843-7142, 2743-8072; http://uvita.info; ⊙ 9am-1pm & 2-6pm Mon-Sat) is a fine place to book tours and transport.

You can find bus schedules, an area map and other useful info at www.marinoballena.org.

Also keep an eye out for the free print magazine *Ballena Tales*, a wonderful resource for visitors, with bilingual articles, tide charts and listings of local businesses from Dominical to the Osa Peninsula.

DANGERS & ANNOYANCES

When enjoying the local beaches, be aware that personal possessions that are left unattended have been known to melt away into the jungles that fringe the shorelines.

In fact, it's best not to bring anything valuable to the beach with you. Until recently, petty theft was the worst problem around the national park and area beaches, and unfortunately, a few in-person (nonviolent) robberies have taken place in the not-so-distant past. Get the latest word from the staff at your accommodations.

❶ Getting There & Away

Most buses depart from the sheltered bus stops on the Costanera in the main village.

Dominical US$1, 30 minutes, nine daily between 4:45am and 5:30pm.

Quepos US$4, two hours, departs 5:30am, 11:40am, 1pm and 4pm.

San José US$9.17, 3½ hours, departs 5:30am, 11:30am, 1pm and 4pm.

Private shuttle companies – Grayline, Easy Ride and Monkey Ride – offer pricier transfers from Uvita to Dominical, San José, Quepos, Jacó, Puerto Jiménez and other popular destinations.

Parque Nacional Marino Ballena

This stunner of a **marine park** (☎ 2743-8141; US$6; ⊙ 7am-4pm), created in 1989, protects coral and rock reefs surrounding several offshore islands. Its name comes not only from the humpback whales that breed here but also because of the Punta Uvita 'Whale Tail,' a distinctive sandbar extending into a rocky reef that, at low tide, forms the shape of a whale's tail. Despite its small size, the importance of this area cannot be overstated, especially since it protects migrating humpback and pilot whales, three types of dolphin and

nesting sea turtles, not to mention colonies of seabirds and several terrestrial reptiles.

Although Ballena was once off the radar of many coastal travelers, its rewards have recently lured an increasing number of beach-lovers and wildlife-watchers. Beat the crowds by arriving early – you might even see dolphins in the surf or a humpback breaching.

🏃 Activities

Swimming

The beaches at Parque Nacional Marino Ballena are a stunning combination of golden sand and polished rock. All of them are virtually deserted and perfect for peaceful swimming and sunbathing.

Diving & Snorkeling

The coral reefs around the offshore islands are a good place to experience the park's underwater world, unlike the coral reefs near the shore that were heavily damaged by sediment runoff from the construction of the coastal highway. To delve into the underwater beauty of the park, go on a diving or snorkeling trip with Mad About Diving (p398).

Wildlife-Watching

Heading southeast from Punta Uvita, the park includes mangrove swamps, estuaries and rocky headlands. In the early morning, before other visitors arrive, you'll have the best opportunity for good birdwatching.

The park is home to, or frequently visited by, a number of wildlife species, including common, bottlenose and pantropical spotted dolphins and a variety of lizards. The offshore islands are important nesting sites for frigate birds, brown boobies and brown pelicans, and from May to November, with a peak in September and October, olive ridley and hawksbill turtles bury their eggs in the sand nightly. However, the star attraction are the pods of humpback whales that pass through the national park from July to November and December to April, as well as occasional pilot whales.

Scientists are unsure as to why humpback whales migrate here, though it's possible that Costa Rican waters may be one of only a few places in the world where the whales mate. There are actually two different groups of humpbacks that pass through the park – whales seen in the fall migrate from Californian waters, while those seen in the spring originate from Antarctica and come here to breed and rear their babies.

Whale- and dolphin-watching trips are run by several tour companies in Uvita, including highly professional Bahía Aventuras (p398).

❶ Information

There are four entrances to the park, the most commonly used being the **ranger station** (☑ 2743-8141; ⊙ 7am-4pm) in Playa Uvita (follow the main road through Uvita), followed by the one along a dirt road that runs past Flutterby House in Uvita; there is now a ranger station (read: wooden shack) there also. All park entrances are open from 7am to 4pm.

DANGERS & ANNOYANCES

The beaches of Parque Nacional Marina Balleno are notorious for bag-snatchings. Leave your bag on the sand near the bushes for a second and you're unlikely to ever see it again. Local residents are putting pressure on the park authorities to improve security in the park and also to provide working toilet facilities.

Another annoyance are the enterprising parking touts who charge visitors US$4 to park near the main entrance to the park. If you park on the street, you're not legally obliged to pay them anything. Better still, park nearby and walk to the entrance.

❶ Getting There & Away

Parque Nacional Marino Ballena is best accessed from Uvita or Ojochal, by private vehicle, a quick taxi ride or by walking.

Ojochal

Of the trio of villages – Dominical, Uvita and Ojochal – that make up the Costa Ballena, this laid-back, spread-out village is the culinary epicenter, with a multicultural expat population. Its friendly, well-integrated vibe has a distinctly different feel from that of surfer-dominated Dominical, although just north of Ojochal the largely undiscovered wilderness beach of Playa Tortuga is home to occasional bouts of decent surf.

Its excellent dining scene aside, Ojochal also serves as a convenient base for exploring nearby Parque Nacional Marino Ballena, and despite its small size there are plenty of accommodations in and around the village to choose from. Wildlife lovers may wish to linger a while to learn more about the locally based turtle conservation project.

◉ Sights

Playa Ventanas   BEACH
(☑ 8946-7134; parking US$3) Tucked behind a grove of coco palms, this crescent-shaped, sand-and-pebble beach has elaborate rock formations at either end, and is called *ventanas* (windows) because on the northern side there are a couple of caves large enough to walk into. The ocean roars and crashes through the caves as the tide comes in, which pretty spectacular to watch. There are no services here, but you can pick up some roadside coconut water and *ceviche* on the way.

Reserva Playa Tortuga   NATURE RESERVE
(☑ 2786-5200; www.reservaplayatortuga.org; ⊙ 9am-3pm Mon-Fri) FREE Set up in 2009 by Costa Rican scientists, this excellent program conducts several important projects, including an inventory of local mammals, a monitoring of scarlet macaw and crocodilian populations in the reserve, a butterfly garden and educational outreach to children on the importance of protecting wildlife. Volunteers are welcome. The reserve office is along the public road to Playa Tortuga.

⛏ Sleeping

There are a number of places to stay in Ojochal village, and more sleeping options spread out along the Costanera Sur. Accommodations in this area lean toward high end.

Hotel El Mono Feliz   HOTEL $
(☑ 2786-5146; www.elmonofeliz.com; r incl breakfast US$45-55, bungalow US$75-110; ❄ �"◎ ") Around 3km inland from Ojochal's entrance, this sweet little spot is under new ownership and at the time of research was undergoing renovation, with shiny new bathrooms, flooring and a yoga deck all in the works. The forested property is hemmed in by a trickling brook and offers tidy, fan-cooled rooms, higher-end bungalows with forest views and a relaxing pool.

A couple of the units are geared toward families, with rooms sharing a bathroom.

Diquis del Sur   B&B $$
(☑ 2786-5012; www.diquis.com; r from US$63; ⓟ ❄ ⌂ ◎ ") In Ojochal proper, around 1.5km in, this B&B is like a home away from home. Accommodations are in a variety of fairly modest rooms, though some have kitchenettes conducive to self-catering. There's also a good restaurant onsite (only open in the

BRINGING BACK THE OJOCHE TREE

Ojochal's namesake, once on the verge of extinction in the area, is making a slow comeback. Though the tall, leafy *ojoche* tree *(Brosimum alicastrum)* takes about 30 years to mature, making this a long-term project, the local community has begun putting the *ojoche* back into Ojochal.

As Ojochal's population grew through the 1950s, most stands of *ojoche* were felled for cattle grazing and lumber. But in the same decade the tree's starchy fruit provided nourishment to many local families during severe drought. The pulp of the fruit can be eaten raw, boiled, or made into flour. The fruit (also known as the 'Maya nut,' though not a true nut) has a low glycemic index and high protein content, and is rich in fiber, fat, folate, iron and antioxidants.

Around 2009 the grassroots community group Comité de Ojoche began to replant *ojoche* trees in the area in an effort to reestablish Ojochal's connection with its roots (so to speak), and to save the tree from local extinction while reforesting the area with a nutritious and culturally valuable food source.

Hotel Villas Gaia offers a self-guided walking tour of the 'Ojoche Route,' and you can buy *ojoche* flour from the local women's entrepreneurial association, which helps to fund the *ojoche*-revival project.

high season), and the well-maintained property is landscaped with flowers and fruit trees. There are also villas for long-term rental. An interesting side fact: the property is named after the 'Diquis Spheres,' which are mysterious pre-Columbian stone balls, many of which were found in this area.

Can organize kid-friendly tours.

★ **El Castillo** BOUTIQUE HOTEL **$$$**
(☑2786-5543; www.elcastillocr.com; r US$275-395, ste US$525; P🌺🛜🏊) Even the most jaded of guests will give an involuntary gasp of surprise when faced with the tremendous view from the infinity pool at this bluff-top hotel. Comprising just five rooms and three suites, decked out with four-poster beds and rain showers, this intimate place organizes outings to a private island. Planning to propose to your sweetie? Do it here.

There's also an excellent restaurant, Azul (p404), open to nonguests.

★ **La Cusinga** LODGE **$$$**
(☑2770-2549; www.lacusingalodge.com; Interamericana Km 166, Finca Tres Hermanas; r incl breakfast US$190; P) 🌿 This lovely ecolodge with breezy wood-and-stone rooms is a model of sustainable practices. It's also a relaxing place to unplug – in place of TVs there are yoga classes. Located on a private reserve, it has access to hiking, birdwatching, snorkeling and swimming in the Parque Nacional Marino Ballena. Wholesome meals feature mostly organic produce. It's about 5km south of Uvita.

In 2017 the hotel opened up its restaurant, Aracari, to the public.

Hotel Villas Gaia CABINA **$$$**
(☑2786-5044; www.villasgaia.com; villa US$85-101, casa from US$153, all incl breakfast; P@🛜🏊) 🌿 Around 500m north of the Ojochal entrance is this beautifully kept collection of shiny wooden cabins with shaded porches, set in tranquil forested grounds. An excellent restaurant serves a variety of international standards, and the hilltop pool boasts a panoramic view of Playa Tortuga. The beach is a pleasant 20-minute hike along a dirt path that winds down the hillside.

Lookout at Playa Tortuga BOUTIQUE HOTEL **$$$**
(☑2786-5074; www.hotelcostarica.com; Interamericana Km 175; d US$130-180; P🌺@🛜🏊) This beautiful hilltop sanctuary is home to a dozen brightly painted bungalows awash in calming pastels. The grounds are traversed by a series of paths overlooking the beaches below, but the highlight is the large deck in a tower above the pool. Here you can pursue some early-morning birdwatching, or perhaps some late-afternoon slothful lounging.

🍴 Eating

Ojochal is *the* culinary enclave along the Costa Ballena, with influences ranging from Mediterranean to Indonesian, and it's home to a patisserie, a pizzeria and a farmers' market. Restaurants are well signposted throughout the village.

Ballena Bistro
FUSION $

(☑ 2786-5407; www.ballenabistro.com; Costanera Sur, Km 169; mains US$5-12; ⊙11am-4pm Tue-Sun; 🛜✍) The main attraction of a multiuse, barnlike structure topped with a scrap-metal goat sculpture, this bistro offers welcome, diverse fodder for your belly and your Instagram feed. Feast on garlic hummus, chèvre-orange salad, pulled-pork burgers and Brazilian coconut fish soup. Wraps, fresh juices and local beers round out the menu. It's a smashing spot to break up a long drive.

★ Exotica
INTERNATIONAL $$

(☑ 2786-5050; mains US$10-23; ⊙5-9pm Mon-Sat) This phenomenal gourmet restaurant is worth planning your evening around. In a sultry, jungle ambience with orchids everywhere, the nouveau-French dishes each emphasize a breadth of ingredients brought together in masterful combinations. Some of the highlights include Tahitian fish carpaccio, wild-duck breast with port-pineapple reduction and its signature dessert – the chili-tinged chocolate Devil's Fork. Reservations recommended.

★ Azul
FUSION $$

(☑ 2786-5543; El Castillo; lunch mains US$10-26, 2-/3-course dinner US$30/60; ⊙noon-10pm; 🛜✍) At this chic little restaurant inside El Castillo (p403), with killer views of the Pacific coast, your tastebuds will be singing praises when you treat them to innovative, Tico-style potato skins, goat-cheese ravioli and expertly seared steak. There's terrific attention to presentation and taste, and the Mediterranean-style three-course dinners are worth a splurge. Great cocktails and wine list too.

Restaurante Terraba
COSTA RICAN $$

(☑ 4702-9896; mains US$7-12; ⊙11am-9pm Wed-Mon) This unassuming roadside eatery offers local cuisine with giant flavors at tiny prices (relative to the rest of Ojochal). How did this happen? Well, the kind owners picked up their kitchen skills in some of the area's top restaurants before opening this one.

Spring for a steak dish or one of the *casados* (set meal), and pair with a refreshing fruit smoothie.

★ Ylang-Ylang
INDONESIAN $$$

(☑ 2786-5054; www.facebook.com/YlangYlang Restaurant; mains US$25; ⊙5-9pm Wed-Sat early Dec-early May; 🛜✍) The only Indonesian restaurant in Central America, this characterful expat-run place is immensely popular for the authentic, fiery flavors of its dishes (the owners grow their own Asian herbs). Dishes such as *daging rendang* (beef simmered with spices in coconut milk) and *ikan ketcap* (snapper with galangal and tamarind) are meant to be shared. With only 12 guests per night, advance reservations are essential.

🍷 Drinking & Nightlife

Bamboo Room
COCKTAIL BAR

(☑ 2786-5295; www.almacr.com; ⊙noon-9pm Mon-Sat) This new hilltop bar and restaurant, housed in the Alma de Ojochal hotel, has raised the bar for nightlife in an otherwise food-focused beach enclave. Sunset views are a beautiful thing here, particularly with a signature Bamboozle cocktail in hand, and live music (including things like dueling pianos) goes on nightly.

ℹ Getting There & Away

Daily buses between Dominical and Palmar can drop you off near any of the places along the highway and also at the entrance of Ojochal village. However, to reach most places in Ojochal proper, it's best to have a car.

Gray Line, Easy Ride and Monkey Ride shuttles connect Ojochal with popular destinations along the Pacific coast and the Península de Osa.

Southern Costa Rica & Península de Osa

Best Ecolodges

→ Danta Corcovado Lodge
(p449)

→ Casa Corcovado Jungle
Lodge (p434)

→ Playa Nicuesa Rainforest
Lodge (p458)

→ La Paloma Lodge (p430)

Best off the Beaten Track

→ Parque Internacional La
Amistad (p424)

→ Reserva Indígena Boruca
(p420)

→ Playas San Josecito,
Nicuesa & Cativo (p458)

→ Dos Brazos (p446)

→ Zancudo (p454)

Why Go?

From the chilly heights of Cerro Chirripó (3820m) to the steamy coastal jungles of the Península de Osa, this sector of Costa Rica encompasses some of the country's least-explored and least-developed land. Vast tracts of wilderness remain untouched in Parque Internacional La Amistad, and the country's most visible indigenous groups – the Bribrí, Cabécar, Boruc and Ngöbe – maintain traditional ways of living in their remote territories.

Quetzal sightings around San Gerardo de Dota are frequent, and scarlet-macaw appearances are the norm along the coast. Monkeys, sloths and coatis roam the region's abundant parks and reserves, and in Parque Nacional Corcovado there's also the rare chance to spy on slumbering tapir. Meanwhile, the rugged coasts of the Golfo Dulce and Península de Osa captivate travelers with abandoned wilderness beaches, world-class surf and opportunities for rugged exploration. This is the land for intrepid travelers yearning for something truly wild.

When to Go

From December to March is the best time for trekking in Corcovado, and also up Cerro Chirripó.

Surfing is at its best in Pavones from April through October, though there are beginner waves year-round.

Best time for quetzal sightings is February to May; this also coincides with the fruiting of the wild avocado, their favorite food.

Southern Costa Rica & Península de Osa Highlights

① **Parque Nacional Corcovado** (p434) Hiking the coast and rich rainforest in the country's premier wilderness experience.

② **Cerro Chirripó** (p416) Climbing atop Costa Rica's tallest peak to watch the sunrise.

③ **Bahía Drake** (p427) Snorkeling, hiking and wildlife-spotting along the wild coast.

④ **San Gerardo de Dota** (p409) Looking for resplendently feathered quetzal in the cool highlands.

⑤ **Pavones** (p455) Catching a ride on one of the world's longest left breaks at this surfing paradise.

⑥ **Fiesta de los Diablitos** (p420) Celebrating this vibrant festival at the Reserva Indígena Boruca.

⑦ **Parque Nacional Isla del Coco** (p458) Exploring the underwater environs of a far-flung island.

⑧ **Dos Brazos** (p446) Immersing yourself in rural tourism at a gold-mining villages.

⑨ **Sitio Arqueológico Finca 6** (p426) Contemplating the pre-Columbian stone spheres.

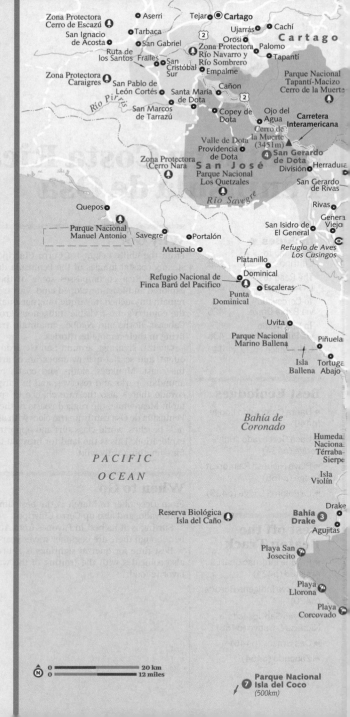

History

Costa Rica's indigenous population was almost entirely wiped out through both the direct and indirect effects of colonization. Spanish conquistadors eventually gave way to Catholic missionaries, though the end result was the same, namely the complete disruption of pre-Columbian life in the New World.

Even as late as the 20th century, indigenous groups were actively disenfranchised from the Spanish-dominated society. In fact, citizenship was not granted to the indigenous population until 1949, and reservations were not organized until 1977. In the intervening decades, indigenous groups have been allowed to engage in their traditional languages and customs.

On the Osa, the vast majority of the peninsula was never populated or developed by Ticos. In fact, because of the remoteness of the region, commercial logging was not a threat until the early 1960s. Although this tumultuous decade saw the destruction of much of Costa Rica's remaining primary forests, Osa was largely spared. By 1975, however, international companies were greedily eyeing the peninsula's timber and gold. Fortunately, these ambitions were halted when researchers petitioned President Daniel Oduber to establish a national park.

In recent years the peninsula has attracted the attention of wealthy foreigners, who have snatched up some prime real estate, but there's hope that development will be more sustainable in this part of the country, particularly since there is a vested interest in keeping the peninsula green.

Parks & Reserves

As the country's premier ecotourism destination, the Península de Osa has a plethora of parks, reserves and wildlife refuges. Beyond the Osa, the southern zone has its own wealth of less-visited protected lands. The following is only a list of absolute highlights.

Parque Internacional La Amistad (p424) This enormous binational park is shared with Panama and protects a biological corridor of incredible ecological significance.

Parque Nacional Chirripó (p416) Home to Costa Rica's highest and most famous peak, Cerro Chirripó, which on a clear day offers views of both the Pacific and the Caribbean.

Parque Nacional Corcovado (p434) Osa's shining crown jewel, and one of Costa Rica's last true wilderness areas.

Reserva Biológica Isla del Caño (p429) A tiny but spectacular marine and terrestrial park, popular with snorkelers, divers and biologists.

ⓘ Getting There & Away

The main towns in the region are well connected by buses, with the exception of Puerto Jiménez, Bahía Drake, Zancudo and Pavones, which each have only a couple of bus connections daily. To explore southern Costa Rica in depth, it's best to have your own 4WD. That said, it's fairly easy to connect via bus to departure points for Amistad and Chirripó. Note that addresses in this part of the country are virtually nonexistent, and the numbered posts (counting the kilometers from San José) along the Carretera Interamericana are used to locate places.

Getting to Osa requires one of two things: lots of patience or flying in. Given the reasonable cost of flights, a good option for exploring the peninsula is to fly if your time is limited (you can then rent a vehicle in Puerto Jiménez). If you choose to drive, you'll need a 4WD and plenty of confidence: many roads in Osa are extremely poor and there are river crossings involved.

Easy Ride shuttles connect Puerto Jiménez to San José and popular destinations along the Pacific coast.

Sansa (☑ 2290-4100, in USA 877-767-2672; www.flysansa.com) serves Palmar, which is a jumping-off point for the southern zone. Prices vary according to season and availability.

THE ROAD TO CHIRRIPÓ

Traveling south from San José, the road to Parque Nacional Chirripó passes through gorgeous countryside redolent of coffee plantations and cool, misty cloud forest. It bisects the Zona de los Santos, a collection of highland villages that bear sainted names: San Pablo de León Cortés, San Marcos de Tarrazú, San Cristóbal Sur, San Gerardo de Dota, Santa María de Dota – the last renowned for its superb, ecologically produced coffee. Further south in the Valle de El General, family-run *fincas* (farms) dot the fertile valley, though the action tends to center on San Isidro de El General, southern Costa Rica's largest town and major transportation hub.

Travelers aiming for this region tend to have one of two goals in mind: hiking up Cerro Chirripó, Costa Rica's tallest mountain and challenging high-altitude hike; or trying to spot the resplendent quetzal in the dense cloud forest that cloaks Cerro de La Muerte.

San Gerardo de Dota

POP 500 / ELEV 2194M

San Gerardo de Dota is unlike any other place in Costa Rica – a bucolic mountain village run through by a clear, rushing river and surrounded by forested hills that more resemble the alps than the tropics. It's set deep within a mountain valley; the air is crisp and fresh, and chilly at night, and the orchard-lined Savegre basin hosts numerous high-altitude bird species, including the eye-catching and beloved resplendent quetzal, that draw birdwatchers from around the world.

🏃 Activities

One of the best places to go birdwatching and hiking in the area is Parque Nacional Los Quetzales, though you're just as likely to spot the elusive quetzal along the private trails in the grounds of Savegre Hotel (p410) and Paraíso Quetzal Lodge (p411), the latter a little way from San Gerardo (both allow access to nonguests for a fee), or at a particular spot along the river (ask your lodgings where it is), which gets crowded with binocular-bearing twitchers at dawn. Your accommodations can arrange a birding guide for Parque Nacional Los Quetzales to maximize your chances of spotting the likes of collared trogons and emerald toucanets, as well as the quetzal. One particularly excellent local guide and quetzal expert who speaks perfect English is Raul Chacón

(☑8920-9987; jrfc01@gmail.com; quetzal tour for up to 5 people US$70).

Quetzals are easily spotted every April and May (during breeding season) and are fairly common throughout the rest of the year. An especially nice place to photograph them and other birds is the lovely **Batsù Garden** (☑8395-0115; www.batsucr.com; US$20; ☺5am-8pm).

For those interested in hiking, a challenging 9km trail runs up from San Gerardo to Cerro de la Muerte; the trailhead is in the Savegre Hotel grounds. It's easier to hike down (five hours), but best done with a guide as the trailhead down is not as easy to find as the one going up. Those who wish to do extensive hiking in the area are advised to collect maps before they arrive, and those less ambitious can enjoy an easy 1km trail that rambles along the Río Savegre to a pretty waterfall at the south end of the San Gerardo valley.

🛏 Sleeping

Ranchos la Isla CAMPGROUND $
(☑2740-1009; campsite per person US$10; 🅿) This attractive property just across from Cabinas El Quetzal offers a handful of campsites on metal-roofed platforms alongside a small river. The accommodating Chinchilla families arrange guided hikes to nearby waterfalls in the hope of spotting the elusive quetzal.

★ Trogon Lodge LODGE $$$
(☑2293-8181; www.trogonlodge.com; s/d incl breakfast from US$127/153) Hemmed in by cloud forest and with the Río Savegre crossing the property, Trogon Lodge is home to over 175 bird species, including that feathered prize – the quetzal – found along the marked hiking trails. Beautifully landscaped

---

DON'T MISS

COOPEDOTA

Coopedota (☑2541-2828; www.coopedota.com; tours per person US$25; ☺tours 9:30am, 1:30pm & 3pm Mon-Fri, by prior reservation Sat & Sun) gives you the complete picture of where your caffeine fix comes from, either in a 1½-hour tour of the production facility or a half-day experience that takes guests to a coffee farm, visits the production facility and offers tastings. Harvest season (November to March) is the best time to visit. It's on the south side of the Coopedota Building, across from the soccer field.

Coopedota is the first coffee co-op in the world to be certified carbon-neutral by the British Standards Institution, and you'll learn about the steps it takes to reduce its environmental impact during the course of the tour. You can buy bags of freshly roasted coffee at the cafe next to the processing facility.

gardens, an excellent restaurant and delightful little touches, such as hot-water bottles delivered to your cabin, make this a superb choice.

★ **Savegre Hotel** LODGE $$$
(☑2740-1028, in USA & Canada 866-549-1178; www.savegre.com; r from US$134; P@🛜) Operated by the Chacón family since 1957, this lodge is beautifully landscaped and hugely popular with birdwatchers, since quetzals nest along the 30km of trails on the 400-hectare property. The gorgeous, wood-paneled rooms and suites have wrought-iron chandeliers and wooden furniture surrounding a stone fireplace. The onsite spa provides pampering and the professional guides organize birding, horseback riding and hiking outings.

The trail network is open to nonguests (US$10 per person).

Dantica Cloud Forest Lodge LODGE $$$
(☑2740-1067; www.dantica.com; r/ste incl breakfast from US$101/287; P✱🛜) The most elegant place in San Gerardo, this upscale lodge consists of lovely stucco bungalows with colorful Colombian architectural accents. The modern comforts – leather sofas, plasma TVs, Jacuzzis and track lighting – are nice, but the stunning vistas over the cloud forest steal the scene. The rooms used to get cold at night in spite of ethanol-burning stoves, but newly installed heaters fixed that problem.

A nature reserve complete with private trails is just steps away, as is a spa for posthike pampering. If the price tag is too steep, you can just stop by to browse the gallery's collection of art from all over Latin America, visit the gift store or book a romantic dinner at the Restaurant Le Tapir, which serves delicious food.

Cabinas El Quetzal CABINA $$$
(☑2740-1036; www.cabinaselquetzal.com; per person incl 2 meals US$140; P🛜) This simple cluster of four family-run, riverside *cabinas* (some with wood-burning stoves) has a homespun feel. The included meals are lovingly prepared – naturally, fresh trout is on offer. The rooms are without frills (tile floors, small sitting areas, no TVs), but they're clean, comfortable and stocked with a pile of blankets in the likely event of a chilly night.

✖ Eating

Restaurante Los Lagos COSTA RICAN $
(☑2740-1009; mains US$7-10; ☺7am-7pm Sun-Fri, to 8pm Sat) Set amid gardens, ponds and a splashing fountain, this is the place to catch your own trout and have it seasoned, lightly breaded and then deep-fried for lunch, alongside some french fries made from locally grown potatoes. The complimentary dessert, *papaya chilena* (sweet glacé papaya), is also a regional favorite and is served with a scoop of ice cream.

Café Kahawa CAFE $
(☑2740-1081; mains US$5-10; ☺7:30am-5:30pm; P) With alfresco tables sitting above the river, funky skull art and sparkling fish tanks filled with fingerling trout, this atmospheric spot prepares trout in many excellent ways (and there are a few nonfishy dishes). Variations on the theme – such as trout in coconut sauce and trout *ceviche* – can't be found just anywhere. Located toward the southern end of the valley.

La Comida Típica Miriam COSTA RICAN $
(☑2740-1049; www.miriamquetzals.com/restaurant.html; meals US$6-10; ☺7am-7pm; P) One of the first places you will pass in San Gerardo, about 6km from the Interamericana, is this cozy house advertising *comida típica* (regional specialties). Eating here is almost like receiving a personal invitation to dine in a Tico home: the food is delicious and abundant, and the hospitality even more so.

Miriam also rents a few cabins (US$40) in the woods behind the restaurant: a modest but comfortable place to spend a night or two.

★ **Restaurant Le Tapir** COSTA RICAN $$
(☑2740-1069; Dantica Cloud Forest Lodge; mains US$11-23; ☺7am-9pm) With 270-degree views of the valley, this glass-encased restaurant specializes in homemade pasta, rainbow trout and mouthwatering steaks, all garnished with organic herbs fresh from the onsite garden. The breakfast is fabulous, and the blackberry tenderloin with ground pepper and rosemary is the kind of dish you continue thinking of a decade after you've eaten it.

ⓘ Getting There & Away

If you're driving, the turnoff to San Gerardo de Dota is near Km 80 on the Interamericana. From here, the steep road down into the valley alter-

PARQUE NACIONAL LOS QUETZALES

Spread along both banks of the Río Savegre, Parque Nacional Los Quetzales officially became a national park in 2005. At an altitude of 2000m to 3000m, Los Quetzales covers 50 sq km of rainforest and cloud forest lying along the slopes of the Cordillera de Talamanca.

The park's lifeblood is the Río Savegre, which starts high up on the Cerro de la Muerte and feeds several glacial lakes before pouring into the Pacific. This region is remarkably diverse – the Savegre watershed contains approximately 20% of the country's registered bird species.

True to the park's name, the beautiful quetzal is here (best spotted during the March–June nesting season), along with trogons, hummingbirds and sooty robins. Avians aside, the park is home to endangered species including jaguars, Baird's tapirs and squirrel monkeys. The park also has premontane forests, the second-most-endangered life zone in Costa Rica.

nates between paved and dirt; it's best to have a 4WD. Take it slowly, as two-way traffic necessitates a bit of negotiation. Buses between San José and San Isidro de El General can drop you at the turnoff, but bear in mind that the village spreads along 9km of road, so you may have a fair hike ahead of you.

Cerro de La Muerte

Between Empalme and San Isidro de El General, the Interamericana reaches its highest point along the famed Cerro de la Muerte (3451m). The 'Hill of Death' received its moniker during its prehighway days, when crossing the mountains required travel on foot or horseback and many travelers succumbed to exposure.

It's still a harrowing journey, snaking the fog-shrouded spine along a path riddled with blind corners, hair-raising cliffs and careless drivers who take huge risks to overtake slower road users. The upside? Exquisite panoramic views of the Cordillera de Talamanca.

Cerro de la Muerte marks the northernmost extent of the *páramo,* a highland shrub and tussock grass habitat typical of the southern zone. This Andean-style landscape is rich in wildlife and home to many of the same species found in nearby Parque Nacional Chirripó. On the way to San Isidro the road also descends through cloud forests, montane and premontane forest.

Sleeping & Eating

There are several lodges spread out along this stretch of highway. Note that addresses in this part of Costa Rica are nonexistent, so accommodations tend to be listed by their 'Km' distance marker.

★ **Paraíso Quetzal Lodge**　　　LODGE $$
(☏ 2200-0241; www.paraisoquetzal.com; Interamericana Km 70; r incl breakfast from US$88, half-board from US$112) Birders rave about this lodge, surrounded by 13km of walking trails that provide an excellent chance of spotting the resplendent quetzal during the 6am tours. The scattering of wooden cabins is kept warm by a generous collection of space heaters and woollen blankets. Superior cabins come with Jacuzzis and superb valley views, ideal for canoodling with your sweetie.

Bosque del Tolomuco　　　B&B $$
(☏ 8847-7207; www.bosquedeltolomuco.com; Interamericana Km 118; cabin from US$65; P🛜❄) Named for the sly tayra (tree otter) spotted on the grounds, this cutesy B&B is run by a lovely, chatty expat couple. There are five spacious, light-filled cabins, the most charming of which is the secluded 'Hummingbird Cabin.' The grounds offer 5km of hiking trails, ample opportunities to indulge in birdwatching and some magnificent views of Los Cruces and Chirripó.

Breakfast is $8. A made-to-order gourmet dinner is available with advance notice. Day hikers who want to stretch their legs and get off the road can hike the network of trails for US$3.

Mirador Valle del General　　　LODGE $$
(☏ 2200-5465; www.valledelgeneral.com; Interamericana Km 119; r/bungalow incl breakfast US$50/ 100; P🛜) This aptly named lodge features a panoramic view from its charming

reception area and restaurant, which serves up local specialties such as fried trout. Below, spotless rooms and bungalows built from cultivated wood are brightened by colorful indigenous tapestries and also offer spectacular valley views. Nature trails through the cloud forest often receive visits from tanagers and other feathered life.

Mirador de Quetzales
CABINA $$

(☎ 8381-8456, 2200-4185; www.quetzalesdecosta rica.com; Interamericana Km 70; d incl 2 meals US$82; P) About 1km west of the Interamericana, this excellent option consists of a cluster of wooden cabins, warmed by electric heaters. Prices also include an early-morning 'quetzal quest' along the 4km trail shaded by immense cypress trees – the feathered beauties reside in these forested hills year-round. Nonguests can wander the system of trails for US$7.

❶ Getting There & Away

Frequent buses running between San José and San Isidro de El General can drop you off near the lodges.

San Isidro de El General

POP 45,000

Although it's a place where few travelers choose to linger, San Isidro de El General is the fastest-growing urban area outside the capital and a sprawling, utilitarian market town at the crossroads between some of Costa Rica's prime destinations.

'El General' (often referred to as Pérez Zeledón, the name of the municipality) is the region's largest population center and major transportation hub. If you're traveling to the southern Pacific beaches or Chirripó, a brief stop is inevitable. Some accommodations options just outside the town environs are worthy destinations in their own right.

🎊 Festivals & Events

Agricultural Festival
CULTURAL

(☺ early Feb) This fair is a chance for local farmers to strut their stuff – and that they do, by taking over the agricultural showgrounds 4km south of the city with regional culinary delights. There are also bullfights (well, bull-teasing), horsemanship events, an orchid exhibition, livestock competitions and concerts in the evening.

🛏 Sleeping

Hotel Chirripó
HOTEL $

(☎ 2771-0529; Av 2 btwn Calles Central & 1; s/d US$30/41, without bathroom US$20/25; P❋🛜) Let's put it bluntly: if you're traveling through town, weary and cash-poor, this is *the* choice. Popular with discerning budget travelers, this centrally located hotel is a two-minute stroll from the bus station and filled with bare, whitewashed rooms that are barren but utterly dirt- and grime-free.

Talari Mountain Lodge
LODGE $$

(☎ 2771-0341; www.talari.co.cr; Rivas; s/d incl breakfast US$70/92; P🛜🏊) This secluded mountain lodge is a birdwatcher's haven, with over 200 species of bird spotted along the three well-maintained trails on the riverside property. Accommodations are in simple wooden cabins hemmed in by the forest, and there's also a pool and a tennis court. To get here from San Isidro, follow the road to San Gerardo de Rivas for 7km; the driveway will be on the right.

Best Western Hotel Zima
HOTEL $$

(☎ 2770-1114; www.hotelzima.net; Interamericana; s/d incl breakfast US$87/107; P❋🛜🏊) This Best Western benefits from a central location yet is far enough from the main highway to avoid the traffic noise. The rooms are of a standard, not hugely memorable, business variety, but comfortable and very clean, and the staff are friendly and eager to please.

★ Hacienda AltaGracia
RESORT $$$

(☎ 2105-3000, in USA 815-812-2212; http://alta gracia.aubergeresorts.com; Santa Teresa de Cahón, Pérez Zeledón; r US$525-1495; P❋🛜🏊) A hillside hacienda overlooking the lush Valle de General, this Auberge Resort consists of self-contained *casitas* (cottages) and suites, their decor stylish and understated (neutral shades, dark leather), surrounded by 350 hectares – ideal for hiking, horseback riding and observing from the air from one of the resort's own ultralights. Dining focuses on the farm-to-table concept, and there's a world-class spa.

🍽 Eating & Drinking

★ Urban Farm Cafe
INTERNATIONAL $

(☎ 2771-2442; Calle Central; mains US$5-7; ☺ 7am-7pm Mon-Sat; 🛜🍴) With its 'from farm to table' motto, this delightful cafe singlehandedly pushes San Isidro's dining scene

San Isidro de El General

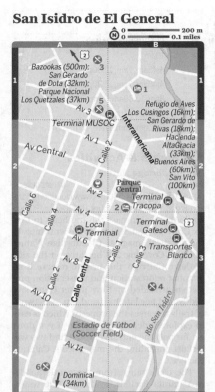

San Isidro de El General

🛏 Sleeping
1	Best Western Hotel Zima	B1
2	Hotel Chirripó	B2

✖ Eating
3	Bazookas	A1
4	Farmers' Market	B3
5	Kafe de la Casa	A1
6	Urban Farm Cafe	A4

🍷 Drinking & Nightlife
7	Bar El Balcón	A2

day morning and usually winds down by early afternoon on Friday; organic produce, prepared foods and goods are bountiful.

Kafe de la Casa   CAFE $
(📞 2770-4816; Av 3 btwn Calles 2 & 4; meals US$7-13; ☺ 7am-7pm Mon-Sat; 🖥🚲) Set in an old Tico house, this bohemian cafe features eclectic artwork, an open kitchen and breezy garden seating. The menu has excellent breakfasts, light lunches, gourmet dinners and plenty of coffee drinks. Veggie options include salads and sandwiches.

Bar El Balcón   BAR
(📞 2771-1112; cnr Calle 2 & Av 2; ☺ 11am-midnight) On an open 2nd-floor corner spot in the heart of town, this spacious bar brings in a largely local crowd at night.

ℹ Getting There & Away

AIR
Sansa (📞 2290-4100, in USA 877-767-2672; www.flysansa.com) has flights on Tuesday, Friday and Sunday between San José and San Isidro for about US$70 one way.

BUS
In San Isidro the **local bus terminal** (🖥; known as Mercado) is on Av 6 and serves nearby villages. The bus to San Gerardo de Rivas (for Parque Nacional Chirripó; US$4, 1½ hours) departs from the local terminal five times daily from 5:45am.

Local buses from **Terminal Gafeso** (📞 2771-1523) serve Buenos Aires, with onward connections to Reserva Biológica Dúrika.

Long-distance buses leave from points near the Interamericana and are frequently packed, so buy tickets early. Note that buses heading south to Golfito or Ciudad Neily will go through Palmar Norte.

up a big notch. Breakfast options range from 'Hawaiian-style' macadamia pancakes with banana to veggie omelettes and falafel, while its lunchtime wraps and salads are just overflowing with fresh vegetables. Wash it down with a delectable fruit smoothie.

Bazookas   INTERNATIONAL $
(www.bazookasrestaurant.com; Interamericana; mains US$5-15; ☺ 7am-10pm; 🅿🖥) Toward the north exit from San Isidro and memorable for its bubblegum pink signage, this diner caters to hungry travelers with a good mix of Tico dishes (decent *gallo pinto*), vast breakfast platters involving bacon, eggs and pancakes, and more robust dinner mains, such as the tender rack of ribs the size of a cow, and slabs of steak.

Farmers Market   MARKET $
(off Calle 3) The largest *feria* (fair) in the region, this farmers market starts early Thurs-

BUSES FROM TERMINAL TRACOPA

DESTINATION	COST (US$)	DURATION	FREQUENCY (DAILY)
Golfito	8	4hr	10am
Neily	8	4hr	4:45am, 7am, 12:30pm, 3pm
Palmar Norte	6	2½	4:45am, 7am, 12:30pm, 3pm
Paso Canoas	9	4½	8am, 10:30am, 4pm, 6:30pm, 9:30pm
San José	6.50	3	hourly
San Vito	6.50	3½	5:30am, 9am, 11am, 2pm, 7pm

Terminal Tracopa

You will find **Terminal Tracopa** (☑2771-0468) on the Interamericana, just southwest of Av Central, and **Terminal Musoc** (☑2771-0414), which only serves San José, just beside Kafe de la Casa. If heading for Paso Canoas, Golfito or Palmar Norte, try to catch a bus that originates from San Isidro, or risk standing room only.

Terminal Quepos

Transportes Blanco (☑2771-4744) is on the side street west of the Interamericana. Desinations include the following:

Domenical (US$3, 1½ hours, daily 8am, 9am, 11:30am, 3.30pm and 4pm)

Puerto Jiménez (via Palmar Norte; US$9.60, five hours, daily 6:30am, 11am and 3pm)

Quepos (US$4.90, 2½ hours, daily 8am, 11:30am and 3.30pm)

Uvita (US$3.60, two hours, daily 9am and 4pm)

San Gerardo de Rivas

POP 400 / ELEV 1219M

If you have plans to climb Chirripó, you're in the right place – the tiny, tranquil, spread-out town of San Gerardo de Rivas is at the doorstep of the national park. This is a place to get supplies, a good night's rest and a hot shower before and after the trek.

With a new online reservation system, hiking permits recently became much easier to obtain. For those who don't have the time or energy to summit Chirripó, there are also lovely, less difficult hikes in private nature reserves, and rural tourism aplenty, from the local trout farm to local cheese- and chocolate-makers in nearby Canaán. San Gerardo's bird-filled alpine scenery certainly makes it a beautiful place to linger.

The road to San Gerardo de Rivas winds its way 22km up the valley of the Río Chirripó from San Isidro.

◉ Sights & Activities

★ **Cloudbridge Nature**
Reserve NATURE RESERVE

(☑in USA 917-494-5408; www.cloudbridge.org; admission by donation, tours US$10-30; ☉6am-6pm) About 2km past the trailhead to Cerro Chirripó you will find the entrance to the mystical, magical Cloudbridge Nature Reserve. Covering 283 hectares on the side of Cerro Chirripó, this private reserve is an ongoing reforestation and preservation project spearheaded by New Yorker Genevieve Giddy and her late husband Ian. A network of trails traverses the property, which is easy to explore independently. Even if you don't get far past the entrance, you'll find two waterfalls, including the magnificent Catarata Pacifica.

The trails range from the gentle Sendero Catarata Pacifica, leading to the waterfalls, to the steep uphill Sendero Montaña that joins the main trail up Cerro Chirripó. Guided tours, including birdwatching, night hikes and strolls through old-growth forest, have set times and English-speaking guides, and must be booked at least a full day in advance.

Volunteer reforestation and conservation opportunities are listed on the reserve's website.

Talamanca Reserve NATURE RESERVE

(☑2742-5080; www.talamancareserve.com) With over 4000 acres of primary and secondary cloud forest, this private reserve has numerous hiking trails, the longest being a seven-hour trek, and another leading to its 11 waterfalls. Talamanca is doing its best to promote itself as an alternative to Parque Nacional Chirripó, and nonguests are welcome to hike its trails for a day fee of US$25. All-terrain vehicle (ATV) tours are available both to guests and nonguests.

Jardines Secretos
GARDENS

(🖉8451-3001, 2742-5086; US$5; ⊙7am-5pm) These not-so-secret gardens make for a tranquil pre- or post-Chirripó pastime as the owners talk you through their collection of orchids and other tropical plants. Find the turnoff just before the ranger station.

Thermal Hot Springs
HOT SPRINGS

(Aguas Termales; 🖉2742-5210; Herradura; US$7; ⊙7am-5:30pm) Between the ranger station and upper San Gerardo lies a bridge; before the bridge, a road forks to the left. Take this and walk for about 1km on a paved road, then turn right and take the suspension bridge over the river. A switchback trail lead for 1km to a house with a *soda* (place serving counter meals), the entrance to the hot springs – two pools popular with soaking locals.

🎊 Festivals & Events

Carrera Chirripó
SPORTS

(www.carrerachirripo.com; ⊙Feb) This grueling race from San Gerardo de Rivas to Crestones Base Lodge and back (34km) takes place at the end of February, with up to 225 participants. If you're trekking up the mountain you may be disheartened to know that the fastest man and woman have covered the distance in three hours four minutes, and four hours 19 minutes, respectively.

🛏 Sleeping

★Hostel Cabaña Mis Ojos
GUESTHOUSE $

(🖉8349-6842; www.facebook.com/MisOjos2015/; r incl breakfast US$25) This charming wooden cottage overlooks the river, and has been a favorite with groups and families. The main draws are the tranquil atmosphere and the tasty meals prepared by the owner Laura, who lives onsite, speaks decent English and personally retrieves her guests from the bus station.

★Casa Mariposa
HOSTEL $

(🖉2742-5037; www.hotelcasamariposa.net; dm US$16, d US$40-60; 🅿@) 🍴 Just 50m from the park entrance, this adorable hostel is built into the side of the mountain and is characterized by the warmth and knowledge of owners John and Jill. Traveler-oriented benefits – warm clothes to borrow for the hike, laundry service, assistance with booking the Chirripó lodge and tips on alternative activities in the area – make it ideal.

In the evening, guests gather around the wood stove in the communal living room to read, plan hikes and welcome weary hikers returning from the summit. There's a tidy kitchen, a lookout with hammocks on the roof and a stone soaking tub. There's only space for 20 guests, so advance booking is recommended. Parking here is $2 per night.

Casa Hostel Chirripó
HOSTEL $

(🖉2742-5020; www.casachirripo.com; dm US$15, r with/without bathroom US$40/35; 🛜) Near the football field, this colorful newer hostel gives guests a space to cook and socialize, and post-hike provides cozy rooms and dorms to lay down their weary heads. Taxis to the trailhead cost $10, which can be split among groups.

Hotel Roca Dura
CABINA $

(🖉2742-5071; r US$25-45; 🅿) Located in the center of town just opposite the soccer field, this hip hostel is built right into the side of a giant boulder, lending a *Flintstones* ambience to the quarters. Wall murals brighten the smallest stone rooms, while pricier rooms have tree-trunk furniture and fixtures plus views of forested hillsides. There's also a great **restaurant** (mains from US$6; ⊙8am-9pm).

Hotel Uran
HOSTEL $

(🖉2742-5003; www.hoteluran.com; s/d US$36/57, without bathroom US$20/40; 🅿🛜) Just 70m below the trailhead, these no-nonsense budget digs are a longtime mecca for hikers heading to/from Chirripó. Budget-friendly rooms are fine for a restful snooze, while the onsite restaurant and laundry facility cater to the shoestring set. Note that it's possible to buy beer here (the *pulpería* in town doesn't sell alcohol).

Casa de los Celtas
B&B $$

(🖉8707-2921, 2770-3524; www.casaceltas.com; s/d US$55/70; 🅿🛜) Overlooking 4 acres of native greenery and brightened by Sheelagh's orchid collection, this delightful B&B is run by two retired expat travelers, whose genuine warmth and knowledge of the area greatly enhances your stay. Choose between a twin room or a compact, self-contained cottage and feast on Sheelagh's gourmet cooking (two-course dinner US$18). Extensive breakfasts feature plenty of fresh fruit.

The property is located slightly outside of San Gerardo proper (roughly halfway between San Gerardo and San Isidro de El

General), so confirm location before you arrive.

Hotel de Montaña El Pelícano   HOTEL $$

(☑ 2742-5050; www.hotelpelicano.net; r & ste US$72-116; P 🛜 🐾) 🍴 About 300m below the ranger station, steeply uphill from the main road, this simple, functional lodge, surrounded by gorgeous vegetation, has a collection of spartan but spotless rooms that overlook the river valley. The highlight of the property is the gallery of the owner, a late-blooming artist who sculpts whimsical wood pieces.

★ Talamanca Reserve   HOTEL $$$

(☑ 2742-5080; www.talamancareserve.com; r & ste US$118-220; P 🛜) 🍴 Set within the private Talamanca Reserve, uphill from the ranger station, is a scattering of appealing garden and river cabins – all with terraces and beautifully embellished wood and tile interiors. There's a good onsite restaurant, but the biggest attraction is access to the reserve's many trails.

The accommodations and hiking tours are managed by the friendly, bilingual Kenneth, who was born and raised on the reserve, and whose family still maintains the gardens, fruit trees, trails and a reforestation project here.

Río Chirripó Retreat   HOTEL $$$

(☑ 2742-5109; www.riochirripo.com; d/cabin/ casita incl breakfast US$106/142/217; P 🍴 🛜 🐾) This upscale lodge, 1.5km from San Gerardo, in Canaán, is centered on a yoga studio overlooking the river, and an open-air, Santa Fe–style communal area. You can hear the rush of the river from 10 secluded cabins, where woven blankets and stenciled walls evoke the southwest USA.

On the grounds are a private reserve with a 30-minute hiking trail, a couple of pools (one heated and one surrounded by rocks adjacent to the river), a hot tub and a relaxing spa.

✕ Eating

★ Antojos de Maíz   COSTA RICAN $

(☑ 2772-4381; chorreadas US$3; ⊙ 8am-8pm Wed-Mon) For all things corn, stop at this traditional roadside restaurant on your way to or from the mountain. Our favorite here is the *chorreada*, a traditional sweet pancake made with fresh white or yellow corn and served with sour cream. Pairs very well with strong, organic coffee.

Restaurante Rio   PIZZA $

(☑ 2742-5110; mains from US$8; ⊙ 11am-10pm; 🍴) Not far from the soccer field, this place serves surprisingly good pizzas; we particularly like the one topped with pepperoni, bacon and ham. Generous portions, and several pizza options are meat-free.

ℹ Information

The **Chirripó Ranger Station** (Sinac; ☑ 905-244-7747, in the USA 506-2742-5348; ⊙ 8am-noon & 1-4:30pm) is 1km below the soccer field, at the entrance to San Gerardo de Rivas. If you're here to hike up Cerro Chirripó, you must stop by before you start the hike to confirm your permit. If you haven't booked your park permit in advance, there's a slim chance of availability.

Your lodgings at Crestones Base Lodge (p419) will also need to be booked in advance. At the time of research, the way to do that was through Consorcio Aguas Eternas; see p417 for details.

ℹ Getting There & Away

Arriving via public transportation requires a connection through San Isidro. Buses to San Isidro depart from the soccer field six times daily (three daily on Sunday) between 5:15am and 6:45pm (US$2, 1½ hours).

Driving from San Isidro, head south on the Interamericana and cross Río San Isidro south of town. About 500m further on, cross the unsigned Río Jilguero and take the first, steep turn up to the left, about 300m beyond the Jilguero. Note that this turnoff is not marked (if you miss the turn, it is signed from the northbound side).

The ranger station is about 18km up this road from the Interamericana. The road passes through Rivas village and is paved as far as the entrance to San Gerardo de Rivas. It is passable for ordinary cars, but a 4WD is recommended if you are driving to Hotel Urán or to Cloudbridge Nature Reserve, as the unpaved road is steep and truly hideous.

Parque Nacional Chirripó

Costa Rica's mountainous spine runs the length of the country in four distinct mountain ranges, of which the Cordillera de Talamanca is the highest, longest and most remote. The cordillera's highlight and the focus of the high-altitude Parque Nacional Chirripó is Costa Rica's highest peak, **Cerro Chirripó** (3820m).

The only way up Chirripó is on foot. Although the trekking routes are challenging, watching the sunrise from such lofty heights is one of the country's undeniable highlights.

Parque Nacional Chirripó is a welcome respite from lowland heat. Above 3400m, the landscape is *páramo*, comprising scrubby trees and grasslands. Rocky outposts punctuate the otherwise barren hills, and feed a series of glacial lakes that earned the park its iconic name: Chirripó means 'Eternal Waters.'

The bare *páramo* contrasts with the lush cloud forest, which dominates the hillsides between 2500m and 3400m. Oak trees tower over the dense undergrowth and the evergreen canopy.

🏃 Activities

Wildlife-Watching

The varying altitude means an amazing diversity of fauna in Parque Nacional Chirripó. Particularly famous for its extensive birdlife, the national park is home to several endangered species, including the harpy eagle (the largest, most powerful raptor in the Americas) and the resplendent quetzal (especially visible between March and May). Even besides these highlights, you might see highland birds including the three-wattled bellbird, black guan and tinamou. The Andean-like *páramo* guarantees volcano junco, sooty robin, slaty finch, large-footed finch and the endemic volcano hummingbird, which is found only in Costa Rica's highlands.

In addition to the prolific birdlife, the park is home to some unusual high-altitude reptiles, such as the green spiny lizard and the highland alligator lizard. Mammals include pumas, Baird's tapirs, spider monkeys, capuchin monkeys, and – at higher elevations – Dice's rabbits and the coyotes that feed on them.

Although spotting rarer animals is never a guaranteed proposition, here are a few tips to maximize your chances: pumas stick to the savanna areas and use the trails at dawn and dusk to move about; Baird's tapirs gravitate to various highland lagoons, mainly in the rainy season, so stake out the muddy edges at dawn or dusk if you see recent tracks; and at nighttime, coyotes can be seen feeding at the rubbish bins near Crestones Base Lodge.

Climbing Chirripó

The park entrance is at San Gerardo de Rivas, which lies 1219m above sea level; the altitude at the summit is 3820m, which makes it 2.6km straight up! A well-marked 19.6km trail leads all the way to the top, with trail markers every kilometer, and no technical

ADVANCE PLANNING

Hiking up Chirripó requires a bit of planning, though the process became significantly easier in 2016 when Sistema Nacional de Areas de Conservación (Sinac) created an online booking system for park permits, which can be found at https://serviciosenlinea. sinac.go.cr. You'll need to set up an account to purchase your permits for each day you'll be in the park, which can be done up to six months in advance and must be secured with a credit card. You'll also be able to reserve a bed at Crestones Base Lodge, and at the time of research it was Consorcio Aguas Eternas that had the concession to handle lodgings within the park (this is subject to change, and you can get the most current information on the Sinac website). Payment must be carried out with **Consorcio Aguas Eternas** (Consortium Office; ☎ 2742-5097, 2742-5200; infochirriposervicios@gmail. com; ⊘ 8am-5pm Mon-Sat, from 9am Sun) via email, over the phone or possibly in person. You must arrange your payment within 10 days of making the reservation then send a receipt with your reservation number to info@chirripo.org. Otherwise, your reservation for the lodge will be cancelled.

The dry season (from late December to April) is the most popular time to visit Chirripó. February and March are the driest months with the clearest skies, though it may still rain. On weekends, and especially during holidays, the trails can get a bit crowded with Tico hiking groups. The park is now open year-round, and the early months of the rainy season are good for climbing as it usually doesn't rain in the morning.

In any season, temperatures can drop below freezing at night, so warm clothes (including hat and gloves) and rainwear are necessary. Wear sturdy boots and bring good second-skin blister plasters. In exposed areas, high winds seem even colder. The ranger station in San Gerardo de Rivas is a good place to check on the weather conditions.

Chirripó's trails are well marked and do not require maps.

climbing is required. It would be nearly impossible to get lost.

Altitude sickness can be an issue as you get higher up. Watch out for nausea, shortness of breath, headaches and exhaustion. If you start feeling unwell, rest for a little while; if the symptoms persist, descend immediately.

The amount of time it takes to get up varies greatly – it can take as little as five and as many as 12 hours to cover the 14.5km from the start of the trail to the Crestones Base Lodge, depending on how fit you are; bank on at least seven hours. From the lodge it's another 5.1km to the summit, which takes around two hours one way.

Most hikers start the hike between 4am and 5am, though there's nothing to stop you from leaving earlier. The actual entrance to the park is 4km from the start of the trail in San Gerardo, which is 70m beyond Hotel Urán (and about 4km from the ranger station).

The first 6km or so are mostly uphill, over uneven, rocky ground, with some relatively flat stretches. You pass through dense cloud forest, so keep an eye out for quetzals.

Then there's a gentle descent toward the shelter at Llano Bonito (7.5km), which is a good place for a break. Here you can stock up on drinking water, use the flushing toilets and buy snacks and even aspirin. This place is intended for emergency use, not overnight stays, however.

Just beyond begins the Cuesta de los Arrepentidos ('Hill of the Repentants') and boy, will you repent! (At this point, try not to think about the long-distance runners

who run from San Gerardo to Crestones and back again in around four hours.) It's a steep uphill slog until you reach the top of Monte Sin Fe (which translates as 'Mountain Without Faith'), a preliminary crest that reaches 3200m at around Km 10. By then you're on exposed ground, flanked by stunted tree growth, with gorgeous mountain views around you. The trail then descends gently for around 1.5km, making you grind your teeth, since what goes down must come up! The last section is an interminable, steep ascent before you see the green roofs of the Crestones Base Lodge just downhill from you; breathe a sigh of relief before descending to 3400m.

Reaching the lodge is the hardest part. From here the hike to the **summit** is 5.1km on relatively flatter terrain (although the last 100m is very steep). Carry a warm jacket, rain gear, water, snacks and a flashlight just in case, but leave anything you don't need at the lodge. From the summit on a clear day, the vista stretches to both the Caribbean Sea and the Pacific Ocean. The deep-blue lakes and the plush-green hills carpet the Valle de las Morenas in the foreground.

Most hikers reach the lodge around lunchtime and spend the rest of the day recuperating before leaving for the summit at around 3am to arrive in time to watch the sunrise – a spectacular experience.

For most people, a minimum of two days is needed to climb from the ranger station in San Gerardo to the summit and back, leaving no time for exploration. During peak season you're allowed to book a maximum of two nights at the lodge, and at all other

---

ⓘ DAY HIKING CHIRRIPÓ

The masochistically inclined and the superfit may be thrilled to know that it's feasible to summit Chirripó and return to town in a single day. But whatever you do, don't underestimate the mountain.

It's a 39.2km round trip that involves a climb of 2000m into high-altitude territory and is an exhausting uphill slog most of the way. The summit is more likely to be cloudy in the afternoons than early in the morning, meaning you probably won't get much of a view, and summiting and returning on the same day almost invariably means descending at least part of the way in the dark.

But if you're determined to do it, make sure you take food, water, a flashlight with spare batteries and warm clothes. And start early – around 1am or 2am. That way you can get to Crestones Base Lodge midmorning, have time to rest, summit, and then head back down again in the afternoon. Walking part of the way in the dark is not a problem, since the trail is clearly marked and it's almost impossible to get lost. But if you have any doubts about your fitness, consider a long day hike in the Cloudbridge Nature Reserve (p414) instead.

times the max is three nights. This gives you extra time to explore the trails around the summit and/or the Base Lodge.

Hiking Other Trails

There are several attractive destinations that are accessible by trails from the Crestones Base Lodge. These will require at least another day and real topographical maps. An alternative, longer route between the Base Lodge and the summit goes via **Cerro Terbi** (3760m), as well as **Los Crestones**, the moonlike rock formations that adorn many postcards. If you are hanging around for a few days, the glorious, grassy **Sabana de los Leones** is a popular destination that offers a stark contrast to the otherwise alpine scenery. Peak-baggers will want to visit **Cerro Ventisqueros** (3812m), which is also within a day's walk of Crestones. These trails are fairly well maintained, but it's worth inquiring about conditions before setting out.

For hard-core adventurers, an alternative route is to take a guided three- or five-day loop trek that begins in the nearby village of Herradura and spends a day or two traversing cloud forest and *páramo* on the slopes of Fila Urán. Hikers ascend **Cerro Urán** (3600m) before the final ascent of Chirripó and then descend through San Gerardo. This trip requires bush camping and carrying a tent. **Costa Rica Trekking Adventures** (☎2771-4582; www.chirripo.com) can make arrangements for this tour, although Cerro Urán was temporarily closed to hikers at the time of research.

🛏 Sleeping & Eating

Crestones Base Lodge (☎2742-5097; www.chirripo.org/hospedaje/; dm US$35; 🛜) is the only accommodations in the park. Visitors may stay a maximum of three nights most of the year, and only two nights during peak season.

Space is at a premium during holiday periods and on weekends during the dry season. Your chances of getting a last-minute place are best when you have days to spare or come in low season.

There's a good cafeteria serving three meals per day (US$10 to US$13 per meal) at Crestones Base Lodge. Hikers are not permitted to cook their own meals but they may bring cold food and snacks.

DON'T MISS

QUESO PACHECO

Queso is not Costa Rica's strong suit, but the little cheese operation **Queso Pacheco** (☎2541-3126, 8434-0654; www.facebook.com/quesopacheco; ⊙hours vary), run by a former president's son, is one example to the contrary. Abel Pacheco has been living on this remote farm with his wife since the '80s, honing his craft and hand-producing the tastiest dry-aged Swiss around.

The schedule is extremely variable, but ring up Pacheco and you might just luck into a farm tour that also includes an old insider's commentary on the history and politics of Costa Rica. Ask for very specific directions – this is not an easy place to find.

At the time of research, there was talk of opening up a geodesic dome on the property for stays.

ℹ Information

It is essential that you stop at the ranger station (p416) in San Gerardo de Rivas at least one day before you intend to climb Chirripó to confirm your park permit (bring your reservation and proof of payment). After you've done that, you have to confirm your Crestones Base Lodge reservation at the Consorcio Aguas Eternas (p417). Park fees are now US$18 per day. You can also make arrangements at the ranger station to hire a porter (a fixed fee of US$100 for up to 15kg of luggage), though it's now less necessary than ever. Since Crestones offers meals and includes bedding in the accommodations price, you can travel light, without cooking gear or a sleeping bag.

ℹ Getting There & Around

Travelers connect to the trails via the mountain village of San Gerardo de Rivas, which is also home to the ranger station. From opposite the ranger station, in front of Cabinas El Bosque, there is free transportation to the trailhead at 5am. Also, several hotels offer early-morning trailhead transportation for their guests.

While supplies are brought to Crestones Base Lodge by horse, the only way you can get up and down the mountain is on your own two legs (don't underestimate the challenge).

THE ROAD TO LA AMISTAD

From San Isidro de El General, the Interamericana winds its way southeast through glorious rolling hills and coffee and pineapple plantations backed by striking mountain facades, towering as much as 3350m above. Along this stretch, a series of narrow, steep, dirt roads leads to some of the country's most remote areas – some nearly inaccessible due to the prohibitive presence of the Cordillera de Talamanca. But it's worth enduring the thrilling road for the chance to visit Parque Internacional La Amistad, a true wilderness of epic scale. This part of the country is rich in indigenous culture, and Italian immigrants have left their mark on the mountain town of San Vito, which has the best dining in the area.

Reserva Indígena Boruca

The picturesque valley of the Río Grande de Térraba cradles several mostly indigenous villages that comprise the reserve of Boruca (Brunka) peoples. At first glance it is difficult to differentiate these towns from typical Tico villages, aside from a few artisans selling their handiwork. These towns hardly cater to the tourist trade, which is one of the main reasons why traditional Boruca life has been able to continue without much distraction. The best way to engage with the community is to come here on a culturally sensitive tour, or else contact the community directly to arrange an overnight stay and activities.

Be thoughtful when visiting these communities – avoid taking photographs of people without asking permission, and respect the fact that these communities are struggling to maintain traditional culture in a changing world.

Tours

Galería Namu (p94) in San José can arrange eco-ethno tours of the Boruca area, which include homestays, hiking to waterfalls, handicraft demonstrations and storytelling. These cost US$85 per person per day, and include meals, but not transportation to the village itself, which is relatively simple to work out by bus or taxi via Buenos Aires. Visit the website for more details.

Festivals & Events

Fiesta de los Diablitos CULTURAL
This raucous three-day festival, held in Boruca (December 30 to January 2) and Curré (February 5 to 8), symbolizes the historical struggle between the Spanish and the indigenous population. Villagers wearing wooden devil masks and burlap costumes role-play the native peoples in their fight against the Spanish conquerors and the festival culminates in a choreographed battle, which the Spanish lose.

Fiesta de los Negritos RELIGIOUS
(⊙Dec) This festival is held during the second week of December to celebrate the Virgin of the Immaculate Conception. Traditional indigenous music (mainly drumming and bamboo flutes) accompanies dancing and costumes.

Sleeping & Eating

Travelers can find rooms to rent by inquiring locally in Boruca village. **Mileni Gonzalez** (☎2730-5178; www.boruca.org), a local community organizer, can help arrange rustic *cabina* and traditional *rancho* accommodations and also homestays, which are an excellent way to connect with the community and contribute to the local economy.

Shopping

The Boruca are celebrated craftspeople and their traditional art plays a leading role in the survival of their culture. While most make their living from agriculture, some Boruca began producing fine handicrafts for tourists a couple of decades ago, at the initiative of a female community leader; many carvers are women.

The tribe is most famous for its ornate masks featuring jungle birds and animals as well as devil faces, carved from balsa or cedar, and often colored with natural dyes and acrylics. Boruca women also use pre-Columbian backstrap looms to weave colorful, natural cotton bags, placemats and other textiles. These crafts are available along the Pacific coast, in the Península de Osa and the capital, with particularly good selections at Hotel Cristal Ballena (p400) in Uvita, Jagua Arts & Crafts (p445) in Puerto Jiménez and Galería Namu (p94) in San José.

Curré is about 30km south of Buenos Aires, right on the Interamericana. Drivers can stop to visit a small **cooperative** (⊙9am-

5pm Mon-Fri, 2-5pm Sat) that sells handicrafts. In Boruca, local artisans post signs outside their homes advertising their handmade balsa masks and woven bags, but the best selection of masks and woven goods is found at **Bisha Cra** (☑ 8366-8606, 2730-0854; www.bishacra.jimdo.com; ☺ 10am-5pm), near the entrance to the village if you're taking the road south of Curré.

ℹ Information

The community operates an excellent website, www.boruca.org, with historical information and more. Community leader Mileni Gonzalez (p420) is an excellent source of local information.

ℹ Getting There & Away

Buses (US$1.70, one hour) leave the central market in Buenos Aires at noon and 3:30pm daily, traveling to Boruca via a bumpy, partially paved road. The bus returns at 6am and 11am the following morning, which makes an overnight stay necessary if you're relying on public transportation. A taxi from Buenos Aires to Boruca is about US$30.

Drivers will find a better road that leaves the Interamericana about 3km south of Curré; look for the sign to Boruca. This dusty, unpaved route climbs a ridgeline and affords spectacular views of the valleys below. It's about 8km to Boruca from Curré, though the going is slow, and a 4WD is recommended, though not strictly necessary. If you're heading toward San Isidro or Buenos Aires, you can follow this road all the way through the village of Térraba, with more glimpses of indigenous community life along the way.

Palmar

POP 4900

At the intersection of the country's two major highways, this crossroads town serves as a gateway to the Península de Osa and Golfo Dulce. This functional banana-growing settlement makes a convenient base for exploring the Sierpe area if you have a particular interest in pre-Columbian stone spheres (which the area is newly famous for), and the Festival de la Luz in December is worth stopping for.

Palmar is actually split in two – to get from Palmar Norte to Palmar Sur, take the Interamericana southbound over the Río Grande de Térraba bridge, then take the first right. Most facilities are in Palmar Norte, clustered around the intersection of the Carretera Interamericana and the Costanera Sur; if you're heading to Bahía Drake via Sierpe, this is your last chance to hit an ATM. Palmar Sur is home to the airstrip and a little park with an excellent example of a stone sphere.

🛏 Sleeping & Eating

Self-caterers will want to hit the **Supermercado BM** (☑ 2786-6556; ☺ 7am-9pm Mon-Sat, 8am-8pm Sun), 200m north of the Interamericana–Costanera intersection, before heading to the Osa, as shopping opportunities are limited in Bahía Drake. The nicest place to eat is the onsite restaurant at Brunka Lodge.

Hotel El Teca HOTEL $
(☑ 8950-8562, 2786-8010; www.hotelelteca.com; Ruta 2; s/d from US$28/35; ⓟ❋⌗) Run by a sweet, hospitable local family, this small hotel offers a clutch of tidy, tiled rooms, complete with coffee makers and mini-fridges. The owners can provide information on the pre-Columbian stone spheres and where best to find them, and also organize trips to Parque Nacional Corcovado, Térraba mangroves and more. The hotel is 25m west of the Red Cross building.

Brunka Lodge HOTEL $$
(☑ 2786-7489; s/d from US$40/50; ⓟ❋⌗⛱) The Brunka Lodge is undoubtedly the most inviting option in Palmar Norte. Sun-filled,

SOUTHERN COSTA RICA & PENÍNSULA DE OSA PALMAR

BUSES FROM PALMAR

DESTINATION	COST (US$)	DURATION	FREQUENCY (DAILY)
Dominical	2	1½hr	8:20am, 1:20pm, 3:45pm
Golfito	3.20	1½hr	11:20am, 12:30pm
Neily	3.20	1½hr	12 daily 5:10am-6pm
Paso Canoas	3.80	2hr	6 daily 10:30am-8:30pm
San Isidro	6.36	2½hr	8:30am, noon, 2:45pm, 5pm, 6:15pm
San José	9.09	5½hr	16-19 daily 4:45am-6:30pm
Sierpe	0.63	40min	7 daily 5am-5:15pm

clean-swept, brightly painted bungalows are clustered around a swimming pool and a popular, pleasant open-air restaurant, and all rooms have hot-water bathrooms, cable TV and high-speed internet. The suite is particularly nice as it has a private entrance to the pool.

Getting There & Away

Departing from San José, **Sansa** (☎ 2290-4100, in USA 877-767-2672; www.flysansa.com) has daily flights to the Palmar airstrip. Prices vary according to season and availability, though you can expect to pay around US$100 to/from San José.

Taxis meet incoming flights and charge up to US$10 to Palmar Norte and US$15 to US$30 to Sierpe. Otherwise, the infrequent Palmar Norte–Sierpe bus goes through Palmar Sur – you can board it if there's space available.

BUS

Buses to San José and San Isidro stop on the east side of the Interamericana. Other buses leave from in front of the Pirola's Pizza and Seafood restaurant or the Tracopa window across the street. Buses to Sierpe depart from in front of the Gollo store.

Neily

POP 17,250

Although it's southern Costa Rica's second-largest 'city,' Ciudad Neily has retained the friendly atmosphere of a rural town. At just 50m above sea level, steamy Neily serves as a regional transportation hub and agricultural center, but is decidedly lacking in tourist appeal.

If you wind up stranded here, the one good option is **Hotel Andrea** (☎ 2783-3784; www.hotelandreacr.com; r with/without air-con US$50/30; P ◉ ❄ ❁).

Getting There & Away

Buses leave from **Terminal Tracopa** (☎ 2221-4214), which is attached to a *mercado* (market) with a clutch of busy *sodas*, two blocks east of Hwy 237. Destinations include the following:

Paso Canoas

POP 9550

The main port of entry between Costa Rica and Panama is hectic, slightly seedy and completely devoid of charm. Fortunately, the border crossing itself is straightforward. As you might imagine, most travelers leave Paso Canoas with little more than a passing glance at their passport stamp.

ⓘ Information

If leaving Costa Rica, you'll be charged an exit tax of $8 here ($7 for the actual exit tax, $1 'commission' because you didn't pay through a national bank before you arrived at the border). You'll pay this tax at a window across from the Migración & Aduana office.

BCR (Banco de Costa Rica; ☎ 2732-2613; ◉ 9am-4pm Mon-Sat, 9am-1pm Sun) has ATM near the Migración & Aduana office. Street vendors' rates for converting excess colones into dollars are not great. Colones are accepted at the border, but are difficult to get rid of further into Panama.

The **Autoridad de Turismo de Panamá** (☎ 507-526-7000; ◉ 8am-4pm), in the Panamanian immigration post, has basic information on travel to Panama.

ⓘ Getting There & Away

Tracopa buses leave for San José (US$17.69, 7½ hours) at 4am, 8am, 8:30am, 9am, 1pm, 4:30pm and 4:40pm. The **Tracopa bus terminal** (☎ 2732-2119; ◉ 7am-4pm), a window really, is north of the border post, on the east side of the main road. Sunday-afternoon buses are full of weekend shoppers, so buy tickets as early as possible. Buses for Neily (US$0.70, 30 minutes)

BUSES FROM NEILY

DESTINATION	COST (US$)	DURATION	FREQUENCY
Golfito	1.12	1½hr	hourly 5:20am-7:30pm
Palmar	1.16	1½hr	12 daily 4:45am-5:45pm
Paso Canoas	0.70	30min	every 30min
San Isidro	7.60	4hr	9 daily
San José	12.80	7hr	11 daily
San Vito	1.28	1½hr	4 daily 6am-5pm

leave from the **Terminal de Buses Transgolfo** at least once an hour from 5am to 6:30pm. Taxis to Neily cost about US$10.

Just across the border, buses run to David, the nearest city in Panama, from where there are onward connections to Panama City and elsewhere.

San Vito

POP 5500

Although the Italian immigrants who founded little San Vito in the 1850s are long gone, this hillside village proudly bears traces of their legacy in linguistic, cultural and culinary echoes. As such, the town serves as a base for travelers in need of a steaming plate of pasta and a good night's sleep.

The proximity of the town to the Reserva Indígena Guaymí de Coto Brus means that indigenous peoples pass through this region (groups of Ngöbe – also known as Guaymí – move back and forth across the border with Panama). You might spot women in traditional clothing – long, solid-colored *nagua* dresses trimmed in contrasting hues – riding the bus or strolling the streets.

Tucked in between the Cordillera de Talamanca and the Fila Costeña, the Valle de Coto Brus offers some glorious geography, featuring the green, rolling hills of coffee plantations backed by striking mountain facades.

◉ Sights

★ **Wilson Botanical Garden**   GARDENS
(Las Cruces Biological Station; ☑ 2773-4004; www.ots.ac.cr/lascruces; US$8, half-/full-day guided tours US$39/54; ⏱ 7am-5pm) Covering 10 hectares and surrounded by 355 hectares of natural forest, world-class Wilson Botanical Garden, established by Robert and Catherine Wilson in 1963 and thereafter becoming internationally known for its collection, lies 6km south of San Vito.

A trail map is available for self-guided walks amid exotic species such as orchids, bromeliads and medicinal plants; birdwatchers can look for rare birds here.

In 1973 the area came under the auspices of the Organization for Tropical Studies (OTS) and today the well-maintained garden – part of Las Cruces Biological Station – holds more than 1000 genera of plants from about 200 families and over 2000 native Costa Rican species. Species threatened with extinction are preserved here for possible reforestation in the future.

The botanical garden is a choice spot for birders, as it draws hundreds of Costa Rican and migrating species, as well numerous butterfly species.

If you want to stay overnight at the botanical garden, make reservations well in advance: facilities often fill with researchers. Accommodations are in comfortable cabins (singles/doubles including meals and a tour US$95/180) in the midst of the gorgeous grounds. The rooms are simple, but they each have a balcony with an amazing view.

Buses between San Vito and Neily (via Agua Buena not Cañas Gordas) pass the entrance to the garden.

Finca Cántaros   PARK
(☑ 2773-5530, 2773-3760; www.fincacantaros.com; adult/child 12-17yr $6/3; ⏱ 6:30am-5pm) About 3km south of San Vito, Finca Cántaros is a recreation center and reforestation project. Over 17 acres of grounds – formerly coffee plantations and pastureland – are now a lovely nature reserve with trails, picnic areas and a dramatic lookout over the city. Especially interesting are the pre-Columbian cemetery and a large petroglyph that was discovered on the property in 2009. Though its meaning and age are unclear, the petroglyph is estimated to be around 1600 years old.

Another point of interest, reachable by self-guided hike, is the 3000-year-old Laguna Zoncho: picnic at one of the small shelters and watch for rare birds; if birders wish to visit the *finca* before 6:30am, arrangements can be made in advance. The reserve's reception contains a small but carefully chosen selection of local and South American crafts.

Camping on the property is allowed (US$10 per person); call ahead if arriving on a Sunday.

⌂ Sleeping & Eating

★ **Casa Botania**   B&B **$$**
(☑ 8711-3008, 2773-4217; www.casabotania.com; s/d incl breakfast US$62/75; ❋ 🖂) 🌿 The freshest B&B in the region is exquisitely run by a sweet young couple. It hits every note with pitch-perfect elegance, from the modern, beautifully adorned rooms with stellar views, to the library of birdwatching guides, to the gourmet vegetarian meals served on a

deck overlooking the lush foliage of the valley below. It's 5km south of San Vito.

The three-course, locally sourced, ever-changing dinner menu includes smart Costa Rican and European-inspired fare, though you can only enjoy it as a guest. The property also contains 3 hectares of forest, with trails throughout.

Cascata del Bosco BUNGALOW $$
(☑2773-3208; www.cascatasanvito.com; campsites US$20, r from US$65; ℗⊛) The four round cabins at Cascata del Bosco overlook the forested valley below and enclose guests in tree-house-like comfort. Each cabin has a terrace, skylight, kitchenette and bamboo-and-tile interior. Several nature trails wind through the property, and the roadside restaurant is a convivial gathering spot for locals and expats, serving delicious barbecue. Located just north of Wilson Botanical Garden.

🛈 Getting There & Away

The drive north from Neily is a scenic one, with superb views of the lowlands dropping away as the road winds up the hillside. The paved road is steep, narrow and full of hairpin turns. You can also get to San Vito from San Isidro via the Valle de Coto Brus – an incredibly scenic and less used route with fantastic views of the Cordillera de Talamanca to the north and the lower Fila Costeña to the south.

BUS

The main **Tracopa bus terminal** (☑2773-3410) is about 150m down the road to Sabalito from downtown. Destinations include San Isidro (US$7, three hours, daily 6:45am and 1:30pm) and San José (US$13, seven hours, daily 5am, 7am, 7:30am, 10am and 3pm).

A local bus terminal at the northwest end of town runs buses to Neily (US$1.75, 1½ hours, eight daily) and other destinations.

Parque Internacional La Amistad

The 4070-sq-km Parque Internacional La Amistad – by far the largest protected area in Costa Rica – is an enormous patch of green sprawling across the borders of Panama and Costa Rica (hence its Spanish name La Amistad – 'Friendship'). Standing as a testament to the possibilities of international cooperation and environmental conservation, the park was established in 1982 and declared a Unesco World Heritage site in 1990. It then became part of the greater Mesoamerican Biological Corridor, which protects a great variety of endangered habitats and animals. Its cultural importance is also significant as it includes several scattered indigenous reserves.

The largest chunk of the park is high up in the Cordillera de Talamanca, and remains virtually inaccessible. There's very little tourist infrastructure within the park, although hard-core exploration of some of the country's most rugged terrain is possible with an experienced guide.

🏃 Activities

Hiking

Except for the specialized guided hikes, park visitors are pretty much limited to the two trails that leave from the Altamira Ranger Station: **Sendero Gigantes del Bosque** and **Sendero Valle del Silencio**.

Contact the association of guides, Aso-ProLA, to inquire about arrangements for guided hikes. Rates vary depending on the size of your party and your intended course.

Wildlife-Watching

Although most of Parque Internacional La Amistad is inaccessible terrain high up in the Talamanca, the park is home to a recorded 90 mammal species and more than 400 bird species. The park has the nation's largest population of Baird's tapirs, as well as giant anteaters, all six species of neotropical (and endangered) cats – jaguar, puma (mountain lion), margay, ocelot, oncilla (tiger cat) and jaguarundi – and many more common mammals.

Bird species (49 unique) that have been sighted – more than half of the total in Costa Rica – include the majestic but extremely rare harpy eagle, now feared extinct in the country. In addition, the park protects 115 species of fish, 215 different reptiles and amphibians, as well as innumerable insect species.

🛏 Sleeping & Eating

AsoProLA Lodge LODGE $
(☑8651-7324; www.asoprola.com; r incl breakfast from US$22; ℗) The AsoProLA guiding association runs a simple lodge and restaurant in the village of Altamira, and can also make arrangements for lodging in local homes in Altamira for US$18 per person, breakfast included. Homestays are a great way to get an

intimate look at the lives of people living on the fringes of the rainforest.

Altamira Ranger Station
CAMPGROUND $

(☑ 8616-1647; campsite per person US$6) The Altamira Ranger Station offers camping facilities, with drinking water, cold-water showers, toilets and electricity. All food and supplies must be packed in and out.

Heladería Biolley
ICE CREAM $

(☑ 8515-9267; ice cream US$1-3; ⊘9am-6pm) This purple-and-green, mushroom-shaped, artisanal ice-cream shop is a hilariously weird installment near the AsoProLa Lodge. The ice cream is all-natural and flavored with fruit grown nearby.

ⓘ Information

The primary jumping-off point by which visitors launch into the deepest parts of the park is the tiny mountain town of Altamira, 25km northwest of San Vito. There are three other official entrances to the park: one near Buenos Aires, one near Helechales, and one near San Vito. But Estación Altamira is the only year-round, staffed facility, and the other entrances are accessed by horrifically bad roads.

To make reservations to camp, call the park headquarters at Estación Altamira directly. This is the best-developed area of the park, with a camping area, showers, drinking water, electricity and a lookout tower.

Altamira Ranger Station (☑ 8616-1647; park fee per person per day US$10; ⊘8am-4pm) Collects entrance fees and provides information on the park.

AsoProLA (☑ 8651-7324, 8616-1647, 8621-5559; www.asoprola.com; Altamira; ⊘7am-8pm) Can arrange guided hikes within the park.

ⓘ Getting There & Away

To reach Altamira, you can take any bus that runs between San Isidro and San Vito and get off in the town of Guácimo (often called Las Tablas). From Guácimo buses generally depart at 1pm and 5pm for El Carmen; if the road conditions permit, they continue 4km to the village of Altamira. From the village of Altamira, follow the Minae sign (near the church) leading to the steep 2km hike to the ranger station.

It's considerably more convenient to explore the area by 4WD rather than with public transportation; the roads are rough and bumpy and the buses are not hugely reliable. The turnoff for the park is signposted after the town of Guácimo if you're driving from San Vito. The park entrance at Altamira is 21km (around an hour's drive) along the unpaved, bone-jarring road from Hwy 237.

TO CORCOVADO VIA BAHÍA DRAKE

On the western side of the Península de Osa, the Bahía Drake route is one of two principal ways to reach Parque Nacional Corcovado. The route starts in the town of Sierpe in the Valle de Diquís, at the northern base of the peninsula, from where the Río Sierpe flows out to Bahía Drake. Most travelers opt for the exhilarating boat ride through the mangroves between Sierpe, Drake and Corcovado, with a potential detour via the Humedal Nacional Térraba-Sierpe. Alternatively, there's a rough road to Drake via the former gold-mining settlement of Rancho Quemado, which allows for a spot of *agroturismo* along the way. Either way, the Bahía Drake route offers a chance to experience rural Tico life and also a greater share of creature comforts in the many wilderness lodges.

Sierpe
POP 4000

This sleepy village on the Río Sierpe is the gateway to Bahía Drake, and if you've made a reservation with any of the jungle lodges further down the coast, you will be picked up here by boat. Beyond its function as a transit point, there is little reason to spend any more time here than necessary, though it's well worth taking a peek at one of the celebrated pre-Columbian stone spheres in the main square. If you're visiting the excellent Sitio Arqueológico Finca 6 near Sierpe, you can stop here for lunch. Mangrove cruises can also be arranged in town.

⌴ Sleeping

Veragua River House
B&B $$

(☑ 2788-1460; www.hotelveragua.com/en; s/d incl breakfast US$50/60; ❐✳❖) Run by an accommodating Italian-Tico couple, this memorable B&B is set on a pair of riverside gardens lovingly planted with fruit trees and tropical flowers. Guests stay in the four garden bungalows, built in a uniquely Costa Rican Victorian architectural style. The B&B is located 3km north of Sierpe. Lunch and dinner (US$15 to US$20) are also available with prior notice.

Hotel Oleaje Sereno
HOTEL $$

(☑ 2788-1111; s/d incl breakfast from US$30/50; ❐✳❖) This motel overlooking the Río

WORTH A TRIP

SIERPE SPHERES

The Diquís Delta is believed to have been the most developed and historically significant part of Costa Rica, heavily populated in pre-Columbian times and playing an important role as a trading post between the other important cultures in Latin America (the Incas to the south and the Maya to the north) – jade and gold artifacts found in the delta and created elsewhere suggest that this was so. But while other pre-Columbian cultures left behind vast pyramid-like monuments, unparalleled stonework and sophisticated languages, the Diquís left behind immense stone spheres and little else.

It is known that the civilization invested great efforts in their creation (over 300 spheres have been found in the Diquís Delta), crafting them out of sandstone, limestone, gabbro and granodiorite from the Costeña coastal range using nothing but stone tools, and transporting them great distances, including over water (some have been found on Isla del Caño). Their function remains unclear, though theories suggest that those spheres found in sets or alignments may represent celestial phenomena or function as solar calendars, while others have been interpreted as territorial markers or symbols of an individual's power (the bigger the sphere, the more powerful the individual). Spheres range from a few centimeters to 2.54m in diameter; the largest and heaviest found at the El Silencio site weighs a staggering 24 tons. Smaller spheres have been found in some graves, presumed to be of particularly important chiefs.

In 2014 the Diquís spheres were included on Unesco's list of World Heritage sites, and efforts are under way to excavate other significant sites in the Diquís Delta and to educate both visitors and the local population about the region's unique history. Communities also hope that this Unesco endorsement will bring more tourism to the Delta and revitalize the area.

While a number of spheres were whisked away from the area in the past to be used as decorative elements in people's gardens, and the most important archaeological finds grace San José museums, there are a few excellent examples of these spheres that can easily be seen in parks in Palmar Sur and Sierpe.

Sitio Arqueológico Finca 6 (☑ 2100-6000; finca6@museocostarica.go.cr; 4km north of Sierpe; US$6; ⊙ 8am-4pm Tue-Sun) offers the best opportunity to view these mysterious spheres, and the onsite museum screens a good video on the spheres' significance and purpose. The site on which the Finca 6 museum is located is thought to have been a large settlement in pre-Columbian times, with trade links throughout the region.

Sierpe has rather unloved, dusty rooms with wooden floors, sturdy furniture and a restaurant popular with boat-catching gringos. Wi-fi comes and goes like a stray cat.

ℹ Information

La Perla del Sur (☑ 2788-1082; info@perla delsur.net; ⊙ 6am-10pm; 🕾) This info center and open-air restaurant next to the boat dock is the hub of Sierpe – arrange your long-term parking (US$6 per night), book a tour and take advantage of the free wi-fi before catching your boat to Drake.

ℹ Getting There & Away

Scheduled flights and charters fly into Palmar Sur, 14km north of Sierpe. If you are heading to Bahía Drake, most upmarket lodges will arrange the boat transfer. Should things go awry or if you're traveling independently, there's no shortage of water taxis milling about – be prepared to negotiate a fair price. Regularly scheduled *colectivo* (shared) boats depart Sierpe for Drake at 11:30am (US$15) and 4:30pm (US$20).

Buses to Palmar Norte (US$0.70, 40 minutes) depart from in front of Pulpería Fenix at 5:30am, 8:30am, 10:30am, 12:30pm, 3:30pm and 6pm. A shared taxi to Palmar costs about US$10 per person.

Humedal Nacional Térraba-Sierpe

The Ríos Térraba and Sierpe begin on the southern slopes of the Talamanca mountains and, nearing the Pacific Ocean, they form a network of channels and waterways that weave around the country's largest mangrove swamp. This river delta comprises the Humedal Nacional Térraba-Sierpe, which protects approximately 330 sq km of wetland and is home to red, black and tea mangrove species. The reserve also protects a plethora of birdlife, especially waterbirds such as herons, egrets and cormorants, and larger denizens of the murky waters and tangled vegetation such as caimans and boas. An exploration of this watery world by boat gives you a unique insight into this very special and fragile ecosystem.

ℹ Information

The Térraba-Sierpe reserve has no facilities for visitors, though lodges and tour companies can organize tours to help you explore the wetlands. Bahía Aventuras (p398) in Uvita offers half-day boat trips (US$85 per person) in the mangroves, as does Corcovado Expeditions (p429) in Bahía Drake (US$110 per person).

Bahía Drake

POP 1000

One of Costa Rica's most isolated destinations, Bahía Drake (drah-kay) is a veritable Lost World, bordered by Parque Nacional Corcovado to the south. In the rainforest canopy, howler monkeys greet the rising sun with their haunting bellows, while pairs of macaws soar between the treetops, filling the air with their cacophonous squawking. Offshore in the bay, pods of migrating dolphins glide through turquoise waters near the beautiful Isla del Caño marine reserve.

One of the reasons why Bahía Drake is brimming with wildlife is that it remains largely cut off from the rest of the country. Life is centered around the sedate village of Agujitas, the area's transport hub, which attracts increasing numbers of backpackers and nature lovers with inexpensive digs and plenty of snorkeling, diving and wildlife-watching opportunities. The more remote corners of Bahía Drake are home to some of Costa Rica's best (and priciest) wilderness lodges.

🏃 Activities

Canoeing & Kayaking

Río Agujitas   KAYAKING

The idyllic Río Agujitas attracts a huge variety of birdlife and lots of reptiles. The river conveniently empties out into the bay, which is surrounded by hidden coves and sandy beaches ideal for exploring in a sea kayak, best done at high tide. Some accommodations have kayaks and canoes for rent; or else kayaks can be rented along Agujitas beach (around US$15 per hour).

Hiking & Wildlife-Watching

All of the lodges and most tour companies offer tours to Parque Nacional Corcovado, usually a full-day trip to San Pedrillo or Sirena Ranger Stations (from US$85 to US$150 per person), including boat transportation, lunch and guided hikes.

Some travelers, however, come away from these tours disappointed, particularly with boating into Sirena, which takes quite a while and can be treacherous if the sea is rough. In addition, the trails around Sirena attract many groups of people, which inhibit animal sightings, and because most tours arrive at the park well after sunrise, activity in the rainforest has already quieted down. Overnighting in the park is a better bet if you have your heart set on seeing wildlife.

All park visitors are now required to be accompanied by a guide certified by the ICosta Rican Tourism Board (ICT): exploring the beaches and jungles with an eagle-eyed guide will reveal much more than you would likely discover on your own. One of the best in the area is **Everest Cerdas** (📞8584-5199; www.ontourwitheverest.com; 1/2 nights per person from US$300/580).

If you'd prefer to hike independently, the easiest and most obvious route is the 17km coastal trail from Agujitas to San Pedrillo (p433). A determined, reasonably fit hiker could make it all the way to San Pedrillo Ranger Station in six to seven hours (though visitors intending to enter or spend the night in the park must have secured reservations in advance and be accompanied by a guide). An alternative is getting a tour company to drop you off by boat near San Pedrillo and then hiking back to Agujitas; remember that sunset descends swiftly at around 5:30pm. You don't have to hike the entire trail – there are plenty of beaches along the way.

👉 Tours

Adventure

Original Canopy Tour   TOURS

(📞8371-1598, 2291-4465; www.jinetesdeosa.com/ canopy_tour.htm; US$35; ⊗8am-4pm) At Hotel Jinetes de Osa, the Original Canopy Tour has nine platforms, six cables and one 20m observation deck from where you can get a new perspective on the rainforest. Tours take two to three hours.

Birding & Wildlife-Watching

With almost 400 species recorded in the area, Bahía Drake and nearby Corcovado are hands down the best places to spot Costa Rica's Pacific lowland rainforest species, including such feathered beauties as scarlet macaws, chestnut-mandibled toucans, honeycreepers, hawk-eagles and the black-cheeked ant tanager (endemic to the Península de Osa). All upscale lodges organize birding walks, as do the bay's independent tour operators and specialist birding guides.

★ Pacheco Tours   WILDLIFE

(☎ 8906-2002; www.pachecotours.com) Very competent all-rounder organizing snorkeling tours to Isla del Caño, day trips to Corcovado, daylong tours combining jungle trekking with waterfall swimming (US$65), and whale-watching excursions.

★ Tracie the Bug Lady   WILDLIFE

(☎ 8701-7462, 8701-7356; www.thenighttour.com; tours per person US$40; ⊙ 7:30-10:15pm) Tracie the 'Bug Lady' has created quite a name for

Bahía Drake & Around

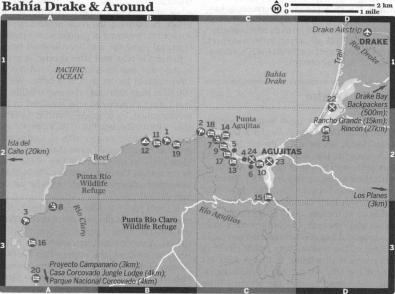

Southern Costa Rica & Península de Osa Bahía Drake

Bahía Drake & Around

herself with this fascinating nighttime walk in the jungle that takes in bugs, reptiles and birds. Tracie is a walking encyclopedia on bug facts – one of her fields of research is the military use of insects! Her naturalist-photographer husband Gian also leads the night tours; reserve in advance.

Corcovado Info Center WILDLIFE
(☑ 2775-0916, 8846-4734; www.corcovadoinfo-center.com; whale-watching/Corcovado day tours US$110/90) Leading tours into Corcovado and Isla del Caño, all guides with this outfit are local, bilingual and ICT-certified. They're at the beach end of the main road in Agujitas.

Corcovado Expeditions TOURS
(☑ 2775-0916, 8846-4734; www.corcovadoexpeditions.net; tours US$45-85) Offers competitively priced tours to Corcovado and Isla del Caño, as well as a wide variety of specialty hikes including unique excursions to look for rare tropical birds and poison-dart frogs. The office is located between the clinic and the school.

Dolphin- and Whale-Watching

Bahía Drake is rife with marine life, including more than 20 species of dolphin and whale that pass through on their migrations throughout the year. This area is uniquely suited for whale-watching: humpback whales come from both the northern and the southern hemispheres to calve, resulting in the longest humpback-whale season in the world. Humpbacks can be spotted in Bahía Drake from December to March, and then from July until October.

Several of the lodges are involved with programs that protect and preserve marine life in Bahía Drake, and offer tourists a chance for a close encounter, as do independent, knowledgeable operators in Agujitas. Tours generally start at about US$100 per person.

Diving

About 20km west of Agujitas, Isla del Caño is one of Costa Rica's top spots for diving, with attractions including intricate rock and coral formations and an amazing array of underwater life. Divers report that the schools of fish swimming overhead are often so dense that they block the sunlight from filtering down. Lodges offer day trips to the island (from US$80 per person), usually in-

WORTH A TRIP

RESERVA BIOLÓGICO ISLA DEL CAÑO

The centerpiece of **Reserva Biológica Isla del Caño** (US$10, diving charge US$4) is a 326-hectare island – the tip of numerous underwater rock formations. Some 15 different species of coral are here, as well as threatened species including the Panulirus lobster and giant conch. The sheer numbers of fish attract dolphins and whales, as well as hammerhead sharks, manta rays and sea turtles.

cluding the park fee, snorkeling equipment and lunch on Playa San Josecito. The clarity of the ocean and the variety of the fish fluctuate according to water and weather conditions: it's worth inquiring before booking.

A two-tank dive runs from US$110 to US$150 depending on the site. Several upscale lodges have onsite dive centers, and there are several dive centers in Agujitas.

Bajo del Diablo DIVING
(Devil's Rock) While Bahía Drake is rich with dive sites, a local highlight is undoubtedly the Bajo del Diablo, an astonishing formation of submerged mountains that attracts an incredible variety of fish species, including jack, snapper, barracuda, puffer, parrotfish, moray eel and shark.

Osa Divers DIVING
(☑ 8994-9309; www.osadivers.com) Competitively priced, recommended diving outfit whisking divers (and snorkelers) off for underwater adventures around Isla del Caño. Snorkeling tours cost US$80; two-/three-tank dives are US$120/160. Equipment could be newer, though, and the dive masters don't have too much patience with novices.

🛏 Sleeping

Agujitas has an ever-growing number of budget and midrange options, though Bahía Drake accommodations are skewed toward the top end. This area is off the grid, so a few places do not have 24/7 electricity. Reservations are recommended in the dry season (mid-December to mid-April).

SOUTHERN COSTA RICA & PENÍNSULA DE OSA BAHÍA DRAKE

For more accommodations check out the stretch of coastline from Bahía Drake to Corcovado.

★ Martina's Place
GUESTHOUSE $

(⌨ 8720-0801; www.puravidadrakebay.com; dm/s/d from US$14/30/40; 🛜) With a few fan-cooled dorms and rooms with air-con, this budget spot also provides access to a clean, thoroughly equipped communal kitchen and a friendly and economical place to lay your head in the middle of Agujitas. It's also an excellent spot to meet other travelers, tap into Martina's wealth of Corcovado intel and arrange a variety of local tours.

Drake Bay Backpackers
HOSTEL $

(⌨ 2775-0726, 8981-5519; www.drakebaybackpackers.com; campsite per person US$5, dm/r from US$15/40; P ✳ 🛜) This excellent nonprofit, off-the-beaten-track hostel is a boon for budget travelers wanting to connect with the local community. Competitively priced local tours can be arranged, there's a nice hangout area and a BBQ patio. It's in the village of El Progreso, near the airstrip, straight after the river crossing.

★ Finca Maresia
BUNGALOW $$

(⌨ 8888-1625, 2775-0279; www.fincamaresia.com; Camino a Los Planes; incl breakfast s US$35-85, d US$45-100) The globe-trotting owners have created this absolute gem of a *finca* hotel that stretches across a series of hills. Budget travelers are drawn by the excellent value-to-price ratio and superb wildlife-watching opportunities. All rooms and the open-air communal area are exposed to an audio track of jungle sounds, and manager Juan is a phenomenal host.

Sunset Lodge
CABIN $$

(⌨ 2775-9068; cabin incl breakfast US$85; P) Comprising just two wooden cabins up a punishingly steep flight of steps on the hillside, this newish spot is run by a young, enthusiastic Tico owner whose family were some of the original pioneers who came to settle in Bahía Drake. The views of said bay from the terraces are absolutely stellar and we're assured that wi-fi is coming.

Casita Corcovado
B&B $$

(⌨ 8996-8987, 2775-0627; www.casitacorcovado.com; r incl breakfast from US$85; ☺ ✳ 🛜) Jamie and Craig's lovely little ocean-facing home has three rooms, all sharing a bathroom and with comfortable orthopedic beds. Guests have access to two breezy patios and plenty of hammocks, with the amenities of the village at the doorstep, but it's the warmth and helpfulness of your hosts that sets this place apart. Delicious, home-cooked meals are also available.

If you rent the whole house, children of all ages are welcome. If you go for the B&B option, day care is available on request.

★ Drake Bay Getaway Resort
BOUTIQUE HOTEL $$$

(⌨ 6003-7253; www.drakebaygetaway.com; r US$540-880; P 🛜) 🦋 The five luxurious cabins in this glorious bluff-top location catch the breeze and expansive views of Drake Bay from private decks. The chef uses organic produce from the property's gardens to serve each guest individually crafted dishes, never repeating himself once during your stay. The service is wonderfully attentive and a full range of tours of the area is available.

Aguila de Osa
LODGE $$$

(⌨ 2296-2190, in USA 866-924-8452; www.aguiladeosa.com; s/d 3-night package incl all meals per person from US$1243; P ✳ 🛜) On the east side of the Río Agujitas, this swanky lodge offers spacious rooms with cathedral ceilings and private decks with expansive ocean views. Diving and sportfishing charters are available to guests, and the dedicated staff and knowledgeable wildlife guides are the icing on the cake. Rates include an Isla del Caño tour and a Corcovado tour.

The hotel restaurant offers delicious, four-course meals (US$45 per person) that make use of fresh fruits and veggies from the property's hydroponic garden.

Drake Bay Wilderness Resort
CABIN $$$

(⌨ 2775-1716; www.drakebay.com; 4-day package per person US$865; ✳ 🛜 ⛱) Sitting pretty on Punta Agujitas, Drake's oldest resort comprises comfortable cabins with mural-painted walls and ocean-view terraces, more functional than luxurious. Naturalists will be won over by the lovely landscaping, from flowering trees to the rocky oceanfront out-croppings, while history buffs will appreciate the memorial to Drake's landing. The views are terrific but some guests have been underwhelmed by the food.

La Paloma Lodge
LODGE $$$

(⌨ 2775-1684, 2293-7502; www.lapalomalodge.com; 3-/4-/5-day package per person from US$1085/1350/1620; ✳ 🛜 ⛱) This hillside lodge provides guests with an incredible panorama of ocean and forest, all from the comfort of the sumptuous, stylish quarters. Rooms feature queen-sized orthopedic beds and ocean-view balconies, while shoulder-high walls in the bathrooms offer rainforest views. Popular with vacationing families. Three-day minimum; rates include a tour to both Isla del Caño and Corcovado.

Hotel Jinetes de Osa HOTEL **$$$**
(☑ 8996-6161, in USA 866-553-7073; www.jinetes deosa.com; s/d from US$103/110, ste US$180, all incl breakfast; ☎) Ideal for divers, the reasonably priced Jinetes de Osa boasts a choice bayside location that is literally steps from the ocean. Jinetes also has a canopy tour, as well as one of the peninsula's top Professional Association of Diving Instructors (PADI) dive facilities. Just outside of Agujitas, this sweet collection of rooms strikes the perfect balance between village and jungle.

✗ Eating

⭐ **Heladería Popis** ICE CREAM **$**
(⊙ 1-9pm) In hot and dusty Bahía Drake, there isn't a more refreshing or perfect midday treat than a vanilla milkshake from this incredible ice-cream parlor. It also does banana splits, coffee and ice cappuccinos.

⭐ **Drake's Kitchen** COSTA RICAN **$**
(Casa el Tortugo; ☑ 2775-1405, 6161-3193; mains from US$7; ⊙ noon-9pm; ℗) Excellent, small local restaurant along the main dirt road from Agujitas to the airstrip. The casados (set meals), such as catch of the day with fried plantains and avocado, are clearly prepared by a capable and passionate chef, the fresh juices are stellar and the ambience mellow.

Soda Mar y Bosque COSTA RICAN **$**
(☑ 6015-4981, 5002-7554; mains US$5-16; ⊙ 5:30am-9pm; ☎) This restaurant up the hill in Agujitas serves typical Tico cuisine and an array of desserts; it even has free wi-fi. From the spacious terrace and a recently added upstairs seating area, it's possible to catch a cool breeze and spot pairs of scarlet macaws coasting over the sea.

Los Coquitos SEAFOOD **$$**
(☑ 2775-9049; mains US$12-18; ⊙ 10am-9pm) Just off the beach on a covered terrace, this delicious restaurant serves up the freshest fish around. The red snapper and marlin

get high marks from travelers, as do the typical Costa Rican *casado* plates, which come with a meat (beef, chicken or fish), beans, rice and a surprisingly tasty salad. Friendly service, too.

❶ Getting There & Away

AIR
Departing from San José, **NatureAir** (☑ 2735-5062; www.natureair.com) and **Sansa** (☑ 2290-4100, in USA 877-767-2672; www.flysansa.com) have daily flights to the Drake airstrip, which is 2km north of Agujitas. Prices vary according to season and availability, though you can expect to pay around US$80 to US$120 one way.

Alfa Romeo Aero Taxi (☑ 8632-8150; www.alfaromeoair.com) offers charter flights connecting Drake to Puerto Jiménez (US$430), Carate (US$450) and Sirena (US$420). Flights are best booked at the airport in person; if there are several of you, one-way fares can be less than US$100.

Most lodges provide transportation to/from the airport or Sierpe, which involves a jeep or a boat or both, but advance reservation is necessary.

BOAT
An exhilarating boat ride from Sierpe is one of the true thrills of visiting the area. Boats travel along the river through the rainforest and the mangrove estuary. Captains then pilot boats through tidal currents and surf the river mouth into the ocean. All of the hotels offer boat transfers between Sierpe and Bahía Drake with prior arrangements. Most hotels in Drake have beach landings, so wear appropriate footwear.

If you have not made advance arrangements with your lodge for a pickup, two *colectivo* boats depart daily from Sierpe at 11:30am and 4:30pm, and from Bahía Drake back to Sierpe at 7:15am (US$15) and 2:30pm (US$20).

BUS

A bus to La Palma (where you can connect to a bus to Puerto Jiménez) picks passengers up along the beach road and in front of the supermarkets at around 8am and 1:30pm (US$10, two hours). The return journey from La Palma is at 11am and 4:30pm. Double-check departure times locally.

CAR

Rincón, on the main road between Puerto Jiménez and the Interamericana, is linked to Agujitas in Bahía Drake by a decent dirt road, although a 4WD is absolutely necessary for this route, which can be impassable during the rainy season as there are several river crossings. The most hazardous crossing is the Río Drake – locals fish many a water-logged vehicle out of the river. Even high-clearance 4WD vehicles have difficulty after it's been raining. If in doubt, wait until a local car appears, watch where it crosses and follow its lead. The construction of a bridge has been approved, but it may be some years yet until it's actually built.

Between Rincón and Rancho Quemado there's also a very narrow bridge with no safety railings; proceed with caution.

Fill up your tank before driving to Drake; there is no gas station here, though in a pinch you can buy some pricey gas at the supermarket.

Once in Agujitas, you will likely have to abandon your car as most places are accessible only by boat or by foot. Park your car in a secure place, such as a guesthouse. There are several small supermarkets where the management will be happy to watch over your 4WD for a nice tip.

Rancho Quemado

POP 200

For much of its existence, this small village, founded by gold miners in the 1940s some 15km east of Bahía Drake, has relied on farming and cattle raising for its existence, especially when gold mining dried up and became illegal, though some gold-panning still goes on in the nearby rivers. As production prices fell, bringing unemployment and associated problems – poaching, illegal deforestation – the community began to look at rural tourism as an alternative means of making a living, and for protecting the natural environment at the same time. Part of the Caminos de Osa project, these locals enthusiastically welcome visitors, who come here to learn about gold-panning and farming, or to just enjoy some terrific rural hospitality and hearty Tico food, en route to or from Bahía Drake.

⊙ Sights

Trapiche Don Carmen FARM
(☑ 8455-9742; tours per person US$25) Johnny and his family show visitors around their sugarcane mill. You get to see (and taste) the fresh sugarcane juice when the stalks pass through the grinder, watch Johnny boil the juice and cool it down in special molds, and then behold the finished product – delicious cane sugar.

☞ Tours

Finca Las Minas de Oro CULTURAL
(☑ 8621-6531; adult/child under 12yr US$25/12) A two-hour tour at this farm brings visitors to a creek where they are shown how to pan for gold, and they get to try their luck at this time-honored profession. The lunch here, consisting of fresh, typical Costa Rican cuisine served atop grape leaves, is enormous and outstanding.

🛏 Sleeping & Eating

Rancho Verde CABIN $
(☑ 8646-5431; per person US$25) Right by the road winding through Rancho Quemado, this welcoming little place has a couple of tidy guest cabins, and the friendly proprietor cooks up monumental portions of grilled pork or fish with rice, beans and plantains (meals US$10). Discounts are available for groups and volunteers.

Soda Edward COSTA RICAN $
(meals US$6; ⊙ hours vary, call ahead) In central Rancho Quemado, across from the soccer field, this typical *soda* cooks up ample helpings of Tico standards.

ℹ Information

If you want to book any activities or lodgings in Rancho Quemado in advance, it's best to call either Jessica (Spanish only), Katie (English and Spanish) or Alice (English and Spanish) from **Rancho Quemado information** (☑ Alice 8646-5431, Jessica 8667-2535, Katie 8504-1606; www.visitranchoquemado.com) to make arrangements.

ℹ Getting There & Away

Twice-daily buses leave La Palma for Rancho Quemado and Bahía Drake at 11:30am and 4:30pm Monday to Saturday (US$4, one hour). Low-season buses can run less frequently. If you're driving, you'll need a 4WD to get here as there are a couple of shallow rivers to cross.

Bahía Drake to Corcovado

This craggy stretch of coastline is home to sandy inlets that disappear at high tide, leaving only the rocky outcroppings and luxuriant rainforest. Virtually uninhabited and undeveloped beyond a few tourist lodges, the setting here is magnificent and wild. If you're looking to spend a bit more time along the shores of Bahía Drake before penetrating the depths of Parque Nacional Corcovado, consider a night or two in some of the country's most remote accommodations, with plenty of wildlife sightings in the surrounding jungle.

The only way to get around the area is by boat or by foot, which means that travelers are more or less dependent on their lodges unless they're close to Agujitas.

◎ Sights

Playa Cocalito   BEACH
Just west of Punta Agujitas, a short detour off the main trail leads to the picturesque Playa Cocalito, a secluded cove perfect for sunning, swimming and body surfing.

Playa Caletas   BEACH
A recommended spot for snorkeling, situated in front of Las Caletas Lodge.

Playa San Josecito   BEACH
South of Río Claro, Playa San Josecito is the longest stretch of white-sand beach on this side of the Península de Osa. It is popular with swimmers, snorkelers and sunbathers, though you'll only find it crowded at lunchtime since it's the favorite post-snorkeling picnic spot for tour companies coming back from Isla del Caño. Watch out for capuchin monkeys!

⚡ Activities

★ Agujitas–Corcovado Trail   HIKING
This 17km public trail follows the coastline from Agujitas to the San Pedrillo Ranger Station for the entire spectacular stretch, and it's excellent for wildlife-spotting (particularly early in the morning), beach-hopping and canoe tours with Río Claro Tours. Tour operators can drop you off by boat at a point of your choosing and you can walk back to Agujitas.

★ Río Claro Tours   CANOEING
(☑ 8931-1345; 1/2/3hr tour per person US$20/30/40) A 20-minute hike toward Agu-

jitas from Playa San Josecito, a hermit called Ricardo ('Clavito') lives by the Río Claro and runs hugely entertaining canoeing tours that start with a rope-swing plunge and continue to some waterfalls with refreshing plunge pools. Various tour operators can drop you off by boat, leaving you to walk back to Agujitas afterward.

⌂ Sleeping

Reservations are recommended in the dry season (mid-December to mid-April). Some places in this area don't have 24-hour electricity (pack a flashlight) or hot water.

With prior arrangements, accommodations provide transportation (free or for a charge) from Agujitas, Sierpe or the airstrip in Drake.

Life for Life Hostel   HOSTEL $
(☑ 4702-7209; http://hostelindrake.com; Playa San Josecito; dm or tent incl breakfast/full board US$20/50) This new hostel and turtle-conversation project is beachfront, jungle-shrouded and beloved by travelers for the relaxed atmosphere, home-cooked meals and proximity to local wildlife. The activity of choice is relaxing in a hammock as exotic birds and monkeys stop by, though hanging at the beach, hiking and visiting waterfalls are also popular.

Dorms are basic but adequate, and there's no wi-fi whatsoever, which is pretty fantastic.

Turtle-project volunteers are accepted to excavate nests, rebury eggs, input data, patrol the beach, do hatchery maintenance and participate in turtle releases. Those who stay more than five days pay just US$25 per night for a room and full board.

★ Las Caletas Lodge   LODGE $$
(☑ 8863-9631, 8826-1460, 2560-6602; www. caletas.cr; Playa Caletas; tent/r per person from US$80/95; ◉ 🏠) 🍃 This adorable lodge consists of cozy wooden cabins and safari tents perched above the picturesque beach of the same name. The expat and local owners are warm hosts who established this convivial spot before there was phone access or electricity (now mostly solar- and hydro-powered). The food is delicious and bountiful, the staff friendly and the environment beautifully chill.

Some of the rooms are geared toward families and there's a 50% discount for four- to 11-year-olds. Wi-fi exists but it can be sluggish.

★**Proyecto Campanario** CAMPGROUND $$$
(📞 2289-8694, 2289-8708; www.campanario.org; 4-day package per person US$511, minimum 2 people) 🏊 This biological reserve is an education center rather than a tourist facility, aimed at those wanting to learn about the importance of various tropical ecosystems, as evidenced by the dormitory, library and field station. Ecology courses and conservation camps are scheduled throughout the year, attracting individuals passionate about these issues, from university students and field biologists to concerned tourists.

★**Casa Corcovado Jungle Lodge** LODGE $$$
(📞 2256-3181, in USA 888-896-6097; www.casacorcovado.com; 4-day package adult/child from US$1680/1115; 🛜🏊) 🏊 A spine-tingling boat ride takes you to this luxurious lodge on 175 hectares of rainforest bordering Parque Nacional Corcovado . Each bungalow is tucked away in its own private tropical garden, and artistic details include antique Mexican tiles and handmade stained-glass windows. Guests can stretch their legs on the lodge's extensive network of trails, which pass a number of watering holes.

Onsite, the Margarita Sunset Bar lives up to its name, serving up frosty margaritas and great sunset views over the Pacific. Discounts are available for longer stays.

Copa de Arbol LODGE $$$
(📞 8935-1212, in the USA 831-246-4265; www.copadearbol.com; Playa Caletas; s/d from US$380/600; ❄🛜🏊) Though they look a bit rustic from the outside with their thatch roofs and stilts, these 10 hillside *cabinas* are gorgeously outfitted inside – built with sustainably grown wood and recycled materials, and each with private terraces overlooking the sea. Steps from the beach, the lodge offers laid-back luxury and a top-notch infinity pool. Paddleboards and kayaks are free for guests.

Guaria de Osa LODGE $$$
(📞 2235-4313, in USA 510-235-4313; www.guariadeosa.com; r per person incl full board from US$150; 🛜) Cultivating a New Age ambience, this Asian-style retreat center offers yoga, tai chi and 'Sentient Experiential' events, along with the more typical rainforest activities. The lovely grounds include an ethnobotanical garden, which features exotic local species. The architecture of this place is unique: the centerpiece is the Lapa Lapa Lounge, a spacious multistory pagoda built entirely from reclaimed hardwood. Three-night minimum.

Corcovado Adventures Tent Camp CAMPGROUND $$$
(📞 8386-2296, in USA 866-498-0824; www.corcovado.com; 2-day package per person from US$299; 🛜) Less than an hour's walk from Agujitas brings you to this rugged spot run by long-time expat Larry. Spacious safari tents with beds are set up on covered platforms, 20 hectares of rainforest offer plenty of opportunity for exploration, and the beachfront setting is excellent for kayaking, snorkeling and bodyboarding (equipment use is free). Backpacker digs are in the works.

Parque Nacional Corcovado

This national park takes up 40% of the Península de Osa and is the last great original tract of tropical rainforest in Pacific Central America. The bastion of biological diversity is home to *half* of Costa Rica's species, including the largest population of scarlet macaws, as well as countless other endangered species, including Baird's tapir, the giant anteater and the world's largest bird of prey, the harpy eagle.

Corcovado's amazing biodiversity as well as the park's demanding, multiday hiking trails have long attracted a devoted stream of visitors who descend from Bahía Drake and Puerto Jiménez to see the wildlife and experience a bona fide jungle adventure.

🏃 Activities

Hiking
There are three main trails in the park that are open to visitors, as well as shorter trails around the ranger stations. Trails are primitive and the hiking is hot, humid and insect-ridden, but the challenge of the trek and the interaction with wildlife at Corcovado are thrilling. Carry plenty of food, water and insect repellent.

One trail traverses the park from Los Patos to Sirena, then exits the park at La Leona (or vice versa). This allows hikers to begin and end their journey in or near Puerto

POISON DARTS & HARMLESS ROCKETS

Traversed by many streams and rivers, Corcovado is a hot spot for exquisitely beautiful poison-dart frogs. Two species here, the granular poison-dart frog and the Golfo Dulce poison-dart frog, are Costa Rican endemics – the latter only occurs in and around Corcovado. A search of the leaf litter near Sirena Ranger Station readily turns up both species, as well as the more widespread green and black poison-dart frog.

You might also find some other members of the family that have one important difference: they're not poisonous! Called rocket frogs because of their habit of launching themselves into streams when disturbed, they are essentially poison-dart frogs without the poisonous punch.

The difference is likely in their diets. Poison-dart frogs have a diet dominated by ants, which are rich in alkaloids, and are thought to give rise to their formidable defenses. Rocket frogs also eat ants but in lower quantities, and rely instead on their astounding leaps to escape predators. They also lack the dazzling warning colors of their toxic cousins.

Costa Rica's poison-dart frogs are not dangerous to humans unless their toxins come into contact with a person's bloodstream or mucous membranes. It's probably best to admire their cautionary colors without touching.

Jiménez, offering easy access to La Leona and Los Patos.

The most popular trail, however, is still La Leona to Sirena, with an additional trail section running parallel to the beach trail for those who don't want to expose themselves to the relentless sun. The toughest day trek is from La Tarde to Sirena via Los Patos – a whopping 30km.

An El Tigre trail loop has been added that starts in Dos Brazos and dips into the park but doesn't join up with the rest of the trail network; you still have to pay the full park fee to hike it, though.

Hiking is best in the dry season (from December to April), when there is still regular rain but all of the trails are open. It remains muddy, but you won't sink quite as deep.

La Leona to Sirena   HIKING
The largely flat 16km hike (five to seven hours) follows the shoreline through coastal forest and along deserted beaches. Take plenty of water, a hat and sunscreen. It involves one major river crossing at Río Claro, just south of Sirena, and there's an excellent chance of seeing monkeys, tapirs and scarlet macaws en route. La Leona is an additional 3.5km to Carate.

A trail running parallel to this trail allows you to avoid the sizzling tramp along the beach.

Sirena to Los Patos   HIKING
This trail goes 18km through the heart of Corcovado, passing through primary and secondary forest, and is relatively flat for the first 12km. After you wade through two river tributaries before reaching the Laguna Corcovado, the route undulates steeply (mostly uphill!) for the remaining 6km. It's less punishing to do this trek in the opposite direction.

The largest herds of peccaries are reportedly on this trail. Local guides advise that peccaries sense fear, but they will back off if you act aggressively. Alternatively, if you climb up a tree – about 2m off the ground – you'll avoid being bitten or trampled in the event of running into a surly bunch. Fun fact: peccary herds emit a strong smell of onions, so you usually have a bit of a heads-up before they come crashing through the bush.

La Tarde to Los Patos   HIKING
This 5km hike starts outside the Corcovado park boundary, and consists of fairly steep downhills through dense secondary forest, where you're likely to see different monkey species, numerous birds and the Golfo Dulce poison-dart frog, endemic to Costa Rica. A little way past Los Patos Ranger Station there's an enticing waterfall with a deep pool to swim in.

Sendero El Tigre   HIKING
Part of this 8km loop trail passes through Parque Nacional Corcovado, so a guide is mandatory. It's a fairly rugged trail, part of which passes through an ancient indigenous burial ground; be prepared to spend the best

Hiking in Parque Nacional Corcovado

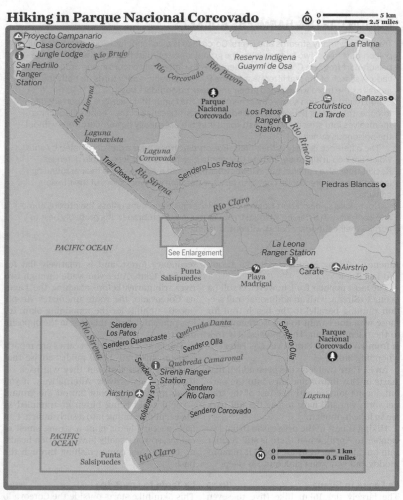

part of a day hiking it. It's doable as a day trip yet gives you a good taste of the park.

Wildlife-Watching

Corcovado is home to a staggering 370 species of bird, 140 species of mammals and thousands of insect species, with more still waiting to be discovered. The best wildlife-watching in Corcovado is around Sirena, but the coastal trails have two advantages: they are more open, and the constant crashing of waves covers the sound of noisy walkers. This can allow up-close encounters with the likes of the white-faced capuchin

monkey, red-tailed squirrel, collared peccary, white-nosed coati, tapir and northern tamandua.

The coastal trail from Carate to Sirena produces an endless pageant of birds. Sightings of scarlet macaws are guaranteed, as the tropical almond trees lining the coast are a favorite food. The sections along the beach shelter mangrove black hawks by the dozens and numerous waterbird species.

The Los Patos–Sirena trail attracts lowland rainforest birds such as great curassows, chestnut-mandibled toucans, fiery-billed aracaris and rufous pihas. Encounters with mixed flocks are common. Mammals are similar to those near coastal trails, but Los Patos is better for primates and white-lipped peccaries. If you spend a night at Ecoturístico La Tarde before hiking to Los Patos, it's an excellent place to see snakes and frogs.

For wildlife-watchers frustrated by the difficulty of seeing rainforest mammals, a stay at Sirena Ranger Station is a must. Baird's tapirs are practically assured – a statement that can be made at few other places in the world. This endangered and distant relative of the rhinoceros is frequently spotted grazing along the airstrip after dusk. Sirena is excellent for other herbivores, particularly red brocket (especially on the Los Patos–Sirena trail) and both species of peccary. Agouti and tayra are also common.

Jaguars are rarely spotted, as their population in the Osa is suspected to be in the single digits. At night look for kinkajous and crab-eating skunks (especially at the mouth of the Río Sirena). Ocelots represent your best chance for observing a cat, but again, don't get your hopes up.

Corcovado is one of the few national parks in Costa Rica with all four of the country's primate species. Spider monkeys, mantled howlers and white-faced capuchins can be encountered anywhere, while the Los Platos–Sirena trail is best for the fourth and most endangered species, the Central American squirrel monkey. Sirena also has fair chances for the extremely hard-to-find silky anteater, a nocturnal animal that frequents the beachside forests between the Río Claro and the station.

The Río Sirena is a popular spot for American crocodiles, three-toed sloths and bull sharks.

☞ Tours

All visitors to Corcovado must be accompanied by an ICT-certified guide. Besides their intimate knowledge of the trails, local guides are amazingly informed about flora and fauna, including the best places to spot various species. Most guides also carry telescopes, allowing for up-close views of wildlife.

Guides are most often hired through the Área de Conservación Osa park office (p445) in Puerto Jiménez, or through hotels and tour operators. Two recommended local offices are the super-reliable, locally run Osa Wild (p442) in Puerto Jiménez and Corcovado Info Center (p429) in Bahía Drake. Prices vary considerably depending on the season, availability, size of your party and type of expedition you want to arrange. In any case, you will need to negotiate a price that includes park fees, meals and transportation.

🛏 Sleeping & Eating

Camping costs US$6 per person per day at the San Pedrillo and La Leona Ranger Stations, but is no longer allowed elsewhere in the park. Facilities include potable water and latrines. Remember to bring a flashlight or a headlamp, as the campsites are dark at night.

Note that all visitors are required to pack out all of their trash.

Sirena Ranger Station (dm US$30) serves large meals (US$20 to US$25 per meal) by advance reservation only and there are no cooking facilities. All other ranger stations have drinking water, but you have to bring your own provisions.

★ **Ecoturístico La Tarde**   LODGE **$$**
(☑2200-9617; www.ecoturisticolatarde.com; per person incl 3 meals US$80; ☎) ⌖ This wonderful, farm-based rural-tourism project is run by Eduardo and his hospitable family. There are various nature trails on the property, and it's a great place to stay if you're looking to hike to Sirena in Parque Nacional Corcovado. Accommodations are either in a dorm, rustic cabins or an en suite cabin (no electricity; no wi-fi).

A resident herpetologist leads excellent night tours (US$40) in search of rare frogs and fer-de-lance snakes.

ℹ Information

DANGERS & ANNOYANCES
The main danger in the park comes from the wildlife. The San Pedrillo to Sirena trail remains closed indefinitely, since it runs largely along the beach and hikers were tackling it at night, when predatory wildlife is most active. Also, there is no way to cross the Río Llorona except by swimming – and the river estuary is home to both crocodiles and bull sharks.

Guides no longer run night hikes around Sirena because if anyone gets a snakebite there is no way to fly them to a hospital in the dark. Don't get too close to peccaries because they are very aggressive; climb a tree if in doubt.

TOURIST INFORMATION

Information and maps are available at the office of Área de Conservación Osa (p445) in Puerto Jiménez, where you also have to pay your park entry fee of US$15 per day. If you hire a guide through a tour agency, the agency will make all the arrangements for you and include the required fees in the package price. If you hire a guide independently, you may have to make the reservations for lodging and meals yourself. Be sure to make these arrangements a few days in advance, especially in the dry season, as there's a daily limit to the number of visitors allowed in the park and facilities often hit their maximum capacity. Note that you cannot secure a permit more than 30 days in advance.

Park headquarters are at Sirena Ranger Station on the coast in the middle of the park. Other ranger stations are located on the park boundaries: San Pedrillo in the northwest corner on the coast; and La Leona in the southeast corner on the coast (near the village of Carate). The newest ranger station in is Dos Brazos village, and the rebuilt Los Patos Ranger Station is actually just outside the park boundary, closest to La Tarde.

ℹ Getting There & Away

AIR

Alfa Romeo Aero Taxi (☑ 8632-8150; www. alfaromeoair.com) offers charter flights connecting Puerto Jiménez, Drake and Golfito to Carate and Sirena. Sample flights from Puerto Jiménez or Carate to Sirena cost US$390, but if a pilot is dropping passengers off in Sirena and leaving empty, and you're too exhausted to hike out, there's certainly room for negotiation, and if there's a group of you, it works out more reasonably. Note that long-term parking is not available at any of these locations, so it's best to make prior arrangements if you need to leave your car somewhere.

FROM BAHÍA DRAKE

From Bahía Drake, you can walk the coastal trail that leads to San Pedrillo station (about seven hours from Agujitas). Many lodges and tour companies run day tours here, with a boat ride to San Pedrillo (30 minutes to an hour, depending on the departure point) or Sirena (one to 1½ hours). You can make camping reservations at San Pedrillo or Sirena stations.

FROM CARATE

In the southeast, the closest point of access is Carate, from where La Leona station is a one-hour, 3.5km hike west along the beach.

Carate is accessible from Puerto Jiménez via a poorly maintained, 45km dirt road. This journey is an adventure in itself, and often allows for some good wildlife-spotting along the way.

A 4WD *colectivo* travels this route twice daily for US$9, departing Puerto Jiménez for Carate at 6am and 1:30pm, returning at 8:30am and 3:30pm. Otherwise you can hire a 4WD taxi for around US$80.

If you have your own car, the *pulpería* (mini-mart) in Carate is a safe place to park for a few days, though you'll have some extra peace of mind if you tip the manager before setting out.

FROM LA PALMA

From the north, the closest point of access is the town of La Palma, from where you can catch a bus or taxi south to Puerto Jiménez or north to San José.

Heading to Los Patos station, you might be able to find a taxi to take you partway; however, the road is only passable to 4WD vehicles (and not always), so be prepared to hike the 14km to the ranger station. The road crosses the river about 20 times in the last 6km, so not only do you need a rugged vehicle, but you have to be experienced at driving through rivers.

A far more sensible option is to drive to La Tarde (where the road divides; the branch going uphill leads to La Tarde, whereas the lower branch leads to Los Patos) and hike to Los Patos from there, especially since there's nowhere to stay at Los Patos and you have to either limit yourself to a day hike or walk all the way to Sirena.

If you have a car, it's best to leave it with a hotel or lodge in La Palma.

FROM DOS BRAZOS

Dos Brazos is a short drive from Puerto Jiménez; it's 10km to the El Tigre turnoff from where Dos Brazos is signposted along a dirt road. The trailhead is signposted in the Dos Brazos village.

TO CORCOVADO VIA PUERTO JIMÉNEZ

Of the two principal overland routes to Parque Nacional Corcovado, the Puerto Jiménez route on the eastern side of the peninsula is much more 'developed.' Of course, as this is Osa, development doesn't amount to much more than a single road and a sprinkling of villages along the coast of Golfo Dulce. The landscape is cattle pastures and palm-oil plantations, while the Reserva Forestal Golfo Dulce protects much of the inland area and encompasses the former gold-mining community of Dos Brazos, now the newest entrance to Corcovado and *agroturismo* epicenter. The largest settlement in the area is the town of Puerto Jiménez, which has transitioned from a boomtown for gold miners to an ecotourism hot spot. South of Jiménez, the surfer haven of Cabo Matapalo and the jungle lodges of Carate beckon travelers in search of nature and solitude.

Carate

If you make it all the way here, congratulations. A bone-rattling 45km south of Puerto Jiménez, this is where the dirt road rounds the peninsula and comes to an abrupt dead end. There's literally nothing more than an airstrip, a long strip of wild beach and a *pulpería*. Carate is not a destination in itself, but it is the southwestern gateway for anyone hiking into Sirena Ranger Station in Parque Nacional Corcovado.

A handful of well-designed wilderness lodges in the area make a good night's rest for travelers heading to/from Corcovado or those in search of a quiet retreat surrounded by jungle. The ride from Puerto Jiménez to Carate is also its own adventure as the narrow, bumpy dirt road winds its way around dense rainforest, through gushing rivers and across windswept beaches. Birds and other wildlife are prolific along this stretch: keep your eyes peeled and hang on tight.

🛏 Sleeping & Eating

Some places in Carate don't have 24-hour electricity or hot water. Reservations are recommended in the dry season – communication is often through Puerto Jiménez, so messages may not be retrieved every day. For shoestringers, the best option is to camp in the yard in front of the *pulpería;* the expat owner charges US$5 a day. All accommodations provide meals.

★ Finca Exotica   BUNGALOW $$$
(☑ 8359-8408; http://fincaexotica.com; tent per person from US$80, bungalow from US$130, all incl breakfast) 🍃 To stay at Finca Exotica is to glamp in a tropical Eden, surrounded by 90 hectares of farmland that include more than 125 species of fruit and vegetables, a henhouse, a duck house and a pig enclosure. Guests sleep in open-air, designer cabins and tents, feast on organic, communal meals and relax in hammocks overlooking mountains and the sea.

It's all at the foot of Parque Nacional Corcovado, and visitors can also go on farm tours that include edible plant tastings.

Luna Lodge   LODGE $$$
(☑ 2206-5859, in USA & Canada 888-760-0760; www.lunalodge.com; tent/r/bungalow per person incl all meals US$248/345/433; 🅿🛜🏊) 🍃 A steep road crisscrosses the Río Carate and up the valley to this enchanting mountain retreat on the border of Parque Nacional Corcovado. Accommodations range from tent cabins to thatched bungalows with open-air garden showers and private terraces, all with stunning views of the pristine jungle rolling down to the ocean. This is the farthest-flung of Carate's accommodations.

The open-air restaurant is a marvelous place to indulge in the expansive views, while a rooftop yoga deck provides an even higher vantage point. Lana, the founder and owner of the lodge, is passionate about conservation and sustainability and has made the lodge a working practice in both. There are accommodations discounts for under-12s.

La Leona Eco-Lodge   LODGE $$$
(☑ 2735-5704; www.laleonaecolodge.com; tents per person half/full board from US$89/99; 🏊) 🍃 On the edge of Parque Nacional Corcovado, this friendly lodge offers all the thrills of camping, without the hassles. The 16 fully screened forest-green tents with beds are nestled between palm trees, with decks facing the beach and allowing frequent wildlife sightings. Solar power provides electricity in the restaurant.

All guests must hike the 2.5km in from the Carate airstrip, but the lodge offers a new base camp in Carate where guests may drop their bags. From here, the bags are transported via horse-drawn carriage so guests can hike the beach with a lighter load.

Lookout Inn   GUESTHOUSE $$$
(☑ 2735-5431; www.lookout-inn.com; r per person all-inclusive from US$125; 🅿@🏊) Near the airstrip and perched up the side of a steep hill overlooking the ocean, Lookout Inn attracts younger travelers with its comfortable, open-air quarters with mural-painted walls and unbeatable views. Accommodations are accessible by a wooden walkway winding through the trees. The 'Stairway to Heaven' (360 steps) leads up to four observation platforms and a waterfall trail.

More traditional rooms are available in the main building. Interesting gimmick: if you don't spot a scarlet macaw during your stay, your lodging is free!

Getting There & Away

AIR
Alfa Romeo Aero Taxi (☑ 8632-8150; www.alfaromeoair.com) offers charter flights from Puerto Jiménez. Prices are dependent on the number of passengers, so if you're with others, the rate can be as low as US$60 per person.

BUS
The *colectivo* (US$9) departs Puerto Jiménez for Carate at 6am and 1:30pm, returning at 8:30am and 3:30pm. Note that it often fills up on its return trip to Puerto Jiménez, especially during the dry season. Arrive at least 30 minutes ahead of time or you might find yourself stranded. Alternatively, catch a taxi from Puerto Jiménez (US$80).

CAR
If you're driving you'll need a 4WD, even in the dry season, as there are several streams to ford, as well as a river. Assuming you don't have valuables in sight, you can leave your car at the *pulpería* (per night US$5) and hike to La Leona station (1½ hours).

Cabo Matapalo

If you didn't know that it was here, you would hardly suspect that the jungle-obscured community of Matapalo existed. There isn't much to the southern tip of the Península de Osa save some surfing digs and homes at the entrance to the Golfo Dulce. Matapalo lies just 17km south of Puerto Jiménez, but this heavily forested and beach-fringed cape is a vastly different world. A network of trails traverses the foothills, uninhabited except for migrating wildlife from the Reserva Forestal Golfo Dulce. Along the coastline, miles of beaches are virtually empty, except for a few surfers in the know.

Cabo Matapalo is home to wilderness lodges that cater to travelers searching for seclusion and wildlife. Scarlet macaws, brown pelicans and herons are frequently sighted on the beaches, while all four species of Costa Rican monkey, several wildcat species, plus sloths, coatis, agoutis and anteaters roam the woods.

Activities

Playa Matapalo   SURFING
There are three excellent right point breaks off this beach, not far from Encanta La Vida.

If there's a south or west swell this is the best time to hit the waves.

Playa Pan Dulce   SURFING
Good for beginners and intermediate surfers, Pan Dulce gets some nice longboard waves most days. You can also go swimming here, but be careful of rip tides.

Tours

★Psycho Tours   ADVENTURE
(Everyday Adventures; ☑ 8428-3904; www.psychotours.com; tours US$55-130) Witty, energetic naturalist Andy Pruter runs Psycho Tours, which offers high-adrenaline adventures in Cabo Matapalo. His signature tour is tree climbing (US$65 per person): scaling a 60m ficus tree, aptly named 'Cathedral.' Also popular – and definitely adrenaline-inducing – is waterfall rappelling (US$95) down cascades ranging from 15m to 30m. The best one? The tree-climbing/waterfall combo tour (US$130).

Sleeping

Ojo del Mar   BUNGALOW $$
(☑ 8378-5246; www.ojodelmar.com; road to Carate, Km 16; tents s/d US$25/50, bungalows s/d from US$100/150, all incl breakfast; P 🕏) Tucked in amid a good surfing beach and lush jungle, the six beautifully handcrafted, thatch-roofed bamboo bungalows are entirely open-air, allowing for all the natural sounds and scents to seep in. Surfers chill in palm-strung hammocks, and Nico – co-owner and cook – serves an excellent, all-organic dinner. Yoga classes (US$15) are offered periodically.

★Lapa Ríos   LODGE $$$
(☑ 2735-5130; www.laparios.com; road to Carate, Km 17; r per person incl 3 meals US$560; P 🞧) One of Costa Rica's best all-inclusive wilderness lodges, Lapa Ríos combines luxury with a rustic, tropical ambience. It comprises 17 spacious, thatched bungalows, all decked out with king- and queen-sized beds, bamboo furniture, garden showers and private decks with panoramic views (no wi-fi/TV). An extensive trail system allows exploration of the 400-hectare reserve, while swimming, snorkeling and surfing are within easy reach.

★Encanta La Vida   LODGE $$$
(☑ 8376-3209; www.encantalavida.com; Cabo Matapalo; cabins per person US$145-210; P 🕏 🞧)

The enchanted life, indeed. Gorgeous breeze-cooled, wood-beamed structures – from round tree houses to romantic, free-standing *casitas* – are scattered at the foot of a jungle-clad backdrop. The food is brilliant and the location a perfect base for exploring the cape. An ocean-view yoga terrace is available, there are surfboards for rent, and tours can be arranged by the accommodating staff.

Howlers and spider monkeys regularly travel the treetops, while pairs of great currasows stroll shyly below.

Bosque del Cabo
BUNGALOW $$$

(☎2735-5206; www.bosquedelcabo.com; per person all-inclusive rate US$270-295, rental houses without food US$595; P🅿❄🛜❄) 🌿 On this expansive property tucked away on Cabo Matapalo, dreamy, far-flung cabins overlook the jungle and sea, and meals are taken in a central *rancho*. Although the grounds feel a bit manicured in comparison to wilder, neighboring properties, a vast system of hiking trails brings guests into contact with an abundance of local wildlife.

Blue Osa Yoga Retreat
BOUTIQUE HOTEL $$$

(☎in USA 917-400-9797; www.blueosa.com; r from US$292; P🅿❄🛜❄) 🌿 With an emphasis on rejuvenation, this intimate oceanfront eco-resort attracts those looking to unwind, through yoga, swimming in the chemical-free pool or getting pampered in the solar-powered eco-spa. Communal meals include organic produce from the onsite garden and lodgings are harmonious, with rustic furnishings and screened windows. There's a definite camaraderie among guests.

It's located halfway between Puerto Jiménez and Matapalo.

El Remanso Lodge
LODGE $$$

(☎2735-5569; www.elremanso.com; road to Carate, Km 21; s/d from US$185/195; P🅿🛜❄) 🌿 Set on 72 hectares of rainforest, this blufftop lodge is run by the daughter of Greenpeace activists. Constructed from fallen tropical hardwoods, the secluded, spacious and sumptuous cabins have mesh instead of glass, and guests are taken ziplining, birding and hiking by knowledgeable guides. Private trails lead through jungle to the beach, a waterfall and tide pools.

Kapú Rancho Almendros
CABINA $$$

(☎8622-6366, 8692-4692; http://home.earthlink.net/~kapu; Cabo Matapalo; r per person with/without meals from US$80/50; P🅿🛜) This is the end of the line on Cabo Matapalo, where the road stops pretending and turns into a sandy beach path. The property includes three cozy *cabañas* equipped with solar power, large screened windows, full kitchens and garden showers. Well suited to surfers and self-sufficient types, these *cabañas* are practically steps from the beach and allow for self-catering.

❶ Getting There & Away

If you are driving, a 4WD is essential even in the dry season, as roads frequently get washed out. There are several streams and a river to cross on the way here. From the Puerto Jiménez–Carate road, the poorly marked turnoff for Cabo Matapalo is on the left-hand side, then through a crumbling cement gate (called 'El Portón Blanco').

Otherwise, the *colectivo* (US$6) will drop you here; it passes by at about 7:15am and 2:45pm heading to Carate, and 9:15am and 4:15pm heading back to Jiménez. A taxi will come here from Puerto Jiménez for about US$55.

Puerto Jiménez

POP 1800

Sliced in half by the swampy, overgrown Quebrada Cacao, and flanked on one side by the emerald waters of the Golfo Dulce, the vaguely Wild West outpost of Puerto Jiménez is shared by local residents and wildlife. While walking through the dusty streets of Jiménez (as it's known to locals), it's not unusual to spot scarlet macaws roosting on the soccer field, or white-faced capuchins traversing the treetops along the main street.

On the edge of Parque Nacional Corcovado, Jiménez is the preferred jumping-off point for travelers heading to the famed Sirena Ranger Station, and a great place to organize an expedition, stock up on supplies, eat a hot meal and get a good night's rest before hitting the trails.

Despite the region's largest and most diverse offering of hotels, restaurants and other tourist services, this town at its core is a close-knit Tico community.

☞ Tours

Puerto Jiménez has a host of tour operators, taxi drivers and touts hungry for the tourist dollar. Ask lots of questions, consult with fellow travelers and choose carefully.

★ **Osa Wild**   TOURS
(☏ 2735-5848, 8376-1152, 8709-1083; www.osa wildtravel.com; tours from US$30, 1-day Corcovado tour US$85; ⊗ 8am-noon & 2-7pm Mon-Fri, 9am-noon &1-4pm Sat & Sun) ✐ Osa Wild is *the* way to connect with Corcovado park and Osa. It's just what the area so desperately needed: a resource for travelers to connect with community-oriented initiatives that go to the heart of the real Osa through homestays, farm tours and sustainable cultural exchanges. It also offers more typical stuff like kayaking tours and guided trips through Corcovado.

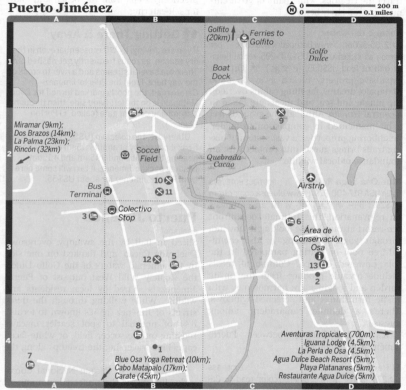

Puerto Jiménez

DAY-TRIPPER

You've got a free day in Puerto Jiménez and you don't want to hang around town? Here's what you can do:

➡ Take a trip to meet a local farmer or learn about rainforest medicine with Osa Wild (p442).

➡ Kayak through the mangrove estuary to look for caimans, birds and monkeys with Aventuras Tropicales.

➡ Indulge your sweet tooth; see (and taste) where chocolate comes from at Finca Köbö (p447).

➡ Slow down and get some sun; have a picnic on the deserted wilderness beach of Playa Blanca (p447).

➡ Head to Dos Brazos (p446) for a seven-hour tramp along the newer forest trail.

Run by university-trained biologist Ifi and her husband Daniel, Osa Wild's focus on sustainability, environmental protection and community development put it in a league of its own. It also sets up volunteer programs.

It's located 80m west of Corcovado BM Supermarket

Osa Aventura ADVENTURE
(📞 8372-6135, 2735-5670; www.osaaventura.com) 🖉 Run by Mike Boston, a biologist with a real passion for nature, Osa Aventura aims to introduce travelers to the beauty of rainforest life and to raise awareness of the need to preserve Corcovado's unique environment. Adventures vary from three-day treks through Corcovado to a tour that focuses on Golfo Dulce's rural communities. Custom tours also available.

Surcos Tours TOURS
(📞 8603-2387, 2237-4189; www.surcostours.com) 🖉 A trio of excellent guides make Surcos the best company tours into Osa that focus on wildlife and birdwatching. Tours vary from day hikes in Corcovado and Matapalo to multiday experiences in Corcovado and specialized birding tours.

Arrangements for tours are made through its website.

Osa Corcovado ADVENTURE
(📞 8632-8150; www.soldeosa.com; Hwy 245; ⏰ 7am-4pm Mon-Fri) Operator offering anything from three-day Corcovado hikes to kayaking in the mangroves, sunset kayak dolphin-watching tours on the Golfo Dulce (US$75) and Matapalo day hikes.

Aventuras Tropicales ADVENTURE
(📞 2735-5195; www.aventurastropicales.com) This is a professional, Tico-run operation that offers all sorts of active adventures. Some of its most popular excursions include kayaking tours of the mangroves, which cost US$45 per person. Located 2km east on the road to Platanares.

🛏 Sleeping

Puerto Jiménez is fairly quiet most times of the year, though reservations are always a good idea on weekends and during holidays. You'll find the greatest diversity of accommodations at the budget and midrange levels here, more so than in other parts of the Osa. Top-end options tend to be located on the outskirts of town.

Lunas Hostel HOSTEL $
(📞 2735-6007; www.lunashostelpuertojimenezcr. com; dm/d without bathroom US$12/14; ❊ 🛜) A backpacker haven presided over by friendly and helpful owner Alex, who's been a guardian angel to more than one traveler in distress. While the fan-cooled dorms and rooms are can't-swing-a-cat size, the handmade furniture and excellent mattresses are a boon. Shared bathrooms only. Alex can arrange Corcovado tours, though there have been mixed reports about the guide he works with.

Cabinas Back Packer GUESTHOUSE $
(📞 2735-5181; s/d without bathroom with air-con US$30/40, without air-con US$15/30; ❊ 🛜) One of the better budget digs – it's squeaky clean, relatively quiet as it's a couple of blocks from the main street, and comes with a front

garden strung with hammocks. Rooms share clean bathrooms and there are bicycles for guest use. There's even a brightly tiled kitchen, available for a US$5 fee.

Cabinas Marcelina   HOTEL $

(☑ 2735-5007; www.jimenezhotels.com/cabinasmarcelina; r with/without air-con US$42/38; P ✳ ☎) Marcelina's place is a long-standing favorite among budget travelers looking for a peaceful night's sleep. The concrete building is painted salmon pink and is surrounded by blooming trees, lending it a homey atmosphere. Rooms have modern furniture, fluffy towels and tile bathrooms. The owner is largely AWOL, though, so this is not the place to book excursions.

★ Cabinas Jiménez   CABINA $$

(☑ 2735-5090; www.cabinasjimenez.com; s/d from US$45/60, cabinas US$80-120; P ✳ ☎ ☀) Cabinas Jiménez is hands down the nicest place to stay in Jiménez proper. Rooms come with fridges and jungle scenes painted on the walls, and poolside rooms come with chillout patios. Pricier *cabinas* have kitchenettes and fantastic views of the lagoon. Bikes and kayaks are free for guests' use, and the bilingual staff are friendly and helpful.

Agua Dulce Beach Resort   RESORT $$

(☑ 8599-9499, 8310-6304; www.aguadulcehotel.com; Playa Platanares; r/ste/bungalow incl breakfast from US$89/159/299; P ✳ ☎ ☀) Literally a stone's throw from Playa Platanares, this resort is centered on a pool and has an appealing open-air restaurant that specializes in excellent pasta dishes. The spacious beachfront bungalows benefit from views of the Golfo Dulce, and even the cheapest garden rooms are sizable and come with private decks. Monkeys and macaws haunt the jungle around the hotel.

Cabinas Tropicales   CABINA $$

(☑ 2735-5298, 8997-1445; www.cabinas-tropicales.com; s/d from US$45/50; P ✳ ☎) Six tidy rooms at Cabinas Tropicales range from simple standards to roomy lofts and a deluxe suite, some of which have lovely outdoor showers. Each is unique, but they all have sturdy furniture, air-con and access to the gorgeous gardens and well-stocked open-air kitchen. Your host, Mark, is both personable and knowledgeable. One of the best-value options in town.

Cacao Monkeys   CABINA $$

(☑ 2735-5248; www.cacaomonkeys.com; s/d from US$40/60; P ☎) On the fringes of downtown on a cacao farm, this jungle joint has a set of five brightly painted wooden *cabinas* – one with a kitchen and two geared toward families. There's also a shared kitchen for all guests. It's removed from town noise, feels junglelike, and monkeys and iguanas stop by for a visit.

One of the bungalows is specially furnished to accommodate a family with two children.

★ Iguana Lodge   HOTEL $$$

(☑ 8848-0752, in USA & Canada 800-259-9123; www.iguanalodge.com; d incl breakfast US$188, casitas per person incl 2 meals from US$229, villa US$676; P ☎ ☀) This luxurious lodge fronting Playa Platanares has the most architecturally alluring cabins in the area: four two-story bungalows with breezy decks, bamboo furniture, orthopedic beds draped in mosquito netting, and lovely stone bathrooms with garden showers. The three-story beach house is ideal for families, and there's a spa and exclusive onsite restaurant serving three delectable meals a day.

The restaurant, with a daily changing menu, is open to nonguests with prior reservations. On the premises there's also a more casual eatery. There are beachfront *palapas* (shelters with thatched, palm-leaf roofs and open sides), hammocks and a volleyball court, and a tennis court was being constructed at the time of research.

✗ Eating

★ Restaurante Monka   COSTA RICAN $

(☑ 2735-5051; mains US$5-7; ⊙ 6am-8pm; ☎ ✿) Bright and airy and the best breakfast spot in town, Monka does excellent cold coffee drinks, smoothies and extensive breakfast platters, from American-style, involving bacon and pancakes, to Mexican-style huevos rancheros. The rest of the day you can fill up on good, inexpensive *casados*. Several breakfast options and *casados* are vegetarian.

Restaurant y Bar Lozaari   COSTA RICAN $

(☑ 8795-6861; mains US$3-10; ⊙ 6am-9pm; ☎) This adorable little Costa Rican restaurant is tucked back in a plaza, filled with plants and adorned with pretty paper lanterns. The breakfast is super-cheap and delicious, and best taken at a picnic table in the lush garden out back. Favorites include *gallo pinto* (beans and rice) with eggs, fried plantains and natural fruit juices.

Soda Valeria
COSTA RICAN **$**
(☑2735-6180; mains US$4-8; ⏰6am-8pm Mon-Sat, 7am-3pm Sun) Clean, cute and smack-dab in the middle of town, this *soda* is a dream – the kind of place you know is good because the local government workers all pile in at lunch. The heaping, fresh *casados* change daily and are delivered with fresh, home-made tortillas and sided with fresh fruit. Considerate, quick service is an extra boon.

Restaurante Agua Dulce
INTERNATIONAL **$$**
(www.aguadulcehotel.com; Agua Dulce Beach Resort, Playa Platanares; mains from US$8; ⏰7am-10pm; 🛜🅿) This breezy restaurant is a trusted spot for imaginative pasta dishes, grilled fish and ample breakfasts, although the service is positively languid. There are various vegetarian pasta dishes and salads.

La Perla de Osa
INTERNATIONAL **$$**
(☑8829-5865; mains US$10-17; ⏰11am-8pm; 🅿🛜🅿) On the grounds of Iguana Lodge, this jungle-fringed restaurant-bar is locally (and justifiably) famous for its cocktails, accompanied by such delectable nibbles as pulled-pork tacos, grilled Asian-style tuna and shrimp plates. Very popular with locals on weekends, and there are also vegetarian soups, salads and meat-free pasta mains.

Il Giardino
ITALIAN **$$**
(☑2735-5129; www.ilgiardinoitalianrestaurant. com; meals US$11-16; ⏰7am-10pm) While the possibly overextended menu touts steaks and sushi as offerings, Il Giardino shines when it sticks to Italian specialties – home-made pasta, gnocchi and pizza. Although the service and cuisine can be somewhat inconsistent, there's a reliably romantic and candlelit waterfront ambience. The restaurant also contains three well-kept rooms (US$40 including breakfast) with views of a mangrove swamp.

🛍 Shopping

★ Jagua Arts & Crafts
ARTS & CRAFTS
(☑2735-5267; ⏰7am-3pm Mon-Sat) A terrific, well-stocked crafts shop, featuring local art and jewelry, a wonderful collection of high-quality, colorful Boruca masks and black-and-ocher Guaitil pottery, as well as woven goods by the Emberá and Wounaan

people. Kuna weavings technically belong across the border in Panama, but they make excellent gifts.

❶ Information

Área de Conservación Osa (ACOSA; Osa Conservation Area Headquarters; ☑2735-5036; Corcovado park fee per person per day US$15; ⏰8am-4pm Mon-Fri) Information about Parque Nacional Corcovado, Isla del Caño, Parque Nacional Marino Ballena and Golfito parks and reserves.

Banco Nacional (☑2735-5020; ⏰8:30am-3:45pm Mon-Fri) Has an ATM.

BCR (Banco de Costa Rica; ☑2735-5260; ⏰9am-4pm Mon-Fri) Across from the church; it also has an ATM.

Police Near the soccer field.

Post office (☑2735-5045; ⏰8am-noon & 1-5pm Mon-Fri) Near the soccer field.

❶ Getting There & Away

AIR
The airstrip is to the east of town. During research it was closed for maintenance, but should have reopened by now.

NatureAir (☑2735-5062; www.natureair. com) and **Sansa** (☑2735-5890; www.flysansa. com) have flights to/from San José (50 minutes, up to four daily); one-way flights are anywhere from US$59 to US$129. NatureAir also does the puddle jumper to Golfito (10 minutes, daily).

Alfa Romeo Aero Taxi (☑8632-8150, 2735-5353; www.alfaromeoair.com) has light aircraft (for three and five passengers) for charter flights to Golfito, Carate, Drake, Sirena, Palmar Sur, Quepos and Limón. Prices are dependent on the number of passengers, so it's best to try to organize a larger group if you're considering this option. Sometimes, if there's already a trip planned into the park, the cost can be as low as US$60 per person.

BOAT
Several fast **ferries** (☑8632-8672, 2735-5095) travel to Golfito (US$6, 30 minutes), departing at 6am, 8:45am, 11:30am, 2pm and 4pm daily. Double-check current schedules, as they change often and without notice. On Sundays, ferries depart less frequently.

Alternatively, you could opt to hire a private water taxi to shuttle you across to Golfito or Zancudo. You will have to negotiate, but prices are generally reasonable, especially considering that you set the schedule. Osa Corcovado (p443) has a list of private boat operators.

BUS

Most buses arrive at the blue **terminal** (☑2735-5189) behind the green paint store on the west side of town. Destinations include Neily (US$4.60, three hours, daily 5:30am and 2pm), La Palma (US$2.60, one hour, at least once hourly), San Isidro de El General (US$10, 5½ hours, daily 1pm) and San José (US$13, eight hours, daily 5am and 9am).

CAR

Puerto Jiménez is now connected to the rest of the country by a beautifully paved road. You can rent a vehicle from **Solid Car Rental** (☑2735-5777; www.solidcarrental.com; ☺7am-4pm). If you're driving to Carate or Matapalo, you'll need a 4WD; be sure to fill up at the gas station in Jiménez.

TAXI

The *colectivo* (shared truck taxi) runs daily to Cabo Matapalo (1½ hours, US$5) and Carate (2½ hours, US$9) on the southern tip of the national park. Departures are from the **colectivo stop** (☑8832-8680) at Soda Deya at 6am and 1:30pm, returning at 8:30am and 4pm.

Otherwise, you can call and hire a 4WD taxi. Taxis usually charge from US$60 for the ride to Carate and from US$70 for the ride to Matapalo, and more than US$120 for the overland trek to Bahía Drake.

Dos Brazos

POP 300

Clustered along two branches of Río Tigre (which gives the village its full name: Dos Brazos de Río Tigre), this appealing village that lives on 'Tico time' is surrounded by secondary forest near the edge of Parque Nacional Corcovado. In the 1970s there was a gold rush here, with miners coming from all over to seek their fortune. But while small-scale gold-panning still goes on, Dos Brazos is now looking toward rural tourism and ecotourism as the way forward for its close-knit community, and is part of the Caminos de Osa project.

🏃 Activities

A rugged 8km trail loop with a trailhead in Dos Brazos passes through part of Corcovado, Sendero El Tigre (p435). It opened in early 2015, bringing with it new visitors, and all profits are invested in the local community. It's probably the least expensive way of experiencing the national park (US$150 for two people) and is the only part of Corcovado that can be easily seen on a day trip.

👉 Tours

The well-organized tourist office, Dos Brazos Oficina de Turismo, arranges night tours, horseback-riding tours (half-day US$150 for two people) and gold-panning tours (US$30 per person), with local gold-seekers showing you how it's done. Also on offer are birding tours (US$30 per person), guided hikes to a local waterfall (US$20 per person) and more.

🛏 Sleeping & Eating

All accommodations provide meals on request. Some offer cooking facilities.

⭐ Bolita Rainforest Hostel
HOSTEL $

(☑8549-9898; www.bolita.org; dm/cabinas US$12/30) For total immersion in rural life, stay at this semi-sustainable rustic farmhouse in the midst of 61 acres of rainforest. There's no electricity, so you'll be up with the howler monkeys and eating dinner by candlelight. Rooms come with mosquito nets and there are 15km of walking trails (and waterfalls) to explore. The office in the village provides walking directions.

There are solar-powered USB charging stations for cameras and phones.

Los Mineros Guesthouse
GUESTHOUSE $

(☑8721-8087; www.losminerosguesthouse.com; per person hut/cabina US$16/21) This is the most characterful place to stay in the village, with a historical bar frequented by miners during the gold rush. The *cabinas*? Most were part of the village brothel; one was the town jail. Or you can bed down in one of the rustic bamboo-and-corrugated-iron huts with a strangely alpine feel. The multilingual owners can provide meals (US$8 to US$15).

Amazonita
BUNGALOW $$

(☑8501-9608; amazonitaecolodge@gmail.com; cabinas US$70-80, house US$100) A five-minute walk from the Sendero El Tigre trailhead, on a steep hillside, Amazonita consists of two *cabinas* and a house open to the wilderness and dwarfed by towering trees. Mosquito nets protect the beds and the kitchens are fully equipped. Nearby are 14km of walking trails, or you can just swing in your hammock in tropical isolation.

Bosque del Río Tigre
LODGE $$$

(☑8705-3729; www.osaadventures.com; s/d US$195/330, 4-day package per person US$640;

P) 🕊 In the midst of a 13-hectare private reserve, this ecolodge is a birdwatcher's paradise; guests can opt for unlimited birding and herping packages. Liz and Abraham are effusive hosts, the food is outstanding and wildlife comes up to your door. Four well-appointed guest rooms and one private cabin have huge windows for wildlife-watching.

Getting here involves driving through a river that can become impassable in the wet season.

ℹ Information

There's a helpful tourist office, **Dos Brazos Oficina de Turismo** (☑ 8691-4545; info@dos brazosderiotigre.com; ⊙ 6am-6pm) near the entrance to the village. Here visitors can book various tours, pay the park entry fee (US$15) if they wish to hike the Sendero El Tigre, and book a guide – mandatory for hiking inside the national park.

The comprehensive website www.dosbrazos deriotigre.com offers plenty of useful info on what to do and where to stay in the village.

ℹ Getting There & Away

A minibus runs from Puerto Jiménez to Dos Brazos twice daily on weekdays at 11am and 4pm (US$4, 30 minutes); it departs from in front of the Grupo Materiales hardware store, and returns to Puerto Jiménez at 6am and noon. If driving, Río Tigre is well signposted off the main highway, around 10km north of Puerto Jiménez.

Reserva Forestal Golfo Dulce

The northern shore of the Golfo Dulce is home to this vast forest reserve, which links Parque Nacional Corcovado to the Parque Nacional Piedras Blancas. This connecting corridor plays an important role in preserving the biodiversity of the peninsula, and in allowing the wildlife to migrate to the mainland. Although much of the reserve is not easily accessible, there are several lodges in the area doing their part to preserve this natural resource by protecting their own little pieces of this wildlife wonderland.

◉ Sights

Playa Blanca   BEACH
The beautiful sand-and-coral beach known as Playa Blanca, at the east end of La Palma, is a low-key scene popular with Ticos and an excellent place to go sea kayaking.

Finca Köbö   FARM
(☑ 8398-7604; www.fincakobo.com; 2hr tour US$32; P) 🕊 About 8km south of La Palma, Finca Köbö is a chocolate-lover's dream come true (in fact *köbö* means 'dream' in Ngöbere). The 20-hectare *finca* is dedicated to the organic cultivation of fruits and vegetables and – the product of choice – cacao. Tours in English give a comprehensive overview of the life cycle of cacao plants and the production of chocolate (with degustation!). More than half of the territory is dedicated to protecting and reforesting natural ecosystems.

To really experience the beauty and vision of this *finca*, you can stay in simple, comfortable teak cabins and bungalows (US$95 to US$155, including breakfast; dinner costs US$8 to US$15), with lovely open-air bathrooms and quality linens. Those who stay longer can hike the surrounding forest trails and speak with local farmers. The onsite gift store sells toasted cocoa nibs – great for energy! – and locally produced organic jam.

🏃 Activities

Kayaking

Playa Blanca is ideal for sea kayaking. The owner of Lapamar (p448) also arranges independent sea-kayaking outings, and this ecolodge is an overnight stop for participants in multiday kayaking trips run by Tropical Sea Kayaking.

Tropical Sea Kayaking   KAYAKING
(☑ 2249-0666, in USA 719-581-9891; www.trop icalseakayaking.com; 3/6/8/10 days per person from US$599/1295/1849/2399) This experienced, reliable operator organizes in-depth sea-kayaking adventures on the Golfo Dulce, looking for wildlife in the mangroves and dolphin-spotting along the way, stopping on tiny islands and Playa Blanca, seeking out secret spots that few visitors get to see and staying in lodges only accessible by water. Prices include accommodations, meals, kayaking and more.

The kayaking operation is based at El Chontal hotel in the town of Rincón.

Wildlife-Watching

Most travelers skip the northern part of the peninsula and beeline for Puerto Jiménez to get to Parque Nacional Corcovado. If you have time to dawdle, though, there's lots of DIY wildlife-watching to be had. About 9km southeast of Rincón, the town of **La Palma**

KNOWING THE NGÖBE

The earliest inhabitants of Costa Rica's far southern corner were the Ngöbe, historically referred to as the Guaymí. The name Guaymí was a Spanish transliteration of what another indigenous group had dubbed the Ngöbe – and while 'Guaymí' is not considered offensive, necessarily, the Ngöbe rightly prefer the name that they call themselves.

Having migrated over generations from neighboring Panama, the Ngöbe now inhabit indigenous reserves in the Valle de Coto Brus, the Península de Osa and southern Golfo Dulce; however, they retain some seminomadic ways and are legally allowed to pass freely over the border into Panama. This occurs frequently during the coffee-harvesting season, when many travel to work on plantations.

More so than many tribes in Costa Rica, the Ngöbe have been able to preserve their customs and culture, and it is not unusual to see women wearing the traditional brightly colored, ankle-length *nagua* dress. Unlike other indigenous groups, the Ngöbe still speak Ngöbere, their native language, and teach it in local schools.

One reason the culture has been able to preserve its traditional ways is that the Ngöbe reserves are largely inaccessible. But as tourism filters into the furthest reaches of the country, the growing interest in indigenous traditions and handicrafts may actually encourage their preservation, so long as it is managed with community participation and visitor respect.

The easiest way to visit a Ngöbe reserve is to head to the visitor center at La Casona or the community museum (open 8am to 5pm) at Villa Palacios in the Coto Brus reserve, about 8km north of San Vito and another 8km off the Interamericana (the turnoff is marked by a hard-to-miss statue of a woman in Ngöbe dress).

To get the full-on immersion experience (and fully off the beaten track), stay for a few nights at **Tamandu Lodge** (☑8821-4525; www.tamandu-lodge.com; r per person incl meals US$65) on the northern Península de Osa.

is the origin of the rough road that turns into the trail to Corcovado's Los Patos Ranger Station. If you're through-hiking Corcovado, this will likely be the start or end point of your trek.

Río Nuevo is a hamlet reachable via a 16km unpaved road from a turnoff just before entering Puerto Jiménez. A good trail network leads to spectacular mountain viewpoints, some with views of the gulf. Birdwatching is excellent around Rio Nuevo.

☞ Tours

**Reserva Indígena
Guaymí de Osa**　　　　CULTURAL
The Reserva Indígena Guaymí de Osa is southwest of La Palma town, on the border of Parque Nacional Corcovado. If you're interested in learning more about the indigenous culture, it's possible to arrange a homestay with a Ngöbe family, who will meet you in La Palma for the journey into the reserve.

🛏 Sleeping

Manglares del Golfo　　　　CABIN $
(☑8989-7246; tent US$5, cabin per person US$13) Fronting Playa Blanca, its quirky restaurant decorated with nautical flotsam and jetsam, this friendly place has two types of shoe-stringer digs: mosquito-mesh tents with beds inside, or simple wooden cabins. The proprietor cooks up some wonderfully fresh fish.

Lapamar　　　　CABINA $$
(☑8339-1458, 2735-3047; r per person incl breakfast US$30; ℗) The owner of this ecolodge on Playa Blanca runs excellent sea-kayaking tours (US$25 per person) and is very knowledgeable about local wildlife. Scarlet macaw sightings are a guarantee as they nest in the tree above the basic but comfy guest cabins. If you call ahead when arriving by bus you can get picked up from the Playa Blanca turnoff.

Suital Lodge　　　　LODGE $$
(☑2200-4662; www.suital.com; s/d US$51/71) Lots of love has gone into this tiny clutch

of six *cabinas* on the northern shores of Golfo Dulce. It's situated 15km northeast of Rincón on 30 hectares of hilly, forested property (not a single tree has been felled). Guests can take advantage of a network of birdwatching trails that winds through the property and down to the beach.

★ **Danta Corcovado Lodge**   LODGE **$$$**
(☑ 2735-1111; www.dantalodge.com; d/bungalow incl breakfast US$108/137; ℙ 🛜) ✒ Midway between the Los Patos Ranger Station and La Palma, this low-key lodge offers tours and activities, including day trips to Corcovado. Winding through this family-run property are 4km of trails, and its delightful room and bungalow designs are dreamed up by the staff, from comfortable wood cabins to a funky concrete dome, with open-air, hot-water bathrooms.

Tours to Los Patos are conducted in a special high-clearance, open-air contraption with benches that's attached to a tractor – the best way to navigate the rough road crisscrossed by a river and ideal for wildlife-viewing.

❶ Getting There & Away

The easiest way to travel on the eastern coast of the peninsula is by car. Otherwise, frequent buses ply the sole road between La Palma and Puerto Jiménez (US$2.50, 30 minutes).

GOLFO DULCE

While the Golfo Dulce is certainly less celebrated than the Península de Osa, an increasing number of travelers are making the arduous journey in search of one of the world's longest left-hand breaks, at Pavones. The region is also home to Parque Nacional Piedras Blancas, a stunning tract of rainforest that used to be part of Corcovado, and still protects the same amazing biodiversity, with some wonderful wilderness lodges on its outskirts. This far corner of Costa Rica is also home to significantly large indigenous populations, who live in the Reserva Indígena Guaymí de Conte Burica near Pavones.

Golfito

POP 7900

With a long and sordid history, spread-out Golfito is a rough-around-the-edges port that stretches out along the Golfo Dulce.

The town was built on bananas – the United Fruit Company moved its regional headquarters here in the '30s. In the 1980s, declining markets, rising taxes, worker unrest and banana diseases forced the company's departure.

In an attempt to boost the region's economy, the federal government built the duty-free Zona Americana in Golfito. The surreal shopping mall Depósito Libre attracts Ticos and expats from around the country, who descend on the otherwise decaying town for 24-hour shopping sprees. There other attractions, such as hiking or horseback riding in a wildlife refuge or kayaking to nearby mangrove forests and islands, but Golfito is largely a transportation hub for hikers heading to Corcovado, surfers heading to Pavones and sportfishers.

◉ Sights

**Refugio Nacional de
Vida Silvestre Golfito**   NATURE RESERVE
(☑ 2775-1210, Sinac office in Golfito 2775-2620; US$10; ☉ 8am-4pm) This small, 28-sq-km reserve encompasses most of the steep hills surrounding Golfito, though it's easy to miss. There are no facilities for visitors, save some poorly maintained trails. About 2km south of the center of Golfito, a gravel road heads inland, past a soccer field, and winds 7km up to some radio towers (Las Torres) 486m above sea level. A very steep hiking trail (two hours), almost opposite the Samoa del Sur hotel, brings you out near the radio towers.

Playa Cacao   BEACH
Just a quick trip across the bay, this small beach offers a prime view of Golfito, with the rainforest as a backdrop. It's a pleasant spot to spend the day, and there are a couple of tasty seafood shacks where you can have lunch. To reach the beach, catch a water taxi from Golfito for around US$6 per person. You can also get to Playa Cacao by taking the 6km dirt road west and then south from the airport – a 4WD is recommended.

🏃 Activities

Golfito is home to several full-service marinas that attract coastal-cruising yachties. If you didn't bring your own boat, you can hire local sailors for tours of the gulf at any of the docks. You can fish year-round, but the best season for the sought-after Pacific sailfish is from November to May.

Banana Bay Marina FISHING
(☑2775-0255, in USA 512-431-4187; www.ba
nanabaymarinagolfito.com) Charters can be
arranged, and a full day of all-inclusive inshore fishing starts at US$650; all-inclusive
offshore fishing starts at US$800.

🛏 Sleeping

Domestic tax-free shoppers usually spend
the night in Golfito, so hotel rooms can be
in short supply on weekends and during
holiday periods. The digs aren't particularly
appealing, with the exception of Hostal Del
Mar, but there are some lovely ecolodges
along the nearby coastline.

Note that the area around the soccer field
in town is Golfito's red-light district.

★ Hostal Del Mar HOSTEL $
(☑4700-0510; www.hostaldelmargolfito.com; dm
US$23, r US$45-55, all incl breakfast; P❀🤶)
This labyrinthine castle-like abode overlooking the Golfo Dulce is run by a sweet
proprietor with tons of local knowledge and
connections to local tour operators. The
rooms are simple, fan-cooled and immaculate, and there's an open-air kitchen for
guests, along with kayaks (US$10 for the
first hour, US$5 per hour thereafter) to ex-
plore a tiny, nearby island.

From the main Hwy 14 into Golfito, take a
left turn along the unpaved road right by El
Ceibo restaurant.

Cabinas Princesa de Golfito CABINA $
(☑2775-0442; s/d US$21/36; P❀🤶) If you're
watching your budget, this cozy little red-
roofed house is the best option. The rooms
aren't too fancy – they have fans and tile
floors, firm beds and mismatched linens –
but it is safe, homey and secure. The *cabinas* are located in the southern part of town,
on Rte 14. They're on the bay side, opposite
the Banco Nacional.

Samoa del Sur HOTEL $$
(☑2775-0233; www.samoadelsur.com; s/d incl
breakfast US$79/85; P❀🤶🔲) This orange,
hard-to-miss facility offers dated rooms outfitted with tiled floors, wood furniture and
thick towels. The bar, with its huge dome
ceiling, is a popular spot in the evenings,
and the restaurant serves typical Tico fare
as well as French specialties like mussels
Provençal. There's a children's pool and a
canopy tour and nature walk suitable for
older children.

Casa Roland Marina Resort RESORT $$$
(☑2775-0180; www.casarolandgolfito.com; s/d
from US$125/140; P❀🤶🔲) Golfito's swishest
hotel primarily caters to duty-free shoppers
looking for an amenity-laden base. You can
expect to find such facilities as a swimming
pool, a restaurant, a bar and a health spa.
But the hotel is overpriced, the basement
rooms are dark and the low ceilings suggest
that they're meant for hobbits.

🍴 Eating

The small, walkable district of the Pueblo
Civil has about a dozen *sodas* of reputable
quality, but the seafood shacks over at Playa
Cacao serve delicious food.

★ Restaurante Buenos Días COSTA RICAN $
(☑2775-1124; meals US$6-10; ☺6am-10pm;
P❀🤶) Rare is the visitor who passes
through Golfito without stopping at this
cheerful spot opposite the Muellecito (Small
Dock). Brightly colored booths, bilingual
menus and a convenient location ensure a
constant stream of guests – whether for an
ample early breakfast, a typical Tico *casado*
or a good old-fashioned burger, accompanied by tamarind and other fresh juices.

Banana Bay Marina INTERNATIONAL $$
(☑2775-0383; mains US$6-15; ☺6am-10pm; 🤶)
Haunted by (mostly) American yachties
and expat duty-free shoppers, the open-air
restaurant at the marina specializes in hu-
mongous plates of American, international
and Tico dishes. Come with a supersized appetite to tackle platters of buffalo wings, potato skins and Veracruz-style snapper, while
football is shown on the big screen.

ℹ Orientation

The southern part of town is where you'll find
most of the bars and businesses, including a
seedy red-light district. Nearby is the so-called
Muellecito (Small Dock), from where the daily
ferry to Puerto Jiménez departs. The northern
part of town was the old United Fruit Company
headquarters, and it retains a languid air with
its large, veranda-decked homes. Now, the
Zona Americana is home to the airport and the
duty-free zone.

ℹ Getting There & Away

AIR
The airport is 4km north of the town center near
the duty-free zone. **NatureAir** (☑2735-5062;

www.natureair.com) and **Sansa** (☎ 2290-4100, in USA 877-767-2672; www.flysansa.com) have daily flights to/from San José. One-way tickets can be as little as US$50.

BOAT

There are two main boat docks for passenger service: the **Muellecito** is the main dock in the southern part of town. There is a smaller dock north of the Muelle Bananero (opposite the ICE building) where you'll find the **Asociación de Boteros** (Abocap; ☎ 8878-1220, 8879-8184, 8426-1345; www.facebook.com/boterosdegolfito), an association of water taxis that can provide services anywhere in the Golfo Dulce area.

Fast ferries travel to Puerto Jiménez from the Muellecito (US$6, 30 minutes), departing at 7am, 10am, 11:30am, 1pm, 3pm and 5pm daily. This schedule is subject to change, so it's best to check for current times at the dock; in any event, show up early to ensure a spot.

You can also take a private water taxi to Puerto Jiménez. You'll have to negotiate, but prices are usually between US$25 and US$30 per person (sometimes with a US$60 minimum).

At research time there was no scheduled shared *lancha* (small motorboat) to Zancudo, but you can negotiate with loitering boatmen to run you over for around US$30 per person. If you're staying at a coastal lodge north of Golfito and you've made prior arrangements for transportation, the lodge will pick you up at the docks.

BUS

Most buses stop at the depot opposite the small park in the southern part of town. Tracopa buses depart from the **stop** (☎ 2775-0365) across from the fire station. Destinations include Neily (US$3, 1½ hours, every 30 minutes 6am to 7pm), Pavones (US$4, 2½ hours, 10am and 3pm), San José via San Isidro de El General and the Costanera (Tracopa; US$15, seven hours, 5am and 1:30pm, 2pm Sun) and Zancudo (US$4, three hours, 10am and 3pm).

Parque Nacional Piedras Blancas

One of the last remaining stretches of lowland rainforest on the Pacific, Piedras Blancas is home to a mindboggling array of flora and fauna, including many of Costa Rica's most exciting animals: pumas, jaguars, monkeys, two-toed sloths and numerous species of bats. Dozens of species of migrating birds stop by here also. According to a study conducted at the biological station at La Gamba, the biodiversity of trees in Piedras Blancas is the densest in all of Costa Rica, even surpassing Corcovado.

Consisting of parcels of land purchased by benefactors as diverse as the Nature Conservancy and the Austrian government, this national park was established in 1992 as an extension of Parque Nacional Corcovado, though it's now an independent entity. Piedras Blancas has 120 sq km of undisturbed tropical primary rainforest, as well as 20 sq km of secondary forests, pastureland, coastal cliffs and beaches.

🛏 Sleeping

★ **Finca Bellavista**   TREEHOUSE **$$**
(www.fincabellavista.com; tree house US$50-275)
🌿 Costa Rica's most ambitious tree-house project is the 600-acre Finca Bellavista, an upscale community of arboreal abodes in the vicinity of Parque Nacional Piedras Blancas (the exact location is emailed to guests once they've booked). Canopy dwellings are individually owned and rented out when unoccupied, and dinner is grown in a garden on the rainforest floor below.

Many of the homes offer kitchens, electricity and running water, and the rainforest and waterfall hikes around the property are a nature-lover's dream. There's a two-night minimum, and bookings are handled through the website.

Esquinas Rainforest Lodge   LODGE **$$$**
(☎ 2741-8001; www.esquinaslodge.com; s/d incl meals US$146/260; P🐾❄) 🌿 Esquinas consists of 16 spacious, high-ceilinged, fan-cooled cabins with indigenous textiles on the walls. The lodge's extensive grounds comprise a network of well-marked trails and a stream-fed pool. It was founded by the nonprofit Rainforest of the Austrians, vital in the establishment of Piedras Blancas as a national park. It's in Gamba, 7km west of Km 37 on the Interamericana.

❶ Getting There & Away

Piedras Blancas is best accessed from the Esquinas Rainforest Lodge, which has an extensive trail network onsite and can easily arrange guided hikes deeper into the park. If you don't have your own transportation, any bus heading north from Golfito can drop you off at the lodge.

If you're staying at any of the coastal lodges north of Golfito, you can inquire about transportation to/from the park as well as guided hikes into the interior.

1. Harpy eagle
This rare eagle can be spotted in Parque Nacional Chirripó (p416), Parque Internacional La Amistad (p424) and Parque Nacional Corcovado (p434).

2. Cerro Chirripó (p416)
Costa Rica's highest peak is a difficult but rewarding climb.

3. Parque Nacional Chirripó (p416)
Cloud forest dominates the hillsides of the national park; the cool undergrowth harbors mushrooms and other plant life.

4. Parque Internacional La Amistad (p424)
The largest protected area in Costa Rica protects a range of animals and habitats.

Zancudo

POP 450

Occupying a slender finger of land that juts into the Golfo Dulce, the tiny village of Zancudo is about as laid-back a beach destination as you'll find in Costa Rica. On the west side of town, gentle, warm Pacific waters lap onto black sands, and seeing more than a handful of people on the beach means it's crowded. On the east side, a tangle of mangrove swamps attracts birds, crocodiles and plenty of fish, which in turn attract fishers hoping to reel them in.

Unlike nearby Pavones, a surf destination, Zancudo is content to remain a far-flung village in a far-flung corner of Costa Rica.

🏃 Activities

The main activities at Zancudo are undoubtedly swinging on hammocks, strolling on the beach and swimming in the aqua-blue waters of the Golfo Dulce. Here, the surf is gentle, and at night the water sometimes sparkles with bioluminescence – tiny phosphorescent marine plants and plankton that light up if you sweep a hand through the water. The effect is like underwater fireflies.

🛏 Sleeping & Eating

Be aware that life goes into hibernation mode in low season – accommodations are discounted up to 50% and there's even less going on than usual. Those seeking solitude and a little self-sufficiency will find Zancudo to be just the thing.

Cabinas Coloso Del Mar   CABINA **$**
(☑2776-0050; www.colosodelmar.com; r US$40-49; P�) It's the little touches that make Coloso stand out – matching sheets, shiny hardwood floors and coffee makers. Bigger-picture attractions include its ideal location steps from the surf, a cute cafe, JC the stellar manager, Edwin who mixes a mean cocktail, and friendly dogs underfoot.

Sol y Mar   CABINA **$**
(☑2776-0014; www.zancudo.com; cabins US$35-56; P@) This popular hangout offers various lodging options, from smallish cheapies further from the water to private deluxe units with fancy tile showers and unobstructed ocean views. Even if you're not staying here, the open-air restaurant, serving fish burgers and chicken cordon bleu (mains US$3 to US$12), and thatched bar are Zancudo favorites.

Cabinas Pura Vida   HOSTEL **$**
(☑2776-0029; www.cabinaspuravida.com; ⊙dm US$10) This Zancudo cheapie proves that Costa Rica is still a friend to backpackers, while providing a fun gathering spot for travelers from the far reaches of the Earth. Dorm rooms are simple but adequate, and the group dinners on weekends (and drinks thereafter) can get rowdy.

Cabinas Au Coeur du Soleil   CABINA **$$**
(☑2776-0112; www.aucoeurdusoleil.com; cabins US$50-80; P�) These three brightly painted, lovingly maintained cabins have fans, fridges and kitchenettes, hammock-strewn porches and tons of homey charm. Young French-Canadian hosts Joanne and Daniel are warm and gregarious, and offer guests the use of bikes for cruising around Zancudo and kayaks and bodyboards for hitting the sea.

Cabinas Los Cocos   CABINA **$$**
(☑2776-0012; www.loscocos.com; cabins US$85; P) Los Cocos, run by the ever-helpful Susan, is home to two historical cabins that used to be banana-company homes in Palmar but were transported to Zancudo and completely restored. The other two more *rancho* cabins are also charming, with hardwood floors and loft sleeping areas under palm-frond roofs. Boat taxi to Golfito (US$60) can be arranged.

★ Zancudo Lodge   LODGE **$$$**
(☑2776-0008; www.zancudolodge.com; r/ste from US$352/446; P❄�☕) The most luxurious retreat in Zancudo by a long shot, this 16-room lodge sits amid landscaped grounds, complete with trickling water features, bamboo stockades, and spacious, tranquil rooms fitted out with fine linens and other creature comforts. The open-sided gourmet restaurant (open to nonguests) is known for its devotion to ultrafresh produce. Sportfishing outings and boat pickup from Golfito arranged.

★ Gamefisher Restaurant   INTERNATIONAL **$$**
(mains US$10-25; ⊙11am-10pm; �☑) This terrific open-sided restaurant inside the Zancudo Lodge prides itself on its commitment to super-fresh produce and creativity, and it shows – in the best fish tacos for miles around, the tuna smoked in-house and the fine-dining experience in the evenings that makes the most of locally available ingredients.

ℹ Getting There & Away

BOAT

The boat dock is near the north end of the beach on the inland, estuary side. In the high season, the public water ferry is reliable and frequent, but the price varies. Cabinas and hotels in Zancudo can also arrange private water taxis at the time of your choosing, starting at US$60 for two people and becoming cheaper per person as the group size increases. For US$80, a boat captain will take you to Puerto Jiménez.

BUS

A bus to the border at Paso Canoas passes through Zancudo at around 6am each morning (US$42.75, two hours). In Conte, passengers may switch to a bus to Golfito. Those continuing to the border will exit the bus at Laurel and catch a collective taxi the rest of the way.

CAR

From both Golfito and Paso Canoas, roads to Zancudo are well signposted. The main roads are paved, but as you get closer to Zancudo, long stretches of road are not. Outside of the dry season, a 4WD is recommended. There are two ways of getting from Zancudo to Pavones: the bumpy coastal road that requires a 4WD as it crosses several creeks, and the main unpaved road (retrace your steps to the fork). It takes around 1¼ hours to drive from Golfito and about 45 minutes to drive to Pavones.

Pavones

POP 2750

Pavones is a legendary destination for surfers the world over. As this is Costa Rica's southernmost point, you'll need to work hard to get down here. However, the journey is an adventure in its own right, especially since the best months for surfing coincide with the rainy season.

The village remains relatively off the beaten path, and though both foreigners and Ticos are transforming Pavones from its days as a relative backwater, Pavones' few streets are still unpaved, the pace of life is slow and the overall atmosphere is tranquil and New Agey.

🏃 Activities

Surfing

Pavones is legendary among surfers for being one of the longest left breaks in the world (up there with a 2km-long break in Chicama, Peru, and an even longer sand-bottomed left in Namibia's Skeleton Bay).

On the best days, your ride can last over two minutes!

Conditions are best with a southern swell, usually during the rainy season from April to October, but the rest of the year the waves are ideal for beginners. **Sea Kings Surf Shop** (☏2776-2015; www.seakingssurfshop.com; ⊙9am-5pm Mon-Sat) has boards for rent and arranges surfing lessons.

When Pavones has nothing (or when it's too crowded), head south to Punta Banco, a reef break with decent rights and lefts. The best conditions are at mid- or high tide, especially with swells from the south or west.

Yoga

Surfing goes hand in hand with yoga, and there are several yoga studios in Pavones where you can stretch your knotted limbs.

Shooting Star Studio   YOGA
(☏2776-2107, 8829-2409; www.yogapavones.com; drop-in class US$15) Only 30m from the beach, this yoga studio is open-air and offers several classes per week, including a specialized 'Yoga for Surfers.' To get here, you have to go all the way to Punta Banco, and then take the steep road uphill (best walked).

Pavones Yoga Center   YOGA
(☏in USA 937-474-2387; www.pavonesyogacenter.com; Calle Altamira; drop-in class US$10) Classes at this teacher-training facility tend to be Vinyasa yoga, and also 'Surfers' Therapeutic Yoga' to help you unwind after long sessions in the water; find the class schedule on its website. It's 800m along Calle Altamira – the steep, unpaved road going uphill from the Río Claro grocery store crossroads; if driving, you need a 4WD.

🛏 Sleeping

Accommodations are scattered along the main road in Playa Río Claro and along the coastal road to Punta Banco. Some budget places tend to operate on a first-come, first-served basis. Some shoestringers and locals camp along the coastal road to Punta Banco.

🛏 Playa Río Claro

Cabinas & Café de la Suerte   GUESTHOUSE **$**
(☏2776-2388; r/house US$75/100; ❄ 🐾) Run by a friendly surfer couple (who also run the vegetarian restaurant on the premises), this colorful three-room guesthouse is just 50m from the beach and comes with a hammock-hung terrace shared by the

upstairs rooms and a secluded garden corner for the downstairs one. Rooms have fridges. From the supermarket crossroads, follow the beach road to the left.

Surf House
HOSTEL $

(☎8508-7779; www.facebook.com/pavones rooms/; dm US$20, r from US$40; P🖥🛜) 🍴 A new crash pad for surfers, this funky hostel is right near the beach and offers comfy beds, a chill atmosphere and plenty of eco-friendliness. (The meals are vegan and management makes a show of composting and recycling.) Accommodations vary, with dorms and private rooms, some sharing bathrooms, some featuring air conditioning.

Cabinas Mira Olas
CABINA $

(☎2776-2006, 8393-7742; www.miraolas.com; d/tr from US$38/48; P🛜) This 4.5-hectare farm is full of wildlife and fruit trees, with a lookout at the top of a hill. A sweet duplex with comfortable tiled cabins has a terrace in front, while the 'Jungle Deluxe' is a beautiful, open-air lodging with a huge balcony, kitchen and elegant cathedral ceiling. It's signposted off the Río Claro road, before the bridge.

Riviera Riverside Villas
VILLA $$$

(☎2776-2396; www.pavonesriviera.com; r/house US$110/160; P🖥🛜) This clutch of upmarket *cabinas* and homes in Pavones proper offers fully equipped kitchens, cool tile floors and attractive hardwood ceilings. Big shady porches overlook the landscaped fruit gardens, which are visited by birds and monkeys and offer a degree of intimacy and privacy found at few other places in town. There are also boards for rent.

🛏 Punta Banco

★ Rancho Burica
LODGE $

(☎2776-2223; www.ranchoburica.com; dm US$15, s/d US$40/70, without bathroom US$25/45; P🖥🛜) This legendary Dutch-run outpost is literally the end of the road in Punta Banco, and it's where surfers gather to socialize in the evenings. Rooms are cooled with fans, and hammocks are interspersed around the property, which has convivial common areas, a restaurant and a trail to a romantic jungle lookout. Meals are family-style; guests aren't allowed to cook.

Clientele mainly includes surfers, but those interested in relaxation, wildlife and yoga will also land well here, as there's a newly constructed yoga deck and lots of rare

birds flitting around. The owners are also involved in a community turtle conservation project.

Lanzas de Fuego Surf & Adventure Lodge
LODGE $$

(☎2776-2014, 8634-0739; www.lanzasdefuego. com; per person US$45; ❇🛜) Run by cheerful South African owner Rainy, this hillside lodge organizes multiday surfing, birding and sportfishing packages, with its own boat to whisk surfers to the best hot spots. It's an intimate, friendly place, with three cabins to accommodate eight guests, a huge thatched-roofed hangout space and a restaurant serving wholesome Tico meals. Cross the bridge and carry on until the signpost.

Yoga Farm
LODGE $$

(www.yogafarmcostarica.org; dm/r/cabin incl meals & yoga US$43/50/65) 🍴 This tranquil retreat has simple rooms and dorms, three vegetarian meals prepared with ingredients from the organic garden, and daily yoga classes in an open-air studio overlooking the ocean. It's an uphill 15-minute walk from road's end at Rancho Burica: take the uphill road and go through the first gate on the left. No wi-fi or phones; rejuvenation is key.

★ Tiskita Jungle Lodge
LODGE $$$

(☎2296-8125; www.tiskita.com; r/ste incl all meals from US$285/380; P🖥❇) Set amid extensive gardens and orchards, this lodge is arguably the most beautiful and intimate in all of Golfo Dulce. Accommodations are in various stunning wooden cabins accented by stone garden showers that allow you to freshen up while birdwatching. Guided birding walks, horseback riding, night tours and surfing lessons are available. Advance reservations required; three-night minimum.

Multiple cabin rooms are geared toward families, and the nature walks and horse-riding tours are suitable for children.

Rancho Cannatella
VILLA $$$

(☎2776-2228; www.pavonesranchocannatella. com; rancho US$495, 5-night minimum; P🛜❇) About 2km toward Punta Banco, this former surfer's haven has been turned into a luxurious four-room retreat, complete with maid service, fully stocked chef's kitchen, outdoor shower for one of the rooms, balconies with ocean views and hammocks around the pool. Ideal for a family or group of friends. Surfing and paddleboarding lessons can be arranged.

Castillo de Pavones BOUTIQUE HOTEL $$$
(2776-2191; ste/villa from US$125/400;
P❂☎) This hillside stone mansion with
a wrought-iron staircase overlooks the
Pavones point break from its lofty perch.
Cross the bridge and follow the rough road
until the signpost. Accommodations are in
four individually decorated and furnished
suites and a self-contained four-bedroom
villa; our favorite suite is the split-level Aves.
Fantasic food, revitalising packages, sport-
fishing and surfing are on offer, too.

One of the split-level suites is specifically
furnished to accommodate a family.

✖ Eating

Soda Doña Dora COSTA RICAN $
(2776-2021; meals US$4-8; ☻6am-10pm)
This long-standing family-run spot serves
up huge breakfasts of *gallo pinto,* eggs
and toast; banana pancakes; *casados* with
fresh seafood; burgers and fries; and cheap
beer. Look for the Bar La Plaza sign just
inland from the football field; the *soda* and
bar share this space. If driving, take the
beach road from the supermarket
crossroads.

Café de la Suerte CAFE $
(2776-2388; meals US$4-9; ☻8am-5pm Mon-
Sat; ☎✎) Filling breakfasts, omelets and
veggie dishes dominate the menu, the chef
makes her own hummus, and there's usually
a daily special (veggie burgers, lasagna) –
all to be washed down with a tropical-fruit
smoothie. If you have a sweet tooth, there
are gooey brownies on offer.

★ La Bruschetta ITALIAN $$
(La Piña; 2776-2174; mains US$7-12; ☻10am-
10pm; ☎✎) A couple of kilometers along
the beach road to Punta Banco, this cheerful
place decked out with fairy lights is the most
happenin' spot in town. The lovely owner
serves ample portions of homemade pasta,
wood-fired pizza and Italian desserts, all
made with care and authentic ingredients.
The sign says 'La Piña' and many locals still
call it that.

❶ Orientation

The name Pavones is used to refer to both Playa
Río Claro de Pavones and Punta Banco, which is
6km south.

The road into Pavones first arrives at Río Claro,
where you'll find a crossroads with two small
supermarkets. One road leads straight to the
beach, with a couple of eateries and a surf rental
shop. The road leading to the left crosses a
bridge and carries straight on; Playa Río Claro's
accommodations are located along and off this
road. Straight after the bridge, another road
heads right and runs parallel to the waterfront
for 6km to Punta Banco where, as the locals say,
'the bad road ends and the good life begins' –
the rest of the accommodations are spread out
along this coastal road.

❶ Information

We cannot stress this enough: Pavones has no
bank or gas station, so make sure you have plenty of money and gas prior to arrival. Very few
places accept credit cards and the nearest ATM
and gas station are in Laurel, an hour's drive
away. In an emergency, you can buy gas at the
grocery store (for a high price).

❶ Getting There & Away

AIR

NatureAir (2735-5062; www.natureair.com),
Sansa (2290-4100, in USA 877-767-2672;
www.flysansa.com) and **Alfa Romeo Aero Taxi**
(8632-8150; www.alfaromeoair.com) offer
charter flights. Prices are dependent on the
number of passengers, so it's best to try to
organize a larger group if you're considering this
option.

BUS

Two daily buses go to Golfito (US$3.80, two
hours). The first leaves at 5:15am, departing
from the end of the road in Punta Banco and
stopping by the two supermarkets. The second
leaves at 12:30pm from the school. You can also
pick up the early bus in Pavones; check locally
for the current bus stops.

CAR

The turnoff to Pavones and Zancudo is well
signposted from the main road leading south
from Golfito to Laurel. The main road is partially
paved; the 32km of minor road that leads to
Pavones is not. There's a rough coastal road
connecting Pavones to Zancudo that requires a
4WD as it crosses several creeks; alternatively,
retrace your steps to the fork in the road. It takes
around 1¼ hours to drive from Golfito and about
45 minutes to drive to Zancudo.

TAXI

A 4WD taxi will charge about US$80 from Golf-
ito, and US$70 from Paso Canoas. One of the
locals operates a shared-van service to Paso
Canoas and Golfito on demand for US$16 per
person; ask around to see if it's operating during
your visit.

PLAYAS SAN JOSECITO, NICUESA & CATIVO

Idyllic deserted beaches, backed by the pristine rainforest of Parque Nacional Piedras Blancas, define the northeastern shore of the Golfo Dulce. The appeal of this area is only enhanced by its inaccessibility: part of the charm is that very few people make it to this untouched corner of Costa Rica. If you're looking for a romantic retreat or a secluded getaway, all of the lodges along this stretch of coastline are completely isolated and serve as perfect spots for quiet reflection.

They also provide kayaks for maritime exploration and transport to **Casa Orquideas** (self-guided tour US$10), a vibrant botanical garden only accessible by boat, along with direct access to the wilds of Piedras Blancas. Miles of trails lead to secluded beaches, cascading waterfalls and other undiscovered attractions.

Playa Nicuesa Rainforest Lodge (☏2258-8250, in USA 866-504-8116; www.nicuesa lodge.com; Playa Nicuesa; s/d from US$305/490; ☏) Nestled into a 65-hectare private reserve, this place is part retreat, part activity center. The dreamy accommodations come with canopied beds, indigenous textile spreads and garden showers. Meals are served in a thatched *rancho* and owners Michael and Donna have activities for all the family, from sportfishing to rainforest adventures. Two-night minimum stay.

Dolphin Quest (☏8669-4688, 8811-2099; www.dolphinquestcostarica.com; Playa San Josecito; s/d campsite US$60/100, cabin US$85/160, house US$110/200; P ☏) This jungle lodge offers a mile of beach and 750 secluded acres of mountainous rainforest, with accommodations in round, thatched-roof cabins. Meals – featuring organic ingredients from the garden – are served in an open-air pavilion near the shore. Beachcombing, horseback riding, snorkeling and fishing are on offer, and there's a real timelessness to the place. The hotel is only reachable by private boat.

PARQUE NACIONAL ISLA DEL COCO

A tiny speck of green amid the endless Pacific, Isla del Coco looms large in the imagination of the adventurer: jagged mountains and tales of treasure, a pristine and isolated ecosystem filled with wildlife and some of the world's best diving. Remember the opening aerial shot of *Jurassic Park,* where the helicopter sweeps over the sea to a jungle-covered island? That was here.

As beautiful as the island may be, its terrestrial environs pale in comparison to what lies beneath. Named by PADI as one of the world's top 10 dive spots, the surrounding waters of Isla del Coco harbor abundant pelagics, including one of the largest known schools of hammerhead sharks in the world.

Isla del Coco (aka Cocos Island) is around 500km southwest of the mainland in the middle of the eastern Pacific, making it Costa Rica's most remote destination.

History

In 1526 Spanish explorer Joan Cabezas stumbled onto Isla del Coco, though it wasn't noted on maps until its second discovery by French cartographer Nicolás Desliens in 1541; prior to being 'discovered' by Europeans, Isla del Coco received pre-Columbian seafaring visitors from Latin America. In the centuries that followed, heavy rainfall attracted the attention of sailors, pirates and whalers, who frequently stopped by for fresh water, seafood and coconuts.

Between the late 17th and early 19th centuries, Isla del Coco became a way station for pirates who are rumored to have hidden countless treasures here. The most famous was the storied Treasure of Lima, a trove of gold and silver ingots, gold laminae scavenged from church domes and a solid-gold, life-sized sculpture of the Virgin Mary. 'X marks the spot,' right? Not really. More than 400 treasure-hunting expeditions have found only failure. In fact, in 1869 the government of Costa Rica organized an official treasure hunt. They didn't find anything, but the expedition resulted in Costa Rica taking possession of the island, a treasure in itself, and it was declared a national park in 1978.

German settlers arrived on the island in the late 19th and early 20th centuries, though their stay on Isla del Coco was short-lived. However, they did leave behind a host of invasive plants and domestic animals that have since converted into feral populations of pigs, goats, cats and rats – all of which threaten the natural wildlife.

🏃 Activities

Diving

The diving is excellent, and is regarded by most as the main attraction of the island. But strong oceanic currents can lead to treacherous underwater conditions, and Isla del Coco can only be recommended to intermediate and advanced divers with sufficient experience. Divers are wise to bring gloves to cling onto the rocks.

The island has two large bays with safe anchorages and sandy beaches: Chatham Bay is located on the northeast side and Wafer Bay is on the northwest.

The island's marine life is hugely varied, with more than a dozen species of coral, more than 50 types of crustaceans and more than 270 species of fish. Sea turtles, manta rays, marble rays, dolphins and sharks are also abundant. Just off Cocos are a series of smaller basaltic rocks and islets, which constitute some of the best dive sites.

Isla Manuelita is a prime spot, home to a wide array of fish, rays and eels, as well as schools of manta rays. Eleven species of shark also inhabit these waters, including huge schools of scalloped hammerheads as well as whitetips, which are best spotted at night. Dirty Rock is another main attraction – a spectacular rock formation that harbors all kinds of sea creatures.

Diving is possible year-round, and tiger sharks, Galapagos sharks and whitetip sharks are always around, but the best time to see hammerhead sharks is the May–November rainy season.

Undersea Hunter   DIVING
(☎ 2228-6613, in the USA 800-203-2120; www.underseahunter.com) Runs liveaboard 10- and 12-day land and sea expeditions to Isla del Coco from Puntarenas, with room for 14 to 18 people, from US$5645 per person. Undersea Hunter passengers can also experience life at 1000ft below the ocean's surface, in the **DeepSee Submersible** (☎ 2228-6613, in USA 800-203-2120; 80/300m dive US$1450/1850).

Aggressor   DIVING
(☎ in USA & Canada 800-348-2628; www.aggressor.com) Operates a fleet of liveaboard diving boats in different destinations around the world. Offers eight- and 10-day land and sea expedition charters on *Okeanos Aggressor I*

OFF THE BEATEN TRACK

BIOLLEY

Below the wilderness of Parque Internacional La Amistad, a network of rural villages is signposted by Gaudí-esque mosaic navigation markers made by a local artist. These farming villages went about their business mostly unperturbed by tourists until 1997, when an enterprising group of local women in the village of Biolley (pronounced *bee-oh-lay*; named for a Swiss biologist who settled here) set up a cooperative, Asociación de Mujeres Organizadas de Biolley (Asomobi). It has 37 members and is designed to promote rural tourism in the area and to generate funds for the cooperative's various sustainable projects, such as organic coffee growing.

Asomobi (☎ 8916-4638, 2200-4250; www.asomobi-costarica.com) organizes coffee tours that let you visit the *beneficio* (processing plant) in Biolley that processes delicious locally grown coffee. It uses ecofriendly methods that conserve water and compost organic waste for use as fertilizer.

Other tours are on offer, from birding outings and hot-springs tours to hiking the Valle del Silencio in Parque Internacional La Amistad. Arrange in advance.

Asomobi can arrange inexpensive accommodations in a Biolley homestay with a friendly local family. The cooperative operates a hotel, **Posada Cerro Biolley** (☎ 2200-4250; http://asomobi-costarica.com; Biolley; per person incl breakfast $20; P 🛜), which was rebuilt after a fire destroyed it in 2012. Down the road, **Hotel Finca Palo Alto** (☎ 2743-1063, 2743-1062; www.hotelfincapaloalto.com; Biolley; dm/r US$30/57; P 🌊) is also a decent place to stay.

Biolley is 6km west of the crossroads in Altamira village, but the way there zigzags and is poorly signed; get detailed directions at AsoProLA (p425) or by calling Asomobi if traveling independently.

and *Okeanos Aggressor II* from Puntarenas to Isla del Coco from US$5299 per person.

Hiking

Even though this is the turf of hard-core divers, making landfall and exploring is worth the time and effort.

Rugged, heavily forested and punctuated by cascading waterfalls, Cocos is ringed and transected by an elaborate network of trails. The highest point is at **Cerro Iglesias** (575m), where you can soak up spectacular views of the lush, verdant island and the deep blue Pacific.

Note that visitors to the island must first register with the park rangers, though your tour company will most likely make all the necessary arrangements well in advance.

Because of its remote location, Isla del Coco is the most pristine national park in the country and one of Costa Rica's great wildlife destinations. Since the island was never linked to the Americas during its comparatively short geological history, Cocos is home to a very large number of rare endemic species.

Heading inland from the coastal forests up to the high-altitude cloud forests, it is possible to find around 235 unique species of flowering plants, 30% of which are found only on the island. This incredible diversity of flora supports more than 400 known

insect species – 65 endemics, as well as a striking range of butterflies and moths, are included in this count. Scientists believe that more remain to be discovered.

Of the 87 recorded bird species on the island and neighboring rocks, the most pronounced are the aquatic birds: brown and red-footed boobies, great frigatebirds, white terns and brown noddies. There are also three terrestrial endemics, namely the Cocos cuckoo, Cocos flycatcher and Cocos finch.

ℹ Information

In order to protect the conservation status of the island, all visitors must apply for a permit at the **Área de Conservación Marina Isla del Coco** (Acmic; Map p72; ✆ in San José 2250-7295, 2258-8750; ⊙ 8am-3pm Mon-Fri) in San José (which costs a whopping US$70 per day). However, unless you're sailing to the island on a private boat, tour operators will make all the necessary arrangements for you.

ℹ Getting There & Away

The only way to get here is via a liveaboard diving boat. With advance reservations, both of the liveaboard diving tour companies in Puntarenas will arrange transfers from either San José or Liberia to Puntarenas, which is the embarkation/disembarkation point for tours. It takes 32 hours by boat from Puntarenas to Isla del Coco.

Understand
Costa Rica

Costa Rica Today

Costa Rica remains one of the more prosperous and stable countries in Central America. It's also one of the only nations in the region without an army. Sound environmental management is a prominent issue, and green proposals were recurring themes in political campaigns during the lead-up to the 2018 general election. Agriculture is one of Costa Rica's main industries, but tourism is its economic backbone.

Best on Film

El Regreso (The Return; 2011) Featuring a realistic, contemporary plot, this is the first Tico film to earn international acclaim; Hernán Jiménez wrote, directed, starred in and crowdfunded it.

Agua Fría de Mar (Cold Ocean Water; 2010) Directed by Paz Fábrega, this social commentary unfolds at a paradisiacal Pacific beach; the film won several international awards.

Caribe (Caribbean; 2004) The first Costa Rican film ever to be submitted for Oscar consideration; it's a drama set in Limón.

Best in Print

Tropical Nature: Life and Death in the Rain Forests of Central and South America (Adrian Forsyth and Ken Miyata; 1987) Easy-to-digest natural-history essays on rainforest phenomena, written by two biologists.

There Never Was a Once Upon a Time (Carmen Naranjo; 1989) Ten stories, narrated by children and adolescents, by Costa Rica's most widely translated novelist.

Costa Rica: A Traveler's Literary Companion (Barbara Ras, foreword by Óscar Arias; 1994) Collection of stories reflecting distinct regions of Costa Rica.

Carbon Neutrality

Costa Rica has long had a reputation for being green, but, to paraphrase Kermit, it ain't easy. In 2009, then-president Óscar Arias set a big goal: that Costa Rica would achieve carbon neutrality by the year 2021. Achieving this would make Costa Rica the world's first carbon-neutral country and would coincide auspiciously with its bicentennial.

Some measures have not yet been implemented as scheduled, and the numbers suggest that the 2021 target may have been overly ambitious. Proposed changes for the energy sector, for example, include transitioning buses and taxis to natural gas, electric and hybrid vehicles, and imposing stricter emissions regulations on these companies. Agricultural changes include government-sponsored training programs for smaller farms, teaching them to implement organic methods such as composting, using biochar and creating biodigester systems to trap methane gases and use them as on-site fuel. For larger-scale agriculture, such as the country's sprawling banana plantations, government incentives encourage reforestation and conservation of existing rainforest in order to offset carbon-dioxide emissions (most of which are generated from overseas shipping).

In 2016 Costa Rica produced 98% of its electricity from renewables. That same year, the nation ran without fossil fuel–generated electricity for 271 days, including a 110-day run between 17 June and 6 October. This feat was achieved using hydro, wind and geothermal power to deliver electricity to homes. However, despite Costa Rica's best efforts, it has an oil-reliant transport infrastructure, so in big-picture terms nonrenewables make up most of the country's energy use.

Costa Rica's Elections

On April 1, 2018, Costa Rica elected a new president, Carlos Alvarado Quesada, of the center-left Citizen Action Party (PAC). Although polls predicted the run-off would be a close race, it wasn't. Alvarado – a 38-year-old novelist, musician and former cabinet minister – won more than 60% of the vote, handily defeating Fabricio Alvarado Munoz (a right-wing former TV anchor and evangelical preacher from the National Restoration Party). The decisive victory was particularly good news for progressives and proponents of gay rights. Key challenges the new president faces include an escalating murder rate and a widening national deficit.

Joining Alvarado in structuring Costa Rica's future is economist and politician Epsy Campbell Barr, who became the first female vice president of African descent in Latin America.

Alvarado took the reins from former President Luis Guillermo Solís, also a member of PAC. Solís was Costa Rica's first president in half a century not to come from the two-party system, under which the social-democratic National Liberation Party and the center-right Social Christian Unity Party took turns holding power.

Relations with Nicaragua

The Río San Juan forms the eastern stretch of the border between Costa Rica and Nicaragua. This quiet waterway has been the source of much discord between the two countries, and the International Court of Justice (ICJ) has had to preside over several legal disputes in the last 20 years.

The latest flap started with Nicaragua dredging Isla Calero's river delta in late 2010. This involved trees being felled and earth being dumped into the river. Nicaraguan soldiers were present during the process and the Costa Rican government decided to claim invasion – the situation deteriorated from there. In March 2011, when the ICJ considered the case and reiterated the validity of the Cañas-Jerez Treaty, both sides interpreted the language as a win.

Subsequently, then-president of Costa Rica Laura Chinchilla called for emergency funds to begin construction of a road along the Costa Rican bank of the river, without proper environmental or engineering reviews. This caused consternation about the road's environmental and political impact, not only in Nicaragua but also in Costa Rica. Nicaraguan president Daniel Ortega, for his part, has also proposed the construction of a trans-oceanic canal in the Río San Juan. In December 2015 the ICJ ruled that Costa Rica has sovereignty over the 3km patch of wetlands in Río San Juan, and Nicaragua promised to abide by the ruling.

POPULATION: **4.87 MILLION**

AREA: **51,100 SQ KM**

ADULT LITERACY: **97%**

POPULATION LIVING BELOW THE POVERTY LINE: **20.5%**

CARBON-DIOXIDE EMISSIONS: **1.6 METRIC TONS PER PERSON PER YEAR**

if Costa Rica were 100 people

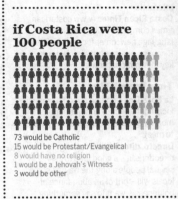

73 would be Catholic
15 would be Protestant/Evangelical
8 would have no religion
1 would be a Jehovah's Witness
3 would be other

race
(% of population)

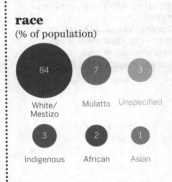

84 White/Mestizo
7 Mulatto
3 Unspecified
3 Indigenous
2 African
1 Asian

Population per Sq Mile

COSTA RICA   NICARAGUA   USA

🚶 ≈ 30 people

Gringo Media

The Tico Times (www.ticotimes.net) Costa Rica's biggest English-language newspaper stopped its print run in 2012; it's now available online only.

Radio Dos Broadcasting across the country on 99.5FM, Radio 2 spins an amazing selection of US Top-40 music spanning several decades; it's probably most appealing to Gen X and older. It's officially a Spanish-language station, but much of the music is international.

Costa Rican Times (www.costarican times.com) This online, English-language newcomer focuses on Costa Rican happenings but also features key international news.

Tico Travel Tips

La hora Tica Don't be put off if your local host views an appointment as more of a ballpark suggestion of when to meet.

Directo, directo When asking directions, it's a good idea to ask several people along the way, as some locals will – out of an abundance of politeness – want to say something helpful even if they're not sure how to get there.

Church as compass All Costa Rican churches face west, which is very useful when you're trying to navigate your way around a town.

Sadly, tensions escalated again in late 2015, this time in relation to Cuban immigrants. Hundreds of Cubans were trying to cross Central America to reach the US, fearing that the thawing of relations between Cuba and the US would soon mean an end to their right to asylum in the latter. Costa Rica was granting short-term visas to Cubans, but they were being turned back at the Nicaraguan border in spite of appeals by the Costa Rican government that they be granted a 'humanitarian corridor' through the region. In early 2016, talks with Nicaragua broke down. Hundreds of Cuban immigrants were instead flown from Costa Rica to Mexico, from where they would have to make their way to the US border.

However, since then the relationship between the US and Cuba has improved further, and in January 2017 former US president Barack Obama scrapped the historic 'wet foot, dry foot' policy that granted Cubans immigrant status. Fearing that they would become alternative destinations for Cubans, Costa Rica and Panama followed Nicaragua in turning Cubans away.

At the beginning of 2017 the Costa Rican government filed a new case with the ICJ concerning continued Nicaraguan military presence on its territory. It also asked for a new deadline and a compensation amount for the 2015 settlement to be issued.

History

Like other Central American countries, Costa Rica's history remains a loose sketch during the reign of its pre-Columbian tribes, and European 'discovery' of the New World was followed by the subjugation and evangelization of Costa Rica's indigenous peoples. But in the mid-20th century, Costa Rica radically departed from the standard Central American playbook by abolishing its army, diversifying its economy and brokering peace in the region, paving the way for today's stable and environmentally friendly nation.

Lost Worlds of Ancient Costa Rica

The coastlines and rainforests of Central America have been inhabited by humans for at least 10,000 years, but ancient civilizations in Costa Rica are largely the subject of speculation. It is thought that the area was something of a backwater straddling the two great civilizations of the Andes and Mesoamerica, with the exception of the Diquís Valley along the Pacific coast, where archaeological finds suggest that a great deal of trading took place between early inhabitants of Costa Rica and their more powerful neighbors. On the eve of European discovery some 500 years ago, an estimated 400,000 people were living in today's Costa Rica.

Unlike the massive pyramid complexes found throughout other parts of Latin America, the ancient towns and cities of Costa Rica (with the exception of Guayabo) were loosely organized and had no centralized government or ceremonial centers. The settlements fought among each other, but for the purpose of getting slaves rather than to extend their territory. Not known for building edifices that would stand the test of time, Costa Rica's early inhabitants did, however, leave behind mysterious relics: enormous stone spheres, liberally scattered around the Diquís Valley.

Pre-Colombian Sites

Monumento Nacional Arqueológico Guayabo (Turrialba)

Hacienda Barú (Dominical)

Sitio Arqueológico Finca 6 (Sierpe)

Finca Cántaros (San Vito)

Heirs of Columbus

On his fourth and final voyage to the New World in 1502, Christopher Columbus was forced to drop anchor near present-day Puerto Limón after a hurricane damaged his ship. While waiting for repairs, Columbus ventured into the verdant terrain and exchanged gifts with hospitable and welcoming chieftains. He returned from this encounter claiming to have

TIMELINE	11,000 BC	1000 BC	100 BC
	The first humans occupy Costa Rica and populations quickly flourish due to the rich land and marine resources found along both coastlines.	The Huetar power base in the Central Valley is solidified following the construction and habitation of the ancient city of Guayabo, continuously inhabited until its mysterious abandonment in AD 1400.	Costa Rica becomes part of an extensive trade network that moves gold and other goods and extends from present-day Mexico down through to the Andean empires.

seen 'more gold in two days than in four years in Española.' Columbus dubbed the stretch of shoreline from Honduras to Panama 'Veraguas,' but it was his excited descriptions of *costa rica* (the 'rich coast') that gave the region its lasting name. At least that's how the popular story goes.

Anxious to claim the country's bounty, Columbus petitioned the Spanish Crown to have himself appointed governor. But by the time he returned to Seville, his royal patron Queen Isabella was on her deathbed, which prompted King Ferdinand to award the prize to Columbus' rival, Diego de Nicuesa. Although Columbus became a very wealthy man, he never returned to the New World. He died in 1506 after being worn down by ill health and court politics.

To the disappointment of his conquistador heirs, Columbus' tales of gold were mostly lies and the locals were considerably less than affable.

PRE-COLUMBIAN COSTA RICA

The early inhabitants of Costa Rica were part of an extensive trading zone that extended as far south as Peru and as far north as Mexico. The region hosted roughly 20 small tribes, organized into chiefdoms with a *cacique* (permanent leader), who sat atop a hierarchical society that included shamans, warriors, toilers and slaves.

Adept at seafaring, the Carib dominated the Atlantic coastal lowlands and served as a conduit of trade with the South American mainland. In the northwest, several tribes were connected to the great Mesoamerican cultures. Aztec religious practices and Maya jade and craftsmanship are in evidence in the Península de Nicoya, while Costa Rican quetzal feathers and golden trinkets have turned up in Mexico. In the southwest, three chiefdoms showed such influence of Andean indigenous cultures as coca leaves, yucca and sweet potatoes.

There is also evidence that the language of the Central Valley, Huetar, was known by all of Costa Rica's indigenous groups, which may be an indication of their power and influence. The Central Valley is home to Guayabo, the only major archaeological site uncovered in Costa Rica thus far.

Thought to be an ancient ceremonial center, Guayabo once featured paved streets, an aqueduct and decorative gold. Here archaeologists uncovered exquisite gold ornaments and unusual life-size stone statues of human figures, as well as distinctive types of pottery and *metates* (stone platforms that were used for grinding corn). Today the site consists of little more than ancient hewed rock and stone, though Guayabo continues to stand as testament to a once-great civilization of the New World.

Still a puzzle, however, are the hundreds of hand-sculpted, monolithic stone spheres that dot the landscape of the Diquís Valley in Palmar and the Isla del Caño. Weighing up to 16 tons and ranging from the size of a baseball to the size of a Volkswagen, the spheres have inspired many theories: an ancient calendar, symbols of power, extraterrestrial meddling or pieces of a giant game.

1502	1540	1562	1563
Christopher Columbus docks off the coast and, due to all the gold he sees, dubs it *costa rica* ('rich coast'). The name sticks.	The Kingdom of Guatemala is established by the Spanish and includes much of Central America: Costa Rica, Nicaragua, Honduras, El Salvador, Guatemala and the Mexican state of Chiapas.	Spanish conquistador Juan Vásquez de Coronado arrives in Costa Rica under the title of governor, determined to move the fringe communities of Spanish settlers to the more hospitable Central Valley.	The first permanent Spanish colonial settlement in Costa Rica is established in Cartago by Juan Vásquez de Coronado, who chooses the site based on its rich and fertile volcanic soils.

Nicuesa's first colony in present-day Panama was abruptly abandoned when tropical disease and warring tribes decimated its ranks. Successive expeditions launched from the Caribbean coast also failed as pestilent swamps, oppressive jungles and volcanoes made Columbus' paradise seem more like a tropical hell.

A bright moment in Spanish exploration came in 1513 when Vasco Núñez de Balboa heard rumors about a large sea and a wealthy, gold-producing civilization across the mountains of the isthmus – these almost certainly referred to the Inca empire of present-day Peru. Driven by equal parts ambition and greed, Balboa scaled the continental divide, and on September 26, 1513, he became the first European to set eyes upon the Pacific Ocean. Keeping up with the European fashion of the day, Balboa immediately proceeded to claim the ocean and all the lands it touched for the king of Spain.

The thrill of discovery aside, the conquistadors now controlled a strategic western beachhead from which to launch their conquest of Costa Rica. In the name of God and king, aristocratic adventurers plundered indigenous villages, executed resisters and enslaved survivors throughout the Península de Nicoya. However, none of these bloodstained campaigns led to a permanent presence, as intercontinental germ warfare caused outbreaks of feverish death on both sides. The indigenous people mounted a fierce resistance to the invaders, which included guerrilla warfare, destroying their own villages and killing their own children rather than letting them fall into Spanish hands.

New World Order

It was not until the 1560s that a Spanish colony was firmly established in Costa Rica. Hoping to cultivate the rich volcanic soil of the Central Valley, the Spanish founded the village of Cartago on the banks of the Río Reventazón. Although the fledgling colony was extremely isolated, it miraculously survived under the leadership of its first governor, Juan Vásquez de Coronado. Some of Costa Rica's demilitarized present was presaged in its early colonial government: preferring diplomacy over firearms to counter the indigenous threat, Coronado used Cartago as a base to survey the lands south to Panama and west to the Pacific, and secured deed and title over the colony.

Though Coronado was later lost in a shipwreck, his legacy endured. Costa Rica was an officially recognized province of the Virreinato de Nueva España (Viceroyalty of New Spain), which was the name given to the viceroy-ruled territories of the Spanish empire in North America, Central America, the Caribbean and Asia.

For roughly three centuries, the Captaincy General of Guatemala (also known as the Kingdom of Guatemala), which included Costa Rica,

The indigenous people of Costa Rica make up only about 1% of the population. They represent several ethnic groups (the Boruca, Bribrí, Cabécar, Chorotega, Huetar, Kèköldi, Maleku, Ngöbe and Térraba) and six surviving languages.

HISTORY NEW WORLD ORDER

December 1823	April 1823	1821	1737
The United Provinces of Central America is formed; it includes Costa Rica, El Salvador, Guatemala, Nicaragua and Honduras.	The Costa Rican capital officially moves to San José after intense skirmishes with the conservative residents of Cartago, who take issue with the more liberal longings of the power-hungry *josefinos*.	Following a unanimous declaration by Mexico on behalf of all of Central America, Costa Rica finally gains its independence from Spain after centuries of colonial occupation.	The future capital of San José is established, sparking a rivalry with neighboring Cartago that will culminate in a civil war between the two dominant cities.

British explorer, government-sponsored pirate and slaver Sir Francis Drake is believed to have anchored in Bahía Drake in 1579. Rumor has it that he buried some of his plundered treasure here, but the only solid memorial to the man is a monument that looks out to his namesake bay.

Nicaragua, Honduras, El Salvador, Guatemala and the Mexican state of Chiapas, was a loosely administered colony in the vast Spanish empire. Since the political and military headquarters of the kingdom were in Guatemala, Costa Rica became a minor provincial outpost that had little if any strategic significance or exploitable riches.

As a result of its status as a swampy, largely useless backwater, Costa Rica's colonial path diverged from the typical pattern in that a powerful landholding elite and slave-based economy never gained prominence. Instead of large estates, mining operations and coastal cities, modest-sized villages of smallholders developed in the interior Central Valley. According to national lore, the stoic, self-sufficient farmer provided the backbone for 'rural democracy' as Costa Rica emerged as one of the only egalitarian corners of the Spanish empire.

Equal rights and opportunities were not extended to the indigenous groups, and as Spanish settlement expanded, the local population decreased dramatically. From 400,000 at the time Columbus first sailed, the population was reduced to 20,000 a century later, and to 8000 a century after that. While disease was the main cause of death, the Spanish were relentless in their effort to exploit the natives as an economic resource by establishing the *encomienda* system that applied to indigenous males and gave the Spaniards the right to demand free labor, with many worked to death. Central Valley groups were the first to fall, though outside the valley several tribes managed to survive a bit longer under forest cover, staging occasional raids. However, as in the rest of Latin America, repeated military campaigns eventually forced them into submission and slavery, though throughout that period many clergymen protested the brutal treatment of indigenous subjects and implored the Spanish Crown to protect them.

Fall of an Empire

Spain's costly Peninsular War with France from 1808 to 1814 – and the political turmoil, unrest and power vacuums that it caused – led Spain to lose all its colonial possessions in the first third of the 19th century.

In 1821 the Americas wriggled free of Spain's imperial grip following Mexico's declaration of independence for itself as well as the whole of Central America. Of course, the Central American provinces weren't too keen on having another foreign power reign over them and subsequently declared independence from Mexico. However, all of these events hardly disturbed Costa Rica, which learned of its liberation a month after the fact.

The newly liberated colonies pondered their fate: stay together in a United States of Central America or go their separate national ways. At first they came up with something in between, namely the Central Amer-

1838	1856	1889	1900
Costa Rica becomes entirely independent.	Costa Rica quashes the expansionist aims of hawks in the US by defeating William Walker and his invading army at the epic Battle of Santa Rosa.	Costa Rica's first democratic elections are held – a monumental event given the long history of colonial occupation – though the black population and women are prohibited from voting.	The population of Costa Rica reaches 50,000 as the country begins to develop and prosper due to the increasingly lucrative international coffee and banana trades.

ican Federation (CAF), though it could neither field an army nor collect taxes. Accustomed to being at the center of things, Guatemala also attempted to dominate the CAF, alienating smaller colonies and hastening the CAF's demise. Future attempts to unite the region would likewise fail.

Meanwhile, an independent Costa Rica was taking shape under Juan Mora Fernández, the first head of state (1824–33). He tended toward nation building, and organized new towns, built roads, published a newspaper and coined a currency. His wife even partook in the effort by designing the country's flag.

Life returned to normal, unlike in the rest of the region, where post-independence civil wars raged on. In 1824 the Nicoya-Guanacaste region seceded from Nicaragua and joined its more easygoing southern neighbor, defining the territorial borders. In 1852 Costa Rica received its first diplomatic emissaries from the US and Great Britain.

> Thirty-three out of 44 Costa Rican presidents prior to 1970 were descended from just three original colonizing families.

Coffee Rica

In the 19th century, the riches that Costa Rica had long promised were uncovered when farmers realized that the soil and climate of the Central Valley highlands were ideal for coffee cultivation. Costa Rica led Central America in introducing the caffeinated bean, which transformed the impoverished country into the wealthiest in the region.

When an export market was discovered, the government actively promoted coffee to farmers by providing free saplings. At first Costa Rican producers exported their crop to nearby South Americans, who processed the beans and re-exported the product to Europe. By the 1840s, however, local merchants had already built up domestic capacity and

THE LITTLE DRUMMER BOY

During your travels through the countryside, you may notice statues of a drummer boy from Alajuela named Juan Santamaría. He is one of Costa Rica's most beloved national heroes.

In April 1856 the North American mercenary William Walker and his ragtag army attempted to invade Costa Rica during an ultimately unsuccessful campaign to conquer all of Central America. Walker had already managed to seize control of Nicaragua, taking advantage of the civil war that was raging there. It didn't take him long after that to decide to march on Costa Rica, though Costa Rican president Juan Rafael Mora Porras guessed Walker's intentions and managed to recruit a volunteer army of 9000 civilians. They surrounded Walker's army as they lay waiting in an old hacienda in present-day Parque Nacional Santa Rosa. The Costa Ricans won the battle and Walker was forever expelled from Costa Rican soil. During the fighting, Santamaría was killed while daringly setting fire to Walker's defenses – and a national legend was born.

1914	1919	1948	1949
Costa Rica is given an economic boost following the opening of the Panama Canal. The canal was forged by 75,000 laborers, many thousands of whom died during construction.	Federico Tinoco Granados is ousted as the dictator of Costa Rica in one of the few violent episodes in an otherwise peaceful political history.	Conservative and liberal forces clash, resulting in a six-week civil war that leaves 2000 Costa Ricans dead and many more wounded, and destroys much of the country's fledgling infrastructure.	Hoping to heal old wounds and look forward, the temporary government enacts a new constitution abolishing the army, desegregating the country, and granting women and black people the right to vote.

learned to scope out their own overseas markets. Their big break came when they persuaded the captain of HMS *Monarch* to transport several hundred sacks of Costa Rican coffee to London, percolating the beginning of a beautiful friendship.

The Costa Rican coffee boom was on. The drink's quick fix made it popular among working-class consumers in the industrializing north. The aroma of riches lured a wave of enterprising German immigrants, enhancing technical and financial skills in the business sector. By century's end, more than one-third of the Central Valley was dedicated to coffee cultivation, and coffee accounted for more than 90% of all exports and 80% of foreign-currency earnings.

The coffee industry in Costa Rica developed differently from those in the rest of Central America. As elsewhere, there arose a group of coffee barons – elites who reaped the rewards of the export bonanza – but Costa Rican coffee barons lacked the land and labor to cultivate the crop. Coffee production is labor intensive, with a long and painstaking harvest season. Costa Rica's small farmers became the principal planters, and the coffee barons monopolized processing, marketing and financing. The coffee economy in Costa Rica created a wide network of high-end traders and small-scale growers, whereas in the rest of Central America a narrow elite controlled large estates worked by tenant laborers.

Coffee wealth became a power resource in politics. Costa Rica's traditional aristocratic families were at the forefront of the enterprise. At mid-century, three-quarters of the coffee barons were descended from just two colonial families. The country's leading coffee exporter at this time was President Juan Rafael Mora Porras (1849–59), whose lineage went back to the colony's founder, Juan Vásquez de Coronado. Mora was overthrown by his brother-in-law after the president proposed to form a national bank independent of the coffee barons. The economic interests of the coffee elite would thereafter become a priority in Costa Rican politics.

Coffee-processing cooperative Coopedota, located in Costa Rica's Valley of the Saints (famous for growing delicious highland coffee), launched the country's first carbon-neutral coffee in 2011, certified to the British Standards Institution's PAS2060 specifications for carbon neutrality.

Banana Empire

The coffee trade unintentionally gave rise to Costa Rica's next export boom: bananas. Getting coffee out to world markets necessitated a rail link from the central highlands to the coast, and Limón's deep harbor made an ideal port. Inland was dense jungle and insect-infested swamps, which prompted the government to contract the task to Minor Keith, the nephew of an American railroad tycoon.

The project was a disaster. Malaria and accidents churned through workers as Tico recruits gave way to US convicts and Chinese indentured servants, who were in turn replaced by freed Jamaican slaves. To entice Keith to continue, the government turned over 3200 sq km of land along

1963	1977	1987	1994
Reserva Natural Absoluta Cabo Blanco at the tip of the Península de Nicoya becomes Costa Rica's first federally protected conservation area through the efforts of Swedish and Danish conservationists.	The Indigenous Law of 1977 is passed, protecting indigenous communities' right to ownership of their territories.	President Óscar Arias Sánchez wins the Nobel Peace Prize for his work on the Central American peace accords, which brought about greater political freedom throughout the region.	The indigenous people of Costa Rica are finally granted the right to vote.

the route and provided a 99-year lease to run the railroad. In 1890 the line was finally completed and running at a loss.

Keith had begun to grow banana plants along the tracks as a cheap food source for the workers. Desperate to recoup his investment, he shipped some bananas to New Orleans in the hope of starting a side venture. He struck gold, or rather yellow. Consumers went crazy for the elongated finger fruit. By the early 20th century, bananas surpassed coffee as Costa Rica's most lucrative export and the country became the world's leading banana exporter. Unlike in the coffee industry, the profits were exported along with the bananas.

Costa Rica was transformed by the rise of Keith's banana empire. He joined another American importer to found the infamous United Fruit Company, known locally as Yunai, which was soon the largest employer in Central America. To locals it was known as *el pulpo* (the octopus) – its tentacles stretched across the region, becoming entangled with the local economy and politics. United Fruit owned huge swaths of lush lowlands, much of the transportation and communication infrastructure, and bunches of bureaucrats. The company drew a wave of migrant laborers from Jamaica, changing the country's ethnic complexion and provoking racial tensions. In its various incarnations as the United Brands Company and, later, Chiquita, Yunai was virulently anti-union and maintained control over its workforces by paying them in redeemable scrip rather than cash for many years. Amazingly, the marks that *el pulpo* left on Costa Rica are still present, including the rusting train tracks and a locomotive engine in Palmares.

For details on the role of Minor Keith and the United Fruit Company in lobbying for a CIA-led coup in Guatemala, pick up a copy of the highly readable *Bitter Fruit* by Stephen Schlesinger and Stephen Kinzer.

Birth of a Nation

The inequality of the early 20th century led to the rise of José Figueres Ferrer, a self-described farmer-philosopher. The son of Catalan immigrant coffee planters, Figueres excelled in school and went to Boston's MIT to study engineering. Upon returning to Costa Rica to set up his own coffee plantation, he organized the hundreds of laborers on his farm into a utopian socialist community and appropriately named the property La Luz Sin Fin (The Struggle Without End).

In the 1940s Figueres became involved in national politics as an outspoken critic of President Calderón. In the midst of a radio interview in which he bad-mouthed the president, police broke into the studio and arrested Figueres. He was accused of having fascist sympathies and was banished to Mexico. While in exile he formed the Caribbean League, a collection of students and democratic agitators from all over Central America who pledged to bring down the region's military dictators. When he returned to Costa Rica, the Caribbean League, now 700 men strong, went with him and helped protest against those in power.

2000	2006	2007	2010
The population of Costa Rica tops four million, though many believe the number is far greater due to burgeoning illegal settlements on the fringes of the capital.	Óscar Arias Sánchez is elected president for the second time in his political career on a pro-Cafta (Central American Free Trade Agreement) platform, though he wins by an extremely narrow margin.	A national referendum narrowly passes Cafta. Opinion remains divided as to whether opening up trade with the USA will be beneficial for Costa Rica in the long run.	Costa Rica elects its first female president, National Liberation Party candidate Laura Chinchilla.

When government troops descended on the farm with the intention of arresting Figueres and disarming the Caribbean League, it sparked a civil war. The moment had arrived: the diminutive farmer-philosopher now played the man on horseback. Figueres emerged victorious from the brief conflict and seized the opportunity to put into place his vision of Costa Rican social democracy. After dissolving the country's military, Figueres quoted HG Wells: 'The future of mankind cannot include the armed forces.'

As head of a temporary junta government, Figueres enacted nearly a thousand decrees. He taxed the wealthy, nationalized the banks and built a modern welfare state. His 1949 constitution granted full citizenship and voting rights to women, African Americans, indigenous groups and Chinese minorities. Today Figueres' revolutionary regime is regarded as the foundation of Costa Rica's unarmed democracy.

The American Empire

Throughout the 1970s and '80s, the sovereignty of the small nations of Central America was limited by their northern neighbor, the US. Big sticks, gunboats and dollar diplomacy were instruments of a Yankee policy to curtail socialist politics, especially the military oligarchies of Guatemala, El Salvador and Nicaragua.

In 1979 the rebellious Sandinistas toppled the American-backed Somoza dictatorship in Nicaragua. Alarmed by the Sandinistas' Soviet and Cuban ties, fervently anticommunist president Ronald Reagan decided it was time to intervene. Just like that, the Cold War arrived in the hot tropics.

The organizational details of the counterrevolution were delegated to Oliver North, an eager-to-please junior officer working out of the White House basement. North's can-do creativity helped to prop up the famed Contra rebels to incite civil war in Nicaragua. While both sides invoked the rhetoric of freedom and democracy, the war was really a turf battle between left-wing and right-wing forces.

Under intense US pressure, Costa Rica was dragged in. The Contras set up camp in northern Costa Rica, from where they staged guerrilla raids. Not-so-clandestine CIA operatives and US military advisors were dispatched to assist the effort. A secret jungle airstrip was built near the border to fly in weapons and supplies. To raise cash for the rebels, North allegedly used this covert supply network to traffic illegal narcotics through the region.

The war polarized Costa Rica. From conservative quarters came a loud call to re-establish the military and join the anticommunist crusade, which was largely underwritten by the US Pentagon. In May 1984 more than 20,000 demonstrators marched through San José to give peace a

Prior to his re-election, Óscar Arias Sánchez founded the Arias Foundation for Peace and Human Progress (www.arias.or.cr).

2011	2013	2014	2014
Central American drug wars encroach on Costa Rica's borders, and the country is listed among the US' major drug-trafficking centers.	The murder of 26-year-old environmentalist Jairo Mora Sandoval in Limón province brings international attention to the dangers and lack of police protection that conservationists face on the Caribbean coast.	Luis Guillermo Solís is elected president by default when his opponent withdraws from the race.	Volcán Poás, one of the most visited attractions in Costa Rica, erupts, prompting park closures until further notice.

chance, though the debate didn't climax until the 1986 presidential election. The victor was 44-year-old Óscar Arias Sánchez, who, despite being born into coffee wealth, was an intellectual reformer in the mold of José Figueres Ferrer, his political patron.

Once in office, Arias affirmed his commitment to a negotiated resolution and reasserted Costa Rican national independence. He vowed to uphold his country's pledge of neutrality and to vanquish the Contras from the territory. The sudden resignation of the US ambassador around this time was suspected to be a result of Arias' strong stance. In a public ceremony, Costa Rican schoolchildren planted trees on top of the CIA's secret airfield. Most notably, Arias became the driving force in uniting Central America around a peace plan, which ended the Nicaraguan war and earned him the Nobel Peace Prize in 1987.

In 2006 Arias once again returned to the presidential office, winning the popular election by a 1.2% margin and subsequently ratifying the controversial Central American Free Trade Agreement (Cafta), which Costa Rica entered in 2009.

When Laura Chinchilla became the first female president of Costa Rica in 2010, she promised to continue with Arias' free-market policies, in spite of the divisive Cafta agreement (the referendum in 2007 barely resulted in a 'yes' vote at 51%). She also pledged to tackle the rise of violent crime and drug trafficking, on the increase due to Costa Rica's being used as a halfway house by Colombian and Mexican cartels. Ironically, a month after discussing the drug-cartel problem with then-US president Barack Obama during his visit to Costa Rica, Chinchilla herself became embroiled in a drug-related scandal over the use of a private jet belonging to a man under investigation by Costa Rican intelligence for possible links to international drug cartels.

2015	2015	2016	2017
A Costa Rican judge grants a common-law marriage to a same-sex couple, a first in Costa Rica and in Central America.	The International Court of Justice in The Hague settles the long-standing land dispute between Costa Rica and Nicaragua in Costa Rica's favor.	Volcán Turrialba erupts, engulfing the country's major cities in a toxic ash cloud. The national park is closed until further notice.	The Costa Rican government files a new case with the International Court of Justice concerning Nicaraguan military presence on its territory.

The Tico Way of Life

Blessed with natural beauty and a peaceful, army-less society, it's no wonder Costa Rica has long been known as the Switzerland of Central America. While nowadays the country is certainly challenged by its lofty eco-conscious goals and modern intercontinental maladies (such as drug trafficking and a wealth disparity between the haves and have-nots), the Tico (Costa Rican) attitude remains sunny and family-centered, with a good balance between work and quality of life.

One of the most comprehensive and complete books on Costa Rica history and culture is *The Ticos: Culture and Social Change in Costa Rica*, by Mavis, Richard and Karen Biesanz.

The Pura Vida

Pura vida – pure life – is more than just a slogan that rolls off the tongues of Ticos and emblazons souvenirs. In the laid-back tone in which it is constantly uttered, the phrase is a bona fide mantra for the Costa Rican way of life. Perhaps the essence of the pure life is something better lived than explained, but hearing '*pura vida*' again and again while traveling across this beautiful country – as a greeting, a stand-in for goodbye, 'cool,' and an acknowledgement of thanks – makes it evident that the concept lives deep within the DNA of this country.

The living seems particularly pure when Costa Rica is compared with its Central American neighbors such as Nicaragua and Honduras; there's little poverty, illiteracy or political tumult, the country is crowded with ecological jewels, and the standard of living is high. What's more, Costa Rica has flourished without an army for the past 60 years. The sum of the parts is a country that's an oasis of calm in a corner of the world that has been continuously degraded by warfare. And though the Costa Rican people are justifiably proud hosts, a compliment to the country is likely to be met simply with a warm smile and an enigmatic two-word reply: *pura vida*.

Daily Life

With its lack of war, long life expectancy and relatively sturdy economy, Costa Rica enjoys the highest standard of living in Central America. For the most part, Costa Ricans live fairly affluent and comfortable lives, even by North American standards.

As in many places in Latin America, the family unit in Costa Rica remains the nucleus of life. Families socialize together and extended families often live near each other. When it's time to party it's also largely a family affair; celebrations, vacations and weddings are a social outlet for rich and poor alike, and those with relatives in positions of power – nominal or otherwise – don't hesitate to turn to them for support.

Given this mutually cooperative environment, it's no surprise that life expectancy in Costa Rica is slightly higher than in the US. In fact, most Costa Ricans are more likely to die of heart disease or cancer as opposed to the childhood diseases that plague many developing nations. A comprehensive socialized health-care system and excellent sanitation systems account for these positive statistics, as do a generally stress-free lifestyle, tropical weather and a healthy and varied diet – the *pura vida*.

Still, the divide between rich and poor is evident. The middle and upper classes largely reside in San José, as well as in the major cities of the Central Valley highlands (Heredia, Alajuela and Cartago), and enjoy a level of comfort similar to their economic brethren in Europe and the US. City dwellers are likely to have a maid and a car or two, and the lucky few have a second home on the beach or in the mountains.

The home of an average Tico is a one-story construction built from concrete blocks, wood or a combination of both. In the poorer lowland areas, people often live in windowless houses made of *caña brava* (a local cane). For the vast majority of *campesinos* (farmers) and *indígenas* (people of indigenous origin), life is harder than in the cities, poverty levels are higher and standards of living are lower than in the rest of the country. This is especially true along the Caribbean coast, where the descendants of Jamaican immigrants have long suffered from lack of attention from the federal government, and in indigenous reservations. However, although poor families have few possessions and little financial security, every member assists with working the land or contributing to the household, which creates a strong safety net.

As in the rest of the world, globalization is having a dramatic effect on Costa Ricans, who are increasingly mobile, international and intertwined in the global economy – for better or for worse. These days, society is increasingly geographically mobile – the Tico who was born in Puntarenas might end up managing a lodge on the Península de Osa. And, with the advent of better-paved roads, cell coverage and the increasing presence of North American and European expats (and the accompanying malls and big box stores), the Tico family unit is subject to the changing tides of a global society.

THE TICO WAY OF LIFE WOMEN IN COSTA RICA

The expression *matando la culebra* (meaning 'to be idle' or 'to waste time' – literally 'killing the snake') originates with *peones* (laborers) from banana plantations. When foremen would ask what they were doing, the response would be '*¡Matando la culebra!*'

Women in Costa Rica

By the letter of the law, Costa Rica's progressive stance on women's issues makes the country stand out among its Central American neighbors. A 1974 family code stipulated equal duties and rights for men and women. Women can draw up contracts, assume loans and inherit property. Sexual harassment and sex discrimination are also against the law, and in 1996 Costa Rica passed a landmark law against domestic violence that was one of the most progressive in Latin America. With women holding more and more roles in political, legal, scientific and medical fields, Costa Rica has been home to some historic firsts: in 1998 both vice presidents (Costa Rica has two) were women, and in February 2010 Arias Sánchez's former vice president, Laura Chinchilla, became the first female president.

Still, the picture of sexual equality is much more complicated than the country's bragging rights might suggest. Byproducts of the legal prostitution trade include illicit underground activities such as child prostitution and the trafficking of women. Despite the cultural reverence for the

In conjunction with two indigenous women, Juanita Sánchez and Gloria Mayorga, Paula Palmer wrote *Taking Care of Sibö's Gifts*, an inspiring account of the intersection between the spiritual and environmental values of the Bribrí.

SAME-SEX RELATIONSHIPS

Since 1998 there have been laws on the books to protect 'sexual option,' and discrimination is generally prohibited in most facets of society, including employment. However, though the country is becoming increasingly gay friendly, this traditional culture has not always been quick to adopt equal protection.

Legal recognition of same-sex partnerships has been a hot topic since 2006 and was a major point of contention in the 2010 presidential race. In January 2012 Costa Rica's primary newspaper, *La Nación,* conducted a poll in which 55% of the respondents believed that same-sex couples should have the same rights as heterosexual couples. Then in July 2013 the Costa Rican legislature 'accidentally' passed a law legalizing gay marriage, due to a small change in the bill's wording. In 2015 a Costa Rican judge granted a same-sex common-law marriage, making Costa Rica the first country in Central America to recognize gay relationships. The current president, Luis Guillermo Solís, has expressed support for gay rights, and he even flew the rainbow flag at the presidential house.

matriarch (Mother's Day is a national holiday), traditional Latin American machismo is hardly a thing of the past and anti-discrimination laws are rarely enforced. Particularly in the countryside, many women maintain traditional societal roles: raising children, cooking and running the home.

Sports

From scrappy little matches that take over the village pitch to the breathless exclamations of 'Goal!' that erupt from San José bars on the day of a big game, no Costa Rican sporting venture can compare with *fútbol* (soccer). Every town has a soccer field (which usually serves as the most conspicuous landmark) where neighborhood aficionados play heated matches.

The *selección nacional* (national selection) team is known affectionately as La Sele. Legions of Tico fans still recall La Sele's most memorable moments, including an unlikely showing in the quarterfinals at the 1990 World Cup in Italy and a solid (if not long-lasting) performance in the 2002 World Cup. More recently, La Sele's failure to qualify for the 2010 World Cup led to a top-down change in leadership and the reinstatement of one-time coach Jorge Luis Pinto, a Colombian coach who has had mixed results on the international stage. Pinto seemed to be a good fit for the team's ferocious young leaders such as record-setting scorer Álvaro Saborío, goalkeeper Keylor Navas and forward Bryan Ruiz. In fact, Pinto led the team to qualify for the 2014 World Cup in Brazil, where the team reached the quarterfinals, making them national heroes. At the time of research Costa Rica's national team was battling it out in the 2018 World Cup qualifiers.

With such perfect waves, surfing has steadily grown in popularity among Ticos, especially those who grow up in surf towns. Costa Rica hosts numerous national and international competitions annually that are widely covered by local media, and holds regular local competitions such as the weekly contest at Playa Hermosa (south of Jacó).

For a nation that values its wildlife, it may be surprising that the controversial sport of bullfighting is still popular, particularly in the Guanacaste region, though the bull isn't killed in the Costa Rican version of the sport. More aptly described, bullfighting is really a ceremonial opportunity to watch an often tipsy cowboy run around with a bull. Travelers should consider the ethics of the spectacle when deciding to attend.

Get player statistics and game schedules and find out everything you ever needed to know about La Sele, the Costa Rican national soccer team, at www.fedefutbol. com.

NEW NATIONAL STADIUM, NEW TRADE RELATIONSHIP

As in many Latin American nations, *fútbol* dominates the sports conversation in Costa Rica. So imagine the wonderment when a brand-new, state-of-the-art national stadium was proposed – and at no cost to Costa Rica.

China was the font of this magnanimity, asking in return that Costa Rica establish trade relations with the Asian giant while cutting ties with Taiwan. As recently as 2003, the Costa Rican and Taiwanese governments were the closest of allies, with the Taiwanese funding the construction of the Puente de la Amistad (Friendship Bridge) in Puntarenas. That was a trade, too, for fishing rights. With the new stadium, Taiwan is out and China is in. Ironic commentators have now dubbed the structure Puente de la Apuñalada (Backstabbing Bridge).

The fact that the new stadium was built entirely with Chinese materials and labor (800 workers in all), and violated Costa Rican labor law in the forced overtime of workers, did not sit well with all in the country. One worker died during construction.

Costa Rica is now China's second-biggest trading partner, right behind the USA. China has used this 'stadium diplomacy' to forge friendships across Latin America, the Caribbean, Asia and Africa, most recently erecting brand-new stadia for the last few African Cups.

For most Costa Ricans, though, the stadium has been a bonus – a nice new place to watch the national team play world-class competition like Argentina, Brazil and Spain. Miley Cyrus, the Red Hot Chili Peppers, Paul McCartney, Shakira and Guns N' Roses have all played shows there.

COSTA RICA BY THE BOOK

Tycoon's War, by Stephen Dando-Collins, is a well-told tale of US business tycoon Cornelius Vanderbilt's epic struggle to maintain his economic stranglehold over the Central American isthmus. There are hair-raising battle scenes and intriguing personal sketches of protagonists Vanderbilt and William Walker.

Bananas: How United Fruit Company Shaped the World, by Peter Chapman, tells the story of the meteoric rise and inevitable collapse of the megalith known to locals as '*el pulpo*' (the octopus) for its far reach into the echelons of power in Costa Rica and Central America.

Nation Thief, by Robert Houston, is a novelistic telling of William Walker's excursions into Central America, narrated by several of his 'immortals' in the vernacular of the time.

Green Phoenix, by William Allen, details the ultimate victory of a cohort of Costa Rican and US scientists and volunteers in halting deforestation and establishing the 600-plus-square-mile Guanacaste Conservation Area.

Walking with Wolf, by Kay Chornook and Wolf Guindon, recounts the life of one of Monteverde's pioneering Quakers and his decades-long dedication to preserving and sharing his adopted cloud-forest home.

Cocorí, by Joaquín Guitiérrez, is an illustrated tapestry of life lessons gleaned by a young boy in the rainforest. Recounted by Costa Rica's most famous author, this children's book, first published in 1947 and translated worldwide, is required reading for Tico students. Note that some Afro-Caribbean Costa Ricans find the portrayal of the young protagonist offensive and racist.

Guanacaste: Rutas de Viaje (Travel Routes), by Luciano Capelli and Yazmin Ross, is a stunning coffee-table book of the province's festivals, farmers, and frogs, among other things. It's a lovely record of your trip here. You'll find it at the airport.

Arts

Literature

Costa Rica has a relatively young literary history and few works of Costa Rican writers or novelists are available in translation. Carlos Luis Fallas (1909–66) is widely known for *Mamita Yunai* (1940), an influential 'proletarian' novel that took the banana companies to task for their labor practices, and he remains very popular among the Latin American left.

Carmen Naranjo (1928–2012) is one of the few contemporary Costa Rican writers to have risen to international acclaim. She was a novelist, poet and short-story writer who also served as ambassador to India in the 1970s, and a few years later as minister of culture. In 1996 she was awarded the prestigious Gabriela Mistral medal by the Chilean government. Her collection of short stories, *There Never Was a Once Upon a Time*, is widely available in English. Two of her stories can also be found in *Costa Rica: A Traveler's Literary Companion*.

José León Sánchez (b 1929) is an internationally renowned memoirist of Huetar descent, from the border of Costa Rica and Nicaragua. After being convicted for stealing from the Basílica de Nuestra Señora de Los Ángeles in Cartago, he was sentenced to serve his term at Isla San Lucas, one of Latin America's most notorious jails. Illiterate when he was incarcerated, Sánchez taught himself how to read and write, and clandestinely authored one of the continent's most poignant books: *La isla de los hombres solos* (called *God Was Looking the Other Way* in the translated version).

Music & Dance

Although there are other Latin American musical hotbeds of more renown, Costa Rica's central geographical location and colonial history have resulted in a varied musical culture that incorporates elements from North and South America and the Caribbean islands.

San José features a regular lineup of domestic and international rock, folk and hip-hop artists, but regional sounds also survive, each with their own special rhythms, instruments and styles. For instance, the Península de Nicoya has a rich musical history, most of its sound made with guitars, maracas and marimbas. The common sounds on the Caribbean coast are reggae, reggaetón (a newer version of reggae mixed with hip-hop beats) and calypso, which has roots in Afro-Caribbean slave culture.

Popular dance music includes Latin dances, such as salsa, merengue, bolero and *cumbia*. Guanacaste is also the birthplace of many traditional dances, most of which depict courtship rituals. The most famous dance – sometimes considered the national dance – is the *punto guanacasteco*. What keeps it lively is the *bomba,* a funny (and usually racy) rhymed verse shouted by the male dancers during the musical interlude.

Visual Arts

The visual arts in Costa Rica first took on a national character in the 1920s, when Teodórico Quirós, Fausto Pacheco and their contemporaries began painting landscapes that differed from traditional European styles, depicting the rolling hills and lush forest of the Costa Rican countryside, often sprinkled with characteristic adobe houses.

The contemporary scene is more varied and it's difficult to define a unique Tico style. The work of several artists has garnered acclaim, including the magical realism of Isidro Con Wong, the surreal paintings and primitive engravings of Francisco Amighetti and the mystical female figures painted by Rafa Fernández. The Museo de Arte y Diseño Contemporáneo (p66) in San José is the top place to see this type of work, and its permanent collection is a great primer.

Many galleries are geared toward tourists and specialize in 'tropical art': brightly colored, whimsical folk paintings depicting flora and fauna that evoke the work of French artist Henri Rousseau.

Folk art and handicrafts are not as widely produced or readily available here as in other Central American countries. However, the dedicated souvenir hunter will have no problem finding the colorful Sarchí oxcarts that have become a symbol of Costa Rica. Indigenous crafts, which include intricately carved and painted masks made by the Boruca indigenous people, as well as handwoven bags and linens and colorful Chorotega pottery, can also be found in San José and more readily along Costa Rica's Pacific coast.

Film

Artistically, while film is not a new medium in Costa Rica, young filmmakers have been upping the country's ante in this arena. Over the last decade or so, a handful of Costa Rican filmmakers have submitted their work for Oscar consideration, and many others have received critical acclaim for their pictures nationally and internationally. These films range from adaptations of Gabriel García Márquez's magical-realism novel *Del amor y otro demonios* (Of Love and Other Demons, 2009), directed by Hilda Hidalgo, and a comedic coming-of-age story of young Ticos on the cusp of adulthood in contemporary Costa Rica in *El cielo rojo* (The Red Sky, 2008), written and directed by Miguel Alejandro Gomez, to the light-hearted story of a Costa Rican farmer who embarks on the journey to Europe to raise money to avoid losing his farm in *Maikol Yordan de viaje perdido* (Maikol Yordan Traveling Lost, 2014), also directed by Gomez.

A film-festival calendar has also been blossoming in Costa Rica, though dates vary. Sponsored by the Ministerio de Cultura y Juventud, the Costa Rica Festival Internacional de Cine (www.facebook.com/CostaRicaCine Fest) takes place in San José (check for current dates) and features international films fitting the year's theme. The Costa Rica International Film Festival (CRIFF; www.filmfestivallife.com) takes place in early June, with an associated documentary film festival the week afterwards.

Little of his work is translated into English, but poet Alfonso Chase is a Fulbright scholar and a contemporary literary hero. In 2000 he won the nation's highest literary award, the Premio Magón.

Landscapes & Ecology

Despite its diminutive size – at 51,100 sq km, it's slightly smaller than West Virginia in the US – Costa Rica's land is an astounding collection of habitats. On one coast are the breezy skies and big waves of the Pacific, while only 119km away lie the languid shores of the Caribbean. In between there are active volcanoes, alpine peaks and crisp high-elevation forest. Few places on earth can compare with this little country's spectacular interaction of natural, geological and climatic forces.

The Land
The Pacific Coast

Two major peninsulas hook out into the ocean along the 1016km-long Pacific coast: Nicoya in the north and Osa in the south. Although they look relatively similar from space, on the ground they could hardly be more different. Nicoya is one of the driest places in the country and holds

Above: Volcán Arenal (p254)

some of Costa Rica's most developed tourist infrastructure; Osa is wet and rugged, run through by wild, seasonal rivers and rough dirt roads that are always under threat from the creeping jungle.

Just inland from the coast, the Pacific lowlands are a narrow strip of land backed by mountains. This area is equally dynamic, ranging from dry deciduous forests and open cattle country in the north to misty, mysterious tropical rainforests in the south.

Central Costa Rica

Move a bit inland from the Pacific coast and you immediately ascend the jagged spine of the country: the majestic Cordillera Central in the north and the rugged, largely unexplored Cordillera de Talamanca in the south. Continually being revised by tectonic activity, these mountains are part of the majestic Sierra Madre chain that runs north through Mexico.

Home to active volcanoes, clear trout-filled streams and ethereal cloud forest, these mountain ranges generally follow a northwest to southeast line, with the highest and most dramatic peaks in the south near the Panamanian border. The highest peak in the country is windswept Cerro Chirripó (3820m).

In the midst of this powerful landscape, surrounded on all sides by mountains, are the highlands of the Meseta Central – the Central Valley. This fertile central plain, some 1000m above sea level, is the agricultural heart of the nation and enjoys abundant rainfall and mild temperatures. It includes San José and cradles three more of Costa Rica's five largest cities, accounting for more than half of the country's population.

The Caribbean Coast

Cross the mountains and drop down the eastern slope and you'll reach the elegant line of the Caribbean coastline – a long, straight 212km along low plains, brackish lagoons and waterlogged forests. A lack of strong tides allows plants to grow right over the water's edge along coastal sloughs. Eventually, these create the walls of vegetation along the narrow, murky waters that characterize much of the region. As if taking cues from the slow-paced, Caribbean-influenced culture, the rivers that rush out of the central mountains take on a languid pace here, curving through broad plains toward the sea.

While there are smoothly paved main roads along the southern Caribbean coast, the northern Caribbean is still largely inaccessible except by boat or plane.

The Geology

If all this wildly diverse beauty makes Costa Rica feel like the crossroads between vastly different worlds, that's because it is. As it's part of the thin strip of land that separates two continents with hugely divergent wildlife and topographical character, and right in the middle of the world's two largest oceans, it's little wonder that Costa Rica boasts such a colorful collision of climates, landscapes and wildlife.

> Costa Rica's national tree is the guanacaste, commonly found in the lowlands of the Pacific slope.

> Few organizations are as involved in building sustainable rainforest-based economies as the Rainforest Alliance (www.rainforest-alliance.org); see the website for special initiatives in Costa Rica.

DON'T DISTURB THE DOLPHINS

Swimming with dolphins has been illegal since 2006, although shady tour operators out for a quick buck may encourage it. Research indicates that in some heavily touristed areas, dolphins are leaving their natural habitat in search of calmer seas. When your boat comes across these amazing creatures of the sea, avoid the temptation to jump in with them – you can still have an awe-inspiring experience peacefully observing them without disturbing them.

Playa Blanca (p162), Cahuita

The country's geological history began when the Cocos Plate, a tectonic plate that lies below the Pacific, crashed headlong into the Caribbean Plate, which is off the isthmus' east coast. Since the plates travel about 10cm every year, the collision might seem slow by human measure, but it was a violent wreck by geological standards, creating the area's subduction zone. The plates continue to collide, with the Cocos Plate pushing the Caribbean Plate toward the heavens and making the area prone to earthquakes and ongoing volcanic activity.

Despite all the violence underfoot, these forces have blessed the country with some of the world's most beautiful and varied tropical landscapes.

Coral Reefs

Compared with the rest of the Caribbean, the coral reefs of Costa Rica are not a banner attraction. Heavy surf and shifting sands along most of the Caribbean coast produce conditions that are unbearable to corals. The exceptions are two beautiful patches of reef in the south that are protected on the rocky headlands of Parque Nacional Cahuita and Refugio Nacional de Vida Silvestre Gandoca-Manzanillo. These diminutive but vibrant reefs are home to more than 100 species of fish and many types of coral and make for decent snorkeling and diving.

Unfortunately, the reefs themselves are in danger due to global warming and increased water temperatures, tourism (divers and snorkelers damaging the reefs), and pollutants, like sediments washing downriver from logging operations and toxic chemicals that wash out of nearby agricultural fields. Although curbed by the government, these factors persist. Along with these threats, a major earthquake in 1991 lifted the reefs as much as 1.5m, stranding and killing large portions of this fragile ecosystem.

Owl butterfly, Parque Nacional Tortuguero (p149)

Wildlife

Nowhere else are so many types of habitats squeezed into such a tiny area, and species from different continents have been commingling here for millennia. Costa Rica has the world's largest number of species per 10,000 sq km – a whopping 615. This simple fact alone makes Costa Rica the premier destination for nature-lovers.

The large number of species here is also due to the country's relatively recent appearance. Roughly three million years ago, Costa Rica rose from the ocean and formed a land bridge between North and South America. As species from these two vast biological provinces started to mingle, the number of species essentially doubled in the area where Costa Rica now sits.

Flora

Simply put, Costa Rica's floral biodiversity is mind-blowing – there are more than 500,000 species in total, including close to 12,000 species of vascular plant, and the list gets more and more crowded each year. Orchids alone account for about 1400 species. The diversity of habitats created when this many species mix is a wonder to behold.

Mangroves can survive in highly saline environments by secreting salt via the surface of their leaves, filtering it at the root level and accumulating it in bark and leaves that eventually fall off.

Rainforest

The humid, vibrant mystery of the tropical rainforest connects acutely with a traveler's sense of adventure. These forests, far more dense with plant life than any other environment on the planet, are leftover scraps of the prehistoric jungles that once covered the continents. Standing in the midst of it and trying to take it all in can be overwhelming: tropical rainforests contain more than half of the earth's known living organisms. Naturally, this riotous pile-on of life requires lots of water – the forest typically gets between 5m and 6m of rainfall annually (yes, that's *meters!*).

Classic rainforest habitats are well represented in the parks of southwestern Costa Rica or in the mid-elevation portions of the central mountains. Here you will find towering trees that block out the sky, long, looping vines and many overlapping layers of vegetation. Large trees often show buttresses – wing-like ribs that extend from their trunks for added structural support. And plants climb atop other plants, fighting for a bit of sunlight. The most impressive areas of primary forest – a term designating completely untouched land that has never been disturbed by humans – exist on the Península de Osa.

Cloud Forest

Visiting the unearthly terrain of a cloud forest is a highlight for many visitors; there are amazing swaths of it in Monteverde, along the Cerro de la Muerte and below the peaks of Chirripó. In these regions, fog-drenched trees are so thickly coated in mosses, ferns, bromeliads and orchids that you can hardly discern their true shapes. These forests are created when humid trade winds off the Caribbean blow up into the highlands, cool and condense to form thick, low-hanging clouds. With constant exposure to wind, rain and sun, the trees here are crooked and stunted.

Cloud forests are widespread at high elevations throughout Costa Rica and any of them warrant a visit. Be forewarned, however, that in these habitats the term 'rainy season' has little meaning because it's always dripping wet from the fog – humidity in a cloud forest often hovers around 100%.

Due to deforestation it is best to avoid products made from tropical hardwoods if you're uncertain of their origin.

Tropical Dry Forest

Along Costa Rica's northwestern coast lies the country's largest concentration of tropical dry forest – a stunningly different scene to the country's wet rainforests and cloud forests. During the dry season many trees drop their foliage, creating carpets of crackling, sun-drenched leaves and a sense of openness that is largely absent in other Costa Rican habitats. The large trees here, such as Costa Rica's national tree, the guanacaste, have broad, umbrella-like canopies, while spiny shrubs and vines or cacti dominate the understory. At times, large numbers of trees erupt into spectacular displays of flowers, and at the beginning of the rainy season everything is transformed with a wonderful flush of new, green foliage.

This type of forest was native to Guanacaste and the Península de Nicoya, though it suffered generations of destruction for its commercially valuable lumber. Most was clear-cut or burned to make space for ranching. Guanacaste and Santa Rosa national parks are good examples of the dry forest and host some of the country's most accessible nature hiking.

Mangroves

Along brackish stretches of both coasts, mangrove swamps are a world unto themselves. Growing on stilts out of muddy tidal flats, five species of tree crowd together so densely that no boats and few animals can penetrate. Striking in their adaptations for dealing with salt, mangroves thrive where no other land plant dares tread and are among the world's most relentless colonizers. Mangrove seeds are heavy and fleshy, blooming into flowers in the spring before falling off to give way to fruit. By the time the fruit falls, it is covered with spiky seedlings that anchor in the soft mud of low tides. In only 10 years, a seedling has the potential to mature into an entire new colony.

Above: Nosara (p313)

Left: Parque Nacional Manuel Antonio (p384)

Parque Nacional Volcán Poás (p109)

Mangrove swamps play extremely important roles in the ecosystem. Not only do they buffer coastlines from the erosive power of waves but also they have high levels of productivity because they trap nutrient-rich sediment and serve as spawning and nursery areas for innumerable species of fish and invertebrate. The brown waters of mangrove channels – rich with nutrients and filled with algae, shrimp, crustaceans and caimans – form tight links in the marine food chain and are best explored in a kayak, early in the morning.

There are miles of mangrove channels along the Caribbean coast, and a vast mangrove swamp on the Pacific, near Bahía Drake.

Fauna

Though tropical in nature – with a substantial number of tropical animals such as poison-dart frogs and spider monkeys – Costa Rica is also the winter home for more than 200 species of migrating bird that arrive from as far away as Alaska and Australia. Don't be surprised to see one of your familiar backyard birds feeding alongside trogons and toucans. Birds are one of the primary attractions for naturalists, who scan endlessly for birds of every color, from strawberry-red scarlet macaws to the iridescent jewels called violet sabrewings (a type of hummingbird). Because many birds in Costa Rica have restricted ranges, you are guaranteed to find different species everywhere you travel.

Visitors will almost certainly see one of Costa Rica's four types of monkey or two types of sloth, but there are an additional 230 types of mammal awaiting the patient observer. More exotic sightings might include the amazing four-eyed opossum or the silky anteater, while a lucky few might spot the elusive tapir or have a jaguarundi cross their path. The extensive network of national parks, wildlife refuges and other protected areas are prime places to spot wildlife.

Two-toed sloths descend from the trees once a week to defecate.

La Paz Waterfall Gardens (p110), Central Valley

If you are serious about observing birds and animals, the value of a knowledgeable guide cannot be underestimated. Their keen eyes are trained to notice the slightest movement in the forest, and they recognize the many exotic sounds. Most professional bird guides are proficient in the dialects of local birds, greatly improving your chances of hearing or seeing these species.

No season is a bad one for exploring Costa Rica's natural environment, though most visitors arrive during the peak dry season, when trails are less muddy and more accessible. A bonus of visiting between December and February is that many of the wintering migrant birds are still hanging around. A trip after the peak season means fewer birds, but this is a stupendous time to see dry forests transform into vibrant greens and it's also when resident birds begin nesting.

Endangered Species

The world-famous Organization for Tropical Studies (www.ots.ac.cr) runs three field stations and offers numerous classes for students seriously interested in tropical ecology.

As expected in a country with unique habitats and widespread logging, there are numerous species whose populations are declining or in danger of extinction. Currently, the number-one threat to most of Costa Rica's endangered species is habitat destruction, followed closely by hunting and trapping.

Costa Rica's four species of sea turtle – olive ridley, leatherback, green and hawksbill – deservedly get a lot of attention. All four species are classified as endangered or critically endangered, meaning they face an imminent threat of extinction. While populations of some species are increasing, thanks to various protection programs along both coasts, the risk for these *tortugas* (turtles) is still very real.

Destruction of habitat is a huge problem. With the exception of the leatherbacks, all of these species return to their natal beach to nest, which means that the ecological state of the beach directly affects that turtle's ability to reproduce. All of the species prefer dark, undisturbed beaches, and any sort of development or artificial lighting (including flashlights) will inhibit nesting.

Hunting and harvesting eggs are two major causes of declining populations. Green turtles are hunted for their meat. Leatherbacks and olive ridleys are not killed for meat, but their eggs are considered a delicacy – an aphrodisiac, no less. Hawksbill turtles are hunted for their unusual shells, which are sometimes used to make jewelry and hair ornaments. Of course, any trade in tortoiseshell products and turtle eggs and meat is illegal, but a significant black market exists.

The ultra-rare harpy eagle and the legendary quetzal – the birds at the top of every naturalist's must-see list – teeter precariously as their home forests are felled at an alarming rate. Seeing a noisy scarlet macaw could be a birdwatching highlight in Costa Rica, but trapping for the pet trade has extirpated these magnificent birds from much of their former range. Although populations are thriving on the Península de Osa, the scarlet macaw is now extinct over most of Central America, including the entire Caribbean coast.

A number of Costa Rica's mammals are highly endangered, including the elusive jaguar and the squirrel monkey, both due to destruction of habitat. The two survive in the depths of Parque Nacional Corcovado, with the latter also found in some numbers in Parque Nacional Manuel Antonio.

Harassment and intimidation of conservationists in Costa Rica is nothing new, and although the brutal murder (p145) of 26-year-old environmentalist Jairo Mora Sandoval in Limón Province in 2013 brought the issue to international attention, those accused of his murder were initially acquitted. In 2015, seven men were accused of Sandoval's murder. Four of the men were not convicted of murder but of assault, kidnapping and aggravated robbery for a crime that took place after Mora's murder. Then in 2016, after an appeal, the not-guilty verdict was overturned. Each of the men is serving 50 years in prison, the maximum sentence in Costa Rica.

National Parks & Protected Areas

The national-park system began in the 1960s, and has since been expanded into the Sistema Nacional de Areas de Conservación (National System of Conservation Areas; Sinac), with an astounding 186 protected areas, including 27 national parks, eight biological reserves, 32 protected zones, 13 forest reserves and 58 wildlife refuges. At least 10% of the land is strictly protected and another 17% is included in various multiple-use preserves. Costa Rican authorities take pride in the statistic that more than 27% of the country has been set aside for conservation, but multiple-use zones still allow farming, logging and other exploitation, so the environment within them is not totally protected. The smallest number might be the most amazing of all: Costa Rica's parks are a safe haven to approximately 5% of the world's wildlife species.

In addition to the system of national preserves, there are hundreds of small, privately owned lodges, reserves and haciendas (estates) that have been set up to protect the land. Many belong to longtime Costa Rican expats who decided that this country was the last stop in their journey along the 'gringo trail' in the 1970s and '80s. The abundance of foreign-owned protected areas is a bit of a contentious issue with Ticos. Although these are largely nonprofit organizations with keen interests in conservation, they are private and often cost money to enter. There's also a number of animal rescue and rehabilitation centers (also largely set up by expats), where injured and orphaned animals and illegal pets

The eight species of poison-dart frog in Costa Rica are beautiful but have skin secretions of varying toxicity that cause paralysis and death if they get into your bloodstream.

Parque Nacional Volcán Poás (p109)

are rehabilitated and released into the wild, or looked after for life if they cannot be released.

Although the national-park system appears glamorous on paper, the Sinac authority still sees much work to be done. A report from several years ago amplified the fact that much of the protected area is, in fact, at risk. The government doesn't own all of this land – almost half of the areas are in private hands – and there isn't the budget to buy it. Technically, the private lands are protected from development, but there have been reports that many landowners are finding loopholes in the restrictions and selling or developing their properties, or taking bribes from poachers and illegal loggers in exchange for access.

On the plus side is a project by Sinac that links national parks and reserves, private reserves and national forests into 13 conservation areas. This strategy has two major effects. First, these 'megaparks' allow greater numbers of individual plants and animals to exist. Second, the administration of the national parks is delegated to regional offices, allowing a more individualized management approach. Each conservation area has regional and subregional offices charged with providing effective education, enforcement, research and management, although some regional offices play what appear to be only obscure bureaucratic roles.

In general, support for land preservation remains high in Costa Rica because it provides income and jobs to so many people, plus important opportunities for scientific investigation.

Excellent, contemplative books on birds by the esteemed Dr Alexander Skutch include *A Naturalist in Costa Rica* and *The Minds of Birds*.

Environmental Issues

No other tropical country has made such a concerted effort to protect its environment, and a study published by Yale and Columbia Universities in 2012 ranked Costa Rica in the top five nations for its overall environmental performance. At the same time, as the global leader in

Catarata de Río Celeste (p217), Parque Nacional Volcán Tenorio

the burgeoning ecotourism economy, Costa Rica is proving to be a case study in the pitfalls and benefits of this kind of tourism. The pressures of overpopulation, global climate change and dwindling natural resources have also made it a key illustration of the urgency of environmental protection.

Deforestation

Sometimes, when the traffic jams up around the endless San José sprawl, it is hard to keep in mind that this place was once covered in a lush, unending tropical forest. Tragically, after more than a century of clearing for plantations, agriculture and logging, Costa Rica lost about 80% of its forest cover before the government stepped in with a plan to protect what was left. Through its many programs of forest protection and reforestation, 54% of the country is forested once again – a stunning accomplishment.

Despite protection for two-thirds of the remaining forests, cutting trees is still a major problem for Costa Rica, especially on private lands that are being cleared by wealthy landowners and multinational corporations. Even within national parks, some of the more remote areas are being logged illegally because there is not enough money for law enforcement.

Apart from the loss of tropical forests and the plants and animals that depend on them, deforestation leads directly or indirectly to a number of other severe environmental problems. Forests protect the soil beneath them from the ravages of tropical rainstorms. After deforestation, much of the topsoil is washed away, lowering the productivity of the land and silting up watersheds and downstream coral reefs.

Cleared lands are frequently planted with a variety of crops, including acres of bananas, the production of which entails the use of

Tales of the green turtle's resurgence in Tortuguero are told by Archie Carr in *The Windward Road: Adventures of a Naturalist on Remote Caribbean Shores*.

pesticides as well as blue plastic bags to protect the fruit. Both the pesticides and the plastic end up polluting the environment. Cattle ranching has been another historical motivator for clear-cutting. It intensified during the 1970s, when Costa Rican coffee exports were waning in the global market.

Because deforestation plays a role in global warming, there is much interest in rewarding countries such as Costa Rica for taking the lead in protecting their forests. The US has forgiven millions of dollars of Costa Rica's debt in exchange for increased efforts to preserve rainforests. The Costa Rican government itself sponsors a program that pays landowners for each hectare of forest they set aside, and has petitioned the UN for a global program that would pay tropical countries for their conservation efforts. Travelers interested in taking part in projects that can help protect Costa Rica's trees should look to volunteer opportunities (p514) in conservation and forestry.

Tourism

The other great environmental issue facing Costa Rica comes from the country being loved to death, directly through the passage of around two million foreign tourists a year, and less directly through the development of extensive infrastructure to support this influx. For years, resort hotels and lodges continued to pop up, most notably on formerly pristine beaches or in the middle of intact rainforest. Too many of these projects were poorly planned, and they necessitate additional support systems, including roads and countless vehicle trips, with much of this activity unregulated and largely unmonitored.

As tourism continues to become a larger piece of the Costa Rican economy, the bonanza invites more and more development. Taking advantage of Costa Rica's reputation as a green destination, developers promote mass tourism by building large hotels and package tours that, in turn, drive away wildlife, hasten erosion and strain local sewer and water systems. The irony is painful: these businesses threaten to ruin the very environment that they're selling.

It's worth noting that many private lodges and reserves are also doing some of the best conservation work in the country, and it's heartening to run across the ever-increasing homespun efforts to protect Costa Rica's environment, spearheaded by hardworking families or small organizations tucked away in some quiet corner of the country. These include projects to boost rural economies by raising native medicinal plants, efforts by villagers to document their local biodiversity, and resourceful fundraising campaigns to purchase endangered lands.

Sustainable Travel

Costa Rica's visitors presently account for the largest sector of the national economy and thus have unprecedented power to protect this country. How? By spending wisely, asking probing questions about sustainability claims and simply avoiding businesses that threaten Costa Rica's future.

In its purest form, sustainable tourism simply means striking the ideal balance between the traveler and their surrounding environment. This often includes being conscientious about energy and water consumption, and treading lightly on local environments and communities. Sustainable tourism initiatives support their communities by hiring local people for decent wages, furthering women's and civil rights, and supporting local schools, artists and food producers.

On the road, engage with the local economy as much as possible; for example, if a local artisan's handiwork catches your eye, make the purchase – every dollar infuses the micro-economy in the most direct (and rewarding) way.

For maps and descriptions of the national parks, visit www.costarica-nationalparks.com.

The tallest tree in the rainforest is usually the ceiba (silk-cotton tree); the most famous example is a 77m elder in Corcovado.

Green Phoenix, by science journalist William Allen, is an absorbing account of his efforts, alongside scientists and activists, to conserve and restore the rainforest in Guanacaste.

Above: Parque Nacional Tortuguero (p149)

Right: Cattleya orchid

IMAGES ETC LTD/GETTY IMAGES ©

Hiking near San José

Ecofriendly Credentials

Interpreting the jargon – 'green,' 'sustainable,' 'low carbon footprint,' 'ecofriendly' etc – can be confusing when every souvenir stall and tour operator claims to be ecofriendly. Since sustainable travel has no universal guidelines, here are some things to look for:

➡ For hotels and restaurants, obvious recycling programs, effective management of waste water and pollutants, and alternative energy systems and natural illumination, at a bare minimum.

➡ A high rating from a legitimate sustainability index. In Costa Rica, the government-sanctioned Certificado para la Sostenibilidad Turística (CST; www.turismo-sostenible.co.cr) offers a 'five-leaf' rating system. Factors considered by the CST include physical-biological parameters, infrastructure and services, and socioeconomic environment, including interaction with local communities. Its website has a complete directory.

➡ Partnership with environmental conservation programs, education initiatives, or regional or local organizations that work on solving environmental problems.

➡ Grassroots connections: sourcing a majority of employees from the local population, associating with locally owned businesses, providing places where local handicrafts can be displayed for sale, serving foods that support local markets, and using local materials and products in order to maintain the health of the local economy.

The National Biodiversity Institute (www.inbio.ac.cr) is a clearinghouse of information on both biodiversity and efforts to conserve it.

ONDREJ PROSICKY/SHUTTERSTOCK ©

Costa Rica Wildlife Guide

Costa Rica's reputation as a veritable Eden precedes it – with its iconic blue morpho butterflies, four species each of monkey and sea turtle, scarlet and great green macaws, two- and three-toed sloths, a rainbow of poison-dart frogs, mysterious tapirs and cute coatis.

Contents
➡ Birds
➡ Reptiles & Amphibians
➡ Marine Animals
➡ Land Mammals
➡ Insects & Arachnids

Above: Keel-billed toucan

JORGE A. RUSSELL/SHUTTERSTOCK ©

1. Roseate spoonbill 2. Respendent quetzal 3. Scarlet macaw
4. Green violetear hummingbirds

Birds

Toucan

Six species of this classic rainforest bird are found in Costa Rica. Huge bills and vibrant plumage make the commonly sighted chestnut-mandibled toucan and keel-billed toucan hard to miss. Listen for the keel-billed's song: a repetitious 'carrrick!'

Scarlet Macaw

Of more than a dozen parrot species in Costa Rica, none is as spectacular as the scarlet macaw. Unmistakable for its large size, bright-red body and ear-splitting squawk, it's common in Parque Nacional Carara and the Península de Osa. Macaws have long, monogamous relationships and can live for 50 years.

Resplendent Quetzal

The most dazzling bird in Central America, the quetzal once held great ceremonial significance for the Aztecs and the Maya. Look for its iridescent-green body, red breast and long green tail at high elevations and near Parque Nacional Los Quetzales.

Roseate Spoonbill

This wading bird has a white head and a distinctive spoon-shaped bill, and feeds by touch. It's common around the Península de Nicoya, Pacific lowlands and on the Caribbean side at the Refugio Nacional de Vida Silvestre Caño Negro.

Tanager

There are 42 species of tanager in the country – many are brightly colored and all have bodies about the size of an adult fist. Look for them everywhere except at high elevation. Their common name in Costa Rica is *viuda* (widow).

Hummingbird

More than 50 species of hummingbird have been recorded – and most live at high elevations. The largest is the violet sabrewing, with a striking violet head and body and dark-green wings.

1. Eyelash viper 2. Red-eyed tree frog 3. Green iguana
4. Strawberry poison-dart frog

BRANDON ALMS/SHUTTERSTOCK ©

Reptiles & Amphibians

Green Iguana

The stocky green iguana is regularly seen draping its 2m-long body along a branch. Despite their enormous bulk, iguanas are vegetarians, and prefer to eat young shoots and leaves. You'll see them just about everywhere in Costa Rica – in fact, if you're driving, beware of iguanas sunning themselves on or skittering across the roads.

Red-eyed Tree Frog

The unofficial symbol of Costa Rica, the red-eyed tree frog has red eyes, a green body, yellow and blue side stripes, and orange feet. Despite this vibrant coloration, they're well camouflaged in the rainforest and rather difficult to spot. Their presence is widespread apart from on the Península de Nicoya, which is too dry for them. You have a particularly good chance of seeing them at Estación Biológica La Selva.

Poison-dart Frog

Among the several species found in Costa Rica, the blue-jeans or strawberry poison-dart frog is the most commonly spotted, from Arenal to the Caribbean coast. These colorful, wildly patterned frogs' toxic excretions were once used to poison indigenous arrowheads. The Golfo Dulce poison-dart frog is endemic to Costa Rica.

Crocodile

Impressive specimens can be seen from Crocodile Bridge on the central Pacific coast or in a more natural setting on boat trips along the Tortuguero canals. Avoid swimming in these areas.

Viper

Three serpents you'll want to avoid are the fer-de-lance pit viper, which lives in agricultural areas of the Pacific and Caribbean slopes, the black-headed bushmaster (endemic to Costa Rica) and the beautiful eyelash pit viper, which lives in low-elevation rainforest. To avoid serious or fatal bites, watch your step and look before you grab onto any vines when hiking.

1. Olive ridley turtle hatchling 2. Bottlenose dolphins 3. Whale shark 4. Hammerhead shark

PHOTOBOTOS IMAGE/GETTY IMAGES ©

Marine Animals

Olive Ridley Turtle

The smallest of Costa Rica's sea turtles, the olive ridley is easy to love – it has a heart-shaped shell. Between September and October they arrive to nest at Ostional beach in Guanacaste province and near Ojochal on the Pacific coast.

Leatherback Turtle

The gigantic 360kg leatherback sea turtle is much, much bigger than the olive ridley, and is distinguished by its soft, leathery carapace, which has seven ridges. It nests on the Pacific beaches of the Osa and Nicoya peninsulas.

Whale

Migrating whales, which arrive from both the northern and southern hemispheres, include orca, blue and sperm whales and several species of relatively unknown beaked whale. Humpback whales are commonly spotted along the Pacific coast and off the Península de Osa.

Bottlenose Dolphin

These charismatic, intelligent cetaceans are commonly sighted, year-round residents of Costa Rica. Keep a lookout for them on the boat ride to Bahía Drake.

Whale Shark

Divers may encounter this gentle giant in the waters off Reserva Biológica Isla del Caño, the Golfo Dulce or Isla del Coco. The world's biggest fish, whale sharks can reach 6m long and more than 2000kg in weight.

Manta Ray

With wings that can reach 7m, the elegant manta ray is common in warm Pacific waters, especially off the coast of Guanacaste and around the Bat and Catalina islands.

Hammerhead Shark

The intimidating hammerhead has a unique cephalofoil that enables it to maneuver with incredible speed and precision. Divers can see enormous schools of hammerheads around the remote Isla del Coco.

1. White-nosed coati **2.** Baby sloth **3.** Jaguar **4.** Squirrel monkeys

JONATHAN FIFE/GETTY IMAGES ©

Land Mammals

Sloth

Costa Rica is home to the brown-throated, three-toed sloth and Hoffman's two-toed sloth (nocturnal). Both species tend to hang seemingly motionless from branches, their coats growing moss. Look for them in Parque Nacional Manuel Antonio.

Howler Monkey

The loud vocalizations of a male mantled howler monkey can carry for more than 1km even in dense rainforest, and they echo through many of the country's national parks.

White-faced Capuchin

The small and inquisitive white-faced capuchin has a prehensile tail that is typically carried with the tip coiled – one is likely to steal your lunch near Volcán Arenal or Parque Nacional Manuel Antonio.

Squirrel Monkey

The adorable, diminutive squirrel monkey travels in small- to medium-sized groups during the day, in search of insects and fruit. They live only along the Pacific coast and are common in Parque Nacional Manuel Antonio and on the Península de Nicoya.

Jaguar

The king of Costa Rica's big cats, the jaguar is extremely rare, shy and well camouflaged, so the chance of seeing one is virtually nil (but the likeliest place is Parque Nacional Corcovado).

White-nosed Coati

A frequently seen member of the raccoon family, with a longer, slimmer and lighter body than your average raccoon. It has a distinctive pointy, whitish snout and a perky striped tail.

Baird's Tapir

A large browsing mammal related to the rhinoceros, the tapir has a characteristic prehensile snout and lives deep in forests ranging from the Península de Osa to Parque Nacional Santa Rosa.

Blue morpho butterfly

Insects & Arachnids

Blue Morpho Butterfly

The blue morpho butterfly flutters along tropical rivers and through openings in the forests. When it lands, the electric-blue upper wings close, and only the mottled brown underwings become visible, an instantaneous change from outrageous display to modest camouflage.

Leaf-cutter Ant

Long processions of busy leaf-cutter ants traverse the forest floors and trails of Costa Rica, appearing like slow-moving rivulets of green leaf fragments. Leaf-cutter ants are actually fungus farmers – in their underground colonies, the ants chew the harvested leaves into a pulp to precipitate the growth of fungus, which feeds the colonies. Don't confuse them with the predatory army ants!

Tarantula

Easily identified by its enormous size and hairy appendages, the Costa Rican red tarantula is an intimidating arachnid that can take down a mouse, but although its bite may cause as much pain as a bee sting, its venom is harmless to humans. They are most active at night while foraging and seeking mates.

Hercules Beetle

Turn on your flashlight while visiting one of Costa Rica's old-growth forests and you might draw out the Hercules beetle, one of the largest bugs in the world, a terrifying-looking but utterly harmless scarab beetle that can be as big as a cake plate. Fun fact: it can carry over 100 times its own body weight.

Survival Guide

Directory A–Z

Accommodations

Accommodations come at every price and comfort level: from luxurious ecolodges and sparkling all-inclusive resorts and backpacker palaces to spartan rooms with little more than a bed and four cinderblock walls. The variety and number of rooms on offer, coupled with online booking, means that advance booking is not usually required.

Note that the term *cabina* (cabin) is a catchall that can define a wide range of prices and amenities, from very rustic to very expensive.

Booking Services

Costa Rica Innkeepers Association (www.costaricainnkeepers. com) A nonprofit association of B&Bs, small hotels, lodges and inns.

Escape Villas (www.villascosta rica.com) High-end accommodations across Costa Rica, most near Parque Nacional Manuel Antonio, which are suitable for families and honeymooners looking for luxury.

Lonely Planet (www.lonely planet.com/costa-rica/hotels) Recommendations and bookings.

Apartments & Villas

The network of long-term rentals has grown dramatically in recent years. These can be an excellent option for families, as they typically include a kitchen and several bedrooms. In many beach towns, vacation villas and apartments of varying quality are rented by the week, month or longer, and some come with resort access, beach toys and other amenities. Many restaurants now offer rooms in the back, and some are surprisingly nice.

B&Bs

Generally speaking, B&Bs in Costa Rica tend to be midrange to top-end affairs, often run by resident European and North American expats. You can find B&Bs listed in the *Tico Times*. Many homeowners now list their properties on airbnb.com, to the chagrin of tax-paying hoteliers.

Camping

➡ Camping on Costa Rica's coasts is not legal but is widely tolerated. Many local families camp at the beach during the holidays.

➡ Most major tourist destinations have at least one campground and most budget hotels outside San José accommodate campers on their grounds. Although these sites usually include toilets, cold showers and basic self-catering facilities (sink and barbecue pit), they can be crowded and noisy.

➡ In most national parks, campsites are usually of excellent quality and rigorously cleaned and maintained by staff. As a rule, you will need to carry in all of your food and supplies, and carry out all of your trash.

➡ Theft is a major concern; don't leave anything in your tent unattended. Camp in a group if possible.

➡ Don't camp near riverbanks, which are prone to flooding and home to snakes.

➡ Mosquito nets and repellent with DEET are often essential.

Hostels

Although there is still a handful of Hostelling International (HI) hostels left in Costa Rica, the backpacker scene has gone increasingly upmarket; the era of the 'resort hostel', complete with bars, pools and entertainment centers, is in full swing. Compared to other destinations in Central America, hostels in Costa Rica tend to be fairly expensive, though the quality of service and accommodations is unequaled. Expect to pay between US$10 and US$15 for a dorm bed.

Hotels

→ It's always advisable to ask to see a room – including the bathroom – before committing to a stay, especially in budget lodgings. Rooms within a single hotel can vary greatly.

→ Some pricier hotels will require confirmation of a reservation with a credit card. Before doing so, note that some top-end hotels require a 50% to 100% deposit up front when you reserve. This rule is not always clearly communicated.

→ In most cases reservations can be canceled and refunded with enough notice. Ask the hotel about its cancellation policy before booking. It is often easier to make the reservation than to unmake it.

→ Many hotels charge a hefty service fee for credit-card use.

→ Have the hotel fax or email you a confirmation. Hotels often get overbooked, and if you don't have a confirmation, you could be out of a room.

→ To compete with online booking services, some hotels offer a discount if you book direct, or if you pay in cash.

Prices & Accommodations

Many lodgings lower their prices during the low (rainy, aka 'green' season), season, from May to November. Prices change quickly and many hotels charge per person rather than per room – read rates carefully and always

check ahead. US dollars are the preferred currency for listing rates in Costa Rica. However, colones are accepted everywhere and are usually exchanged at current rates without an additional fee. Paying with a credit card sometimes incurs a surcharge and cash discounts are sometimes on offer.

BUDGET

→ Budget accommodations in the most popular regions of the country are much sought after and need to be booked well in advance during high season.

→ The cheapest places generally have shared bathrooms, but it's still possible to get a double with a bathroom for US$25 in towns off the tourist trail.

→ At the top end of the budget scale, rooms will frequently include a fan and a bathroom with hot water.

→ Hot water in showers is often supplied by electric showerheads (don't touch!), which will dispense hot water if the pressure is kept low.

→ Most budget hotels also have a few midrange options with more amenities, including air-con and TV.

→ Wi-fi is increasingly available at budget accommodations, particularly in popular tourist destinations, but sometimes only in the main lobby area.

MIDRANGE

→ Midrange rooms will be more comfortable than budget options, and will

generally include a bathroom with gas-heated hot water, a choice between fans and air-con, and cable or satellite TV.

→ Most midrange hotels have wi-fi, though it's sometimes limited to the area near reception or the office.

→ Many midrange places offer tour services, and will have an onsite restaurant or bar and a swimming pool or Jacuzzi.

→ Hotels in this price range often offer kitchenettes or even full kitchens. Some offer complimentary breakfast.

TOP END

→ Top-end accommodations include many ecolodges, all-inclusive resorts, and business and chain hotels, in addition to a strong network of intimate boutique hotels, remote jungle camps and upmarket B&Bs.

→ Costa Rica's top-end lodgings adhere to the same standards of quality and service as similarly priced accommodations in North America and Europe.

→ Staff will likely speak English.

→ Many top-end lodgings include amenities such as hot-water bathtubs, Jacuzzis, private decks, satellite TV and air-con, as well as concierge, tour and spa services.

→ A typical breakfast is usually *gallo pinto* (a stir-fry of rice and beans). This national breakfast dish is usually served with eggs, cheese or *natilla* (sour

Climate

San José

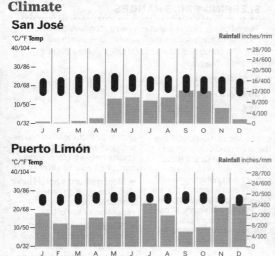

Puerto Limón

Puntarenas

cream). Tropical-style continental breakfasts are also offered.

Customs Regulations

➜ All travelers over the age of 18 are allowed to enter the country with 5L of wine or spirits and 500g of processed tobacco (roughly 400 cigarettes or 50 cigars).

➜ Camera gear, binoculars, and camping, snorkeling and other sporting equipment are readily allowed into the country.

➜ Dogs and cats are permitted entry providing they have obtained both general-health and rabies-vaccination certificates.

➜ Pornography and illicit drugs are prohibited.

Discount Cards

Note that discount cards are not universally accepted at museums and parks.

Costa Rica Discount+ (http://costaricadiscount.com; from US$20/50 for six/60 days) Discounts on car rental, activities and hotels of up to 20%. One card is valid for up to eight people and one vehicle. Buy it online and print it.

International Student Identity Card (ISIC; www.isic.org; around US$20 depending on country of origin) Discounts on museum

and tour fees for any full-time student.

International Student Exchange (ISE; www.isecard.com; around US$25 depending on country of origin) Discounts on museums and tour fees for full-time students between 12 and 26 years old.

Electricity

120V/60Hz

120V/60Hz

Embassies & Consulates

Australia and New Zealand do not have consular representation in Costa Rica; their closest embassies are in Mexico City. Most countries are represented in San José. Mornings are the best time to go to embassies and consulates.

Canadian Embassy (☎2242-4400; www.costarica.gc.ca; Oficentro Ejecutivo La Sabana, 3rd fl, Edificio 5, Sabana Sur; ☺7:30am-4pm Mon-Thu, to 1pm Fri) Behind La Contraloría.

Dutch Embassy (☎2296-1490; www.nederlandwereldwijd.nl/landen/costa-rica; Oficentro La Sabana, Edificio 3, 3rd fl, Sabana Sur; ☺7:30am-4:30pm Mon-Thu, to 12:30pm Fri)

French Embassy (☎2234-4167; www.ambafrance-cr.org; Av 22, Curridabat; ☺7:30am-12:30pm Mon-Fri) On the A022, off the D022 (a smaller road off Rte 2, the road to Curridabat).

German Embassy (☎2290-9091; www.san-jose.diplo.de; 8th fl, Edificio Torre Sabana, Sabana Norte; ☺8am-noon Mon-Fri) Northwest of Parque Metropolitano La Sabana.

Guatemalan Embassy (☎2220-1297, 2291-6172; www.minex.gob.gt; Calle 64, Sabana Sur; ☺9am-1pm Mon-Fri) Southwest Parque Metropolitano La Sabana.

Honduran Embassy (☎2231-1642; www.embajadahonduras.co.cr; Blvr Rohrmoser; ☺9am-noon & 1:30-4pm Mon-Fri)

Israeli Embassy (☎2221-6444; 11th fl, Edificio Colón, Paseo Colón btwn Calles 38 & 40; ☺9am-noon Mon-Fri)

Italian Embassy (☎2224-6574, 2224-1082; www.ambsanjose.esteri.it; Calle 43, Los Yoses; ☺9am-noon Mon-Fri) Between Avs 2 and 8.

Mexican Embassy (☎2257-0633; https://embamex.sre.gob.mx/costarica/; Av 7 btwn Calles 13 & 15; ☺8am-5pm Mon-Fri) Northwest of Parque National.

Nicaraguan Embassy (☎2221-2884, 2233 8001; Av Central 2540 btwn Calles 25 & 27; ☺9am-5pm Mon & Wed-Fri) On the corner of 25A, in Carmen (San José).

Panamanian Embassy (☎2281-2442; www.facebook.com/EmbajadadePanamaenCostaRica/; cnr Av 10 & Calle 69, Barrio La Granja; ☺9am-2pm Mon-Fri) A block north of Parque El Retiro in San Pedro (San José).

Spanish Embassy (☎2222-1933, 2222-5745; www.exteriores.gob.es; Calle 32 btwn Paseo Colón & Av 2; ☺8am-3pm Mon-Fri)

Swiss Embassy (☎2221-4829; www.eda.admin.ch/sanjose; 10th fl, Edificio Centro Colón, Paseo Colón btwn Calles 38 & 40; ☺9am-noon Mon-Fri)

UK Embassy (☎2258-2025; www.gov.uk/government/world/organisations/british-embassy-in-costa-rica; 11th fl, Edificio Centro Colón, Paseo Colón btwn Calles 38 & 40; ☺8am-noon & 12:15-4pm Mon-Thu, 8am-1pm Fri)

US Embassy (☎2519-2000; https://cr.usembassy.gov; cnr Av Central & Calle 120; ☺8am-noon & 1-4pm Mon-Fri) Opposite Centro Comercial del Oeste in Pavas (San José).

Health

Travelers to Central America need to be vigilant about food- and mosquito-borne infections. Most of the illnesses most frequently caught while on holiday here are not life threatening, but they can certainly ruin your trip. Besides getting the proper vaccinations, it's important to use a good insect repellent and exercise care in what you eat and drink.

Before You Go

HEALTH INSURANCE

High-risk adventure activities or water sports such as diving are not covered on all travel policies, so make sure you pay for the appropriate level of insurance coverage. Yours may cover basic activities, such as walking, but not ziplining or surfing; if diving, some companies may only cover you up to a certain number of dives or a certain depth. If unsure, check with your insurer before leaving your home country.

A list of medical evacuation and travel-insurance companies can be found on the US State Department (www.travel.state.gov) website under the 'Before You Go' tab.

RECOMMENDED VACCINATIONS

➡ Get necessary vaccinations four to eight weeks before departure.

➡ Ask your doctor for an International Certificate of Vaccination (otherwise known as the 'yellow booklet'), which will list all the vaccinations you've received. This is mandatory for countries that require proof of yellow-fever vaccination upon entry (Costa Rica only requires such proof if you are entering from a country that carries a risk of yellow fever).

In Costa Rica

AVAILABILITY & COST OF HEALTH CARE

➡ Good medical care is available in most major cities but may be limited in rural areas.

➡ For an extensive list of physicians, dentists and hospitals, visit https://cr.usembassy.gov and look under 'U.S. Citizen Services/ Medical Assistance/Medical Practitioners List.'

➡ Most pharmacies are well supplied and a handful are open 24 hours. Pharmacists are licensed to prescribe medication. If you're taking any medication on a regular basis, make sure you know its generic (scientific) name, since many pharmaceuticals go under different names in Costa Rica.

ENVIRONMENTAL HAZARDS

Animal bites Do not attempt to pet, handle or feed any animal. Any bite or scratch by a mammal, including bats, should be promptly and thoroughly cleansed with large amounts of soap and water, and an antiseptic such as iodine or alcohol should be applied. Contact a local health authority in the event of such an injury. Rabies cases are rare but do happen.

Insect bites No matter how much you safeguard yourself, getting bitten by mosquitoes is part of every traveler's experience here. The best prevention is to stay covered up – wear long pants, long sleeves, a hat, and shoes, not sandals. Invest in a good insect repellent, preferably one containing DEET. Apply to exposed skin and clothing (but not to eyes, mouth, cuts, wounds or irritated skin). Compounds containing DEET should not be used on children under the age of two and should be used sparingly on children under 12. Invest in a bug net to hang over beds (along with a few thumbtacks or nails with which to hang it). Many hotels in Costa Rica don't have windows (or screens), and a cheap little net will save you

plenty of nighttime aggravation. The mesh size should be less than 1.5mm. Dusk is the worst time for mosquitoes, so take extra precautions then.

Sun Stay out of the midday sun, wear sunglasses and a wide-brimmed hat, and apply sunblock with SPF 15 or higher, with both UVA and UVB protection and reapply often, especially if getting in the sea or rivers. Drink plenty of fluids and avoid strenuous exercise when the temperature is high.

INFECTIOUS DISEASES

Dengue fever (breakbone fever) Dengue is transmitted by *Aedes aegypti* mosquitoes, which often bite during the daytime and are usually found close to human habitations, often indoors. Dengue is especially common in densely populated urban environments. It usually causes flu-like symptoms including fever, muscle aches, joint pains, headaches, nausea and vomiting, often followed by a rash. Most cases resolve uneventfully in a few days. There is no treatment for dengue fever except taking analgesics such as acetaminophen/paracetamol (Tylenol) and drinking plenty of fluids. Severe cases may require hospitalization for intravenous fluids and supportive care. There is no vaccine. The key to prevention is taking insect-protection measures.

Hepatitis A The second most common travel-related infection (after traveler's diarrhea). It's a viral infection of the liver that is usually acquired by ingestion of contaminated water, food or ice, though it may also be acquired by direct contact with infected persons. Symptoms may include fever, malaise, jaundice, nausea, vomiting and abdominal pain. Most cases resolve without complications, though hepatitis A occasionally causes severe liver damage. There is no treatment. The vaccine for hepatitis A is extremely safe and highly effective.

Leishmaniasis This is transmitted by sand flies. Most cases occur in newly cleared forest or areas of secondary growth; the

highest incidence is in Talamanca. It causes slow-growing ulcers over exposed parts of the body. There is no vaccine. To protect yourself from sand flies, follow the same precautions as for mosquitoes.

Malaria Malaria is very rare in Costa Rica, occurring only occasionally in rural parts of Limón Province. It's transmitted by mosquito bites, usually between dusk and dawn. Taking malaria pills is not necessary unless you are making a long stay in the province of Limón (not Puerto Limón). Protection against mosquito bites is most effective.

Traveler's diarrhea Tap water is safe and of high quality in Costa Rica, but when you're far off the beaten path it's best to avoid tap water unless it has been boiled, filtered or chemically disinfected (with iodine tablets). To prevent diarrhea, be wary of dairy products that might contain unpasteurized milk and be highly selective when eating food from street vendors. If you develop diarrhea, be sure to drink plenty of fluids, preferably with an oral rehydration solution containing lots of salt and sugar. If diarrhea is bloody or persists for more than 72 hours, or is accompanied by fever, shaking chills or severe abdominal pain, seek medical attention.

Typhoid Caused by ingestion of food or water contaminated with a species of salmonella known as *Salmonella typhi*. Fever occurs in virtually all cases. Other symptoms may include headache, malaise, muscle aches, dizziness, loss of appetite, nausea and abdominal pain. Possible complications include intestinal perforation, intestinal bleeding, confusion, delirium or (rarely) coma. A pretrip vaccination is recommended.

Zika virus At the time of research, pregnant women are advised against traveling to Costa Rica, as the virus may be linked to microcephaly, a birth defect that affects a baby's brain development. Zika is primarily transmitted by mosquitoes, but it can also be transmitted by a man to his sexual partner or by a woman to her fetus. Be aware that symptoms are usually mild in adults, and many people may not realize that they are infected.

Chikungunya virus The newest mosquito-borne viral disease was accidentally introduced to Costa Rica from Africa, and carried from *Aedes albopictus* or Tiger mosquitoes. The symptoms are similar to those of dengue fever (high fever, joint inflammation, a skin rash, headache, muscle aches, nausea), and so are the treatments – replace fluids, reduce fever and wait it out. Unlike dengue, it's very unlikely to be fatal, and once you get it you'll probably develop an immunity. The best prevention is to cover up with long sleeves and DEET.

TAP WATER

➡ It's generally safe to drink tap water in Costa Rica, except in the most rural and undeveloped parts of the country. However, if you prefer to be cautious, buying bottled water is your best bet.

➡ If you have the means, vigorous boiling for one minute is the most effective means of water purification. At altitudes greater than 2000m, boil for three minutes.

➡ Another option is to disinfect water with iodine pills: add 2% tincture of iodine to 1L of water (five drops to clear water, 10 drops to cloudy water) and let stand for 30 minutes. If the water is cold, longer times may be required.

➡ Alternatively, carry a SteriPen that destroys most bacteria, viruses and protozoa with UV light.

Insurance

It's vital that travelers purchase the right type of travel insurance before coming to Costa Rica. Basic insurance tends to cover medical expenses, baggage loss, trip cancellation, accidents and personal liability, but it's worth spending extra to

make sure you're covered in the event of natural disasters. If you intend to take part in adventure sports, make sure that those particular sports are covered by your policy; for divers, some policies only cover you up to a certain depth.

Worldwide travel insurance is available at www. lonelyplanet.com/travel-insurance. You can buy, extend and claim online anytime – even if you're already on the road.

Internet Access

➡ The number of internet cafes in Costa Rica has greatly decreased with the advent of smartphones, and wi-fi in restaurants and cafes.

➡ Expect to pay US$1 to US$2 per hour at internet cafes in San José and tourist towns.

➡ Wi-fi is common in all midrange and top-end hotels, and in the vast majority of budget hotels and hostels. Some hostels still have computers for guest use and/or wi-fi.

Language Courses

➡ Spanish-language schools operate all over Costa Rica and charge by the hour for instruction.

➡ Many courses can be found in central San José and the suburb of San Pedro, and the Central Valley.

➡ It's best to arrange classes in advance. A good clearinghouse is the **Institute for Spanish Language Studies** (ISLS; ☑505-404-0736, in USA 866-391-0394; www.isls.com), which has eight schools in Costa Rica.

Legal Matters

➡ If you are arrested your embassy can offer limited assistance. Embassy officials

will not bail you out and you are subject to Costa Rican laws, not the laws of your own country.

➡ The use of recreational substances other than tobacco and alcohol is illegal in Costa Rica and punishable by imprisonment.

LGBT Travelers

In Costa Rica the situation facing gay and lesbian travelers is better than in most Central American countries, and some areas of the country – particularly Quepos and Parque Nacional Manuel Antonio – have been gay vacation destinations for two decades. Homosexual acts are legal, and in 2015 Costa Rica became the first country in Central America to recognize gay relationships. Still, most Costa Ricans are tolerant of homosexuality only at a 'don't ask, don't tell' level. Same-sex couples are unlikely to be the subject of harassment, though public displays of affection might attract unwanted attention.

The undisputed gay and lesbian capital of Costa Rica is Manuel Antonio; while there, you can pick up an issue of *Playita* (www. gaymanuelantonio.com/ playita-magazine.html). The Spanish-language magazine *Gente 10* (www.gente10. com) is available at gay bars in San José.

Agua Buena Human Rights Association (☑2280-3548; www.aguabuena.org) This noteworthy nonprofit organization has campaigned steadily for fairness in medical treatment for people living with HIV/AIDS in Costa Rica.

Center of Investigation & Promotion of Human Rights in Central America (CIPAC; ☑2280-7821; www.cipacdh. org) The leading gay activist organization in Costa Rica.

Toto Tours (☑800-565-1241, in USA 773-274-8686; www. tototours.com) Gay-travel specialist that organizes regular trips to Costa Rica, among other destinations.

Maps

Unfortunately, detailed maps are hard to come by in Costa Rica, so it's best to purchase one online before your trip.

➡ The excellent, water-resistant 1:350,000 *Costa Rica Adventure Map* published by National Geographic also has an inset map of San José. Available online or in various book and gift shops in San José.

➡ Another quality option is the 1:330,000 *Costa Rica* sheet produced by International Travel Map, which is waterproof and includes a San José inset.

➡ **Fundación Neotrópica** (☎2253-2130; www.neotropica. org) publishes a 1:500,000 map showing national parks and other protected areas; it's available online and in San José bookstores.

➡ The Instituto Costarricense de Turismo (ICT; Costa Rican Tourism Board) publishes a 1:700,000 *Costa Rica* map with a 1:12,500 *Central San José* map on the reverse; it's free at the ICT office in San José.

➡ Maptak (www.maptak. com) has maps of Costa Rica's seven provinces and their capitals.

➡ Few national-park offices or ranger stations have maps for hikers.

➡ **Instituto Geográfico Nacional** (IGN; ☎2202-0777; 215, Zapote; ⊙8:30am-3:30pm Mon-Fri) in San José has topographical maps available for purchase.

➡ Incafo formerly published the *Mapa-Guía de la Naturaleza Costa Rica*, an atlas that included 1:200,000 topographical sheets, as well as English and Spanish descriptions of Costa Rica's natural areas. Used copies can be purchased online.

Money

ATMs

ATMs are ubiquitous, typically dispensing colones; many dispense US dollars. They are not easily found in rural and remote areas.

Bargaining

➡ A high standard of living along with a stream of international tourist traffic means that the Latin American tradition of haggling is uncommon in Costa Rica.

➡ Negotiating prices at outdoor markets is acceptable, as is bargaining when arranging informal tours or hiring long-distance taxis.

Cash & Currency

➡ The Costa Rican currency is the colón (plural colones), named after Cristóbal Colón (Christopher Columbus).

➡ Bills come in 1000-, 2000-, 5000-, 10,000-, 20,000- and 50,000-colón notes, while coins come in denominations of five, 10, 20, 25, 50, 100 and 500 colones.

➡ Paying for things in US dollars is common, and at times is encouraged, since the currency is viewed as being more stable than the colón.

➡ In US-dollar transactions the change will usually be given in colones.

➡ Newer US dollars are preferred throughout Costa Rica; if your note has a rip in it, it may not be accepted.

➡ When paying in US dollars at a local restaurant, bar or shop the exchange rate can be unfavorable.

Changing Money

All banks will exchange US dollars, and some will exchange euros and British pounds; other currencies are more difficult. Most banks have excruciatingly long lines, especially at the state-run institutions (Banco Nacional, Banco de Costa Rica, Banco Popular), though they don't charge commissions on cash exchanges. Private banks (Banex, Banco Interfin, Scotiabank) tend to be faster. Make sure the bills you want to exchange are in good condition or they may be refused.

WHAT'S THAT ADDRESS?

Though some larger cities have streets that have been dutifully named, signage is rare in Costa Rica and finding a Tico who knows what street they are standing on is even rarer. Everybody uses landmarks when providing directions; an address may be given as 200m south and 150m east of a church. A city block is *cien metros* – literally 100m – so 250 *metros al sur* means '2½ blocks south,' regardless of the distance. Churches, parks, office buildings, fast-food joints and car dealerships are the most common landmarks used – but these are often meaningless to the foreign traveler, who will have no idea where the Subaru dealership is to begin with. Even more confusingly, Ticos frequently refer to landmarks that no longer exist. In San Pedro, outside San José, locals still use the site of an old fig tree (*el antiguo higuerón*) to provide directions.

Confused? Get used to it...

DOLLARS VERSUS COLONES

While colones are the official currency of Costa Rica, US dollars are virtually legal tender. Case in point: most ATMs in large towns and cities will dispense both currencies. However, it pays to know where and when you should be paying with each currency.

In Costa Rica you can use US dollars to pay for hotel rooms, midrange to top-end meals, admission fees for sights, tours, domestic flights, international buses, car hire, private shuttle buses and big-ticket purchases. Local meals and drinks, domestic bus fares, taxis and small purchases should be paid for in colones.

Credit Cards

➡ Cards are widely accepted at midrange and top-end hotels, as well as at top-end restaurants and many travel agencies; they are less likely to be accepted in small towns and in remote areas.

➡ A transaction fee (around 3% to 5%) on all international credit-card purchases is often added.

➡ Holders of credit and debit cards can buy colones in some banks, though expect to pay a high transaction fee.

➡ All car-rental agencies require drivers to have a credit card. It's possible to hire a car with just a debit card, but only on the condition that you pay for full insurance and leave a deposit for traffic violations.

Taxes & Refunds

Travelers will notice a 13% sales tax at hotels and restaurants, although many smaller budget and midrange businesses have been known to waive the tax if you pay in cash.

Tipping

Restaurants Your bill will usually include a 10% service charge. If not, you might leave a small tip.

Hotels Tip the bellhop/porter US$1 to US$5 per service and the housekeeper US$1 to US$2 per day in top-end hotels, less in budget places.

Taxis Tip only if some special service is provided.

Guides Tip US$5 to US$15 per person per day. Tip the tour driver about half of what you tip the guide.

Traveler's Checks

With the popularity of ATMs and credit cards, traveler's checks are increasingly uncommon in Costa Rica and difficult to exchange outside big cities. They can be exchanged at banks, typically only for US dollars or Costa Rican colones.

Opening Hours

The following are high-season opening hours; hours will generally shorten in the shoulder and low seasons. Generally, sights, activities and restaurants are open daily.

Banks 9am to 4pm Monday to Friday, sometimes 9am to noon Saturday

Bars and clubs 8pm to 2am

Government offices 8am and 5pm Monday to Friday; often closed between 11:30am and 1:30pm

Restaurants 7am to 9pm; upscale places may open only for dinner, and in remote areas even the small *sodas* (inexpensive eateries) might open only at specific meal times

Shops 8am to 6pm Monday to Saturday

Photography

➡ Always ask permission to take someone's photo.

➡ With the prominence of digital cameras, it is increasingly difficult to purchase high-quality film in Costa Rica.

➡ *Lonely Planet's Guide to Travel Photography* is full of helpful tips for photography while on the road.

Post

➡ Mailing smaller parcels (less than 2kg) internationally is quite reliable; for example, a 1kg package costs upwards of US$30 to ship to North America and takes one to two weeks to arrive.

➡ EMS (Express Mail Service) courier service costs a bit more but includes tracking and is speedier.

Public Holidays

Días feriados (national holidays) are taken seriously in Costa Rica. Banks, public offices and many stores close. During these times, public transport is tight and hotels are heavily booked. Many festivals coincide with public holidays.

New Year's Day January 1

Semana Santa (Holy Week; March or April) The Thursday and Friday before Easter Sunday is the official holiday, though most businesses shut down for the whole week. From Thursday to Sunday bars are closed and alcohol sales are prohibited; on Thursday and Friday buses stop running.

Día de Juan Santamaría (April 11) Honors the national hero who died fighting William Walker in 1856; major events are held in Alajuela, his hometown.

Labor Day May 1

Día de la Madre (Mother's Day; August 15) Coincides with the annual Catholic Feast of the Assumption.

Independence Day September 15

Día de la Raza (Columbus Day) October 12.

PRACTICALITIES

Media

La Nación (www.nacion.com) Spanish-language daily newspaper.

La Prensa Libre (www.laprensalibre.cr) Launched in 1889, this is the oldest continually published daily newspaper in Costa Rica. Spanish language.

Tico Times (www.ticotimes.net) Costa Rica's online English-language newspaper. It's high quality, though news and views are often geared toward the expat community.

Costa Rican Times (www.costaricantimes.com) This online, English-language newcomer focuses on Costa Rican happenings but also features international news.

DVDs In Costa Rica DVDs are region 4.

Weights & Measures

Costa Ricans use the metric system for weights, distances and measures.

Christmas Day (December 25) Christmas Eve is also an unofficial holiday.

Last week in December The week between Christmas and New Year is an unofficial holiday; businesses close and beach hotels are crowded.

Safe Travel

Costa Rica is a largely safe country, but petty crime (bag snatchings, car break-ins etc) is common and muggings do occur, so it's important to be vigilant.

➸ Many of Costa Rica's dangers are nature related: riptides, earthquakes and volcanic eruptions are among them.

➸ Predatory and venomous wildlife can also pose a threat, so a wildlife guide is essential if trekking in the jungle.

Earthquakes & Volcanic Eruptions

Costa Rica lies on the edge of active tectonic plates, so it is decidedly earthquake prone. Recent major quakes occurred in 1990 (7.1 on the Richter scale), 1991 (7.4) and 2012 (7.6). Smaller quakes and tremors happen quite often (one area that sees particularly frequent seismic activity is the Península de Nicoya), cracking roads and knocking down telephone lines.

Two of the most popular volcanoes in Costa Rica, Poás and Turrialba, have been very active recently with a number of eruptions of varying degrees since 2014 and 2015. Due to safety concerns, the national parks surrounding these protected sites were closed at the time of research. Check the status of each before you visit.

Hiking Hazards

Hikers setting out into the wilderness should be adequately prepared.

➸ Know your limits and don't set out to do a hike you can't reasonably complete.

➸ Carry plenty of water, even on very short trips.

➸ Carry maps, extra food and a compass.

➸ Let someone know where you are going, so they can narrow the search area in the event of an emergency.

➸ Be aware that Costa Rica's wildlife can pose a threat to hikers, particularly in Parque Nacional Corcovado.

Riptides

Each year Costa Rican waters see more than 100 drownings, the majority of which are caused by riptides (strong currents that pull the swimmer in different directions). Many deaths due to riptides are caused by panicked swimmers struggling to the point of exhaustion. If you are caught in a riptide, do not struggle. Swim parallel to shore; eventually the riptide will dissipate. Alternatively, you can float until the riptide dissipates, then swim parallel to shore and back in where there is no riptide.

Thefts & Muggings

The biggest danger that most travelers face is theft, primarily from pickpockets, but also when personal possessions are left in parked cars. There is a lot of petty crime in Costa Rica, so keep an eye on your belongings and your surroundings at all times.

Telephone

➸ Mobile service now covers most of the country and nearly all of the country that is accessible to tourists.

➸ Public phones are found all over Costa Rica, and chip or Colibrí phone cards are available in 1000-, 2000- and 3000-colón denominations.

➸ Chip cards are inserted into the phone and scanned. Colibrí cards (more common) require you to dial a toll-free number (199) and enter an access code. Instructions are provided in English or Spanish.

➸ The cheapest international calls from Costa Rica are direct-dialed using a phone card. To make international calls, dial '00' followed by the country code and number.

➸ Pay phones cannot receive international calls.

➜ To call Costa Rica from abroad, use the country code (506) before the eight-digit number.

➜ Due to the widespread popularity of voice-over IP services such as Skype, and more reliable ethernet connections, traveling with a smartphone or tablet can be the cheapest and easiest way to call internationally.

Time

Costa Rica is six hours behind GMT, so Costa Rican time is equivalent to Central Time in North America. There is no daylight saving time.

Toilets

➜ Public restrooms are rare, but most restaurants and cafes will let you use their facilities, sometimes for a small charge – never more than 500 colones.

➜ Bus terminals and other major public buildings usually have toilets, also at a charge.

➜ Don't flush your toilet paper. Costa Rican plumbing is often poor and has very low pressure.

➜ Dispose of toilet paper in the rubbish bin inside the bathroom.

Tourist Information

➜ The government-run Costa Rica Tourism Board, the ICT (www.ict.go.cr/en), has an office in the capital; English is spoken.

➜ The ICT can provide you with free maps, a master bus schedule, information on road conditions in the hinterlands, and a helpful brochure with up-to-date emergency numbers for every region.

➜ Consult the ICT's English-language website for information.

Travelers with Disabilities

Independent travel in Costa Rica is difficult for anyone with mobility constraints. Although Costa Rica has an equal-opportunity law, the law applies only to new or newly remodeled businesses and is loosely enforced. Therefore, very few hotels and restaurants have features specifically suited to wheelchair use. Many don't have ramps, and room or bathroom doors are rarely wide enough to accommodate a wheelchair.

Streets and sidewalks are potholed and poorly paved, making wheelchair use frustrating at best. Public buses don't have provisions to carry wheelchairs, and most national parks and outdoor tourist attractions don't have trails suited to wheelchair use. Notable exceptions include Parque Nacional Volcán Poás (p109) – closed at the time of research due to volcanic activity – and the Rainforest Adventures aerial tram (p140).

Download Lonely Planet's free Accessible Travel guide from http://lptravel.to/AccessibleTravel.

Visas

Passport-carrying nationals of the following countries are allowed 90 days' stay with no visa: Argentina, Australia, Canada, Chile, Iceland, Ireland, Israel, Japan, Mexico, New Zealand, Panama, South Africa, the US and most Western European countries.

Most other visitors require a visa from a Costa Rican embassy or consulate.

For the latest info on visas, check the websites of the ICT (www.ict.go.cr/en) or the Costa Rican Embassy (www.costarica-embassy.org).

Extensions

➜ Extending your stay beyond the authorized 30 or 90 days is time-consuming; it's easier to leave the country for 72 hours and then re-enter.

➜ Extensions can be handled by **migración offices** (⌨ in Juan Santamaria International Airport 2299-8001, in Puerto Limón 2798-2097, in Puntarenas

---

GOVERNMENT TRAVEL ADVICE

The following government websites offer travel advisories and information on current hot spots.

Australian Department of Foreign Affairs (www.smarttraveller.gov.au)

British Foreign Office (www.gov.uk/foreign-travel-advice)

Canadian Department of Foreign Affairs (www.dfait-maeci.gc.ca)

Dutch government (www.nederlandwereldwijd.nl)

German Federal Foreign Office (www.auswaertiges-amt.de/de)

Japanese Ministry of Foreign Affairs (www.anzen.mofa.go.jp)

New Zealand government (www.safetravel.govt.nz)

US State Department (http://travel.state.gov)

2661-1445, in San José 2299-8100; www.migracion.go.cr).

➡ Requirements for extensions change, so allow several working days.

Volunteering

Costa Rica offers a huge number of volunteer opportunities. Word of mouth is a powerful influence on future participants, so the majority of programs in Costa Rica are very conscientious about pleasing their volunteers. Almost all placements require a commitment of two weeks or more.

Lonely Planet does not vouch for any organization that we do not work with directly, and we strongly recommend travelers always investigate a volunteer opportunity themselves to assess the standards and suitability of the project.

Teaching English
Amerispan Study Abroad (www.amerispan.com) Offers a variety of educational travel programs in specialized areas.

Sustainable Horizon (www.sustainablehorizon.com) Arranges volunteering trips such as guest-teaching spots.

Forestry Management
Cloudbridge Nature Reserve (www.cloudbridge.org) Trail building, construction, tree planting and projects monitoring the recovery of the cloud forest are offered to volunteers, who pay for their own housing with a local family. Preference is given to biology students, but all enthusiastic volunteers can apply.

Tropical Science Center (www.cct.or.cr) This long-standing NGO offers volunteer placement at Reserva Biológica Bosque Nuboso Monteverde. Projects can include trail maintenance and conservation work.

Fundación Corcovado (www.corcovadofoundation.org) An impressive network of people and organizations committed to preserving Parque Nacional Corcovado.

Monteverde Institute (www.monteverde-institute.org) A nonprofit educational institute offering training in tropical biology, conservation and sustainable development.

Organic Farming
WWOOF Costa Rica (www.wwoofcostarica.org) This loose network of farms is part of the large international network of Willing Workers on Organic

SEX TRADE

Exit the baggage claim at the international airport in San José and you'll be welcomed by a sign that reads 'In Costa Rica sex with children under 18 is a serious crime. Should you engage in it we will drive you to jail.' For decades, travelers have arrived in Costa Rica in search of sandy beaches and lush mountainscapes; unfortunately, an unknown percentage of them also come in search of sex – not all of it legal.

Prostitution by men and women over the age of 18 is legal. With the tourist juggernaut of the last few decades has come unwanted illicit activities at its fringes – namely child prostitution and human trafficking. Sex with a minor in Costa Rica is illegal, carrying a penalty of up to 10 years in jail, but child prostitution has nonetheless grown. In fact, a number of aid groups, along with the country's national child-welfare agency (Patronato Nacional de la Infancia; PANI), estimate that there may be more than 3000 child prostitutes in San José alone. In turn, this has led to women and children being trafficked for the purpose of sexual exploitation, as documented in a 2008 report issued by the US Department of State.

Alarm over the problem has increased steadily since 1999, when the UN Committee on Human Rights issued a statement saying that it was 'deeply concerned' about child-sex tourism in Costa Rica. Since then, the government has established national task forces to combat the problem, trained the police force in how to deal with issues of child exploitation and formed a coalition against human trafficking. But enforcement remains weak – largely due to lack of personnel and lack of funding. Meanwhile the US – the principal source of sex tourists to Costa Rica – has made it a prosecutable crime for Americans to have sex with minors anywhere in the world.

Along with Thailand and Cambodia, Costa Rica is one of the most popular sex-tourism destinations in the world, according to Ecpat International, a nonprofit dedicated to ending child prostitution. The phenomenon has been magnified by the internet: entire sex-tourism websites chronicle – in detail – where and how to find sex. In all of these, Costa Rica figures prominently.

Various organizations fight the sexual exploitation of children in Costa Rica. See the websites of Ecpat International (www.ecpat.org) and Cybertipline (www.cybertipline.com) to learn more about the problem or to report any incidents you encounter.

Farms (WWOOF). Placements are incredibly varied. WWOOF Mexico, Costa Rica, Guatemala and Belize have a joint US$33 membership, which gives potential volunteers access to all placement listings.

Reserva Biológica Dúrika (www.durika.org) A sustainable community on an 85-sq-km biological reserve.

Finca La Flor de Paraíso (www.la-flor.org) Offers programs in a variety of disciplines from animal husbandry to medicinal-herb cultivation.

Punta Mona (www.puntamona.org) An organic farm and retreat center that focuses on organic permaculture and sustainable living.

Rancho Margot (www.ranchomargot.com) This self-proclaimed life-skills university offers a natural education emphasizing organic farming and animal husbandry.

Wildlife Conservation

Be aware that conservationists in Costa Rica occasionally face harassment or worse from local poachers and that police are pretty ineffectual in following up incidents.

Earthwatch (www.earthwatch.org) This broadly recognized international volunteer organization works in sea-turtle conservation in Costa Rica.

Sea Turtle Conservancy (www.conserveturtles.org) From March to October, this Tortuguero organization hosts 'eco-volunteer adventures' working with sea turtles and birds.

Profelis (www.grafischer.com/profelis) A feline-conservation program that takes care of confiscated wild cats, both big and small.

Reserva Playa Tortuga (www.reservaplayatortuga.org) Assist with olive-ridley-turtle conservation efforts near Ojochal.

Asociacion Salvemos las Tortugas de Parismina (ASTOP, Save the Turtles of Parismina; ☏2798-2220; homestays per night incl 3 meals & patrols US$28, registration fee US$35; ☺by arrangement Mar-Sep) ✐ Help protect turtles and their eggs, and help improve quality of life for villagers in this tiny community.

Women Travelers

Most female travelers experience little more than a *mi amor* ('my love') or an appreciative glance from the local men. But, in general, Costa Rican men consider foreign women to have looser morals and to be easier conquests than Ticas (female Costa Ricans). Men will often make flirtatious comments to single women, particularly blondes, and women traveling together are not exempt. The best response is to do what Ticas do: ignore it completely. Women who firmly resist unwanted verbal advances from men are normally treated with respect.

➡ In small highland towns, dress is usually conservative. Women rarely wear shorts, but belly-baring tops are all the rage. On the beach, skimpy bathing suits are OK, but topless and nude bathing is not.

➡ Solo women travelers should avoid hitchhiking.

➡ Do not take unlicensed 'pirate' taxis (licensed taxis are red and have medallions) as there have been reports of assaults on women by unlicensed drivers.

Work

It is difficult for foreigners to find work in Costa Rica. The only foreigners legally employed in Costa Rica are those who work for their own businesses, possess skills not found in the country, or work for companies that have special agreements with the government.

Getting a bona fide job necessitates obtaining a work permit, which can be a time-consuming and difficult process. The most likely source of paid employment is as an English teacher at one of the language institutes, or working in the hospitality industry in a hotel or resort. Naturalists or river guides may also be able to find work with private lodges or adventure travel operators, though you shouldn't expect to make more than survival wages.

Transportation

GETTING THERE & AWAY

Costa Rica can be reached via frequent, direct international flights from the US and Canada and from other Central American countries. You can also cross a land border into Costa Rica from Panama or Nicaragua. Flights, cars and tours can be booked online at lonelyplanet.com/bookings.

Entering the Country

➡ Entering Costa Rica is mostly free of hassle, with the exception of some long queues at the airport.

➡ The vast majority of travelers enter the country by plane, and most international flights arrive at Aeropuerto Internacional Juan Santamaría, outside San José.

➡ Liberia is a growing destination for international flights; it is in the Guanacaste province and serves travelers heading to the Península de Nicoya.

➡ Overland border crossings (p517) are straightforward and travelers can move freely between Panama to the south and Nicaragua to the north.

➡ Some foreign nationals will require a visa (p513). Be aware that you cannot get a visa at the border.

Passports

➡ Citizens of all nations are required to have a passport that is valid for at least six months beyond the dates of their trip.

➡ The law requires that you carry your passport at all times; if you're driving, you must have your passport handy, but otherwise the law is seldom enforced.

Onward Ticket

➡ Officially, travelers are required to have a ticket out of Costa Rica before they are allowed to enter. This is rarely and erratically enforced.

➡ Those arriving overland with no onward ticket can purchase one from international bus companies in Managua (Nicaragua) and Panama City (Panama).

Air

Costa Rica is well connected by air to other Central and South American countries, as well as the US.

Airports & Airlines

Aeropuerto Internacional Juan Santamaría (☏2437-2400; www.fly2sanjose.com) International flights arrive here, 17km northwest of San José, in the town of Alajuela.

Aeropuerto Internacional Daniel Oduber Quirós (LIR; www.liberiacostaricaairport.net) This

---

CLIMATE CHANGE & TRAVEL

Every form of transport that relies on carbon-based fuel generates CO_2, the main cause of human-induced climate change. Modern travel is dependent on airplanes, which might use less fuel per kilometer per person than most cars but travel much greater distances. The altitude at which aircraft emit gases (including CO_2) and particles also contributes to their climate change impact. Many websites offer 'carbon calculators' that allow people to estimate the carbon emissions generated by their journey and, for those who wish to do so, to offset the impact of the greenhouse gases emitted with contributions to portfolios of climate-friendly initiatives throughout the world. Lonely Planet offsets the carbon footprint of all staff and author travel.

airport in Liberia also receives international flights from the US, the Americas and Canada. It serves a number of American and Canadian airlines and some charters from London, as well as regional flights from Panama and Nicaragua.

Avianca (part of the Central American airline consortium Grupo TACA; www.avianca.com). The Colombian-owned airline is regarded as the national airline of Costa Rica and flies to the US and Latin America, including Cuba.

Tickets

Airline fares are usually more expensive during the Costa Rican high season (from December through April); December and January are the most expensive months to travel.

TO/FROM CENTRAL AMERICA

➜ **American Airlines** (www. aa.com), **Delta** (www. delta.com) and **United** (www.united.com) have connections to Costa Rica from many Central and Latin American countries. Avianca usually offers the most flights on these routes.

➜ **Nature Air** (www. natureair.com) flies from Liberia to Managua (Nicaragua). Note that rates vary considerably according to season and availability.

➜ **Avianca** offers direct flights to Caracas (Venezuela), Guatemala City (Guatemala), Panama City (Panama) and San Salvador (El Salvador). TACA and Mexicana have daily flights to Mexico City, and COPA also has multiple flights a day to Panama City. Rates vary considerably according to season and availability.

TO/FROM OTHER COUNTRIES

➜ Flights from Houston, Miami or New York are most common.

➜ From Canada, most travelers to Costa Rica

DEPARTURE TAX

➜ There is a US$29 departure tax on all international outbound flights, payable in dollars or colones, though most carriers now include it in the ticket price.

➜ At the Juan Santamaría and Liberia airports this tax can be paid in cash or by credit card; Banco de Costa Rica has an ATM by the departure-tax station. Note that credit-card payments are processed as cash advances, which often carry hefty fees.

➜ If fees are not included in your ticket, travelers will not be allowed through airport security without paying.

connect through US gateway cities, though Air Canada has direct flights from Toronto.

➜ From the UK, Costa Rica is served by British Airways and Virgin, typically with at least one stop.

➜ Flights from the UK and Europe connect either in the US, Mexico City or Toronto. High-season fares may still apply during the northern summer, even though this is the beginning of the Costa Rican rainy season.

➜ From Australia and New Zealand, routes usually go through the US or Mexico. Fares are highest in June and July, even though this is the beginning of the rainy season in Costa Rica.

Land
Border Crossings

Costa Rica shares land borders with Nicaragua and Panama. There is no fee for travelers to enter Costa Rica, but visas (p513) may be required for certain nationalities. There have also been reports of towns adding their own entry and exit fees, usually US$1.

NICARAGUA

A land border crossing opened in 2015 linking Los Chiles (Nicaragua) to Las Tablillas (Costa Rica). A bridge crosses the Río San Juan just north of the Nicaraguan border.

➜ The **Los Chiles–Las Tablillas border crossing** (☎2471-1233) is open from 8am to 4pm daily .

➜ Hourly buses connect Los Chiles and Las Tablillas (US$1, 15 minutes). There are also direct buses from San José and Ciudad Quesada (San Carlos).

➜ A Costa Rican land exit fee of US$7 is payable at immigration by credit or debit card only (no cash).

➜ After walking across the border, you'll go through Nicaraguan immigration. The entrance fee is US$12, payable in US dollars or cordobas.

➜ After exiting immigration, you can catch a boat up the river or hop on a bus or a *collectivo* (shared transport) to San Carlos (roughly US$2.50, 30 minutes).

➜ It's also still possible to cross this border by boat, which is a slower but more pleasant way of doing it. There is no scheduled service; boats depart Los Chiles when there's sufficient demand. Fares are approximately US$10 to US$15 per person, but if you have time constraints it may be possible to pay more and leave more quickly. You'll avoid the Costa Rican land exit fee, but you'll still have to pay US$12 to enter Nicaragua.

➜ If you are entering Costa Rica from Nicaragua, there

are three lines in Nicaragua: one for payment (go there first and pay the US$3 municipal tax/exit tax), one for entrance, and one for exiting the country. Situated on the Interamericana, Sapoá–Peñas Blancas is a heavily trafficked border station between Nicaragua and Costa Rica.

➧ The **Sapoá–Peñas Blancas border crossing** (☑2677-0230) is open from 6am to 10pm.

➧ This is the only official border between Nicaragua and Costa Rica that you can drive across.

➧ Waiting times at this border can be several hours. Plan on at least an hour's wait.

➧ You cannot cross into Nicaragua with a rental car; however, you can leave it at the customs office if you're just going for a quick visit – it'll cost US$10 per day to have your vehicle watched. However, don't leave anything of value inside.

➧ You'll pay a US$7 Costa Rican land exit tax to cross the border (via credit/debit card) and then US$2 municipal tax (in dollars; colones are not accepted – bring some cash in small bills with you).

➧ After walking a few hundred meters, you will also pay US$7 to enter Nicaragua. Keep your passport handy but stowed safely away – officials from both countries may ask to see it.

➧ Do not pay anyone for customs forms; this is a scam. The forms are free, but do bring your own pen to avoid the hassle of borrowing one. As at any border, there are shady operators acting as 'tour guides' and such. Keep your eyes peeled and on your luggage.

➧ After you cross you can catch a Nicaraguan bus or taxi for the 30-minute ride to Rivas (bus fares are approximately US$1), the

key transit point for other Nicaraguan destinations. You can also take a taxi to San Juan del Sur (US$25, 30 minutes). A new road to this Nicaraguan beach town was being paved at the time of research.

➧ Theoretically, if you stay for 90 days in Costa Rica, you're supposed to stay in Nicaragua three days before returning to Costa Rica, but in practice many foreigners (expats who live in Costa Rica but do not yet have residence) stay only three hours. Coming back into Costa Rica, you'll pay a US$3 municipal tax/exit tax. Costa Rican officials may query you about how long you plan to stay and base your visa (60 or 90 days) on this information. Importantly, you should have a return ticket home or out of Costa Rica, dated within 90 days.

➧ **Tica Bus** (☑2296-9788, in Nicaragua 2298-5500, in Panama 314-6385; www.ticabus.com), **Nica Bus** (☑2221-2679, in Nicaragua 2222-2276; www.nicabus.com.ni) and **TransNica** (Map p64; ☑2223-4242; www.transnica.com; Calle 22 btwn Avs 3 & 5) all have daily buses that serve points north and south. Regular buses depart Peñas Blancas, on the Costa Rican side, for La Cruz, Liberia and San José.

➧ Note that Peñas Blancas is only a border post, not a town, so there is nowhere to stay.

PANAMA
Note that Panamanian time is one hour ahead of Costa Rican time.

At the time of writing, entry to Panama required proof of US$500 (per person), proof of onward travel from Panama (including a bus ticket from Panama back to Costa Rica, if you're not flying out of Panama) and a passport valid for at least six months. If you don't have an onward plane ticket yet, buy a refundable one originating

in Panama, print the itinerary and then cancel the ticket.

The Carretera Interamericana (Pan-American Hwy) at **Paso Canoas** (☑2732-2150) is by far the most frequently used entry and exit point with Panama, and it's open 6am to 10pm Monday to Friday, and to 8pm on weekends.

➧ The border crossing in either direction is at times chaotic and slow.

➧ Get an exit stamp from Costa Rica at the immigration office before entering Panama; do the same on the Panamanian side when entering Costa Rica.

➧ There is no charge for entering Costa Rica. Entry to Panama costs US$1.

➧ The departure tax in Costa Rica is US$7, but you will be charged US$8 at the border because the company that handles the transaction takes a US$1 commission. You pay this through the window of a storage container across the highway from the Costa Rica Migration office. Panama has no departure tax.

➧ Northbound buses usually stop running at 6pm. Travelers without a private vehicle should arrive during the day.

➧ Those with a private vehicle are likely to encounter long lines.

➧ Tica Bus travels from Panama City to San José (US$42 to US$58, 15 hours) daily and Tracopa (www.tracopacr.com) has a route from San José to David (US$21), both crossing this border post. In David, Tracopa has one bus daily from the main terminal to San José (nine hours). In David you'll also find frequent buses to the border at Paso Canoas.

➧ Situated on the Caribbean coast, **Guabito–Sixaola** (☑2754-2044) is a fairly tranquil and hassle-free border crossing open between 7am and 5pm.

➡ If you're coming from Bocas del Toro in Panama, you'll first have to take the frequent boat to Almirante (around US$2), then a public bus or shuttle to Changuinola (roughly 40 minutes), from where you can take a quick taxi to the border or to the bus station (roughly US$5).

➡ One daily bus travels between Changuinola and San José at 10am (approximately US$16, eight hours). Otherwise, you can walk over the border and catch one of the hourly buses that go up the coast from Sixaola.

➡ **Río Sereno–San Vito** (☑ 2784-0130) is a rarely used crossing in the Cordillera de Talamanca. The border is open 8am to 4pm on the Costa Rican side and 9am to 5pm on the Panamanian side. The small village of Río Sereno on the Panamanian side has a hotel and a place to eat; there are no facilities on the Costa Rican side.

➡ Regular buses depart Concepción and David in Panama for Río Sereno. Local buses (around US$1.60, 40 minutes, six daily) and taxis (about US$30) go from the border to San Vito.

➡ For travelers departing Costa Rica, there is a US$7 exit tax, plus a US$1 admin fee, payable at a kiosk at the border crossing.

Bus

➡ If crossing a border by bus, note that international buses may cost slightly more than taking a local bus to the border, then another local bus onward from the border, but they're worth it. These companies are familiar with border procedures and will tell you what's needed to cross efficiently.

➡ There will be no problems crossing borders provided your papers are in order. If

you are on an international bus, you'll have to exit the bus and proceed through both border stations. Bus drivers will wait for everyone to be processed before heading on.

➡ If you choose to take local buses, it's advisable to get to border stations early in the day to allow time for waiting in line and processing. Note that onward buses tend to wind down by the afternoon.

➡ International buses go from San José to Changuinola (Bocas del Toro), David and Panama City in Panama; Guatemala City in Guatemala; Managua in Nicaragua; San Salvador in El Salvador; and Tegucigalpa in Honduras.

Car & Motorcycle

The cost of insurance, fuel and border permits makes a car journey significantly more expensive than buying an airline ticket. To enter Costa Rica by car, you'll need the following items:

➡ valid registration and proof of ownership

➡ valid driver's license or International Driving Permit

➡ valid license plates

➡ recent inspection certificate

➡ passport

➡ multiple photocopies of all these documents in case the originals get lost

Before departing, check that the following elements are present and in working order:

➡ blinkers and head- and taillights

➡ spare tire

➡ jerrycan for extra gas (petrol)

➡ well-stocked toolbox including parts, such as belts, that are harder to find in Central America

➡ emergency flares and roadside triangles

Insurance from foreign countries isn't recognized in Cos-

ta Rica, so you'll have to buy a policy locally. At the border it will cost about US$12 to US$36 a month. In addition, you'll have to pay a fumigation fee of about US$5. If you have an accident you must leave your car where the accident occurred and call the police or your insurance will be invalid.

You are not allowed to sell the car in Costa Rica. If you need to leave the country without the car, it must be left in a customs warehouse in San José.

Sea

Cruise ships stop in Costa Rican ports and enable passengers to make a quick foray into the country. Typically, ships dock at either the Pacific ports of Caldera, Puntarenas, Quepos and Bahía Drake, or the Caribbean port of Puerto Limón.

It is also possible to arrive in Costa Rica by private yacht.

GETTING AROUND

Air

Airlines in Costa Rica

➡ Costa Rica's domestic airlines are **Nature Air** (☑ 2299-6000, in USA 1-800-235-9272; www.natureair.com) and **Sansa** (☑ 2290-4100, in USA 877-767-2672; www.flysansa.com). Sansa is linked with the Grupo TACA consortium.

➡ Both airlines fly small passenger planes; check your allowance, as some allow no more than 12kg.

➡ Space is limited and demand is high in the dry season, so reserve and pay for tickets in advance.

➡ The following all depart from San José:

Domestic Air Routes

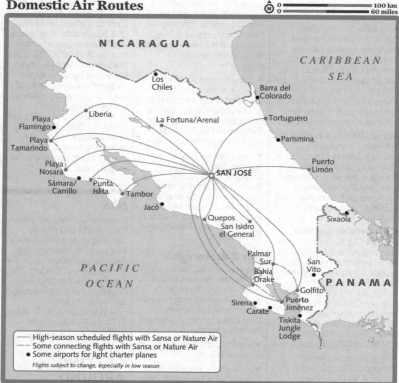

High-season scheduled flights with Sansa or Nature Air
— — Some connecting flights with Sansa or Nature Air
• Some airports for light charter planes
Flights subject to change, especially in low season

DESTINATION	AIRLINE
Arenal	Nature Air
Bahía Drake	Nature Air, Sansa
Bocas del Toro	Nature Air
Golfito	Nature Air, Sansa
Liberia	Nature Air, Sansa
Limón	Sansa
Palmar Sur	Sansa
Playa Nosara	Nature Air
Puerto Jiménez	Nature Air, Sansa
Quepos	Nature Air, Sansa
San Isidro	Sansa
Tamarindo	Nature Air, Sansa
Tambor	Sansa
Tortuguero	Nature Air, Sansa

Charters

➡ Travelers on a larger budget or in a larger party should consider chartering a private plane, which is by far the quickest way to travel around the country.

➡ It takes under 90 minutes to fly to most destinations, though weather conditions can significantly speed up or extend travel time.

➡ The two main charter companies in the country are **Nature Air** (☑2299-6000, in USA 1-800-235-9272; www.natureair.com) and **Alfa Romeo Aero Taxi**

(☑2735-5353, 8632-8150; www.alfaromeoair.com). Both can be booked directly through the company, a tour agency or some high-end accommodation.

➡ Luggage space on charters is extremely limited.

Bicycle

With an increasingly large network of paved secondary roads and heightened awareness of cyclists, Costa Rica is emerging as one of Central America's most comfortable cycle-touring destinations. That said, many roads are narrow, potholed and winding and there are no designated cycle lanes, so there's an element of risk involved.

Mountain bikes and beach cruisers can be rented in towns with a significant tourist presence for US$10 to US$20 per day. A few companies organize bike tours around Costa Rica.

Boat

➡ In Costa Rica there are some regular coastal services, and safety standards are generally good.

➡ Ferries cross the Golfo de Nicoya, connecting the central Pacific coast with the southern tip of the Península de Nicoya.

➡ The **Coonatramar** (☑2661-1069; www.coonatramar.com; adult/child/bicycle/motorcycle/car US$2/1/4/6/18) ferry links the port of Puntarenas with Playa Naranjo five times daily. The ferry **Naviera Tambor** (☑2661-2084; www.navieratambor.com; adult/child/bicycle/motorcycle/car US $1.65/1/4/7/23) travels between Puntarenas and Paquera six times a day, for a bus connection to Montezuma.

➡ On the Golfo Dulce a daily passenger ferry links Golfito with Puerto Jiménez on the Península de Osa. On the other side of the Península de Osa, water taxis connect Bahía Drake with Sierpe.

➡ On the Caribbean coast there are various bus and boat services that run several times a day, linking Cariari and Tortuguero via La Pavona, while another links Parismina and Siquirres (transfer in Caño Blanco).

➡ Boats ply the canals that run along the coast from Moín to Tortuguero; although no regular service exists, tourists can prebook water taxis to transport them around these waterways. Costa Rica and Nicaragua have disputed the San Juan as territory, so take your passport if you want

to explore these waters. You can try to arrange boat transportation for Barra del Colorado from Tortuguero.

Bus
Local Buses
➡ Local buses are a cheap and reliable way of getting around Costa Rica. Fares range from less than US$1 to around US$20.

➡ San José is the transportation center for the country, though there is no central terminal. Bus offices are scattered around the city: some large bus companies have big terminals that sell tickets in advance, while others have little more than a stop – sometimes unmarked.

➡ Buses can be very crowded but don't usually pass up passengers on account of being too full. Note that there are usually no buses from Thursday to Saturday before Easter Sunday.

➡ There are two types of bus: *directo* and *colectivo*. The *directo* buses should go from one destination to the next with few stops; the *colectivos* make more stops and are very slow going.

➡ Trips longer than four hours usually include a rest stop as buses do not have toilets.

➡ Space is limited on board, so if you have to check luggage be watchful. Theft from overhead racks is rampant, though it's much

less common than in other Central American countries.

➡ Bus schedules fluctuate wildly, so always confirm the time when you buy your ticket. If you are catching a bus that picks you up somewhere along a road, get to the roadside early.

➡ For information on departures from San José, see www.visitcostarica.com/en/costa-rica/bus-itinerary for a reasonably up-to-date copy of the master schedule, or check www.thebusschedule.com/cr for route planning.

Shuttle Buses
The tourist-van shuttle services (aka gringo buses) are a pricier alternative to the standard intercity buses. Shuttles are provided by **Gray Line** (☑2220-2126, in US 800-719-3905; www.graylinecostarica.com), **Easy Ride** (☑8812-4012, in USA 703-879-2284; www.easyridecostarica.com), **Monkey Ride** (☑2787-0454; www.monkeyridecr.com), **Tropical Tours** (☑2640-1900; www.tropicaltourshuttles.com) and **Interbus** (☑6050-6500, 4100-0888; www.interbusonline.com).

➡ All four companies run overland transportation from San José to the most popular destinations, as well as directly between other destinations (see the websites for the comprehensive list).

➡ These services will pick you up at your hotel, and reservations can be made online or through local travel agencies and hotel owners.

FATAL NATURE AIR ACCIDENTS

In late 2017, in separate incidents, two planes operated by the Costa Rican airline Nature Air crashed, resulting in a total of 14 deaths. The Civil Aviation Administration temporarily suspended the airline shortly after the second crash, reportedly due to personnel shortages and route changes. Nature Air began flying passengers again in February 2018, and at the time of research, investigations into the causes of the crashes were ongoing.

➡ Popular destinations include Quepos, Monteverde/Santa Elena, Manuel Antonio, Jacó, Dominical, Uvita, Puerto Jiménez, Arenal, Montezuma and Mal País.

➡ Easy Ride offers international services directly from Jacó, Tamarindo and Liberia to Granada and Managua in Nicaragua and from Monteverde to Managua.

Car & Motorcycle

➡ Foreign drivers in Costa Rica are required to have a valid driver's license from their home country. Many places will also accept an International Driving Permit (IDP), issued by the automobile association in your country of origin. After 90 days, however, you will need to get a Costa Rican driver's license.

➡ Gasoline (petrol) and diesel are widely available, and 24-hour service stations are along the Interamericana. At the time of research, fuel prices averaged US$1.02 per liter.

➡ In more remote areas, fuel will be more expensive and might be sold at the neighborhood *pulpería* (corner store).

➡ Spare parts may be hard to find, especially for vehicles with sophisticated electronics and emissions-control systems.

Rental & Insurance

➡ There are car-rental agencies in San José and in popular tourist destinations on the Pacific coast.

➡ All of the major international car-rental agencies have outlets in Costa Rica, though you can sometimes get better deals from local companies.

➡ Due to road conditions, it's necessary to invest in a 4WD unless travel is limited to the Interamericana.

➡ Many agencies will insist on 4WD in the rainy season, when driving through rivers is a matter of course.

➡ To rent a car you'll need a valid driver's license, a major credit card and a passport. The minimum age for car rental is 21 years. It's possible to rent with a debit card, but only if you agree to pay full insurance and leave a deposit for traffic violations.

➡ Carefully inspect rented cars for minor damage and make sure that any damage is noted on the rental agreement. If your car breaks down, call the rental company. Don't attempt to get the car fixed yourself – most companies won't reimburse expenses without prior authorization.

➡ Prices vary considerably; on average you can expect to pay more than US$200 per week for a standard SUV, including *kilometraje libre* (unlimited mileage). Economy cars are much cheaper: as little as US$80 a week.

➡ Costa Rican insurance is mandatory, even if you have insurance at home. Expect to pay about US$10 to US$30 per day. Many rental companies won't rent you a car without it. The basic insurance that all drivers must buy is from a government monopoly, the Instituto Nacional de

---

DRIVING THROUGH RIVERS

Driving in Costa Rica will likely necessitate a river crossing at some point. Unfortunately, too many travelers have picked up their off-road skills from watching TV, and every season Ticos get a good chuckle out of the number of dead vehicles they help wayward travelers fish out of waterways.

If you're driving through water, follow the rules below:

Only do this in a 4WD, with 4WD turned on Don't drive through a river in a car. (It may seem ridiculous to have to say this, but it's attempted all the time.) Getting out of a steep, gravel riverbed requires a 4WD. Besides, car engines flood very easily.

Check the depth of the water before driving through To accommodate an average rental 4WD, the water should be no deeper than above the knee. In a sturdier vehicle (Toyota 4Runner or equivalent), water can be waist deep. If you're nervous, wait for a local car to come along, and follow their lead.

The water should be calm If the river is gushing so that there are white crests on the water, do not try to cross. The force of the water will not only flood the engine but could also sweep the car away.

Drive very, very slowly The pressure of driving through a river too quickly will send the water right into the engine and will impair the electrical system. Keep steady pressure on the accelerator so that the tailpipe doesn't fill with water, but go slowly; if driving a stick shift, go in first gear.

Err on the side of caution Car-rental agencies in Costa Rica do not insure for water damage, so ruining a car in a river can come at an extremely high cost.

Seguros. This insurance does not cover your rental car at all, only damages to other people and their car or property. It is legal to drive with this insurance only, but it can be difficult to negotiate with a rental agency to allow you to drive away with just this minimum standard. Full insurance through the rental agency can be up to US$50 a day.

➡ Some roads in Costa Rica are rough and rugged, meaning that minor accidents or car damage are common.

➡ Note that if you pay basic insurance with a gold or platinum credit card, the card company may take responsibility for damage to the car, in which case you can forgo the cost of the full insurance. Make sure you verify this with your credit-card company ahead of time.

➡ Most insurance policies do not cover damage caused by flooding or driving through a river, so be aware of the extent of your policy.

➡ Rental rates fluctuate wildly, so shop around. Some agencies offer discounts for extended rentals. Note that rental offices at the airport charge a 12% fee in addition to regular rates.

➡ Thieves can easily recognize rental cars. Never leave anything in sight in a parked car – nothing! – and remove all luggage from the trunk overnight. If possible, park the car in a guarded parking lot rather than on the street.

➡ Motorcycles (including Harley-Davidsons) can be rented in San José and Escazú, but considering the condition of the roads it's not recommended.

Road Conditions & Hazards

➡ The quality of roads varies, from the quite smoothly paved Interamericana to the barely passable,

FLAT-TIRE SCAM
....
For years Aeropuerto Internacional Juan Santamaría has suffered from a scam involving sudden flat tires on rental cars. Though it's commonly reported, it continues to happen.

It goes like this: after you pick up a rental car and drive out of the city, the car gets a flat; as you pull over to fix it, the disabled vehicle is approached by a group of locals, ostensibly to help. There is inevitably some confusion with the changing of the tire, and in the commotion you are relieved of your wallet, luggage or other valuables.

This incident has happened enough times to suggest that you should be very wary if somebody pulls over to help after you get a flat on a recently rented car. Keep your wallet and passport on your person whenever you get out of a car.

bumpy, potholed, rural back roads. Any can suffer from landslides, sudden flooding and fog.

➡ Many roads are single lane and winding; mountain roads have huge gutters at the sides and lack hard shoulders; other roads are rock-strewn, dirt-and-mud affairs that traverse rivers.

➡ Drive defensively and expect a variety of obstructions, from cyclists and pedestrians to broken-down cars and cattle. Unsigned speed bumps are placed on some stretches of road.

➡ Roads around major tourist areas are adequately marked; all others are not.

➡ Always ask about road conditions before setting out, especially in the rainy season, when a number of roads become impassable.

Road Rules

➡ There are speed limits of 100km/h to 120km/h or less on highways; limits will be posted. The minimum driving speed on highways is 40km/h. The speed limit is 60km/h or less on secondary roads.

➡ Traffic police use radar, and speed limits are

sometimes enforced with speeding tickets.

➡ Tickets are issued to drivers operating vehicles without a seat belt.

➡ It's illegal to stop in an intersection or make a right turn on a red.

➡ At unmarked intersections, yield to the car on your right.

➡ Drive on the right. Passing is allowed only on the left.

➡ If you are issued with a ticket, you have to pay the fine at a bank; instructions are given on the ticket. If you are driving a rental car, the rental company may be able to arrange your payment for you – the amount of the fine should be on the ticket. A portion of the money from these fines goes to a children's charity.

➡ Police have no right to ask for money, and they shouldn't confiscate a car unless the driver cannot produce a license and ownership papers, the car lacks license plates, the driver is drunk or the driver has been involved in an accident causing serious injury.

➡ If you are driving and see oncoming cars with headlights flashing, it often means that there is a road problem or a radar speed trap ahead. Slow down immediately.

Hitchhiking

Hitchhiking is never entirely safe, and we don't recommend it. Travelers who hitchhike should understand that they are taking a small but potentially serious risk. People who do hitchhike will be safer if they travel in pairs and let someone know where they are planning to go. Solo women should use even greater caution.

Hitchhiking in Costa Rica is unusual on main roads that have frequent buses. On minor rural roads, hitchhiking is more common. To get picked up, most locals wave down passing cars. If you get a ride, offer to pay when you arrive by saying '¿Cuánto le debo?' (How much do I owe you?). Your offer may be waved aside, or you may be asked to help with money for gas.

Local Transportation

Bus

Local buses operate chiefly in San José, Puntarenas, San Isidro de El General, Golfito and Puerto Limón, connecting urban and suburban areas. Most local buses pick up passengers on the street and on main roads. For years these buses were converted school buses imported from the US, but they have slowly been upgraded and are now mainly coaches.

Taxi

In San José, taxis have marías (meters) and it is illegal for drivers not to use them. Outside San José, however, most taxis don't have meters and fares tend to be agreed upon in advance. Bargaining is quite acceptable.

In some towns there are colectivos (taxis that several passengers are able to share). Although colectivos are becoming increasingly difficult to find, the basic principle is that the driver charges a flat fee (usually about US$1) to take passengers from one end of town to the other.

In rural areas, 4WDs are often used as taxis and are a popular means for surfers (and their boards) to travel from their accommodations to the break. Prices vary wildly depending on how touristy the area is, though generally speaking a 10-minute ride costs between US$5 and US$20.

Taxi drivers are not normally tipped unless they assist with your luggage or have provided an above-average service.

Language

Spanish pronunciation is easy, as most sounds have equivalents in English. Also, Spanish spelling is phonetically consistent, meaning that there's a clear and consistent relationship between what you see in writing and how it's pronounced. If you read our colored pronunciation guides as if they were English, you'll be understood. Note that kh is a throaty sound (like the 'ch' in the Scottish *loch*), v and b are like a soft English 'v' (between a 'v' and a 'b'), and r is strongly rolled. The stressed syllables are in italics in our pronunciation guides.

The polite form is used in this chapter; where both polite and informal options are given, they are indicated by the abbreviations 'pol' and 'inf'. Where necessary, both masculine and feminine forms of words are included, separated by a slash and with the masculine form first, eg *perdido/a* (m/f).

BASICS

Hello.	Hola.	o·la
Goodbye.	Adiós.	a·dyos
How are you?	¿Cómo va? (pol)	ko·mo va
	¿Cómo vas? (inf)	ko·mo vas
Fine, thanks.	Bien, gracias.	byen gra·syas
Excuse me.	Con permiso.	kon per·mee·so
Sorry.	Perdón.	per·don
Please.	Por favor.	por fa·vor

WANT MORE?

For in-depth language information and handy phrases, check out Lonely Planet's *Latin American Spanish Phrasebook*. You'll find it at **shop.lonelyplanet.com**, or you can buy Lonely Planet's iPhone phrasebooks at the Apple App Store.

Thank you.	Gracias.	gra·syas
You're welcome.	Con mucho gusto.	kon moo·cho goo·sto
Yes.	Sí.	see
No.	No.	no

My name is ...
Me llamo ... — me ya·mo ...

What's your name?
¿Cómo se llama Usted? — ko·mo se ya·ma oo·ste (pol)
¿Cómo te llamas? — ko·mo te ya·mas (inf)

Do you speak English?
¿Habla inglés? — a·bla een·gles (pol)
¿Hablas inglés? — a·blas een·gles (inf)

I don't understand.
Yo no entiendo. — yo no en·tyen·do

ACCOMMODATIONS

Do you have a ... room?
Tiene una habitación ...? — tye·ne oo·na a·bee·ta·syon ...

| single | sencilla | sen·see·ya |
| double | doble | do·ble |

How much is it per night/person?
¿Cuánto es por noche/persona? — kwan·to es por no·che/per·so·na

Is breakfast included?
¿Incluye el desayuno? — een·kloo·ye el de·sa·yoo·no

campsite	área para acampar	a·re·a pa·ra a·kam·par
hotel	hotel	o·tel
hostel	hospedaje	os·pe·da·khe
guesthouse	casa de huéspedes	ka·sa de wes·pe·des
youth hostel	albergue juvenil	al·ber·ge khoo·ve·neel

TIQUISMOS

These colloquialisms and slang terms (*tiquismos*) are frequently heard, and are for the most part used only in Costa Rica.

¡Adiós! – Hi! (used when passing a friend in the street, or anyone in remote rural areas; also means 'Farewell!' but only when leaving for a long time)

bomba – gas station

buena nota – OK/excellent (literally 'good note')

chapulines – a gang, usually of young thieves

chunche – thing (can refer to almost anything)

cien metros – one city block

¿Hay campo? – Is there space? (on a bus)

machita – blonde woman (slang)

mae – buddy (pronounced 'ma' as in 'mat' followed with a quick 'eh'; it's mainly used by boys and young men)

mi amor – my love (used as a familiar form of address by both men and women)

pulpería – corner grocery store

¡Pura vida! – Super! (literally 'pure life,' also an expression of approval or even a greeting)

sabanero – cowboy, especially one who hails from Guanacaste Province

salado – too bad; tough luck

soda – cafe or lunch counter

¡Tuanis! – Cool!

¡Upe! – Is anybody home? (used mainly in rural areas at people's homes, instead of knocking)

vos – you (singular and informal, same as *tú*)

air-con	aire acondicionado	ai·re a·kon·dee·syo·na·do
bathroom	baño	ba·nyo
bed	cama	ka·ma
window	ventana	ven·ta·na

DIRECTIONS

Where's ...?
¿Adónde está ...?   a·don·de es·ta ...

What's the address?
¿Cuál es la dirección?   kwal es la dee·rek·syon

Could you please write it down?
¿Podría escribirlo?   po·dree·a es·kree·beer·lo

Can you show me (on the map)?
¿Me puede enseñar (en el mapa)?   me pwe·de en·se·nyar (en el ma·pa)

at the corner	en la esquina	en la es·kee·na
at the traffic lights	en el semáforo	en el se·ma·fo·ro
behind ...	detrás de ...	de·tras de ...
far	lejos	le·khos
in front of ...	en frente de ...	en fren·te de ...
left	a la izquierda	a la ees·kyer·da
near	cerca	ser·ka
next to ...	a la par de ...	a la par de ...
opposite ...	opuesto a ...	o·pwes·to a ...
right	a la derecha	a la de·re·cha
straight ahead	aquí directo	a·kee dee·rek·to

EATING & DRINKING

Can I see the menu, please?
¿Puedo ver el menú, por favor?   pwe·do ver el me·noo por fa·vor

What would you recommend?
¿Qué me recomienda?   ke me re·ko·myen·da

Do you have vegetarian food?
¿Tienen comida vegetariana?   tye·nen ko·mee·da ve·khe·ta·rya·na

I don't eat (red meat).
No como (carne roja).   no ko·mo (kar·ne ro·kha)

That was delicious!
¡Estuvo delicioso!   es·too·vo de·lee·syo·so

Cheers!
¡Salud!   sa·lood

The bill, please.
La cuenta, por favor.   la kwen·ta por fa·vor

I'd like a table for ...	Quisiera una mesa para ...	kee·sye·ra oo·na me·sa pa·ra ...
(eight) o'clock	las (ocho)	las (o·cho)
(two) people	(dos) personas	(dos) per·so·nas

Key Words

appetisers	aperitivos	a·pe·ree·tee·vos
bar	bar	bar
bottle	botella	bo·te·ya
bowl	plato hondo	pla·to on·do
breakfast	desayuno	de·sa·yoo·no
cafe	café	ka·fe
(too) cold	(muy) frío	(mooy) free·o
dinner	cena	se·na

food	comida	ko·mee·da
fork	tenedor	te·ne·dor
glass	vaso	va·so
hot (warm)	caliente	kal·yen·te
knife	cuchillo	koo·chee·yo
lunch	almuerzo	al·mwer·so
main course	plato fuerte	pla·to fwer·te
market	mercado	mer·ka·do
menu	menú	me·noo
plate	plato	pla·to
restaurant	restaurante	res·tow·ran·te
spoon	cuchara	koo·cha·ra
supermarket	supermercado	soo·per·mer·ka·do
with/without	con/sin	kon/seen

Meat & Fish

beef	carne de vaca	kar·ne de va·ka
chicken	pollo	po·yo
duck	pato	pa·to
fish	pescado	pes·ka·do
lamb	cordero	kor·de·ro
pork	cerdo	ser·do
turkey	pavo	pa·vo
veal	ternera	ter·ne·ra

Fruit & Vegetables

apple	manzana	man·sa·na
apricot	albaricoque	al·ba·ree·ko·ke
asparagus	espárragos	es·pa·ra·gos
banana	banano	ba·na·no
bean	frijol	free·khol
cabbage	repollo	re·po·yo
carrot	zanahoria	sa·na·o·rya
cherry	cereza	se·re·sa
corn	maíz	ma·ees
cucumber	pepino	pe·pee·no
fruit	fruta	froo·ta
grapes	uvas	oo·vas
lemon	limón	lee·mon
lentils	lentejas	len·te·khas
lettuce	lechuga	le·choo·ga
mushroom	hongo	on·go
nuts	nueces	nwe·ses
onion	cebolla	se·bo·ya
orange	naranja	na·ran·kha
peach	melocotón	me·lo·ko·ton
pea	petipoa	pe·tee·po·a

pepper (bell)	pimentón	pee·men·ton
pineapple	piña	pee·nya
plum	ciruela	seer·we·la
potato	papa	pa·pa
pumpkin	calabaza	ka·la·ba·sa
spinach	espinaca	es·pee·na·ka
strawberry	fresa	fre·sa
tomato	tomate	to·ma·te
vegetable	vegetal	ve·khe·tal
watermelon	sandía	san·dee·a

Other

bread	pan	pan
butter	mantequilla	man·te·kee·ya
cheese	queso	ke·so
egg	huevo	we·vo
honey	miel	myel
jam	jalea	kha·le·a
oil	aceite	a·sey·te
pastry	pastel	pas·tel
pepper	pimienta	pee·myen·ta
rice	arroz	a·ros
salt	sal	sal
sugar	azúcar	a·soo·kar
vinegar	vinagre	vee·na·gre

Drinks

beer	cerveza	ser·ve·sa
coffee	café	ka·fe
(orange) juice	jugo (de naranja)	khoo·go (de na·ran·kha)
milk	leche	le·che
tea	té	te
(mineral) water	agua (mineral)	a·gwa (mee·ne·ral)
(red/white) wine	vino (tinto/ blanco)	vee·no (teen·to/ blan·ko)

SIGNS

Abierto	Open
Cerrado	Closed
Entrada	Entrance
Hombres/Varones	Men
Mujeres/Damas	Women
Prohibido	Prohibited
Salida	Exit
Servicios/Baños	Toilets

EMERGENCIES

Help!   ¡Socorro!   so·ko·ro
Go away!   ¡Váyase!   va·ya·se

Call ...!   ¡Llame a ...!   ya·me a ...
  a doctor   un doctor   oon dok·tor
  the police   la policía   la po·lee·see·a

I'm lost.
Estoy perdido/a.   es·toy per·dee·do/a (m/f)
I'm ill.
Estoy enfermo/a.   es·toy en·fer·mo/a (m/f)
It hurts here.
Me duele aquí.   me dwe·le a·kee
I'm allergic to (antibiotics).
Soy alérgico/a a   soy a·ler·khee·ko/a a
(los antibióticos).   (los an·tee·byo·tee·kos) (m/f)
Where are the toilets?
¿Dónde está el   don·de es·ta el
baño?   ba·nyo

SHOPPING & SERVICES

I'd like to buy ...
Quiero comprar ...   kye·ro kom·prar ...
I'm just looking.
Sólo estoy viendo.   so·lo es·toy vyen·do
Can I look at it?
¿Lo puedo ver?   lo pwe·do ver
How much is it?
¿Cuánto cuesta?   kwan·to kwes·ta
That's too expensive.
Está muy caro.   es·ta mooy ka·ro
Can you lower the price?
¿Podría bajarle   po·dree·a ba·khar·le
el precio?   el pre·syo
There's a mistake in the bill.
Hay un error   ai oon e·ror
en la cuenta.   en la kwen·ta

ATM   cajero   ka·khe·ro
  automático   ow·to·ma·tee·ko
credit card   tarjeta de   tar·khe·ta de
  crédito   kre·dee·to

QUESTION WORDS

How?   ¿Cómo?   ko·mo
What?   ¿Qué?   ke
When?   ¿Cuándo?   kwan·do
Where?   ¿Dónde?   don·de
Who?   ¿Quién?   kyen
Why?   ¿Por qué?   por ke

market   mercado   mer·ka·do
post office   correo   ko·re·o
tourist office   oficina   o·fee·see·na
  de turismo   de too·rees·mo

TIME & DATES

What time is it?   ¿Qué hora es?   ke o·ra es
It's (10) o'clock.   Son (las diez).   son (las dyes)
It's half past (one).   Es (la una) y media.   es (la oo·na) ee me·dya

morning   mañana   ma·nya·na
afternoon   tarde   tar·de
evening   noche   no·che
yesterday   ayer   a·yer
today   hoy   oy
tomorrow   mañana   ma·nya·na

Monday   lunes   loo·nes
Tuesday   martes   mar·tes
Wednesday   miércoles   myer·ko·les
Thursday   jueves   khwe·ves
Friday   viernes   vyer·nes
Saturday   sábado   sa·ba·do
Sunday   domingo   do·meen·go

January   enero   e·ne·ro
February   febrero   fe·bre·ro
March   marzo   mar·so
April   abril   a·breel
May   mayo   ma·yo
June   junio   khoon·yo
July   julio   khool·yo
August   agosto   a·gos·to
September   septiembre   sep·tyem·bre
October   octubre   ok·too·bre
November   noviembre   no·vyem·bre
December   diciembre   dee·syem·bre

TRANSPORTATION

boat   barco   bar·ko
bus   bús   boos
plane   avión   a·vyon
train   tren   tren

first   primero   pree·me·ro
last   último   ool·tee·mo
next   próximo   prok·see·mo

A ... ticket, please.	Un pasaje de ..., por favor.	oon pa·sa·khe de ... por fa·vor
1st-class	primera clase	pree·me·ra kla·se
2nd-class	segunda clase	se·goon·da kla·se
one-way	ida	ee·da
return	ida y vuelta	ee·da ee vwel·ta

I want to go to ...
Quisiera ir a ... kee·sye·ra eer a ...

Does it stop at ...?
¿Hace parada en ...? a·se pa·ra·da en ...

What stop is this?
¿Cuál es esta parada? kwal es es·ta pa·ra·da

What time does it arrive/leave?
¿A qué hora llega/ sale? a ke o·ra ye·ga/ sa·le

Please tell me when we get to ...
Por favor, avíseme cuando lleguemos a ... por fa·vor a·vee·se·me kwan·do ye·ge·mos a ...

I want to get off here.
Quiero bajarme aquí. kye·ro ba·khar·me a·kee

airport	aeropuerto	a·e·ro·pwer·to
aisle seat	asiento de pasillo	a·syen·to de pa·see·yo
bus stop	parada de autobuses	pa·ra·da de ow·to·boo·ses
cancelled	cancelado	kan·se·la·do
delayed	atrasado	a·tra·sa·do
platform	plataforma	pla·ta·for·ma
ticket office	taquilla	ta·kee·ya
timetable	horario	o·ra·ryo
train station	estación de trenes	es·ta·syon de tre·nes
window seat	asiento junto a la ventana	a·syen·to khoon·to a la ven·ta·na

I'd like to hire a ...	Quiero alquilar ...	kye·ro al·kee·lar ...
4WD	un cuatro por cuatro	oon kwa·tro por kwa·tro
bicycle	una bicicleta	oo·na bee·see·kle·ta
car	un carro	oon ka·ro
motorcycle	una moto- cicleta	oo·na mo·to- see·kle·ta

NUMBERS

1	uno	oo·no
2	dos	dos
3	tres	tres
4	cuatro	kwa·tro
5	cinco	seen·ko
6	seis	seys
7	siete	sye·te
8	ocho	o·cho
9	nueve	nwe·ve
10	diez	dyes
20	veinte	veyn·te
30	treinta	treyn·ta
40	cuarenta	kwa·ren·ta
50	cincuenta	seen·kwen·ta
60	sesenta	se·sen·ta
70	setenta	se·ten·ta
80	ochenta	o·chen·ta
90	noventa	no·ven·ta
100	cien	syen
1000	mil	meel

child seat	asiento de seguridad para niños	a·syen·to de se·goo·ree·da pa·ra nee·nyos
diesel	diesel	dee·sel
helmet	casco	kas·ko
mechanic	mecánico	me·ka·nee·ko
petrol/gas	gasolina	ga·so·lee·na
service station	bomba	bom·ba
truck	camión	ka·myon

Is this the road to ...?
¿Por aquí se va a ...? por a·kee se va a ...

(How long) Can I park here?
¿(Cuánto tiempo) Puedo parquear aquí? (kwan·to tyem·po) pwe·do par·ke·ar a·kee

The car has broken down (at ...).
El carro se varó en ... el ka·ro se va·ro en ...

I've had an accident.
Tuve un accidente. too·ve oon ak·see·den·te

I've run out of petrol.
Me quedé sin gasolina. me ke·de seen ga·so·lee·na

I have a flat tyre.
Se me estalló una llanta. se me es·ta·yo oo·na yan·ta

GLOSSARY

adiós – means 'goodbye' universally, but used as a greeting in rural Costa Rica

alquiler de automóviles – car rental

apartado – post-office box (abbreviated 'Apdo')

artesanía – handicrafts

ATH – *a toda hora* (open all hours); used to denote ATMs

automóvil – car

avenida – avenue

avión – airplane

bahía – bay

barrio – district or neighborhood

biblioteca – library

bomba – short, funny verse; also means 'gas station' and 'bomb'

bosque – forest

bosque nuboso – cloud forest

buena nota – excellent, OK; literally 'good note'

caballo – horse

cabaña – cabin; see also *cabina*

cabina – cabin; see also *cabaña*

cajero automático – ATM

calle – street

cama, cama matrimonial – bed, double bed

campesino – peasant, farmer or person who works in agriculture

carreta – colorfully painted wooden oxcart, now a form of folk art

carretera – road

casado – inexpensive set meal; also means 'married'

casita – cottage or apartment

catedral – cathedral

caverna – cave; see also *cueva*

cerro – mountain or hill

Chepe – affectionate nickname for José; also used when referring to San José

cine – cinema

ciudad – city

cocina – kitchen or cooking

colectivo – bus, minivan or car operating as shared taxi

colibrí – hummingbird

colina – hill

colón – Costa Rican unit of currency; plural colones

cordillera – mountain range

correo – mail service

Costarricense – Costa Rican; see also *Tico/a*

cruce – crossing

cruda – often used to describe a hangover; literally 'raw'

cueva – cave; see also *caverna*

culebra – snake; see also *serpiente*

Dios – God

directo – direct; refers to long-distance bus with few stops

edificio – building

estación – station, eg ranger station or bus station; also means 'season'

farmacia – pharmacy

fauna silvestre – wildlife

fiesta – party or festival

finca – farm or plantation

floresta – forest

frontera – border

fútbol – soccer (football)

garza – cattle egret

gasolina – gas (petrol)

gracias – thanks

gringo/a (m/f) – US or European visitor; can be affectionate or insulting, depending on the tone used

hacienda – rural estate

hielo – ice

ICT – Instituto Costarricense de Turismo; Costa Rica Tourism Board

iglesia – church

indígena – indigenous

Interamericana – Pan-American Hwy; the nearly continuous highway running from Alaska to Chile (it breaks at the Darién Gap between Panama and Colombia)

invierno – winter; the rainy season in Costa Rica

isla – island

jardín – garden

josefino/a (m/f) – resident of San José

lago – lake

lavandería – laundry facility, usually offering dry-cleaning services

librería – bookstore

llanura – tropical plain

machismo – an exaggerated sense of masculine pride

macho – literally 'male'; figuratively also 'masculine,' 'tough.' In Costa Rica *macho/a* (m/f) also means 'blonde.'

maría – local name for taxi meter

mercado – market

mercado central – central town market

Meseta Central – Central Valley or central plateau

mestizo/a (m/f) – person of mixed descent, usually Spanish and indigenous

metate – flat stone platform, used by Costa Rica's pre-Columbian populations to grind corn

migración – immigration

Minae – Ministerio de Ambiente y Energía; Ministry of Environment and Energy, in charge of the national park system

mirador – lookout point

mole – rich chocolate sauce

mono – monkey

mono tití – squirrel monkey

motocicleta – motorcycle

muelle – dock

museo – museum

niño – child

normal – refers to long-distance bus with many stops

obeah – sorcery rituals of African origin

ola(s) – wave(s)

OTS – Organization for Tropical Studies

pájaro – bird

palapa – shelter with a thatched, palm-leaf roof and open sides

palenque – indigenous settlement

páramo – habitat with highland shrub and tussock grass

parque – park

parque central – central town square or plaza

parque nacional – national park

perezoso – sloth

perico – mealy parrot

playa – beach

posada – country-style inn or guesthouse

puente – bridge

puerto – port

pulpería – corner grocery store

punta – point

pura vida – super; literally 'pure life'

quebrada – stream

rana – frog or toad

rancho – small house or house-like building

río – river

sabanero – cowboy from Guanacaste

selva – jungle

Semana Santa – the Christian Holy Week that precedes Easter

sendero – trail or path

serpiente – snake

Sinac – Sistema Nacional de Areas de Conservación; National System of Conservation Areas

supermercado – supermarket

telenovela – Spanish-language soap opera

Tico/a (m/f) – Costa Rican; see also *Costarricense*

tienda – store

tiquismos – typical Costa Rican expressions or slang

tortuga – turtle

valle – valley

verano – summer; the dry season in Costa Rica

volcán – volcano

zoológico – zoo

Food Glossary

a la plancha – grilled or pan-fried

agua – water

agua de sapo – literally 'toad water,' a lemonade made with fresh ginger and brown sugar

agua dulce – sugarcane juice

aguacate – avocado

almuerzo – lunch

almuerzo ejecutivo – literally 'executive lunch'; a more expensive version of a set meal or *casado*

arroz – rice

batido – fruit shake made with milk or water

bocas – small savory dishes served in bars; tapas

café – coffee

camaron – shrimp

carambola – starfruit

cas – a type of tart guava

casado – inexpensive set meal; also means 'married'

cena – dinner

cerveza – beer; also known as birra

ceviche – seafood marinated in lemon or lime juice, garlic and seasonings

chan – drink made from chia seeds

chuleta – pork chop

comida típica – typical local food

desayuno – breakfast

dorado – mahi-mahi

empanada – savory turnover stuffed with meat or cheese

ensalada – salad

frito – fried

gallo pinto – stir-fry of rice and beans

guanabana – soursop or cherimoya

guaro – local firewater made from sugarcane

leche – milk

linaza – drink made from flaxseeds

lomito – fillet; tenderloin

macrobiótica – health-food store

maracuya – passion fruit

mariscos – seafood

melón – cantaloupe

mora – blackberry

natilla – sour cream

olla de carne – beef stew

palmito – heart of palm

pargo – red snapper

pan – bread

pan tostada – toast

panadería – bakery

pastelería – pastry shop

patacones – twice-fried green plantains

patí – Caribbean version of empanada

pescado – fish

piña – pineapple

pipa – young green coconut; harvested for refreshing coconut water

plátanos maduros – ripe plantain cut in slices lengthwise and baked or broiled with butter, brown sugar and cinnamon

pollo – chicken

queso – cheese

resbladera – sweet barley and rice drink

ron – rum

rondón – seafood gumbo

Salsa Lizano – Costa Rican version of Worcestershire sauce; a key ingredient in *gallo pinto*

sandía – watermelon

soda – informal lunch counter or inexpensive eatery

tamarindo – fruit of the tamarind tree

tapa de dulce – brown sugar

vino – wine

Behind the Scenes

SEND US YOUR FEEDBACK

We love to hear from travelers – your comments keep us on our toes and help make our books better. Our well-traveled team reads every word on what you loved or loathed about this book. Although we cannot reply individually to your submissions, we always guarantee that your feedback goes straight to the appropriate authors, in time for the next edition. Each person who sends us information is thanked in the next edition – the most useful submissions are rewarded with a selection of digital PDF chapters.

Visit **lonelyplanet.com/contact** to submit your updates and suggestions or to ask for help. Our award-winning website also features inspirational travel stories, news and discussions.

Note: We may edit, reproduce and incorporate your comments in Lonely Planet products such as guidebooks, websites and digital products, so let us know if you don't want your comments reproduced or your name acknowledged. For a copy of our privacy policy visit lonelyplanet.com/privacy.

OUR READERS

Ashley Garver, Bridget Bero, David Callow, Deborah Weisinger, Edward Stiel, Federica Peruzzi, Iris Köster, Jean-Sebastien Goupil, Joan Mcconnell, John Shepherd, Kimberly Hayward, Marc Van-pé, Monika Schindler, Pascale Braam, Rebecca Kass, Shawn Smith, Susana Jimeno, Tommy Crabeels

AUTHOR THANKS

Ashley Harrell

Thanks to: editor Bailey Freeman for her kindness/wisdom, co-authors Jade Bremner and Brian Kluepfel for general awesomeness, Ronni and Mack Harrell for the support/dog-sitting, Adele Fox for being the best Gumpy, Genna Marie and Sean Davis for the helpful info/endless entertainment/undying friendship, Alejandro López-Meoño for the time/expertise, Andy Lavender for stalking quetzals and cheesemakers with me, Jonathan Harris for his kindness and his genius, and finally, the knowledgeable/hilarious/eternally accommodating Stacey Auch for leading me up mountains and beyond. Love you.

Jade Bremner

Gracias to helpful destination editor Bailey Freeman for her quick responses and support. Thanks also to local experts Ludrick Mcloud, for his informative guiding services, Gregg from Costa Rica Surf School, for showing me the Caribbean's best breaks, and Harriet Sinclair for her impressive 4WD driving skills. Plus, Nelson Torres and Julia Vaughns for their endless contacts book and helpfulness, and to everyone working hard behind the scenes – Cheree Broughton, Dianne and Jane, and Neill Coen.

Brian Kluepfel

To Paula Paz, my wife, you were there, even though you weren't, you know?

Muchas gracias to Wilfredo de Cabuya, Marlon y Pippa de Bijagua, Ernesto y Joel de Cano Negro, Sonia de La Fortuna, Lieke de Junquillal (¡Viva Mandela!), Carole and Sjull de Quebec and Holland, Tony de Avellanas, Mariano de Tamarindo for fixing my computer, and my great LP colleagues, Bailey, Jade and Ashley.

And to the Flying Taco of Samara and La Fortuna Pub – thanks for letting me sing in your bars.

ACKNOWLEDGEMENTS

Climate map data adapted from Peel MC, Finlayson BL & McMahon TA (2007) 'Updated World Map of the Köppen-Geiger Climate Classification', *Hydrology and Earth System Sciences*, 11, 163344.

Cover photograph: Red-eyed tree frog, Marco Simoni/AWL ©

THIS BOOK

This 13th edition of Lonely Planet's *Costa Rica* guidebook was researched and written by Ashley Harrell, Jade Bremner and Brian Kluepfel. This guidebook was produced by the following:

Destination Editor Bailey Freeman

Product Editors Kate James, Saralinda Turner

Senior Cartographer Corey Hutchison

Assisting Cartographer James Leversha

Book Designer Jessica Rose

Assisting Editors Sarah Bailey, Katie Connolly, Lucy Cowie, Melanie Dankel, Andrea Dobbin, Emma Gibbs, Charlotte Orr, Tamara Sheward

Cover Researcher Naomi Parker

Thanks to Carolyn Boicos, Hannah Cartmel, Andi Jones, Claire Naylor, Karyn Noble

Index